Exploring Business Version 2.1

By
Karen Collins

P-1658819-BW

9 781453 366585

Exploring Business Version 2.1

Karen Collins

Published by:

Flat World Knowledge, Inc.
1111 19th St NW, Suite 1180
Washington, DC 20036

Brief Contents

Contents

About the Author

KAREN COLLINS

Dr. Karen Collins is professor emerita of accounting at Lehigh University in Bethlehem, Pennsylvania. She has a Ph.D. in accounting from Virginia Tech. Dr. Collins coordinated the college's freshman-level Introduction to Business course. *Exploring Business* has evolved based on Dr. Collin's innovative and successful approach to Lehigh's Introduction to Business course. She was honored with an Innovation in Teaching Award for the course from the Middle Atlantic Association of Colleges and Business Administration.

Dr. Collins's research interests include upward mobility of women in accounting, quality of life issues, stress, and ethnic diversity in the accounting profession. She has published articles in journals such as *Accounting, Organizations and Society, Accounting Horizons, Journal of Accountancy, Journal of Vocational Behavior*, and *Journal of Occupational Health Psychology*.

Dr. Collins won numerous teaching awards while at Lehigh, including the Deming Lewis Faculty Award (for the faculty member who had the strongest influence on the ten-year graduating class); the Faculty Recognition Award (from the Dean of Students Office); and the Andersen Consulting Faculty Fellowship for Excellence in Teaching.

Acknowledgments

The author would like to thank the following colleagues who have reviewed the text and provided comprehensive feedback and suggestions for improving the material:

- Tim Allwine, Lower Columbia College
- Douglas Antola Crowe, Bradley University
- Vondra Armstrong, Pulaski Technical College
- April Bailey, Shippensburg University of Pennsylvania
- Michael Baran, South Puget Sound Community College
- Ruby Barker, Tarleton State University
- Murray Brunton, Central Ohio Technical College
- Laura Bulas, Central Community College
- Leon Chickering, South Puget Sound Community College
- Glenn Doolittle, Santa Ana College
- Amy Epplin, Rend Lake College
- Andrea Foster, John Tyler Community College
- Joseph Fox, Asheville-Buncombe Technical Community College
- Leatrice Freer, Pitt Community College
- George Generas, University of Hartford
- Connie Golden, Lakeland Community College
- David Gilliss, San Jose State University
- Alfredo Gomez, Broward College
- Madeline Grant, Santa Ana College
- Graham Harvey, Athivia College
- Graham Henning, Adelphi University
- Gail Jacobs, LA College International
- Francis Krcmarik, Mott Community College
- Elaine Madden, Anne Arundel Community College
- Timothy March, Kaskaskia College
- Marian Matthews, Central NM Community College
- Gina McConoughey, Illinois Central College
- Tom McFarland, Mt. San Antonio College
- Bill McPherson, Indiana University of Pennsylvania
- Diane Minger, Cedar Valley College
- Jennifer Morton, Ivy Tech Community College of Indiana
- John Olivo, Bloomsburg University of Pennsylvania
- Lauren Paisley, Genesee Community College
- Col. Stephen Pomeroy, Norwich University
- Anthony Racka, Oakland Community College
- Nancy Ray-Mitchell, McLennan Community College
- P. Gerard Shaw, Dean College
- Martin St. John, Westmoreland County Community College
- John Striebich, Monroe Community College
- Frank Titlow, St. Petersburg College
- Bob Urell, Irvine Valley College
- Dean Williamson, Brewton-Parker College #2004
- John Wolford, LaBrae High School

In addition, a select group of instructors assisted the development of this material by actually using it in their classrooms. Their input, along with their students' feedback, has provided us critical confirmation that the material is effective and impactful in the classroom:

- Nikolaos Adamou, Borough of Manhattan CC
- April Bailey, Shippensburg University of Pennsylvania
- Michael Davis, Yavaipai College
- Andrea Foster, John Taylor Community College
- Frank Markham, Mesa State
- Donn Miller-Kermani, Florida Institute of Technology
- Diane Minger, Cedar Valley College
- Tony Racka, Oakland Community College
- P. Gerard Shaw, Dean College
- Dean Williamson, Brewton-Parker College
- David Woolgar, Santa Ana College

I am sincerely grateful to Jeff Shelstad, Eric Frank and Sharon Koch-Schwarzmiller for their confidence in me and in the project. Thanks to Becky Knauer and Scott Marinaro for their support, positive attitude, hard work and dedication to the project. Thanks to my project manager, Becky Knauer, for her hard work, dedication to quality, constant support, and positive attitude. Thanks also to several very special friends who made substantial contributions to the textbook project: Ron Librach, Joseph Manzo, Judy Minot, and Eleanore Stinner.

Thanks to the members of the Introduction to Business faculty team at Lehigh University who were a constant source of ideas and advice. Their excitement about the course and dedication to our students created a positive and supportive teaching environment. I enjoyed the hours we spent in the "bullpen" sharing teaching tips, brainstorming ways to improve the course, and just having fun.

Finally, I thank my husband, Bill, my sons, Don and Mark, and their wives, Courtney and Tara, for their support and encouragement during this project. They, along with my five wonderful grandchildren, are the best of my world.

Dedication

To the memory of Dave Jones, a very special teacher and dear friend, who was devoted to his students in Lehigh's Introduction to Business course.

I, along with the other members of the BUS 01 team, will miss you forever.

Preface

My desire in writing this text was to provide faculty with a fully developed teaching package that allows them to enhance student learning and introduce students to business in an exciting way. *Exploring Business* is designed to be a *powerful but simple-to-use teaching tool*. I've devised a broad range of features that allow instructors to introduce students to business in an exciting way, but also worked to fashion material that's straightforward, current, relevant, and easy to teach from. The text is purposely brief and covers business essentials without burdening students or faculty with unnecessary detail.

OVERVIEW OF TEXTBOOK PACKAGE

I've tried to build a textbook package that's as *supportive* as possible to both students and faculty. The textbook package supports learning through content and teaching materials designed to help students master topics and assess their learning. The sixteen chapters are written using a modular format with self-contained sections. Each module ends with a detailed summary and relevant exercises written to assist students as they learn from the text.

Using FlatWorld's fast and easy online editor, you can easily customize your book to suit your needs and those of your students. You can add, delete or rearrange content to create the perfect text for your class and improve student success.

As in other Introduction to Business books, this text uses a wide variety of company-specific examples. However, I improve on the traditional approach by adding an *optional* case study of a dynamic organization that can easily be integrated into the text. The company chosen for this purpose is Nike. I have also included an *optional* business plan project.

I have designed this textbook package to be *flexible* and meet the needs of four groups of instructors—those who want to

- teach the course using the textbook alone;
- teach the course using the comprehensive, optional Nike case (or a company of their choice);
- teach the course using the optional business plan project; or
- teach the course by incorporating both a company case study and the business plan project.

ENHANCED LEARNING

> "Tell me and I forget. Teach me and I remember. Involve me and I learn."

I believe that this quote summarizes an important goal of this textbook package: *to encourage students to be active learners*. Thus I've designed the textbook to facilitate the attainment of this goal. To give you a flavor of the purpose of these online materials, let's take a quick tour of the features available for each chapter:

- Active Figures—which simulate the process that a faculty member goes through in class when diagramming a concept on the board, one piece at a time.
- Active Exercises—which engage students in active learning and help them master key concepts.
- Active Assessment Questions—which provide students with instant feedback and reinforce learning.

In addition, I strive to enhance student learning through thought-provoking questions, problems, and cases that ask students to do more than merely regurgitate information from the text. Most of these exercises require students to gather information, assess a situation, think about it critically, and reach a conclusion. Many are based on current business situations involving well-known companies of interest to students. Each chapter presents a number of Questions and Problems as well as five cases on areas of skill and knowledge endorsed by the Association to Advance Collegiate Schools of Business (AACSB): Learning on the Web, Career Opportunities, The Ethics Angle, Team-Building Skills, and The Global View. The questions are challenging and stimulating, and most are appropriate for in-class discussions. More than 70 percent of our items help students build skills in areas designated as critical by AACSB, including analytical skills, ethical awareness and reasoning abilities, multicultural understanding and globalization, use of information technology, and communications and team-oriented skills.

AUTHOR-PREPARED INSTRUCTOR'S MANUAL

For twelve years, I developed, coordinated and taught an Introduction to Business course in which first-year students were introduced to business through the study of Nike and the preparation of a business plan. During this twelve-year period, more than 3,500 students took the course. Over the years, sections of the course were taught by a mix of permanent faculty, graduate students, business executives, other adjuncts, and even the dean. Each semester, I oversaw the course and guided approximately ten instructors as they taught their sections—a task that was made possible through the development and continuous improvement of extensive teaching materials.

Because I feel strongly that well-structured and easily understood teaching materials are vital to the success of this course, I have personally written the Instructor's Manual. In doing this, I relied on the experiences that I've gained in developing these materials for my faculty team. The Instructor's Manual includes comprehensive teaching notes that integrate material from the chapter, material geared toward the optional Nike case study, and material dedicated to the optional business plan project. The easy-to-use notes include teaching tips and ample in-class activities. The Instructor's Manual also contains author-prepared solutions to all questions, problems and cases.

TEST ITEM FILE AND POWERPOINT SLIDES

The teaching package includes an extensive Test Item File designed to assess students' understanding of each of the learning objectives. The Test Item File is grouped by module. In addition, there are about thirty-five to forty PowerPoint slides per chapter.

NIKE: AN INTEGRATED CASE STUDY

A Nike case study is available for those instructors who decide to introduce their students to business using an exciting case—one which is updated yearly. Through an in-depth study of a real company, students can learn not only about the functional areas of business, but how these functional areas fit together. Studying a dynamic organization on a real-time basis allows students to discover the challenges that it faces and exposes them to critical issues affecting the business, such as globalization, ethics and social responsibility, diversity, sustainability, product innovation, supply chain management, social medial marketing, and e-business.

Students learn about Nike by reading a case study based on extensive research and executive interviews. The case is broken down into 26 individual case notes, which are linked to the appropriate sections of the text. Each provides a real-world example to help students master a particular business topic. For example, after reading about the ways companies promote their products, students are directed to a Nike case note that traces the evolution of the company's promotional strategies, including its well-known sports-marketing efforts. After reading chapter materials on the pros and cons of doing business in a global environment, students can read a Nike case note that examines both the benefits that Nike derives from its international operations and the responsibilities that it has to the countries in which it operates.

Current (and sometimes controversial) topics can be woven into the class through Nike-related memo or e-mail writing (or debating) assignments accompanying each chapter. These assignments, which are updated frequently, provide students with an opportunity to strengthen their writing skills and form opinions on current issues affecting Nike.

I've found that, by studying Nike, students willingly participate in classroom discussions. Why? Because Nike is on just about everybody's radar screen. Students enjoy discussing the opportunities and challenges faced by Nike and speculating on what the company intends to do about them, now and in the future.

BUSINESS PLAN PROJECT

I'm convinced that having students develop a business plan as a component of an Introduction to Business course has considerable academic value. A business plan project introduces students to the excitement and challenges of starting a business and helps them discover how the functional areas of business interact. Thus this textbook package includes an *optional* business plan project that's *fully integrated* into the book. The business plan project is modeled after one used and refined by me and my teaching team over the past twelve years. During this time period, more than 800 student teams have prepared and presented business plans using this approach.

If their instructor elects to assign the business plan project, students begin the project early in the course by reviewing a document describing the business plan project. In chapters that follow, students are asked to complete another section of the 10-part business plan project. By the time they've reached the end of the course they're shown how to integrate each of these individual sections into a final version of the plan. Because the project is carefully coordinated with the presentation of course materials, students are able to apply what they're learning, as they're learning it, to the practical process of preparing a business plan.

Because I understand that preparing the financial section of the business plan can be difficult for students, we furnish students with an Excel template that simplifies the process of preparing financial reports for their proposed businesses. They don't even need to be competent in Excel to use it; it's designed to be simple to use, and we provide detailed instructions.

INTRODUCTION TO BUSINESS COMMUNITY

Those teaching Introduction to Business come from varied backgrounds but share common goals of exciting students about business and sparking their interest in future business courses. I wrote this text to provide members of this community with a fully developed teaching package that enhances the learning environment and helps them introduce students to business in an exciting way. My hope is that by sharing my materials, experiences and approach to teaching with others, they will enjoy the course as much as I have.

Karen Collins

CHAPTER 1
The Foundations of Business

WHY IS APPLE SUCCESSFUL?

In 1976, Steve Jobs and Steve Wozniak created their first computer, the Apple I.[1] They invested a mere $1,300 and set up business in Jobs's garage. Three decades later, their business—Apple Inc.—has become one of the world's most influential and successful companies. Did you ever wonder why Apple flourished while so many other young companies failed? How did it grow from a garage start-up to a company generating $171 billion in sales? How was it able to transform itself from a nearly bankrupt firm to a multinational corporation with locations all around the world? You might conclude that it was the company's products, such as the Mac, the iPod, iTunes, the iPad, and the wildly popular iPhone. Or you might decide that it was its people: its dedicated employees and loyal customers. Perhaps you will decide it was luck—Apple simply was in the right place at the right time. Or maybe you will attribute the company's success to management's willingness to take calculated risks. Perhaps you will attribute Apple's initial accomplishments and reemergence to its cofounder, the late Steve Jobs. After all, Jobs was instrumental in the original design of the Apple I and, after being ousted from his position with the company, returned to save the firm from destruction and lead it onto its current path.

Before we decide what made Apple what it is today and what will propel it into a successful future, let's see if you have all the facts about the possible choices: its products, its customers, luck, willingness to take risks, or Steve Jobs. We're confident that you're aware of Apple's products and understand that "Apple customers are a loyal bunch. Though they're only a small percentage of all computer users, they make up for it with their passion and outspokenness."[2] We believe you can understand the role that luck or risk taking could play in Apple's success. But you might like to learn more about Steve Jobs, the company's cofounder and former CEO, before arriving at your final decision.

Growing up, Jobs had an interest in computers. He attended lectures at Hewlett-Packard after school and worked for the company during the summer months. He took a job at Atari after graduating from high school and saved his money to make a pilgrimage to India to search for spiritual enlightenment. Following his India trip, he attended Steve Wozniak's "Homebrew Computer Club" meetings, where the idea for building a personal computer surfaced.[3] "Many colleagues describe Jobs as a brilliant man who could be a great motivator and positively charming. At the same time his drive for perfection was so strong that employees who do not meet his demands are faced with blistering verbal attacks."[4] Not everyone at Apple appreciated Jobs's brilliance and ability to motivate. Nor did they all go along with his willingness to do whatever it took to produce an innovative, attractive, high-quality product. So at age thirty, Jobs found himself ousted from Apple by John Sculley, whom Jobs himself had hired as president of the company several years earlier. It seems that Sculley wanted to cut costs and thought it would be easier to do so without Jobs around. Jobs sold

Following the iPad's release in 2010, it has become popular for a variety of uses including use by students.

©Thinkstock

$20 million of his stock and went on a two-month vacation to figure out what he would do for the rest of his life. His solution was to start a new personal computer company called NextStep. In 1993, he was invited back to Apple (a good thing, because neither his new company nor Apple was doing well).

Steve Jobs was definitely not humble, but he was a visionary and had a right to be proud of his accomplishments. Some have commented that "Apple's most successful days have occurred with Steve Jobs at the helm."[5] Jobs did what many successful CEOs and managers do: he learned, adjusted, and improvised.[6] Perhaps the most important statement that can be made about him is this: he never gave up on the company that once turned its back on him. So now you have the facts. Here's a multiple-choice question that you'll likely get right: Apple's success is due to (a) its products, (b) its customers, (c) luck, (d) willingness to take risks, (e) Steve Jobs, or (f) some combination of these options.

1. INTRODUCTION

As the story of Apple suggests, today is an interesting time to study business. Advances in technology are bringing rapid changes in the ways we produce and deliver goods and services. The Internet and other improvements in communication (such as smartphones, video conferencing, and social networking) now affect the way we do business. Companies are expanding international operations, and the workforce is more diverse than ever. Corporations are being held responsible for the behavior of their executives, and more people share the opinion that companies should be good corporate citizens. Plus—and this is a big plus—businesses today are facing the lingering effects of what many economists believe was the worst financial crisis since the Great Depression.[7] Economic turmoil that began in the housing and mortgage industries as a result of troubled subprime mortgages quickly spread to the rest of the economy. In 2008, credit markets froze up and banks stopped making loans. Lawmakers tried to get money flowing again by passing a $700 billion Wall Street bailout, yet businesses and individuals were still denied access to needed credit. Without money or credit, consumer confidence in the economy dropped and consumers cut back their spending. Businesses responded by producing fewer products, and their sales and profits dropped. Unemployment rose as troubled companies shed the most jobs in five years, and 760,000 Americans marched to the unemployment lines.[8] The stock market reacted to the financial crisis and stock prices dropped by 44 percent while millions of Americans watched in shock as their savings and retirement accounts took a nose dive. In fall 2008, even Apple, a company that had enjoyed strong sales growth over the past five years, began to cut production of its popular iPhone. Without jobs or cash, consumers would no longer flock to Apple's fancy retail stores or buy a prized iPhone.[9] Things have turned around for Apple, which reported blockbuster sales for 2013 in part because of continued strong customer response to the iPhone. And things have turned around (somewhat) for the country: the economy is recovering at a slow pace, consumer confidence is rebounding, home prices are rising, and the unemployment rate is slowly decreasing (though long-term unemployment has increased).

As you go through the course with the aid of this text, you'll explore the exciting world of business. We'll introduce you to the various activities in which businesspeople engage—accounting, finance, information technology, management, marketing, and operations. We'll help you understand the roles that these activities play in an organization, and we'll show you how they work together. We hope that by exposing you to the things that businesspeople do, we'll help you decide whether business is right for you and, if so, what areas of business you'd like to study further.

2. GETTING DOWN TO BUSINESS

LEARNING OBJECTIVES

1. Identify the main participants of business.
2. Describe the functions that most businesses perform.
3. Identify the external forces that influence business activities.

A **business** is any activity that provides goods or services to consumers for the purpose of making a profit. When Steve Jobs and Steve Wozniak created Apple in Jobs's family garage, they started a business. The product was the Apple I, and the company's founders hoped to sell their computers to customers for more than it cost to make and market them. If they were successful (which they were), they'd make a **profit**.

Before we go on, let's make a couple of important distinctions concerning the terms in our definitions. First, whereas Apple produces and sells *goods* (Mac, iPhone, iPod, iPad), many businesses provide *services*. Your bank is a service company, as is your Internet provider. Hotels, airlines, law firms, movie theaters, and hospitals are also service companies. Many companies provide both goods and services. For example, your local car dealership sells goods (cars) and also provides services (automobile repairs).

Second, some organizations are not set up to make profits. Many are established to provide social or educational services. Such **not-for-profit (or nonprofit) organizations** include the United Way of America, Habitat for Humanity, the Boys and Girls Clubs, the Sierra Club, the American Red Cross, and many colleges and universities. Most of these organizations, however, function in much the same way as a business. They establish goals and work to meet them in an effective, efficient manner. Thus, most of the business principles introduced in this text also apply to nonprofits.

business

Activity that provides goods or services to consumers for the purpose of making a profit.

profit

Difference between the revenue that a company brings in from selling goods and services and the costs of generating this revenue.

not-for-profit (or nonprofit) organization

Organization that has a purpose other than returning profits to owners.

2.1 Business Participants and Activities

Let's begin our discussion of business by identifying the main participants of business and the functions that most businesses perform. Then we'll finish this section by discussing the external factors that influence a business's activities.

Participants

Every business must have one or more *owners* whose primary role is to invest money in the business. When a business is being started, it's generally the owners who polish the business idea and bring together the resources (money and people) needed to turn the idea into a business. The owners also hire *employees* to work for the company and help it reach its goals. Owners and employees depend on a third group of participants—*customers*. Ultimately, the goal of any business is to satisfy the needs of its customers in order to generate a profit for the owners.

2.2 Functional Areas of Business

The activities needed to operate a business can be divided into a number of *functional areas*: management, operations, marketing, accounting, and finance. Let's briefly explore each of these areas.

Management

Managers are responsible for the work performance of other people. **Management** involves planning for, organizing, staffing, directing, and controlling a company's resources so that it can achieve its goals. Managers *plan* by setting goals and developing strategies for achieving them. They *organize* activities and resources to ensure that company goals are met. They *staff* the organization with qualified employees and *direct* them to accomplish organizational goals. Finally, managers design *controls* for assessing the success of plans and decisions and take corrective action when needed.

Operations

All companies must convert resources (labor, materials, money, information, and so forth) into goods or services. Some companies, such as Apple, convert resources into *tangible* products—Macs, iPhones, iPods, iPads. Others, such as hospitals, convert resources into *intangible* products—health care. The person who designs and oversees the transformation of resources into goods or services is called an **operations manager**. This individual is also responsible for ensuring that products are of high quality.

Marketing

Marketing consists of everything that a company does to identify customers' needs and designs products to meet those needs. Marketers develop the benefits and features of products, including price and quality. They also decide on the best method of delivering products and the best means of promoting them to attract and keep customers. They manage relationships with customers and make them aware of the organization's desire and ability to satisfy their needs.

Accounting

Managers need accurate, relevant, timely financial information, and accountants provide it. **Accountants** measure, summarize, and communicate financial and managerial information and advise other managers on financial matters. There are two fields of accounting. *Financial accountants* prepare financial statements to help users, both inside and outside the organization, assess the financial strength of the company. *Managerial accountants* prepare information, such as reports on the cost of materials used in the production process, for internal use only.

Finance

Finance involves planning for, obtaining, and managing a company's funds. Finance managers address such questions as the following: How much money does the company need? How and where will it get the necessary money? How and when will it pay the money back? What should it do with its funds? What investments should be made in plant and equipment? How much should be spent on research and development? How should excess funds be invested? Good financial management is particularly important when a company is first formed, because new business owners usually need to borrow money to get started.

FIGURE 1.1

Hospitals specialize in an intangible product—health care.

© 2010 Jupiterimages Corporation

management

Process of planning for, organizing, directing, and controlling a company's resources so that it can achieve its goals.

operations manager

Person who designs and oversees the process that converts resources into goods or services.

marketing

Marketing is the activity, set of institutions, and processes for creating, communicating, delivering, and exchanging offerings that have value for customers, clients, partners, and society at large.

accountant

Financial advisor responsible for measuring, summarizing, and communicating financial and managerial information.

finance

Activities involved in planning for, obtaining, and managing a company's funds.

FIGURE 1.2 Business and Its Environment

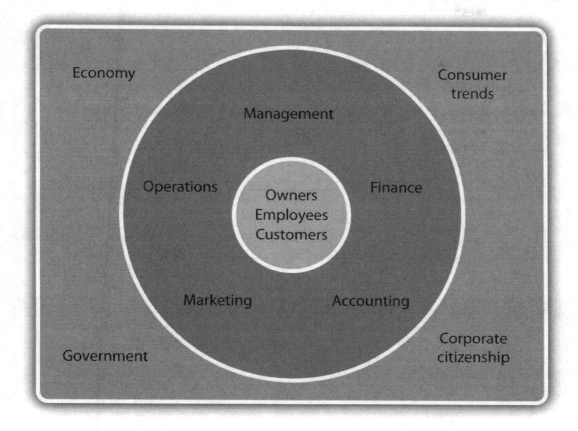

2.3   External Forces that Influence Business Activities

Apple and other businesses don't operate in a vacuum: they're influenced by a number of external factors. These include the economy, government, consumer trends, and public pressure to act as good corporate citizens. Figure 1.2 sums up the relationship among the participants in a business, its functional areas, and the external forces that influence its activities. One industry that's clearly affected by all these factors is the fast-food industry. A strong *economy* means people have more money to eat out at places where food standards are monitored by a *government* agency, the Food and Drug Administration. Preferences for certain types of foods are influenced by *consumer trends* (eating fried foods might be OK one year and out the next). Finally, a number of decisions made by the industry result from its *desire to be a good corporate citizen*. For example, several fast-food chains have responded to environmental concerns by eliminating Styrofoam containers.[10] As you move through this text, you'll learn more about these external influences on business. (Section 3 will introduce in detail one of these external factors—the economy.)

What Activities Do Managers Perform?

Take a few minutes to complete an exercise that reinforces what you've learned about the activities managers perform.

- The main participants in a business are its owners, employees, and customers.
- Businesses are influenced by such external factors as the economy, government, consumer trends, and public pressure to act as good corporate citizens.
- The activities needed to run a business can be divided into five functional areas:
    1. **Management** involves planning, organizing, staffing, directing, and controlling resources to achieve organizational goals.
    2. **Operations** transforms resources (labor, materials, money, and so on) into products.
    3. **Marketing** works to identify and satisfy customers' needs.
    4. **Finance** involves planning for, obtaining, and managing company funds.
    5. **Accounting** entails measuring, summarizing, and communicating financial and managerial information.

Before going to the next section of this chapter, take a few minutes to test your knowledge of the material covered in this section. Quizzes can be found under the "Resources" tab, "Study Aids: Quizzes."

EXERCISES

1. The Martin family has been making guitars out of its factory in Nazareth, Pennsylvania, for more than 150 years. In 2004, Martin Guitar was proud to produce its millionth instrument. Go to the Martin Guitar Web site (http://www.martinguitar.com) and read about the company's long history. You'll discover that, even though it's a family-run company with a fairly unique product, it operates like any other company. Identify the main activities or functions of Martin Guitar's business and explain how each activity benefits the company.
2. Name four external factors that have an influence on business. Give examples of the ways in which each factor can affect the business performance of two companies: Wal-Mart and Ford Motor Company.

3. WHAT IS ECONOMICS?

LEARNING OBJECTIVES

1. Define "economics."
2. Identify the factors of production businesses use to produce goods and services.
3. Identify the three key economics questions and explain how economists answer these three questions.
4. Compare and contrast the following economic systems: planned system (communism and socialism) and free market system (capitalism).

To appreciate how a business functions, we need to know something about the economic environment in which it operates. We begin with a definition of economics and a discussion of the resources used to produce goods and services.

3.1   Resources: Inputs and Outputs

Economics is the study of the production, distribution, and consumption of goods and services. **Resources** are the *inputs* used to produce *outputs*. Resources may include any or all of the following:

- Land and other natural resources
- Labor (physical and mental)
- Capital, including buildings and equipment
- Entrepreneurship

Resources are combined to produce goods and services. Land and natural resources provide the needed raw materials. Labor transforms raw materials into goods and services. Capital (equipment, buildings, vehicles, cash, and so forth) are needed for the production process. Entrepreneurship provides the skill and creativity needed to bring the other resources together to produce a good or service to be sold to the marketplace.

Because a business uses resources to *produce* things, we also call these resources **factors of production**. The factors of production used to produce a shirt would include the following:

- The land that the shirt factory sits on, the electricity used to run the plant, and the raw cotton from which the shirts are made
- The laborers who make the shirts
- The factory and equipment used in the manufacturing process, as well as the money needed to operate the factory
- The entrepreneurship skill used to coordinate the other resources to initiate the production process and the distribution of the goods or services to the marketplace

3.2   Input and Output Markets

Many of the factors of production (or resources) are provided to businesses by households. For example, households provide businesses with labor (as workers), land and buildings (as landlords), and capital (as investors). In turn, businesses pay households for these resources by providing them with income, such as wages, rent, and interest. The resources obtained from households are then used by businesses to produce goods and services, which are sold to the same households that provide businesses with revenue. The revenue obtained by businesses is then used to buy additional resources, and the cycle continues. This circular flow is described in Figure 1.3, which illustrates the dual roles of households and businesses:

- Households not only provide factors of production (or resources) but also consume goods and services.
- Businesses not only buy resources but also produce and sell both goods and services.

economics

Study of how scarce resources are used to produce outputs—goods and services—that are distributed among people.

Resources

Inputs used to produce outputs.

factors of production

Resources consisting of land, labor, capital (money, buildings, equipment), and entrepreneurial skills combined to produce goods and services.

FIGURE 1.3 The Circular Flow of Inputs and Outputs

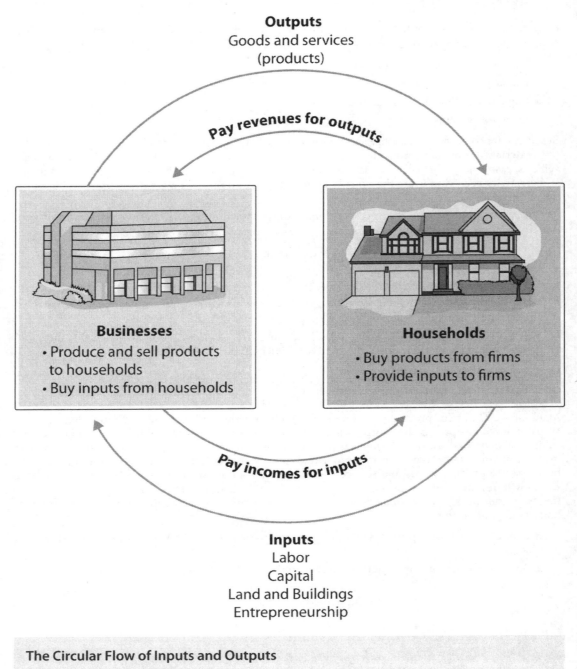

Outputs
Goods and services
(products)

Pay revenues for outputs

Businesses
- Produce and sell products to households
- Buy inputs from households

Households
- Buy products from firms
- Provide inputs to firms

Pay incomes for inputs

Inputs
Labor
Capital
Land and Buildings
Entrepreneurship

The Circular Flow of Inputs and Outputs

Click on this link to experience an active version of this figure.

3.3   The Questions Economists Ask

Economists study the interactions between households and businesses and look at the ways in which the factors of production are combined to produce the goods and services that people need. Basically, economists try to answer three sets of questions:

1. *What goods and services should be produced to meet consumers' needs?* In what quantity? When should they be produced?

2. *How should goods and services be produced?* Who should produce them, and what resources, including technology, should be combined to produce them?

3. *Who should receive the goods and services produced?* How should they be allocated among consumers?

3.4   Economic Systems

The answers to these questions depend on a country's **economic system**—the means by which a society (households, businesses, and government) makes decisions about allocating resources to produce products and about distributing those products. The degree to which individuals and business owners, as opposed to the government, enjoy freedom in making these decisions varies according to the type of economic system. Generally speaking, economic systems can be divided into two systems: *planned systems* and *free market systems*.

Planned Systems

In a planned system, the government exerts control over the allocation and distribution of all or some goods and services. The system with the highest level of government control is **communism**. In theory, a communist economy is one in which the government owns all or most enterprises. Central planning by the government dictates which goods or services are produced, how they are produced, and who will receive them. In practice, pure communism is practically nonexistent today, and only a few countries (notably North Korea and Cuba) operate under rigid, centrally planned economic systems.

Under **socialism**, industries that provide essential services, such as utilities, banking, and health care, may be government owned. Other businesses are owned privately. Central planning allocates the goods and services produced by government-run industries and tries to ensure that the resulting wealth is distributed equally. In contrast, privately owned companies are operated for the purpose of making a profit for their owners. In general, workers in socialist economies work fewer hours, have longer vacations, and receive more health care, education, and child-care benefits than do workers in capitalist economies. To offset the high cost of public services, taxes are generally steep. Examples of socialist countries include Sweden and France.

Free Market System

The economic system in which most businesses are owned and operated by individuals is the **free market system**, also known as **capitalism**. As we will see next, in a free market, *competition* dictates how goods and services will be allocated. Business is conducted with only limited government involvement. The economies of the United States and other countries, such as Japan, are based on capitalism.

How Economic Systems Compare

In comparing economic systems, it's helpful to think of a continuum with communism at one end and pure capitalism at the other, as in Figure 1.4. As you move from left to right, the amount of government control over business diminishes. So, too, does the level of social services, such as health care, child-care services, social security, and unemployment benefits.

FIGURE 1.4 The Spectrum of Economic Systems

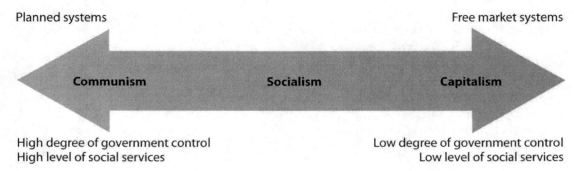

Planned systems   Free market systems

Communism   Socialism   Capitalism

High degree of government control   Low degree of government control
High level of social services   Low level of social services

economic system

Means by which a society makes decisions about allocating resources to produce and distribute products.

communism

Economic system featuring the highest level of government control over allocation and distribution.

socialism

Economic system falling between communism and capitalism in terms of government control over allocation and distribution.

free market system

Economic system in which most businesses are owned and operated by individuals.

capitalism

Economic system featuring the lowest level of government control over allocation and distribution.

Mixed Market Economy

mixed market economy

Economic system that relies on both markets and government to allocate resources.

privatization

Process of converting government-owned businesses to private ownership.

Though it's possible to have a pure communist system, or a pure capitalist (free market) system, in reality many economic systems are mixed. A **mixed market economy** relies on both markets and the government to allocate resources. We've already seen that this is what happens in socialist economies in which the government controls selected major industries, such as transportation and health care, while allowing individual ownership of other industries. Even previously communist economies, such as those of Eastern Europe and China, are becoming more mixed as they adopt capitalistic characteristics and convert businesses previously owned by the government to private ownership through a process called **privatization**.

The U.S. Economic System

Like most countries, the United States features a mixed market system: though the U.S. economic system is primarily a free market system, the federal government controls some basic services, such as the postal service and air traffic control. The U.S. economy also has some characteristics of a socialist system, such as providing social security retirement benefits to retired workers.

The free market system was espoused by Adam Smith in his book *The Wealth of Nations*, published in 1776.[11] According to Smith, competition alone would ensure that consumers received the best products at the best prices. In the kind of competition he assumed, a seller who tries to charge more for his product than other sellers won't be able to find any buyers. A job-seeker who asks more than the going wage won't be hired. Because the "invisible hand" of competition will make the market work effectively, there won't be a need to regulate prices or wages.

Almost immediately, however, a tension developed among free market theorists between the principle of *laissez-faire*—leaving things alone—and government intervention. Today, it's common for the U.S. government to intervene in the operation of the economic system. For example, government exerts influence on the food and pharmaceutical industries through the Food and Drug Administration, which protects consumers by preventing unsafe or mislabeled products from reaching the market.

To appreciate how businesses operate, we must first get an idea of how prices are set in competitive markets. Thus, Section 4 begins by describing how markets establish prices in an environment of *perfect competition*.

Comparing Economic Systems

Take a few minutes to complete an exercise that reinforces your understanding of the characteristics of different economic systems.

KEY TAKEAWAYS

- **Economics** is the study of the production, distribution, and consumption of goods and services.
- Economists address these three questions: (1) What goods and services should be produced to meet consumer needs? (2) How should they be produced, and who should produce them? (3) Who should receive goods and services?
- The answers to these questions depend on a country's **economic system**. The primary economic systems that exist today are planned and free market systems.
- In a planned system, such as **communism** and **socialism**, the government exerts control over the production and distribution of all or some goods and services.
- In a **free market system**, also known as **capitalism**, business is conducted with only limited government involvement. Competition determines what goods and services are produced, how they are produced, and for whom.

Before going to the next section of this chapter, take a few minutes to test your knowledge of the material covered in this section. Quizzes can be found under the "Resources" tab, "Study Aids: Quizzes."

4. PERFECT COMPETITION AND SUPPLY AND DEMAND

LEARNING OBJECTIVES

1. **Describe a free market system.**
2. **Identify four types of competition.**
3. **Define the following terms: supply, demand, and equilibrium price.**
4. **Describe perfect competition, and explain how supply and demand interact to set prices in a free market system.**

Under a mixed economy, such as in the United States, businesses make decisions about which goods to produce or services to offer and how they are priced. Because there are many businesses making goods or providing services, customers can choose among a wide array of products. The competition for sales among businesses is a vital part of our economic system. Economists have identified four types of competition—*perfect competition*, *monopolistic competition*, *oligopoly*, and *monopoly*. We'll introduce the first of these—perfect competition—in this section and cover the remaining three in Section 5.

4.1 Perfect Competition

Perfect competition exists when there are many consumers buying a standardized product from numerous small businesses. Because no seller is big enough or influential enough to affect price, sellers and buyers accept the going price. For example, when a commercial fisher brings his fish to the local market, he has little control over the price he gets and must accept the going market price.

4.2 The Basics of Supply and Demand

To appreciate how perfect competition works, we need to understand how buyers and sellers interact in a market to set prices. In a market characterized by perfect competition, price is determined through the mechanisms of *supply* and *demand*. Prices are influenced both by the supply of products from sellers and by the demand for products by buyers.

To illustrate this concept, let's create a *supply and demand schedule* for one particular good sold at one point in time. Then we'll define *demand* and create a *demand curve* and define *supply* and create a *supply curve*. Finally, we'll see how supply and demand interact to create an *equilibrium price*—the price at which buyers are willing to purchase the amount that sellers are willing to sell.

Demand and the Demand Curve

Demand is the quantity of a product that buyers are willing to purchase at various prices. The quantity of a product that people are willing to buy depends on its price. You're typically willing to buy *less* of a product when prices *rise* and *more* of a product when prices *fall*. Generally speaking, we find products more attractive at lower prices, and we buy more at lower prices because our income goes further.

FIGURE 1.5

Produce, like these apples, is a standardized product available from numerous businesses.

© 2010 Jupiterimages Corporation

perfect competition

Market in which many consumers buy standardized products from numerous small businesses.

demand

Quantity of a product that buyers are willing to purchase at various prices.

FIGURE 1.6 The Demand Curve

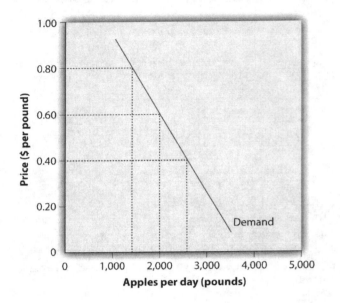

Using this logic, we can construct a **demand curve** that shows the quantity of a product that will be demanded at different prices. Let's assume that the diagram in Figure 1.6 represents the daily price and quantity of apples sold by farmers at a local market. Note that as the price of apples goes down, buyers' demand goes up. Thus, if a pound of apples sells for $0.80, buyers will be willing to purchase only fifteen hundred pounds per day. But if apples cost only $0.60 a pound, buyers will be willing to purchase two thousand pounds. At $0.40 a pound, buyers will be willing to purchase twenty-five hundred pounds.

demand curve

Graph showing the quantity of a product that will be bought at certain prices.

Supply and the Supply Curve

Supply is the quantity of a product that sellers are willing to sell at various prices. The quantity of a product that a business is willing to sell depends on its price. Businesses are *more* willing to sell a product when the price *rises* and *less* willing to sell it when prices *fall*. Again, this fact makes sense: businesses are set up to make profits, and there are larger profits to be made when prices are high.

supply

Quantity of a product that sellers are willing to sell at various prices.

FIGURE 1.7 The Supply Curve

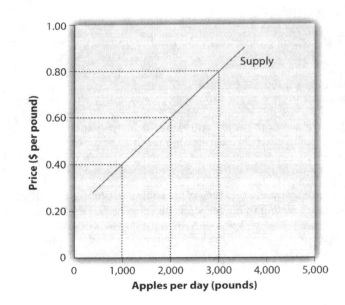

Now we can construct a **supply curve** that shows the quantity of apples that farmers would be willing to sell at different prices, regardless of demand. As you can see in Figure 1.7, the supply curve goes in the opposite direction from the demand curve: as prices rise, the quantity of apples that farmers are willing to sell also goes up. The supply curve shows that farmers are willing to sell only a thousand pounds of apples when the price is $0.40 a pound, two thousand pounds when the price is $0.60, and three thousand pounds when the price is $0.80.

Equilibrium Price

We can now see how the market mechanism works under perfect competition. We do this by plotting both the supply curve and the demand curve on one graph, as we've done in Figure 1.8. The point at which the two curves intersect is the **equilibrium price**. At this point, buyers' demand for apples and sellers' supply of apples is in equilibrium.

FIGURE 1.8   The Equilibrium Price

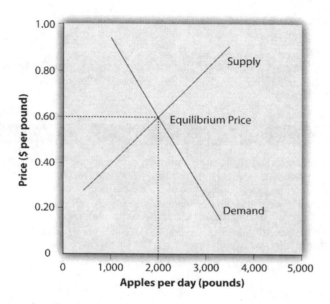

You can see in Figure 1.8 that the supply and demand curves intersect at the price of $0.60 and quantity of two thousand pounds. Thus, $0.60 is the equilibrium price: at this price, the quantity of apples demanded by buyers equals the quantity of apples that farmers are willing to supply. If a farmer tries to charge more than $0.60 for a pound of apples, he won't sell very many and his profits will go down. If, on the other hand, a farmer tries to charge less than the equilibrium price of $0.60 a pound, he will sell more apples but his profit per pound will be less than at the equilibrium price.

What have we learned in this discussion? We've learned that without outside influences, markets in an environment of perfect competition will arrive at an equilibrium point at which both buyers and sellers are satisfied. But we must be aware that this is a very simplistic example. Things are much more complex in the real world. For one thing, markets rarely operate without outside influences. Sometimes, sellers supply more of a product than buyers are willing to purchase; in that case, there's a *surplus*. Sometimes, they don't produce enough of a product to satisfy demand; then we have a *shortage*.

Circumstances also have a habit of changing. What would happen, for example, if income rose and buyers were willing to pay more for apples? The demand curve would change, resulting in an increase in equilibrium price. This outcome makes intuitive sense: as demand increases, prices will go up. What would happen if apple crops were larger than expected because of favorable weather conditions? Farmers might be willing to sell apples at lower prices. If so, the supply curve would shift, resulting in another change in equilibrium price: the increase in supply would bring down prices.

supply curve

Graph showing the quantity of a product that will be offered for sale at certain prices.

equilibrium price

Price at which buyers are willing to buy exactly the amount that sellers are willing to sell.

KEY TAKEAWAYS

- In a free market system, buyers and sellers interact in a market to set prices.
- When the market is characterized by **perfect competition**, many small companies sell identical products. Because no company is large enough to control price, each simply accepts the market price. The price is determined by supply and demand.
- **Supply** is the quantity of a product that sellers are willing to sell at various prices.
- **Demand** is the quantity of a product that buyers are willing to purchase at various prices.
- The quantity of a product that people will buy depends on its price: they'll buy more when the price is low and less when it's high.
- Price also influences the quantity of a product that producers are willing to supply: they'll sell more of a product when prices are high and less when they're low.
- In a competitive market, the decisions of buyers and sellers interact until the market reaches an **equilibrium price**—the price at which buyers are willing to buy the same amount that sellers are willing to sell.

Before going to the next section of this chapter, take a few minutes to test your knowledge of the material covered in this section. Quizzes can be found under the "Resources" tab, "Study Aids: Quizzes."

EXERCISE

You just ran across three interesting statistics: (1) the world's current supply of oil is estimated by some to be 1.3 trillion barrels; (2) the worldwide use of oil is thirty billion barrels a year; and (3) at this rate of consumption, we'll run out of oil in forty-three years. Overcoming an initial sense of impending catastrophe, you remember the discussion of supply and demand in this chapter and realize that things aren't as simple as they seem. After all, many factors affect both the supply of oil and the demand for products made from it, such as gasoline. These factors will influence when (and if) the world runs out of oil. Answer the following questions, and provide explanations for your answers:

a. What's the major factor that affects the *supply* of oil? (*Hint*: It's the same major factor affecting the *demand* for oil.)

b. If producers find additional oil reserves, what will happen to the price of oil?

c. If producers must extract oil from more-costly wells, what will happen to the price that you pay to fill up your gas tank?

d. If China's economy continues to expand rapidly, what will happen to the price of oil?

e. If drivers in the United States start favoring fuel-efficient cars over SUVs, will gas be cheaper or more expensive?

f. In your opinion, will oil producers be able to supply enough oil to meet the increasing demand for oil-related products, such as gasoline?

5. MONOPOLISTIC COMPETITION, OLIGOPOLY, AND MONOPOLY

LEARNING OBJECTIVES

1. Describe monopolistic competition, oligopoly, and monopoly.
2. Define natural monopolies and legal monopolies, and provide examples of both.

Economists have identified four types of competition—*perfect competition, monopolistic competition, oligopoly,* and *monopoly*. Perfect competition was discussed in the last section; we'll cover the remaining three types of competition here.

5.1 Monopolistic Competition

In **monopolistic competition**, we still have many sellers (as we had under perfect competition). Now, however, they don't sell identical products. Instead, they sell *differentiated* products—products that differ somewhat, or are *perceived* to differ, even though they serve a similar purpose. Products can be differentiated in a number of ways, including quality, style, convenience, location, and brand name. Some people prefer Coke over Pepsi, even though the two products are quite similar. But what if there was a substantial price difference between the two? In that case, buyers could be persuaded to switch from one to the other. Thus, if Coke has a big promotional sale at a supermarket chain, some Pepsi drinkers might switch (at least temporarily).

How is product differentiation accomplished? Sometimes, it's simply geographical; you probably buy gasoline at the station closest to your home regardless of the brand. At other times, perceived differences between products are promoted by advertising designed to convince consumers that one product is different from another—and better than it. Regardless of customer loyalty to a product, however, if its price goes too high, the seller will lose business to a competitor. Under monopolistic competition, therefore, companies have only limited control over price.

monopolistic competition
Market in which many sellers supply differentiated products.

5.2 Oligopoly

Oligopoly means few sellers. In an oligopolistic market, each seller supplies a large portion of all the products sold in the marketplace. In addition, because the cost of starting a business in an oligopolistic industry is usually high, the number of firms entering it is low.

Companies in oligopolistic industries include such large-scale enterprises as automobile companies and airlines. As large firms supplying a sizable portion of a market, these companies have some control over the prices they charge. But there's a catch: because products are fairly similar, when one company lowers prices, others are often forced to follow suit to remain competitive. You see this practice all the time in the airline industry: When American Airlines announces a fare decrease, Continental, United Airlines, and others do likewise. When one automaker offers a special deal, its competitors usually come up with similar promotions.

oligopoly
Market in which a few sellers supply a large portion of all the products sold in the marketplace.

5.3 Monopoly

In terms of the number of sellers and degree of competition, monopolies lie at the opposite end of the spectrum from perfect competition. In perfect competition, there are many small companies, none of which can control prices; they simply accept the market price determined by supply and demand. In a **monopoly**, however, there's only one seller in the market. The market could be a geographical area, such as a city or a regional area, and doesn't necessarily have to be an entire country.

There are few monopolies in the United States because the government limits them. Most fall into one of two categories: *natural* and *legal*. **Natural monopolies** include public utilities, such as electricity and gas suppliers. Such enterprises require huge investments, and it would be inefficient to duplicate the products that they provide. They inhibit competition, but they're legal because they're important to society. In exchange for the right to conduct business without competition, they're regulated. For instance, they can't charge whatever prices they want, but they must adhere to government-controlled prices. As a rule, they're required to serve all customers, even if doing so isn't cost efficient.

A **legal monopoly** arises when a company receives a patent giving it exclusive use of an invented product or process. Patents are issued for a limited time, generally twenty years.[12] During this period, other companies can't use the invented product or process without permission from the patent holder. Patents allow companies a certain period to recover the heavy costs of researching and developing products and technologies. A classic example of a company that enjoyed a patent-based legal monopoly is Polaroid, which for years held exclusive ownership of instant-film technology.[13] Polaroid priced the product high enough to recoup, over time, the high cost of bringing it to market. Without competition, in other words, it enjoyed a monopolistic position in regard to pricing.

monopoly
Market in which there is only one seller supplying products at regulated prices.

natural monopoly
Monopoly in which, because of the industry's importance to society, one seller is permitted to supply products without competition.

legal monopoly
Monopoly in which one seller supplies a product or technology to which it holds a patent.

Types of Competition

Take a moment to complete an exercise that reinforces what you've learned about the characteristics of various forms of competition.

Before going to the next section of this chapter, take a few minutes to test your knowledge of the material covered in this section. Quizzes can be found under the "Resources" tab, "Study Aids: Quizzes."

EXERCISE

Identify the four types of competition, explain the differences among them, and provide two examples of each. (Use examples different from those given in the text.)

6. MEASURING THE HEALTH OF THE ECONOMY

LEARNING OBJECTIVES

1. Understand the criteria used to assess the status of the economy.
2. Identify the three major goals shared by all economies, and indicate how they are measured.
3. Distinguish between inflation and deflation.
4. Explain how the consumer price index (CPI) is calculated and what it measures.
5. Define the terms "leading indicator" and "lagging indicator," and provide an example of each indicator.

Every day, we are bombarded with economic news. We're told that the economy is improving but at a mediocre rate; unemployment is decreasing, but those unemployed more than six months are having a very hard time finding jobs; home prices are rising; and consumer confidence is heading up. As a student learning about business, and later as a business manager, you need to understand the nature of the U.S. economy and the terminology that we use to describe it. You need to have some idea of where the economy is heading, and you need to know something about the government's role in influencing its direction.

6.1 Economic Goals

All the world's economies share three main goals:

1. Growth
2. High employment
3. Price stability

Let's take a closer look at each of these goals, both to find out what they mean and to show how we determine whether they're being met.

Economic Growth

One purpose of an economy is to provide people with goods and services—cars, computers, video games, houses, rock concerts, fast food, amusement parks. One way in which economists measure the performance of an economy is by looking at a widely used measure of total output called **gross domestic product (GDP)**. GDP is defined as the market value of all goods and services produced by the economy in a given year. In the United States, it's calculated by the Department of Commerce. GDP includes only those goods and services produced domestically; goods produced outside the country are excluded. GDP also includes only those goods and services that are produced for the final user; intermediate products are excluded. For example, the silicon chip that goes into a computer (an intermediate product) would not count, even though the finished computer would.

By itself, GDP doesn't necessarily tell us much about the state of the economy. But *change* in GDP does. If GDP (after adjusting for inflation) goes up, the economy is growing. If it goes down, the economy is contracting.

The Business Cycle

The economic ups and downs resulting from expansion and contraction constitute the **business cycle**. A typical cycle runs from three to five years but could last much longer. Though typically irregular, a cycle can be divided into four general phases of *prosperity*, *recession*, *depression* (which the cycle generally skips), and *recovery*:

- During *prosperity*, the economy expands, unemployment is low, incomes rise, and consumers buy more products. Businesses respond by increasing production and offering new and better products.
- Eventually, however, things slow down. GDP decreases, unemployment rises, and because people have less money to spend, business revenues decline. This slowdown in economic activity is called a **recession**. Economists often say that we're entering a recession when GDP goes down for two consecutive quarters.
- Generally, a recession is followed by a *recovery* in which the economy starts growing again.
- If, however, a recession lasts a long time (perhaps a decade or so), while unemployment remains very high and production is severely curtailed, the economy could sink into a **depression**. Though not impossible, it's unlikely that the United States will experience another severe depression like that of the 1930s. The federal government has a number of economic tools (some of which we'll discuss shortly) with which to fight any threat of a depression.

Full Employment

To keep the economy going strong, people must spend money on goods and services. A reduction in personal expenditures for things like food, clothing, appliances, automobiles, housing, and medical care could severely reduce GDP and weaken the economy. Because most people earn their spending money by working, an important goal of all economies is making jobs available to everyone who wants one. In principle, **full employment** occurs when everyone who wants to work has a job. In practice, we say that we have "full employment" when about 95 percent of those wanting to work are employed.

The Unemployment Rate

The U.S. Department of Labor tracks unemployment and reports the **unemployment rate**—the percentage of the labor force that's unemployed and actively seeking work. The unemployment rate, which was 6.7 percent in March 2014, is an important measure of economic health. It goes up during recessionary periods because companies are reluctant to hire workers when demand for goods and services is low. Conversely, it goes down when the economy is expanding and there is high demand for products and workers to supply them. Figure 1.10 traces the U.S. unemployment rate between 1970 and 2013.

gross domestic product (GDP)

Measure of the market value of all goods and services produced by a nation's economy in a given year.

business cycle

Pattern of expansion and contraction in an economy.

recession

Economic slowdown measured by a decline in gross domestic productivity.

FIGURE 1.9

© *Thinkstock*

depression

Severe, long-lasting recession.

full employment

Condition under which about 95 percent of those who want to work are employed.

unemployment rate

Percentage of the total labor force that's currently unemployed and actively seeking work.

FIGURE 1.10   The U.S. Unemployment Rate, 1970–2013

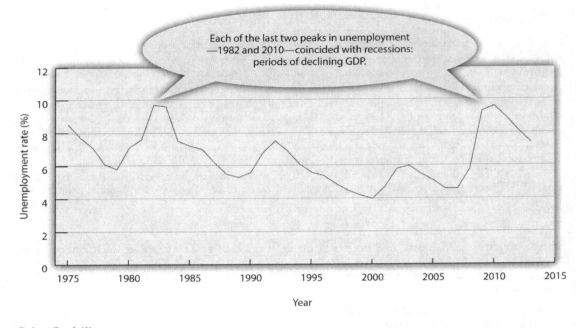

Price Stability

A third major goal of all economies is maintaining **price stability**. Price stability occurs when the average of the prices for goods and services either doesn't change or changes very little. Rising prices are troublesome for both individuals and businesses. For individuals, rising prices mean you have to pay more for the things you need. For businesses, rising prices mean higher costs, and, at least in the short run, businesses might have trouble passing on higher costs to consumers. When the overall price level goes up, we have **inflation**. Figure 1.11 shows inflationary trends in the U.S. economy since 1960. When the price level goes down (which rarely happens), we have **deflation**.

FIGURE 1.11   The U.S. Inflation Rate, 1960–2013

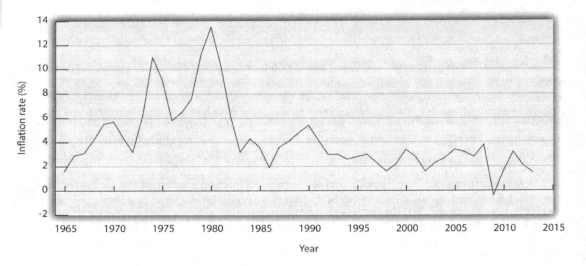

The Consumer Price Index

The most widely publicized measure of inflation is the **consumer price index (CPI)**, which is reported monthly by the Bureau of Labor Statistics. The CPI, which stood at 1.5 percent in March 2014, measures the rate of inflation by determining price changes of a hypothetical basket of goods, such as food, housing, clothing, medical care, appliances, automobiles, and so forth, bought by a typical household.

The CPI base period is 1982 to 1984, which has been given an average value of 100. Table 1.1 gives CPI values computed for selected years. The CPI value for 1950, for instance, is 24. This means that $1 of typical purchases in 1982 through 1984 would have cost $0.24 in 1950. Conversely, you would have needed $2.37 to purchase the same $1 worth of typical goods in 2014. The difference registers the effect of inflation over more than thirty years. In fact, that's what an *inflation rate* is—*the percentage change in a price index.*

TABLE 1.1 Selected Inflation Rates, 1960–2014

Year	1960	1970	1980	1990	2000	2001	2002	2003	2004	2005
CPI	29.1	38.8	82.4	130.7	172.2	177.1	179.9	184.0	188.9	195.3
Year	2006	2007	2008	2009	2010	2011	2012	2013	2014	
CPI	201.6	207.3	215.3	214.2	218.1	224.9	229.6	233.0	237.1	

6.2 Economic Forecasting

In Section 1.6, we introduced several measures that economists use to assess the performance of the economy at a given time. By looking at changes in GDP, for instance, we can see whether the economy is growing. The CPI allows us to gauge inflation. These measures help us understand where the economy stands today. But what if we want to get a sense of where it's headed in the future? To a certain extent, we can forecast future economic trends by analyzing several leading economic indicators.

Economic Indicators

An **economic indicator** is a statistic that provides valuable information about the economy. There's no shortage of economic indicators, and trying to follow them all would be an overwhelming task. Thus, economists and businesspeople track only a select few, including those that we'll now discuss.

economic indicator

Statistic that provides information about trends in the economy.

Lagging and Leading Indicators

Statistics that report the status of the economy a few months in the past are called **lagging economic indicators**. One such indicator is *average length of unemployment*. If unemployed workers have remained out of work for a long time, we may infer that the economy has been slow. Indicators that predict the status of the economy three to twelve months in the future are called **leading economic indicators**. If such an indicator rises, the economy is likely to expand in the coming year. If it falls, the economy is likely to contract.

lagging economic indicator

Statistical data that measure economic trends after the overall economy has changed.

leading economic indicator

Statistical data that predict the status of the economy three to twelve months in the future.

To predict where the economy is headed, we obviously must examine several leading indicators. It's also helpful to look at indicators from various sectors of the economy—labor, manufacturing, and housing. One useful indicator of the outlook for future jobs is the number of new *claims for unemployment insurance*. This measure tells us how many people recently lost their jobs. If it's rising, it signals trouble ahead because unemployed consumers can't buy as many goods and services as they could if they had paychecks.

To gauge the level of goods to be produced in the future (which will translate into future sales), economists look at a statistic called *average weekly manufacturing hours*. This measure tells us the average number of hours worked per week by production workers in manufacturing industries. If it's on the rise, the economy will probably improve. For assessing the strength of the housing market, *building permits* is often a good indicator. An increase in this statistic—which tells us how many new housing units are being built—indicates that the economy is improving. Why? Because increased building brings money into the economy not only through new home sales but also through sales of furniture and appliances to furnish them.

Finally, if you want a measure that combines all these economic indicators, as well as others, a private research firm called the Conference Board publishes a U.S. *leading index.*

Consumer Confidence Index

The Conference Board also publishes a **consumer confidence index** based on results of a monthly survey of five thousand U.S. households. The survey gathers consumers' opinions on the health of the economy and their plans for future purchases. It's often a good indicator of consumers' future buying intent. Consumer confidence rose to its highest level in six years in March 2014, a sign that consumers are optimistic about the economy's future and that spending will increase.[14]

consumer confidence index

Measure of optimism that consumers express about the economy as they go about their everyday lives.

KEY TAKEAWAY

1. All economies share three goals: growth, high employment, and price stability.

   - *Growth*. An economy provides people with goods and services, and economists measure its performance by studying the **gross domestic product (GDP)**—the market value of all goods and services produced by the economy in a given year.
   - If GDP goes up, the economy is growing; if it goes down, the economy is contracting.
   - *High employment*. Because most people earn their money by working, a goal of all economies is making jobs available to everyone who wants one.
   - The U.S. government reports an **unemployment rate**—the percentage of the labor force that's unemployed and actively seeking work.
   - The unemployment rate goes up during recessionary periods and down when the economy is expanding.
   - *Price stability*. When the average prices of products either don't change or change very little, **price stability** occurs.
   - When overall prices go up, we have **inflation**; when they go down, we have **deflation**.
   - The **consumer price index (CPI)** measures inflation by determining the change in prices of a hypothetical basket of goods bought by a typical household.
   - To get a sense of where the economy is headed in the future, we use statistics called **economic indicators**.
   - Indicators that, like *average length of unemployment*, report the status of the economy a few months in the past are **lagging economic indicators**.
   - Those, like *new claims for unemployment insurance*, that predict the status of the economy three to twelve months in the future are **leading economic indicators**.

Before going to the next section of this chapter, take a few minutes to test your knowledge of the material covered in this section. Quizzes can be found under the "Resources" tab, "Study Aids: Quizzes."

EXERCISES

1. Congratulations! You entered a sweepstakes and won a fantastic prize: a trip around the world. There's only one catch: you have to study the economy of each country (from the list below) that you visit, and identify the current phase of its business cycle. Be sure to explain your responses.

   - *Country 1*. While the landscape is beautiful and the weather is superb, a lot of people seem unhappy. Business is slow, and production has dropped steadily for the past six months. Revenues are down, companies are laying off workers, and there's less money around to spend.
   - *Country 2*. Here, people are happily busy. Almost everyone has a job and makes a good income. They spend freely, and businesses respond by offering a steady outflow of new products.
   - *Country 3*. Citizens of this country report that, for a while, life had been tough; lots of people were jobless, and money was tight. But things are getting much better. Workers are being called back to their jobs, production is improving, and people are spending again.
   - *Country 4*. This place makes you so depressed that you can't wait to get back home. People seem defeated, mostly because many have been without jobs for a long time. Lots of businesses have closed down, and those that have managed to stay open are operating at reduced capacity.

2. What are the three main economic goals of most economies, including the economy of the United States? What economic measures do we examine to determine whether or how well these goals are being met?

7. GOVERNMENT'S ROLE IN MANAGING THE ECONOMY

LEARNING OBJECTIVES

1. Discuss the government's role in managing the economy.
2. Distinguish between monetary policy and fiscal policy, and explain how each type of policy is used to influence the United States' economic performance.
3. Identify the actions taken by the Federal Reserve (Fed) to counter inflation.
4. Identify and describe the type of policy used by the Fed to pull the country out of a recession.
5. Define the terms "surplus" and "deficit."
6. Explain the difference between macroeconomics and microeconomics.

In every country, the government takes steps to help the economy achieve the goals of growth, full employment, and price stability. In the United States, the government influences economic activity through two approaches: monetary policy and fiscal policy. Through **monetary policy**, the government exerts its power to regulate the money supply and level of interest rates. Through **fiscal policy**, it uses its power to tax and to spend.

monetary policy

Efforts exerted by the Federal Reserve System ("the Fed") to regulate the nation's money supply.

fiscal policy

Governmental use of taxation and spending to influence economic conditions.

7.1 Monetary Policy

Monetary policy is exercised by the Federal Reserve System ("the Fed"), which is empowered to take various actions that decrease or increase the money supply and raise or lower short-term interest rates, making it harder or easier to borrow money. When the Fed believes that inflation is a problem, it will use *contractionary policy* to decrease the money supply and raise interest rates. When rates are higher, borrowers have to pay more for the money they borrow, and banks are more selective in making loans. Because money is "tighter"—more expensive to borrow—demand for goods and services will go down, and so will prices. In any case, that's the theory.

To counter a recession, the Fed uses *expansionary policy* to increase the money supply and reduce interest rates. With lower interest rates, it's cheaper to borrow money, and banks are more willing to lend it. We then say that money is "easy." Attractive interest rates encourage businesses to borrow money to expand production and encourage consumers to buy more goods and services. In theory, both sets of actions will help the economy escape or come out of a recession.

FIGURE 1.12

The Fed will typically tighten or decrease the money supply during inflationary periods, making it harder to borrow money.

7.2 Fiscal Policy

Fiscal policy relies on the government's powers of spending and taxation. Both taxation and government spending can be used to reduce or increase the total supply of money in the economy—the total amount, in other words, that businesses and consumers have to spend. When the country is in a recession, the appropriate policy is to increase spending, reduce taxes, or both. Such expansionary actions will put more money in the hands of businesses and consumers, encouraging businesses to expand and consumers to buy more goods and services. When the economy is experiencing inflation, the opposite policy is adopted: the government will decrease spending or increase taxes, or both. Because such contractionary measures reduce spending by businesses and consumers, prices come down and inflation eases.

© 2010 Jupiterimages Corporation

7.3 The National Debt

If, in any given year, the government takes in more money (through taxes) than it spends on goods and services (for things such as defense, transportation, and social services), the result is a budget *surplus*. If, on the other hand, the government spends more than it takes in, we have a budget *deficit* (which the government pays off by borrowing through the issuance of Treasury bonds). Historically, deficits have occurred much more often than surpluses; typically, the government spends more than it takes in. Consequently, the U.S. government now has a total **national debt** of more than $14 *trillion*.

national debt

Total amount of money owed by the federal government.

As you can see in Figure 1.13, this number has risen dramatically in the last seventy years. The significant jump that starts in the 1980s reflects several factors: a big increase in government spending (especially on defense), a substantial rise in interest payments on the debt, and lower tax rates. As of this writing, your share is $58,333. If you want to see what the national debt is today—and what your current share is—go on the Web to the U.S. National Debt Clock (http://www.brillig.com/debt_clock).

FIGURE 1.13 The U.S. National Debt, 1940–2013

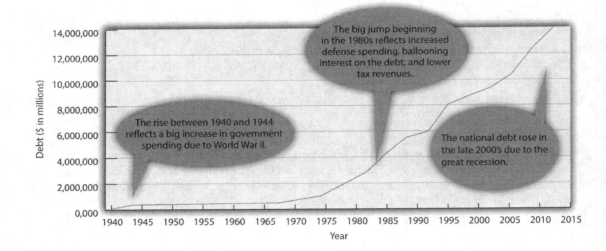

7.4 Macroeconomics and Microeconomics

In the preceding discussion, we've touched on two main areas in the field of economics: (1) *macroeconomics*, or the study of the economy as a whole, and (2) *microeconomics*, or the study of the economic choices made by individual consumers or businesses. Macroeconomics examines the economy-wide effect of inflation, while microeconomics considers such decisions as the price you're willing to pay to go to college. Macroeconomics investigates overall trends in imports and exports, while microeconomics explains the price that teenagers are willing to pay for concert tickets. Though they are often regarded as separate branches of economics, we can gain a richer understanding of the economy by studying issues from both perspectives. As we've seen in this chapter, for instance, you can better understand the overall level of activity in an economy (a macro issue) through an understanding of supply and demand (a micro issue).

KEY TAKEAWAYS

- The U.S. government uses two types of policies—monetary policy and fiscal policy—to influence economic performance. Both have the same purpose: to help the economy achieve growth, full employment, and price stability.
- **Monetary policy** is used to control the money supply and interest rates.
- It's exercised through an independent government agency called the Federal Reserve System ("the Fed"), which has the power to control the money supply and interest rates.
- When the Fed believes that inflation is a problem, it will use *contractionary policy* to decrease the money supply and raise interest rates. To counter a recession, it will use *expansionary policy* to increase the money supply and reduce interest rates.
- **Fiscal policy** uses the government's power to spend and tax.
- When the country is in a recession, the government will increase spending, reduce taxes, or do both to expand the economy.
- When we're experiencing inflation, the government will decrease spending or increase taxes, or both.
- When the government takes in more money in a given year (through taxes) than it spends, the result is a *surplus*.
- When the opposite happens—government spends more money than it takes in—we have a *deficit*.
- The cumulative sum of deficits is the **national debt**—the total amount of money owed by the federal government.

Before going to the next chapter, take a few minutes to test your knowledge of the material covered in this section. Quizzes can be found under the "Resources" tab, "Study Aids: Quizzes."

EXERCISES

1. Let's say that you're the Fed chairperson and that the country is in a recession. What actions should the Fed take to pull the country out of the recession? What would you advise government officials to do to improve the economy? Justify your recommendations.

2. Browsing through your college's catalog, you notice that all business majors must take two economics courses: macroeconomics and microeconomics. Explain what's covered in each of these courses. In what ways will the things you learn in each course help you in the future?

8. CASES AND PROBLEMS

LEARNING ON THE WEB

The "Economy" section of the CNNMoney Web site provides current information on a number of economic indicators. Go to http://money.cnn.com and click on "Economy" and then on "Jobs," and find answers to the following questions:

1. You read in the chapter that an important goal of all economies is to make jobs available to everyone who wants one. Review the discussion on job growth in "An Economy that Works: Job Creation and America's Future" (http://www.mckinsey.com/insights/employment_and_growth/ an_economy_that_works_for_us_job_creation), and then answer the following questions:

    a. Is the current level of unemployment rising or falling?

    b. What do economists expect will happen to unemployment rates in the near future?

    c. Is the current level of unemployment a burden or an asset to the economy? In what ways?

2. Do you remember the first dollar you earned? Maybe you earned it delivering newspapers, shoveling snow, mowing lawns, or babysitting. How much do you think that dollar is worth today? Go to the WestEgg site at http://www.westegg.com/inflation and find the answer to this question. After determining the current value of your first dollar, explain how the calculator was created. (Hint: Apply what you know about CPI.)

CAREER OPPORTUNITIES

Is a Career in Economics for You?

Are you wondering what a career in economics would be like? Go to the U.S. Department of Labor Web site (http://www.bls.gov/ooh/life-physical-and-social-science/economists.htm) and review the occupational outlook for economists. Look for answers to the following questions:

1. What issues interest economists?

2. What kinds of jobs do government economists perform? What about those who work in private industry? In education?

3. What educational background and training is needed for these jobs?

4. What is the current job outlook for economists?

5. What is the entry-level salary for an economist with a bachelor's degree? With a master's degree?

ETHICS ANGLE

How Much Is That CD in the Window?

The early 1990s were a good time to buy CDs, mainly because discounters such as Wal-Mart and Best Buy were accumulating customers by dropping prices from $15 to $10. They were losing money, but they figured that the policy still made good business sense. Why? They reasoned that while customers were in the store to shop for CDs, they'd find other, more profitable products.

The policy was a windfall for CD buyers, but a real problem for traditional music retailers such as Tower Records. With discounters slashing prices, CD buyers were no longer willing to pay the prices asked by traditional music retailers. Sales plummeted and companies went out of business.

Ultimately, the discounters' strategy worked: stores such as Wal-Mart and Best Buy gained customers who once bought CDs at stores like Tower Records.

Let's pause at this point to answer the following questions:

1. Does selling a product at below cost make business sense?
2. Whom does it hurt? Whom does it help?
3. Is it ethical?

Let's continue and find out how traditional music retailers responded to this situation.

They weren't happy, and neither were the record companies. Both parties worried that traditional retailers would put pressure on them to reduce the price that they charged for CDs so that retailers could lower their prices and compete with discounters. The record companies didn't want to lower prices. They just wanted things to return to "normal"—to the world in which CDs sold for $15 each.

Most of the big record companies and several traditional music retailers got together and made a deal affecting every store that sold CDs. The record companies agreed with retail chains and other CD outlets to charge a minimum advertised price for CDs. Any retailer who broke ranks by advertising below-price CDs would incur substantial financial penalties. Naturally, CD prices went up.

Now, think about the following:

1. Does the deal made between the record companies and traditional retailers make business sense?
2. Whom does it hurt? Whom does it help?
3. Is it ethical?
4. Is it legal?

TEAM-BUILDING SKILLS

Get together in groups of four selected by your instructor and pick any three items from the following list:

- Pint of milk
- Gallon of gas
- Roundtrip airline ticket between Boston and San Francisco
- Large pizza
- Monthly cost of an Internet connection
- CD by a particular musician
- Two-day DVD rental
- Particular brand of DVD player
- Quarter-pound burger

Outside of class, each member of the team should check the prices of the three items, using his or her own sources. At the next class meeting, get together and compare the prices found by team members. Based on your findings, answer the following questions as a group:

1. Are the prices of given products similar, or do they vary?
2. Why do the prices of some products vary while those of others are similar?
3. Can any price differences be explained by applying the concepts of supply and demand or types of competition?

THE GLOBAL VIEW

Life Is Good in France (if You Have *Le Job***)**

A strong economy requires that people have money to spend on goods and services. Because most people earn their money by working, an important goal of all economies is making jobs available to everyone who wants one. A country has "full employment" when 95 percent of those wanting work are employed. Unfortunately, not all countries achieve this goal of full employment. France, for example, often has a 10 percent unemployment rate overall and a 20 percent unemployment rate among young people.

Does this mean that France isn't trying as hard as the United States to achieve full employment? A lot of people in France would say yes.

Let's take a quick trip to France to see what's going on economically. The day is March 19, 2006, and more than a million people are marching through the streets to protest a proposed new employment law that would make it easier for companies to lay off workers under the age of twenty-six during their first two years of employment. Granted, the plan doesn't sound terribly youth-friendly, but, as usual, economic issues are never as clear-cut as they seem (or as we'd like them to be).

To gain some further insight into what's going on in France, go to a *BusinessWeek* Web site (http://www.businessweek.com/globalbiz/content/mar2006/gb20060321_896473.htm) and read the article "Job Security Ignites Debate in France." Then answer the following questions:

1. Why does the French government support the so-called First Employment Contract? Who's supposed to be helped by the law?

2. Which two groups are most vocal in protesting the law? Why?

3. If you were a long-time worker at a French company, would you support the new law? Why, or why not?

4. If you were a young French person who had just graduated from college and were looking for your first job, would you support the law? Why, or why not?

5. What do you think of France's focus on job security? Does the current system help or hurt French workers? Does it help or hurt recent college graduates?

6. Does the French government's focus on job security help or hinder its economy? Should the government be so heavily involved in employment matters?

ENDNOTES

1. This vignette is based on an honors thesis written by Danielle M. Testa, "Apple, Inc.: An Analysis of the Firm's Tumultuous History, in Conjunction with the Abounding Future" (Lehigh University), November 18, 2007.

2. Ellen Lee, "Faithful, Sometimes Fanatical Apple Customers Continue to Push the Boundaries of Loyalty," *San Francisco Chronicle*, March 26, 2006.

3. Lee Angelelli, "Steve Paul Jobs," http://ei.cs.vt.edu/~history/Jobs.html (accessed April 21, 2014).

4. Lee Angelelli, "Steve Paul Jobs," http://ei.cs.vt.edu/~history/Jobs.html (accessed April 21, 2014).

5. Cyrus Farivar, "Apple's First 30 Years: Three Decades of Contributions to the Computer Industry," *Macworld*, June 2006, 2.

6. Dan Barkin, "He Made the iPod: How Steve Jobs of Apple Created the New Millennium's Signature Invention," *Knight Ridder Tribune Business News*, December 3, 2006, 1.

7. Jon Hilsenrath, Serena Ng, and Damian Paletta, "Worst Crisis Since '30s, With No End Yet in Sight," *Wall Street Journal*, Markets, September 18, 2008, http://online.wsj.com/news/articles/SB122169431617549947 (accessed April 21, 2014).

8. "How the Economy Stole the Election," *CNN.com*, http://money.cnn.com/galleries/2008/news/0810/gallery.economy_election/index.html (accessed April 21, 2014).

9. Dan Gallagher, "Analyst Says Apple Is Cutting Back Production as Economy Weakens," *MarketWatch*, November 3, 2008, http://www.marketwatch.com/news/story/apple-cutting-back-iphone-production/story.aspx?guid={7F2B6F99-D063-4005-87AD-D8C36009F29B}&dist=msr_1 (accessed April 21, 2014).

10. David Baron, "Facing-Off in Public," *Stanford Business*, April 15, 2006, https://www.stanford.edu/group/knowledgebase/cgi-bin/2003/08/15/facing-off-in-public (accessed April 21, 2014).

11. According to many scholars, *The Wealth of Nations* not only is the most influential book on free-market capitalism but remains relevant today.

12. United States Patent and Trademark Office, *General Information Concerning Patents*, April 15, 2006, http://www.uspto.gov/web/offices/pac/doc/general/index.html#laws (accessed April 21, 2014).

13. Mary Bellis, "Inventors-Edwin Land-Polaroid Photography-Instant Photography/Patents," April 15, 2006, http://inventors.about.com/library/inventors/blpolaroid.htm (accessed April 21, 2014).

14. Katherine Peralta, "Consumer Confidence in U.S. Rises to Six-Year High," *Bloomberg News*, March 25, 2014, http://www.bloomberg.com/news/2014-03-25/consumer-confidence-index-in-u-s-increased-to-82-3-in-march.html (accessed April 22, 2014).

CHAPTER 2

Business Ethics and Social Responsibility

"MOMMY, WHY DO YOU HAVE TO GO TO JAIL?"

The one question Betty Vinson would prefer to avoid is "Mommy, why do you have to go to jail?"[1] Vinson gradu-ated with an accounting degree from Mississippi State and married her college sweetheart. After a series of jobs at small banks, she landed a midlevel accounting job at WorldCom, at the time still a small long-distance provider. Sparked by the telecom boom, however, WorldCom soon became a darling of Wall Street, and its stock price soared. Now working for a wildly successful company, Vinson rounded out her life by reading legal thrillers and watching her twelve-year-old daughter play soccer.

Her moment of truth came in mid-2000, when company executives learned that profits had plummeted. They asked Vinson to make some accounting adjustments to boost income by $828 million. She knew that the scheme was unethical (at the very least) but gave in and made the adjustments. Almost immediately, she felt guilty and told her boss that she was quitting. When news of her decision came to the attention of CEO Bernard Ebbers and CFO Scott Sullivan, they hastened to assure Vinson that she'd never be asked to cook any more books. Sullivan explained it this way: "We have planes in the air. Let's get the planes landed. Once they've landed, if you still want to leave, then leave. But not while the planes are in the air."[2] Besides, she'd done nothing illegal, and if anyone asked, he'd take full responsibility. So Vinson decided to stay. After all, Sullivan was one of the top CFOs in the country; at age thirty-seven, he was already making $19 million a year.[3] Who was she to question his judgment?[4]

Six months later, Ebbers and Sullivan needed another adjustment—this time for $771 million. This scheme was even more unethical than the first: It entailed forging dates to hide the adjustment. Pretty soon, Vinson was making adjustments on a quarterly basis—first for $560 million, then for $743 million, and yet again for $941 million. Even-tually, Vinson had juggled almost $4 billion, and before long, the stress started to get to her: She had trouble sleep-ing, lost weight, looked terrible, and withdrew from people at work. But when she got a promotion and a $30,000 raise, she decided to hang in.

By spring 2002, however, it was obvious that adjusting the books was business as usual at WorldCom. Vinson finally decided that it was time to move on, but, unfortunately, an internal auditor had already put two and two to-gether and blown the whistle. The Securities and Exchange Commission charged WorldCom with fraud amounting to $11 billion—the largest in U.S. history. Seeing herself as a valuable witness, Vinson was eager to tell what she knew. The government, however, regarded her as more than a mere witness. When she was named a co-conspirat-or, she agreed to cooperate fully and pleaded guilty to criminal conspiracy and securities fraud. And that's why Betty Vinson spent five months in jail. But she wasn't the only one who did time: Scott Sullivan (who claimed he was innocent) was sent to jail for five years, and Bernie Ebbers (who swore he was innocent also) is locked up for twenty-five years.[5]

WorldCom Inc.'s former director of management, Betty Vinson, leaves Federal Court after pleading guilty to securities fraud October 10, 2002, in New York City.

Photo by Adam Rountree/Getty Images

So where did Betty Vinson, mild-mannered midlevel executive and mother, go wrong? How did she manage to get involved in a scheme that not only bilked investors out of billions but also cost seventeen thousand people their jobs?[6] Ultimately, of course, we can only guess. Maybe she couldn't say no to her bosses; maybe she believed that they'd take full responsibility for her accounting "adjustments." Possibly she was afraid of losing her job. Perhaps she didn't fully understand the ramifications of what she was doing. What we *do* know is that she disgraced herself and headed for jail.[7]

1. MISGOVERNING CORPORATIONS: AN OVERVIEW

LEARNING OBJECTIVES

1. Explain why it's in a company's best interest to act ethically.
2. Define "business ethics," and explain what it means to act ethically in business.
3. Compare and contrast business ethics and social responsibility.
4. Explain how you can recognize an ethical organization.
5. Discuss what is needed for you to act ethically in business situations.
6. Explain why it is important to study business ethics.

The WorldCom situation is not an isolated incident. The boom years of the 1990s were followed by revelations of massive corporate corruption, including criminal schemes at companies such as Enron, Adelphia, and Tyco. In fall 2001, executives at Enron, an energy supplier, admitted to accounting practices concocted to overstate the company's income over a period of four years. In the wake of the company's collapse, stock prices plummeted from $90 to $1 a share, inflicting massive financial losses on the investment community. Thousands of employees lost not only their jobs but their retirement funds, as well.[8] Before the Enron story was off the front pages, officials at Adelphia, the nation's sixth-largest cable company, disclosed that founder and CEO John Rigas had treated the publicly owned firm as a personal piggy bank, siphoning off billions of dollars to support his family's extravagant lifestyle and bankrupting the company in the process.[9] Likewise, CEO Dennis Koslowzki of conglomerate Tyco International was apparently confused about what was his and what belonged to the company. Besides treating himself to a $30 million estate in Florida and a $7 million Park Avenue apartment, Koslowzki indulged in a taste for expensive office accessories—such as a $15,000 umbrella stand, a $17,000 traveling toilette box, and a $2,200 wastebasket—that eventually drained $600 million from company coffers.[10]

As crooked as these CEOs were, Bernie Madoff, founder of Bernard L. Madoff Investment Securities and former chairman of the NASDAQ stock exchange, makes them seem like dime-store shoplifters.[11] Madoff is alleged to have run a giant Ponzi scheme[12] that cheated investors of up to $65 billion. His wrongdoings won him a spot at the top of *Time Magazine*'s Top 10 Crooked CEOs. According to the SEC charges, Madoff convinced investors to give him large sums of money. In return, he gave them an impressive 8 percent to 12 percent return a year. But Madoff never really invested their money. Instead, he kept it for himself. He got funds to pay the first investors their return (or their money back if they asked for it) by bringing in new investors. Everything was going smoothly until the fall of 2008, when the stock market plummeted and many of his investors asked for their money back. As he no longer had their money, the game was over and he had to admit that the whole thing was just one big lie. Thousands of investors, including many of his wealthy friends, not-so-rich retirees who trusted him with their life savings, and charitable foundations, were financially ruined. All those harmed by Madoff either directly or indirectly were pleased when he was sentenced to jail for one-hundred and fifty years.

Are these cases merely aberrations? A *Time*/CNN poll conducted in the midst of all these revelations found that 72 percent of those surveyed don't think so. They believe that breach of investor and employee trust represents an ongoing, long-standing pattern of deceptive behavior by officials at a large number of companies.[13] If they're right, then a lot of questions need to be answered. Why do such incidents happen (and with such apparent regularity)? Who are the usual suspects? How long until the next corporate bankruptcy record is set? What action can be taken—by individuals, organizations, and the government—to discourage such behavior?

1.1   The Idea of Business Ethics

It's in the best interest of a company to operate ethically. Trustworthy companies are better at attracting and keeping customers, talented employees, and capital. Those tainted by questionable ethics suffer from dwindling customer bases, employee turnover, and investor mistrust.

Let's begin this section by addressing one of the questions that we posed previously: What can individuals, organizations, and government agencies do to foster an environment of ethical and socially responsible behavior in business? First, of course, we need to define two terms: *business ethics* and *social responsibility*. They're often used interchangeably, but they don't mean the same thing.

What Is Ethics?

You probably already know what it means to be **ethical**: to know right from wrong and to know when you're practicing one instead of the other. At the risk of oversimplifying, then, we can say that **business ethics** is the application of ethical behavior in a business context. Acting ethically in business means more than simply obeying applicable laws and regulations: It also means being honest, doing no harm to others, competing fairly, and declining to put your own interests above those of your company, its owners, and its workers. If you're in business, you obviously need a strong sense of what's right and what's wrong (not always an easy task). You need the personal conviction to *do* what's right, even if it means doing something that's difficult or personally disadvantageous.

ethical

Ability and willingness to distinguish right from wrong and when you're practicing one or the other.

business ethics

Application of ethical behavior in a business context.

1.2   What Is Social Responsibility?

Corporate social responsibility deals with actions that affect a variety of parties in a company's environment. A socially responsible company shows concern for its **stakeholders**—anyone who, like owners, employees, customers, and the communities in which it does business, has a "stake" or interest in it. We'll discuss corporate responsibility later in the chapter. At this point, we'll focus on ethics.

corporate social responsibility

Approach that an organization takes in balancing its responsibilities toward different stakeholders when making legal, economic, ethical, and social decisions.

stakeholders

Parties who are interested in the activities of a business because they're affected by them.

1.3   How Can You Recognize an Ethical Organization?

One goal of anyone engaged in business should be to foster ethical behavior in the organizational environment. How do we know when an organization is behaving ethically? Most lists of ethical organizational activities include the following criteria:

- Treating employees, customers, investors, and the public fairly
- Making fairness a top priority
- Holding every member personally accountable for his or her action
- Communicating core values and principles to all members
- Demanding and rewarding integrity from all members in all situations[14]

Whether you work for a business or for a nonprofit organization, you probably have a sense of whether your employer is ethical or unethical. Employees at companies that consistently make *Business Ethics* magazine's list of the "100 Best Corporate Citizens" regard the items on the previous list as business as usual in the workplace. Companies that routinely win good-citizenship awards include Intel, Starbucks, and Cisco Systems.[15]

By contrast, employees with the following attitudes tend to suspect that their employers aren't as ethical as they should be:

- They consistently feel uneasy about the work they do.
- They object to the way they're treated.
- They're uncomfortable about the way coworkers are treated.
- They question the appropriateness of management directives and policies.[16]

FIGURE 2.1

In the early 1990s, many Sears automotive customers were surprised by hefty repair bills. Their complaints raised red flags with law-enforcement officials and forced Sears to refund $60 million.

© 2010 Jupiterimages Corporation

In the early 1990s, many workers in Sears automotive service centers shared suspicions about certain policies, including the ways in which they were supposed to deal with customers. In particular, they felt uncomfortable with a new compensation plan that rewarded them for selling alignments, brake jobs, shock absorbers, and other parts and services. Those who met quotas got bonuses; those who didn't were often fired. The results shouldn't be surprising: In their zeal to meet quotas and keep their jobs, some employees misled customers into believing they needed parts and services when, in fact, they were not needed. Before long, Sears was flooded with complaints from customers—as were law-enforcement officials—in more than forty states. Sears denied any intent to deceive customers but was forced not only to eliminate sales commissions but also to pay out $60 million in refunds.

The Cost of Doing Business Unethically

Take a moment to complete an exercise that lets you gain a sense of the cost of unethical and irresponsible behavior to companies and the environment.

1.4 Why Study Ethics?

Ideally, prison terms, heavy fines, and civil suits should put a damper on corporate misconduct, but, unfortunately, many experts suspect that this assumption may be a bit optimistic. Whatever the condition of the ethical environment in the near future, one thing seems clear: The next generation entering business—which includes most of you—will find a world much different than the one that waited for the previous generation. Recent history tells us in no uncertain terms that today's business students, many of whom are tomorrow's business leaders, need a much sharper understanding of the difference between what is and isn't ethically acceptable. As a business student, one of your key tasks is learning how to recognize and deal with the ethical challenges that will confront you.

Moreover, knowing right from wrong will make you more marketable as a job candidate. Asked what he looked for in a new hire, Warren Buffet, the world's most successful investor, replied: "I look for three things. The first is personal integrity, the second is intelligence, and the third is a high energy level." He paused and then added: "But if you don't have the first, the second two don't matter."[17]

KEY TAKEAWAYS

- It's in a company's best interest to act ethically. Trustworthy companies are better able to attract and keep customers, talented employees, and capital.
- **Business ethics** is the application of ethical behavior in a business context.
- Acting ethically in business means more than just obeying laws and regulations. It also means being honest, doing no harm to others, competing fairly, and declining to put your own interests above those of your employer and coworkers.
- To act ethically in business situations, you need a good idea of what's right and wrong (not always an easy task).
- You also need the personal conviction to do what's right even if it means doing something that's difficult or personally disadvantageous.
- Ethical organizations treat employees, customers, investors, and the public fairly. They make fairness a top priority, communicate core values to those in the organization, and demand and reward integrity from all members while holding them accountable for their actions.

Before going to the next section of this chapter, take a few minutes to test your knowledge of the material covered in this section. Quizzes can be found under the "Resources" tab, "Study Aids: Quizzes."

Is Honesty Academic?

Just as businesses have codes of conduct for directing employee behavior in job-related activities, so, too, do colleges and universities have codes of conduct to guide students' academic behavior. They're called various things—*honor codes, academic integrity policies, policies on academic honesty, student codes of conduct*—but they all have the same purpose: to promote academic integrity and to create a fair and ethical environment for all students.

At most schools, information on academic integrity is available from one of the following sources:

- The school Web site (probably under the tab "Dean of Students" or "Student Life")
- The student handbook
- Printed materials available through the Dean of Students' office

Assignment

Locate information on your school's academic integrity policies and answer the following questions:

1. What behaviors violate academic integrity?
2. What happens if you're accused of academic dishonesty?
3. What should you do if you witness an incident of academic dishonesty?

2. THE INDIVIDUAL APPROACH TO ETHICS

LEARNING OBJECTIVES

1. **Compare and contrast the following terms: "ethical dilemma," "ethical decision," and "ethical lapse."**
2. **Specify the steps that you'd take to solve an ethical dilemma and make an ethical decision.**
3. **Identify the questions you should ask yourself to improve your odds of making an ethical choice.**

Betty Vinson didn't start out at WorldCom with the intention of going to jail. She undoubtedly knew what the right behavior was, but the bottom line is that she didn't *do* it. How can you make sure that you do the right thing in the business world? How should you respond to the kinds of challenges that you'll be facing? Because your actions in the business world will be strongly influenced by your moral character, let's begin by assessing your current moral condition. Which of the following best applies to you (select one)?

1. I'm always ethical.
2. I'm mostly ethical.
3. I'm somewhat ethical.
4. I'm seldom ethical.
5. I'm never ethical.

Now that you've placed yourself in one of these categories, here are some general observations. Few people put themselves below the second category. Most of us are ethical most of the time, and most people assign themselves to category number two—"I'm *mostly* ethical." Why don't more people claim that they're *always* ethical? Apparently, most people realize that being ethical all the time takes a great deal of moral energy. If you placed yourself in category number two, ask yourself this question: How can I change my behavior so that I can move up a notch? The answer to this question may be simple. Just ask yourself an easier question: How would I like to be treated in a given situation?[18]

Unfortunately, practicing this philosophy might be easier in your personal life than in the business world. Ethical challenges arise in business because business organizations, especially large ones, have multiple stakeholders and because stakeholders make conflicting demands. Making decisions that affect multiple stakeholders isn't easy even for seasoned managers; and for new entrants to the business world, the task can be extremely daunting. Many managers need years of experience in an organization before they feel comfortable making decisions that affect various stakeholders. You can, however, get a head start in learning how to make ethical decisions by looking at two types of challenges that you'll encounter in the business world: *ethical dilemmas* and *ethical decisions*.

2.1 Addressing Ethical Dilemmas

An **ethical dilemma** is a morally problematic situation: You have to pick between two or more acceptable but often opposing alternatives that are important to different groups. Experts often frame this type of situation as a "right-versus-right" decision. It's the sort of decision that Johnson & Johnson (known as J&J) CEO James Burke had to make in 1982.[19] On September 30, twelve-year-old Mary Kellerman of Chicago died after her parents gave her Extra-Strength Tylenol. That same morning, twenty-seven-year-old Adam Janus, also of Chicago, died after taking Tylenol for minor chest pain. That night, when family members came to console his parents, Adam's brother and his wife took Tylenol from the same bottle and died within forty-eight hours. Over the next two weeks, four more people in Chicago died after taking Tylenol. The actual connection between Tylenol and the series of deaths wasn't made until an off-duty fireman realized from news reports that every victim had taken Tylenol. As consumers panicked, J&J pulled Tylenol off Chicago-area retail shelves. Researchers discovered Tylenol capsules containing large amounts of deadly cyanide. Because the poisoned bottles came from batches originating at different J&J plants, investigators determined that the tampering had occurred after the product had been shipped.

So J&J wasn't at fault. But CEO Burke was still faced with an extremely serious dilemma: Was it possible to respond to the tampering cases without destroying the reputation of a highly profitable brand? Burke had two options:

- He could recall only the lots of Extra-Strength Tylenol that were found to be tainted with cyanide. This was the path followed by Perrier executives in 1991 when they discovered that cases of bottled water had been poisoned with benzine. This option favored J&J financially but possibly put more people at risk.

- Burke could order a nationwide recall of all bottles of Extra-Strength Tylenol. This option would reverse the priority of the stakeholders, putting the safety of the public above stakeholders' financial interests.

Burke opted to recall all 31 million bottles of Extra-Strength Tylenol on the market. The cost to J&J was $100 million, but public reaction was quite positive. Less than six weeks after the crisis began, Tylenol capsules were reintroduced in new tamper-resistant bottles, and by responding quickly and appropriately, J&J was eventually able to restore the Tylenol brand to its previous market position. When Burke was applauded for moral courage, he replied that he'd simply adhered to the long-standing J&J credo that put the interests of customers above those of other stakeholders. His only regret was that the tamperer was never caught.[20]

If you're wondering what your thought process should be if you're confronted with an ethical dilemma, you could do worse than remember the mental steps listed in Figure 2.2—which happen to be the steps that James Burke took in addressing the Tylenol crisis:

1. **Define the problem:** How to respond to the tampering case without destroying the reputation of the Tylenol brand.

2. **Identify feasible options:** (1) Recall only the lots of Tylenol that were found to be tainted with cyanide or (2) order a nationwide recall of all bottles of Extra-Strength Tylenol.

3. **Assess the effect of each option on stakeholders:** Option 1 (recalling only the tainted lots of Tylenol) is cheaper but puts more people at risk. Option 2 (recalling all bottles of Extra-Strength Tylenol) puts the safety of the public above stakeholders' financial interests.

4. **Establish criteria for determining the most appropriate action:** Adhere to the J&J credo, which puts the interests of customers above those of other stakeholders.

5. **Select the best option based on the established criteria:** In 1982, Option 2 was selected, and a nationwide recall of all bottles of Extra-Strength Tylenol was conducted.

FIGURE 2.2 How to Face an Ethical Dilemma

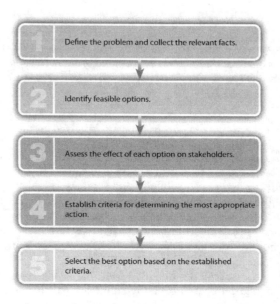

2.2 Making Ethical Decisions

In contrast to the "right-versus-right" problem posed by an ethical dilemma, an **ethical decision** entails a "right-versus-wrong" decision—one in which there is a right (ethical) choice and a wrong (unethical or illegal) choice. When you make a decision that's unmistakably unethical or illegal, you've committed an **ethical lapse**. Betty Vinson, for example, had an ethical lapse when she caved in to her bosses' pressure to cook the WorldCom books. If you're presented with what appears to be this type of choice, asking yourself the questions in Figure 2.3 will increase your odds of making an ethical decision.

ethical decision

Decision in which there is a right (ethical) choice and a wrong (unethical or illegal) choice.

ethical lapse

Situation in which an individual makes a decision that's unmistakably unethical or illegal.

FIGURE 2.3 How to Avoid an Ethical Lapse

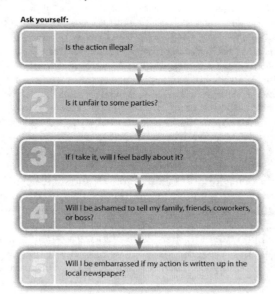

To test the validity of this approach, let's take a point-by-point look at Betty Vinson's decisions:

1. Her actions were clearly illegal.

2. They were unfair to the workers who lost their jobs and to the investors who suffered financial losses (and also to her family, who shared her public embarrassment).

3. She definitely felt bad about what she'd done.

4. She was embarrassed to tell other people what she had done.

5. Reports of her actions appeared in her local newspaper (and just about every other newspaper in the country).

So Vinson could have answered our five test questions with five yeses. To simplify matters, remember the following rule of thumb: If you answer yes to *any one of these five questions*, odds are that you're about to do something you shouldn't.

Revisiting Johnson & Johnson

As discussed earlier in this section, Johnson & Johnson received tremendous praise for the actions taken by its CEO, James Burke, in response to the 1982 Tylenol catastrophe. But things change. To learn how a company can destroy its good reputation, let's fast forward to 2008 and revisit J&J and its credo, which states, "We believe our first responsibility is to the doctors, nurses and patients, to mothers and fathers and all others who use our products and services. In meeting their needs everything we do must be of high quality."[21] How could a company whose employees believed so strongly in its credo find itself under criminal and congressional investigation for a series of recalls due to defective products?[22] In a three-year period, the company recalled twenty-four products, including Children's, Infants' and Adults' Tylenol, Motrin, and Benadryl;[23] 1-Day Acuvue TruEye contact lenses sold outside the U.S.;[24] and hip replacements.[25]

Unlike the 1982 J&J Tylenol recall, no one died from the defective products, but customers were certainly upset to find they had purchased over-the-counter medicines for themselves and their children that were potentially contaminated with dark particles or tiny specks of metal;[26] contact lenses that contained a type of acid that caused stinging or pain when inserted in the eye;[27] and defective hip implants that required patients to undergo a second hip replacement.[28]

Who bears the responsibility for these image-damaging blunders? We'll identify two individuals who were at least partially responsible for the decline of J&J's reputation: The first is the current CEO—William Weldon—who has been criticized for being largely invisible and publicly absent during the recalls.[29] Additionally, he admitted that he did not understand the consumer division where many of the quality control problems originated.[30] Some members of the board of directors were not pleased with his actions (or inactions) and were upset at the revenue declines from the high-profile recalls. Consequently, Weldon was given only a 3 percent raise for 2011, and his end-of-year bonus was cut by 45 percent. But don't cry for him: His annual compensation for the year (including salary, bonus, and stock options) was $23 million—down from $26 million in the previous year.[31]

The second individual who was at least partially responsible for the decline of J&J's reputation is Colleen Goggins, Worldwide Chairman of J&J's Consumer Group, who was in charge of the factories that produced many of the recalled products. She was heavily criticized by fellow employees for her excessive cost-cutting measures and her propensity to replace experienced scientists with new hires.[32] In addition, she was implicated in an unbelievably foolish and extremely unethical behavior to avoid publically disclosing another J&J recall of a defective product.

Here is the story behind the unethical scheme: After learning that J&J had released packets of Motrin that did not dissolve correctly, the company hired contractors to go into convenience stores and secretly buy up every pack of Motrin on the shelves. The instructions given to the contractors were the following: "You should simply 'act' like a regular customer while making these purchases. THERE MUST BE NO MENTION OF THIS BEING A RECALL OF THE PRODUCT!"[33] In May 2010, when Goggins appeared before a congressional committee investigating the "phantom recall," she testified that she was not aware of the behavior of the contractors[34] and that she had "no knowledge of instructions to contractors involved in the phantom recall to not tell store employees what they were doing." In her September 2010 testimony to the House Committee on Oversight and Government Reform, she acknowledged that the company wrote those instructions. She also told the committee she was retiring. This had to be a major disappointment for her. Before J&J started falling apart, she was a contender to take over as CEO when Weldon retired. But, as is true with Weldon, don't shed too many tears for her. Goggins departed from J&J a wealthy woman after cashing in one-third of her shares of company stock for $3 million.[35]

From a right-versus-wrong point of view, both Weldon and Goggins acted inappropriately. Their actions caused harm to others, including consumers, employees, and investors. They most likely felt badly about what happened, were embarrassed to discuss the situation with others, and regretted the fact that almost every newspaper in the country carried the story of J&J's downfall.

Regardless of whom is to blame, the bottom line is this: What was once an admired company is tarnished. J&J went from a most admired company to a struggling company that will require more than a Band-Aid to heal its business wounds.[36] Whether J&J can regain the public's trust is a question that no one can answer at this time. At this point, consumers have a right to ask the questions: Should I pay a premium for J&J products given the company's recent track record of poor quality control?

What to Do When the Light Turns Yellow

Like our five questions, some ethical problems are fairly straightforward. Others, unfortunately, are more complicated, but it will help to think of our five-question test as a set of signals that will warn you that you're facing a particularly tough decision—that you should think carefully about it and perhaps consult someone else. The situation is like approaching a traffic light. Red and green lights are easy; you know what they mean and exactly what to do. Yellow lights are trickier. Before you decide which pedal to hit, try posing our five questions. If you get a single yes, you'll be much better off hitting the brake.[37]

KEY TAKEAWAYS

- Businesspeople face two types of ethical challenges: ethical dilemmas and ethical decisions.
- An **ethical dilemma** is a morally problematic situation in which you must choose between two or more alternatives that aren't equally acceptable to different groups.
- Such a dilemma is often characterized as a "right-versus-right" decision and is usually solved in a series of five steps:
    1. Define the problem and collect the relevant facts.
    2. Identify feasible options.
    3. Assess the effect of each option on **stakeholders** (owners, employees, customers, communities).
    4. Establish criteria for determining the most appropriate option.
    5. Select the best option, based on the established criteria.
- An **ethical decision** entails a "right-versus-wrong" decision—one in which there's a right (ethical) choice and a wrong (unethical or downright illegal) choice.
- When you make a decision that's unmistakably unethical or illegal, you've committed an **ethical lapse**.
- If you're presented with what appears to be an ethical decision, asking yourself the following questions will improve your odds of making an ethical choice:
    1. Is the action illegal?
    2. Is it unfair to some parties?
    3. If I take it, will I feel bad about it?
    4. Will I be ashamed to tell my family, friends, coworkers, or boss about my action?
    5. Would I want my decision written up in the local newspaper?

If you answer yes to any one of these five questions, you're probably about to do something that you shouldn't.

Before going to the next section of this chapter, take a few minutes to test your knowledge of the material covered in this section. Quizzes can be found under the "Resources" tab, "Study Aids: Quizzes."

EXERCISE

Explain the difference between an ethical dilemma and an ethical decision. Then provide an example of each. Describe an ethical lapse and provide an example.

Picture Yourself in This Situation

Take a few minutes to test your responses to an ethical dilemma involving a sports team. Click here to complete the exercise.

3. IDENTIFYING ETHICAL ISSUES

LEARNING OBJECTIVES

1. Identify ethical issues that you might face in business.
2. Distinguish a bribe from an acceptable gift.
3. Describe a situation that gives rise to a conflict of interest.
4. Explain how you would choose between loyalty to your employer and loyalty to a friend or family member.
5. Define "whistle-blower" and describe the challenges whistle-blowers face.
6. Identify rationalizations used to justify unethical conduct.

Make no mistake about it: When you enter the business world, you'll find yourself in situations in which you'll have to choose the appropriate behavior. How, for example, would you answer questions like the following?

- Is it OK to accept a pair of sports tickets from a supplier?
- Can I buy office supplies from my brother-in-law?
- Is it appropriate to donate company funds to my local community center?
- If I find out that a friend is about to be fired, can I warn her?
- Will I have to lie about the quality of the goods I'm selling?
- Can I take personal e-mails and phone calls at work?
- What do I do if I discover that a coworker is committing fraud?

Obviously, the types of situations are numerous and varied. Fortunately, we can break them down into a few basic categories: *bribes, conflicts of interest, conflicts of loyalty, issues of honesty and integrity*, and *whistle-blowing*. Let's look a little more closely at each of these categories.

3.1 Bribes versus Gifts

It's not uncommon in business to give and receive small gifts of appreciation. But when is a gift unacceptable? When is it really a bribe? If it's OK to give a bottle of wine to a corporate client during the holidays, is it OK to give a case of wine? If your company is trying to get a big contract, is it appropriate to send a gift to the key decision maker? If it's all right to invite a business acquaintance to dinner or to a ball game, is it also all right to offer the same person a fully paid weekend getaway?

There's often a fine line between a gift and a bribe. The questions that we've just asked, however, may help in drawing it, because they raise key issues in determining how a gesture should be interpreted: the cost of the item, the timing of the gift, the type of gift, and the connection between the giver and the receiver. If you're on the receiving end, it's a good idea to refuse any item that's overly generous or given for the purpose of influencing a decision. But because accepting even small gifts may violate company rules, the best advice is to check on company policy.

JCPenney's "Statement of Business Ethics," for instance, states that employees can't accept any cash gifts or any noncash gifts except those that have a value below $50 and that are generally used by the giver for promotional purposes. Employees can attend paid-for business functions, but other forms of entertainment, such as sports events and golf outings, can be accepted only if it's practical for the Penney's employee to reciprocate. Trips of several days can't be accepted under any circumstances.[38]

3.2 Conflicts of Interest

conflict of interest

Situation in which an individual must choose between the promotion of personal interests and the interests of others.

Conflicts of interest occur when individuals must choose between taking actions that promote their personal interests over the interests of others or taking actions that don't. A conflict can exist, for example, when an employee's own interests interfere with, or have the potential to interfere with, the best interests of the company's stakeholders (management, customers, owners). Let's say that you work for a company with a contract to cater events at your college and that your uncle owns a local bakery. Obviously, this situation could create a conflict of interest (or at least give the appearance of one—which, by the way, is a problem in itself). When you're called on to furnish desserts for a luncheon, you might be tempted to throw some business your uncle's way even if it's not in the best interest of the catering company that you work for.

What should you do? You should probably disclose the connection to your boss, who can then arrange things so that your personal interests don't conflict with the company's. You may, for example, agree that if you're assigned to order products like those that your uncle makes, you're obligated to find another supplier. Or your boss may make sure that someone else orders bakery products.

The same principle holds that an employee shouldn't use private information about an employer for personal financial benefit. Say that you learn from a coworker at your pharmaceutical company that one of its most profitable drugs will be pulled off the market because of dangerous side effects. The recall will severely hurt the company's financial performance and cause its stock price to plummet. Before the news becomes public, you sell all the stock you own in the company. What you've done isn't merely unethical: It's called **insider trading**, it's illegal, and you could go to jail for it.

> **insider trading**
>
> Practice of buying or selling of securities using important information about the company before it's made public.

3.3   Conflicts of Loyalty

Sometimes you find yourself in a bind between being loyal either to your employer or to a friend or family member. Perhaps you just learned that a coworker, a friend of yours, is about to be downsized out of his job. You also happen to know that he and his wife are getting ready to make a deposit on a house near the company headquarters. From a work standpoint, you know that you shouldn't divulge the information. From a friendship standpoint, though, you feel it's your duty to tell your friend. Wouldn't he tell you if the situation were reversed? So what do you do? As tempting as it is to be loyal to your friend, you shouldn't. As an employee, your primary responsibility is to your employer. You might be able to soften your dilemma by convincing a manager with the appropriate authority to tell your friend the bad news before he puts down his deposit.

3.4   Issues of Honesty and Integrity

Master investor Warren Buffet once told a group of business students the following:

> *I cannot tell you that honesty is the best policy. I can't tell you that if you behave with perfect honesty and integrity somebody somewhere won't behave the other way and make more money. But honesty is a good policy. You'll do fine, you'll sleep well at night and you'll feel good about the example you are setting for your coworkers and the other people who care about you.*[39]

If you work for a company that settles for its employees' merely obeying the law and following a few internal regulations, you might think about moving on. If you're being asked to deceive customers about the quality or value of your product, you're in an ethically unhealthy environment.

Think about this story:

> *A chef put two frogs in a pot of warm soup water. The first frog smelled the onions, recognized the danger, and immediately jumped out. The second frog hesitated: The water felt good, and he decided to stay and relax for a minute. After all, he could always jump out when things got too hot (so to speak). As the water got hotter, however, the frog adapted to it, hardly noticing the change. Before long, of course, he was the main ingredient in frog-leg soup.*[40]

So, what's the moral of the story? Don't sit around in an ethically toxic environment and lose your integrity a little at a time; get out before the water gets too hot and your options have evaporated.

Fortunately, a few rules of thumb can guide you. We've summed them up in Figure 2.4.

FIGURE 2.4 How to Maintain Honesty and Integrity

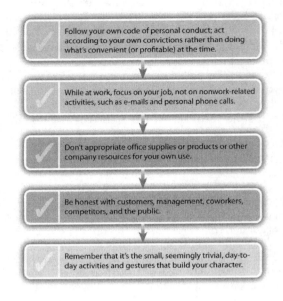

Follow your own code of personal conduct; act according to your own convictions rather than doing what's convenient (or profitable) at the time.

While at work, focus on your job, not on nonwork-related activities, such as e-mails and personal phone calls.

Don't appropriate office supplies or products or other company resources for your own use.

Be honest with customers, management, coworkers, competitors, and the public.

Remember that it's the small, seemingly trivial, day-to-day activities and gestures that build your character.

3.5 Whistle-Blowing

whistle-blower

Individual who exposes illegal or unethical behavior in an organization.

As we've seen, the misdeeds of Betty Vinson and her accomplices at WorldCom didn't go undetected. They caught the eye of Cynthia Cooper, the company's director of internal auditing. Cooper, of course, could have looked the other way, but instead she summoned up the courage to be a **whistle-blower**—an individual who exposes illegal or unethical behavior in an organization. Like Vinson, Cooper had majored in accounting at Mississippi State and was a hardworking, dedicated employee. Unlike Vinson, however, she refused to be bullied by her boss, CFO Scott Sullivan. In fact, she had tried to tell not only Sullivan but also auditors from the huge Arthur Andersen accounting firm that there was a problem with WorldCom's books. The auditors dismissed her warnings, and when Sullivan angrily told her to drop the matter, she started cleaning out her office. But she didn't relent. She and her team worked late each night, conducting an extensive, secret investigation. Two months later, Cooper had evidence to take to Sullivan, who told her once again to back off. Again, however, she stood up to him, and though she regretted the consequences for her WorldCom coworkers, she reported the scheme to the company's board of directors. Within days, Sullivan was fired and the largest accounting fraud in history became public.

As a result of Cooper's actions, executives came clean about the company's financial situation. The conspiracy of fraud was brought to an end, and though public disclosure of WorldCom's problems resulted in massive stock-price declines and employee layoffs, investor and employee losses would have been greater without Cooper's intervention.

Even though Cooper did the right thing, the experience wasn't exactly gratifying. A lot of people applauded her action, but many coworkers shunned her; some even blamed *her* for the company's troubles. She's never been thanked by any senior executive at WorldCom. Five months after the fraud went public, new CEO Michael Capellas assembled what was left of the demoralized workforce to give them a pep talk on the company's future. The senior management team mounted the stage and led the audience in a rousing rendition of "If you're happy and you know it, clap your hands!" Cynthia Cooper wasn't invited.[41]

Whistle-blowing often means career suicide. A survey of two hundred whistle-blowers conducted by the National Whistleblower Center found that half of them had been fired for blowing the whistle.[42] Even those who get to keep their jobs experience painful repercussions. As long as they stay, some people will treat them (as one whistle-blower puts it) "like skunks at a picnic"; if they leave, they're frequently blackballed in the industry.[43] On a positive note, there's the 2002 Sarbanes-Oxley Act, which protects whistle-blowers under federal law.

For her own part, Cynthia Cooper doesn't regret what she did. As she told a group of students at Mississippi State: "Strive to be persons of honor and integrity. Do not allow yourself to be pressured. Do what you know is right even if there may be a price to be paid."[44] If your company tells employees to do whatever it takes, push the envelope, look the other way, and "be sure that we make our numbers," you have three choices: go along with the policy, try to change things, or leave. If your personal integrity is part of the equation, you're probably down to the last two choices.[45]

FIGURE 2.5 Cynthia Cooper

3.6 Refusing to Rationalize

Despite all the good arguments in favor of doing the right thing, why do many reasonable people act unethically (at least at times)? Why do good people make bad choices? According to one study, there are four common rationalizations for justifying misconduct:[46]

1. *My behavior isn't really illegal or immoral.* Rationalizers try to convince themselves that an action is OK if it isn't downright illegal or blatantly immoral. They tend to operate in a gray area where there's no clear evidence that the action is wrong.

2. *My action is in everyone's best interests.* Some rationalizers tell themselves: "I know I lied to make the deal, but it'll bring in a lot of business and pay a lot of bills." They convince themselves that they're expected to act in a certain way, forgetting the classic parental parable about jumping off a cliff just because your friends are.[47]

3. *No one will find out what I've done.* Here, the self-questioning comes down to "If I didn't get caught, did I really do it?" The answer is yes. There's a simple way to avoid succumbing to this rationalization: Always act as if you're being watched.

4. *The company will condone my action and protect me.* This justification rests on a fallacy. Betty Vinson may honestly have believed that her actions were for the good of the company and that her boss would, therefore, accept full responsibility (as he promised). When she goes to jail, however, she'll go on her own.

Here's another rule of thumb: If you find yourself having to rationalize a decision, it's probably a bad one. Over time, you'll develop and hone your ethical decision-making skills.

What to Do When You're Partners in Crime

Take a moment to test your response to an ethical question on the submission of a term paper. Click here to complete the exercise.

KEY TAKEAWAYS

- When you enter the business world, you'll find yourself in situations in which you'll have to choose the appropriate behavior.
- You'll need to know how to distinguish a bribe from an acceptable gift.
- You'll encounter situations that give rise to a **conflict of interest**—situations in which you'll have to choose between taking action that promotes your personal interest and action that favors the interest of others.
- Sometimes you'll be required to choose between loyalty to your employer and loyalty to a friend or family member.
- In business, as in all aspects of your life, you should act with honesty and integrity.
- At some point in your career, you might become aware of wrongdoing on the part of others and will have to decide whether to report the incident and become a **whistle-blower**—an individual who exposes illegal or unethical behavior in an organization.
- Despite all the good arguments in favor of doing the right thing, some businesspeople still act unethically (at least at times). Sometimes they use one of the following rationalizations to justify their conduct:

  1. The behavior isn't really illegal or immoral.
  2. The action is in everyone's best interests.
  3. No one will find out what I've done.
  4. The company will condone my action and protect me.

Before going to the next section of this chapter, take a few minutes to test your knowledge of the material covered in this section. Quizzes can be found under the "Resources" tab, "Study Aids: Quizzes."

EXERCISE

1. You own a tax-preparation company with ten employees who prepare tax returns. In walking around the office, you notice that several of your employees spend a lot of time making personal use of their computers, checking personal e-mails, or shopping online. After doing an Internet search on employer computer monitoring, respond to the following questions:

   - Is it unethical for your employees to use their work computers for personal activities?
   - Is it ethical for you to monitor computer usage?
   - Do you have a legal right to do it?
   - If you decide to monitor computer usage in the future, what rules would you make and how would you enforce them?

4.   THE ORGANIZATIONAL APPROACH TO ETHICS

LEARNING OBJECTIVES

1. **Specify actions that managers can take to create and sustain ethical organizations.**
2. **Define culture, and indicate how it promotes ethical (or unethical) behavior.**
3. **Explain the role played by top management in letting members of the organization know what's considered acceptable behavior and what happens if it's violated.**
4. **Explain the purpose of a formal code of conduct.**

Ethics is more than a matter of individual behavior; it's also about organizational behavior. Employees' actions aren't based solely on personal values alone: They're influenced by other members of the organization, from top managers and supervisors to coworkers and subordinates. So how can ethical companies be created and sustained? In this section, we'll examine some of the most reasonable answers to this question.

4.1   Ethical Leadership

Organizations have unique *cultures*—ways of doing things that evolve through shared values and beliefs. An organization's culture is strongly influenced by senior executives, who tell members of the organization what's considered acceptable behavior and what happens if it's violated. In theory, the tone set at the top of the organization promotes ethical behavior, but sometimes (as at Enron) it doesn't.

Before its sudden demise, Enron fostered a growth-at-any-cost culture that was defined by the company's top executives. Said one employee, "It was all about taking profits now and worrying about the details later. The Enron system was just ripe for corruption." Coupled with the relentless pressure to generate revenue—or at least to look as if you were generating it—was a climate that discouraged employees from questioning the means by which they were supposed to do it. There may have been chances for people to speak up, but no one did. "I don't think anyone started out with a plan to defraud the company," reflects another ex-employee. "Everything at Enron seemed to start out right, but somewhere something slipped. People's mentality switched from focusing on the future good of the company to 'let's just do it today.'"[48]

4.2   Exercising Ethical Leadership

Leaders should keep in constant touch with subordinates about ethical policies and expectations. They should be available to help employees identify and solve ethical problems, and should encourage them to come forward with concerns. They're responsible for minimizing opportunities for wrongdoing and for exerting the controls needed to enforce company policies. They should also think of themselves as role models. Subordinates look to their supervisors to communicate policies and practices regarding ethical behavior, and as a rule, actions speak more loudly than words: If managers behave ethically, subordinates will probably do the same.

This is exactly the message that senior management at Martin Marietta (now a part of Lockheed Martin) sent to members of their organization. A leading producer of construction components, the company at the time was engaged in a tough competitive battle over a major contract. Because both Martin Marietta and its main competitor were qualified to do the work, the job would go to the lower bid. A few days before bids were due, a package arrived at Martin Marietta containing a copy of the competitor's bid sheet (probably from a disgruntled employee trying to sabotage his or her employer's efforts). The bid price was lower than Martin Marietta's. In a display of ethical backbone, executives immediately turned the envelope over to the government and informed the competitor. No, they didn't change their own bid in the meantime, and, no, they didn't get the job. All they got was an opportunity to send a clear message to the entire organization.[49]

By the same token, leaders must be willing to hold subordinates accountable for their conduct and to take appropriate action. The response to unethical behavior should be prompt and decisive. One CEO of a large company discovered that some of his employees were "dumpster diving" in the trash outside a competitor's offices (which is to say, they were sifting around for information that would give them a competitive advantage). The manager running the espionage operation was a personal friend of the CEO's, but he was immediately fired, as were his "operatives." The CEO then informed his competitor about the venture and returned all the materials that had been gathered. Like the top managers at Martin Marietta, this executive sent a clear message to people in his organization: namely, that deviations from accepted behavior would not be tolerated.[50]

It's always possible to send the wrong message. In August 2004, newspapers around the country carried a wire-service story titled "Convicted CEO Getting $2.5 Million Salary While He Serves Time." Interested readers found that the board of directors of Fog Cutter Capital Group had agreed to pay CEO Andrew Wiederhorn (and give him a bonus) while he served an eighteen-month federal-prison term for bribery, filing false tax returns, and financially ruining his previous employer (from which he'd also borrowed $160 million). According to the board, they couldn't afford to lose a man of Wiederhorn's ability. The entire episode ended up on TheStreet.com's list of "The Five Dumbest Things on Wall Street This Week."[51]

4.3   Tightening the Rules

In response to the recent barrage of corporate scandals, more large companies have taken additional steps to encourage employees to behave according to specific standards and to report wrongdoing. Even companies with excellent reputations for integrity have stepped up their efforts.

Codes of Conduct

code of conduct

Statement that defines the principles and guidelines that employees must follow in the course of all job-related activities.

Like many firms, Hershey Foods now has a formal **code of conduct**: a document describing the principles and guidelines that all employees must follow in the course of all job-related activities. It's available on the company intranet and in printed form and, to be sure that everyone understands it, the company offers a training program. The Hershey code covers such topics as the use of corporate funds and resources, conflict of interest, and the protection of proprietary information. It explains how the code will be enforced, emphasizing that violations won't be tolerated. It encourages employees to report wrongdoing and provides instructions on reporting violations (which are displayed on posters and printed on wallet-size cards). Reports can be made through a Concern Line, by e-mail, or by regular mail; they can be anonymous; and retaliation is also a serious violation of company policy.[52]

KEY TAKEAWAYS

- Ethics is more than a matter of individual behavior; it's also about organizational behavior. Employees' actions aren't based solely on personal values; they're also influenced by other members of the organization.
- Organizations have unique *cultures*—ways of doing things that evolve through shared values and beliefs.
- An organization's culture is strongly influenced by top managers, who are responsible for letting members of the organization know what's considered acceptable behavior and what happens if it's violated.
- Subordinates look to their supervisors as role models of ethical behavior. If managers act ethically, subordinates will probably do the same.
- Those in positions of leadership should hold subordinates accountable for their conduct and take appropriate action.
- Many organizations have a formal **code of conduct** that describes the principles and guidelines that all members must follow in the course of job-related activities.

Before going to the next section of this chapter, take a few minutes to test your knowledge of the material covered in this section. Quizzes can be found under the "Resources" tab, "Study Aids: Quizzes."

EXERCISES

1. You're the CEO of a company that sells golf equipment, including clubs, bags, and balls. When your company was started and had only a handful of employees, you were personally able to oversee the conduct of your employees. But with your current workforce of nearly fifty, it's time to prepare a formal code of conduct in which you lay down some rules that employees must follow in performing job-related activities. As a model for your own code, you've decided to use Macy's Code of Business Conduct and Ethics. Go to the company's Web site (http://www.federated-fds.com/for-investors/corporate-governance/default.aspx) and click on "Code of Conduct" to view its posted code of business conduct. Your document won't be as thorough as Macy's, but it will cover the following areas: (1) conflicts of interest; (2) acceptance of gifts, services, or entertainment; (3) protection of confidential information; (4) use of company funds or assets for personal purposes; (5) competing fairly and ethically; and (6) adherence to code. Draw up a code of conduct for your company.

2. Think of someone whom you regard as an ethical leader. It can be anyone connected with you—a businessperson, educator, coach, politician, or family member. Explain why you believe the individual is ethical in his or her leadership.

5.   CORPORATE SOCIAL RESPONSIBILITY

LEARNING OBJECTIVES

1. Define "corporate social responsibility," and identify a company's stakeholders.
2. Discuss the responsibilities a company's managers have to its owners.
3. Explain the responsibilities managers have to the company's employees.
4. Identify the benefits of valuing a diverse workforce.
5. Explain the ethical and legal responsibilities sellers have to their customers, and identify the rights of consumers.
6. Discuss the responsibilities companies have to the communities in which they produce and sell their goods and services.

Corporate social responsibility refers to the approach that an organization takes in balancing its responsibilities toward different stakeholders when making legal, economic, ethical, and social decisions. What motivates companies to be "socially responsible" to their various stakeholders? We hope it's because they want to do the right thing, and for many companies, "doing the right thing" is a key motivator. The fact is, it's often hard to figure out what the "right thing" is: What's "right" for one group of stakeholders isn't necessarily just as "right" for another. One thing, however, is certain: Companies today are held to higher standards than ever before. Consumers and other groups consider not only the quality and price of a company's products but also its character. If too many groups see a company as a poor corporate citizen, it will have a harder time attracting qualified employees, finding investors, and selling its products. Good corporate citizens, by contrast, are more successful in all these areas.

Figure 2.6 presents a model of corporate responsibility based on a company's relationships with its *stakeholders*. In this model, the focus is on managers—not owners—as the principals involved in all these relationships. Here, owners are the stakeholders who invest risk capital in the firm in expectation of a financial return. Other stakeholders include employees, suppliers, and the communities in which the firm does business. Proponents of this model hold that customers, who provide the firm with revenue, have a special claim on managers' attention. The arrows indicate the two-way nature of corporation-stakeholder relationships: All stakeholders have some claim on the firm's resources and returns, and it's management's job to make decisions that balance these claims.[53]

> **corporate social responsibility**
>
> Approach that an organization takes in balancing its responsibilities toward different stakeholders when making legal, economic, ethical, and social decisions.

FIGURE 2.6 The Corporate Citizen

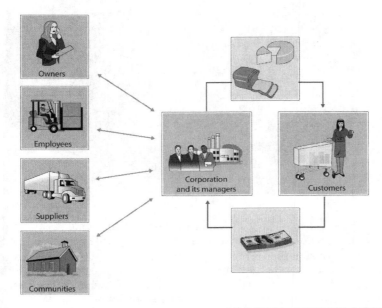

The Corporate Citizen

Click on this link to experience an active version of this figure.

Let's look at some of the ways in which companies can be "socially responsible" in considering the claims of various stakeholders.

5.1 Owners

Owners invest money in companies. In return, the people who run a company have a responsibility to increase the value of owners' investments through profitable operations. Managers also have a responsibility to provide owners (as well as other stakeholders having financial interests, such as creditors and suppliers) with accurate, reliable information about the performance of the business. Clearly, this is one of the areas in which WorldCom managers fell down on the job. Upper-level management purposely deceived shareholders by presenting them with fraudulent financial statements.

Fiduciary Responsibilities

fiduciary responsibility

Duty of management to safeguard a company's assets and handle its funds in a trustworthy manner.

Finally, managers have a **fiduciary responsibility** to owners: They're responsible for safeguarding the company's assets and handling its funds in a trustworthy manner. This is a responsibility that was ignored by top executives at both Adelphia and Tyco, whose associates and families virtually looted company assets. To enforce managers' fiduciary responsibilities for a firm's financial statements and accounting records, the Sarbanes-Oxley Act of 2002 requires CEOs and CFOs to attest to their accuracy. The law also imposes penalties on corporate officers, auditors, board members, and any others who commit fraud.

Employees

Companies are responsible for providing employees with safe, healthy places to work—as well as environments that are free from sexual harassment and all types of discrimination. They should also offer appropriate wages and benefits. In the following sections, we'll take a closer look at each of these areas of responsibility.

Safety and Health

FIGURE 2.7 Workplace Deaths by Event or Exposure, 2010

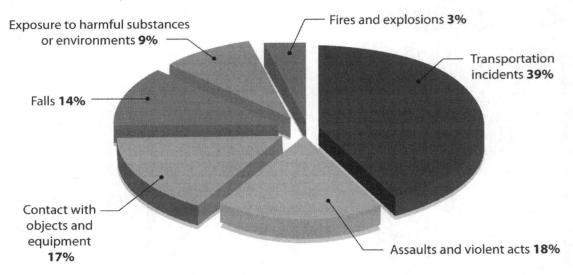

Though it seems obvious that companies should guard workers' safety and health, a lot of them simply don't. For over four decades, for example, executives at Johns Manville suppressed evidence that one of its products, asbestos, was responsible for the deadly lung disease developed by many of its workers.[54] The company concealed chest X-rays from stricken workers, and executives decided that it was simply cheaper to pay workers' compensation claims (or let workers die) than to create a safer work environment. A New Jersey court was quite blunt in its judgment: Johns Manville, it held, had made a deliberate, cold-blooded decision to do nothing to protect at-risk workers, in blatant disregard of their rights.[55]

About four in one hundred thousand U.S. workers die in workplace "incidents" each year. The Department of Labor categorizes deaths caused by conditions like those at Johns Manville as "exposure to harmful substances or environments." How prevalent is this condition as a cause of workplace deaths?

See Figure 2.7, which breaks down workplace fatalities by cause. Some jobs are more dangerous than others. For a comparative overview based on workplace deaths by occupation, see Figure 2.8.

FIGURE 2.8   Workplace Deaths by Industry, 2010

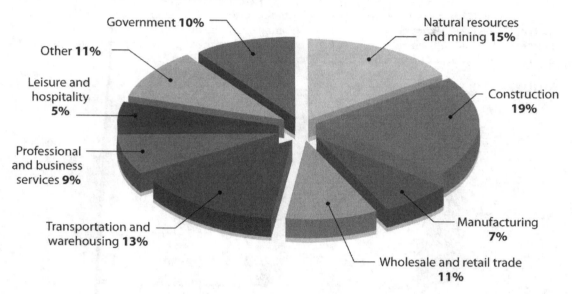

For most people, fortunately, things are better than they were at Johns Manville. Procter & Gamble (P&G), for example, considers the safety and health of its employees paramount and promotes the attitude that "Nothing we do is worth getting hurt for." With nearly one hundred thousand employees worldwide, P&G uses a measure of worker safety called "total incident rate per employee," which records injuries resulting in loss of consciousness, time lost from work, medical transfer to another job, motion restriction, or medical treatment beyond first aid. The company attributes the low rate of such incidents—less than one incident per hundred employees—to a variety of programs to promote workplace safety.[56]

Freedom from Sexual Harassment

What is *sexual harassment*? The law is quite precise:

- Sexual harassment occurs when an employee makes "unwelcome sexual advances, requests for sexual favors, and other verbal or physical conduct of a sexual nature" to another employee who doesn't welcome the advances.

- It's also sexual harassment when "submission to or rejection of this conduct explicitly or implicitly affects an individual's employment, unreasonably interferes with an individual's work performance or creates an intimidating, hostile or offensive work environment."[57]

To prevent sexual harassment—or at least minimize its likelihood—a company should adopt a formal anti-harassment policy describing prohibited conduct, asserting its objections to the behavior, and detailing penalties for violating the policy.[58] Employers also have an obligation to investigate harassment complaints. Failure to enforce anti-harassment policies can be very costly. In 1998, for example, Mitsubishi paid $34 million to more than three hundred fifty female employees of its Normal, Illinois, plant to settle a sexual harassment case supported by the Equal Employment Opportunity Commission. The EEOC reprimanded the company for permitting an atmosphere of verbal and physical abuse against women, charging that female workers had been subjected to various forms of harassment, ranging from exposure to obscene graffiti and vulgar jokes to fondling and groping.[59]

Equal Opportunity and Diversity

People must be hired, evaluated, promoted, and rewarded on the basis of merit, not personal characteristics. This, too, is the law—namely, Title VII of the 1964 Civil Rights Act. Like most companies, P&G has a formal policy on hiring and promotion that forbids discrimination based on race, color, religion, gender, age, national origin, citizenship, sexual orientation, or disability. P&G expects all employees to support its commitment to equal employment opportunity and warns that those who violate company policies will face strict disciplinary action, including termination of employment.[60]

FIGURE 2.9

Requiring workers to wear protective clothing like gloves, hard hats, and goggles cuts down on accidents. It also helps the firm reduce time lost from work due to injuries.

© 2010 Jupiterimages Corporation

Equal Pay and the Wage Gap

The Equal Pay Act of 1963 requires equal pay for both men and women in jobs that entail equal skill, equal effort, equal responsibility, or similar working conditions. What has been the effect of the law after forty years? In 1980, women earned, on average, $0.60 for every $1 earned by men. By 2014, that difference—which we call the wage gap—has been closed to $0.77 for every $1, or approximately 77 percent.[61] Figure 2.10 provides some interesting numbers on the differences in annual earnings based not only on gender but on race, as well. Figure 2.11 throws further light on the wage and unemployment gap when education is taken into consideration.

FIGURE 2.10 Median Annual Earnings by Gender and Race

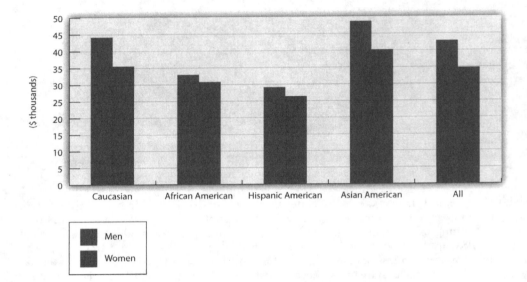

What accounts for the difference, despite the mandate of federal law? For one thing, the jobs typically held by women tend to pay less than those typically held by men. Also, women work fewer hours than men, often to give them more time to care for their children. In addition, men often have better job opportunities. For example, a man newly hired at the same time as a woman will often get a higher-paying assignment at the entry level. Coupled with the fact that the same sort of discrimination applies when it comes to training and promotions, women are usually relegated to a lifetime of lower earnings.

FIGURE 2.11 Median Annual Earnings by Level of Education

Education pays in higher earnings and lower unemployment rates. Note: Data are 2010 annual averages for persons age 25 and over. Earnings are for full-time wage and salary workers.

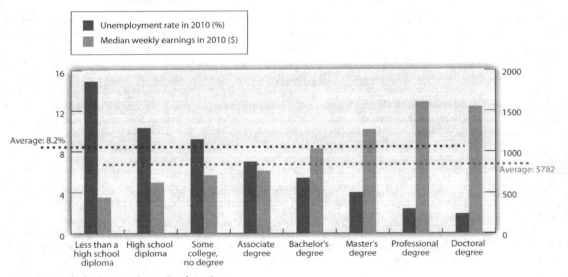

Source: Bureau of Labor Statistics, Current Population Survey.

Median Annual Earnings

Click on this link to experience an active version of this figure.

Building Diverse Workforces

In addition to complying with equal employment opportunity laws, many companies make special efforts to recruit employees who are underrepresented in the workforce according to sex, race, or some other characteristic. In helping to build more diverse workforces, such initiatives contribute to competitive advantage for two reasons: (1) People from diverse backgrounds bring new talents and fresh perspectives to an organization, typically enhancing creativity in the development of new products. (2) By reflecting more accurately the changing demographics of the marketplace, a diverse workforce improves a company's ability to serve an ethnically diverse population.

Wages and Benefits

At the very least, employers must obey laws governing minimum wage and overtime pay. A minimum wage is set by the federal government, though states can set their own rates. The current federal rate, for example, is $7.25, while the rate in the state of Washington is $9.32. When there's a difference, the higher rate applies.[62] By law, employers must also provide certain benefits—social security (which provides retirement benefits), unemployment insurance (which protects against loss of income in case of job loss), and workers' compensation (which covers lost wages and medical costs in case of on-the-job injury). Most large companies pay most of their workers more than minimum wage and offer considerably broader benefits, including medical, dental, and vision care, as well as pension benefits.

5.2   Customers

The purpose of any business is to satisfy customers, who reward businesses by buying their products. Sellers are also responsible—both ethically and legally—for treating customers fairly. The rights of consumers were first articulated by President John F. Kennedy in 1962 when he submitted to Congress a presidential message devoted to consumer issues.[63] Kennedy identified four consumer rights:

1. *The right to safe products.* A company should sell no product that it suspects of being unsafe for buyers. Thus, producers have an obligation to safety-test products before releasing them for public consumption. The automobile industry, for example, conducts extensive safety testing before introducing new models (though recalls remain common).

2. *The right to be informed about a product.* Sellers should furnish consumers with the product information that they need to make an informed purchase decision. That's why pillows have labels identifying the materials used to make them, for instance.

3. *The right to choose what to buy.* Consumers have a right to decide which products to purchase, and sellers should let them know what their options are. Pharmacists, for example, should tell patients when a prescription can be filled with a cheaper brand-name or generic drug. Telephone companies should explain alternative calling plans.

4. *The right to be heard.* Companies must tell customers how to contact them with complaints or concerns. They should also listen and respond.

Companies share the responsibility for the legal and ethical treatment of consumers with several government agencies: the Federal Trade Commission (FTC), which enforces consumer-protection laws; the Food and Drug Administration (FDA), which oversees the labeling of food products; and the Consumer Product Safety Commission, which enforces laws protecting consumers from the risk of product-related injury.

5.3   Communities

For obvious reasons, most communities see getting a new business as an asset and view losing one—especially a large employer—as a detriment. After all, the economic impact of business activities on local communities is substantial: They provide jobs, pay taxes, and support local education, health, and recreation programs. Both big and small businesses donate funds to community projects, encourage employees to volunteer their time, and donate equipment and products for a variety of activities. Larger companies can make greater financial contributions. Let's start by taking a quick look at the philanthropic activities of a few U.S. corporations.

Financial Contributions

Many large corporations donate a percentage of sales or profits to worthwhile causes. Retailer Target, for example, donates about $4 million per week to schools, neighborhoods, and local projects across the country; its store-based grants underwrite programs in early childhood education, the arts, and family-violence prevention. The company is on track to give $1 billion for education by 2015.[64] The late actor Paul Newman donated 100 percent of the profits from "Newman's Own" foods (salad dressing, pasta sauce, popcorn, and more than ninety other products). His company continues his legacy of donating all profits and distributing them to thousands of organizations, including the Hole in the Wall Gang camps for seriously ill children.[65]

Volunteerism

Many companies support employee efforts to help local communities. Patagonia, for example, a maker of outdoor gear and clothing, lets employees leave their jobs and work full-time for any environmental group for two months—with full salary and benefits; so far, more than 850 employees have taken advantage of the program.[66]

Supporting Social Causes

Companies and executives often take active roles in initiatives to improve health and social welfare in the United States and elsewhere. Microsoft's former CEO Bill Gates intends to distribute more than $3 billion through the Bill and Melinda Gates Foundation, which funds education initiatives in the United States and global health, agriculture, and family-planning initiatives[67] in undeveloped countries.[68] Noting that children from low-income families have twice as many cavities and often miss school because of dental-related diseases, P&G invested $1 million a year to set up "cavity-free zones" for 3.3 million economically disadvantaged children at Boys and Girls Clubs nationwide. In addition to giving away toothbrushes and toothpaste, P&G provided educational programs on dental hygiene. At some locations, the company even maintained clinics providing affordable oral care to poor children and their families.[69] Proctor & Gamble committed to provide more than two billion liters of clean drinking water to adults and children living in poverty in developing countries. The company believes that this initiative will save an estimated ten thousand lives.[70]

KEY TAKEAWAYS

- **Corporate social responsibility** refers to the approach that an organization takes in balancing its responsibilities toward different stakeholders when making legal, economic, ethical, and social decisions.
- Companies are socially responsible to their various stakeholders—owners, employees, customers, and the communities in which they conduct business.
- Owners invest money in companies. In return, the people who manage companies have a responsibility to increase the value of owners' investments through profitable operations.
- Managers have a responsibility to provide owners and other stakeholders with accurate, reliable financial information.
- They also have a **fiduciary responsibility** to safeguard the company's assets and handle its funds in a trustworthy manner.
- Companies have a responsibility to guard workers' safety and health and to provide them with a work environment that's free from sexual harassment.
- Businesses should pay appropriate wages and benefits, treat all workers fairly, and provide equal opportunities for all employees.
- Many companies have discovered the benefits of valuing diversity. People with diverse backgrounds bring new talents and fresh perspectives, and improve a company's ability to serve an ethically diverse population.
- Sellers are responsible—both ethically and legally—for treating customers fairly. Consumers have certain rights: to use safe products, to be informed about products, to choose what to buy, and to be heard.
- Companies also have a responsibility to the communities in which they produce and sell their products. The economic impact of businesses on local communities is substantial. Companies have the following functions:

    1. Provide jobs
    2. Pay taxes
    3. Support local education, health, and recreation activities
    4. Donate funds to community projects
    5. Encourage employees to volunteer their time
    6. Donate equipment and products for a variety of activities

Before going to the next section of this chapter, take a few minutes to test your knowledge of the material covered in this section. Quizzes can be found under the "Resources" tab, "Study Aids: Quizzes."

EXERCISES

1. Nonprofit organizations (such as your college or university) have social responsibilities to their stakeholders. Identify your school's stakeholders. For each category of stakeholder, indicate the ways in which your school is socially responsible to that group.

2. Pfizer is the largest research-based pharmaceutical company in the world. It's in the business of discovering, developing, manufacturing, and marketing prescription drugs. While it's headquartered in New York, it sells products worldwide, and its corporate-responsibility initiatives are also global. Go to the "Corporate Responsibility" section of the Pfizer Web site (http://www.pfizer.com/responsibility/global_health/global_health.jsp) and read about the firm's global corporate-citizenship initiatives. Write a brief report describing the focus of Pfizer's efforts and identifying a few key programs. In your opinion, why should U.S. companies direct corporate-responsibility efforts at people in countries outside the United States?

6. ENVIRONMENTALISM

Today, virtually everyone agrees that companies must figure out how to produce products without compromising the right of future generations to meet their own needs. Clearly, protecting natural resources is the right thing to do, but it also has become a business necessity. Companies' customers demand that they respect the environment. Let's identify some key environmental issues and highlight the ways in which the business community has addressed them.

6.1 Land Pollution

The land we live on has been polluted by the dumping of waste and increasing reliance on agricultural chemicals. It's pockmarked by landfills stuffed with the excess of a throwaway society. It's been strip-mined and deforested, and urban sprawl on every continent has squeezed out wetlands and farmlands and destroyed wildlife habitats.

FIGURE 2.12

Did you know your cozy fleece jacket is most likely made from recycled plastic bottles?

© 2010 Jupiterimages Corporation

Protecting the land from further damage, then, means disposing of waste in responsible ways (or, better yet, reducing the amount of waste). At both national and global levels, we must resolve the conflicts of interest between those who benefit economically from logging and mining and those who argue that protecting the environment is an urgent matter. Probably municipalities must step in to save open spaces and wetlands.

Clothing manufacturer Patagonia has for years been at the forefront of efforts to protect the land. Each year, the company pledges 1 percent of sales revenue to protect and restore the natural environment.[71] According to its mission statement, Patagonia exists as a business to "inspire and implement solutions to the environmental crisis." Instead of traditional materials for making clothes (such as regular cotton and fleece), Patagonia relies on organically grown cotton, which is more expensive, because it doesn't require harmful chemicals.[72] Its fleece products are made with *postconsumer recycled* (PCR) fleece, which is actually made with recycled plastic bottles. So far, the company's efforts to build a more sustainable system has saved eighty-six million plastic bottles from ending up in landfills.[73]

6.2 Air Pollution

It's amazing what we can do to something as large as the atmosphere. Over time, we've managed to pollute the air with emissions of toxic gases and particles from factories, power plants, office buildings, cars, trucks, and even farms. In addition, our preferred method of deforestation is burning, a major source of air pollution. In some places, polluted air causes respiratory problems, particularly for the young and elderly. Factory emissions, including sulfur and other gases, mix with air and rain to produce *acid rain*, which returns to the earth to pollute forests, lakes, and streams. Perhaps most importantly, many experts—scientists, government officials, and businesspeople—are convinced that the heavy emission of carbon dioxide is altering the earth's climate. Predictions of the effect of unchecked global warming include extreme weather conditions, flooding, oceanic disruptions, shifting storm patterns, droughts, reduced farm output, and even animal extinctions.[74]

Curbing global warming will require international cooperation. More than 194 nations (though not the United States) have stated their support for this initiative by endorsing the Kyoto Protocol, an agreement to slow global warming by reducing worldwide carbon-dioxide emissions.

What can business do? They can reduce greenhouse emissions by making vehicles, factories, and other facilities more energy efficient. In response to a government ban on chlorofluorocarbons, which damage the ozone layer, DuPont has cut its own greenhouse emissions by 72 percent over the last twenty years through improvements in manufacturing processes and a commitment to increased energy efficiency.[75]

U.S., Japanese, and other automobile manufacturers are doing their part to reduce air pollution by offering hybrid gas-electric and electric plug-in cars as alternatives to cars propelled by gas alone. There are now seven million hybrid cars on the road along with a growing number of electric plug-in cars.[76] General Electric has designed more energy-efficient appliances[77] and is investing heavily to research wind power.[78]

6.3   Water Pollution

Water makes up more than 70 percent of the earth's surface, and it's no secret that without it we wouldn't be here. Unfortunately, that knowledge doesn't stop us from polluting our oceans, rivers, and lakes and generally making our water unfit for use. Massive pollution occurs when such substances as oil and chemicals are dumped into bodies of water. The damage to the water, to the marine ecosystem, and to coastal wildlife from the accidental spilling of oil from supertankers and offshore drilling operations can be disastrous, and the cleanup can cost billions. Most contaminants, however, come from agricultural fertilizers, pesticides, wastewater, raw sewage, and silt that make their way into water systems over time.[79] In some parts of the world—including the American Southwest—water supplies are dwindling, partly because of diminishing rainfall and partly because of increased consumption.[80]

The Environmental Protection Agency (EPA) has been a major force in cleaning up U.S. waters. Companies are now held to stricter standards in the discharge of wastes into water treatment systems. In some places, particularly where water supplies are dangerously low, such as the Southwest, local governments have instituted conservation programs. In Arizona (which suffers a severe shortage), Home Depot works with governmental and nongovernmental agencies on a water-conservation campaign. From its stores nationwide, the company runs weekend workshops to educate consumers on conservation basics, including drought-resistant gardening techniques.[81]

6.4   Sustainability

Did you ever read (or have read to you) *The Lorax*, a well-known children's book, written by Dr. Seuss in 1971?[82] It tells the story of how a business owners' greed destroyed an ecosystem. To manufacture and sell a product that the owner argued everyone needed, he cut down the trees in the forest, polluted the river, and fouled the air. These actions destroyed the habitat for the bears that lived on the fruit that fell from the trees, the fish that swam in the streams and the birds that flew high up in the sky. In 1971, these actions were not viewed negatively; business owners believed that the purpose of business was to make a profit without regard for the effect on the environment.

This book was written for young people, but it sends an important message to today's business executives. When it was written in 1971, few business people listened to its message. But, they seem to be listening now. Over the past ten to fifteen years, most of our large corporations have adopted measures that would have pleased environmentalists. These initiatives fall under the umbrella called "sustainability." But what does sustainability mean? There are, of course, many definitions, but here is one that should work for us: **sustainability**—the principle of providing products today that don't compromise the ability of future generations to meet their needs.[83] Companies that undertake sustainability initiatives believe that meeting business needs and protecting the environment are not mutually exclusive. They must do both.

How would you like a job in the sustainability field? Well twenty-six-year-old Robyn Beavers had one (before she left for an even cooler job). As Google's chief sustainability officer, she ran the company's "Green Biz Ops" (Green Business Operations). She was responsible for reducing Google's impact on the environment by overseeing the installation of 9,200 solar panels at the company's corporate headquarters (the world's biggest solar power system).[84] The solar panels reduce the company's use of electricity supplied from fossil fuels. When she wasn't finding ways to reduce Google's footprint on the world, she kept busy making sure Google's offices were green—energy efficient, built with cradle-to-cradle products, and healthy. She got to pick out carpeting that could be returned to the manufacturer when it was worn out so that it could be ground up and used to make other rugs, rather than sit in a landfill decaying. She approved of window shades and other textiles used in the cubicles only after she was assured they were toxin-free. And she made sure there was plenty of filtered water for everyone and 90 percent fresh air coming into the building during the day. Although she had a lot of leeway in making decisions, each project had to be reviewed to be sure it added value and made financial sense.

Google, like many other companies who are proactive in environmental and social responsibility issues often have a "triple bottom line" focus. They believe that the current reporting model of one

sustainability

The principle of providing products today that don't compromise the ability of future generations to meet their needs.

bottom line—profit—does not capture all the dimensions of performance. They argue instead that companies should measure performance using three separate bottom lines: profit, people, and planet (or the 3Ps). In addition to reporting *profit* through their income statement, companies should also report their progress in being socially responsible to other *people* (stakeholders, including employee, customers, owners) and to the *planet* (the environment).[85]

KEY TAKEAWAYS

- Companies bear a responsibility to produce products without compromising the right of future generations to meet their needs.

- Customers demand that companies respect the environment. Our land, air, and water all face environmental threats.

- Land is polluted by the dumping of waste and an increasing reliance on agricultural chemicals. It's pockmarked by landfills, shredded by strip mining, and laid bare by deforestation.

- Urban sprawl has squeezed out wetlands and farmlands and destroyed wildlife habitats.

- To protect the land from further damage, we must dispose of waste in responsible ways, control strip mining and logging, and save open spaces and wetlands.

- Emissions of toxic gases and particles from factories, power plants, office buildings, cars, trucks, and even farms pollute the air, which is also harmed by the burning associated with deforestation.

- Many experts believe that the heavy emission of carbon dioxide by factories and vehicles is altering the earth's climate: carbon dioxide and other gases, they argue, act as a "greenhouse" over the earth, producing global warming—a heating of the earth that could have dire consequences. Many companies have taken actions to reduce air pollution.

- Water is polluted by such substances as oil and chemicals. Most of the contaminants come from agricultural fertilizers, pesticides, wastewater, raw sewage, and silt.

- Also of concern is the dwindling supply of water in some parts of the world brought about by diminishing rainfall and increased consumption.

- The Environmental Protection Agency has been a major force in cleaning up U.S. waters.

- Many companies have joined with governmental and nongovernmental agencies alike in efforts to help people protect and conserve water.

- Sustainability can be defined as the principle of providing products today that don't compromise the ability of future generations to meet their needs.

- Companies that undertake sustainability initiatives believe that meeting business needs and protecting the environment are not mutually exclusive. They must do both.

- Those who support a "triple bottom line" approach to corporate performance evaluation believe that the current reporting model of one bottom line—profit—does not capture all the dimensions of performance. They argue instead that companies should measure performance using three separate bottom lines: profit, people, and planet (or the 3Ps).

Before going to the next section of this chapter, take a few minutes to test your knowledge of the material covered in this section. Quizzes can be found under the "Resources" tab, "Study Aids: Quizzes."

EXERCISE

After building their ice cream company with a focus on social responsibility, Ben & Jerry's founders—Ben Cohen and Jerry Greenfield—found themselves in an unfriendly situation: Unilever—a very large Dutch-British company that owns three ice cream brands—wanted to buy Ben & Jerry's, against the founders' wishes. To make matters worse, most of the Ben & Jerry's stockholders (owners) sided with Unilever. They had little confidence in the ability of Ben Cohen and Jerry Greenfield to continue managing the company and were frustrated with the firm's social-mission focus. The stockholders (owners) liked Unilever's offer to buy their Ben & Jerry's stock at almost twice its current market price and wanted to take their profits and run. Unilever won, and Ben & Jerry's was acquired by Unilever in a hostile takeover.

Read a case produced by Daniels Fund Ethics Initiative at the University of New Mexico, called "Managing Social Responsibility and Growth at Ben & Jerry's" (http://danielsethics.mgt.unm.edu/pdf/ben-and-jerry-case-.pdf), and then answer the following questions:

1. Earlier in the chapter, you learned that companies should show concern for their stakeholders: owners (stockholders), employees, customers, and the communities in which they do business. Identify several ways in which Ben & Jerry's management showed concern for its employees, customers, and the communities in which it did business.

2. Did Ben Cohen and Jerry Greenfield's passion for using company funds for social issues conflict with their responsibilities to the company's owners and stockholders?

3. If you were either Ben Cohen or Jerry Greenfield, would you devote as much time and money on social issues, even at the risk of losing your company?

7. STAGES OF CORPORATE RESPONSIBILITY

LEARNING OBJECTIVE

1. List the stages of corporate responsibility.

We expect companies to recognize issues of social importance and to address them responsibly. The companies that do this earn reputations as good corporate citizens and enjoy certain benefits, such as the ability to keep satisfied customers, to attract capital, and to recruit and retain talented employees. But companies don't become good corporate citizens overnight. Learning to identify and develop the capacity to address social concerns takes time and requires commitment. The task is arduous because so many different issues are important to so many different members of the public—issues ranging from the environment, to worker well-being (both at home and abroad), to fairness to customers, to respect for the community in which a company operates.

7.1 The Five Faces of Corporate Responsibility

Faced with public criticism of a particular practice, how does a company respond? What actions does it take to demonstrate a higher level of corporate responsibility? According to Harvard University's Simon Zadek, exercising greater corporate responsibility generally means going through the series of five different stances summarized in Figure 2.13.[86]

FIGURE 2.13 Stages of Corporate Responsibility

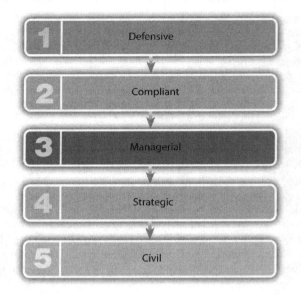

1. *Defensive.* When companies are first criticized over some problem or issue, they tend to take a defensive, often legalistic stance. They reject allegations of wrongdoing and refuse to take responsibility, arguing that fixing the problem or addressing the issue isn't their job.

2. *Compliant.* During this stage, companies adopt policies that acknowledge the wishes of the public. As a rule, however, they do only what they have to do to satisfy their critics, and little more. They're acting mainly to protect brands or reputations and to reduce the risk of litigation.

3. *Managerial.* When it becomes clear that the problem won't go away, companies admit that they need to take responsibility and action, so they look for practical long-term solutions.

4. *Strategic.* At this point, they may start to reap the benefits of acting responsibly. They often find that responding to public needs gives them a competitive edge and enhances long-term success.

5. *Civil.* Ultimately, many companies recognize the importance of getting other companies to follow their lead. They may promote participation by other firms in their industries, endorsing the principle that the public is best served through collective action.

7.2 Here's Your Salad—How About Fries?

Several years ago, McDonald's found itself in a public relations nightmare. The fast-food giant faced massive public criticism for serving unhealthy food that contributed to a national epidemic of obesity. Let's look at McDonald's responses to these criticisms and assess how far along the five-stage process the company has progressed.

The Defensive Stage

As the documentary film *Super Size Me* demonstrated, a steady diet of McDonald's burgers and fries will cause you to gain weight. It was certainly inevitable that one day the public would make a connection between the rising level of obesity in the United States and a diet heavy in fat-laden fast foods. McDonald's fast food/obesity link got a lot of attention in 2002 when obese adults and teenagers filed suits against the company, claiming it was responsible for their excess pounds. McDonald's reaction to the public outcry against the company's menu items was defensive. For example, an owner of seven McDonald's in midtown Manhattan said, "We offer healthy choices. It is up to individuals to set limits and to be informed.…McDonald's discloses nutritional information about its foods in its restaurants."[87]

The Compliant Stage

In early 2004, the public's attention was drawn to McDonald's "super-size" options. Despite the fact that a super-sized meal delivered more than fifteen hundred calories, one in ten customers went for the upgrade. McDonald's faced daily criticisms on its super-sizing campaign, from nutritionists, doctors, advocacy groups, and lawyers who held it up as a "grossly overweight" poster child for U.S. obesity concerns. And the company feared public criticism would escalate when the movie *Super Size Me* hit the theaters. The documentary tells the story of a young man who gained twenty-four pounds and wrecked his health by eating only McDonald's food for a month. Even worse, one scene shows him getting sick in his car after trying to wolf down a super-size meal. So McDonald's immediately moved from the defensive stage to the compliant stage and announced that it was eliminating its super-size option by the end of 2004. The move, though small, was in the right direction. It was touted by the company as a "menu simplification" process, but a spokesman did state, "It certainly is consistent with and on a parallel path with our ongoing commitment to a balanced lifestyle."[88]

The Managerial Stage

Criticism of McDonald's continued as customers stayed away and its profits plummeted. The company searched for ways to win back customers and keep them long-term. To do this, it would have to come up with a healthier menu. Though McDonald's had served salads for years, they weren't very good. The company got serious about salads and introduced new, improved "premium salads," complete with Newman's Own salad dressing (a nice public relations touch, as all profits on the salad dressings are donated to charities). The company also improved the Happy Meal by letting kids substitute apple slices and low-fat milk for the usual fries and soda. Oprah Winfrey's personal trainer was brought in to promote an adult version of the Happy Meal, called the GoActive meal, which includes a salad, a bottle of water, a book on nutrition, and a clip-on pedometer that measures the number of steps you take. The fat calories in Chicken McNuggets were lowered by coming out with all-white-meat McNuggets. And to appease those between-meal munchies, the company added a fruit-and-walnut salad to its menu. McDonald's goal was to convince customers that it had turned a corner and would forever more offer healthy choices to both adults and children.

The Strategic Stage

The new focus on healthy choices worked, and customers started returning. McDonald's salads were well received and accounted for about 10 percent of sales. Overall, things improved financially for the company: Sales increased and profits rose. To complete the transition to a healthier image, McDonald's came up with a new theme: helping adults and children live a balanced, active lifestyle. To go along with the theme, it launched a new active-life public-awareness campaign with the tagline "It's what I eat and what I do…I'm lovin' it." McDonald's demonstrated its concern for the health of its customers through permanent menu changes and an emphasis on the value of physical fitness. Even Ronald McDonald, the company's mascot, helped out by shooting hoops with NBA basketball star Yao Ming. The company launched a program called GoActive to help people find fun ways to build physical activity and fitness into their daily lives.

The Civil Stage

McDonald's hasn't advanced to the final stage yet; it hasn't enlisted the cooperation of other fast-food companies in encouraging children and adults to eat healthier foods. It's difficult to predict whether it will assume this role in the future, or even whether the company will stick with its healthier lifestyle theme. Indeed, it's hard to reconcile McDonald's commitment to helping people eat healthier with a promotion in the Chicago area that gave a free forty-two-ounce "super-size" soda to anyone buying a Big Mac and fries. Given that a Big Mac and medium fries deliver 910 calories, it's hard to justify encouraging customers to pile on an additional 410 calories for a big drink (at least, it's hard to justify this if you're promoting yourself as a company helping people eat better).[89]

KEY TAKEAWAYS

Faced with public criticism of a particular practice, a company is likely to progress through five different stages:

1. *Defensive.* When first criticized over some problem, companies take a defensive stance. They reject allegations of wrongdoing and refuse to take responsibility.

2. *Compliant.* During this stage, companies do only what they have to do to satisfy their critics, protect brands or reputations, and reduce the risk of litigation.

3. *Managerial.* When it's clear that the problem won't go away, companies take responsibility and look for long-term solutions.

4. *Strategic.* At this point, they may start to reap the benefits of acting responsibly. Responding to public needs gives them a competitive edge and enhances long-term success.

5. *Civil.* Ultimately, companies recognize the importance of getting other companies to follow their lead. They enlist the cooperation of other companies in supporting the issue of concern to the public.

Before going to the next chapter, take a few minutes to test your knowledge of the material covered in this section. Quizzes can be found under the "Resources" tab, "Study Aids: Quizzes."

EXERCISE

This chapter discusses a five-stage process that companies go through in responding to public criticism. Consider the situation in which McDonald's found itself when it faced massive public criticism for serving unhealthy food that contributed to a national epidemic of obesity. Given what you know about the company's reaction, identify the steps that it took in response to this criticism. In particular, show how its responses do or don't reflect the five stages of corporate responsibility outlined in the chapter. In your opinion, how far along the five-stage process has McDonald's progressed?

---

8.   CASES AND PROBLEMS

LEARNING ON THE WEB

Lessons in Community Living

Executives consider it an honor to have their company named one of *Business Ethics* magazine's "100 Best Corporate Citizens." Companies are chosen from a group of one thousand, according to how well they serve their stakeholders—owners, employees, customers, and the communities with which they share the social and natural environment. Being in the top one hundred for five years in a row is cause for celebration. Two of the twenty-nine companies that enjoy this distinction are Timberland and the New York Times Company.

The two companies are in very different industries. Timberland designs and manufactures boots and other footwear, apparel, and accessories; the New York Times Company is a media giant, with nineteen newspapers (including the *New York Times* and the *Boston Globe*), eight television stations, and more than forty Web sites. Visit the Timberland Web site (http://shop.timberland.com/home/index.jsp), and scroll to the bottom of the page to look at several social responsibility issues. Then follow the arrow to the next page, which expands its discussion of social responsibility. Then go to the New York Times Company Web site (http://www.nytco.com/social-responsibility/environmental-stewardship/), and click on the items under "Social Responsibility" to learn how each, in its own way, supports the communities with which it shares the social and natural environment. Look specifically for information that will help you answer the following questions:

1. How does each company assist its community? To what organizations does each donate money? How do employees volunteer their time? What social causes does each support?

2. How does each company work to protect the natural environment?

3. Are the community-support efforts of the two companies similar or dissimilar? In what ways do these activities reflect the purposes of each organization?

4. In your opinion, why do these companies support their communities? What benefits do they derive from being good corporate citizens?

CAREER OPPORTUNITIES

Is "WorldCom Ethics Officer" an Oxymoron?

As you found out in this chapter, WorldCom's massive accounting scandal cost investors billions and threw the company into bankruptcy. More than one hundred employees who either participated in the fraud or passively looked the other way were indicted or fired, including accountant Betty Vinson, CFO Scott Sullivan, and CEO Bernard Ebbers. With the name "WorldCom" indelibly tarnished, the company reclaimed its previous name, "MCI." It was put on court-imposed probation and ordered to follow the directives of the court. One of those directives called for setting up an ethics office. Nancy Higgins, a corporate attorney and onetime vice president for ethics at Lockheed Martin, was brought in with the title of chief ethics officer.

Higgins's primary responsibility is to ensure that MCI lives up to new CEO Michael Capellas's assertion that the company is dedicated to integrity and its employees are committed to high ethical standards. Her tasks are the same as those of most people with the same job title, but she's under more pressure because MCI can't afford any more ethical lapses. She oversees the company's ethics initiatives, including training programs and an ethics hotline. She spends a lot of her time with employees, listening to their concerns and promoting company values.

Higgins is a member of the senior executive team and reports to the CEO and board of directors. She attends all board meetings and provides members with periodic updates on the company's newly instituted ethics program (including information gleaned from the new ethics hotline).

Answer the following questions:

1. Would you be comfortable in Higgins's job? Does the job of ethics officer appeal to you? Why, or why not?
2. Would you find it worthwhile to work in an ethics office for a few years at some point in your career? Why, or why not?
3. What qualities would you look for if you were hiring an ethics officer?
4. What factors will help (or hinder) Higgins's ability to carry out her mandate to bolster integrity and foster ethical standards?
5. Would the accounting scandals have occurred at WorldCom if Higgins had been on the job back when Vinson, Sullivan, and Ebbers were still there? Explain your opinion.

TEAM-BUILDING SKILLS

What Are the Stakes When You Play with Wal-Mart?

In resolving an ethical dilemma, you have to choose between two or more opposing alternatives, both of which, while acceptable, are important to different groups. Both alternatives may be ethically legitimate, but you can act in the interest of only one group.

This project is designed to help you learn how to analyze and resolve ethical dilemmas in a business context. You'll work in teams to address three ethical dilemmas involving Wal-Mart, the world's largest company. Before meeting as a group, every team member should go to the *BusinessWeek* Web site (http://www.businessweek.com/magazine/content/03_40/b3852001_mz001.htm) and read "Is Wal-Mart Too Powerful?" The article discusses Wal-Mart's industry dominance and advances arguments for why the company is both admired and criticized.

Your team should then get together to analyze the three dilemmas that follow. Start by reading the overview of the dilemma and any assigned material. Then debate the issues, working to reach a resolution through the five-step process summarized in Figure 2.2:

1. Define the problem and collect the relevant facts.
2. Identify feasible options.
3. Assess the effect of each option on stakeholders.
4. Establish criteria for determining the most appropriate action.
5. Select the best option based on the established criteria.

Finally, prepare a report on your deliberations over each dilemma, making sure that each report contains all the following items:

- The team's recommendation for resolving the dilemma
- An explanation of the team's recommendation
- A summary of the information collected for, and the decisions made at, each step of the dilemma-resolution process

THREE ETHICAL DILEMMAS

Ethical Dilemma 1: Should Wal-Mart Close a Store because It Unionizes?

Scenario:

In February 2005, Wal-Mart closed a store in Quebec, Canada, after its workers voted to form a union. The decision has ramifications for various stakeholders, including employees, customers, and stockholders. In analyzing and arriving at a resolution to this dilemma, assume that you're the CEO of Wal-Mart, but *ignore the decision already made by the real CEO.* Arrive at your own recommendation, which may or may not be the same as that reached by your real-life counterpart.

Before analyzing this dilemma, go to the *Washington Post* Web site (http://www.washingtonpost.com/wp-dyn/articles/A15832-2005Feb10.html) and read the article "Wal-Mart Chief Defends Closing Unionized Store."

Ethical Dilemma 2: Should Levi Strauss Go into Business with Wal-Mart?

Scenario:

For years, the words *jeans* and *Levi's* were synonymous. Levi Strauss, the founder of the company that carries his name, invented blue jeans in 1850 for sale to prospectors in the gold fields of California. Company sales peaked at $7 billion in 1996 but then plummeted to $4 billion by 2003. Management has admitted that the company must reverse this downward trend if it hopes to retain the support of its twelve thousand employees, operate its remaining U.S. factories, and continue its tradition of corporate-responsibility initiatives. At this point, Wal-Mart made an attractive offer: Levi Strauss could develop a low-cost brand of jeans for sale at Wal-Mart. The decision, however, isn't as simple as it may seem: Wal-Mart's relentless pressure to offer "everyday low prices" can have wide-ranging ramifications for its suppliers' stakeholders—in this case, Levi Strauss's shareholders, employees, and customers, as well as the beneficiaries of its various social-responsibility programs. Assume that, as the CEO of Levi Strauss, you have to decide whether to accept Wal-Mart's offer. Again, ignore any decision already made by your real-life counterpart, and instead work toward an independent recommendation.

Before you analyze this dilemma, go to the *Fast Company* Web site (http://www.fastcompany.com/magazine/77/walmart.html) and read the article "The Wal-Mart You Don't Know."

Ethical Dilemma 3: Should You Welcome Wal-Mart into Your Neighborhood?

Scenario:

In 2002, Wal-Mart announced plans to build forty "supercenters" in California—a section of the country that has traditionally resisted Wal-Mart's attempts to dot the landscape with big-box stores. Skirmishes soon broke out in California communities between those in favor of welcoming Wal-Mart and those determined to fend off mammoth retail outlets.

You're a member of the local council of a California city, and you'll be voting next week on whether to allow Wal-Mart to build in your community. The council's decision will affect Wal-Mart, as well as many local stakeholders, including residents, small business owners, and employees of community supermarkets and other retail establishments. As usual, ignore any decisions already made by your real-life counterparts.

Before working on this dilemma, go to the *USA Today* Web site (http://www.usatoday.com/money/industries/retail/2004-03-02-wal-mart_x.htm) and read the article "California Tries to Slam Lid on Big-Boxed Wal-Mart."

THE GLOBAL VIEW

Was Nike Responsible for Compensating Honduran Factory Workers?

Honduras is an impoverished country in which 70 percent of its residents live in poverty. Jobs are scarce, particularly those that pay decent wages along with benefits, such as health care. It is not surprising then that workers at two Honduran factories making products for U.S. companies, including Nike, were extremely upset when their factories closed down and they lost their jobs. Even worse, the owners of the factories refused to pay the 1,800 workers $2 million in severance pay and other benefits due to them by law. Although the factory owners had been paid in full by Nike for the apparel they produced, the workers argued that Nike should be responsible for paying the $2 million in severance that the factory owners had not received.

Nike's original response was to sympathize with the workers but refuse to pay the workers the severance pay they had not received from the factory owners. This stance did not settle well with student groups around the country who rallied in support of the unpaid workers. In the end, Nike gave in to pressure from the students and paid $1.5 million to a relief fund for the employees. In addition, the company said it would provide vocational training and health coverage for the unemployed workers.

To learn more about this case, read the following:

- Nike, "Nike Statement Regarding Vision Tex and Hugger" (press release), April 20, 2010, http://nikeinc.com/news/nike-statement-regarding-vision-tex-and-hugger
- Akito Yoshikane, "Honduran Workers Speak Out against Nike's Labor Violations," *In These Times*, April 21, 2010, http://inthesetimes.org/working/entry/5895/honduran_workers_speak_out_against_nikes_labor_violations
- Steven Greenhouse, "Pressured, Nike to Help Workers in Honduras," *New York Times*, July 26, 2010, http://www.nytimes.com/2010/07/27/business/global/27nike.html
- Tim Padgett, "Just Pay It: Nike Creates Fund for Honduran Workers," *Time*, July 27, 2010, http://content.time.com/time/business/article/0,8599,2006646,00.html
- Nike, "Nike and CGT Statement" (press release), July 26, 2010, http://nikeinc.com/news/nike-and-cgt-statement

Answer the following questions:

1. Do you think Nike was responsible for compensating the workers in Honduras? Why did it change its stance?
2. Did the students, universities, and workers themselves have all the information they needed before becoming involved in the protest? Are their facts accurate?
3. Should students be activists? Do companies such as Nike ignore them at their own peril?

ENDNOTES

1. This case is based on Susan Pulliam, "How Following Orders Can Harm Your Career," *Wall Street Journal*, June 23, 2003, CareerJournal.com, http://www.cfo.com/article.cfm/3010537/c_3036075 (accessed April 23, 2014).

2. Susan Pulliam, "How Following Orders Can Harm Your Career," *Wall Street Journal*, June 23, 2003, CareerJournal.com, http://www.cfo.com/article.cfm/3010537/c_3036075 (accessed April 23, 2014).

3. Amanda Ripley, "The Night Detective," *Time*, December 22, 2002, http://www.time.com/time/personoftheyear/2002 (accessed April 23, 2014).

4. Jeff Clabaugh, "WorldCom's Betty Vinson Gets 5 Months in Jail," *Washington Business Journal*, August 5, 2005, Albuquerque Bizjournals.com, http://www.bizjournals.com/washington/stories/2005/08/01/daily51.html (accessed April 23, 2014).

5. Scott Reeves, "Lies, Damned Lies and Scott Sullivan," *Forbes.com*, February 17, 2005, http://www.forbes.com/2005/02/17/cx_sr_0217ebbers.html (accessed April 23, 2014); David A. Andelman, "Scott Sullivan Gets Slap on the Wrist—WorldCom Rate Race," *Forbes.com*, August 12, 2005, http://www.mindfully.org/Industry/2005/Sullivan-WorldCom-Rat12aug05.htm (accessed April 23, 2014).

6. Susan Pulliam, "How Following Orders Can Harm Your Career," *Wall Street Journal*, June 23, 2003, CareerJournal.com, http://www.cfo.com/article.cfm/3010537/c_3036075 (accessed April 23, 2014).

7. "World-Class Scandal at WorldCom," *CBSNews.com*, June 26, 2002, http://www.cbsnews.com/news/world-class-scandal-at-worldcom (accessed April 23, 2014).

8. Daniel Kadlec, "Enron: Who's Accountable?" *Time*, January 21, 2002, http://content.time.com/time/magazine/article/0,9171,1001636,00.html (accessed April 23, 2014).

9. David Lieberman, "Prosecutors Wrap Up $3.2B Adelphia Case," *USA Today*, June 25, 2004, http://www.usatoday.com/money/industries/telecom/2004-06-25-adelphia_x.htm (accessed April 23, 2014).

10. "Tyco Wants Its Money Back," *CNNMoney*, September 17, 2002, http://money.cnn.com/2002/09/17/news/companies/tyco/index.htm (accessed April 23, 2014).

11. "Top 10 Crooked CEOs," Time Specials, *Time.com*, http://www.time.com/time/specials/packages/article/0,28804,1903155_1903156_1903160,00.html (accessed April 23, 2014).

12. Fred Langan, "The $50-Billion BMIS Debacle: How a Ponzi Scheme Works," *CBSNews*, December 15, 2008, http://www.cbc.ca/news/business/story/2008/12/15/f-langan-bmis.html (accessed April 23, 2014).

13. Nancy Gibbs et al., "Summer of Mistrust," *Time*, July 22, 2002, http://content.time.com/time/nation/article/0,8599,320734,00.html (accessed April 14, 2014).

14. Alan Axelrod, *My First Book of Business Ethics* (Philadelphia: Quirk Books, 2004), 7.

15. "100 Best Corporate Citizens for 2013," *Corporate Responsibility Magazine*, http://www.thecro.com/content/cr-magazine-corporate-citizenship-lists-methodology (accessed April 23, 2014).

16. Alan Axelrod, *My First Book of Business Ethics* (Philadelphia: Quirk Books, 2004), 7.

17. Quoted by Adrian Gostick and Dana Telford, *The Integrity Advantage* (Salt Lake City: Gibbs Smith, 2003), 3–4.

18. John C. Maxwell, *There's No Such Thing as "Business Ethics": There's Only One Rule for Making Decisions* (New York: Warner Books, 2003), 19–21.

19. See Tamara Kaplan, "The Tylenol Crisis: How Effective Public Relations Saved Johnson & Johnson," http://www.aerobiologicalengineering.com/wxk116/TylenolMurders/crisis.html (accessed April 23, 2014).

20. Yaakov Weber, "CEO Saves Company's Reputation, Products," *New Sunday Times*, June 13, 1999, http://adtimes.nstp.com.my/jobstory/jun13.htm (accessed April 24, 2006).

21. Credo, Johnson & Johnson company Web site, http://www.jnj.com/connect/about-jnj/jnj-credo (accessed April 23, 2014).

22. Mina Kimes, "Why J&J's Headache Won't Go Away," *Fortune* (CNNMoney), August 19, 2010, http://money.cnn.com/2010/08/18/news/companies/jnj_drug_recalls.fortune/index.htm (accessed April 23, 2014).

23. McNeil Product Recall Information, http://www.mcneilproductrecall.com (accessed April 23, 2014).

24. Bill Berkrot, "J&J Confirms Widely Expanded Contact Lens Recall," December 1, 2010, http://www.reuters.com/article/2010/12/01/us-jandj-recall-idUSTRE6B05G620101201 (accessed April 23, 2014).

25. *New York Times*, Business Day, August 20, 2010, http://www.nytimes.com/2010/08/27/business/27hip.html (accessed April 23, 2014).

26. Mina Kimes, "Why J&J's Headache Won't Go Away," *Fortune* (CNNMoney), August 19, 2010, http://money.cnn.com/2010/08/18/news/companies/jnj_drug_recalls.fortune/index.htm (accessed April 23, 2014).

27. Jonathan D. Rockoff and Jon Kamp, "J&J Contact Lenses Recalled," *Wall Street Journal*, Health section, August 24, 2010, http://online.wsj.com/article/SB10001424052748703846604575447430303567108.html (accessed April 23, 2014).

28. Natasha Singer, "Johnson & Johnson Recalls Hip Implants," *New York Times*, Business Day, August 20, 2010, http://www.nytimes.com/2010/08/27/business/27hip.html (accessed April 23, 2014).

29. Mina Kimes, "Why J&J's Headache Won't Go Away," *Fortune* (CNNMoney), August 19, 2010, http://money.cnn.com/2010/08/18/news/companies/jnj_drug_recalls.fortune/index.htm (accessed April 23, 2014).

30. Mina Kimes, "Why J&J's Headache Won't Go Away," *Fortune* (CNNMoney), August 19, 2010, http://money.cnn.com/2010/08/18/news/companies/jnj_drug_recalls.fortune/index.htm (accessed April 23, 2014).

31. Matthew Perrone, "J&J CEO Gets 3% Raise, but Bonus Is Cut," *USA Today*, February 25, 2011, http://www.usatoday.com/money/industries/health/2011-02-25-jnj_N.htm (accessed April 23, 2014).

32. Mina Kimes, "Why J&J's Headache Won't Go Away," *Fortune* (CNNMoney), August 19, 2010, http://money.cnn.com/2010/08/18/news/companies/jnj_drug_recalls.fortune/index.htm (accessed April 23, 2014).

33. Mina Kimes, "Why J&J's Headache Won't Go Away," *Fortune* (CNNMoney), August 19, 2010, http://money.cnn.com/2010/08/18/news/companies/jnj_drug_recalls.fortune/index.htm (accessed April 23, 2014).

34. Ed Silverman, "Recall Fallout? Johnson & Johnson's Goggins to Retire," *Pharmalot*, September 16, 2010, http://regator.com/p/244670135/recall_fallout_johnson_johnsons_goggins_to_retire (accessed April 23, 2014).

35. "J&J's Colleen Goggins Sells Nearly $3M in Stock," *Citibizlist*, September 14, 2010, http://philadelphia.citybizlist.com/article/jjs-colleen-goggins-sells-nearly-3m-stock-cbl-1 (accessed April 23, 2014).

36. Mina Kimes, "Why J&J's Headache Won't Go Away," *Fortune* (CNNMoney), August 19, 2010, http://money.cnn.com/2010/08/18/news/companies/jnj_drug_recalls.fortune/index.htm (accessed April 23, 2014).

37. Online Ethics Center for Engineering and Science, "Advice from the Texas Instruments Ethics Office: What Do You Do When the Light Turns Yellow?" Onlineethics.org, http://onlineethics.org/corp/help.html#yellow (accessed April 24, 2006).

38. JCPenney Co., "Statement of Business Ethics for Associates and Officers: The 'Spirit' of This Statement," http://ir.jcpenney.com/phoenix.zhtml?c=70528&p=irol-govconduct (accessed April 23, 2014).

39. Quoted by Adrian Gostick and Dana Telford, *The Integrity Advantage* (Salt Lake City: Gibbs Smith, 2003), 103.

40. Adapted from Adrian Gostick and Dana Telford, The Integrity Advantage (Salt Lake City: Gibbs Smith, 2003), 16.

41. See Adrian Gostick and Dana Telford, *The Integrity Advantage* (Salt Lake City: Gibbs Smith, 2003), 13.

42. National Whistleblower Center, "Labor Day Report: The National Status of Whistleblower Protection on Labor Day, 2002," http://www.whistleblowers.org/labordayreport.htm (accessed April 23, 2014).

43. Paula Dwyer et al., "Year of the Whistleblower," *BusinessWeek Online*, December 16, 2002, http://www.businessweek.com/magazine/content/02_50/b3812094.htm (accessed April 23, 2014).

44. Scott Waller, "Whistleblower Tells Students to Have Personal Integrity," *The (Jackson, MS) Clarion-Ledger*, November 18, 2003, http://www.clarionledger.com/news/0311/18/b01.html (accessed April 24, 2006).

45. Adrian Gostick and Dana Telford, *The Integrity Advantage* (Salt Lake City: Gibbs Smith, 2003), 98–99.

46. Saul W. Gellerman, "Why 'Good' Managers Make Bad Ethical Choices," *Harvard Business Review on Corporate Ethics* (Boston: Harvard Business School Press, 2003), 59.

47. Adrian Gostick and Dana Telford, *The Integrity Advantage* (Salt Lake City: Gibbs Smith, 2003), 12.

48. See especially Tom Fowler, "The Pride and the Fall of Enron," *Houston Chronicle*, October 20, 2002, http://www.chron.com/business/enron/article/Enron-s-corporate-tumble-was-a-long-time-coming-2083723.php (accessed April 23, 2014).

49. Episode recounted by Norm Augustine, "Business Ethics in the 21st Century" (speech, Ethics Resource Center), http://www.ethics.org/resources/speech_detail.cfm?ID=848 (accessed April 24, 2006).

50. Norm Augustine, "Business Ethics in the 21st Century" (speech, Ethics Resource Center), http://www.ethics.org/resources/speech_detail.cfm?ID=848 (accessed April 24, 2006).

51. William McCall, "CEO Will Get Salary, Bonus in Prison," *CorpWatch*, http://www.corpwatch.org/article.php?id=11476 (accessed April 24, 2006).

52. Hershey Foods, "Code of Ethical Business Conduct," http://www.thehersheycompany.com/about/conduct.asp (accessed April 24, 2014).

53. See David P. Baron, *Business and Its Environment*, 4th ed. (Upper Saddle River, NJ: Prentice Hall, 2003), 650–52.

54. Saul W. Gellerman, "Why 'Good' Managers Make Bad Ethical Choices," *Harvard Business Review on Corporate Ethics* (Boston: Harvard Business School Press, 2003), 49–66.

55. Saul W. Gellerman, "Why 'Good' Managers Make Bad Ethical Choices," *Harvard Business Review on Corporate Ethics* (Boston: Harvard Business School Press, 2003), 53.

56. Procter & Gamble, *2003 Sustainability Report*, http://www.pg.com/content/pdf/01_about_pg/corporate_citizenship/sustainability/reports/sustainability_report_2003.pdf (accessed April 24, 2014).

57. U.S. Equal Employment Opportunity Commission, "Facts about Sexual Harassment," http://www.eeoc.gov/facts/fs-sex.html (accessed April 24, 2014).

58. Joanna Grossman, "Sexual Harassment in the Workplace: Do Employers' Efforts Truly Prevent Harassment, or Just Prevent Liability," *Find Laws Legal Commentary, Writ*, http://writ.news.findlaw.com/grossman/20020507.html (accessed April 24, 2014).

59. Joanna Grossman, "Sexual Harassment in the Workplace: Do Employers' Efforts Truly Prevent Harassment, or Just Prevent Liability," *Find Laws Legal Commentary, Writ*, http://writ.news.findlaw.com/grossman/20020507.html (accessed April 24, 2014).

60. Procter & Gamble, "Respect in the Workplace," *Our Values and Policies*, http://www.pg.com/content/pdf/01_about_pg/01_about_pg_homepage/about_pg_toolbar/download_report/values_and_policies.pdf (accessed April 24, 2014).

61. Brenda Cronin, "Male-Female Pay Gap Hasn't Moved Much in Years," *Wall Street Journal*, September 17, 2013, http://blogs.wsj.com/economics/2013/09/17/male-female-pay-gap-hasnt-moved-much-in-years (accessed April 24, 2014).

62. U.S. Department of Labor, "Minimum Wage Laws in the States," http://www.dol.gov/esa/minwage/america.htm (accessed April 24, 2014).

63. Henry A. Waxman, House of Representatives, "Remarks on Proposed Consumer Bill of Rights Day, Extension of Remarks," March 15, 1993, http://thomas.loc.gov/cgi-bin/query/z?r103:E15MR30-90 (accessed April 24, 2006), 1–2.

64. Target Brands Inc., "1 Billion for Education," https://corporate.target.com/corporate-responsibility/education (accessed April 24, 2014).

65. Jennifer Barrett, "A Secret Recipe for Success: Paul Newman and A. E. Hotchner Dish Up Management Tips from Newman's Own," *Newsweek*, November 3, 2003, http://www.highbeam.com/doc/1G1-109357986.html (accessed April 24, 2014); Paul Newman, "Our Story," Newman's Own Web site, http://www.newmansown.com/our-stories (accessed April 24, 2014).

66. "Environmental Internships," Patagonia Web site, http://www.patagonia.com/us/patagonia.go?assetid=80524 (accessed April 24, 2014).

67. Bill and Melinda Gates Foundation, "2011 Annual Letter from Bill Gates," http://www.gatesfoundation.org/annual-letter/2011/Pages/home.aspx (accessed April 24, 2014); Bill and Melinda Gates Foundation, "2013 Annual Letter from Bill Gates," http://www.gatesfoundation.org/Who-We-Are/Resources-and-Media/Annual-Letters-List/Annual-Letter-2013 (accessed April 24, 2014).

68. Dan Ackman, "Bill Gates Is a Genius and You're Not," *Forbes.com*, July 21, 2004, http://www.forbes.com/2004/07/21/cx_da_0721topnews.html (accessed April 24, 2014).

69. Philip Kotler and Nancy Lee, "Best of Breed," *Stanford Social Innovation Review*, Spring 2004, 21.

70. "Social Responsibility, P&G Children's Safe Drinking Water Program," Procter & Gamble Web site, http://www.pg.com/en_US/sustainability/social_responsibility/childrens_safe_water.shtml (accessed April 24, 2014); "Together, We Can Help Save One Life Every Hour," Procter & Gamble Web site, http://www.csdw.org/csdw/index.shtml (accessed April 24, 2014).

71. "1% for the Planet," Environmentalism: What We Do, Patagonia Web site, http://www.patagonia.com/us/patagonia.go?assetid=2047 (accessed April 24, 2014).

72. "Fabric: Organic Cotton," Patagonia Web site, http://www.patagonia.com/us/patagonia.go?assetid=2077 (accessed April 24, 2014).

73. "Fabric: Recycled Polyester," Patagonia Web site, http://www.patagonia.com/us/patagonia.go?assetid=2791 (accessed August 15, 2011).

74. John Carey, "Global Warming," *Business Week*, August 16, 2004, 64.

75. John Carey, "Global Warming," *Business Week*, August 16, 2004, 60; "Reducing DuPont's Footprint," DuPont Web site, Sustainability, http://www2.dupont.com/Sustainability/en_US/Footprint/index.html (accessed April 24, 2014).

76. "Plug-In Electric Vehicles in the United States," *Wikipedia*, http://en.wikipedia.org/wiki/Plug-in_electric_vehicles_in_the_United_States (accessed April 24, 2014).

77. "Make the Change to ENERGY STAR," General Electric Web site, http://www.geappliances.com/energy-star-appliances (accessed April 24, 2014).

78. John Carey, "Global Warming," *Business Week*, August 16, 2004, 64; "Wind Turbines," General Electric Web site, http://www.ge-energy.com/wind (accessed April 24, 2014).

79. David Krantz and Brad Kifferstein, "Water Pollution and Society," University of Michigan, http://www.umich.edu/~gs265/society/waterpollution.htm (accessed April 24, 2006).

80. Frances Weaver, "The Unprecedented Water Crisis of the American Southwest," *The Week*, http://theweek.com/article/index/255814/the-unprecedented-water-crisis-of-the-american-southwest (accessed April 24, 2014).

81. "The Home Depot Hosts Water Conservation Workshops Nationwide," Home Depot Web site, http://ir.homedepot.com/phoenix.zhtml?c=63646&p=RssLanding&cat=news&id=1917532 (accessed April 24, 2014).

82. *The Lorax* was written by Dr. Seuss. It was first published in 1971 by Random House, New York. The copyright was renewed in 1999.

83. For an excellent overview of sustainability, watch a short animated movie explaining sustainability at http://www.youtube.com/watch?v=B5NiTN0chj0 2 min—April 9, 2010—Uploaded by RealEyesvideo and created by RealEyes by Igloo Animations.

84. Bob Keefe, Meet Google's chief sustainability officer (What a Cool Job!), Divine Caroline: Life in your words, at http://www.divinecaroline.com/22277/44799-meet-google-s-chief-sustainability-officer#ixzz1VWmTFINK (accessed April 17, 2011).

85. "Triple Bottom Line: It Consists of Three Ps: Profit, People, and Planet," *The Economist*, November 17, 2009, at http://www.economist.com/node/14301663 (accessed April 24, 2014).

86. Simon Zadek, "The Path to Corporate Responsibility," *Harvard Business Review*, December 2004, 1–9.

87. Chris Burritt, "McDonald's Shrugs Off Obesity Case," *Sina.com*, January 27, 2005, http://english.sina.com/business/1/2005/0127/19504.html (accessed April 24, 2014).

88. Bruce Horovitz, "By Year's End, Regular Size Will Have to Do," *USA Today*, March 4, 2004, http://www.usatoday.com/money/industries/food/2004-03-02-mcdonalds-supersize_x.htm (accessed April 24, 2014).

89. Eric Herman, "McDonald's Giant Drinks Return," *Chicago Sun-Times*, June 17, 2005, http://www.freerepublic.com/focus/f-news/1424786/posts (accessed April 24, 2014).

CHAPTER 3
Business in a Global Environment

IT'S A SMALL WORLD

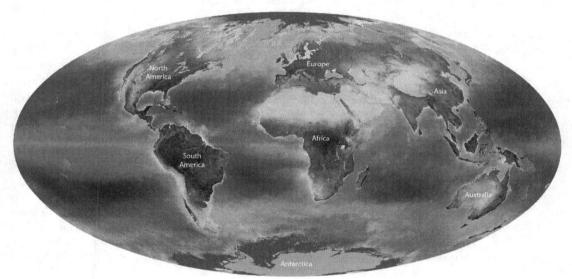

© *Thinkstock*

Do you wear Nike shoes or Timberland boots? Buy groceries at Tops Friendly Markets, Giant Food Stores, or Stop & Shop? Listen to Beyonce, Justin Timberlake, Jay Z, Britney Spears, Rhianna, Taylor Swift, Daft Punk, or the Dave Matthews Band? If you answered yes to any of these questions, you're a global business customer. Both Nike and Timberland manufacture most of their products overseas. The Dutch firm Royal Ahold owns all three supermarket chains. Sony Music, the label that records Beyonce, Rhianna, Taylor Swift, and the other artists mentioned, belongs to a Japanese company. Take an imaginary walk down Orchard Road, the most fashionable shopping area in Singapore. You'll pass department stores such as Tokyo-based Takashimaya and London's very British Marks & Spencer, both filled with such well-known international labels as Ralph Lauren Polo, Burberry, and Chanel. If you need a break, you can also stop for a latte at Seattle-based Starbucks.

Take an imaginary walk down Orchard Road, the most fashionable shopping area in Singapore. You'll pass department stores such as Tokyo-based Takashimaya and London's very British Marks & Spencer, both filled with such well-known international labels as Ralph Lauren Polo, Burberry, Chanel, and Nokia. If you need a break, you can also stop for a latte at Seattle-based Starbucks.

When you're in the Chinese capital of Beijing, don't miss Tiananmen Square. Parked in front of the Great Hall of the People, the seat of Chinese government, are fleets of black Cadillacs, cars made by General Motors in the United States. If you're adventurous enough to find yourself in Faisalabad, a medium-size city in Pakistan, you'll see locals riding donkeys, camels pulling carts piled with agricultural produce, and Hamdard University, located in a refurbished hotel. Step inside its computer labs, and the sensation of being in a faraway place will likely disappear: on the computer screens, you'll recognize the familiar Microsoft flag—the same one emblazoned on screens in Microsoft's hometown of Seattle and just about everywhere else on the planet.

1. THE GLOBALIZATION OF BUSINESS

LEARNING OBJECTIVES

1. Explain why nations and companies participate in international trade.
2. Describe the concepts of absolute and comparative advantage.
3. Explain how trade between nations is measured.
4. Describe the two key indicators a nation looks at to evaluate the impact of its international trade: balance of trade and balance of payments.

The globalization of business is bound to affect you. Not only will you buy products manufactured overseas, but it's highly likely that you'll meet and work with individuals from various countries and cultures as customers, suppliers, colleagues, employees, or employers. The bottom line is that the globalization of world commerce has an impact on all of us. Therefore, it makes sense to learn more about how globalization works.

FIGURE 3.1

World commerce has become increasingly international, so understanding how global business works is key to a successful career.

© 2010 Jupiterimages Corporation

Never before has business spanned the globe the way it does today. But why is international business important? Why do companies and nations engage in international trade? What strategies do they employ in the global marketplace? What challenges do companies face when they do business overseas? How do governments and international agencies promote and regulate international trade? Is the globalization of business a good thing? What career opportunities are there for you in global business? How should you prepare yourself to take advantage of them? These are the questions that we'll be addressing in this chapter. Let's start by looking at the more specific reasons why companies and nations engage in international trade.

1.1 Why Do Nations Trade?

Why does the United States import automobiles, steel, digital phones, and apparel from other countries? Why don't we just make them ourselves? Why do other countries buy wheat, chemicals, machinery, and consulting services from us? Because no national economy produces all the goods and services that its people need. Countries are *importers* when they buy goods and services from other countries; when they sell products to other nations, they're *exporters*. (We'll discuss importing and exporting in greater detail later in the chapter.) The monetary value of international trade is enormous. In 2012, the total value of worldwide trade in merchandise and commercial services was $22.5 *trillion*.[1]

1.2 Absolute and Comparative Advantage

To understand why certain countries import or export certain products, you need to realize that every country (or region) can't produce the same products. The cost of labor, the availability of natural resources, and the level of know-how vary greatly around the world. Most economists use the concepts of *absolute advantage* and *comparative advantage* to explain why countries import some products and export others.

Absolute Advantage

A nation has an **absolute advantage** if (1) it's the only source of a particular product or (2) it can make more of a product using the same amount of or fewer resources than other countries. Because of climate and soil conditions, for example, France had an absolute advantage in wine making until its dominance of worldwide wine production was challenged by the growing wine industries in Italy, Spain, and the United States. Unless an absolute advantage is based on some limited natural resource, it seldom lasts. That's why there are few, if any, examples of absolute advantage in the world today.

Comparative Advantage

How can we predict, for any given country, which products will be made and sold at home, which will be imported, and which will be exported? This question can be answered by looking at the concept of **comparative advantage**, which exists when a country can produce a product at a lower opportunity cost compared to another nation. But what's an *opportunity cost*? Opportunity costs are the products that a country must decline to make in order to produce something else. When a country decides to specialize in a particular product, it must sacrifice the production of another product.

Let's simplify things by imagining a world with only two countries—the Republic of High Tech and the Kingdom of Low Tech. We'll pretend that each country knows how to make two and only two products: wooden boats and telescopes. Each country spends half its resources (labor and capital) on each good. Figure 3.2 shows the daily output for both countries: High Tech makes three boats and nine telescopes while Low Tech makes two boats and one telescope. (They're not highly productive, as we've imagined two *very* small countries.)

FIGURE 3.2 Comparative Advantage in the Techs

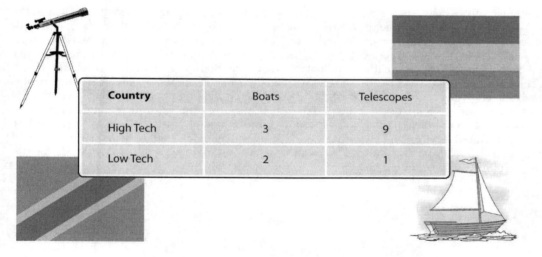

Country	Boats	Telescopes
High Tech	3	9
Low Tech	2	1

First, note that High Tech has an *absolute* advantage (relative to Low Tech) in both boats and telescopes: it can make more boats (three versus two) and more telescopes (nine versus one) than Low Tech can with the same resources. So, why doesn't High Tech make *all* the boats and *all* the telescopes needed for *both* countries? Because it lacks sufficient resources to make all the boats and all the telescopes, High Tech must, therefore, decide how much of its resources to devote to each of the two goods. Let's assume that each country could devote 100 percent of its resources on *either* of the two goods. We'll pick boats as a start. If both countries spend *all* their resources on boats (and make no telescopes), here's what happens:

- When we assumed that High Tech spent half of its time on boats and half of its time on telescopes, it was able to make nine telescopes (see Figure 3.2). If it gives up the opportunity to make the nine telescopes, it can use the time gained by not making the telescopes to make three more boats (the number of boats it can make with half of its time). Because High Tech could make three more boats by giving up the opportunity to make the nine telescopes, the opportunity cost of making each boat is three telescopes (9 telescopes ÷ 3 boats = 3 telescopes).

- When we assumed that Low Tech spent half of its time on boats and half of its time on telescopes, it was able to make only one telescope (Figure 3.2). If it gives up the opportunity to make the telescope, it can use the time gained by not making the telescope to make two more boats. Because Low Tech could make two more boats by giving up the opportunity to make one

---

absolute advantage

Condition whereby a country is the only source of a product or is able to make more of a product using the same or fewer resources than other countries.

comparative advantage

Condition whereby one nation is able to produce a product at a lower opportunity cost compared to another nation.

telescope, the opportunity cost of making each boat is half a telescope (1 telescope ÷ 2 boats = 1/2 of a telescope).

- Low Tech, therefore, enjoys a *lower opportunity cost*: Because it must give up less to make the extra boats (1/2 telescope vs. 3 telescopes), it has a comparative advantage for boats. And because it's better—that is, more efficient—at making boats than at making telescopes, it should specialize in boat making.

Now to telescopes. Here's what happens if each country spends all its time making telescopes and makes no boats:

- When we assumed that High Tech spent half of its time on boats and half of its time on telescopes, it was able to make three boats (Figure 3.2). If it gives up the opportunity to make the three boats, it can use the time gained by not making the boats to make nine more telescopes. Because High Tech could make nine more telescopes by giving up the opportunity to make three boats, the opportunity cost of making each telescope is one-third of a boat (3 boats ÷ 9 telescopes = 1/3 of a boat).

- When Low Tech spent half of its time on boats and half of its time on telescopes, it was able to make two boats. If it gives up the opportunity to make the two boats, it can use the time to make one more telescope. Thus, if High Tech wants to make only telescopes, it could make one more telescope by giving up the opportunity to make two boats. Thus, the opportunity cost of making each telescope is two boats (2 boats ÷ 1 telescope = 2 boats).

- In this case, High Tech has the *lower opportunity cost*: Because it had to give up less to make the extra telescopes (1/3 of a boat vs. 2 boats), it enjoys a comparative advantage for telescopes. And because it's better—more efficient—at making telescopes than at making boats, it should specialize in telescope making.

Each country will specialize in making the good for which it has a comparative advantage—that is, the good that it can make most efficiently, relative to the other country. High Tech will devote its resources to telescopes (which it's good at making), and Low Tech will put its resources into boat making (which it does well). High Tech will export its excess telescopes to Low Tech, which will pay for the telescopes with the money it earns by selling its excess boats to High Tech. Both countries will be better off.

Things are a lot more complex in the real world, but, generally speaking, nations trade to exploit their advantages. They benefit from specialization, focusing on what they do best, and trading the output to other countries for what *they* do best. The United States, for instance, is increasingly an exporter of knowledge-based products, such as software, movies, music, and professional services (management consulting, financial services, and so forth). America's colleges and universities, therefore, are a source of comparative advantage, and students from all over the world come to the United States for the world's best higher-education system.

FIGURE 3.3

Many people study in the United States to take advantage of one of the world's premier education systems.

France and Italy are centers for fashion and luxury goods and are leading exporters of wine, perfume, and designer clothing. Japan's engineering expertise has given it an edge in such fields as automobiles and consumer electronics. And with large numbers of highly skilled graduates in technology, India has become the world's leader in low-cost, computer-software engineering.

1.3   How Do We Measure Trade between Nations?

To evaluate the nature and consequences of its international trade, a nation looks at two key indicators. We determine a country's **balance of trade** by subtracting the value of its imports from the value of its exports. If a country sells more products than it buys, it has a favorable balance, called a **trade surplus**. If it buys more than it sells, it has an unfavorable balance, or a **trade deficit**.

> **balance of trade**
> Difference between the value of a nation's imports and its exports during a specified period.

For many years, the United States has had a trade deficit: we buy far more goods from the rest of the world than we sell overseas. This fact shouldn't be surprising. With high income levels, we not only consume a sizable portion of our own domestically produced goods but enthusiastically buy imported goods. Other countries, such as China and Taiwan, which manufacture primarily for export, have large trade surpluses because they sell far more goods overseas than they buy.

> **trade surplus**
> Condition whereby a country sells more products than it buys, resulting in a favorable trade balance.

Managing the National Credit Card

Are trade deficits a bad thing? Not necessarily. They can be positive if a country's economy is strong enough both to keep growing and to generate the jobs and incomes that permit its citizens to buy the best the world has to offer. That was certainly the case in the United States in the 1990s. Some experts, however, are alarmed at our rapidly accelerating trade deficit. Investment guru Warren Buffet, for example, cautions that no country can continuously sustain large and burgeoning trade deficits. Why not? Because creditor nations will eventually stop taking IOUs from debtor nations, and when that happens, the national spending spree will have to cease. "Our national credit card," he warns, "allows us to charge truly breathtaking amounts. But that card's credit line is not limitless."[2]

> **trade deficit**
> Condition whereby a country buys more products than it sells, resulting in an unfavorable trade balance.

By the same token, trade surpluses aren't necessarily good for a nation's consumers. Japan's export-fueled economy produced high economic growth in the 1970s and 1980s. But most domestically made consumer goods were priced at artificially high levels inside Japan itself—so high, in fact, that many Japanese traveled overseas to buy the electronics and other high-quality goods on which Japanese trade was dependent. CD players and televisions were significantly cheaper in Honolulu or Los Angeles than in Tokyo. How did this situation come about? Though Japan manufactures a variety of goods, many of them are made for export. To secure shares in international markets, Japan prices its exported goods competitively. Inside Japan, because competition is limited, producers can put artificially high prices on Japanese-made goods. Due to a number of factors (high demand for a limited supply of imported goods, high shipping and distribution costs, and other costs incurred by importers in a nation that tends to protect its own industries), imported goods are also expensive.[3]

Balance of Payments

The second key measure of the effectiveness of international trade is **balance of payments**: the difference, over a period of time, between the total flow of money coming into a country and the total flow of money going out. As in its balance of trade, the biggest factor in a country's balance of payments is the money that comes in and goes out as a result of imports and exports. But balance of payments includes other cash inflows and outflows, such as cash received from or paid for foreign investment, loans, tourism, military expenditures, and foreign aid. For example, if a U.S. company buys some real estate in a foreign country, that investment counts in the U.S. balance of payments, but not in its balance of trade, which measures only import and export transactions. In the long run, having an unfavorable balance of payments can negatively affect the stability of a country's currency. Some observers are worried about the U.S. dollar, which has undergone an accelerating pattern of unfavorable balances of payments since the 1970s. For one thing, carrying negative balances has forced the United States to cover its debt by borrowing from other countries.[4] Figure 3.4 provides a brief historical overview to illustrate the relationship between the United States' balance of trade and its balance of payments.

> **balance of payments**
> Difference between the total flow of money coming into a country and the total flow of money going out.

FIGURE 3.4 U.S. Imports, Exports, and Balance of Payments, 1994–2012

Note: Figures are for "goods" only, not "goods and services."

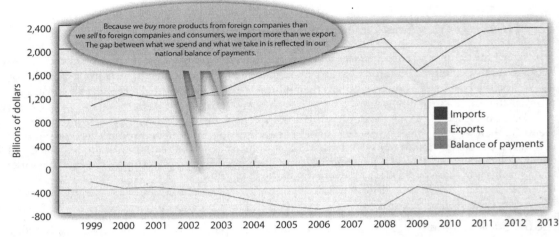

Source: *U.S. Census Bureau, Foreign Trade Division.*

KEY TAKEAWAY

- Nations trade because they don't produce all the products that their inhabitants need.
    1. They import those that they need but don't produce.
    2. To understand why certain countries import or export certain products, you need to realize that not all countries are good at producing or are able to produce the same products.
    3. The cost of labor, the availability of natural resources, and the level of know-how vary greatly around the world.
- To explain how countries decide what products to import and export, economists use the concepts of *absolute* and *comparative advantage*.
    1. A nation has an **absolute advantage** if it's the only source of a particular product or can make more of a product with the same amount of or fewer resources than other countries.
    2. A **comparative advantage** exists when a country can produce a product at a lower *opportunity cost* than other nations.
- Nations trade to exploit their advantages: they benefit from specialization, focusing on what they do best and trading the output to other countries for what *they* do best.
- To evaluate the impact of its international trade, a nation looks at two key indicators: balance of trade and balance of payments.
- We determine a country's **balance of trade** by subtracting the value of its imports from the value of its exports.
    1. If a country sells more products than it buys, it has a favorable balance, called a **trade surplus**.
    2. If it buys more than it sells, it has an unfavorable balance, or a **trade deficit**.
- The **balance of payments** is the difference, over a period of time, between the total flow coming into a country and the total flow going out.
    1. As in its balance of trade, the biggest factor in a country's balance of payments is the money that comes in and goes out as a result of exports and imports.
    2. But balance of payments includes other cash inflows and outflows, such as cash received from or paid for foreign investment, loans, tourism, military expenditures, and foreign aid.

Before going to the next section of this chapter, take a few minutes to test your knowledge of the material covered in this section. Quizzes can be found under the "Resources" tab, "Study Aids: Quizzes."

EXERCISES

1. We use the concepts of absolute and comparative advantage to explain why countries import some products and export others. We can also use them to explain how work can be divided between two persons. Two consultants—Jennifer and John—have a client who needs a company report written and a PowerPoint presentation prepared within the next two weeks. Both Jennifer and John have experience writing reports and preparing presentations, but neither has the time to do both jobs. From past experience, they know how much time each of them needs to complete each type of project:

Consultant	Write a report	Prepare a presentation
John	80 hours	40 hours
Jennifer	150 hours	60 hours

Using the information contained in the grid above, answer each of the following questions:

   a. Does either John or Jennifer have an absolute advantage in (1) writing reports and/or (2) preparing presentations?

   b. Does either have a comparative advantage? (To handle this question, first determine *how many total hours it would take to serve the client if John writes the report and Jennifer prepares the presentation.* Then, determine *how many total hours would be required if, instead, Jennifer writes the report and John prepares the presentation.*)

   c. Based on your analysis, how would you recommend that John and Jennifer divide the work?

   d. Given your answer to the previous question, would you say that John has a comparative advantage in writing reports, in making presentations, or in both? What should John specialize in?

   e. Does Jennifer have a comparative advantage in either task? What should she specialize in?

2. What happens if, during a given year, you spend more money than you take in? What happens if you finance your overspending by running up your credit card balance to some outrageous limit? Would you have trouble borrowing in the future? Would you have to pay higher interest rates? How would you get out of debt?

   Now let's change *you* to *the United States.* The United States has just run up one of the largest one-year trade deficits in history—for 2010 the trade deficit was $540 billion. Respond to the following items:

   a. Define the term *trade deficit* and explain how the United States ended up with such a large one.

   b. Is the trade deficit a good or a bad thing? Why, or why not?

   c. Define the term *balance of payments* and explain whether the United States has a favorable or unfavorable balance of payments.

   d. What will be the consequences if the United States repeatedly runs up a negative balance of payments?

2. OPPORTUNITIES IN INTERNATIONAL BUSINESS

LEARNING OBJECTIVES

1. **Define importing and exporting.**
2. **Explain how companies enter the international market through licensing agreements or franchises.**
3. **Describe how companies reduce costs through contract manufacturing and outsourcing.**
4. **Explain the purpose of international strategic alliances and joint ventures.**
5. **Understand how U.S. companies expand their businesses through foreign direct investments and international subsidiaries.**
6. **Understand the arguments for and against multinational corporations.**

The fact that nations exchange billions of dollars in goods and services each year demonstrates that international trade makes good economic sense. For an American company wishing to expand beyond national borders, there are a variety of ways it can get involved in international business. Let's take a closer look at the more popular ones.

2.1 Importing and Exporting

Importing (buying products overseas and reselling them in one's own country) and **exporting** (selling domestic products to foreign customers) are the oldest and most prevalent forms of international trade. For many companies, importing is the primary link to the global market. American food and beverage wholesalers, for instance, import the bottled water Evian from its source in the pristine French Alps for resale in U.S. supermarkets.[5] Other companies get into the global arena by identifying an international market for their products and become exporters. The Chinese, for instance, are increasingly fond of fast foods cooked in soybean oil. Because they also have an increasing appetite for meat, they need high-protein soybeans to raise livestock.[6] As a result, American farmers now export over $9 billion worth of soybeans to China every year.[7]

2.2 Licensing and Franchising

A company that wants to get into an international market quickly while taking only limited financial and legal risks might consider licensing agreements with foreign companies. An **international licensing agreement** allows a foreign company (the *licensee*) to sell the products of a producer (the *licensor*) or to use its intellectual property (such as patents, trademarks, copyrights) in exchange for royalty fees. Here's how it works: You own a company in the United States that sells coffee-flavored popcorn. You're sure that your product would be a big hit in Japan, but you don't have the resources to set up a factory or sales office in that country. You can't make the popcorn here and ship it to Japan because it would get stale. So you enter into a licensing agreement with a Japanese company that allows your licensee to manufacture coffee-flavored popcorn using your special process and to sell it in Japan under your brand name. In exchange, the Japanese licensee would pay you a royalty fee.

Another popular way to expand overseas is to sell franchises. Under an **international franchise** agreement, a company (the *franchiser*) grants a foreign company (the *franchisee*) the right to use its brand name and to sell its products or services. The franchisee is responsible for all operations but agrees to operate according to a business model established by the franchiser. In turn, the franchiser usually provides advertising, training, and new-product assistance. Franchising is a natural form of global expansion for companies that operate domestically according to a franchise model, including restaurant chains, such as McDonald's and Kentucky Fried Chicken, and hotel chains, such as Holiday Inn and Best Western.

2.3 Contract Manufacturing and Outsourcing

Because of high domestic labor costs, many U.S. companies manufacture their products in countries where labor costs are lower. This arrangement is called **international contract manufacturing** or **outsourcing**. A U.S. company might contract with a local company in a foreign country to manufacture one of its products. It will, however, retain control of product design and development and put its own label on the finished product. Contract manufacturing is quite common in the U.S. apparel business, with most American brands being made in a number of Asian countries, including China, Vietnam, Indonesia, and India.[8]

Thanks to twenty-first-century information technology, nonmanufacturing functions can also be outsourced to nations with lower labor costs. U.S. companies increasingly draw on a vast supply of relatively inexpensive skilled labor to perform various business services, such as software development, accounting, and claims processing. For years, American insurance companies have processed much of their claims-related paperwork in Ireland. With a large, well-educated population with English language skills, India has become a center for software development and customer-call centers for American companies. In the case of India, as you can see in Table 3.1, the attraction is not only a large pool of knowledge workers but also significantly lower wages.

Importing

Practice of buying products overseas and reselling them in one's own country.

exporting

Practice of selling domestic products to foreign customers.

international licensing agreement

Agreement that allows a foreign company to sell a domestic company's products or use its intellectual property in exchange for royalty fees.

international franchise

Agreement in which a domestic company (franchiser) gives a foreign company (franchisee) the right to use its brand and sell its products.

international contract manufacturing

Practice by which a company produces goods through an independent contractor in a foreign country.

outsourcing

Practice of using outside vendors to manufacture all or part of a company's actual products.

TABLE 3.1 Selected Hourly Wages, United States and India

Occupation	U.S. Wage per Hour (per year)	Indian Wage per Hour (per year)
Middle-level manager	$29.40 per hour ($60,000 per year)	$6.30 per hour ($13,000 per year)
Information technology specialist	$35.10 per hour ($72,000 per year)	$7.50 per hour ($15,000 per year)
Manual worker	$13.00 per hour ($27,000 per year)	$2.20 per hour ($5,000 per year)

Source: WageIndicator.com, "Huge Wage Gaps for the Same Work between Countries–June 2011," http://www.wageindicator.org/main/ WageIndicatorgazette/wageindicator-news/huge-wage-gaps-for-the-same-work-between-countries-June-2011.

2.4   Strategic Alliances and Joint Ventures

What if a company wants to do business in a foreign country but lacks the expertise or resources? Or what if the target nation's government doesn't allow foreign companies to operate within its borders unless it has a local partner? In these cases, a firm might enter into a strategic alliance with a local company or even with the government itself. A **strategic alliance** is an agreement between two companies (or a company and a nation) to pool resources in order to achieve business goals that benefit both partners. For example, Viacom (a leading global media company) entered into a strategic alliance with Beijing Television to produce Chinese-language music and entertainment programming.[9]

An alliance can serve a number of purposes:

- Enhancing marketing efforts
- Building sales and market share
- Improving products
- Reducing production and distribution costs
- Sharing technology

Alliances range in scope from informal cooperative agreements to **joint ventures**—alliances in which the partners fund a separate entity (perhaps a partnership or a corporation) to manage their joint operation. Magazine publisher Hearst, for example, has joint ventures with companies in several countries. So, young women in Israel can read *Cosmo Israel* in Hebrew, and Russian women can pick up a Russian-language version of *Cosmo* that meets their needs. The U.S. edition serves as a starting point to which nationally appropriate material is added in each different nation. This approach allows Hearst to sell the magazine in more than fifty countries.[10]

2.5   Foreign Direct Investment and Subsidiaries

Many of the approaches to global expansion that we've discussed so far allow companies to participate in international markets without investing in foreign plants and facilities. As markets expand, however, a firm might decide to enhance its competitive advantage by making a direct investment in operations conducted in another country. **Foreign direct investment (FDI)** refers to the formal establishment of business operations on foreign soil—the building of factories, sales offices, and distribution networks to serve local markets in a nation other than the company's home country. On the other hand, **offshoring** occurs when the facilities set up in the foreign country replace U.S. manufacturing facilities and are used to produce goods that will be sent back to the United States for sale. Shifting production to low-wage countries is often criticized as it results in the loss of jobs for U.S. workers.[11]

FDI is generally the most expensive commitment that a firm can make to an overseas market, and it's typically driven by the size and attractiveness of the target market. For example, German and Japanese automakers, such as BMW, Mercedes, Toyota, and Honda, have made serious commitments to the U.S. market: most of the cars and trucks that they build in plants in the South and Midwest are destined for sale in the United States.

A common form of FDI is the **foreign subsidiary**: an independent company owned by a foreign firm (called the *parent*). This approach to going international not only gives the parent company full access to local markets but also exempts it from any laws or regulations that may hamper the activities of foreign firms. The parent company has tight control over the operations of a subsidiary, but while senior managers from the parent company often oversee operations, many managers and employees are citizens of the host country. Not surprisingly, most very large firms have foreign subsidiaries. IBM and Coca-Cola, for example, have both had success in the Japanese market through their foreign subsidiaries (IBM-Japan and Coca-Cola–Japan). FDI goes in the other direction, too, and many companies operating in the United States are in fact subsidiaries of foreign firms. Gerber Products, for example, is a subsidiary of the Swiss company Novartis, while Stop & Shop and Giant Food Stores belong to the Dutch company Royal Ahold.

strategic alliance

Agreement between two companies (or a company and a nation) to pool resources in order to achieve business goals that benefit both partners.

joint ventures

Alliances in which the partners fund a separate entity (partnership or corporation) to manage their joint operations.

Foreign direct investment (FDI)

Formal establishment of business operations (such as the building of factories or sales offices) on foreign soil.

offshoring

Setting up facilities in a foreign country that replace U.S. manufacturing facilities to produce goods that will be sent back to the United States for sale.

foreign subsidiary

Independent company owned by a foreign firm (called its parent).

Where does most FDI capital end up? Figure 3.6 provides an overview of amounts, destinations (developed or developing countries), and trends.

FIGURE 3.6 Where FDI Goes

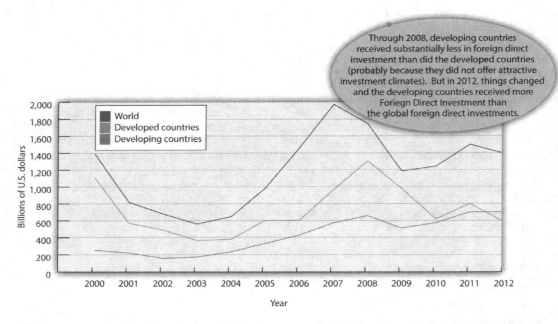

All these strategies have been successful in the arena of global business. But success in international business involves more than merely finding the best way to reach international markets. Doing global business is a complex, risky endeavor. As many companies have learned the hard way, people and organizations don't do things the same way abroad as they do at home. What differences make global business so tricky? That's the question that we'll turn to next.

2.6 Multinational Corporations

multinational corporation (MNC)

Large corporation that operates in many countries.

A company that operates in many countries is called a **multinational corporation (MNC)**. *Fortune* magazine's roster of the top five hundred MNCs in the world speaks for the growth of non-U.S. businesses. In 2013, only two of the top ten multinational companies were headquartered in the United States: Wal-Mart (number 2) and Exxon (number 3). Four others are in the second tier (tenth through twentieth): Chevron, Phillips 66, Berkshire Hathaway, and Apple. The remaining fourteen are non-U.S. firms. Interestingly, of the ten top companies, six are energy suppliers. Figure 3.7 provides a list of these twenty largest MNCs according to revenues.

FIGURE 3.7 The World's Twenty Largest MNCs[12]

Rank	Company	Revenues (in $ millions)	Country —Type of business
1	Royal Dutch Shell	481.7	Netherlands–energy
2	Wal-Mart Stores	469.2	US–retailer
3	Exxon Mobil	449.9	US–energy
4	Sinopec Group	428.2	China–energy
5	China National Petroleum	408.6	China–energy
6	BP	388.3	Britain–energy
7	State Grid	298.4	China–power grid building and operator
8	Toyota Motors	265.7	Japan–automobile manufacturer
9	Volkswagen	247.6	Germany–automobile manufacturer
10	Total	234.3	France–energy
11	Chevron	233.9	US–energy
12	Glencore Xstrata	214.4	Swizerland–mining
13	Japan Post Holdings	190.9	Japan–mail delivery, banking and insurance
14	Samsung Electronics	178.6	South Korean–electronic utility
15	EON	169.8	Britain–energy
16	Phillips66	169.6	US–energy
17	ENI	167.9	Chilé–electric utility
18	Berkshire Hathaway	162.5	US–investment
19	Apple	156.5	US–electronic
20	AXA	154.6	France–insurance

The World's Twenty Largest MNCs

Click on this link to experience an active version of this figure.

MNCs often adopt the approach encapsulated in the motto "Think globally, act locally." They often adjust their operations, products, marketing, and distribution to mesh with the environments of the countries in which they operate. Because they understand that a "one-size-fits-all" mentality doesn't make good business sense when they're trying to sell products in different markets, they're willing to accommodate cultural and economic differences. Increasingly, MNCs supplement their mainstream product line with products designed for local markets. Coca-Cola, for example, produces coffee and citrus-juice drinks developed specifically for the Japanese market.[13] When such companies as Nokia and Motorola design cell phones, they're often geared to local tastes in color, size, and other features. For example, Nokia introduced a cell phone for the rural Indian consumer that has a dust-resistant keypad, antislip grip, and a built-in flashlight.[14] McDonald's provides a vegetarian menu in India, where religious convictions affect the demand for beef and pork.[15] In Germany, McDonald's caters to local tastes by offering beer in some restaurants.[16] It offers a Maharaja Mac in India, a McItaly Burger in Italy, and a Teriyaki McBurger with Seaweed Shaker Fries in Japan.[17]

Likewise, many MNCs have made themselves more sensitive to local market conditions by decentralizing their decision making. While corporate headquarters still maintain a fair amount of control, home-country managers keep a suitable distance by relying on modern telecommunications. Today, fewer managers are dispatched from headquarters; MNCs depend instead on local talent. Not only does decentralized organization speed up and improve decision making, but it also allows an MNC to project the image of a local company. IBM, for instance, has been quite successful in the Japanese market because local customers and suppliers perceive it as a Japanese company. Crucial to this perception is the fact that the vast majority of IBM's Tokyo employees, including top leadership, are Japanese nationals.[18]

Criticism of MNC Culture

The global reach of MNCs is a source of criticism, as well as praise. Critics argue that they often destroy the livelihoods of home-country workers by moving jobs to developing countries where workers are willing to labor under poor conditions and for less pay. They also contend that traditional lifestyles and values are being weakened, and even destroyed, as global brands foster a global culture of American movies; fast food; and cheap, mass-produced consumer products. Still others claim that the demand of MNCs for constant economic growth and cheaper access to natural resources do irreversible damage to the physical environment. All these negative consequences, critics maintain, stem from the abuses of international trade—from the policy of placing profits above people, on a global scale. These views surfaced in violent street demonstrations in Seattle in 1999 and Genoa, Italy, in 2000, and since then, meetings of the International Monetary Fund and World Bank have regularly been assailed by large crowds of protestors who have succeeded in catching the attention of the worldwide media.

In Defense of MNC Culture

Meanwhile, supporters of MNCs respond that huge corporations deliver better, cheaper products for customers everywhere; create jobs; and raise the standard of living in developing countries. They also argue that globalization increases cross-cultural understanding. Anne O. Kruger, first deputy managing director of the IMF, says the following:

> *The impact of the faster growth on living standards has been phenomenal. We have observed the increased well being of a larger percentage of the world's population by a greater increment than ever before in history. Growing incomes give people the ability to spend on things other than basic food and shelter, in particular on things such as education and health. This ability, combined with the sharing among nations of medical and scientific advances, has transformed life in many parts of the developing world. Infant mortality has declined from 180 per 1,000 births in 1950 to 60 per 1,000 births. Literacy rates have risen from an average of 40 percent in the 1950s to over 70 percent. World poverty has declined, despite still-high population growth in the developing world.[19]*

America's Top 20 Trading Partners

Are you any good in geography? Here's your chance not only to find out which countries do the most trading with the United States, but to test yourself on your knowledge of global geography. Click here to complete the exercise.

KEY TAKEAWAYS

- For a company in the United States wishing to expand beyond national borders, there are a variety of ways to get involved in international business.
- **Importing** involves purchasing products from other countries and reselling them in one's own.
- **Exporting** entails selling products to foreign customers.
- Under a **franchise agreement**, a company grants a foreign company the right to use its brand name and sell its products.
- A **licensing agreement** allows a foreign company to sell a company's products or use its intellectual property in exchange for royalty fees.
- Through **international contract manufacturing**, or **outsourcing**, a company has its products manufactured or services provided in other countries.
- A **strategic alliance** is an agreement between two companies to pool talent and resources to achieve business goals that benefit both partners.
- A **joint venture** is a specific type of strategic alliance in which a separate entity funded by the participating companies is formed to manage the alliance.
- **Foreign direct investment (FDI)** refers to the formal establishment of business operations on foreign soil.
- **Offshoring** occurs when a company sets up facilities in a foreign country that replaces U.S. manufacturing facilities to produce goods that will be sent back to the United States for sale. Shifting production to low-wage countries is often criticized as it results in the loss of jobs for U.S. workers.
- A common form of FDI is the **foreign subsidiary**, an independent company owned by a foreign firm.
- A company that operates in many countries is called a **multinational corporation (MNC)**.

Before going to the next section of this chapter, take a few minutes to test your knowledge of the material covered in this section. Quizzes can be found under the "Resources" tab, "Study Aids: Quizzes."

EXERCISES

1. There are four common ways for a firm to expand its operations into overseas markets: importing, exporting, licensing, and franchising. First, explain what each approach entails. Then, select the one that you'd use if you were the CEO of a large company. Why was this approach particularly appealing?

2. You own a company that employs about two hundred people in Maine to produce hockey sticks. Why might you decide to outsource your production to Indonesia? Would closing your plant and moving your operations overseas help or hurt the U.S. economy? Who would be hurt? Who would be helped? Now, armed with answers to these questions, ask yourself whether you would indeed move your facilities or continue making hockey sticks in Maine. Explain your decision.

3. THE GLOBAL BUSINESS ENVIRONMENT

LEARNING OBJECTIVES

1. **Appreciate the business challenges that arise from differences in language, concepts of time and sociability, and communication styles.**
2. **Explain why it's important to understand a nation's level of economic development.**
3. **Be aware of the impact that fluctuations in exchange rates have on a global company's profits.**
4. **Explain how the vast differences in legal and regulatory environments among various countries pose challenges to global companies.**

In the classic movie *The Wizard of Oz*, a magically misplaced Midwest farm girl takes a moment to survey the bizarre landscape of Oz and then comments to her little dog, "I don't think we're in Kansas anymore, Toto." That sentiment probably echoes the reaction of many businesspeople who find themselves in the midst of international ventures for the first time. The differences between the foreign landscape and the one with which they're familiar are often huge and multifaceted. Some are quite obvious, such as differences in language, currency, and everyday habits (say, using chopsticks instead of silverware). But others are subtle, complex, and sometimes even hidden. Success in international business means understanding a wide range of cultural, economic, legal, and political differences between countries. Let's look at some of the more important of these differences.

3.1   The Cultural Environment

culture

System of shared beliefs, values, customs, and behaviors that govern the interactions of members of a society.

Even when two people from the same country communicate, there's always a possibility of misunderstanding. When people from different countries get together, that possibility increases substantially. Differences in communication styles reflect differences in **culture**: the system of shared beliefs, values, customs, and behaviors that govern the interactions of members of a society. Cultural differences create challenges to successful international business dealings. We explain a few of these challenges in the following sections.

Language

English is the international language of business. The natives of such European countries as France and Spain certainly take pride in their own languages and cultures, but nevertheless English is the business language of the European community. Whereas only a few educated Europeans have studied Italian or Norwegian, most have studied English. Similarly, on the South Asian subcontinent, where hundreds of local languages and dialects are spoken, English is the official language. In most corners of the world, English-only speakers—such as most Americans—have no problem finding competent translators and interpreters. So why is language an issue for English speakers doing business in the global marketplace?

In many countries, only members of the educated classes speak English. The larger population—which is usually the market you want to tap—speaks the local tongue. Advertising messages and sales appeals must take this fact into account. More than one English translation of an advertising slogan has resulted in a humorous (and perhaps serious) blunder. Some classics are listed in Table 3.2.

TABLE 3.2   Lost in Translation

In Belgium, the translation of the slogan of an American auto-body company, "Body by Fisher," came out as "Corpse by Fisher."
Translated into German, the slogan "Come Alive with Pepsi" became "Come out of the Grave with Pepsi."
A U.S. computer company in Indonesia translated "software" as "underwear."
A German chocolate product called "Zit" didn't sell well in the United States.
An English-speaking car-wash company in Francophone Quebec advertised itself as a *lavement d'auto* ("car enema") instead of the correct *lavage d'auto.*"
A proposed new soap called "Dainty" in English came out as "aloof" in Flemish (Belgium), "dimwitted" in Farsi (Iran), and "crazy person" in Korea; the product was shelved.
One false word in a Mexican commercial for an American shirt maker changed "When I used this shirt, I felt good" to "Until I used this shirt, I felt good."
In the 1970s, GM's Chevy Nova didn't get on the road in Puerto Rico, in part because *Nova* in Spanish means "It doesn't go."
A U.S. appliance ad fizzled in the Middle East because it showed a well-stocked refrigerator featuring a large ham, thus offending the sensibilities of Muslim consumers, who don't eat pork.

Furthermore, relying on translators and interpreters puts you as an international businessperson at a disadvantage. You're privy only to *interpretations* of the messages that you're getting, and this handicap can result in a real competitive problem. Maybe you'll misread the subtler intentions of the person with whom you're trying to conduct business. The best way to combat this problem is to study foreign languages. Most people appreciate some effort to communicate in their local language, even on the most basic level. They even appreciate mistakes you make resulting from a desire to demonstrate your genuine interest in the language of your counterparts in foreign countries. The same principle goes doubly when you're introducing yourself to non-English speakers in the United States. Few things work faster to encourage a friendly atmosphere than a native speaker's willingness to greet a foreign guest in the guest's native language.

Time and Sociability

Americans take for granted many of the cultural aspects of our business practices. Most of our meetings, for instance, focus on business issues, and we tend to start and end our meetings on schedule. These habits stem from a broader cultural preference: we don't like to waste time. (It was an American, Benjamin Franklin, who coined the phrase "Time is money.") This preference, however, is by no means universal. The expectation that meetings will start on time and adhere to precise agendas is common in parts of Europe (especially the Germanic countries), as well as in the United States, but elsewhere—say, in Latin America and the Middle East—people are often late to meetings.

High- and Low-Context Cultures

Likewise, don't expect businesspeople from these regions—or businesspeople from most of Mediterranean Europe, for that matter—to "get down to business" as soon as a meeting has started. They'll probably ask about your health and that of your family, inquire whether you're enjoying your visit to their country, suggest local foods, and generally appear to be avoiding serious discussion at all costs. For Americans, such topics are conducive to nothing but idle chitchat, but in certain cultures, getting started this way is a matter of simple politeness and hospitality.

If you ever find yourself in such a situation, the best advice is to go with the flow and be receptive to cultural nuances. In **high-context cultures**, the numerous interlocking (and often unstated) personal and family connections that hold people together have an effect on almost all interactions. Because people's personal lives overlap with their business lives (and vice versa), it's important to get to know your potential business partners as human beings and individuals.

By contrast, in **low-context cultures**, such as those of the United States, Germany, Switzerland, and the Scandinavian countries, personal and work relationships are more compartmentalized: you don't necessarily need to know much about the personal context of a person's life to deal with him or her in the business arena.

high-context cultures

Cultures in which personal and family connections have an effect on most interactions, including those in business.

low-context cultures

Cultures in which personal and work relationships are compartmentalized.

The Spectrum of Cultural Contexts

Are you a good judge of culture? How accurate are your impressions of the different ways in which different people behave? Find out by placing several cultures on a spectrum running from low to high context. Click here to complete the exercise.

Intercultural Communication

Different cultures have different communication *styles*—a fact that can take some getting used to. For example, *degrees of animation in expression* can vary from culture to culture. Southern Europeans and Middle Easterners are quite animated, favoring expressive body language along with hand gestures and raised voices. Northern Europeans are far more reserved. The English, for example, are famous for their understated style and the Germans for their formality in most business settings. In addition, the *distance* at which one feels comfortable when talking with someone varies by culture. People from the Middle East like to converse from a distance of a foot or less, while Americans prefer more personal space.

Finally, while people in some cultures prefer to deliver direct, clear messages, others use language that's subtler or more indirect. North Americans and most Northern Europeans fall into the former category and many Asians into the latter. But even within these categories, there are differences. Though typically polite, Chinese and Koreans are extremely direct in expression, while Japanese are indirect: They use vague language and avoid saying "no" even if they do not intend to do what you ask. They worry that turning someone down will result in their "losing face," and so they avoid doing this in public.

This discussion brings up two important points. First, avoid lumping loosely related cultures together. We sometimes talk, for example, about "Asian culture," but such broad categories as "Asian" are usually oversimplifications. Japanese culture is different from Korean, which is different from Chinese. Second, never assume that two people from the same culture will always act in a similar manner. Not all Latin Americans are casual about meeting times, not all Italians use animated body language, and not all Germans are formal.

In summary, learn about a country's culture and use your knowledge to help improve the quality of your business dealings. Learn to value the subtle differences among cultures, but don't allow cultural stereotypes to dictate how you interact with people from *any* culture. Treat each person as an individual and spend time getting to know what he or she is about.

3.2   The Economic Environment

If you plan to do business in a foreign country, you need to know its level of economic development. You also should be aware of factors influencing the value of its currency and the impact that changes in that value will have on your profits.

Economic Development

If you don't understand a nation's level of economic development, you'll have trouble answering some basic questions, such as, Will consumers in this country be able to afford the product I want to sell? How many units can I expect to sell? Will it be possible to make a reasonable profit? A country's level of economic development can be evaluated by estimating the annual income earned per citizen. The World Bank, which lends money for improvements in underdeveloped nations, divides countries into four income categories:[20]

- *High income*—$12,616 or higher (United States, Germany, Japan)
- *Upper-middle income*—$4,086 to $12,615 (China, South Africa, Mexico)
- *Lower-middle income*—$1,036 to $4,085 (Vietnam, Philippines, India)
- *Low income*—$1,035 or less (Kenya, Bangladesh, Haiti)

Note that even though a country has a low annual income per citizen, it can still be an attractive place for doing business. India, for example, is a lower-middle-income country, yet it has a population of 1.2 billion, and a segment of that population is well educated—an appealing feature for many business initiatives.

FIGURE 3.8 Share of GDP, 1970–2010

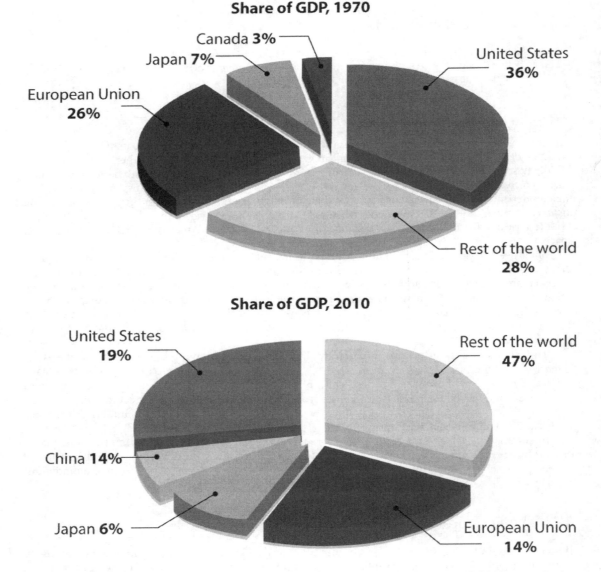

The long-term goal of many countries is to move up the economic development ladder. Some factors conducive to economic growth include a reliable banking system, a strong stock market, and government policies to encourage investment and competition while discouraging corruption. It's also important that a country have a strong *infrastructure*—its systems of communications (telephone, Internet, television, newspapers), transportation (roads, railways, airports), energy (gas and electricity, power plants), and social facilities (schools, hospitals). These basic systems will help countries attract foreign investors, which can be crucial to economic development.

The World's Wealth

Click on this link to experience an active version of this figure.

Currency Valuations and Exchange Rates

If every nation used the same currency, international trade and travel would be a lot easier. Unfortunately, this is not the case. There are about 175 currencies in the world: Some you've heard of, such as the British pound; others are likely unknown to you, such as the *manat*, the official currency of Azerbaijan, a small nation in Southwest Asia. Let's pretend you suddenly find yourself in Azerbaijan and all you have with you is a credit card (which none of the restaurants or hotels will take) and U.S. dollars (which no one wants either). How can you get some Azerbaijani manats so you can buy a good meal and check into a hotel? If it's during the day, you're in luck. Head to the closest bank and ask someone there who speaks English to exchange your dollars for Azerbaijan manats. If you give the bank clerk $300 (all of your travel money), don't expect to get back 300 manats; the two currencies are not equal. To determine how much Azerbaijan money you'll get in exchange for your $300, the bank clerk will look up the day's foreign **exchange rate**—which tells you how much one currency is worth *relative to another currency*. If today were March 25, 2014, the clerk would find an exchange rate of 1 U.S. dollar equals .78 manats (which means that you get 78 manats for every dollar you give to the bank clerk). In other words, when you hand the clerk your $300 you'll get back only 234 manats (.78 × $300). Most likely, the deal does not sound good to you, but you have no choice—that's what the exchange rate is. Plus, you're lucky that it's during the day and the banks are open: sleeping outside in Azerbaijan with an empty stomach doesn't sound like fun, although it would give you time to wonder what would happen if an Azerbaijani traveled to the United States. When the traveler goes to exchange manats for U.S. dollars, he or she will get back $1.27 for each manat. Exchanging 300 manats for U.S. dollars yields $381 in U.S. dollars (1.27 × $300). Well, this doesn't sound fair. Why did you receive fewer manats for your U.S. dollars while the Azerbaijan traveler received more dollars for his or her manats? It is because the U.S. dollar is weak relative to the Azerbaijan manat. There are many reasons for the weakness of the U.S. dollar, but one possible culprit is the huge $17.5 trillion debt (and rising) carried by the United States. And if you are looking for things to get upset about, your share of this huge U.S. debt is about $55,000 (and rising).[21]

Now, we'll look at two business examples. First, let's say that your business is importing watches from Switzerland. Because the watchmaker will want to be paid in Swiss francs, you have to figure out how many U.S. dollars you'll need to buy the francs with which to pay the watchmaker. You'd start by finding out the exchange rate between the Swiss franc and the U.S. dollar.

exchange rate

Value of one currency relative to another.

FIGURE 3.9

Understanding currency values and exchange rates is important to understanding how global business functions.

© 2010 Jupiterimages Corporation

You could simply look in a newspaper or go to any number of Web sites—say, http://www.oanda.com to get the current exchange rate. To keep things simple, let's assume that the exchange rate is 1 Swiss franc = US$1.27 (i.e., 1 Swiss franc is worth $1.27). Let's also assume that you owe the Swiss watchmaker 1,000 francs. Doing some quick math, you figure that it will take $1,270 to buy 1,000 francs (1,000 francs × the exchange rate of 1.27 = $1,270).

Now let's say that you don't have the cash flow to pay the watchmaker for two weeks. When you check the exchange rate two weeks later, you find that it has gone up to 1 Swiss franc = $1.37. Are you better off or worse off? It's easy to check: 1,000 francs × the new exchange rate of 1.37 = $1,370. You've just learned the hard way that when the value of the franc relative to the dollar goes up, it costs you more to buy something from Switzerland. You probably can't help but wonder what would have happened if the value of the franc relative to the dollar had gone *down*—say, to $1.17 per franc. At this rate, you'd need only $1,170 to pay the 1,000 francs (1,000 × 1.17). In other words, when the value of the franc relative to the dollar drops, it costs less to buy goods from Switzerland. In sum, you've learned the following:

- If a foreign currency goes *up* relative to the U.S. dollar, Americans must pay *more* for goods and services purchased from sellers in the country issuing the currency (foreign products are more expensive). This is bad for exporters who have to pay more for the foreign-made goods they buy to bring back to the United States to sell.

- If a foreign currency goes *down* relative to the U.S. dollar, Americans pay *less* for products from the country issuing the currency (foreign products are cheaper).

In the interest of being thorough, let's look at this phenomenon from the perspective of an American seller and a Swiss buyer. First, we need to know the exchange rate for the U.S. dollar relative to the franc, which happens to be .79 francs = US$1. This means that if you want to sell something—let's say your latest painting—for $1,000 U.S. to an art lover in Switzerland, the Swiss buyer will need only 790 francs to get the $1,000 needed to pay you. If the exchange rate went up to .89 francs = US$1, the cost of the painting would be $890. If the exchange rate went down to .69 francs = US$1, the cost of the painting would be $690. So now you also know the following:

- If the U.S. dollar goes *up* relative to a foreign currency, foreign buyers must pay *more* for American goods and services (they become more expensive).

- If the U.S. dollar goes *down* relative to a foreign currency, foreign buyers pay *less* for American products (they become cheaper). This is good for importers as their "cheaper" goods are more attractive to customers in the foreign country.

3.3 The Legal and Regulatory Environment

One of the more difficult aspects of doing business globally is dealing with vast differences in legal and regulatory environments. The United States, for example, has an established set of laws and regulations that provide direction to businesses operating within its borders. But because there is no global legal system, key areas of business law—for example, contract provisions and copyright protection—can be treated in different ways in different countries. Companies doing international business often face many inconsistent laws and regulations. To navigate this sea of confusion, American businesspeople must know and follow both U.S. laws and regulations and those of nations in which they operate.

Business history is filled with stories about American companies that have stumbled in trying to comply with foreign laws and regulations. Coca-Cola, for example, ran afoul of Italian law when it printed its ingredients list on the bottle cap rather than on the bottle itself. Italian courts ruled that the labeling was inadequate because most people throw the cap away. In another case, 3M applied to the Japanese government to create a joint venture with the Sumitomo Industrial Group to make and distribute magnetic tape products in Japan. 3M spent four years trying to satisfy Japan's complex regulations, but by the time it got approval, domestic competitors, including Sony, had captured the market. By delaying 3M, Japanese regulators managed, in effect, to stifle foreign competition.[22]

One approach to dealing with local laws and regulations is hiring lawyers from the host country who can provide advice on legal issues. Another is working with local businesspeople who have experience in complying with regulations and overcoming bureaucratic obstacles.

Foreign Corrupt Practices Act

One U.S. law that creates unique challenges for American firms operating overseas is the Foreign Corrupt Practices Act, which prohibits the distribution of bribes and other favors in the conduct of business. Unfortunately, though they're illegal in this country, such tactics as kickbacks and bribes are business-as-usual in many nations. According to some experts, American businesspeople are at a competitive disadvantage if they're prohibited from giving bribes or undercover payments to foreign officials or businesspeople who expect them; it's like asking for good service in a restaurant when the waiter knows you won't be giving a tip. In theory, because the Foreign Corrupt Practices Act warns foreigners that Americans can't give bribes, they'll eventually stop expecting them.

Where are American businesspeople most likely and least likely to encounter bribe requests and related forms of corruption? Transparency International, an independent German-based organization, annually rates nations according to "perceived corruption," which it defines as "the abuse of public office for private gain." Table 3.3 reports a sampling of the 2012 rankings.

TABLE 3.3 Corruptibility around the World, 2013

Rank	Country	CPI Score*
1	Denmark	9.1
1	New Zealand	9.1
3	Finland	8.9
3	Sweden	8.9
5	Norway	8.6
5	Singapore	8.6
7	Switzerland	8.5
14	United Kingdom	7.6
19	United States	7.3
106	Mexico	3.4
171	Iraq	1.6
175	Afghanistan	0.8
*A score of 10 means that a country is squeaky clean. Anything under 3 means that corruption is rampant.		

Source: Transparency International, "Corruption Perceptions Index 2010 Results," http://www.transparency.org/cpi2013/results.

KEY TAKEAWAYS

- Success in international business means understanding an assortment of cultural, economic, and legal differences between countries.
- Cultural challenges stem from differences in language, concepts of time and sociability, and communication styles.
- If you do business in a foreign country, you need to know the country's level of economic development.
- In dealing with countries whose currency is different from yours, you have to be aware of the impact that fluctuations in **exchange rates** will have on your profits.
- Finally, in doing business globally, you must deal with the challenges that come from the vast differences in legal and regulatory environments.

Before going to the next section of this chapter, take a few minutes to test your knowledge of the material covered in this section. Quizzes can be found under the "Resources" tab, "Study Aids: Quizzes."

EXERCISES

1. After five years at a large sporting-goods company, your boss has asked you to spend six months managing the firm's new office in Rio de Janeiro. It's a good opportunity, but, unfortunately, you know absolutely nothing about life or anything else in Brazil. So, to get some advice on how to work and socialize with Brazilian businesspeople, you decide to do some online research. You're particularly interested in understanding cultural differences in communication styles, dress, time, and sociability. To learn more about Brazilian businesspeople, go to these helpful sites:

   - "Brazil: Language, Culture, Customs and Etiquette," Kwintessential, http://www.kwintessential.co.uk/resources/global-etiquette/brazil-country-profile.html.
   - "Culture of Brazil," Wikipedia, http://en.wikipedia.org/wiki/Culture_of_Brazil.

2. You're a partner in a U.S. engineering firm that's interested in bidding on a water-treatment project in China. You know that firms from two other countries—Malaysia and Italy—will submit bids. The U.S. Foreign Corrupt Practices Act forbids you from making any payment to Chinese officials to enlist their help in getting the job. Unfortunately, the governments of Malaysia and Italy don't prohibit local firms from offering bribes. Are you at a disadvantage? Should the Foreign Corrupt Practices Act be repealed? Why, or why not?

3. You're the CEO of a multinational corporation, and one-fourth of your workforce is infected with AIDS. If you had the means to help your workers and their families, would you do it? This is not strictly a hypothetical question: it's one that's faced by CEOs of multinational corporations with operations in Africa, parts of China, and India. To find out what some of them have decided, go to the *BusinessWeek* Web site (http://www.businessweek.com/stories/2004-08-01/commentary-why-business-should-make-aids-its-business) and read the article "Why Business Should Make AIDS Its Business." Then, answer the following questions:

   a. Why have some multinationals decided to help control AIDS in their workforces?
   b. Why have others failed to help?
   c. From a humanitarian perspective, what's the right thing to do? From a business perspective?
   d. What would you do if you conducted operations in a nation whose government was unwilling or unable to control the spread of AIDS?

Write a brief report to summarize what you learned about cultural differences between U.S. and Brazilian businesspeople.

---

4. TRADE CONTROLS

LEARNING OBJECTIVES

1. Describe the following common types of trade restrictions: tariffs, quotas, embargoes, and dumping.
2. Advance arguments in support of the following opinion: governments should refrain from imposing regulations that restrict the free flow of products between nations.
3. Advance arguments in support of the following competing opinion: governments should impose some level of trade regulation on imported goods and services.

The debate about the extent to which countries should control the flow of foreign goods and investments across their borders is as old as international trade itself. Governments continue to control trade. To better understand how and why, let's examine a hypothetical case. Suppose you're in charge of a small country in which people do two things—grow food and make clothes. Because the quality of both products is high and the prices are reasonable, your consumers are happy to buy locally made food and clothes. But one day, a farmer from a nearby country crosses your border with several wagonloads of wheat to sell. On the same day, a foreign clothes maker arrives with a large shipment of clothes. These two entrepreneurs want to sell food and clothes in your country at prices below those that local consumers now pay for domestically made food and clothes. At first, this seems like a good deal for your consumers: they won't have to pay as much for food and clothes. But then you remember all the people in your country who grow food and make clothes. If no one buys their goods (because the imported goods are cheaper), what will happen to their livelihoods? Will everybody be out of work? And if everyone's unemployed, what will happen to your national economy?

That's when you decide to protect your farmers and clothes makers by setting up trade rules. Maybe you'll increase the prices of imported goods by adding a tax to them; you might even make the tax so high that they're more expensive than your homemade goods. Or perhaps you'll help your farmers grow food more cheaply by giving them financial help to defray their costs. The government payments that you give to the farmers to help offset some of their costs of production are called **subsidies**. These subsidies will allow the farmers to lower the price of their goods to a point below that of imported competitors' goods. What's even better is that the lower costs will allow the farmers to export their own goods at attractive, competitive prices.

The United States has a long history of subsidizing farmers. Subsidy programs guarantee farmers (including large corporate farms) a certain price for their crops, regardless of the market price. This guarantee ensures stable income in the farming community but can have a negative impact on the world economy. How? Critics argue that in allowing American farmers to export crops at artificially low prices, U.S. agricultural subsidies permit them to compete unfairly with farmers in developing countries. A reverse situation occurs in the steel industry, in which a number of countries—China, Japan, Russia, India, and Brazil—subsidize domestic producers. U.S. trade unions charge that this practice gives an unfair advantage to foreign producers and hurts the American steel industry, which can't compete on price with subsidized imports.

Whether they push up the price of imports or push down the price of local goods, such initiatives will help locally produced goods compete more favorably with foreign goods. Both strategies are forms of **trade controls**—policies that restrict free trade. Because they protect domestic industries by reducing foreign competition, the use of such controls is often called **protectionism**. Though there's considerable debate over the pros and cons of this practice, all countries engage in it to some extent. Before debating the issue, however, let's learn about the more common types of trade restrictions: tariffs, quotas, and, embargoes.

4.1 Tariffs

Tariffs are taxes on imports. Because they raise the price of the foreign-made goods, they make them less competitive. The United States, for example, protects domestic makers of synthetic knitted shirts by imposing a stiff tariff of 32.5 percent on imports.[23] Tariffs are also used to raise revenue for a government. Shoe imports are worth $2 billion annually to the federal government.[24]

4.2 Quotas

A **quota** imposes limits on the quantity of a good that can be imported over a period of time. Quotas are used to protect specific industries, usually new industries or those facing strong competitive pressure from foreign firms. U.S. import quotas take two forms. An *absolute quota* fixes an upper limit on the amount of a good that can be imported during the given period. A *tariff-rate quota* permits the import of a specified quantity and then adds a high import tax once the limit is reached.

Sometimes quotas protect one group at the expense of another. To protect sugar beet and sugar cane growers, for instance, the United States imposes a tariff-rate quota on the importation of sugar—a policy that has driven up the cost of sugar to two to three times world prices.[25] These artificially high prices push up costs for American candy makers, some of whom have moved their operations elsewhere, taking high-paying manufacturing jobs with them. Life Savers, for example, were made in the United States for ninety years but are now produced in Canada, where the company saves $6 million annually on the cost of sugar.[26]

An extreme form of quota is the **embargo**, which, for economic or political reasons, bans the import or export of certain goods to or from a specific country. The United States, for example, bans nearly every commodity originating in Cuba.

4.3 Dumping

A common political rationale for establishing tariffs and quotas is the need to combat **dumping**: the practice of selling exported goods below the price that producers would normally charge in their home markets (and often below the cost of producing the goods). Usually, nations resort to this practice to gain entry and market share in foreign markets, but it can also be used to sell off surplus or obsolete goods. Dumping creates unfair competition for domestic industries, and governments are justifiably concerned when they suspect foreign countries of dumping products on their markets. They often retaliate by imposing punitive tariffs that drive up the price of the imported goods.

subsidies
Government payments given to certain industries to help offset some of their costs of production.

trade controls
Government policies that restrict free trade.

protectionism
Use of trade controls to reduce foreign competition in order to protect domestic industries.

Tariffs
Government taxes on imports that raise the price of foreign goods and make them less competitive with domestic goods.

quota
Government-imposed restrictions on the quantity of a good that can be imported over a period of time.

embargo
Extreme form of quota that bans the import or export of certain goods to a country for economic or political reasons.

dumping
Practice of selling exported goods below the price that producers would normally charge home markets.

4.4 The Pros and Cons of Trade Controls

Opinions vary on government involvement in international trade. Some experts believe that governments should support free trade and refrain from imposing regulations that restrict the free flow of goods and services between nations. Others argue that governments should impose some level of trade regulations on imported goods and services.

Proponents of controls contend that there are a number of legitimate reasons why countries engage in protectionism. Sometimes they restrict trade to protect specific industries and their workers from foreign competition—agriculture, for example, or steel making. At other times, they restrict imports to give new or struggling industries a chance to get established. Finally, some countries use protectionism to shield industries that are vital to their national defense, such as shipbuilding and military hardware.

Despite valid arguments made by supporters of trade controls, most experts believe that such restrictions as tariffs and quotas—as well as practices that don't promote level playing fields, such as subsidies and dumping—are detrimental to the world economy. Without impediments to trade, countries can compete freely. Each nation can focus on what it does best and bring its goods to a fair and open world market. When this happens, the world will prosper. Or so the argument goes. International trade hasn't achieved global prosperity, but it's certainly heading in the direction of unrestricted markets.

KEY TAKEAWAYS

- Because they protect domestic industries by reducing foreign competition, the use of controls to restrict free trade is often called **protectionism**.
- Though there's considerable debate over protectionism, all countries engage in it to some extent.
- **Tariffs** are taxes on imports. Because they raise the price of the foreign-made goods, they make them less competitive.
- **Quotas** are restrictions on imports that impose a limit on the quantity of a good that can be imported over a period of time. They're used to protect specific industries, usually new industries or those facing strong competitive pressure from foreign firms.
- An **embargo** is a quota that, for economic or political reasons, bans the import or export of certain goods to or from a specific country.
- A common rationale for tariffs and quotas is the need to combat **dumping**—the practice of selling exported goods below the price that producers would normally charge in their home markets (and often below the costs of producing the goods).
- Some experts believe that governments should support free trade and refrain from imposing regulations that restrict the free flow of products between nations.
- Others argue that governments should impose some level of trade regulations on imported goods and services.

Before going to the next section of this chapter, take a few minutes to test your knowledge of the material covered in this section. Quizzes can be found under the "Resources" tab, "Study Aids: Quizzes."

EXERCISE

Because the United States has placed quotas on textile and apparel imports for the last thirty years, certain countries, such as China and India, have been able to export to the United States only as much clothing as their respective quotas permit. One effect of this policy was spreading textile and apparel manufacture around the world and preventing any single nation from dominating the world market. As a result, many developing countries, such as Vietnam, Cambodia, and Honduras, were able to enter the market and provide much-needed jobs for local workers. The rules, however, have changed: as of January 1, 2005, quotas on U.S. textile imports were eliminated, permitting U.S. companies to import textile supplies from any country they choose. In your opinion, what effect will the new U.S. policy have on each of the following groups:

a. Firms that outsource the manufacture of their apparel
b. Textile manufacturers and workers in the following countries:

  ■ China
  ■ Indonesia
  ■ Mexico
  ■ United States

c. American consumers

---

5. REDUCING INTERNATIONAL TRADE BARRIERS

LEARNING OBJECTIVES

1. Describe the goals and accomplishments of the two most important agreements or organizations set up to monitor trade policies and reduce barriers to trade: General Agreement on Tariffs and Trade (GATT) and the World Trade Organization (WTO).
2. Explain the purposes of the International Monetary Fund (IMF) and the World Bank.
3. Why was the North American Free Trade Association (NAFTA) established, and what has it accomplished?
4. What is the European Union (EU), and why was it formed? What challenges has it faced?

A number of organizations work to ease barriers to trade, and more countries are joining together to promote trade and mutual economic benefits. Let's look at some of these important initiatives.

5.1 Trade Agreements and Organizations

Free trade is encouraged by a number of agreements and organizations set up to monitor trade policies. The two most important are the General Agreement on Tariffs and Trade and the World Trade Organization.

General Agreement on Tariffs and Trade

After the Great Depression and World War II, most countries focused on protecting home industries, so international trade was hindered by rigid trade restrictions. To rectify this situation, twenty-three nations joined together in 1947 and signed the **General Agreement on Tariffs and Trade (GATT)**, which encouraged free trade by regulating and reducing tariffs and by providing a forum for resolving trade disputes. The highly successful initiative achieved substantial reductions in tariffs and quotas, and in 1995 its members founded the World Trade Organization to continue the work of GATT in overseeing global trade.

General Agreement on Tariffs and Trade (GATT)

International trade agreement that encourages free trade by regulating and reducing tariffs and provides a forum for resolving trade disputes.

World Trade Organization

Based in Geneva, Switzerland, with nearly 150 members, the **World Trade Organization (WTO)** encourages global commerce and lower trade barriers, enforces international rules of trade, and provides a forum for resolving disputes. It is empowered, for instance, to determine whether a member nation's trade policies have violated the organization's rules, and it can direct "guilty" countries to remove disputed barriers (though it has no legal power to force any country to do anything it doesn't want to do). If the guilty party refuses to comply, the WTO may authorize the plaintiff nation to erect trade barriers of its own, generally in the form of tariffs.

Affected members aren't always happy with WTO actions. In 2002, for example, the Bush administration imposed a three-year tariff on imported steel. In ruling against this tariff, the WTO allowed the aggrieved nations to impose counter-tariffs on some politically sensitive American products, such as Florida oranges, Texas grapefruits and computers, and Wisconsin cheese. Reluctantly, the administration lifted its tariff on steel.[27]

5.2 Financial Support for Troubled Economies

The key to helping developing countries become active participants in the global marketplace is providing financial assistance. Offering monetary assistance to some of the poorest nations in the world is the shared goal of two organizations: the International Monetary Fund and the World Bank. These organizations, to which most countries belong, were established in 1944 to accomplish different but complementary purposes.

The International Monetary Fund

The **International Monetary Fund (IMF)** loans money to countries with troubled economies, such as Mexico in the 1980s and mid-1990s, Russia and Argentina in the late 1990s, and Turkey and Latin America in the 2000s. There are, however, strings attached to IMF loans: in exchange for relief in times of financial crisis, borrower countries must institute sometimes painful financial and economic reforms. In the 1980s, for example, Mexico received financial relief from the IMF on the condition that it privatize and deregulate certain industries and liberalize trade policies. The government was also required to cut back expenditures for such services as education, health care, and workers' benefits.[28]

The World Bank

The **World Bank** is an important source of economic assistance for poor and developing countries. With backing from wealthy donor countries (such as the United States, Japan, Germany, and the United Kingdom), in 2003 the World Bank committed almost $53 billion in loans, grants, and guarantees to some of the world's poorest nations.[29] Loans are made to help countries improve the lives of the poor through community-support programs designed to provide health, nutrition, education, infrastructure, and other social services.

Criticism of the IMF and the World Bank

In recent years, the International Monetary Fund and the World Bank have faced mounting criticism, though both have their supporters. Some analysts, for example, think that the IMF is often too harsh in its demands for economic reform; others argue that troubled economies can be turned around only with harsh economic measures. Some observers assert that too many World Bank loans go to environmentally harmful projects, such as the construction of roads through fragile rain forests. Others point to the World Bank's efforts to direct funding away from big construction projects and toward initiatives designed to better the lot of the world's poor—educating children, fighting AIDS, and improving nutrition and health standards.[30]

5.3 Trading Blocs

So far, our discussion has suggested that global trade would be strengthened if there were no restrictions on it—if countries didn't put up barriers to trade or perform special favors for domestic industries. The complete absence of barriers is an ideal state of affairs that we haven't yet attained. In the meantime, economists and policymakers tend to focus on a more practical question: Can we achieve the goal of free trade on the *regional* level? To an extent, the answer is yes. In certain parts of the world, groups of countries have joined together to allow goods and services to flow without restrictions across their mutual borders. Such groups are called **trading blocs**. Let's examine two of the most powerful trading blocs—NAFTA and the European Union.

North American Free Trade Association

The **North American Free Trade Association (NAFTA)** is an agreement among the governments of the United States, Canada, and Mexico to open their borders to unrestricted trade. The effect of this agreement is that three very different economies are combined into one economic zone with almost no trade barriers. From the northern tip of Canada to the southern tip of Mexico, each country benefits from the comparative advantages of its partners: each nation is free to produce what it does best and to trade its goods and services without restrictions.

When the agreement was ratified in 1994, it had no shortage of skeptics. Many people feared, for example, that without tariffs on Mexican goods, more U.S. manufacturing jobs would be lost to Mexico, where labor is cheaper. Two decades later, most such fears have not been realized, and, by and large, NAFTA has been a success. Since it went into effect, the value of trade between the United States and Mexico has grown substantially, and Canada and Mexico are now the United States' top trading partners.

North American Free Trade Association (NAFTA)

Agreement among the governments of the United States, Canada, and Mexico to open their borders to unrestricted trade.

The European Union

The forty-plus countries of Europe have long shown an interest in integrating their economies. The first organized effort to integrate a segment of Europe's economic entities began in the late 1950s, when six countries joined together to form the European Economic Community (EEC). Over the next four decades, membership grew, and in the late 1990s, the EEC became the European Union. Today, the **European Union (EU)** is a group of twenty-eight countries that have eliminated trade barriers among themselves (see the map in Figure 3.10).

European Union (EU)

Association of European countries that joined together to eliminate trade barriers among themselves.

FIGURE 3.10   The Nations of the European Union

European Union Member States

At first glance, the EU looks similar to NAFTA. Both, for instance, allow unrestricted trade among member nations. But the provisions of the EU go beyond those of NAFTA in several important ways. Most importantly, the EU is more than a trading organization: it also enhances political and social cooperation and binds its members into a single entity with authority to require them to follow common rules and regulations. It is much like a federation of states with a weak central government, with the effect not only of eliminating internal barriers but also of enforcing common tariffs on trade from outside the EU. In addition, while NAFTA allows goods and services as well as capital to pass between borders, the EU also allows *people* to come and go freely: if you possess an EU passport, you can work in any EU nation.

The Euro

A key step toward unification occurred in 1999, when most (but not all) EU members agreed to abandon their own currencies and adopt a joint currency. The actual conversion occurred in 2002, when a common currency called the *euro* replaced the separate currencies of participating EU countries. The common currency facilitates trade and finance because exchange-rate differences no longer complicate transactions.[31] Its proponents argued that the EU would not only unite economically and politically distinct countries but also create an economic power that could compete against the dominant players in the global marketplace. Individually, each European country has limited economic power, but as a group, they could be an economic superpower. But, over time, the value of the euro has been questioned. Just as is true with the United States today, many of the "euro" countries (Spain, Italy, Greece, Portugal, and Ireland in particular) have been financially irresponsible, piling up huge debts and experiencing high unemployment and problems in the housing market. But because these troubled countries share a common currency with the other "euro" countries, they are less able to correct their economic woes.[32] Many economists fear that the financial crisis precipitated by these financially irresponsible countries threatened the very survival of the euro.[33]

Other Trading Blocs

Other countries have also opted for economic integration. Four historical rivals in South America—Argentina, Brazil, Paraguay, and Uruguay—have established MERCOSUR (for *Mercado Commun del Sur*) to eliminate trade barriers. A number of Asian countries, including Indonesia, Malaysia, the Philippines, Singapore, and Thailand, are cooperating to reduce mutual barriers through ASEAN (the *Association of Southeast Asian Nations*).

Only time will tell whether the trend toward regional trade agreements is good for the world economy. Clearly, they're beneficial to their respective participants; for one thing, they get preferential treatment from other members. But certain questions still need to be answered more fully. Are regional agreements, for example, moving the world closer to free trade on a *global* scale—toward a marketplace in which goods and services can be traded anywhere without barriers?

KEY TAKEAWAY

- Free trade is encouraged by a number of agreements and organizations set up to monitor trade policies.
- The **General Agreement on Tariffs and Trade (GATT)** encourages free trade by regulating and reducing tariffs and by providing a forum for resolving disputes.
- This highly successful initiative achieved substantial reductions in tariffs and quotas, and in 1995, its members founded the **World Trade Organization (WTO)**, which encourages global commerce and lower trade barriers, enforces international rules of trade, and provides a forum for resolving disputes.
- Providing monetary assistance to some of the poorest nations in the world is the shared goal of two organizations: the **International Monetary Fund (IMF)** and the **World Bank**. Several initiatives have successfully promoted free trade on a regional level. In certain parts of the world, groups of countries have joined together to allow goods and services to flow without restrictions across their mutual borders. Such groups are called **trading blocs**.
- The **North American Free Trade Association (NAFTA)** is an agreement among the governments of the United States, Canada, and Mexico to open their borders to unrestricted trade.
- The effect of this agreement is that three very different economies are combined into one economic zone with almost no trade barriers.
- The **European Union (EU)** is a group of twenty-eight countries that have eliminated trade barriers among themselves.

Before going to the next section of this chapter, take a few minutes to test your knowledge of the material covered in this section. Quizzes can be found under the "Resources" tab, "Study Aids: Quizzes."

EXERCISES

1. What is NAFTA? Why was it formed? What has it accomplished?
2. What is the European Union? Why was it formed? What has it accomplished? What challenges has it faced?

---

6. PREPARING FOR A CAREER IN INTERNATIONAL BUSINESS

LEARNING OBJECTIVE

1. **Understand how to prepare for a career in international business.**

No matter where your career takes you, you won't be able to avoid the reality and reach of international business. We're all involved in it. Some readers may want to venture more seriously into this exciting arena. The career opportunities are exciting and challenging, but taking the best advantage of them requires some early planning. Here are some hints.

6.1   Plan Your Undergraduate Education

Many colleges and universities offer strong majors in international business, and this course of study can be good preparation for a global career. In planning your education, remember the following:

- *Develop real expertise in one of the basic areas of business.* Most companies will hire you as much for your skill and knowledge in accounting, finance, information systems, marketing, or management as for your background in the study of international business. Take courses in both areas.
- *Develop your knowledge of international politics, economics, and culture.* Take liberal arts courses that focus on parts of the world that especially interest you. Courses in history, government, and the social sciences offer a wealth of knowledge about other nations and cultures that's relevant to success in international business.
- *Develop foreign-language skills.* If you studied a language in high school, keep up with it. Improve your reading or conversational skills. Or start a new language in college. Recall that your competition in the global marketplace is not just other Americans, but also individuals from countries, such as Belgium, where everyone's fluent in at least two (and usually three) languages. Lack of foreign-language skills often proves to be a disadvantage for many Americans in international business.

6.2   Get Some Direct Experience

Take advantage of study-abroad opportunities, whether offered on your campus or by another college. There are literally hundreds of such opportunities, and your interest in international business will be received much more seriously if you've spent some time abroad. (As a bonus, you'll probably find it an enjoyable, horizon-expanding experience, as well.)

6.3   Interact with People from Other Cultures

Finally, whenever you can, learn about the habits and traits of other cultures, and practice interacting with the people to whom they belong. Go to the trouble to meet international students on your campus and get to know them. Learn about their cultures and values, and tell them about yours. You may initially be uncomfortable or confused in such intercultural exchanges, but you'll find them great learning experiences. By picking up on the details, you'll avoid embarrassing mistakes later and even earn the approval of acquaintances from abroad.

Whether you're committed to a career in global business, curious about the international scene, or simply a consumer of worldwide products and services, you can't avoid the effects of globalization.

Granted, the experience can be frustrating, maybe even troubling at times. More often, however, it's likely to be stimulating and full of opportunities.

KEY TAKEAWAY

- To prepare for a global career, you might want to consider doing some of the following while a student:
    1. Major in international business.
    2. Develop your knowledge of international politics, economics, and culture.
    3. Study a foreign language.
    4. Take advantage of study-abroad opportunities.
    5. Interact with fellow students from other cultures.

EXERCISE

If you had an opportunity to spend a summer working as an intern in a foreign country, which country would you select? Why? In what ways would the internship be valuable to your future career in business? How would you prepare for the internship?

---

7. CASES AND PROBLEMS

LEARNING ON THE WEB

Keeping Current About Currency

On a day-to-day basis, you probably don't think about what the U.S. dollar (US$) is worth relative to other currencies. But there will likely be times when ups and downs in exchange rates will seem extremely important to you in your business career. The following are some hypothetical scenarios that illustrate what these times may be. (*Note*: To respond to the questions raised in each scenario, search Google for a currency converter.)

Scenario 1: Your Swiss Vacation

Your family came from Switzerland, and you and your parents visited relatives there back in 2007. Now that you're in college, you want to make the trip on your own during spring break. While you're there, you also plan to travel around and see a little more of the country. You remember that in 2007, US$1 bought 1.22 Swiss francs (Frs). You estimate that, at this rate, you can finance your trip (excluding airfare) with the $1,200 that you earned this summer. You've heard, however, that the exchange rate has changed. Given the current exchange rate, about how much do you think your trip would cost you? As a U.S. traveler going abroad, how are you helped by a shift in exchange rates? How are you hurt?

Scenario 2: Your British Friends

A few years ago, you met some British students who were visiting the United States. This year, you're encouraging them to visit again so that you can show them around New York City. When you and your friends first talked about the cost of the trip back in 2007, the British pound (£) could be converted into US$1.90. You estimated that each of your British friends would need to save up about £600 to make the trip (again, excluding plane fare). Given today's exchange rate, how much will each person need to make the trip? Have your plans been helped or hindered by the change in exchange rates? Was the shift a plus for the U.S. travel industry? What sort of exchange-rate shift hurts the industry?

Scenario 3: Your German Soccer Boots

Your father rarely throws anything away, and while cleaning out the attic a few years ago, he came across a pair of vintage Adidas soccer boots made in 1955. Realizing that they'd be extremely valuable to collectors in Adidas's home country of Germany, he hoped to sell them for US $5,000 and, to account for the exchange rate at the time, planned to price them at $7,200 in euros. Somehow, he never got around to selling the boots and has asked if you could sell them for him on eBay. If he still wants to end up with US $5,000, what price in euros will you now have to set? Would an American company that exports goods to the European Union view the current rate more favorably or less favorably than it did back in 2007?

CAREER OPPORTUNITIES

Broadening Your Business Horizons

At some point in your life, you'll probably meet and work with people from various countries and cultures. Participating in a college study-abroad program can help you prepare to work in the global business environment, and now is as good a time as any to start exploring this option. Here's one way to go about it:

- Select a study-abroad program that interests you. To do this, you need to decide what country you want to study in and your academic field of interest. Unless you speak the language of your preferred country, you should pick a program offered in English.
  - If your school offers study-abroad programs, choose one that has been approved by your institution.
  - If your school doesn't offer study-abroad programs, locate one through a Web search.
- Describe the program, the school that's offering it, and the country to which it will take you.
- Indicate why you've selected this particular program, and explain how it will help you prepare for your future business career.

ETHICS ANGLE

The Right, Wrong, and Wisdom of Dumping and Subsidizing

When companies sell exported goods below the price they'd charge in their home markets (and often below the cost of producing the goods), they're engaging in *dumping*. When governments guarantee farmers certain prices for crops regardless of market prices, the beneficiaries are being *subsidized*. What do you think about these practices? Is dumping an unfair business practice? Why, or why not? Does subsidizing farmers make economic sense for the United States? What are the effects of farm subsidies on the world economy? Are the ethical issues raised by the two practices comparable? Why, or why not?

TEAM-BUILDING SKILLS

Three Little Words: The China Price

According to business journalists Pete Engardio and Dexter Roberts, the scariest three words that a U.S. manufacturer can hear these days are *the China price*. To understand why, go to the *Business Week* Web site (http://www.businessweek.com/magazine/content/04_49/b3911401.htm) and read its article "The China Price," which discusses the benefits and costs of China's business expansion for U.S. companies, workers, and consumers. Once you've read the article, each member of the team should be able to explain the paradoxical effect of U.S.–Chinese business relationships—namely, that they can hurt American companies and workers while helping American companies and consumers.

Next, your team should get together and draw up two lists: a list of the top five positive outcomes and a list of the top five negative outcomes of recent Chinese business expansion for U.S. businesses, workers, and consumers. Then, the team should debate the pros and cons of China's emergence as a global business competitor and, finally, write a group report that answers the following questions:

1. Considered on balance, has China's business expansion helped or harmed U.S. companies, workers, and consumers? Justify your answers.
2. What will happen to U.S. companies, workers, and consumers in the future if China continues to grow as a global business competitor?
3. How should U.S. companies respond to the threats posed by Chinese competitors in their markets?
4. What can you do as a student to prepare yourself to compete in an ever-changing global business environment?

When you hand in your report, be sure to attach all the following items:

- Members' individually prepared lists of ways in which business relationships with China both hurt and help U.S. businesses, workers, and consumers
- Your group-prepared list of the top five positive and negative effects of Chinese business expansion on U.S. businesses, workers, and consumers

THE GLOBAL VIEW

Go East, Young Job Seeker

How brave are you when it comes to employment? Are you bold enough to go halfway around the world to find work? Instead of complaining about U.S. jobs going overseas, you could take the bull by the horns and grab one job back. It's not that tough to do, and it could be a life-changing experience. U.S. college graduates with business or technical backgrounds are highly sought after by companies that operate in India. If you qualify (and if you're willing to relocate), you could find yourself working in Bangalore or New Delhi for some multinational company like Intel, Citibank, or GlaxoSmithKline (a pharmaceutical company). In addition, learning how to live and work in a foreign country can build self-confidence and make you more attractive to future employers. To get a glimpse of what it would be like to live and work in India, read the articles, "Passage to India" (http://hub.aa.com/en/aw/jeffrey-vanderwerf-high-tech-outsourcing-boom-bangalore-leela-palace) and "Needs Job, Moves to India" (http://money.cnn.com/2004/03/09/pf/workers_to_india). Then, go to the Monster Work Abroad Web site (http://jobsearch.monsterindia.com/return2origin/index.html) and find a job in India that you'd like to have, either right after graduation or about five years into your career. (When selecting the job, ignore its actual location and proceed as if it's in Bangalore.) After you've pondered the possibility of living and working in India, answer the following questions:

1. What would your job entail?
2. What would living and working in Bangalore be like? What aspects would you enjoy? Which would you dislike?
3. What challenges would you face as an expatriate (a person who lives outside his or her native country)? What opportunities would you have?
4. How would the experience of working in India help your future career?
5. Would you be willing to take a job in India for a year or two? Why, or why not?

ENDNOTES

1. World Trade Organization, "Trade to Remain Subdued in 2013 after Sluggish Growth in 2012 as European Economies Continue to Struggle" (Appendix Table 3), news release, April 10, 2013, http://www.wto.org/english/news_e/pres13_e/pr688_e.htm (accessed March 24, 2014).

2. Warren E. Buffet, "Why I'm Not Buying the U.S. Dollar," *Wall Street Week with Fortune*, http://www.pbs.org/wsw/news/fortunearticle_20031026_03.html (accessed March 25, 2014).

3. "Why Are Prices in Japan So Damn High?" *The Japan FAQ*, http://www.thejapanfaq.com/FAQ-Prices.html (accessed March 25, 2014).

4. Warren E. Buffet, "Why I'm Not Buying the U.S. Dollar," *Wall Street Week with Fortune*, http://www.pbs.org/wsw/news/fortunearticle_20031026_03.html (accessed March 25, 2014); "U.S. Trade in Goods and Services—Balance of Payments (BOP) Basis, 1960 thru 2013," March 7, 2014, http://www.census.gov/foreign-trade/statistics/historical/goods.pdf (accessed March 25, 2014).

5. Fine Waters Media, "Bottled Water of France," http://www.finewaters.com/Bottled_Water/France/Evian.asp (accessed March 25, 2014).

6. H. Frederick Gale, "China's Growing Affluence: How Food Markets Are Responding," http://www.worldebooklibrary.org/eBooks/WPLBN0002111649-Amber-Waves (accessed March 25, 2014).

7. American Soybean Association, "ASA Testifies on Importance of China Market to U.S. Soybean Exports," June 22, 2010, http://soygrowers.com/asa-testifies-on-importance-of-china-market-to-u-s-soybean-exports (accessed March 25, 2014).

8. Gary Gereffi and Stacey Frederick, "The Global Apparel Value Chain, Trade and the Crisis: Challenges and Opportunities for Developing Countries," The World Bank, Development Research Group, Trade and Integration Team, April 2010, http://www.iadb.org/intal/intalcdi/PE/2010/05413.pdf (accessed March 25, 214).

9. Viacom International, "TV Production Breakthrough: With Regulations Being Relaxed, Media Giant Viacom Expands Its Presence in China," *Beijing Review*, http://www.bjreview.cn/EN/En-2005/05-17-e/bus-3.htm (accessed March 25, 2014).

10. Liz Borod, "DA! To the Good Life," *Folio*, September 1, 2004, http://www.highbeam.com/doc/1G1-121708402.html (accessed March 25, 2014); Jill Garbi, "Cosmo Girl Goes to Israel," *Folio*, November 1, 2003, http://www.highbeam.com/doc/1G1-109384460.html (accessed March 25, 2014); Liz Borod, "A Passage to India," Folio, August 1, 2004, http://connection.ebscohost.com/c/articles/14194412/passage-india (accessed March 25, 2014); Jill Garbi, "A Sleeping Media Giant?" *Folio*, January 1, 2004, http://www.highbeam.com/doc/1G1-111585651.html (accessed March 25, 2014).

11. Michael Mandel, "The Real Cost of Offshoring," *Bloomberg BusinessWeek*, June 28, 2007, http://www.businessweek.com/magazine/content/07_25/b4039001.htm (accessed March 25, 2014).

12. "Global 500," *Fortune* (CNNMoney), http://money.cnn.com/magazines/fortune/global500/2013/full_list (accessed March 25, 2014).

13. James C. Morgan and J. Jeffrey Morgan, *Cracking the Japanese Market* (New York: Free Press, 1991), 102.

14. "Glocalization Examples—Think Globally and Act Locally," *CaseStudyInc.com*, http://www.casestudyinc.com/glocalization-examples-think-globally-and-act-locally (accessed March 25, 2014).

15. McDonald's India, "Mcdonalds Adapting Globally to Cultures," http://cheek0o.hubpages.com/hub/Mc-Donalds-adapting-globally (accessed March 25, 2014).

16. Susan L. Nasr, "Ten Unusual Items from McDonald's International Menu," *HowStuffWorks*, http://money.howstuffworks.com/10-items-from-mcdonalds-international-menu.htm (accessed March 25, 2014).

17. "Glocalization Examples—Think Globally and Act Locally," *CaseStudyInc.com*, http://www.casestudyinc.com/glocalization-examples-think-globally-and-act-locally (accessed March 25, 2014).

18. James C. Morgan and J. Jeffrey Morgan, *Cracking the Japanese Market* (New York: Free Press, 1991), 117.

19. Anne O. Krueger, "Supporting Globalization" (remarks, 2002 Eisenhower National Security Conference on "National Security for the 21st Century: Anticipating Challenges, Seizing Opportunities, Building Capabilities," September 26, 2002), http://www.imf.org/external/np/speeches/2002/092602a.htm (accessed March 25, 2014).

20. The World Bank, "Country and Lending Groups," http:// http://data.worldbank.org/about/country-classifications/country-and-lending-groups (accessed March 25, 2014).

21. National Debt Clock, http://www.usdebtclock.org (accessed March 25, 2014).

22. David Ricks, *Blunders in International Business* (Malden, MA: Blackwell, 1999), 137.

23. "The Protectionist Swindle: How Trade Barriers Cheat the Poor and Middle Class," *Insider Online*, December 1, 2009, http://www.insideronline.org/feature.cfm?id=270 (accessed August 24, 2011).

24. John Carney, "The Affordable Footwear Act Is a Real Thing," *CNBC NetNet*, June 1, 2011, http://www.cnbc.com/id/43239340/The_Affordable_Footwear_Act_Is_a_Real_Thing.

25. Chris Edwards, "The Sugar Racket," CATO Institute, Tax and Budget, June 2007, http://www.cato.org/pubs/tbb/tbb_0607_46.pdf (accessed March 25, 2014).

26. Dean Reynolds, "Costly Sugar Pushes Candy Plant to Canada," *ABC News*, March 25, 2014, http://abcnews.go.com/Business/story?id=87274 (accessed March 25, 2014).

27. Richard W. Stevenson and Elizabeth Becker, "After 21 Months, Bush Lifts Tariff on Steel Imports,", *New York Times*, March 25, 2014, http://www.nytimes.com/2003/12/05/us/after-21-months-bush-lifts-tariff-on-steel-imports.html (accessed March 25, 2014).

28. Bernard Sanders, "The International Monetary Fund Is Hurting You," *Z Magazine*, July–August 1998, http://www.thirdworldtraveler.com/IMF_WB/IMF_Sanders.html (accessed March 25, 2014).

29. The World Bank, "The World Bank Annual Report 2013," June 2013, http://web.worldbank.org/WBSITE/EXTERNAL/EXTABOUTUS/EXTANNREP/EXTANNREP2013/0,,contentMDK:23461227~pagePK:64168445~piPK:64168309~theSitePK:9304888,00.html (accessed March 25, 2014).

30. Bretton Woods Project, "What Are the Main Concerns and Criticism about the World Bank and IMF?" August 23, 2005, http://www.google.com/search?q=criticisms+of+world+bank+and+imf&ie=utf-8&oe=utf-8&aq=t&rls=org.mozilla:en (accessed March 25, 2014).

31. See Andreas Dombret, "Global Currency Blocs—Is the Euro a Burden or a Competitive Advantage?" *Bank for International Settlements*, December 6, 2013, http://www.bis.org/review/r131206a.htm (accessed March 25, 2014).

32. "Paul Krugman: The Economic Failure of the Euro," *NPR* (National Public Radio), January 25, 2011, http://www.npr.org/2011/01/25/133112932/paul-krugman-the-economic-failure-of-the-euro (accessed March 25, 2014).

33. Willem Buiter, "Three Steps to Survival for Euro Zone," *Wall Street Journal: Agenda*, December 10, 2010, http://online.wsj.com/article/SB10001424052748703766704576009423447485768.html (accessed March 25, 2014).

CHAPTER 4
Selecting a Form of Business Ownership

THE ICE CREAM MEN

Who would have thought it? Two ex-hippies with strong interests in social activism would end up starting one of the best-known ice cream companies in the country—Ben & Jerry's. Perhaps it was meant to be. It seems that Ben Cohen (the "Ben" of Ben & Jerry's) always had a fascination with ice cream. As a child, he made his own ice cream mixtures by smashing his favorite cookies and candies into his ice cream. But it wasn't until his senior year in high school that he became an official "ice cream man," happily driving his truck through neighborhoods filled with kids eager to buy his ice cream pops. After high school, Ben tried college but it wasn't for him. He attended Colgate University for a year and a half before he dropped out to return to his real love: being an ice cream man. He tried college again—this time at Skidmore, where he studied pottery and jewelry making—but, in spite of his selection of courses, still didn't like it.

In the meantime, Jerry Greenfield (the "Jerry" of Ben & Jerry's) was following a similar path. He majored in premed at Oberlin College and hoped to become a doctor. But he had to give up on this goal when he was not accepted into medical school. On a positive note, though, his college education steered him into a more lucrative field: the world of ice cream making. He got his first peek at the ice cream industry when he worked as a scooper in the student cafeteria at Oberlin. So, fourteen years after they met, Ben and Jerry reunited and decided to go into ice cream making big time. They moved to Burlington, Vermont—a college town in need of an ice cream par-lor—and completed a $5 correspondence course from Penn State on making ice cream (they were practically broke at the time so they split the cost). After getting an A in the course—not sur-prising, given that the tests were open book—they took the plunge: with their life savings of $8,000 (plus $4,000 of borrowed funds), they set up an ice cream scoop shop in a made-over gas station on a busy street corner in Burlington. The next big decision was which form of business ownership was best for them. This chapter introduces you to their options.

What's your favorite Ben & Jerry's flavor?

Source: http://en.wikipedia.org/wiki/File:BenJerry-UnitedSquare.jpg.

1. FACTORS TO CONSIDER

LEARNING OBJECTIVE

1. **Identify the questions to ask in choosing the appropriate form of ownership for a business.**

If you're starting a new business, you have to decide which legal form of ownership is best for you and your business. Do you want to own the business yourself and operate as a sole proprietorship? Or, do you want to share ownership, operating as a partnership or a corporation? Before we discuss the pros and cons of these three types of ownership—sole proprietorship, partnership, and corporation—let's address some of the questions that you'd probably ask yourself in choosing the appropriate legal form for your business.

1. What are you willing to do to set up and operate your business? Do you want to minimize the costs of getting started? Do you hope to avoid complex government regulations and reporting requirements?

2. How much control would you like? Do you want to own the company yourself, or do you want to share ownership with other people? Are you willing to share responsibility for running the business?

3. Do you want to be the sole benefactor of your efforts or are you willing to share profits with other people? Do you want to be in charge of deciding how much of the company's profits will be retained in the business?

4. Do you want to avoid special taxes? Do you want to avoid paying "business" income taxes on your business and then paying "personal" income taxes on profits earned by the business?

5. Do you have all the skills needed to run the business? Do you possess the talent and skills to run the business yourself, or would the business benefit from a diverse group of owners? Are you likely to get along with co-owners over an extended period of time?

6. Should it be possible for the business to continue without you? Is it important to you that the business survive you? Do you want to know that other owners can take over if you die or become disabled? Do you want to make it easy for ownership to change hands?

7. What are your financing needs? How do you plan to finance your company? Will you need a lot of money to start, operate, and grow your business? Can you furnish the money yourself, or will you need some investment from other people? Will you need bank loans? If so, will you have difficulty getting them yourself?

8. How much liability exposure are you willing to accept? Are you willing to risk your personal assets—your bank account, your car, maybe even your home—for your business? Are you prepared to pay business debts out of your personal funds? Do you feel uneasy about accepting personal liability for the actions of fellow owners?

No single form of ownership will give you everything you desire. You'll have to make some trade-offs. Because each option has both advantages and disadvantages, your job is to decide which one offers the features that are most important to you. In the following sections, we'll compare the three ownership options (sole proprietorship, partnership, and corporation) on the eight dimensions that we identified previously: setup costs and government regulations, control, profit sharing, income taxes, skills, continuity and transferability, ability to obtain financing, and liability exposure.

KEY TAKEAWAYS

- Some of the questions that you'd probably ask yourself in choosing the appropriate legal form for your business include the following:

  1. *What are you willing to do to set up and operate your business?*
  2. *How much control do you want?*
  3. *Do you want to share profits with others?*
  4. *Do you want to avoid special taxes on your business?*
  5. *Do you have all the skills needed to run the business?*
  6. *Should it be possible for the business to continue without you?*
  7. *What are your financing needs?*
  8. *How much liability exposure are you willing to accept?*

- No single form of ownership—sole proprietorship, partnership, or corporation—will give you everything you want. Each has advantages and disadvantages.

Before going to the next section of this chapter, take a few minutes to test your knowledge of the material covered in this section. Quizzes can be found under the "Resources" tab, "Study Aids: Quizzes."

2. SOLE PROPRIETORSHIP

LEARNING OBJECTIVES

1. Describe the sole proprietorship form of organization, and indicate what percentage of U.S. businesses use this form of ownership.
2. Identify and explain the advantages of a sole proprietorship.
3. Identify and explain the disadvantages of a sole proprietorship.

A **sole proprietorship** is a business owned by only one person. The most common form of ownership, it accounts for about 72 percent of all U.S. businesses.[1] It's the easiest and cheapest type of business to form: if you're using your own name as the name of your business, you just need a license to get started, and once you're in business, you're subject to few government regulations.

sole proprietorship

Business owned by only one person.

2.1 Advantages and Disadvantages of Sole Proprietorships

As sole owner, you have complete control over your business. You make all important decisions, and you're generally responsible for all day-to-day activities. In exchange for assuming all this responsibility, you get all the income earned by the business. Profits earned are taxed as personal income, so you don't have to pay any special federal and state income taxes.

For many people, however, the sole proprietorship is not suitable. The flip side of enjoying complete control, for example, is having to supply all the different talents that may be necessary to make the business a success. And if you die, the business dissolves. You also have to rely on your own resources for financing: in effect, you *are* the business, and any money borrowed by the business is loaned to *you personally*. Even more important, the sole proprietor bears **unlimited liability** for any losses incurred by the business. As you can see from Figure 4.2, the principle of unlimited personal liability means that if the *company* incurs a debt or suffers a catastrophe (say, getting sued for causing an injury to someone), the *owner* is personally liable. As a sole proprietor, you put your personal assets (your bank account, your car, maybe even your home) at risk for the sake of your business. You can lessen your risk with insurance, yet your liability exposure can still be substantial. Given that Ben and Jerry decided to start their ice cream business together (and therefore the business was not owned by only one person), they could not set their company up as a sole proprietorship.

FIGURE 4.1

Sole proprietors enjoy complete control but also face increased risks.

© 2010 Jupiterimages Corporation

unlimited liability

Legal condition under which an owner or investor is personally liable for all debts of a business.

FIGURE 4.2 Sole Proprietorship and Unlimited Liability

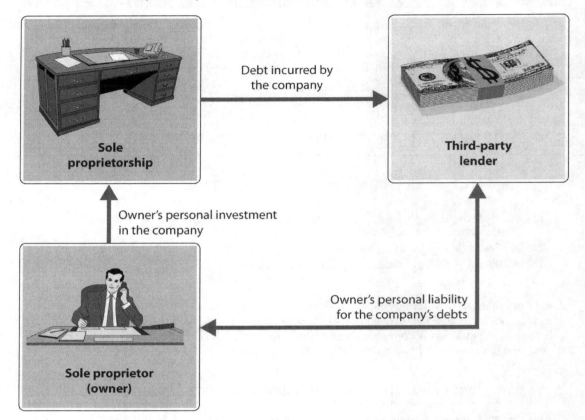

Sole Proprietorship and Unlimited Liability

Click on this link to experience an active version of this figure.

KEY TAKEAWAYS

- A **sole proprietorship** is a business owned by only one person.
- It's the most common form of ownership and accounts for about 72 percent of all U.S. businesses.
- Advantages of a sole proprietorship include the following:
    1. Easy and inexpensive to form; few government regulations
    2. Complete control over your business
    3. Get all the profits earned by the business
    4. Don't have to pay any special income taxes
- Disadvantages of a sole proprietorship include the following:
    1. Have to supply all the different talents needed to make the business a success
    2. If you die, the business dissolves
    3. Have to rely on your own resources for financing
    4. If the company incurs a debt or suffers a catastrophe, you are personally liable (you have unlimited liability)

Before going to the next section of this chapter, take a few minutes to test your knowledge of the material covered in this section. Quizzes can be found under the "Resources" tab, "Study Aids: Quizzes."

> ### EXERCISE
>
> Talk with a sole proprietor about his or her selected form of business ownership. Ask him or her which of the following dimensions (discussed in this section) were important in deciding to operate as a proprietor: setup costs and government regulations, control, profit sharing, income taxes, skills, continuity and transferability, ability to obtain financing, and liability exposure. Write a report detailing what you learned from the business owner.

3. PARTNERSHIP

> ### LEARNING OBJECTIVES
>
> 1. Identify the different types of partnerships.
> 2. Indicate what percentage of U.S. businesses operate as partnerships.
> 3. Explain the importance of a partnership agreement.
> 4. Describe the advantages and disadvantages of the partnership form of organization.
> 5. Describe a limited partnership.

A **partnership (or general partnership)** is a business owned jointly by two or more people. About 10 percent of U.S. businesses are partnerships,[2] and though the vast majority are small, some are quite large. For example, the big four public accounting firms are partnerships. Setting up a partnership is more complex than setting up a sole proprietorship, but it's still relatively easy and inexpensive. The cost varies according to size and complexity. It's possible to form a simple partnership without the help of a lawyer or an accountant, though it's usually a good idea to get professional advice. Professionals can help you identify and resolve issues that may later create disputes among partners.

> **partnership (or general partnership)**
>
> Business owned jointly by two or more people.

3.1 The Partnership Agreement

The impact of disputes can be lessened if the partners have executed a well-planned *partnership agreement* that specifies everyone's rights and responsibilities. The agreement might provide such details as the following:

- Amount of cash and other contributions to be made by each partner
- Division of partnership income (or loss)
- Partner responsibilities—who does what
- Conditions under which a partner can sell an interest in the company
- Conditions for dissolving the partnership
- Conditions for settling disputes

3.2 Unlimited Liability and the Partnership

Figure 4.3 shows that a major problem with partnerships, as with sole proprietorships, is unlimited liability: each partner is personally liable not only for his or her own actions but also for *the actions of all the partners*. In a partnership, it may work according to the following scenario. Say that you're a partner in a dry cleaning business. One day, you return from lunch to find your establishment on fire. You're intercepted by your partner, who tells you that the fire started because he fell asleep while smoking. As you watch your livelihood go up in flames, your partner tells you something else: because he forgot to pay the bill, your fire insurance was canceled. When it's all over, you estimate the loss to the building and everything inside at $1.2 million. And here's the really bad news: if the business doesn't have the cash or other assets to cover losses, *you can be personally sued for the amount owed*. In other words, any party who suffered a loss because of the fire can go after your personal assets.

FIGURE 4.3 General Partnership and Unlimited Liability

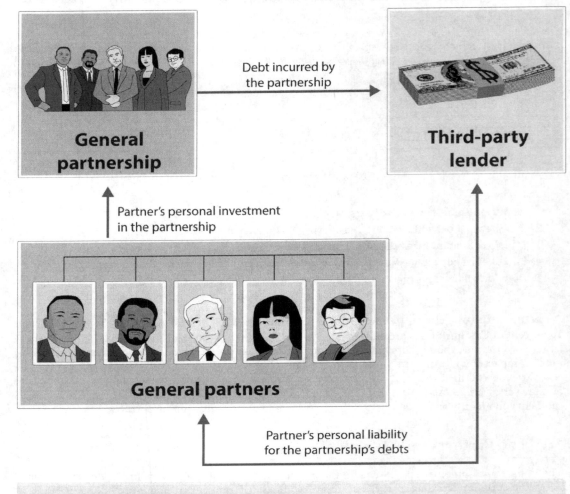

General Partnership and Unlimited Liability

Click on this link to experience an active version of this figure.

3.3 Limited Partnerships

limited partnership

Partnership made up of a single general partner (who runs the business and is responsible for its liabilities) and any number of limited partners.

Many people are understandably reluctant to enter into partnerships because of unlimited liability. Individuals with substantial assets, for example, have a lot to lose if they get sued for a partnership obligation (and when people sue, they tend to start with the richest partner). To overcome this defect of partnerships, the law permits a **limited partnership**, which has two types of partners: a single *general partner* who runs the business and is responsible for its liabilities, and any number of *limited partners* who have limited involvement in the business and whose losses are limited to the amount of their investment.

3.4 Advantages and Disadvantages of Partnerships

The partnership has several advantages over the sole proprietorship. First, it brings together a diverse group of talented individuals who share responsibility for running the business. Second, it makes financing easier: The business can draw on the financial resources of a number of individuals. The partners not only contribute funds to the business but can also use personal resources to secure bank loans. Finally, continuity needn't be an issue because partners can agree legally to allow the partnership to survive if one or more partners die.

Still, there are some negatives. First, as discussed earlier, partners are subject to unlimited liability. Second, being a partner means that you have to share decision making, and many people aren't comfortable with that situation. Not surprisingly, partners often have differences of opinion on how to run a business, and disagreements can escalate to the point of actual conflict; in fact, they can even jeopardize the continuance of the business. Third, in addition to sharing ideas, partners also share profits. This arrangement can work as long as all partners feel that they're being rewarded according to their efforts and accomplishments, but that isn't always the case.

While the partnership form of ownership is viewed negatively by some, it was particularly appealing to Ben Cohen and Jerry Greenfield. Starting their ice cream business as a partnership was inexpensive and let them combine their limited financial resources and use their diverse skills and talents. As friends, they trusted each other and welcomed shared decision making and profit sharing. They were also not reluctant to be held personally liable for each other's actions.

FIGURE 4.4

Partnerships can have many advantages, but there are disadvantages to consider as well.

© 2010 Jupiterimages Corporation

KEY TAKEAWAYS

- A general partnership is a business owned jointly by two or more people.
- About 10 percent of U.S. businesses are partnerships.
- The impact of disputes can be reduced if the partners have a partnership agreement that specifies everyone's rights and responsibilities.
- A partnership has several advantages over a sole proprietorship:
    - It's relatively inexpensive to set up and subject to few government regulations.
    - Partners pay personal income taxes on their share of profits; the partnership doesn't pay any special taxes.
    - It brings a diverse group of people together to share managerial responsibilities.
    - Partners can agree legally to allow the partnership to survive if one or more partners die.
    - It makes financing easier because the partnership can draw on resources from a number of partners.
- A partnership has several disadvantages over a sole proprietorship:
    - Shared decision making can result in disagreements.
    - Profits must be shared.
    - Each partner is personally liable not only for his or her own actions but also for those of all partners—a principle called **unlimited liability**.
- A **limited partnership** has a single general partner who runs the business and is responsible for its liabilities, plus any number of limited partners who have limited involvement in the business and whose losses are limited to the amount of their investment.

Before going to the next section of this chapter, take a few minutes to test your knowledge of the material covered in this section. Quizzes can be found under the "Resources" tab, "Study Aids: Quizzes."

Grand Canyon Helicopter Adventures was started five years ago by Jayden Collins. The business has grown over the years, but is at a standstill now. Jayden would like to expand his business but needs additional funds to do this. Also, he could really use help running the business. Though he is an excellent pilot with a perfect safety record, he's not very good at handling the day-to-day details needed to keep the business running smoothly. A friend of his, Rob Tocci, approached him recently and asked to join him in the business. Rob is fairly wealthy and has considerable business experience. Plus, he knows how to fly choppers—though he has had a few (thankfully nonfatal) mishaps. Jayden is a little apprehensive about sharing responsibility for running the business, but he doesn't mind sharing profits. On the other hand, he recognizes that he alone will not be able to grow the business.

Because Jayden doesn't want to incorporate, he has only two options: continue doing business as a sole proprietorship or find someone to join him in a partnership. You should evaluate these two alternatives, discuss the advantages and disadvantages of each option, and recommend the one you consider most appropriate. If you recommend forming a partnership, distinguish between a limited and a general partnership.

4. CORPORATION

LEARNING OBJECTIVES

1. Describe the corporate form of organization.
2. Indicate what percentage of U.S. businesses use the corporate form of ownership.
3. Explain how corporations are formed and how they operate.
4. Explain how you could become an owner of a corporation.
5. Discuss the advantages of the corporate form of ownership.
6. Describe the legal liability benefit of incorporating.
7. Discuss the disadvantages of the corporate form of ownership.

corporation

Legal entity that is entirely separate from the parties who own it and that is responsible for its own debts.

A **corporation** (sometimes called a *regular* or C-corporation) differs from a sole proprietorship and a partnership because it's a legal entity that is entirely separate from the parties who own it. It can enter into binding contracts, buy and sell property, sue and be sued, be held responsible for its actions, and be taxed. As Figure 4.5 shows, corporations account for 18 percent of all U.S. businesses but generate almost 82 percent of the revenues.[3] Most large well-known businesses are corporations, but so are many of the smaller firms with which you do business.

FIGURE 4.5 Types of U.S. Businesses

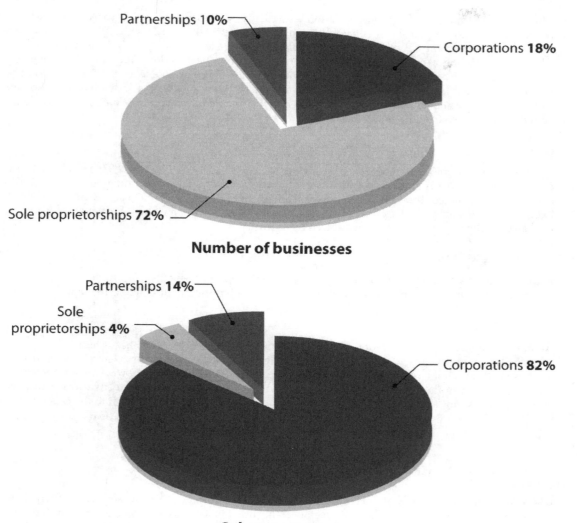

Source: U.S. Census Bureau, "Number of Tax Returns, Receipts, and Net Income by Type of Business," *The 2011 Statistical Abstract: The National Data Book,* http://www.census.gov/compendia/statab/cats/business_enterprise/sole_proprietorships_partnerships_corporations.html (accessed March 30, 2014); U.S. Census Bureau, "Number of Tax Returns and Business Receipts by Size of Receipts," *The 2011 Statistical Abstract: The National Data Book,* http://www.census.gov/compendia/statab/cats/business_enterprise/sole_proprietorships_partnerships_corporations.html (accessed March 30, 2014).

4.1   Ownership and Stock

Corporations are owned by **shareholders** who invest money in the business by buying shares of **stock**. The portion of the corporation they own depends on the percentage of stock they hold. For example, if a corporation has issued 100 shares of stock, and you own 30 shares, you own 30 percent of the company. The shareholders elect a **board of directors**, a group of people (primarily from outside the corporation) who are legally responsible for governing the corporation. The board oversees the major policies and decisions made by the corporation, sets goals and holds management accountable for achieving them, and hires and evaluates the top executive, generally called the CEO (chief executive officer). The board also approves the distribution of income to shareholders in the form of cash payments called **dividends**.

4.2   Benefits of Incorporation

The corporate form of organization offers several advantages, including limited liability for shareholders, greater access to financial resources, specialized management, and continuity.

shareholders

Owners of a corporation.

stock

Share of ownership in a corporation.

board of directors

Group of people who are legally responsible for governing a corporation.

dividends

Earnings distributed to stockholders.

Limited Liability

The most important benefit of incorporation is the **limited liability** to which shareholders are exposed: they are not responsible for the obligations of the corporation, and they can lose *no more than the amount that they have personally invested in the company*. Clearly, limited liability would have been a big plus for the unfortunate individual whose business partner burned down their dry cleaning establishment. Had they been incorporated, the *corporation* would have been liable for the debts incurred by the fire. If the corporation didn't have enough money to pay the debt, the individual shareholders would not have been obligated to pay anything. True, they would have lost all the money that they'd invested in the business, but no more.

Financial Resources

Incorporation also makes it possible for businesses to raise funds by selling stock. This is a big advantage as a company grows and needs more funds to operate and compete. Depending on its size and financial strength, the corporation also has an advantage over other forms of business in getting bank loans. An established corporation can borrow its own funds, but when a small business needs a loan, the bank usually requires that it be guaranteed by its owners.

Specialized Management

Because of their size and ability to pay high sales commissions and benefits, corporations are generally able to attract more skilled and talented employees than are proprietorships and partnerships.

Continuity and Transferability

Another advantage of incorporation is continuity. Because the corporation has a legal life separate from the lives of its owners, it can (at least in theory) exist forever. Transferring ownership of a corporation is easy: shareholders simply sell their stock to others. Some founders, however, want to restrict the transferability of their stock and so choose to operate as a **privately-held corporation**. The stock in these corporations is held by only a few individuals, who are not allowed to sell it to the general public. Companies with no such restrictions on stock sales are called **public corporations**; stock is available for sale to the general public.

4.3 Drawbacks to Incorporation

Like sole proprietorships and partnerships, corporations have both positive and negative properties. In sole proprietorships and partnerships, for instance, the individuals who own and manage a business are the same people. Corporate managers, however, don't necessarily own stock, and shareholders don't necessarily work for the company. This situation can be troublesome if the goals of the two groups differ significantly. Managers, for example, might be more interested in career advancement than the overall profitability of the company. Stockholders might care about profits without regard for the well-being of employees.

Another drawback to incorporation—one that often discourages small businesses from incorporating—is the fact that corporations are costly to set up. When you combine filing and licensing fees with accounting and attorney fees, incorporating a business could set you back by $1,000 to $6,000 or more depending on the size and scope of your business.[4] Additionally, corporations are subject to levels of regulation and governmental oversight that can place a burden on small businesses. Finally, corporations are subject to what's generally called "double taxation." Corporations are taxed by the federal and state governments on their earnings. When these earnings are distributed as dividends, the shareholders pay taxes on these dividends. Corporate profits are thus taxed twice—the corporation pays the taxes the first time and the shareholders pay the taxes the second time.

Five years after starting their ice cream business, Ben Cohen and Jerry Greenfield evaluated the pros and cons of the corporate form of ownership, and the "pros" won. The primary motivator was the need to raise funds to build a $2 million manufacturing facility. Not only did Ben and Jerry decide to switch from a partnership to a corporation, but they also decided to sell shares of stock to the public (and thus become a public corporation). Their sale of stock to the public was a bit unusual: Ben and Jerry wanted the community to own the company, so instead of offering the stock to anyone interested in buying a share, they offered stock to residents of Vermont only. Ben believed that "business has a responsibility to give back to the community from which it draws its support."[5] He wanted the company to be owned by those who lined up in the gas station to buy cones. The stock was so popular that one in every hundred Vermont families bought stock in the company.[6] Eventually, as the company continued to expand, the stock was sold on a national level.

KEY TAKEAWAYS

- A **corporation** (sometimes called a *regular* or C-corporation) is a legal entity that's separate from the parties who own it.
- Corporations are owned by **shareholders** who invest money in them by buying shares of **stock**.
- They elect a **board of directors** that's legally responsible for governing the corporation.
- A corporation has several advantages over a sole proprietorship and partnership:
  - An important advantage of incorporation is **limited liability**: Owners are not responsible for the obligations of the corporation and can lose no more than the amount that they have personally invested in the company.
  - Incorporation also makes it easier to access financing.
  - Because the corporation is a separate legal entity, it exists beyond the lives of its owners.
  - Corporations are generally able to attract skilled and talented employees.
- A corporation has several disadvantages over a sole proprietorship and partnership:
  - The goals of corporate managers, who don't necessarily own stock, and shareholders, who don't necessarily work for the company, can differ.
  - It's costly to set up and subject to burdensome regulations and government oversight.
  - It's subject to "double taxation." Corporations are taxed on their earnings. When these earnings are distributed as dividends, the shareholders pay taxes on these dividends.

Before going to the next section of this chapter, take a few minutes to test your knowledge of the material covered in this section. Quizzes can be found under the "Resources" tab, "Study Aids: Quizzes."

EXERCISE

SolarBike Company was formed as a partnership ten years ago by three sisters-in-law: Peg McLaughlin, Terry McLaughlin, and Joanie McLaughlin. All three worked diligently to design and produce the SolarBike: an electric bicycle propelled by the sun's rays. The good news is that the bike is a big hit with environmentalists and last year's sales reached $2 million. The bad news is that to keep up with growing demand for the bike, the company must expand its capacity at a cost of $1 million. Even though the company is doing well, it's unlikely that the partnership could get the needed $1 million in funds from a bank.

The company's predicament was discussed at a recent partnership meeting. Not only were the three partners unwilling to lend the company any more money, but also they voiced concern about being held responsible for their own actions as well as for all the partners' actions. Peg asked the group to consider incorporating and raising funds through the sale of stock. Joanie supported this idea, but Terry was against it.

The three partners hired you as a consultant to advise them on whether to remain as a partnership or to form a private corporation. In addition to your recommendation, you should discuss the advantages and disadvantages of both forms of organization and explain how they apply to SolarBike Company's situation.

5.   OTHER TYPES OF BUSINESS OWNERSHIP

LEARNING OBJECTIVES

1. Describe the S-corporation, and examine its advantages and disadvantages.
2. Explain why the limited liability company (LLC) is favored by many small businesses.
3. Understand how a cooperative is formed and how it operates.
4. Explain the purpose of a not-for-profit corporation, and describe its favorable tax treatment.

In addition to the three commonly adopted forms of business organization—sole proprietorship, partnership, and regular corporations—some business owners select other forms of organization to meet their particular needs. We'll look at several of these options:

- S-corporations

- Limited-liability companies
- Cooperatives
- Not-for-profit corporations

5.1   Hybrids: S-Corporations and Limited-Liability Companies

To understand the value of S-corporations and limited-liability companies, we'll begin by reviewing the major advantages and disadvantages of the three types of business ownership we've explored so far: sole proprietorship, partnership, and corporation. Identifying the attractive and unattractive features of these three types of business ownership will help us appreciate why S-corporations and limited-liability companies were created.

Attractive and Unattractive Features of Corporations

What feature of corporations do business owners find **most attractive?** The most attractive feature of a corporation is limited liability, which means that the shareholders (owners) cannot be held personally liable for the debts and obligations of the corporation. For example, if a corporation cannot pay its debts and goes bankrupt, the shareholders will not be required to pay the creditors with their own money. Shareholders cannot lose any more than the amount they have invested in the company.

What feature of corporations do business owners find **least attractive?** Most would agree that the least attractive feature of a corporation is "double taxation." Double taxation occurs when the same earnings are taxed twice by the government. Let's use a simple example to show how this happens. You're the only shareholder in a very small corporation. This past year it earned $10,000. It had to pay the government $3,000 corporate tax on the $10,000 earned. The remaining $7,000 was paid to you by the corporation in the form of a dividend. When you filed your personal income tax form, you had to pay personal taxes on the $7,000 dividend. So the $7,000 was taxed twice: the corporation paid the taxes the first time and you (the shareholder) paid the taxes the second time.

Attractive and Unattractive Features of Sole Proprietorships and Partnerships

Now let's turn to the other two types of business ownership: sole proprietorship and partnership. What feature of these forms of business organization do owners find **most attractive?** The most attractive feature is that there is **no** "double taxation" with proprietorships and partnerships. Proprietorships and partnerships do not pay taxes on profits at the business level. The only taxes paid are at the personal level—this occurs when proprietors and partners pay taxes on their share of their company's income. Here are two examples (one for a sole proprietorship and one for a partnership). First, let's say you're a sole proprietor and your business earns $20,000 this year. The sole proprietorship pays no taxes at the "business" level. You pay taxes on the $20,000 earnings on your personal tax return. Second, let's say you're a partner in a three-partner firm (in which each partner receives one-third of the partnership income). The firm earns $90,000 this year. It pays no taxes at the partnership level. Each partner, including you, pays taxes on one-third of the earnings, or $30,000 each. Notice that in both cases, there is no "double taxation." Taxes were paid on the company earnings only once—at the personal level. So the total tax burden is less with sole proprietorships and partnerships than it is with corporations.

What feature of sole proprietorships and partnerships do business owners find **least attractive?** And the answer is...unlimited liability. This feature holds a business owner personally liable for all debts of his or her company. If you're a sole proprietorship and the debts of your business exceed its assets, creditors can seize your personal assets to cover the proprietorship's outstanding business debt. For example, if your business is sued for $500,000 and it does not have enough money to cover its legal obligation, the injured party can seize your personal assets (cash, property, etc.) to cover the outstanding debt. Unlimited liability is even riskier in the case of a partnership. Each partner is personally liable not only for his or her own actions but also for the actions of all the partners. If, through mismanagement by one of your partners, the partnership is forced into bankruptcy, the creditors can go after you for all outstanding debts of the partnership.

The Hybrids

How would you like a legal form of organization that provides the attractive features of the three common forms of organization (corporation, sole proprietorship, and partnership) and avoids the unattractive features of these three organization forms? It sounds very appealing. This is what was accomplished with the creation of two hybrid forms of organization: **S-corporation** and **limited-liability company**. These hybrid organization forms provide business owners with limited liability (the attractive feature of corporations) and no "double taxation" (the attractive feature of sole proprietorships and partnerships). We'll now look at these two hybrids in more detail.

5.2 S-Corporation

In 1970, Karen and Mike Tocci, avid go-kart racing fans, bought a parcel of land in New Hampshire so their son, Rob, and his son's friends could drag race in a safe environment. The Tocci's continued interest in racing resulted in their starting a family-run business called Shannon Dragway. Over time, the business expanded to include a speedway track and a go-kart track and was renamed New Hampshire Motorsports Complex. In selecting their organization form, the Tocci's wanted to accomplish two main goals: (1) limit their personal liability; and (2) avoid having their earnings taxed twice, first at the corporate level and again at the personal level. An S-corporation form of business achieved these goals. They found they were able to meet the following S-corporation eligibility criteria:

- The company has no more than 100 shareholders
- All shareholders are individuals, estates, or certain nonprofits or trusts
- All shareholders are U.S. citizens and permanent residents of the U.S.
- The business is not a bank or insurance company
- All shareholders concur with the decision to form an S-corporation

Deciding to operate as an S-corporation presented the Tocci's with some disadvantages: They had no flexibility in the way profits were divided among the owners. In an S-corporation, profits must be allocated based on percentage ownership. So if an owner/shareholder holds 25 percent of the stock in the S-corporation, 25 percent of the company profits are allocated to this shareholder regardless of the amount of effort he or she exerts in running the business. Additionally, the owners had to follow a number of formal procedures, such as electing a board of directors and holding annual meetings. Finally, they were subjected to heavy recordkeeping requirements. Despite these disadvantages, the Tocci's concluded that on balance the S-corporation was the best form of organization for their business.

5.3 Limited-Liability Company

In 1977, Wyoming was the first state to allow businesses to operate as limited-liability companies. Twenty years later, in 1997, Hawaii was the last state to give its approval to the new organization form. Since then, the limited-liability company has increased in popularity. Its rapid growth was fueled in part by changes in state statutes that permit a limited-liability company to have just one member. The trend to LLCs can be witnessed by reading company names on the side of trucks or on storefronts in your city. It is common to see names such as Jim Evans Tree Care, LLC, and For-Cats-Only Veterinary Clinic, LLC. But LLCs are not limited to small businesses. Companies such as Crayola, Domino's Pizza, Ritz-Carlton Hotel Company, and iSold It (which helps people sell their unwanted belongings on eBay) are operating under the limited-liability form of organization.

In many ways, a limited-liability company looks a lot like an S-corporation. Its owners (called members rather than shareholders) are not personally liable for debts of the company, and its earnings are taxed only once, at the personal level (thereby eliminating double taxation). But there are important differences between the two forms of organizations. For example, an LLC:

1. Has fewer ownership restrictions. It can have as many members as it wants—it is not restricted to a maximum of 100 shareholders.

2. Its members don't have to be U.S. residents or citizens.

3. Profits do not have to be allocated to owners based on percentage ownership. Members can distribute profits in any way they want.

4. Is easier to operate because it doesn't have as many rules and restrictions as does an S-corporation. It doesn't have to elect a board of directors, hold annual meetings, or contend with a heavy recordkeeping burden.

As the approach used to allocate profits is very important (item 3 described previously), let's spend a few minutes going over an example of how the profit allocation process works. Let's say that you and a

S-corporation

Corporation that gives small business owners limited liability protection, but taxes company profits only once, when they are paid out as dividends.

limited-liability company

Corporation whose members are not personally liable for company debts and whose earnings are taxed only once, when they are paid out as dividends. It has fewer rules and restrictions than does an S-corporation.

business partner started a small pet-grooming business at the beginning of the year. Your business partner (who has more money than you do) contributed $40,000 to start up the business and you contributed $10,000 (so your partner's percentage ownership in the business is 80 percent and yours is 20 percent). But your business partner has another job and so you did 90 percent of the work during the past year. Profit for the first year was $100,000. If your company was set up as an S-corporation, you would be required to allocate profits based on percentage ownership. Under this allocation scheme, $80,000 of the profits would be allocated to your business partner and only $20,000 would be allocated to you. This hardly seems fair. Under the limited-liability form of organization, you and your partner can decide what is a "fair" allocation of profits and split the profits accordingly. Perhaps you will decide that you should get 70 percent of the profits (or $70,000) and your business partner should get 30 percent (or $30,000).

Now, let's look at the fourth item—ease of operation. It is true that S-corporations have to deal with more red tape and paperwork and abide by more rules (such as holding annual meetings) than do limited-liability companies. Plus they are more complex to set up. But this does not mean that setting up and operating a limited-liability company is a breeze and should be taken lightly. One essential task that should be carefully attended to is the preparation of an operating agreement. This document, which is completed when the company is formed (and can be revised later), is essential to the success of the business. It describes the rights and responsibilities of the LLC members and spells out how profits or losses will be allocated.

We have touted the benefits of limited liability protection for an LLC (as well as for regular corporations and S-corporations). We now need to point out some circumstances under which an LLC member (or shareholder in a corporation) might be held personally liable for the debts of his or her company. A business owner can be held personally liable if he or she:

- Personally guarantees a business debt or bank loan that the company fails to pay
- Fails to pay employment taxes to the government that were withheld from workers' wages
- Engages in fraudulent or illegal behavior that harms the company or someone else
- Does not treat the company as a separate legal entity, for example, uses company assets for personal uses

As personal loan guarantees are the most common circumstance under which an LLC member is held personally liable for the debts of his or her company, let's explore this topic some more by asking (and answering) two questions:

1. **What is a loan guarantee?** It is a legal agreement made between an individual and a bank that says, "If my company does not repay this loan, I will." It is the same thing as co-signing a loan.
2. **Why would an LLC member give a bank a personal guarantee?** Because it is often the only way a business can get a loan. Bankers understand the concept of limited liability. They know that if the company goes out of business (and the loan is not guaranteed), the bank is stuck with an unpaid loan because the LLC members are not personally liability for the debts of the company. Consequently, banks are reluctant to give loans to companies (particularly those just starting up) unless the loans are guaranteed by an owner.

A final note about hybrid forms of organization. In this section, we have looked at two organization forms that offer business owners limited liability and tax benefits. There are others not covered here such as Professional Limited-Liability Companies (PLLCs), which are set up by doctors, lawyers, accountants, and so on who provide professional services. And it is evident that the variations of organization forms available to businesses will continue to expand in the future.

5.4 Cooperatives

cooperative

A business owned and controlled by those who use its services.

A **cooperative** (also known as a co-op) is a business owned and controlled by those who use its services. Individuals and firms who belong to the cooperative join together to market products, purchase supplies, and provide services for its members. If run correctly, cooperatives increase profits for its producer-members and lower costs for its consumer-members. Cooperatives are common in the agricultural community. For example, some 750 cranberry and grapefruit member growers market their cranberry sauce, fruit juices, and dried cranberries through the Ocean Spray Cooperative.[7] More than three hundred thousand farmers obtain products they need for production—feed, seed, fertilizer, farm supplies, fuel—through the Southern States Cooperative.[8] Co-ops also exist outside agriculture. For example, REI (Recreational Equipment Incorporated), which sells quality outdoor gear, is the largest consumer cooperative in the United States with more than three million active members. The company shares its financial success each year with its members, who get a refund each year based on their eligible purchases.[9]

5.5 Not-for-Profit Corporations

A **not-for-profit corporation** (sometimes called a nonprofit) is an organization formed to serve some public purpose rather than for financial gain. As long as the organization's activity is for charitable, religious, educational, scientific, or literary purposes, it should be exempt from paying income taxes. Additionally, individuals and other organizations that contribute to the not-for-profit corporation can take a tax deduction for those contributions. The types of groups that normally apply for nonprofit status vary widely and include churches, synagogues, mosques, and other places of worship; museums; schools; and conservation groups.

There are more than 1.5 million not-for-profit organizations in the United States.[10] Some are extremely well funded, such as the Bill and Melinda Gates Foundation, which has an endowment of approximately $40 billion and has given away more than $286 billion since its inception.[11] Others are nationally recognized, such as United Way, Goodwill Industries, Habitat for Humanity, and the Red Cross. Yet the vast majority is neither rich nor famous but nevertheless makes significant contributions to society.

> **not-for-profit corporation**
>
> An organization formed to serve some public purpose rather than for financial gain.

Comparing Forms of Ownership

Take a few minutes to complete an exercise that reinforces what you've learned about the advantages and disadvantages of different forms of ownership.

KEY TAKEAWAYS

- The **S-corporation** gives small business owners limited liability protection, but taxes company profits only once, when they are paid out as dividends. It can't have more than one hundred stockholders.
- A **limited-liability company** (LLC) is similar to an S-corporation: its members are not personally liable for company debts and its earnings are taxed only once, when they're paid out as dividends. But it has fewer rules and restrictions than does an S-corporation. For example, an LLC can have any number of members.
- A **cooperative** is a business owned and controlled by those who use its services. Individuals and firms who belong to the cooperative join together to market products, purchase supplies, and provide services for its members.
- A **not-for-profit corporation** is an organization formed to serve some public purpose rather than for financial gain. It enjoys favorable tax treatment.

Before going to the next section of this chapter, take a few minutes to test your knowledge of the material covered in this section. Quizzes can be found under the "Resources" tab, "Study Aids: Quizzes."

EXERCISE

Create a table comparing a regular corporation, an S-corporation, and a limited-liability company on these dimensions: limited-liability protection, double taxation, restrictions on number of stockholders or members, rules, and restrictions. If you and several of your friends owned an ice skating rink, which form of ownership would you select? Why? Which form of ownership would you select for Google?

6. MERGERS AND ACQUISITIONS

LEARNING OBJECTIVES

1. Define "mergers" and "acquisitions."
2. Explain why companies are motivated to merge or acquire other companies.
3. Discuss the reasons companies merge or acquire other companies.
4. Explain what is involved in a hostile takeover.

The headline read, "Wanted: More than 2,000 in Google Hiring Spree."[12] The largest Web search engine in the world was disclosing its plans to grow internally and increase its workforce by more than 2,000 people, with half of the hires coming from the United States and the other half coming from other countries. The added employees will help the company expand into new markets and battle for global talent in the competitive Internet information providers industry. When properly executed, internal growth benefits the firm.

An alternative approach to growth is to merge with or acquire another company. The rationale behind growth through merger or acquisition is that 1 + 1 = 3: the combined company is more valuable than the sum of the two separate companies. This rationale is attractive to companies facing competitive pressures. To grab a bigger share of the market and improve profitability, companies will want to become more cost efficient by combining with other companies.

6.1 Mergers and Acquisitions

merger

The combination of two companies to form a new company.

acquisition

The purchase of one company by another with no new company being formed.

Though they are often used as if they're synonymous, the terms *merger* and *acquisition* mean slightly different things. A **merger** occurs when two companies combine to form a new company. An **acquisition** is the purchase of one company by another with no new company being formed. An example of a *merger* is the merging in 2010 of United Airlines and Continental Airlines. The combined company, the largest carrier in the world, flies under the name United Airlines, but its planes display the Continental Airlines logo. The merger will combine the scale of United Airlines with the management culture of Continental. Another example of a fairly recent *acquisition* is the purchase of Reebok by Adidas for $3.8 billion.[13] The deal was expected to give Adidas a stronger presence in North America and help the company compete with rival Nike. Though Adidas still sells shoes under the Reebok brand, Reebok as a company no longer exists.

6.2 Motives behind Mergers and Acquisitions

Companies are motivated to merge or acquire other companies for a number of reasons, including the following.

Gain Complementary Products

FIGURE 4.6

Do you think by acquiring Reebok, Adidas has had an impact on Nike's command of the running shoe market?

© 2010 Jupiterimages Corporation

Acquiring complementary products was the motivation behind Adidas's acquisition of Reebok. As Adidas CEO Herbert Hainer stated in a conference call, "This is a once-in-a-lifetime opportunity. This is a perfect fit for both companies, because the companies are so complementary....Adidas is grounded in sports performance with such products as a motorized running shoe and endorsement deals with such superstars as British soccer player David Beckham. Meanwhile, Reebok plays heavily to the melding of sports and entertainment with endorsement deals and products by Nelly, Jay-Z, and 50 Cent. The combination could be deadly to Nike."[14]

Attain New Markets or Distribution Channels

Gaining new markets was a significant factor in the 2005 merger of US Airways and America West. US Airways is a major player on the East Coast, the Caribbean, and Europe, while America West is strong in the West. The expectations were that combining the two carriers would create an airline that could reach more markets than either carrier could on its own.[15]

Realize More Efficient Economies of Scale

The purchase of Pharmacia Corporation (a Swedish pharmaceutical company) by Pfizer (a research-based pharmaceutical company based in the United States) in 2003 created the world's largest drug maker and the leading pharmaceutical company, by revenue, in every major market around the globe. The acquisition created an industry giant with more than $48 billion in revenue and a research-and-development budget of more than $7 billion.[16] Each day, almost forty million people around the glove are treated with Pfizer medicines.[17] Its subsequent $68 billion purchase of rival drug maker Wyeth further increased its presence in the pharmaceutical market.[18]

6.3 Hostile Takeover

What happens, though, if one company wants to acquire another company, but that company doesn't want to be acquired? You can end up with a very unfriendly situation. The outcome could be a *hostile takeover*—an act of assuming control that's resisted by the targeted company's management and its board of directors. Ben Cohen and Jerry Greenfield found themselves in one of these unfriendly situations: Unilever—a very large Dutch/British company that owns three ice cream brands—wanted to buy Ben & Jerry's, against the founders' wishes. To make matters worse, most of the Ben & Jerry's stockholders sided with Unilever. They had little confidence in the ability of Ben Cohen and Jerry Greenfield to continue managing the company and were frustrated with the firm's social-mission focus. The stockholders liked Unilever's offer to buy their Ben & Jerry's stock at almost twice its current market price and wanted to take their profits and run. In the end, Unilever won; Ben & Jerry's was acquired by Unilever in a hostile takeover. Despite fears that the company's social mission would end, this didn't happen. Though neither Ben Cohen nor Jerry Greenfield are involved in the current management of the company, they have returned to their social activism roots and are heavily involved in numerous social initiatives sponsored by the company.

KEY TAKEAWAYS

- A **merger** occurs when two companies combine to form a new company.
- An **acquisition** is the purchase of one company by another with no new company being formed.
- Companies merge or acquire other companies to gain complementary products, attain new markets or distribution channels, and realize more-efficient economies of scale.
- A hostile takeover is an act of assuming control that is resisted by the targeted company's management and its board of directors.

Before going to the next chapter, take a few minutes to test your knowledge of the material covered in this section. Quizzes can be found under the "Resources" tab, "Study Aids: Quizzes."

EXERCISE

Go online and research the merger of XM and Sirius. Why did the two satellite radio stations merge? Should this merger have been approved by the Federal Communications Commission? Whom does the merger help? Whom does it hurt? If you were the decision maker, would you approve the merger? Why, or why not?

---

7. CASES AND PROBLEMS

LEARNING ON THE WEB

Do you have an idea for a charitable organization you'd like to start? Think of some cause that's important to you. Then go online and review this article by Joanne Fritz, "How to Incorporate as a Nonprofit: A Check List" located at http://nonprofit.about.com/od/nonprofitbasics/ht/startingsteps.htm. Draft a mission statement for your not-for-profit organization, and indicate the types of people you'd ask to serve on your board of directors. Then list the steps you'd take to set up your not-for-profit organization.

CAREER OPPORTUNITIES

Where Do You Find Happiness?

Have you given much thought to whether you'd be happier working for a small company or for a big one? Here's your chance to compare and contrast the opportunities that small companies and big companies offer. First, read the article "Company Research—Investigate Small Companies" (http://jobsearch.about.com/cs/ employerresearch/a/compresearch.htm). Then read the article "Benefits of Working in a Small Company vs. a Corporation" (http://www.streetdirectory.com/travel_guide/190820/careers_and_job_hunting/benefits_of _working_in_a_small_company_vs_a_corporation.html).[19] Identify five advantages of working for a small company and five advantages of working for a big one. Indicate your choice of employer (small or big company), and explain why you selected this option.

ETHICS ANGLE

Bermuda Is Beautiful, but Should You Incorporate There?

A company can incorporate in any state it chooses. Most small businesses incorporate in the state in which they do business, while larger companies typically hunt around for the state or country that gives them the most favorable treatment (lower taxes, fewer restrictions). A growing number of U.S. companies are incorporating in Bermuda to lower their corporate income taxes while still enjoying the benefits of doing business in the United States. Does this seem right to you? Read these two articles and answer the questions that follow:

- "U.S. Corporations Are Using Bermuda to Slash Tax Bills," by David Cay Johnston, New York Times on the Web, February 18, 2002, http://query.nytimes.com/gst/ fullpage.html?res=9901EEDB1E3FF93BA25751C0A9649C8B63
- "The Hidden Perils of Offshore Tax Havens," by Diane Brady, *BusinessWeek*, August 8, 2002, http://www.businessweek.com/bwdaily/dnflash/aug2002/nf2002088_9533.htm

Questions:

- What advantages do U.S. companies gain by incorporating in Bermuda?
- What disadvantages do U.S. companies incur by incorporating in Bermuda?
- Do you find the practice of incorporating in Bermuda unethical? Why, or why not?

TEAM-BUILDING SKILLS

Legally Speaking

Here's the scenario: You and your team serve as consultants to business owners who need help in deciding which legal form of ownership is best for them. You're currently working with three clients. For each client, you'll evaluate possible legal forms of organization, debate the alternatives, and make a recommendation. Then, you'll write a report to your client, presenting your recommendation and explaining why you arrived at your conclusion.

In addition to learning the basic facts about each company, you've gathered additional information by asking each client the following questions:

- How much control do you want?
- Do you want to share profits with others?
- How much liability exposure are you willing to accept?
- What are your financing needs?
- What are you willing to do to set up and operate your business?
- Should it be possible for the business to continue without you?

The following is the information that you've collected about each client, along with ownership options you should consider.

Client 1: Rainforest Adventures

Rainforest Adventures offers one-day and multiday tours of several locations in Australia. It works both with tourists and with study groups, and its clientele varies from people who want a relaxing experience away from hectic urban life to those who are keenly interested in the exotic environment. The business is dedicated to the preservation of Australia's tropical and wetland preserves. Its guides have many years of experience leading tourists through the rainforests, particularly at night when they come alive.

Rainforest Adventures was started three years ago by Courtney Kennedy, who has fifteen years of experience in the ecotourism industry. She runs the business as a sole proprietorship but is considering a partnership. (She doesn't want the cost or hassle of doing business as a corporation.) In questioning her, you found out the following: Kennedy is dedicated to preserving the Australian wetlands and sees her business as a way of encouraging people to support conservation efforts. However, her guides have displayed an "it's just-a-job" attitude, have become increasingly undependable, and are unwilling to share her commitment. Still, Kennedy has several trusted friends who not only have years of experience as guides, but who also share her enthusiasm for environmental preservation. She's optimistic that they'd be willing to join her in the business. She dreams of expanding her business to offer classes on the ecology of the rainforest but doesn't have enough cash, and she's afraid that a loan application will be turned down by the bank.

Options

Because Kennedy doesn't want to incorporate, she's left with two options: to continue doing business as a sole proprietorship or to find one or more individuals to join her in a partnership. After evaluating these two alternatives, you should recommend the one that you consider most appropriate. You should discuss the pros and cons of both options and explain how each applies to Kennedy's situation. If you recommend forming a partnership, you need to distinguish between a general partnership and a limited partnership, as well as explain what a partnership agreement is, what it covers, and why it's important.

Client 2: Scuffy the Tugboat

Scuffy the Tugboat is a family-run business that makes tugboats. It was formed as a partnership in 1996 by the three McLaughlin brothers—Mick (a naval architect), Jack (an accountant), and Bob (a marine engineer). Their first tugboat is still towing ships in Boston harbor, and over the years, success has allowed them to grow the company by plowing money back into it. Last year's sales were more than $7 million. Now, however, they want to double production by expanding their factory by five thousand square feet. They estimate a cost of about $1 million, yet a bigger facility would enable them to avoid late-delivery penalties that can run up to $2,000 a day. They're not sure, however, about the best way to raise the needed funds. None of the brothers has $1 million on hand, and because lenders are often hesitant to loan money to shipbuilders, even those with good performance records, local banks haven't been encouraging.

Unlike many partners, the three brothers get along quite well. They're concerned, though, about the risks of taking on personal debts for the business. In particular, they don't like being liable not only for their own actions, but also for the actions of all the partners.

Options

You should recommend that Scuffy the Tugboat either remain a partnership or become a privately-held corporation. State the pros and cons of both forms of organization, and explain how they apply to the brothers' situation.

Client 3: Dinner Rendezvous

For three years, owner Peggy Deardon has been operating Dinner Rendezvous, which gives individuals an opportunity to meet others and expand their social networks, in Austin, Texas. Interested clients go to the company's Web site and fill out applications and privacy statements. There's an annual membership fee of $125 and a $15 charge for each dinner attended (plus the cost of dinner and drinks). Deardon sets up all dinners and is onsite at the restaurant to introduce guests and serve complimentary champagne. While the company has a steady clientele, it's not a big moneymaker. If Deardon didn't have a regular full-time job, she couldn't keep the business running. She stays with it because she enjoys it and believes that she provides a good service for Austin residents. Because it's run out of her home, and because her biggest cost is the champagne, it's a low-risk business with no debts. With a full-time job, she also appreciates the fact that it requires only a few hours of her time each week.

Options

Since your client wants advice on whether to incorporate, you should evaluate two options—remaining a sole proprietorship or forming a corporation. In addition to your recommendation, you should state the pros and cons of both forms of organization and explain how they apply to Deardon's situation.

THE GLOBAL VIEW

America for Sale

Our U.S. companies continue to expand by merging with or acquiring other companies. This is acceptable business practice. But what happens when our U.S. companies and other assets are bought up by firms and individuals outside the United States? Is this acceptable business practice or something we should be concerned about? Learn how this is happening by reading this article by Geoff Colvin:

- "America for Sale," *Fortune*, CNNMoney.com, February 6, 2008, http://money.cnn.com/2008/01/30/news/economy/Colvin_recession.fortune/index.htm?postversion=2008020609

Questions:

- Why are foreigners buying U.S. assets?
- Is the current trend in foreign investments in U.S. assets positive or negative for the United States? Whom does it help? Whom does it hurt? Explain.
- What, if anything, can the United States do to stop this trend?
- If you were able, would you limit foreign investment in U.S. assets? Why, or why not?

ENDNOTES

1. "Number of Tax Returns, Receipts, and Net Income by Type of Business," *The 2012 Statistical Abstract: The National Data Book*, January 30, 2011, http://www.census.gov/compendia/statab/cats/business_enterprise/sole_proprietorships_partnerships_corporations.html (accessed March 30, 2014).

2. "Number of Tax Returns, Receipts, and Net Income by Type of Business," *The 2012 Statistical Abstract: The National Data Book*, January 30, 2011, http://www.census.gov/compendia/statab/cats/business_enterprise/sole_proprietorships_partnerships_corporations.html (accessed March 30, 2014).

3. "Number of Tax Returns, Receipts, and Net Income by Type of Business," *The 2012 Statistical Abstract: The National Data Book*, January 30, 2011, http://www.census.gov/compendia/statab/cats/business_enterprise/sole_proprietorships_partnerships_corporations.html (accessed March 30, 2014).

4. "How Much Does It Cost to Incorporate?" *AllBusiness.com*, http://www.allbusiness.com/legal/contracts-agreements-incorporation/2531-1.html (accessed March 30, 2014).

5. Fred Chico Lager, *Ben & Jerry's: The Inside Scoop* (New York: Crown Publishers, 1994), 91.

6. Fred Chico Lager, *Ben & Jerry's: The Inside Scoop* (New York: Crown Publishers, 1994), 103.

7. Ocean Spray, "Our History," http://www.oceanspray.com/Who-We-Are/Heritage/Our-History.aspx (accessed March 30, 2014).

8. Southern States Cooperative, "Our Heritage," http://www.southernstates.com/sscinfo/Our-Heritage/index.aspx (accessed March 30, 2014).

9. Recreational Equipment, Inc., "2012 REI Stewardship Report," http://www.rei.com/stewardship/report.html (accessed March 30, 2014).

10. National Center for Charitable Statistics, "Quick Facts about Nonprofits," http://nccs.urban.org/statistics/quickfacts.cfm (accessed March 30, 2014).

11. Bill and Melinda Gates Foundation, "Foundation Fact Sheet," June 30, 2011, http://www.gatesfoundation.org/Who-We-Are/General-Information/Foundation-Factsheet (accessed March 30, 2014).

12. Alexei Oreskovic, "Wanted: More than 2,000 in Google Hiring Spree," *Reuters*, November 19, 2010, http://www.reuters.com/article/2010/11/19/us-google-idUSTRE6AI05820101119 (accessed March 30, 2014); "Help Wanted: Google Hiring in 2011," *The Official Google Blog*, January 25, 2011, http://googleblog.blogspot.com/2011/01/help-wanted-google-hiring-in-2011.html (accessed March 30, 2014).

13. Theresa Howard, "Adidas, Reebok lace up for run at Nike," *USA Today*, August 3, 2005, http://usatoday30.usatoday.com/money/industries/manufacturing/2005-08-02-adidas-usat_x.htm (accessed March 30, 2014).

14. Theresa Howard, "Adidas, Reebok lace up for run at Nike," *USA Today*, August 3, 2005, http://usatoday30.usatoday.com/money/industries/manufacturing/2005-08-02-adidas-usat_x.htm (accessed March 30, 2014).

15. "America West, US Air in Merger Deal," *CNNMoney.com*, May 20, 2005, http://money.cnn.com/2005/05/19/news/midcaps/airlines/index.htm (accessed March 30, 2014).

16. Robert Frank and Scott Hensley, "Pfizer to Buy Pharmacia For $60 Billion in Stock," *Wall Street Journal Online*, WJS.com, July 15, 2002, http://online.wsj.com/news/articles/SB1026684057282753560 (accessed March 30, 2014).

17. Pfizer Inc., "2003: Pfizer and Pharmacia Merger," http://www.pfizer.com/about/history/pfizer_pharmacia (accessed March 30, 2014).

18. "Pfizer Agrees to Pay $68 Billion for Rival Drug Maker Wyeth," *New York Times*, January 25, 2009, http://www.nytimes.com/2009/01/26/business/26drug.html?pagewanted=2 (accessed March 30, 2014).

19. Alison Doyle, "Company Research: Investigate Small Companies," *About.com: Job Searching*, http://jobsearch.about.com/cs/employerresearch/a/compresearch.htm (accessed March 30, 2014); Tony Jacowsk, "Benefits of Working in a Small Company vs. a Corporation," *Business Resources*, http://www.streetdirectory.com/travel_guide/190820/careers_and_job_hunting/benefits_of_working_in_a_small_company_vs_a_corporation.html (accessed March 30, 2014).

CHAPTER 5
The Challenges of Starting a Business

BUILD A BETTER BABY AND THEY WILL COME

One balmy San Diego evening in 1993, Mary and Rick Jurmain were watching a TV program about teenage pregnancy.[1] To simulate the challenge of caring for an infant, teens on the program were assigned to tend baby-size sacks of flour. Rick, a father of two young children, remarked that trundling around a sack of flour wasn't exactly a true-to-life experience. In particular, he argued, sacks of flour simulated only abnormally happy babies—babies who didn't cry, especially in the middle of the night. Half-seriously, Mary suggested that her husband—a between-jobs aerospace engineer—build a better baby, and within a couple of weeks, a prototype was born. Rick's brainchild was a bouncing 6.5-pound bundle of vinyl-covered joy with an internal computer to simulate infant crying at realistic, random intervals. He also designed a drug-affected model to simulate tremors from withdrawal, and each model monitored itself for neglect or ill treatment.

The Jurmains patented Baby Think It Over (aka BTIO) and started production in 1994 as Baby Think It Over Inc. Their first "factory" was their garage, and the "office" was the kitchen table—"a little business in a house," as Mary put it. With a boost from articles in *USA Today*, *Newsweek*, *Forbes*, and *People*—plus a "Product of the Year" nod from *Fortune*—news of the Jurmains' "infant simulator" eventually spread to the new company's targeted education market, and by 1998, some forty thousand simulators had been babysat by more than a million teenagers in nine countries. By that time, the company had moved to Wisconsin, where it had been rechristened BTIO Educational Products Inc. to reflect an expanded product line that now includes not only dolls and equipment, like the Shaken Baby Syndrome Simulator, but also simulator-based programs like START Addiction Education and Realityworks Pregnancy Profile. BTIO was retired and replaced by the new and improved RealCare Baby and, ultimately, by RealCare Baby II–*plus*, which requires the participant to determine what the "baby" needs when it cries and downloads data to record mishaps (such as missed-care events) and misconduct (like baby shaking). If RealCare Baby II–*plus* shows signs of fatigue, you can plug him or her into the nearest wall outlet. In 2003, the name of the Jurmains' company was changed once again, this time to Realityworks Inc. The change, explains the company Web site, reflects its decision "to focus on what the company does best—providing realistic learning experiences."

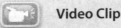

Video Clip

Click here to download The Realityworks Story.

View the video online at: http://www.youtube.com/embed/nLuR9FIIuRk

1. WHAT IS AN ENTREPRENEUR?

LEARNING OBJECTIVES

1. Define "entrepreneur."
2. Describe the three characteristics of entrepreneurial activity.
3. Identify questions you should ask yourself to assess whether you're one of the "right people" to start a business.
4. Identify five potential advantages to starting your own business.
5. Describe a "lifestyle business."

In developing BTIO and Realityworks Inc., the Jurmains were doing what entrepreneurs do (and doing it very well). In fact, Mary was nominated three times for the Ernst & Young Entrepreneur of the Year Award and named 2001 Wisconsin Entrepreneurial Woman of the Year by the National Association of Women Business Owners. So what, exactly, is an *entrepreneur*? What does an entrepreneur do? According to one definition, an entrepreneur is an "individual who starts a new business," and that's true as far as it goes. Another definition identifies an entrepreneur as someone who uses "resources to implement innovative ideas for new, thoughtfully planned ventures,"[2] which is also true as far as it goes. But an important component of a satisfactory definition is still missing. To appreciate fully what it is, let's go back to the story of the Jurmains, for whom entrepreneurship seems to have worked out quite well. We hasten to point out that, in 1993, the Jurmains were both unemployed—Rick had been laid off by General Dynamics Corp., and Mary by the San Diego Gas and Electric Company. While they were watching the show about teenagers and flour sacks, they were living off a loan from her father and the returns from a timely investment in coffee futures. Rick recalls that the idea for a method of creating BTIO came to him while "I was awake in bed, worrying about being unemployed." He was struggling to find a way to feed his family. He had to make the first forty simulators himself, and at the end of the first summer, BTIO had received about four hundred orders—a promising start, perhaps, but, at $250 per baby (less expenses), not exactly a windfall. "We were always about one month away from bankruptcy," recalls Mary.

At the same time, it's not as if the Jurmains started up BTIO simply because they had no "conventional" options for improving their financial prospects. Rick, as we've seen, was an aerospace engineer, and his résumé includes work on space-shuttle missions at NASA. Mary, who has not only a head for business but also a degree in industrial engineering, has worked at the Johnson Space Center. Therefore, the idea of replacing a sack of flour with a computer-controlled simulator wasn't necessarily rocket science for the couple. But taking advantage of that idea—choosing to start a new business and to commit themselves to running it—was a risk. *Risk taking* is the missing component that we're looking for in a definition of *entrepreneurship*, and so we'll define an **entrepreneur** as someone who identifies a business opportunity and assumes *the risk of creating and running a business* to take advantage of it.

entrepreneur

Individual who identifies a business opportunity and assumes the risk of creating and running a business to take advantage of it.

1.1   The Nature of Entrepreneurship

If we look a little more closely at the definition of entrepreneurship, we can identify three characteristics of entrepreneurial activity:[3]

1. *Innovation.* Entrepreneurship generally means offering a new product, applying a new technique or technology, opening a new market, or developing a new form of organization for the purpose of producing or enhancing a product.
2. *Running a business.* A *business*, as we saw in Chapter 1, combines resources to produce goods or services. Entrepreneurship means setting up a business to make a profit.
3. *Risk taking.* The term *risk* means that the outcome of the entrepreneurial venture can't be known. Entrepreneurs, therefore, are always working under a certain degree of *uncertainty*, and they can't know the outcomes of many of the decisions that they have to make. Consequently, many of the steps they take are motivated mainly by their confidence in the innovation and in their understanding of the business environment in which they're operating.

It isn't hard to recognize all three of these characteristics in the entrepreneurial experience of the Jurmains. They certainly had an *innovative* idea. But was it a *good* business idea? In a practical sense, a "good" business idea has to become something more than just an idea. If, like the Jurmains, you're interested in generating income from your idea, you'll probably need to turn it into a *product*—something that you can market because it satisfies a need. If—again, like the Jurmains—you want to develop a product, you'll need some kind of organization to coordinate the resources necessary to make it a reality (in other words, a *business*). Risk enters the equation when, like the Jurmains, you make the decision to start up a business and when you commit yourself to managing it.

1.2   A Few Things to Know about Going into Business for Yourself

So what about you? Do you ever wonder what it would be like to start your own business? Maybe you want to try your hand at entrepreneurship. You could be the next Larry Page or Sergey Brin, cofounders of Google. Or the next David Marcks, a golf course manager who came up with the idea of Geese Police—training dogs to chase geese from golf courses, corporate parks, and municipal playgrounds.[4] Or even the next Pierre Omidyar, the French-born software developer who built an online venue for person-to-person auctions, known as eBay.[5]

You might even turn into a "serial entrepreneur" like Marcia Kilgore.[6] After high school, she moved from Canada to New York City to attend Columbia University. But when her financial aid was delayed, she abandoned her plans to attend college and took a job as a personal trainer (a natural occupation for a former bodybuilder and middleweight title holder). But things got boring in the summer when her wealthy clients left the city for the Hamptons. To keep busy, she took a skin care course at a Manhattan cosmetology institute. As a teenager, she was self-conscious about her bad complexion and wanted to know how to treat it herself. She learned how to give facials and work with natural remedies. Her complexion improved, and she started giving facials to her fitness clients who were thrilled with the results. As demand for her services exploded, she started her first business—Bliss Spa—and picked up celebrity clients, including Madonna, Oprah Winfrey, and Jennifer Lopez. The business went international, and she sold it for more than $30 million.[7]

FIGURE 5.1

Mark Zuckerberg founded Facebook while a student at Harvard and, by age 27, has built up a personal wealth of $27 billion.

Source: Robert Scoble, http://commons.wikimedia.org/wiki/File:Facebook_Press_Conference_4.jpg

But the story doesn't end here; she didn't just sit back and enjoy her good fortune. Instead, she launched two more companies: Soap and Glory, a supplier of affordable beauty products sold at Target, and FitFlops, which sells sandals that tone and tighten your leg muscles as you walk. And by the way, remember how Oprah loved Kilgore's skin care products? She also loves Kilgore's sandals and plugged them on her talk show. You can't get a better endorsement than that. Kilgore never did finish college, but when asked if she would follow the same path again, she said, "If I had to decide what to do all over again, I would make the same choices…I found by accident what I'm good at, and I'm glad I did."

For the sake of argument, let's say that you would like to know a little more about going into business for yourself—in which case, you'll want some answers to questions like the following:

- Should I start a business?
- What are the advantages and disadvantages of starting a business?
- How do I come up with a business idea?
- Should I build a business from scratch, buy an existing business, or invest in a franchise?
- How do I go about planning a business?

- What steps are involved in developing a business plan?
- Where would I find help in getting my business started and operating it through the start-up phase?
- How can I increase the likelihood that I'll succeed?

In this chapter, we'll provide some answers to questions like these.

Why Start Your Own Business?

Small Business Administration (SBA)

Government agency that helps prospective owners set up small businesses, obtain financing, and manage ongoing operations.

Let's say that you are interested in the idea of going into business for yourself. Not everyone, of course, has a desire to take the risks and put in the work involved in starting up a business. What sort of characteristics distinguishes those who do from those who don't want to start a business? Or, more to the point, why do some people actually follow through on the desire to start up their own businesses? According to the **Small Business Administration (SBA)**, a government agency that provides assistance to small businesses, the most common reasons for starting a business are the following:[8]

- To be your own boss
- To accommodate a desired lifestyle
- To achieve financial independence
- To enjoy creative freedom
- To use your skills and knowledge

The Small Business Administration points out, though, that these are likely to be advantages only "for the right person." And how do you know if you're one of the "right people"? The SBA suggests that you assess your strengths and weaknesses by asking yourself a few relevant questions:[9]

- *Am I a self-starter*? You'll need to develop and follow through on your ideas. You'll need to be able to organize your time.
- *How well do I get along with different personalities*? You'll need to develop working relationships with a variety of people, including unreliable vendors and sometimes cranky customers.
- *How good am I at making decisions*? You'll be making decisions constantly—often under pressure.
- *Do I have the physical and emotional stamina*? Can you handle six or seven workdays of as long as twelve hours every week?
- *How well do I plan and organize*? If you can't stay organized, you'll get swamped by the details. In fact, poor planning is the culprit in most business failures.
- *Is my drive strong enough*? You'll need to be highly motivated to withstand bad periods in your business, and simply being responsible for your business's success can cause you to burn out.
- *How will my business affect my family*? Family members need to know what to expect before you begin a business venture, such as financial difficulties and a more modest standard of living.

Later in this chapter, we'll take up the question of why businesses fail, but since we're still talking about the pros and cons of starting a business in the first place, we should consider one more issue: in addition to the number of businesses that start and then fail, a huge number of business ideas never even make it to the grand opening. One business analyst cites four reservations (or *fears*) that prevent people from starting businesses:[10]

- *Money*. Granted, without the cash, you can't get very far. *What to do*: Conduct some research to find out where funding is available.
- *Security*. A lot of people don't want to sacrifice the steady income that comes with the nine-to-five job. *What to do*: Don't give up your day job. At least at first, think about hiring someone to run your business while you're gainfully employed elsewhere.
- *Competition*. A lot of people don't know how to distinguish their business ideas from similar ideas. *What to do*: Figure out how to do something cheaper, faster, or better.
- *Lack of ideas*. Some people simply don't know what sort of business they want to get into. *What to do*: Find out what trends are successful. Turn a hobby into a business. Think about a franchise.

If you're still interested in going into business for yourself, feel free to regard these potential drawbacks as mere obstacles to be overcome by a combination of planning and creative thinking.

Distinguishing Entrepreneurs from Small Business Owners

Though most entrepreneurial ventures begin as small businesses, not all small business owners are entrepreneurs. Entrepreneurs are innovators who start companies to create new or improved products. They strive to meet a need that's not being met, and their goal is to grow the business and eventually expand into other markets.

In contrast, many people either start or buy small businesses for the sole purpose of providing an income for themselves and their families. They do not intend to be particularly innovative, nor do they plan to expand significantly. This desire to operate is what's sometimes called a "lifestyle business."[11] The neighborhood pizza parlor or beauty shop, the self-employed consultant who works out of the home, and even a local printing company—all of these are typical lifestyle businesses. In Section 2, we discuss the positive influences that both lifestyle and entrepreneurial businesses have on the U.S. economy.

Entrepreneurs: Fact and Fiction

Take a few minutes to reinforce what you've learned about entrepreneurs. Click here to complete the exercise.

FIGURE 5.2

These bakers are not entrepreneurs. They run their small bakery for the sole purpose of providing an income for themselves and their families (a salary-substitute firm) or to earn a living while pursuing their hobby of baking (a lifestyle firm).

© 2010 Jupiterimages Corporation

KEY TAKEAWAYS

- An **entrepreneur** is someone who identifies a business opportunity and assumes the risk of creating and running a business to take advantage of it.
- There are three characteristics of entrepreneurial activity:
    1. *Innovating*. An entrepreneur offers a new product, applies a new technique or technology, opens a new market, or develops a new form of organization for the purpose of producing or enhancing a product.
    2. *Running a business*. Entrepreneurship means setting up a business to make a profit from an innovative product or process.
    3. *Risk taking*. Risk means that an outcome is unknown. Entrepreneurs, therefore, are always working under a certain degree of uncertainty, and they can't know the outcomes of many of the decisions that they have to make.
- According to the **SBA**, a government agency that provides assistance to small businesses, there are five advantages to starting a business—"for the right person":
    1. Be your own boss.
    2. Accommodate a desired lifestyle.
    3. Achieve financial independence.
    4. Enjoy creative freedom.
    5. Use your skills and knowledge.
- To determine whether you're one of the "right people" to exploit the advantages of starting your own business, the SBA suggests that you assess your strengths and weaknesses by asking yourself the following questions:
    1. Am I a self-starter?
    2. How well do I get along with different personalities?
    3. How good am I at making decisions?
    4. Do I have the physical and emotional stamina?
    5. How well do I plan and organize?
    6. Is my drive strong enough?
    7. How will my business affect my family?
- Though most entrepreneurial ventures begin as small businesses, not all small business owners are entrepreneurs. Entrepreneurs are innovators who start companies to create new or improved products. In contrast, many people start businesses for the purpose of providing an income for themselves and their families. This type of businesses is sometimes called a "lifestyle business."

Before going to the next section of this chapter, take a few minutes to test your knowledge of the material covered in this section. Quizzes can be found under the "Resources" tab, "Study Aids: Quizzes."

EXERCISE

Do you have what it takes to be an entrepreneur? To find out, start by reviewing the following list of characteristics commonly attributed to entrepreneurs:

- They are creative people who sometimes accomplish extraordinary things because they're passionate about what they're doing.
- They are risk-taking optimists who commit themselves to working long hours to reach desired goals.
- They take pride in what they're doing and get satisfaction from doing something they enjoy.
- They have the flexibility to adjust to changing situations to achieve their goals.

We'll also add that entrepreneurs usually start small. They begin with limited resources and build their businesses through personal effort. At the end of the day, their success depends on their ability to manage and grow the organization that they created to implement their vision.

Now use the following three-point scale to indicate the extent to which each of these attributes characterizes you:

1. It doesn't sound like me.
2. It sounds like me to a certain extent.
3. It sounds a lot like me.

Based on your responses, do you think that you have the attributes of an entrepreneur? Do you think you could be a successful entrepreneur? Why, or why not?

---

2. THE IMPORTANCE OF SMALL BUSINESS TO THE U.S. ECONOMY

LEARNING OBJECTIVES

1. Define a "small business."
2. Explain the importance of small businesses to the U.S. economy.
3. Explain why small businesses tend to foster innovation more effectively than large ones.
4. Describe some of the ways in which small companies work with big ones.

2.1 What Is a "Small Business"?

small business

According to the SBA, a business that is independently owned and operated, is organized for profit, and is not dominant in its field.

To assess the value of small businesses to the U.S. economy, we first need to know what constitutes a small business. Let's start by looking at the criteria used by the Small Business Administration (SBA). According to the SBA's 2014 definition, a **small business** is one that is "independently owned and operated, is organized for profit, and is not dominant in its field." To meet the SBA's definition of a small business, the organization must also be of a certain size, which varies by industry. For example, a manufacturing company would be classified as a small business if it has a maximum range of 500–1,500 employees (depending on the type of product it produces). A service firm would be classified as a small business if its revenues do not exceed $2.5–$21.5 million (depending on the type of service provided).[12]

2.2 Why Are Small Businesses Important?

Small business constitutes a major force in the U.S. economy. There are more than twenty-eight million small businesses in this country, and they generate about 50 percent of our gross domestic product (GDP).[13] The millions of individuals who have started businesses in the United States have shaped the business world as we know it today. Some small business founders like Henry Ford and Thomas

Edison have even gained places in history. Others such as Bill Gates (Microsoft), Sam Walton (Wal-Mart), Steve Jobs (Apple), Michael Dell (Dell), Pierre Omidyar (eBay), Larry Page and Sergey Brin (Google), Jeff Bezos (Amazon.com), Howard Schultz (Starbucks), and Mark Zuckerberg (Facebook) have changed the way business is done today. Still millions of others have collectively contributed to our standard of living.

Aside from contributions to our general economic well-being, founders of small businesses also contribute to growth and vitality in specific areas of economic and socioeconomic development. In particular, small businesses do the following:

- Create jobs
- Spark innovation
- Provide opportunities for many people, including women and minorities, to achieve financial success and independence

In addition, they complement the economic activity of large organizations by providing them with components, services, and distribution of their products.

Let's take a closer look at each of these contributions.

Job Creation

The majority of U.S. workers first entered the business world working for small businesses. Today, half of all U.S. adults either are self-employed or work for small businesses.[14] Although the split between those working in small companies and those working in big companies is about even, small firms hire more frequently and fire more frequently than do big companies.[15] Why is this true? At any given point in time, lots of small companies are started and some expand. These small companies need workers and so hiring takes place. But the survival and expansion rates for small firms is poor, and so, again at any given point in time, many small businesses close or contract and workers lose their jobs. Fortunately, over time more jobs are added by small firms than are taken away, which results in a net increase in the number of workers. Table 5.1 reports the net increase in jobs generated by small firms for the fifteen-year period of 1996 to 2011 and breaks it down into job gains from openings and expansions and job losses from closings and contractions.

TABLE 5.1   Small Firm Job Gains and Losses, 1996–2011 (in Millions of Jobs)

	Job Gains From		Job Losses From	
Net Change	Openings	Expansions	Closings	Contractions
20.7	105.2	398.3	97.7	385.1

The size of the net increase in the number of workers for any given year depends on a number of factors, with the economy being at the top of the list. A strong economy encourages individuals to start small businesses and expand existing small companies, which adds to the workforce. A weak economy does just the opposite: discourages start-ups and expansions, which decreases the workforce through layoffs. Table 5.1 reports the job gains from start-ups and expansions and job losses from business closings and contractions.

Innovation

Given the financial resources available to large businesses, you'd expect them to introduce virtually all the new products that hit the market. According to the SBA, small companies develop more patents per employee than do larger companies. During a recent four-year period, large firms generated 1.7 patents per hundred employees, whereas small firms generated an impressive 26.5 patents per employee.[16] Over the years, the list of important innovations by small firms has included the airplane and air-conditioning, the defibrillator and DNA fingerprinting, oral contraceptives and overnight national delivery, the safety razor, strobe lights, and the zipper.[17]

Small business owners are also particularly adept at finding new ways of doing old things. In 1994, for example, a young computer-science graduate working on Wall Street came up with the novel idea of selling books over the Internet. During the first year of operations, sales at Jeff Bezos's new company—Amazon.com—reached half a million dollars. In twenty years, annual sales had topped $74 billion.[18] Not only did his innovative approach to online retailing make Bezos enormously rich, but it also established a viable model for the e-commerce industry.

Why are small businesses so innovative? For one thing, they tend to offer environments that appeal to individuals with the talent to invent new products or improve the way things are done. Fast decision making is encouraged, their research programs tend to be focused, and their compensation structures typically reward top performers. According to one SBA study, the supportive environments of small firms are roughly thirteen times more innovative per employee than the less innovation-friendly environments in which large firms traditionally operate.[19]

The success of small businesses in fostering creativity has not gone unnoticed by big businesses. In fact, many large companies have responded by downsizing to act more like small companies. Some large organizations now have separate work units whose purpose is to spark innovation. Individuals working in these units can focus their attention on creating new products that can then be developed by the company.

Opportunities for Women and Minorities

Small business is the portal through which many people enter the economic mainstream. Business ownership allows individuals, including women and minorities, to achieve financial success, as well as pride in their accomplishments. While the majority of small businesses are still owned by white males, the past two decades have seen a substantial increase in the number of businesses owned by women and minorities. Figure 5.3 gives you an idea of how many American businesses are owned by women and minorities, and indicates how much the numbers grew between 1982 and 2007.[20]

FIGURE 5.3 Businesses Owned by Women and Minorities

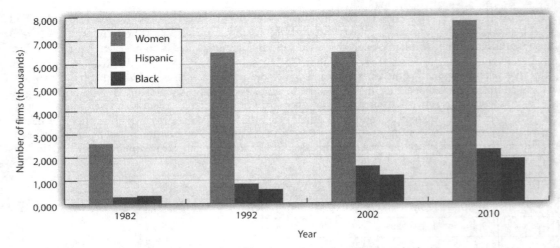

Source: U.S. Census Bureau, "Survey of Business Owners (SBO)," http://www.census.gov/econ/sbo/07menu.html

What Small Businesses Do for Big Businesses

Small firms complement large firms in a number of ways. They supply many of the components needed by big companies. For example, the U.S. automakers depend on more than 1,700 suppliers to provide them with the parts needed to make their cars. While many of the suppliers are large, there are hundreds of smaller companies that provide a substantial portion of the 8,000 to 12,000 parts that go into each vehicle.[21] Small firms also provide large ones with such services as accounting, legal, and insurance. Many small firms provide *outsourcing* services to large firms—that is, they hire themselves out to help with special projects or handle certain business functions. A large firm, for example, might hire a small one to handle its billing or collection services or to manage its health care benefits. A large company might contract with a small information technology firm to manage its Web site or oversee software upgrades.

Small companies provide another valuable service to large companies by acting as sales agents for their products. For example, automobile dealerships, which are generally small businesses, sell vehicles for the big car makers. Local sporting goods stores sell athletic shoes made by industry giants, such as Adidas and Nike. Your corner deli sells products made by large companies, such as Coca-Cola and Frito-Lay.

KEY TAKEAWAY

- According to the SBA, a **small business** is independently owned and operated, organized for profit, and not dominant in its field.

- The nearly twenty-eight million small businesses in the United States generate about 50 percent of our GDP. They also contribute to growth and vitality in several important areas of economic and socioeconomic development. In particular, small businesses do the following:

    1. Create jobs
    2. Spark innovation
    3. Provide opportunities for women and minorities to achieve financial success and independence

- Small businesses tend to foster environments that appeal to individuals with the talent to invent new products or improve the way things are done. They typically make faster decisions, their research programs often are focused, and their compensation structures frequently reward top performers.

- Small firms supply many of the components needed by big companies. They also provide large firms with such services as accounting, legal, and insurance, and many provide *outsourcing* services to large companies—that is, they hire themselves out to help with special projects or handle certain business functions. Small companies (such as automotive dealerships) often act as sales agents for the products of large businesses (for example, car makers).

Before going to the next section of this chapter, take a few minutes to test your knowledge of the material covered in this section. Quizzes can be found under the "Resources" tab, "Study Aids: Quizzes."

EXERCISE

How "small" is a small business? If a substantial portion of small businesses in the United States suddenly closed, what would be the impact on the U.S. economy? How would all these closings affect workers, consumers, and other businesses?

3. WHAT INDUSTRIES ARE SMALL BUSINESSES IN?

LEARNING OBJECTIVES

1. Describe the goods-producing and service-producing sectors of an economy.
2. Identify the industries in which small businesses are concentrated.

If you want to start a new business, you probably should avoid certain types of businesses. You'd have a hard time, for example, setting up a new company to make automobiles or aluminum, because you'd have to make tremendous investments in property, plant, and equipment, and raise an enormous amount of capital to pay your workforce.

Fortunately, plenty of opportunities are still available if you're willing to set your sights a little lower. Many types of businesses require reasonable initial investments, and not surprisingly, these are the ones that usually present attractive small business opportunities.

3.1 Industries by Sector

We'll have more to say about industries and how to analyze them in later chapters. Here, we'll simply define an *industry* as a group of companies that compete with one another to sell similar products, and we'll focus on the relationship between a small business and the industry in which it operates. First, we'll discuss the industries in which small businesses tend to be concentrated. To do this, we'll divide businesses into two broad types of industries, or sectors: the goods-producing sector and the service-producing sector.

FIGURE 5.4

A high percentage of small businesses are in the retail sector.

© 2010 Jupiterimages Corporation

- The **goods-producing sector** includes all businesses that produce tangible goods. Generally speaking, companies in this sector are involved in manufacturing, construction, and agriculture.

- The **service-producing sector** includes all businesses that provide services but don't make tangible goods. They may be involved in retail and wholesale trade, transportation, finance, insurance, real estate, arts, entertainment, recreation, accommodations, food service, education, and such professional activities as technical services, health care, advertising, accounting, and personal services.

About 20 percent of small businesses in the United States are concentrated in the goods-producing sector. The remaining 80 percent are in the service sector.[22] The high concentration of small businesses in the service-producing sector reflects the makeup of the overall U.S. economy. Over the past fifty years, the service-producing sector has been growing at an impressive rate. In 1960, for example, the goods-producing sector accounted for 38 percent of GDP, the service-producing sector for 62 percent. By 2010, the balance had shifted dramatically, with the goods-producing sector accounting for only 23 percent of GDP, while the service-producing sector had grown to 77 percent.[23]

Goods-Producing Sector

The largest areas of the goods-producing sector are construction and manufacturing. Construction businesses are often started by skilled workers, such as electricians, painters, plumbers, and home builders. They tend to be small and generally work on local projects. Though manufacturing is primarily the domain of large businesses, there are exceptions. BTIO/Realityworks, for example, is a manufacturing enterprise (components come from Ohio and China, and assembly is done in Wisconsin).

Another small manufacturer is Reveal Entertainment, which was founded in 1996 to make and distribute board games. Founder Jeffrey Berndt started with a single award-winning game—a three-dimensional finance and real estate game called "Tripoly"—and now boasts a product line of dozens of board games. There are strategy games, like "Squad Seven," which uses a CD soundtrack to guide players through a jungle in search of treasure; children's games, like "Portfolio Junior," which teaches kids the rudiments of personal finances; and party games, like "So Sue Me," in which players get to experience the fun side of suing their neighbors and taking their possessions.[24]

How about making something out of trash? Daniel Blake never followed his mother's advice at dinner when she told him to eat everything on his plate. When he served as a missionary in Puerto Rico, Aruba, Bonaire, and Curacao after his first year in college, he noticed that the families he stayed with didn't follow her advice either. But they didn't throw their uneaten food into the trash. Instead they put it on a compost pile and used the mulch to nourish their vegetable gardens and fruit trees. While eating at an all-you-can-eat breakfast buffet back home at Brigham Young University, Blake was amazed to see volumes of uneaten food in the trash. This triggered an idea: why not turn the trash into money. Two years later, he was running his company—EcoScraps—that collects 40 tons of food scraps a day from 75 grocers (including Costco) and turns it into high-quality potting soil that he sells online and to nurseries and garden supply stores. What's his profit from this venture? Almost half a million dollars on sales of $1.5 million. Beats cleaning your plate. One person's trash is another person's treasure.[25]

Service-Producing Sector

Many small businesses in this sector are *retailers*—they buy goods from other firms and sell them to consumers in stores, by phone, through direct mailings, or over the Internet. In fact, entrepreneurs are turning increasingly to the Internet as a venue for start-up ventures. Take Tony Roeder, for example, who had a fascination with the red Radio Flyer wagons that many of today's adults had owned as children. In 1998, he started an online store through Yahoo! to sell red wagons from his home. In three years, he turned his online store into a million-dollar business.[26] When we talk about Internet entrepreneurs, we have to mention Mark Zuckerberg, the king of Internet entrepreneurship. As is well known, he founded Facebook while a student at Harvard and, by age 27, had built up a personal wealth of $27 billion.[27]

Other small business owners in this sector are wholesalers—they sell products to businesses that buy them for resale or for company use. A local bakery, for example, is acting as a wholesaler when it sells desserts to a restaurant, which then resells them to its customers. A small business that buys flowers from a local grower (the manufacturer) and resells them to a retail store is another example of a wholesaler.

A high proportion of small businesses in this sector provide professional, business, or personal services. Doctors and dentists are part of the service industry, as are insurance agents, accountants, and lawyers. So are businesses that provide personal services, such as dry cleaning and hairdressing.

David Marcks, for example, entered the service industry about fourteen years ago when he learned that his border collie enjoyed chasing geese at the golf course where he worked. Anyone who's been on a golf course recently knows exactly what the goose problem is. While they are lovely to look at, they answer the call of nature on tees, fairways, and greens. That's where Marcks's company, Geese Police, comes in: Marcks employs specially trained dogs to chase the geese away. He now has twenty-seven trucks, thirty-two border collies, and five offices. Golf courses account for only about 5 percent of his business, as his dogs now patrol corporate parks and playgrounds as well.[28]

Figure 5.5 provides a more detailed breakdown of small businesses by industry.

FIGURE 5.5 Small Business by Industry

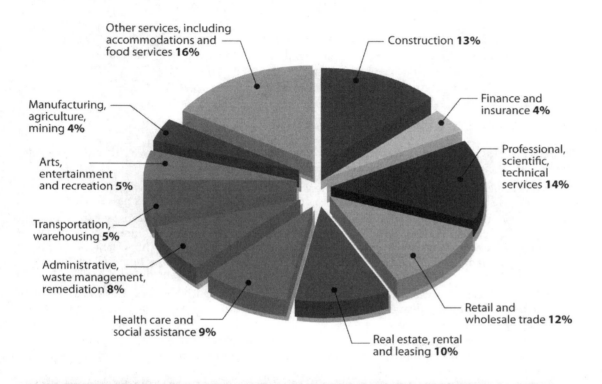

4. ADVANTAGES AND DISADVANTAGES OF BUSINESS OWNERSHIP

L E A R N I N G   O B J E C T I V E S

1. Summarize the advantages and disadvantages of business ownership.
2. Do you want to be a business owner someday? Before deciding, you might want to consider the following advantages and disadvantages of business ownership.[29]

4.1 Advantages of Small Business Ownership

Being a business owner can be extremely rewarding. Having the courage to take a risk and start a venture is part of the American dream. Success brings with it many advantages:

- *Independence.* As a business owner, you're your own boss. You can't get fired. More importantly, you have the freedom to make the decisions that are crucial to your own business success.
- *Lifestyle.* Owning a small business gives you certain lifestyle advantages. Because you're in charge, you decide when and where you want to work. If you want to spend more time on nonwork activities or with your family, you don't have to ask for the time off. If it's important that you be with your family all day, you might decide to run your business from your home. Given today's technology, it's relatively easy to do. Moreover, it eliminates commuting time.
- *Financial rewards.* In spite of high financial risk, running your own business gives you a chance to make more money than if you were employed by someone else. You benefit from your own hard work.
- *Learning opportunities.* As a business owner, you'll be involved in all aspects of your business. This situation creates numerous opportunities to gain a thorough understanding of the various business functions.
- *Creative freedom and personal satisfaction.* As a business owner, you'll be able to work in a field that you really enjoy. You'll be able to put your skills and knowledge to use, and you'll gain personal satisfaction from implementing your ideas, working directly with customers, and watching your business succeed.

4.2 Disadvantages of Small Business Ownership

As the little boy said when he got off his first roller-coaster ride, "I like the ups but not the downs!" Here are some of the risks you run if you want to start a small business:

- *Financial risk.* The financial resources needed to start and grow a business can be extensive. You may need to commit most of your savings or even go into debt to get started. If things don't go well, you may face substantial financial loss. In addition, there's no guaranteed income. There might be times, especially in the first few years, when the business isn't generating enough cash for you to live on.
- *Stress.* As a business owner, you *are* the business. There's a bewildering array of things to worry about—competition, employees, bills, equipment breakdowns, customer problems. As the owner, you're also responsible for the well-being of your employees.
- *Time commitment.* People often start businesses so that they'll have more time to spend with their families. Unfortunately, running a business is extremely time-consuming. In theory, you have the freedom to take time off, but in reality, you may not be able to get away. In fact, you'll probably have less free time than you'd have working for someone else. For many entrepreneurs and small business owners, a forty-hour workweek is a myth; see Figure 5.6. Vacations will be difficult to

take and will often be interrupted. In recent years, the difficulty of getting away from the job has been compounded by cell phones, iPhones, Internet-connected laptops and iPads, and many small business owners have come to regret that they're always reachable.

- *Undesirable duties.* When you start up, you'll undoubtedly be responsible for either doing or overseeing just about everything that needs to be done. You can get bogged down in detail work that you don't enjoy. As a business owner, you'll probably have to perform some unpleasant tasks, like firing people.

In spite of these and other disadvantages, most small business owners are pleased with their decision to start a business. A survey conducted by the *Wall Street Journal* and Cicco and Associates indicates that small business owners and top-level corporate executives agree overwhelmingly that small business owners have a more satisfying business experience. Interestingly, the researchers had fully expected to find that small business owners were happy with their choices; they were, however, surprised at the number of corporate executives who believed that the grass was greener in the world of small business ownership.[30]

FIGURE 5.6   The Entrepreneur's Workweek

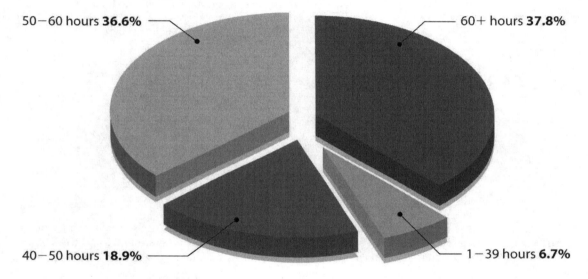

50−60 hours **36.6%**

60+ hours **37.8%**

40−50 hours **18.9%**

1−39 hours **6.7%**

KEY TAKEAWAYS

- There are several advantages that, generally speaking, come with success in business ownership:
  1. *Independence.* As a business owner, you're your own boss.
  2. *Lifestyle.* Because you're in charge, you decide when and where you want to work.
  3. *Financial rewards.* In spite of high financial risk, running your own business gives you a chance to make more money than if you were employed by someone else.
  4. *Learning opportunities.* As a business owner, you'll be involved in all aspects of your business.
  5. *Creative freedom and personal satisfaction.* As a business owner, you'll be able to work in a field that you really enjoy, and you'll gain personal satisfaction from watching your business succeed.

- There are also a number of potential disadvantages to consider in deciding whether to start a small business:
  1. *Financial risk.* The financial resources needed to start and grow a business can be extensive, and if things don't go well, you may face substantial financial loss. In addition, you'll have no guaranteed income.
  2. *Stress.* You'll have a bewildering array of things to worry about—competition, employees, bills, equipment breakdowns, customer problems.
  3. *Time commitment.* Running a business is extremely time-consuming. In fact, you'll probably have less free time than you'd have working for someone else.
  4. *Undesirable duties.* You'll be responsible for either doing or overseeing just about everything that needs to be done, and you'll probably have to perform some unpleasant tasks, like firing people.

Before going to the next section of this chapter, take a few minutes to test your knowledge of the material covered in this section. Quizzes can be found under the "Resources" tab, "Study Aids: Quizzes."

EXERCISES

1. First, identify five advantages of small business ownership. Next, rank these advantages according to their importance to you. Why did you rank them as you did? What factors discourage individuals from small business ownership? Indicate which of these factors might discourage you from starting a business. Explain why.

2. Because you're convinced that the best way to get rich is to work for yourself, you're thinking about starting your own business. You have an idea and $100,000 that you just inherited from a great-aunt. You even have a location: Palo Alto, California, which (according to a *Forbes* magazine article) is the best place in the United States to get rich. But there's a downside: to move to California and start your own business, you'll have to drop out of college. What financial risks should you consider in making your decision? What are your chances of succeeding with your plan? Are you willing to take the financial risk needed to start a business? Why, or why not? Are you really likely to make more money running your own business than working for someone else?

---

5. STARTING A BUSINESS

LEARNING OBJECTIVES

1. **Explain what it takes to start a business.**
2. **Evaluate the advantages and disadvantages of several small business ownership options—starting a business from scratch, buying an existing business, and obtaining a franchise.**

Starting a business takes talent, determination, hard work, and persistence. It also requires a lot of research and planning. Before starting your business, you should appraise your strengths and weaknesses and assess your personal goals to determine whether business ownership is for you.[31]

5.1 Questions to Ask Before You Start a Business

If you're interested in starting a business, you need to make decisions even before you bring your talent, determination, hard work, and persistence to bear on your project. Here are the basic questions you'll need to address:

- What, exactly, is my business idea? Is it feasible?
- What type of business is right for me? What industry do I want to get into? Do I want to be a manufacturer, a retailer, or a wholesaler? Do I want to provide professional or personal services? Do I want to start a business that I can operate out of my home?
- Do I want to run a business that's similar to many existing businesses? Do I want to innovate—to create a new product or a new approach to doing business?
- Do I want to start a new business, buy an existing one, or buy a franchise?
- Do I want to start the business by myself or with others?
- What form of business organization do I want?

After making these decisions, you'll be ready to take the most important step in the entire process of starting a business: you must describe your future business in the form of a **business plan**—a document that identifies the goals of your proposed business and explains how these goals will be achieved. Think of a business plan as a blueprint for a proposed company: it shows how you intend to build the company and how you intend to make sure that it's sturdy. You must also take a second crucial step before you actually start up your business: You need to get financing—the money from individuals, banks, or both, that you'll need to get your business off the ground. (Obviously, if you already have the necessary funds, you're one of the fortunate few who can skip this step.)

5.2 The Business Idea

For some people, coming up with a great business idea is a gratifying adventure. For most, however, it's a daunting task. The key to coming up with a business idea is identifying something that customers want—or, perhaps more importantly, filling an unmet need. Your business will probably survive only if its purpose is to *satisfy its customers*—the ultimate users of its goods or services. In coming up with a business idea, don't ask, "What do we want to sell?" but rather, "What does the customer want to buy?"[32]

To come up with an innovative business idea, you need to be creative. The idea itself can come from various sources. Prior experience accounts for the bulk of new business ideas. Many people generate ideas for industries they're already working in. Past experience in an industry also increases your chances of success. Take Sam Walton, the late founder of Wal-Mart. He began his retailing career at JCPenney and then became a successful franchiser of a Ben Franklin five-and-dime store. In 1962, he came up with the idea of opening large stores in rural areas, with low costs and heavy discounts. He founded his first Wal-Mart store in 1962, and when he died thirty years later, his family's net worth was $25 billion.[33]

Industry experience also gave Howard Schultz, a New York executive for a housewares company, his breakthrough idea. In 1981, Schultz noticed that a small customer in Seattle—Starbucks Coffee, Tea and Spice—ordered more coffeemaker cone filters than Macy's and many other large customers. So he flew across the country to find out why. His meeting with the owner-operators of the original Starbucks Coffee Co. resulted in his becoming part-owner of the company, and changed his life and the life of coffee lovers forever. Schultz's vision for the company far surpassed that of its other owners. While they wanted Starbucks to remain small and local, Schultz saw potential for a national business that not only sold world-class-quality coffee beans but also offered customers a European coffee-bar experience. After attempting unsuccessfully to convince his partners to try his experiment, Schultz left Starbucks and started his own chain of coffee bars, which he called Il Giornale (after an Italian newspaper). Two years later, he bought out the original owners and reclaimed the name Starbucks.[34]

Other people come up with business ideas because of hobbies or personal interests. This was the case with Nike founder Phil Knight, who was an avid runner. He was convinced that it was possible to make high-quality track shoes that cost less than the European shoes dominating the market at the time. His track experience, coupled with his knowledge of business (Knight holds an MBA from Stanford and worked as an accountant), inspired him to start Nike. Michael Dell also turned a personal interest into a business. From a young age, he was obsessed with taking computers apart and putting them back together again, and it was this personal interest that led to his great business idea. At college, instead of attending classes, he spent his time assembling computers and, eventually, founded Dell, Inc.

We will expand on this important topic of idea generation and creativity in other chapters.

Taking Stock of Your Business Personality

Take a moment to complete an exercise that will help you decide if business ownership is right for you.

5.3 Ownership Options

As we've already seen, you can become a small business owner in one of three ways—by starting a new business, buying an existing one, or obtaining a franchise. Let's look more closely at the advantages and disadvantages of each option.

business plan

Formal document describing a proposed business concept, description of the proposed business, industry analysis, mission statement and core values, a management plan, a description of goods or services, a description of production processes, and marketing and financial plans.

Starting from Scratch

FIGURE 5.7

SUBWAY, the largest franchise in the world, grew from a tiny sandwich shop started in 1965 by seventeen-year-old Fred DeLuca hoping to put himself through college.

Source: http://commons.wikimedia.org/wiki/File:Subway_restaurant_Pittsfield_Township_Michigan.JPG

The most common—and the riskiest—option is starting from scratch. This approach lets you start with a clean slate and allows you to build the business the way you want. You select the goods or services that you're going to offer, secure your location, and hire your employees, and then it's up to you to develop your customer base and build your reputation. This is the path taken by Andres Mason, who figured out how to inject hysteria into the process of bargain hunting on the Web. The result is an overnight success story called Groupon.[35] Here is how Groupon (a blend of the words "group" and "coupon") works: A daily e-mail is sent to 34 million people in 175 North American markets and 47 countries offering a deeply discounted deal to buy something or to do something in their city. If the person receiving the e-mail likes the deal, he or she commits to buying it. But, here's the catch, if not enough people sign up for the deal, it is cancelled. Groupon makes money by keeping about half of the revenue from the deal. The company offering the product or service gets exposure. But stay tuned: the "daily deals website isn't just unprofitable—it's bleeding hundreds of millions of dollars."[36] As with all start-ups, cash is always a problem.

Buying an Existing Business

If you decide to buy an existing business, some things will be easier. You'll already have a proven product, current customers, active suppliers, a known location, and trained employees. You'll also find it much easier to predict the business's future success. There are, of course, a few bumps in this road to business ownership. First, it's hard to determine how much you should pay for a business. You can easily determine how much things like buildings and equipment are worth, but how much should you pay for the fact that the business already has steady customers?

In addition, a business, like a used car, might have performance problems that you can't detect without a test drive (an option, unfortunately, that you don't get when you're buying a business). Perhaps the current owners have disappointed customers; maybe the location isn't as good as it used to be. You might inherit employees that you wouldn't have hired yourself. Finally, what if the previous owners set up a competing business that draws away their former—and your current—customers?

Getting a Franchise

franchise

Form of business ownership in which a *franchiser* (a seller) grants a *franchisee* (a buyer) the right to use a brand name and to sell its products or services.

Lastly, you can buy a **franchise**. Under this setup, a *franchiser* (the company that sells the franchise) grants the *franchisee* (the buyer—you) the right to use a brand name and to sell its goods or services. Franchises market products in a variety of industries, including food, retail, hotels, travel, real estate, business services, cleaning services, and even weight-loss centers and wedding services. There are thousands of franchises, many of which are quite familiar—SUBWAY, McDonald's, 7-Eleven, Holiday Inn, Budget Car Rental, RadioShack, and Jiffy Lube.

As you can see from Figure 5.8, franchising has become an extremely popular way to do business. A new franchise outlet opens once every eight minutes in the United States, where one in ten businesses is now a franchise. Franchises employ eight million people (13 percent of the workforce) and account for 17 percent of all sales in this country ($1.3 trillion).[37]

FIGURE 5.8 The Growth of Franchising, 1980–2007

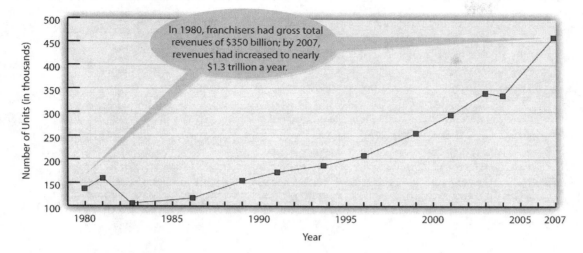

In addition to the right to use a company's brand name and sell its products, the franchisee gets help in picking a location, starting and operating the business, and advertising. In effect, you've bought a prepackaged, ready-to-go business that's proven successful elsewhere. You also get ongoing support from the franchiser, which has a vested interest in your success.

Not surprisingly, these advantages don't come cheaply. Franchises can be very expensive, usually depending on the amount of business that a franchisee is expected to do. KFC franchises, for example, require a total investment of $1.3 million to $2.5 million each. This fee includes the cost of the property, equipment, training, start-up costs, and the *franchise fee*—a one-time charge for the right to operate as a KFC outlet. McDonald's is in the same price range ($1.1 million to $2.2 million). SUBWAY sandwich shops are more affordable, with expected total investment ranging from $86,000 to $263,000. If you'd prefer teaching dance and exercise classes, you could get a Jazzercise franchise for anywhere from $4,000 to $77,000.[38] But be careful in picking a franchise: many go bust. For example, in the mid-1990s dating franchises were a big deal. But then, like lots of relationships, things went sour; those looking for love went to other places, and the dating franchises folded.[39]

In addition to your initial investment, you'll have to pay two other fees on a monthly basis—a *royalty fee* (typically from 3 to 12 percent of sales) for continued support from the franchiser and the right to keep using the company's trade name, plus an *advertising fee* to cover your share of national and regional advertising. You'll also be expected to buy your products from the franchiser.[40]

Why do would-be business owners like franchises? For one thing, buying a franchise lets you start up under fairly safe conditions, with a proven model for running a company and a permanent support team. You can profit from name recognition without having to develop your own image in the marketplace, and you can be your own boss (as long as you comply with the standards set by the franchiser).

But there are disadvantages. The cost of obtaining and running a franchise can be high, and you have to play by the franchiser's rules, even when you disagree with them. The franchiser maintains a great deal of control over its franchisees. For example, if you own a fast-food franchise, the franchise agreement will likely dictate the food and beverages you can sell; the methods used to store, prepare, and serve the food; and the prices you'll charge. In addition, the agreement will dictate what the premises will look like and how they'll be maintained.

Finally, franchisers don't always keep their promises. What do you do if the promised advertising or employee training doesn't materialize? What do you do if you're forced to make unnecessary and costly alterations to your premises, or the franchising company sets up a competing establishment nearby? What if the franchising company gets bad press, which, in turn, hurts your sales? You always have the option of suing the franchiser, but this is time-consuming and costly. As with any business venture, you need to do your homework before investing in a franchise.

KEY TAKEAWAYS

- Before starting a business, you need to ask yourself a few basic questions:

  1. What, exactly, is my *business idea*? Is it feasible?
  2. What type of business is right for me? What *industry* do I want to get into?
  3. Do I want to run a business that's similar to many existing businesses, or do I want to innovate?
  4. Do I want to start a new business, take over an existing one, or buy a franchise?
  5. Do I want to start the business by myself, or do I want company?
  6. What form of *business organization* do I want?

- After you've addressed these basic questions, you'll be ready to describe your future business in the form of a **business plan**—a document that identifies the goals of your proposed business and explains how it will achieve them. Before you actually start up your business, you must also get financing.

- The key to coming up with a business idea is identifying something that customers want. Your business will probably survive only if its "purpose" is *to satisfy its customers*—the ultimate users of its goods or services.

- You can become a small business owner in one of three ways, each of which has advantages and disadvantages:

  1. *Starting from scratch.* This is the most common—and riskiest—option. *Advantage*: You start with a clean slate and build the business the way you want. *Disadvantage*: It's up to you to develop your customer base and build your reputation.
  2. *Buying an existing business.* This option is not as risky as starting a business from scratch, but it has some drawbacks. *Advantages*: You'll already have a proven product, current customers, active suppliers, a known location, and trained employees. *Disadvantages*: It's hard to determine how much to pay for a business; perhaps the current owners have disappointed customers; maybe the location isn't as good as it used to be.
  3. *Buying a franchise.* Under a **franchise** setup, a *franchiser* (the company that sells the franchise) grants the *franchisee* (the buyer) the right to use a brand name and to sell its goods or services. *Advantages*: You've bought a prepackaged, ready-to-go business that's proven successful elsewhere; you also get ongoing support from the franchiser. *Disadvantages*: The cost can be high; you have to play by the franchiser's rules; and franchisers don't always keep their promises.

Before going to the next section of this chapter, take a few minutes to test your knowledge of the material covered in this section. Quizzes can be found under the "Resources" tab, "Study Aids: Quizzes."

EXERCISES

1. If business ownership interests you, you can start a new business, buy an existing one, or obtain a franchise. Evaluate the advantages and disadvantages of each option. Which option do you find most appealing, and why? Describe the business you would probably start.

2. How would you like to spend your summer collecting trash in a used pickup? Doesn't sound very appealing, does it? Would you quit college to do it full time? Probably not. But that's exactly what Brian Scudamore did. And he got very rich doing it. His summer job turned into the company known as 1-800-GOT-JUNK, one of the fastest-growing franchises in the United States and Canada. Go to http://www.1800gotjunk.com to link to the Web site and learn more about the company. After looking at the Web site, answer the following questions (hint: once you are on the company's Web site, click on "Start a Franchise"):

   a. What is the company's business model? What does it do? Where does it do it?
   b. Are you the kind of person the company wants to attract as a franchise partner?
   c. How much would it cost you to buy a franchise? How much total capital would you need?
   d. What kinds of support and services would you receive from the company?
   e. Assuming that you had enough money, would you buy a franchise? Why, or why not?

6. THE BUSINESS PLAN

LEARNING OBJECTIVE

1. Discuss the importance of planning for your business, and identify the key sections of a business plan.

If you want to start a business, you must prepare a business plan. This essential document should tell the story of your business concept, provide an overview of the industry in which you will operate, describe the goods or services you will provide, identify your customers and proposed marketing activities, explain the qualifications of your management team, and state your projected income and borrowing needs.

6.1 Purpose of a Business Plan

The business plan is a plan or blueprint for the company, and it's an indispensable tool in attracting investors, obtaining loans, or both. Remember, too, that the value of your business plan isn't limited to the planning stages of your business and the process of finding start-up money. Once you've acquired start-up capital, don't just stuff your plan in a drawer. Treat it as an ongoing guide to your business and its operations, as well as a yardstick by which you can measure your performance. Keep it handy, update it periodically, and use it to assess your progress.

In developing and writing your business plan, you must make strategic decisions in the areas of management, operations, marketing, accounting, and finance—in short, in all the functional areas of business that we described in Chapter 1. Granted, preparing a business plan takes a lot of time and work, but it's well worth the effort. A business plan forces you to think critically about your proposed business and reduces your risk of failure. It forces you to analyze your business concept and the industry in which you'll be operating, and it helps you determine how you can grab a percentage of sales in that industry.

The most common use of a business plan is persuading investors, lenders, or both, to provide financing. These two groups look for different things. Investors are particularly interested in the quality of your business concept and the ability of management to make your venture successful. Bankers and other lenders are primarily concerned with your company's ability to generate cash to repay loans. To persuade investors and lenders to support your business, you need a professional, well-written business plan that paints a clear picture of your proposed business.

6.2 Sections of the Business Plan

Though formats can vary, a business plan generally includes the following sections: executive summary, description of proposed business, industry analysis, mission statement and core values, management plan, goods or services and (if applicable) production processes, marketing, global issues, and financial plan. Let's explore each of these sections in more detail. (*Note*: More detailed documents and an Excel template are available for those classes in which the optional business plan project is assigned.)

Executive Summary

The **executive summary** is a one- to three-page overview of the business plan. It's actually the most important part of the business plan: it's what the reader looks at first, and if it doesn't capture the reader's attention, it might be the only thing that he or she looks at. It should therefore emphasize the key points of the plan and get the reader excited about the prospects of the business.

Even though the executive summary is the first thing read, it's written *after* the other sections of the plan are completed. An effective approach in writing the executive summary is to paraphrase key sentences from each section of the business plan. This process will ensure that the key information of each section is included in the executive summary.

executive summary

Overview emphasizing the key points of a business plan to get the reader excited about the business's prospects.

Description of Proposed Business

Here, you present a *brief* description of the company and tell the reader why you're starting your business, what benefits it provides, and why it will be successful. Some of the questions to answer in this section include the following:

- What will your proposed company do? Will it be a manufacturer, a retailer, or a service provider?

- What goods or services will it provide?
- Why are your goods or services unique?
- Who will be your main customers?
- How will your goods or services be sold?
- Where will your business be located?

Because later parts of the plan will provide more detailed discussions of many of these issues, this section should provide only an overview of these topics.

Industry Analysis

This section provides a brief introduction to the industry in which you propose to operate. It describes both the current situation and the future possibilities, and it addresses such questions as the following:

- How large is the industry? What are total sales for the industry, in volume and dollars?
- Is the industry mature or are new companies successfully entering it?
- What opportunities exist in the industry? What threats exist?
- What factors will influence future expansion or contraction of the industry?
- What is the overall outlook for the industry?
- Who are your major competitors in the industry?
- How does your product differ from those of your competitors?

Mission Statement and Core Values

This portion of the business plan states the company's *mission statement* and *core values*. The **mission statement** describes the purpose or *mission* of your organization—its reason for existence. It tells the reader what the organization is committed to doing. For example, one mission statement reads, "The mission of Southwest Airlines is dedication to the highest quality of Customer Service delivered with a sense of warmth, friendliness, individual pride, and company spirit."[41]

Core values are fundamental beliefs about what's important and what is (and isn't) appropriate in conducting company activities. Core values are not about profits, but rather about ideals. They should help guide the behavior of individuals in the organization. Coca-Cola, for example, intends that its core values—leadership, collaboration, integrity, accountability, passion, diversity, and quality—will let employees know what behaviors are (and aren't) acceptable.[42]

Management Plan

Management makes the key decisions for the business, such as its legal form and organizational structure. This section of the business plan should outline these decisions and provide information about the qualifications of the key management personnel.

A. Legal Form of Organization

This section identifies the chosen legal form of business ownership: sole proprietorship (personal ownership), partnership (ownership shared with one or more partners), or corporation (ownership through shares of stock).

B. Qualifications of Management Team and Compensation Package

It isn't enough merely to have a good business idea: you need a talented management team that can turn your concept into a profitable venture. This part of the management plan section provides information about the qualifications of each member of the management team. Its purpose is to convince the reader that the company will be run by experienced, well-qualified managers. It describes each individual's education, experience, and expertise, as well as each person's responsibilities. It also indicates the estimated annual salary to be paid to each member of the management team.

C. Organizational Structure

This section of the management plan describes the relationships among individuals within the company, listing the major responsibilities of each member of the management team.

Goods, Services, and the Production Process

To succeed in attracting investors and lenders, you must be able to describe your goods or services clearly (and enthusiastically). Here, you describe all the goods and services that you will provide the marketplace. This section explains why your proposed offerings are better than those of competitors

mission statement

Statement describing an organization's purpose or *mission*—its reason for existence—and telling stakeholders what the organization is committed to doing.

Core values

Statement of fundamental beliefs describing what's appropriate and important in conducting organizational activities and providing a guide for the behavior of organization members.

and indicates what market needs will be met by your goods or services. In other words, it addresses a key question: What *competitive advantage* will the company's goods and services have over similar products on the market?

This section also indicates how you plan to obtain or make your products. Naturally, the write-up will vary, depending on whether you're proposing a service company, a retailer, or a manufacturer. If it's a service company, describe the process by which you'll deliver your services. If it's a retail company, tell the reader where you'll purchase products for resale.

If you're going to be a manufacturer, you must furnish information on product design, development, and production processes. You must address questions such as the following:

- How will products be designed?
- What technology will be needed to design and manufacture products?
- Will the company run its own production facilities, or will its products be manufactured by someone else?
- Where will production facilities be located?
- What type of equipment will be used?
- What are the design and layout of the facilities?
- How many workers will be employed in the production process?
- How many units will be produced?
- How will the company ensure that products are of high quality?

Marketing

This critical section focuses on four marketing-related areas—target market, pricing, distribution, and promotion:

1. *Target market.* Describe future customers and profile them according to age, gender, income, interests, and so forth. If your company will sell to other companies, describe your typical business customer.
2. *Pricing.* State the proposed price for each product. Compare your pricing strategy to that of competitors.
3. *Distribution.* Explain how your goods or services will be distributed to customers. Indicate whether they'll be sold directly to customers or through retail outlets.
4. *Promotion.* Explain your promotion strategy, indicating what types of advertising you'll be using.

In addition, if you intend to use the Internet to promote or sell your products, also provide answers to these questions:

- Will your company have a Web site? Who will visit the site?
- What will the site look like? What information will it supply?
- Will you sell products over the Internet?
- How will you attract customers to your site and entice them to buy from your company?

Global Issues

In this section, indicate whether you'll be involved in international markets, by either buying or selling in other countries. If you're going to operate across borders, identify the challenges that you'll face in your global environment, and explain how you'll meet them. If you don't plan initially to be involved in international markets, state what strategies, if any, you'll use to move into international markets when the time comes.

Financial Plan

In preparing the financial section of your business plan, specify the company's cash needs and explain how you'll be able to repay debt. This information is vital in obtaining financing. It reports the amount of cash needed by the company for start-up and initial operations and provides an overview of proposed funding sources. It presents financial projections, including expected sales, costs, and profits (or losses). It refers to a set of financial statements included in an appendix to the business plan.

Appendices

Here, you furnish supplemental information that may be of interest to the reader. In addition to a set of financial statements, for example, you might attach the résumés of your management team.

The Instant Mission Statement

Take a moment to complete an exercise that will help you learn how to compose a mission statement.

KEY TAKEAWAYS

- A **business plan** tells the story of your business concept, provides an overview of the industry in which you will operate, describes the goods or services you will provide, identifies your customers and proposed marketing activities, explains the qualifications of your management team, and states your projected income and borrowing needs.
- In your business plan, you make strategic decisions in the areas of management, operations, marketing, accounting, and finance. Developing your business plan forces you to analyze your business concept and the industry in which you'll be operating. Its most common use is persuading investors and lenders to provide financing.
- A business plan generally includes the following sections:

  1. **Executive summary**. One- to three-page overview.
  2. *Description of proposed business*. Brief description of the company that answers such questions as what your proposed company will do, what goods or services it will provide, and who its main customers will be.
  3. *Industry analysis*. Short introduction to the industry in which you propose to operate.
  4. *Mission statement and core values*. Declaration of your **mission statement**, which are fundamental beliefs about what's important and what is (and isn't) appropriate in conducting company activities.
  5. *Management plan*. Information about management team qualifications and responsibilities, and designation of your proposed legal form of organization.
  6. *Goods, services, and the production process*. Description of the goods and services that you'll provide in the marketplace; explanation of how you plan to obtain or make your products or of the process by which you'll deliver your services.
  7. *Marketing*. Description of your plans in four marketing-related areas: target market, pricing, distribution, and promotion.
  8. *Global issues*. Description of your involvement, if any, in international markets.
  9. *Financial plan*. Report on the cash you'll need for start-up and initial operations, proposed funding sources, and means of repaying your debt.
  10. *Appendices*. Supplemental information that may be of interest to the reader.

Before going to the next section of this chapter, take a few minutes to test your knowledge of the material covered in this section. Quizzes can be found under the "Resources" tab, "Study Aids: Quizzes."

EXERCISE

Let's start with three givens: (1) college students love chocolate chip cookies, (2) you have a special talent for baking cookies, and (3) you're always broke. Given these three conditions, you've come up with the idea of starting an on-campus business—selling chocolate chip cookies to fellow students. As a business major, you want to do things right by preparing a business plan. First, you identified a number of specifics about your proposed business. Now, you need to put these various pieces of information into the relevant section of your business plan. Using the business plan format described in this chapter, indicate the section of the business plan into which you'd put each of the following:

1. You'll bake the cookies in the kitchen of a friend's apartment.

2. You'll charge $1 each or $10 a dozen.

3. Your purpose is to make the best cookies on campus and deliver them fresh. You value integrity, consideration of others, and quality.

4. Each cookie will have ten chocolate chips and will be superior to those sold in nearby bakeries and other stores.

5. You expect sales of $6,000 for the first year.

6. Chocolate chip cookies are irresistible to college students. There's a lot of competition from local bakeries, but your cookies will be superior and popular with college students. You'll make them close to campus using only fresh ingredients and sell them for $1 each. Your management team is excellent. You expect first-year sales of $6,000 and net income of $1,500. You estimate start-up costs at $600.

7. You'll place ads for your product in the college newspaper.

8. You'll hire a vice president at a salary of $100 a week.

9. You can ship cookies anywhere in the United States and in Canada.

10. You need $600 in cash to start the business.

11. There are six bakeries within walking distance of the college.

12. You'll bake nothing but cookies and sell them to college students. You'll make them in an apartment near campus and deliver them fresh.

---

7.   HOW TO SUCCEED IN MANAGING A BUSINESS

LEARNING OBJECTIVES

1. Discuss ways to succeed in managing a business, and explain why some businesses fail.
2. Identify sources of small business assistance from the Small Business Administration.

7.1   Why Do Businesses Succeed?

Being successful as a business owner requires more than coming up with a brilliant idea and working hard. You need to learn how to manage and grow your business. In the process, you'll face numerous challenges, and your ability to meet them will be a major factor in your success (or failure).[43] To give yourself a fighting chance in making a success of your business, you should do the following:

- *Know your business.* It seems obvious, but it's worth mentioning: successful businesspeople know what they're doing. They're knowledgeable about the industry in which they operate (both as it stands today and where it's headed), and they know who their competitors are. They know how to attract customers and who the best suppliers and distributors are, and they understand the impact of technology on their business.

- *Know the basics of business management.* You might be able to *start* a business on the basis of a great idea, but to *manage* it you need to understand the functional areas of business—accounting, finance, management, marketing, and production. You need to be a salesperson, as well as a decision maker and a planner.

- *Have the proper attitude.* When you own a business, you *are* the business. If you're going to devote the time and energy needed to transform an idea into a successful venture, you need to have a passion for your work. You should believe in what you're doing and make a strong personal commitment to your business.

- *Get adequate funding.* It takes a lot of money to start a business and guide it through the start-up phase (which can last for over a year). You can have the most brilliant idea in the world, the best marketing approach, and a talented management team, yet if you run out of cash, your career as a business owner could be brief. Plan for the long term and work with lenders and investors to ensure that you'll have sufficient funds to get open, stay open during the start-up phase, and, ultimately, expand.

- *Manage your money effectively.* You'll be under constant pressure to come up with the money to meet payroll and pay your other bills. That's why you need to keep an eye on *cash flow*—money coming in and money going out. You need to control costs and collect money that's owed you, and, generally, you need to know how to gather the financial information that you require to run your business.

- *Manage your time efficiently.* A new business owner can expect to work sixty hours a week. If you want to grow a business and have some type of nonwork life at the same time, you'll have to give up some control—to let others take over some of the work. Thus, you must develop time-management skills and learn how to delegate responsibility.

- *Know how to manage people.* Hiring, keeping, and managing good people are crucial to business success. As your business grows, you'll depend more on your employees. You need to develop a positive working relationship with them, train them properly, and motivate them to provide quality goods or services.

- *Satisfy your customers.* You might attract customers through impressive advertising campaigns, but you'll keep them only by providing quality goods or services. Commit yourself to satisfying—or even exceeding—customer needs.

- *Know how to compete.* Find your niche in the marketplace, keep an eye on your competitors, and be prepared to react to changes in the marketplace. The history of business (and much of life) can be summed up in three words: "Adapt or perish."

7.2   Why Do Businesses Fail?

If you've paid attention to the occupancy of shopping malls over a few years, you've noticed that retailers come and go with surprising frequency. The same thing happens with restaurants—indeed, with all kinds of businesses. By definition, starting a business—small or large—is risky, and though many businesses succeed, a large proportion of them don't. One-third of small businesses that have employees go out of business within the first two years. More than half of small businesses have closed by the end of their fourth year, and 70 percent do not make it past their seventh year.[44]

TABLE 5.2   Survival Rate of New Companies

Number of Years after Start-up	Rate of Survival
1	81.2%
2	65.8%
3	54.3%
4	44.4%
5	38.3%
6	34.4%
7	31.2%
Note: Percentages based on a total of 212,182 businesses that started up in the second quarter of 1998.	

Source: "Characteristics of Survival: Longevity of Business Establishments in the Business Employment Dynamics Data: Extension."

http://www.bls.gov/osmr/pdf/st060040.pdf.

As bad as these statistics on business survival are, some industries are worse than others. If you want to stay in business for a long time, you might want to avoid some of these risky industries. Even though your friends think you make the best macaroni and cheese pizza in the world, this doesn't mean you can succeed as a pizza parlor owner. Opening a restaurant or a bar is one of the riskiest ventures (and, therefore, start-up funding is hard to get). You might also want to avoid the transportation industry. Owning a taxi might appear lucrative until you find out what a taxi license costs. It obviously varies by city, but in New York City the price tag is upward of $400,000. And setting up a shop to sell clothing can be challenging. Your view of "what's in" may be off, and one bad season can kill your business. The same is true for stores selling communication devices: every mall has one or more cell phone stores so the competition is steep, and business can be very slow.[45]

Businesses fail for any number of reasons, but many experts agree that the vast majority of failures result from some combination of the following problems:

- *Bad business idea*. Like any idea, a business idea can be flawed, either in the conception or in the execution. If you tried selling snowblowers in Hawaii, you could count on little competition, but you'd still be doomed to failure.

- *Cash problems*. Too many new businesses are underfunded. The owner borrows enough money to set up the business but doesn't have enough extra cash to operate during the start-up phase, when very little money is coming in but a lot is going out.

- *Managerial inexperience or incompetence*. Many new business owners have no experience in running a business; many have limited management skills. Maybe an owner knows how to make or market a product but doesn't know how to manage people. Maybe an owner can't attract and keep talented employees. Maybe an owner has poor leadership skills and isn't willing to plan ahead.

- *Lack of customer focus*. A major advantage of a small business is the ability to provide special attention to customers. But some small businesses fail to seize this advantage. Perhaps the owner doesn't anticipate customers' needs or keep up with changing markets or the customer-focused practices of competitors.

- *Inability to handle growth*. You'd think that a sales increase would be a good thing. Often it is, of course, but sometimes it can be a major problem. When a company grows, the owner's role changes. He or she needs to delegate work to others and build a business structure that can handle the increase in volume. Some owners don't make the transition and find themselves overwhelmed. Things don't get done, customers become unhappy, and expansion actually damages the company.

7.3   Help from the SBA

If you had your choice, which cupcake would you pick—vanilla Oreo, triple chocolate, or latte? In the last few years, cupcake shops are popping up in almost every city. Perhaps the bad economy has put people in the mood for small, relatively inexpensive treats. Whatever the reason, you're fascinated with the idea of starting a cupcake shop. You have a perfect location, have decided what equipment you need, and have tested dozens of recipes (and eaten lots of cupcakes). You are set to go with one giant exception: you don't have enough savings to cover your start-up costs. You have made the round of most local banks, but they are all unwilling to give you a loan. So what do you do? Fortunately, there is help available. It is through your local Small Business Administration (SBA), which offers an array of programs to help current and prospective small business owners. The SBA won't actually loan you the money, but it will increase the likelihood that you will get funding from a local bank by guaranteeing the loan. Here's how the SBA's loan guaranty program works: You apply to a bank for financing. A loan officer decides if the bank will loan you the money without an SBA guarantee. If the answer is no (because of some weakness in your application), the bank then decides if it will loan you the money if the SBA guarantees the loan. If the bank decides to do this, you get the money and make payments on the loan. If you default on the loan, the government reimburses the bank for its loss, up to the amount of the SBA guarantee.

In the process of talking with someone at the SBA, you will discover other programs it offers that will help you start your business and manage your organization. For example, to apply for funding you will need a well-written business plan. Once you get the loan and move to the business start-up phase, you will have lots of questions that need to be answered (including setting up a computer system for your company). And you are sure you will need help in a number of areas as you operate your cupcake shop. Fortunately, the SBA can help with all of these management and technical-service tasks.

This assistance is available through a number of channels, including the SBA's extensive Web site, online courses, and training programs. A full array of individualized services is also available. The **Small Business Development Center (SBDC)** assists current and prospective small business owners with business problems and provides free training and technical information on all aspects of small business management. These services are available at approximately one thousand locations around the country, many housed at colleges and universities.[46]

Small Business Development Center (SBDC)

SBA program in which centers housed at colleges and other locations provide free training and technical information to current and prospective small business owners.

Service Corps of Retired Executives (SCORE)

SBA program in which a businessperson needing advice is matched with a member of a team of retired executives working as volunteers.

If you need individualized advice from experienced executives, you can get it through the **Service Corps of Retired Executives (SCORE)**. Under the SCORE program, a businessperson needing advice is matched with someone on a team of retired executives who work as volunteers. Together, the SBDC and SCORE help more than a million small businesspersons every year.[47]

KEY TAKEAWAYS

- Business owners face numerous challenges, and the ability to meet them is a major factor in success (or failure). As a business owner, you should do the following:
  1. *Know your business.* Successful businesspeople are knowledgeable about the industry in which they operate, and they know who their competitors are.
  2. *Know the basics of business management.* To *manage* a business, you need to understand the functional areas of business—accounting, finance, management, marketing, and production.
  3. *Have the proper attitude.* You should believe in what you're doing and make a strong personal commitment to it.
  4. *Get adequate funding.* Plan for the long term and work with lenders and investors to ensure that you'll have sufficient funds to get open, stay open during the start-up phase, and, ultimately, expand.
  5. *Manage your money effectively.* You need to pay attention *to cash flow*—money coming in and money going out—and you need to know how to gather the financial information that you require to run your business.
  6. *Manage your time efficiently.* You must develop time-management skills and learn how to delegate responsibility.
  7. *Know how to manage people.* You need to develop a positive working relationship with your employees, train them properly, and motivate them to provide quality goods or services.
  8. *Satisfy your customers.* Commit yourself to satisfying—or even exceeding—customer needs.
  9. *Know how to compete.* Find your niche in the marketplace, keep an eye on your competitors, and be prepared to react to changes in your business environment.

- Businesses fail for any number of reasons, but many experts agree that the vast majority of failures result from some combination of the following problems:
  1. *Bad business idea.* Like any idea, a business idea can be flawed, either in the conception or in the execution.
  2. *Cash problems.* Too many new businesses are underfunded.
  3. *Managerial inexperience or incompetence.* Many new business owners have no experience in running a business, and many have limited management skills.
  4. *Lack of customer focus.* Some owners fail to make the most of a small business's advantage in providing special attention to customers.
  5. *Inability to handle growth.* When a company grows, some owners fail to delegate work or to build an organizational structure that can handle increases in volume.

- Services available to current and prospective small business owners from the SBA include assistance in developing a business plan, starting a business, obtaining financing, and managing an organization.
- The **SBDC (Small Business Development Centers)** matches businesspeople needing advice with teams of retired executives who work as volunteers through the SCORE program.

Before going to the next chapter, take a few minutes to test your knowledge of the material covered in this section. Quizzes can be found under the "Resources" tab, "Study Aids: Quizzes."

EXERCISES

1. It's the same old story: you want to start a small business but don't have much money. Go to http://entrepreneurs.about.com/cs/businessideas/a/10startupideas.htm and read the article titled "Business Ideas on a Budget." Identify a few businesses that you can start for $20 or less (that's right—$20 or less). Select one of these business opportunities that interests you. Why did you select this business? Why does the idea interest you? What would you do to ensure that the business was a success? If you needed assistance starting up or operating your business, where could you find help, and what type of assistance would be available?

2. Why do some businesses succeed while others fail? Identify three factors that you believe to be the most critical to business success. Why did you select these factors? Identify three factors that you believe to be primarily responsible for business failures, and indicate why you selected these factors.

8. CASES AND PROBLEMS

LEARNING ON THE WEB

Would You Like to Own a Sub Shop?

How would you like to own your own sandwich shop? You could start one on your own or buy one that's already in business, but an easier way might be buying a franchise from SUBWAY, the largest fast-food franchise in the world (even bigger than McDonald's). SUBWAY began in 1965 when seventeen-year-old Fred DeLuca opened a tiny sandwich shop in Bridgeport, Connecticut, hoping to put himself through college. As it turns out, his venture paid off in more ways than one. By 1974, DeLuca was franchising his business concept, and today, there are more than fifteen thousand SUBWAY franchisees in some seventy-five countries.

Go to http://www.subway.com to link to the SUBWAY Web site, and click on "Own a Franchise" to learn more about franchise opportunities with the company. After reviewing the information provided on the company's Web site, answer the following questions:

1. What do you have to do to get a SUBWAY franchise?
2. How much would it cost to open a SUBWAY shop?
3. What training and support would you receive from SUBWAY?
4. What advantages do you see in buying a SUBWAY franchise rather than starting a business from scratch? What disadvantages do you see?

CAREER OPPORTUNITIES

Do You Want to Be an Entrepreneur?

Want to learn what it's like to be an entrepreneur? To help you decide whether life as an entrepreneur might be for you, go to http://entrepreneurs.about.com/od/interviews; then link to the "Interview with Entrepreneurs" section of the About.com Web site and review the entrepreneur interviews. Select *two* entrepreneurs who interest you and do the following for each:

1. Describe the company that he or she founded.
2. Explain the reasons why he or she became an entrepreneur.
3. Explain what qualities, background, or both, prepared the individual to start a business.

After reading the interviews with these two entrepreneurs, answer the following questions:

1. What aspects of being an entrepreneur are particularly rewarding?
2. What's the downside of being an entrepreneur?
3. What challenges do entrepreneurs face?
4. Is entrepreneurship for you? Why, or why not?

ETHICS ANGLE

Term Papers for Sale

You and some fellow classmates are sitting around over pizza one night when someone comes up with an idea for a business. All of you have old term papers and essays lying around, and a couple of you know how to set up a Web page. What if you combine these two assets and start a business selling term papers over the Internet? Over time, you could collect or buy additional inventory from other students, and since some of you are good at research and others are good writers, you could even offer "student clients" the option of customized papers researched and written just for them. You figure that you can charge $15 for an "off-the-rack" paper, and for customized jobs, $10 per double-spaced page seems reasonable.

You all agree that the idea is promising, and you and a partner volunteer to put together a business plan. You have no difficulty with the section describing your proposed business: you know what your business will do, what products it will offer, who your customers will be, how your products will be sold, and where you'll be located. So far, so good.

Let's pause at this point to consider the following questions:

1. Does selling term papers over the Internet make business sense? Is it a good business idea?
2. Could the venture be profitable?

Let's continue and find out how the business plan proceeds.

Now you're ready to write your section on industry analysis and the first question you need to answer is, who are the players in the industry? To get some answers, you go online, log on to Google, and enter the search term "term papers for sale." Much to your surprise, up pop dozens of links to companies that have beaten you to market. The first company you investigate claims to have a quarter-million papers in stock, plus a team of graduate students on hand to write papers for anyone needing specialized work.

There's also a statement that says something like this: "Our term papers and essays are intended to help students write their own papers. They should be used for research purposes only. Students using our term papers and essays should write their own papers and cite our work."

You realize now that you're facing not only stiff competition but an issue that, so far, you and your partners have preferred to ignore: Is the business that you have in mind even ethical? It occurs to you that you could probably find the answer to this question in at least one of the 8,484 term papers on ethics available on your competitor's Web site, but you decide that it would be more efficient to give the question some thought on your own.

At this point, then, let's pause again to identify a couple of questions that you need to ask yourself as you prepare a report of your findings for your partners:

1. Is the sole purpose of running a business to make a profit, or do you need to be concerned about what your products will be used for? Explain your reasoning.
2. Do you need to consider the ethics of what other people do with your product? Explain your reasoning.

When you report on the problem that you've uncovered, your would-be partners are pretty discouraged, some by the prospect of competition and some by the nagging ethical issue. Just as you're about to dissolve the partnership, one person speaks up: "How about selling software that lets faculty search to see if students have plagiarized material on the Web?"

"Sorry," says someone else. "It's already out there. Two students at Berkeley have software that compares papers to a hundred million Web pages."

TEAM-BUILDING SKILLS

Knowing how to be an effective team member is a vital lifetime skill. It will help you in your academic career, in the business world, and in nonwork activities as well. It takes time and effort to learn how to work in a team. Part of the challenge is learning how to adjust your behavior to the needs of the group. Another part is learning how to motivate members of a group. A well-functioning team allows members to combine knowledge and skills, and this reliance on diverse backgrounds and strengths often results in team decisions that are superior to those made by individuals working alone.

Are You a Team Player?

As a first step, you should do a self-assessment to evaluate whether you possess characteristics that will help you be a successful team member. You can do this by taking a "Team Player" quiz available at the Quintessential Careers Web site. Go to http://www.quintcareers.com/team_player_quiz.html to link to this quiz. You'll get feedback that helps you identify the characteristics you need to work on if you want to improve your teamwork skills.

Working Together as a Team

The best approach to specifying appropriate behavior for team members is for the team to come up with some ground rules. Get together with three other students selected by your instructor, and establish working guidelines for your team. Prepare a team report in which you identify the following:

1. Five things that team members can do to increase the likelihood of group success
2. Five things that team members can do to jeopardize group success

THE GLOBAL VIEW

Global Versions of Groupon

When Andrew Mason founded Groupon in November 2008, he had no idea that he was headed for an overnight success, but two years after he set out on his entrepreneurial adventure (which, admittedly, isn't actually overnight), Groupon had more than fifty million registered users and nine million customers who had purchased at least one "daily deal" (http://www.digital-dd.com/wp-content/uploads/2011/06/groupon-ipo-s-1.pdf).

What's ahead for Groupon? Can its business model be exported to even more locations outside the United States? If you were in charge of global expansion for Groupon, what country would you enter next? What country would you avoid? To identify promising and not-so-promising foreign markets, go to the Groupon Wikipedia article (http://en.wikipedia.org/wiki/Groupon) and click on "Geographic Markets" to obtain a list of counties in which Groupon operates. Also go to http://news.bbc.co.uk/1/hi/country_profiles/default.stm to link to the Country Profiles Web site maintained by BBC News. Study the economic and political profiles of possible overseas locations, and answer the following questions:

1. Why do you think Groupon has been able to expand so quickly in the United States? Cite some of the challenges that it still faces in this country.
2. If you were in charge of global expansion at Groupon, which country would you enter next? Why do you think the Groupon business concept will succeed in this country? What challenges will the company face there?
3. What country would you avoid? Why is it incompatible with the Groupon business concept?

ENDNOTES

1. This vignette is based on the following sources: Realityworks Inc., "About Us," *Reality-works*, http://realityworks.com/about/realityworks-story (accessed May 3, 2014); Realityworks Inc., "RealCare Baby," *Realityworks* (2008), http://www.realityworks.com/products/realcare-baby (accessed May 3, 2014); "Realityworks Infant Simulator and RealCare Parenting Program," *Horizons Solutions Site* (August 17, 2007), http://www.solutions-site.org/node/222 (accessed May 3, 2014); Brenda Bredahl, "Bringing Up Baby," *BNET.com*, Corporate Report Wisconsin, January 2004, http://brendabredahl.blogspot.com/2007/09/business-writing.html (accessed May 3, 2014); "Have a Baby? I Think I'll Think It Over," *Horizons Solutions Site* (1998), http://www.solutions-site.org/kids/stories/KScat3_sol72.htm (accessed May 3, 2014); "'Baby' Helps Teens Think It Over!" *Education World*, May 25, 1998, http://www.education-world.com/a_curr/curr077.shtml (accessed May 3, 2014); Kate Stone Lombardi, "Doll Gives a Taste of Real Life," *New York Times*, May 24, 1998, http://www.nytimes.com/1998/05/24/nyregion/doll-gives-a-taste-of-real-life.html (accessed May 3, 2014); J. F. L., MD, "Dolls from Hell," *Pediatrics* 97, no. 3 (March 1996), http://pediatrics.aappublications.org/content/97/3/317.abstract (accessed May 3, 2014); Deborah L. Cohen, "Bringing Up Baby," *Education Week*, November 16, 1994, http://www.edweek.org/ew/articles/1994/11/16/11baby.h14.html (accessed May 3, 2014); "This Doll Tells the Young to Hold Off," *New York Times*, August 3, 1994, http://www.nytimes.com/1994/08/03/us/this-doll-tells-the-young-to-hold-off.html (accessed May 3, 2014).

2. Canadian Foundation for Economic Education, "Glossary of Terms," *Mentors, Ventures & Plans* (2008), http://www.mvp.cfee.org/en/glossary.html (accessed May 3, 2014).

3. Adapted from Marc J. Dollinger, *Entrepreneurship: Strategies and Resources*, 3rd ed. (Upper Saddle River, NJ: Prentice Hall, 2003), 5–7.

4. Isabel M. Isidro, "Geese Police: A Real-Life Home Business Success Story," *PowerHomeBiz.com* (2008), http://www.powerhomebiz.com/OnlineSuccess/geesepolice.htm (accessed May 3, 2014).

5. See American Academy of Achievement, "Pierre Omidyar," *Academy of Achievement* (November 9, 2005), http://www.achievement.org/autodoc/page/omi0bio-1 (accessed May 3, 2014).

6. Encyclopedia of World Biography, s.v. "Marcia Kilgore: Entrepreneur and spa founder," http://www.notablebiographies.com/newsmakers2/2006-Ei-La/Kilgore-Marcia.html (accessed May 3, 2014).

7. Jessica Bruder, "The Rise Of The Serial Entrepreneur," *Forbes*, August 12, 2010, http://www.forbes.com/2010/08/12/serial-entrepreneur-start-up-business-forbes-woman-entrepreneurs-management.html (accessed May 3, 2014).

8. U.S. Small Business Administration, "First Steps: How to Start a Small Business," http://www.sba.gov/starting/indexsteps.html (accessed April 21, 2006).

9. U.S. Small Business Administration, "Is Entrepreneurship for You?" http://www.sba.gov/content/entrepreneurship-you (accessed May 3, 2014).

10. Shari Waters, "Top Four Reasons People Don't Start a Business," *About.com*, http://retail.about.com/od/startingaretailbusiness/tp/overcome_fears.htm (accessed May 3, 2014).

11. Kathleen Allen, *Entrepreneurship for Dummies* (New York: Wiley, 2001), 14.

12. U.S. Small Business Administration, "What Is SBAs Definition of a Small Business Concern?" http://www.sba.gov/content/what-sbas-definition-small-business-concern (accessed May 4, 2014).

13. Office of Advocacy, U.S. Small Business Administration, *The Small Business Economy*, Appendix A (2012), http://www.sba.gov/advocacy/849/6282 (accessed May 4, 2014).

14. U.S. Small Business Administration, Office of Advocacy, "2014 Edition of Frequently Asked Questions about Small Businesses," *The Small Business Economy* (March 2014), http://www.sba.gov/sites/default/files/FAQ_March_2014_0.pdf (accessed May 4, 2014).

15. U.S. Small Business Administration, Office of Advocacy, "Firm Size Data," http://www.sba.gov/advocacy/849/12162 (accessed May 4, 2014).

16. Anthony Breitzman and Diana Hicks, "An Analysis of Small Business Patents by Industry and Firm Size, Office of Advocacy, Small Business Administration," *U.S. Small Business Administration*, http://archive.sba.gov/advo/research/rs335tot.pdf (accessed May 4, 2014).

17. William J. Baumol, "Small Firms: Why Market-Driven Innovation Can't Get Along without Them" (U.S. Small Business Administration, Office of Advocacy, December 2005), table 8.1, 186, http://www.sba.gov/advo/research/sbe_05_ch08.pdf (accessed May 4, 2014).

18. "Amazon Income Statement," *Yahoo! Finance*, http://finance.yahoo.com/q/is?s=AMZN+Income+Statement&annual (accessed May 4, 2014).

19. William J. Baumol, "Small Firms: Why Market-Driven Innovation Can't Get Along without Them" (U.S. Small Business Administration, Office of Advocacy, December 2005), http://www.sba.gov/advo/research/sbe_05_ch08.pdf (accessed May 4, 2014).

20. U.S. Census Bureau, "Estimates of Business Ownership by Gender, Ethnicity, Race, and Veteran Status: 2007," http://www.census.gov/econ/sbo/#hispanic (accessed May 4, 2014).

21. Bill Canis and Brent D. Yacobucci, "The U.S. Motor Vehicle Industry: Confronting a New Dynamic in the Global Economy, Congressional Research Service," *Federation of American Scientists*, http://www.fas.org/sgp/crs/misc/R41154.pdf (accessed May 4, 2014).

22. U.S. Census Bureau, "Survey of Business Owners (SBO)," http://www.census.gov/econ/sbo/07menu.html (accessed May 4, 2014).

23. "GDP Composition by Sector," The World Fact Book, https://www.cia.gov/library/publications/the-world-factbook/fields/2012.html (accessed August 31, 2011); U.S. Department of Commerce, Bureau of Economic Analysis, "New Quarterly Statistics Detail Industries' Economic Performance" (Table 5), news release, April 25, 2014, http://www.bea.gov/newsreleases/industry/gdpindustry/gdpindnewsrelease.htm (accessed May 4, 2014).

24. Go to Reveal Entertainment at http://www.revealgames.com (accessed May 4, 2014).

25. Jennifer Alsever, "EcoScraps' $1 Million Business Built on Trash," *CNN Money*, http://money.cnn.com/2011/09/23/smallbusiness/ecoscraps (accessed May 4, 2014).

26. Isabel Isidro, "Riding High on the Wave of Success, RedWagons.com," *PowerHomeBiz.com*, http://www.powerhomebiz.com/OnlineSuccess/redwagons.htm (accessed May 4, 2014).

27. "World's Billionaires: Mark Zuckerberg," *Forbes*, http://www.forbes.com/profile/mark-zuckerberg (accessed May 4, 2014).

28. Isabel M. Isidro, "Geese Police: A Real-Life Home Business Success Story," *PowerHomeBiz.com* (2008), http://www.powerhomebiz.com/OnlineSuccess/geesepolice.htm (accessed May 4, 2014); See http://www.youtube.com/watch?v=86veqLldnck (accessed May 4, 2014).

29. Small Business Development Center, "Pros and Cons of Owning a Business," http://www.siu.edu/sbdc/buscheck.htm+pros+and+cons+of+owning+a+business&hl=en&gl=us&ct=clnk&cd=1&ie=UTF-8 (accessed April 21, 2006).

30. Cicco and Associates Inc., "Type E Personality—Happy Days—Entrepreneurs Top Satisfaction Survey," *Entrepreneur.com*, http://www.entrepreneur.com/article/13764 (accessed April 21, 2006).

31. From Kathleen Allen, "Getting Started in Entrepreneurship," in *Entrepreneurship for Dummies* (New York: Wiley, 2001), 46.

32. Scott Thurm and Joann S. Lublin, "Peter Drucker's Legacy Includes Simple Advice: It's All about the People," *Wall Street Journal* (November 14, 2005, B1), http://online.wsj.com/news/articles/SB113192826302796041 (accessed May 4, 2014).

33. Peter Krass, "Sam Walton: 10 Rules for Building a Successful Business," http://www.powerhomebiz.com/vol76/walton.htm (accessed May 4, 2014).

34. Howard Schultz and Dori Jones Yang, *Pour Your Heart into It: How Starbucks Built a Company One Cup at a Time* (New York: Hyperion, 1997), 24–109.

35. Christopher Steiner, "Meet the Fastest Growing Company Ever," *Forbes*, http://www.forbes.com/forbes/2010/0830/entrepreneurs-groupon-facebook-twitter-next-web-phenom.html (accessed May 4, 2014).

36. Joan Lappin, "Two Years after Its Busted IPO, Groupon Still Can't Turn a Profit," *Forbes*, November 1, 2013, http://www.forbes.com/sites/joanlappin/2013/11/11/two-years-after-its-busted-ipo-groupon-still-cant-turn-a-profit (accessed May 4, 2014).

37. U.S. Census Bureau, "Census Bureau's First Release of Comprehensive Franchise Data Shows Franchises Make Up More Than 10 Percent of Employer Businesses," news release, September 14, 2010, http://www.census.gov/newsroom/releases/archives/economic_census/cb10-141.html (accessed May 4, 2014).

38. "2014 Franchise 500 Rankings," *Entrepreneur*, http://www.entrepreneur.com/franchises/rankings/franchise500-115608/2014,-4.html (accessed May 4, 2014).

39. Kara Ohngren Prior, "Franchises that Went Boom or Bust," *Entrepreneur*, http://www.entrepreneur.com/article/204372 (accessed May 4, 2014).

40. Michael Seid and Kay Marie Ainsley, "Franchise Fee—Made Simple," *Entrepreneur.com*, http://www.entrepreneur.com/article/0,4621,299085,00.html (accessed May 4, 2014).

41. Southwest Airlines Co., "About Southwest," http://www.southwest.com/about_swa/mission.html (accessed May 4, 2014).

42. The Coca-Cola Company, "Our Company: Mission, Vision and Values," http://www.coca-colacompany.com/our-company/mission-vision-values (accessed May 4, 2014).

43. D&B Inc., "D&B—The Challenges of Managing a Small Business," http://www.dnbexpress.ca/ChallengesSmallBusiness.html (accessed May 4, 2014).

44. Amy E. Knaup and Merissa C. Piazza, "Characteristics of Survival: Longevity of Business Establishments in the Business Employment Dynamics Data: Extensions," *Bureau of Labor Statistics*, http://www.bls.gov/osmr/pdf/st060040.pdf (accessed May 4, 2014); Amy E. Knaup and Merissa C. Piazza, "Business Employment Dynamics Data: Survival and Longevity, II, Monthly Labor Review • September 2007," *Bureau of Labor Statistics*, http://www.bls.gov/opub/mlr/2007/09/art1full.pdf (accessed May 4, 2014).

45. Maureen Farrell, "Risky Business: 44% of Small Firms Reach Year 4," *Forbes*, February 16, 2007, http://www.msnbc.msn.com/id/16872553/ns/business-forbes_com/t/risky-business-small-firms-reach-year/#.Tl_xVY7CclA (accessed May 4, 2014).

46. U.S. Small Business Administration, "Office of Small Business Development Centers: Entrepreneurial Development," *Services*, http://www.sba.gov/aboutsba/sbaprograms/sbdc/index.html (accessed May 4, 2014).

47. U.S. Small Business Administration, *SCORE—Counselors to America's Small Businesses*, http://www.score.org/index.html (accessed May 4, 2014).

CHAPTER 6
Managing for Business Success

NOTEWORTHY MANAGEMENT

Consider this scenario. You're about halfway through the semester and ready for your first round of midterms. You open up your class notes and declare them "pathetic." You regret scribbling everything so carelessly (and skipping class so many times). You wish you had better notes. That's when it hits you: What if there was a note-taking service on campus? When you were ready to study for a big test, you could buy complete (and completely legible) class notes. You've heard that there are class-notes services at some larger schools, but there's no such thing on your campus. So you ask yourself, why don't I start a note-taking business? My upcoming set of exams may not be salvageable, but after that, I'd always have great notes. And while I was at it, I could learn how to manage a business (isn't that what majoring in business is all about?).

1. WHAT DO MANAGERS DO?

LEARNING OBJECTIVES

1. Define the terms "effective" and "efficient."
2. Identify the four interrelated functions of management (planning, organizing, directing, and controlling), and indicate what each function of management accomplishes.

So you sit down to work on your great business idea. First, you'll hire a bunch of students to take class notes and type them out. Then the notetakers will e-mail the notes to your assistant, who'll get them copied (on a special type of blue paper that can't be duplicated). The last step will be assembling packages of notes and, of course, selling them. You decide to name your company "Notes-4-You."

It sounds like a great idea, but you're troubled by one question: Why does this business need *you*? Do the notetakers need a boss? Couldn't they just sell the notes themselves? This process *could* work, but it would probably work a lot *better* if there was someone to oversee the operations: a manager—someone like you—to make sure that the operations involved in preparing and selling notes were performed in both an effective and an efficient manner. You'd make the process *effective* by ensuring that the right things got done and that they all contributed to the success of the enterprise. You'd make the process *efficient* by ensuring that activities were performed in the right way and used the fewest possible resources. That's the job that you perform as a **manager**: making a group of people more *effective* and *efficient* with you than they would be without you.

Would you be willing to pay someone for a complete set of class notes for this course?

© 2010 Jupiterimages Corporation

manager

Individual in an organization who is responsible for making a group of people more effective and efficient.

Managerial Efficiency and Effectiveness

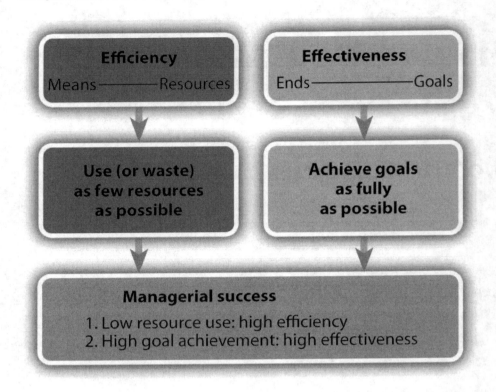

management

Process of planning for, organizing, directing, and controlling a company's resources so that it can achieve its goals.

You'll accomplish this task through **management**: the process of planning, organizing, directing, and controlling resources to achieve specific goals. A *plan* enables you to take your business concept beyond the idea stage. It does not, however, get the work *done*. You have to *organize* things if you want your plan to become a reality. You have to put people and other resources in place to make things happen. And because your note-taking venture is supposed to be better off with you in charge, you need to be a *leader* who can motivate your people to do well. Finally, to know whether things are in fact going well, you'll have to *control* your operations—that is, measure the results and compare them with the results that you laid out in your plan. Figure 6.1 gives you a good idea of the interrelationship between planning and the other functions that managers perform.

FIGURE 6.1 The Role of Planning

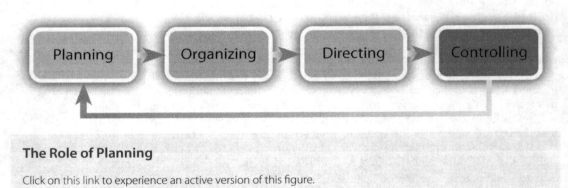

The Role of Planning

Click on this link to experience an active version of this figure.

1.1 Functions of Management

If you visit any small or large company, not-for-profit organization, or government agency, you'll find managers doing the same things you'd be doing to run your note-taking business—*planning, organizing, directing,* and *controlling*. In the rest of the chapter, we'll look at these four interrelated functions in detail.

Before going to the next section of this chapter, take a few minutes to test your knowledge of the material covered in this section. Quizzes can be found under the "Resources" tab, "Study Aids: Quizzes."

EXERCISE

Consider the things that the principal of your old high school had to do to ensure that the school met the needs of its students. Identify these activities and group them by the four functions of management: planning, organizing, directing, and controlling.

2. PLANNING

LEARNING OBJECTIVES

1. Understand the process by which a company develops and implements a strategic plan.
2. Prepare a mission statement that describes the purpose of an organization.
3. Define "core values," and provide some examples.
4. Use SWOT analysis to assess the company's strengths, weaknesses, opportunities, and threats.
5. Discuss the importance of setting goals and objectives, or performance targets, to achieve an organization's mission.
6. Explain how tactical plans are used to implement a company's strategic plan over a period of time.
7. Explain how operational plans, or detailed action steps, are used to implement tactical plans.
8. Understand the importance of crisis management, and provide an example of positive crisis management implementation and a negative implementation.

Without a plan, it's hard to succeed at anything. The reason is simple: if you don't know where you're going, you can't really move forward. Successful managers decide where they want to be and then figure out how to get there. In **planning**, managers set goals and determine the best way to achieve them. As a result of the planning process, everyone in the organization knows what should be done, who should do it, and how it should be done.

planning

Process of setting goals and determining the best way to achieve them.

2.1 Developing a Strategic Plan

Coming up with an idea—say, starting a note-taking business—is a good start, but it's only a start. Planning for it is a step forward. Planning begins at the highest level and works its way down through the organization. Step one is usually called **strategic planning**, which is the process of establishing an overall course of action. To begin this process, you should ask yourself a couple of very basic questions: Why, for example, does the organization exist? What value does it create? Sam Walton posed these questions in the process of founding Wal-Mart: his new chain of stores would exist to offer customers the lowest prices with the best possible service.[1]

strategic planning

Process of establishing an overall plan or course of action for an organization.

After you've identified the purpose of your company, you're ready to take the remaining steps in the strategic-planning process:

- Write a mission statement that tells customers, employees, and others why your organization exists.
- Identify core values or beliefs that will guide the behavior of members of the organization.
- Assess the company's strengths, weaknesses, opportunities, and threats.
- Establish goals and objectives, or performance targets, to direct all the activities that you'll perform to achieve your mission.
- Develop and implement tactical and operational plans to achieve goals and objectives.

In the next few sections, we'll examine these components of the strategic-planning process.

2.2 Mission Statement

As we saw in an earlier chapter, the *mission statement* describes the purpose of your organization—the reason for its existence. It tells the reader what the organization is committed to doing. It can be very concise, like the one from Mary Kay Inc. (the cosmetics company): "To enrich the lives of women around the world."[2] Or it can be as detailed as the one from Harley-Davidson: "We fulfill dreams inspired by the many roads of the world by providing extraordinary motorcycles and customer experiences. We fuel the passion for freedom in our customers to express their own individuality."[3]

FIGURE 6.2

Harley-Davidson has a very focused mission statement—it's all about the motorcycles.

© 2010 Jupiterimages Corporation

What about Notes-4-You? What should your mission statement say? A simple, concise mission statement for your enterprise could be the following: "To provide high-quality class notes to college students." On the other hand, you could prepare a more detailed statement that explains what the company is committed to doing, who its customers are, what its focus is, what goods or services it provides, and how it serves its customers. In that case, your mission statement might be the following:

Notes-4-You is committed to earning the loyalty of college students through its focus on customer service. It provides high-quality, dependable, competitively priced class notes that help college students master complex academic subjects.

2.3   Core Values

Having defined your mission, your next step is to ask, what does this organization stand for? What values will define it? What principles should guide our actions as we build and operate the business? In Chapter 2, we explained that the small set of guiding principles that you identify as crucial to your company are known as *core values*—fundamental beliefs about what's important and what is and isn't appropriate in conducting company activities. Core values affect the overall planning processes and operations. At Volvo, for example, three core values—quality, safety, and environmental care—define the firm's "approach to product development, design and production."[4] Core values should also guide the behavior of every individual in the organization. Coca-Cola, for instance, reports that its stated core values—leadership, collaboration, integrity, accountability, passion, diversity, and quality—tell employees exactly what behaviors are acceptable.[5] How do companies communicate core values to employees and hold them accountable for putting those values into practice? They link core values to performance evaluations and compensation.

In choosing core values for Notes-4-You, you're determined not to fall back on some list of the world's most popular core values: ethics/integrity, accountability, respect for others, and open communication.[6] You want yours to be unique to Notes-4-You. After some thought, you settle on *teamwork, trust,* and *dependability*. Why these three? As you plan your business, you realize that it will need a workforce that functions as a team, trusts each other, and can be depended on to satisfy customers. In building your workforce, you'll seek employees who'll embrace these values.

2.4   Conduct a SWOT Analysis

The next step in the strategic-planning process is to assess your company's fit with its environment. A common approach to *environmental analysis* is matching the strengths of your business with the opportunities available to it. It's called **SWOT analysis** because it calls for analyzing an organization's Strengths, Weaknesses, Opportunities, and Threats. It begins with an examination of *external* factors that could influence the company in either a positive or a negative way. These could include economic conditions, competition, emerging technologies, laws and regulations, and customers' expectations.

One purpose of assessing the external environment is to identify both *opportunities* that could benefit the company and *threats* to its success. For example, a company that manufactures children's bicycle helmets would view a change in federal law requiring all children to wear helmets as an opportunity. The news that two large sports-equipment companies were coming out with bicycle helmets would be a threat.

The next step is to evaluate the company's strengths and weaknesses. *Strengths* might include a motivated workforce, state-of-the-art technology, impressive managerial talent, or a desirable location. The opposite of any of these strengths (poor workforce, obsolete technology, incompetent management, or poor location) could signal a potential *weakness*. Armed with a good idea of external opportunities and threats, as well as internal strengths and weaknesses, managers want to capitalize on opportunities by taking advantage of organizational strengths. Likewise, they want to protect the organization from both external threats and internal weaknesses.

Let's start with our strengths. Now that we know what they are, how do we match them with our available opportunities (while also protecting ourselves from our threats and overcoming our weaknesses)? Here's a possibility: By providing excellent service and price while we're still small (with few customers and low costs), we can solidify our position on campus. When the market grows (as it will, because of the increase in the number of classes—especially those at 8:00 a.m.—and increases in student enrollment), we'll have built a strong reputation and will put ourselves in a position to grow. So even if a competitor comes to campus (a threat), we'll be the preferred supplier of class notes. This strategy will work only if we make sure that our notetakers are dependable and that we don't alienate the faculty or administration.

SWOT analysis

Approach used to assess a company's fit with its environment by analyzing its strengths, weaknesses, opportunities, and threats.

SWOT Analysis

Take a few minutes to test your understanding of SWOT analysis. Click here to complete the exercise.

2.5 Set Goals and Objectives

Goals

Major accomplishments that a company wants to achieve over a long period of time.

Objectives

Intermediate-term performance targets that direct the activities of an organization toward the attainment of a goal.

Your mission statement affirms what your organization is *generally* committed to doing, but it doesn't tell you *how* to do it. So the next step in the strategic-planning process is establishing goals and objectives. **Goals** are major accomplishments that the company wants to achieve over a long period (say, five years). **Objectives** are shorter-term performance targets that direct the activities of the organization toward the attainment of a goal. They should be clearly stated, attainable, and measurable: they should give target dates for the completion of tasks and stipulate who's responsible for taking necessary actions.[7]

An organization will have a number of goals and related objectives. Some will focus on financial measures, such as profit maximization and sales growth. Others will target operational efficiency or quality control. Still others will govern the company's relationships with its employees, its community, its environment, or all three.

Finally, goals and objectives change over time. As a firm reassesses its place in its business environment, it rethinks not only its mission but also its approach to fulfilling it. The reality of change was a major theme when the late McDonald's CEO Jim Cantalupo explained his goal to revitalize the company:

> *The world has changed. Our customers have changed. We have to change too. Growth comes from being better, not just expanding to have more restaurants. The new McDonald's is focused on building sales at existing restaurants rather than on adding new restaurants. We are introducing a new level of discipline and efficiency to all aspects of the business and are setting a new bar for performance.*[8]

This change in focus was accompanied by specific performance objectives—annual sales growth of 3 to 5 percent and income growth of 6 to 7 percent at existing restaurants, plus a five-point improvement (based on customer surveys) in speed of service, friendliness, and food quality.

In setting strategic goals and performance objectives for Notes-4-You, you should keep things simple. Because you know you need to make money to stay in business, you could include a financial goal (and related objectives). Your mission statement promises "high-quality, dependable, competitively priced class notes," so you could focus on the quality of the class notes that you'll be taking and distributing. Finally, because your mission is to serve students, one goal could be customer oriented. When all's said and done, your list of goals and objectives might look like this:

- **Goal 1**: Achieve a 10 percent return on profits in your first five years.
  - *Objective*: Sales of $20,000 and profit of $2,000 for the first twelve months of operations.
- **Goal 2**: Produce a high-quality product.
  - *Objective*: First-year satisfaction scores of 90 percent or higher on quality of notes (based on survey responses to three measures—understandability, readability, and completeness).
- **Goal 3**: Attain 98 percent customer satisfaction by the end of your fifth year.
  - *Objective*: Making notes available within two days after class, 95 percent of the time.

2.6 Develop Tactical and Operational Plans

The planning process begins at the top of the organization, where upper-level managers create a strategic plan, but it doesn't end there. The *execution* of the strategic plan involves managers at all levels.

Tactical Plans

tactical plans

Short-term plans that specify the activities and resources needed to implement a company's strategic plan.

The overall plan is broken down into more manageable, shorter-term components called **tactical plans**. These plans specify the activities and allocation of resources (people, equipment, money) needed to implement the overall strategic plan over a given period. Often, a long-range strategic plan is divided into several tactical plans; a five-year strategic plan, for instance, might be implemented as five one-year tactical plans.

Operational Plans

The tactical plan is then broken down into various **operational plans** that provide detailed action steps to be taken by individuals or groups to implement the tactical plan and, consequently, the strategic plan. Operational plans cover only a brief period—say, a week or a month. At Notes-4-You, for example, notetakers might be instructed to turn in typed class notes five hours earlier than normal on the last day of the semester (an operational guideline). The goal is to improve the customer-satisfaction score on dependability (a *tactical goal*) and, as a result, to earn the loyalty of students through attention to customer service (a *strategic goal*).

operational plans

Detailed action steps to be taken by individuals or groups to implement tactical plans.

2.7 Plan for Contingencies and Crises

Even with great planning, things don't always turn out the way they're supposed to. Perhaps your plans were flawed, or maybe you had great plans but something in the environment shifted unexpectedly. Successful managers anticipate and plan for the unexpected. Dealing with uncertainty requires *contingency planning* and *crisis management*.

Contingency Planning

With **contingency planning**, managers identify those aspects of the business that are most likely to be adversely affected by change. Then, they develop alternative courses of action in case an anticipated change does occur. You probably do your own contingency planning: for example, if you're planning to take in a sure-fire hit movie on its release date, you may decide on an alternative movie in case you can't get tickets to your first choice.

contingency planning

Process of identifying courses of action to be taken in the event that a business is adversely affected by a change.

Crisis Management

Organizations also face the risk of encountering crises that require immediate attention. Rather than waiting until such a crisis occurs and then scrambling to figure out what to do, many firms practice **crisis management**. Some, for instance, set up teams trained to deal with emergencies. Members gather information quickly and respond to the crisis while everyone else carries out his or her normal duties. The team also keeps the public, the employees, the press, and government officials informed about the situation and the company's response to it.[9]

crisis management

Action plans that outline steps to be taken by a company in case of a crisis.

An example of how to handle crisis management involves Wendy's. After learning that a woman claimed she found a fingertip in a bowl of chili she bought at a Wendy's restaurant in San Jose, California, the company's public relations team responded quickly. Within a few days, the company announced that the finger didn't come from an employee or a supplier. Soon after, the police arrested the woman and charged her with attempted grand larceny for lying about how the finger got in her bowl of chili and trying to extort $2.5 million from the company. But the crisis wasn't over for Wendy's. The incident was plastered all over the news as a grossed-out public sought an answer to the question, "Whose finger is (or was) it?" A $100,000 reward was offered by Wendy's to anyone with information that would help the police answer this question. The challenge Wendy's faced was how to entice customers to return to its fifty San Francisco–area restaurants (where sales had plummeted) while keeping a low profile nationally. It accomplished this by giving out free milkshakes and discount coupons to customers in the affected regions and, to avoid calling attention to the missing finger, by making no changes in its national advertising. The crisis-management strategy worked and the story died down (though it flared up temporarily when the police arrested the woman's husband, who allegedly bought the finger from a coworker who had severed it in an accident months earlier).[10]

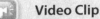

Video Clip

The response to the BP oil spill by its former CEO, Tony Hayward, is an example of poor crisis management.

View the video online at: http://www.youtube.com/embed/MTdKa9eWNFw

Even with crisis-management plans in place, however, it's unlikely that most companies will emerge from a damaging or potentially damaging episode as unscathed as Wendy's did. For one thing, the culprits in the Wendy's case were caught, and the public is willing to forgive an organization it views as a victim. Given the current public distrust of corporate behavior, however, companies whose reputations have suffered due to questionable corporate judgment don't fare as well. These companies include the international oil company, BP, whose CEO, Tony Hayward, did a disastrous job handling the crisis created when a BP controlled oil rig exploded in the Gulf Coast killing eleven workers and creating the largest oil spill in U.S. history. Hayward's lack of sensitivity will be remembered forever; particularly his response to a reporter's question on what he would tell those whose livelihoods were ruined: "We're sorry for the massive disruption it's caused their lives. There's no one who wants this over more than I do. I would like my life back." His comment was obviously upsetting to the families of the eleven men who lost their lives on the rig and had no way to get their lives back.[11]

Then, there are the companies at which executives have crossed the line between the unethical to the downright illegal—Arthur Andersen, Enron, and Bernard L. Madoff Investment Securities, to name just a few. Given the high risk associated with a crisis, it should come as no surprise that contemporary managers spend more time anticipating crises and practicing their crisis-management responses.

KEY TAKEAWAYS

- Successful managers decide where they want the organization to go and then determine how to get there.
- **Planning** for a business starts at the top and works its way down.
- It begins with **strategic planning**—the process of establishing an overall course of action.
- Step one is identifying the purpose of the organization.
- Then, management is ready to take the remaining steps in the strategic planning process:
    1. Prepare a *mission statement* that describes the purpose of the organization and tells customers, employees, and others what it's committed to doing.
    2. Select the *core values* that will guide the behavior of members of the organization by letting them know what is and isn't appropriate and important in conducting company activities.
    3. Use **SWOT analysis** to assess the company's strengths and weaknesses and its fit with the external environment.
    4. Set **goals** and **objectives**, or performance targets, to direct all the activities needed to achieve the organization's mission.
    5. Develop **tactical plans** and **operational plans** to implement objectives.

Before going to the next section of this chapter, take a few minutes to test your knowledge of the material covered in this section. Quizzes can be found under the "Resources" tab, "Study Aids: Quizzes."

EXERCISES

1. Without a plan, it's hard to succeed. Successful managers set goals and determine the best ways to reach them. Successful students do the same thing. Develop a strategic plan for succeeding in this course that includes the following steps:

    1.1. Assess your strengths, weaknesses, opportunities, and threats as they relate to this course.

    1.2. Establish goals and objectives, or performance targets, to direct all the activities that you'll perform to earn a high grade in this course.

    1.3. Describe tactical and operational plans for achieving your stated goals and objectives.

2. If you were the CEO of a large organization, what core values would you want to guide the behavior of your employees? First, assume that you oversee a large company that manufactures and sells medical devices, such as pacemakers, defibrillators, and insulin pumps. Your company was a pioneer in bringing these products to the market. Identify six core values that you would want to guide the behavior of your employees. For each core value, be sure to do the following:

    - Indicate why it's important to the functioning of the organization.
    - Explain how you'll communicate it to your employees and encourage them to embrace it.
    - Outline the approaches that you'll take in holding employees accountable for embracing it.

    Now, repeat the process. This time, however, assume that you're the CEO of a company that rents movies and games at more than eight thousand outlets across the country.

---

3. ORGANIZING

LEARNING OBJECTIVES

1. **Indicate the responsibilities and authority for each of the three levels of management: top managers, middle managers, and first-line managers.**

2. **Develop an organizational structure, or arrangement of people within the organization, that will best achieve company goals.**

3. **Define the terms "specialization" and "departmentalization."**

4. **Discuss the following options for organizing a business: functional, divisional, product, customer, process, or geographical division.**

5. **Understand how to create an organization chart—a diagram showing the reporting relationships of those in the organization.**

6. **Define the following concepts: "chain of command" and "span of control."**

7. **Contrast centralized and decentralized decision making.**

Now that you've developed a strategic plan for Notes-4-You, you need to organize your company so that it can implement your plan. A manager engaged in **organizing** allocates *resources* (people, equipment, and money) to achieve a company's plans. Successful managers make sure that all the activities identified in the planning process are assigned to some person, department, or team and that everyone has the resources needed to perform assigned activities.

organizing

Management process of allocating resources to achieve a company's plans.

3.1   Levels of Management: How Managers Are Organized

A typical organization has several layers of management. Think of these layers as forming a pyramid like the one in Figure 6.3, with top managers occupying the narrow space at the peak, first-line managers the broad base, and middle-managers the levels in between. As you move up the pyramid, management positions get more demanding, but they carry more authority and responsibility (along with more power, prestige, and pay). Top managers spend most of their time in planning and decision making, while first-line managers focus on day-to-day operations. For obvious reasons, there are far more people with positions at the base of the pyramid than there are with jobs at the other two levels (as you get to the top, there are only a few positions). Let's look at each management level in more detail.

FIGURE 6.3 Levels of Management

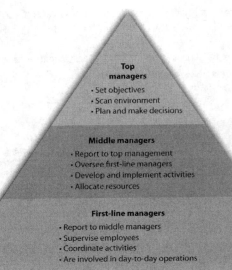

Top Managers

Top managers are responsible for the health and performance of the organization. They set the objectives, or performance targets, designed to direct all the activities that must be performed if the company is going to fulfill its mission. Top-level executives routinely scan the external environment for opportunities and threats, and they redirect company efforts when needed. They spend a considerable portion of their time planning and making major decisions. They represent the company in important dealings with other businesses and government agencies, and they promote it to the public. Job titles at this level typically include *chief executive officer (CEO)*, *chief financial officer (CFO)*, *chief operating officer (COO)*, *president*, and *vice president*.

Middle Managers

As the name implies, **middle managers** are in the "middle" of the management hierarchy: They report to top management and oversee the activities of first-line managers. They're responsible for developing and implementing activities and allocating the resources needed to achieve the objectives set by top management. Common job titles include *operations manager, division manager, plant manager*, and *branch manager*.

First-Line Managers

First-line managers supervise employees and coordinate their activities to make sure that the work performed throughout the company is consistent with the plans of both top and middle management. They're less involved in planning than higher-level managers and more involved in day-to-day operations. It's at this level that most people acquire their first managerial experience. The job titles vary considerably but include such designations as *department head, group leader, office manager, foreman*, and *supervisor*.

Let's take a quick survey of the management hierarchy at Notes-4-You. As president, you are, of course, a member of *top management*, and you're responsible for the overall performance of your company. You spend much of your time setting objectives, or performance targets, to ensure that the company meets the goals you've set for it—increased sales, higher-quality notes, and timely distribution.

Several *middle managers* report to you, including your operations manager. As a middle manager, this individual focuses on implementing two of your objectives: producing high-quality notes and distributing them to customers in a timely manner. To accomplish this task, the operations manager oversees the work of two *first-line managers*—the note-taking supervisor and the copying supervisor. Each first-line manager supervises several non-managerial employees to make sure that their work is consistent with the plans devised by top and middle management.

3.2 Organizational Structure: How Companies Get the Job Done

The organizing process raises some important questions: What jobs need to be done? Who does what? Who reports to whom? What are the formal relationships among people in the organization? You provide answers to these questions by developing an **organizational structure**: an arrangement of positions that's most appropriate for your company at a specific point in time. Remember, given the rapidly changing environment in which businesses operate, a structure that works today might be outdated tomorrow. That's why you hear so often about companies **restructuring**—altering existing organizational structures to become more competitive under conditions that have changed. In building an organizational structure, you engage in two activities: *job specialization* (dividing tasks into jobs) and *departmentalization* (grouping jobs into units). We'll now see how these two processes are accomplished.

Specialization

The first step in designing an organizational structure is twofold:

1. Identifying the activities that need to be performed in order to achieve organizational goals.
2. Breaking down these activities into tasks that can be performed by individuals or groups of employees.

This twofold process of organizing activities into clusters of related tasks that can be handled by certain individuals or groups is called **specialization**. Its purpose is to improve efficiency.

Would specialization make Notes-4-You more efficient? You could have each employee perform all tasks entailed by taking and selling notes. Each employee could take notes in an assigned class, type them up, get them copied, and sell them outside the classroom at the start of the next class meeting. The same person would keep track of all sales and copying costs and give any profit—sales minus copying costs minus compensation—to you. The process seems simple, but is it really *efficient*? Will you earn the maximum amount of profit? Probably not. Even a company as small as Notes-4-You can benefit from specialization. It would function more efficiently if some employees specialized in taking notes, others in copying and packaging them, and still others in selling them. Higher-level employees could focus on advertising, accounting, finance, and human resources.

Obviously, specialization has advantages. In addition to increasing efficiency, for example, it results in jobs that are easier to learn. But it has disadvantages, too. Doing the same thing over and over bores people and will eventually leave employees dissatisfied with their jobs. Before long, you'll notice decreased performance and increased absenteeism and turnover.

Departmentalization

The next step in designing an organizational structure is **departmentalization**—grouping specialized jobs into meaningful units. Depending on the organization and the size of the work units, they may be called *divisions, departments,* or just plain *groups.* Traditional groupings of jobs result in different organizational structures, and for the sake of simplicity, we'll focus on two types—*functional* and *divisional organizations.*

Functional Organization

A **functional organization** groups together people who have comparable skills and perform similar tasks. This form of organization is fairly typical for small to medium-size companies, which group their people by business functions: accountants are grouped together, as are people in finance, marketing and sales, human resources, production, and research and development. Each unit is headed by an individual with expertise in the unit's particular function. The head of an accounting department, for example, will be a senior accountant; the head of a hospital nursing unit will obviously be an experienced nurse. This structure is also appropriate for nonprofits. Think about your school, for instance: mathematics teachers are in the math department, history teachers are in the history department, those who run athletic programs are in the athletic department, and librarians work at the library.

If Notes-4-You adopted a functional approach to departmentalization, jobs might be grouped into four clusters:

- Human resources (hiring, training, and evaluating employees)
- Operations (overseeing notetakers and copiers)
- Marketing (arranging for advertising, sales, and distribution)
- Accounting (handling cash collection and disbursement)

There are a number of advantages to the functional approach. The structure is simple to understand and enables the staff to specialize in particular areas; everyone in the marketing group would probably

---

organizational structure

Organizational arrangement of jobs in an organization that's most appropriate for the company at a specific point in time.

restructuring

Process of altering an existing organizational structure to become more competitive under changing conditions.

specialization

Process of organizing activities into clusters of related tasks that can be handled by specific individuals or groups.

departmentalization

Process of grouping specialized jobs into meaningful units.

functional organization

Form of business organization that groups together people who have comparable skills and perform similar tasks.

have similar interests and expertise. But homogeneity also has drawbacks: it can hinder communication and decision making between units and even promote interdepartmental conflict. The marketing department, for example, might butt heads with the accounting department because marketers want to spend as much as possible on advertising, while accountants want to control costs. Marketers might feel that accountants are too tight with funds, and accountants might regard marketers as spendthrifts.

Divisional Organization

Large companies often find it unruly to operate as one large unit under a functional organizational structure. Sheer size makes it difficult for managers to oversee operations and serve customers. To rectify this problem, most large companies are structured as **divisional organizations** made up of several smaller, self-contained units, or divisions, which are accountable for their own performance. Each division functions autonomously because it contains all the functional expertise (production, marketing, accounting, finance, human resources) needed to meet its objectives. The challenge is to find the most appropriate way of structuring operations to achieve overall company goals. Toward this end, divisions can be formed according to *products, customers, processes,* or *geography.*

Product Division

Product division means that a company is structured according to its product lines. General Motors, for example, has four product-based divisions: Buick, Cadillac, Chevrolet, and GMC.[12] Each division has its own research and development group, its own manufacturing operations, and its own marketing team. This allows individuals in the division to focus all their efforts on the products produced by their division. A downside is that it results in higher costs as corporate support services (such as accounting and human resources) are duplicated in each of the four divisions.

Customer Division

FIGURE 6.4

If you had a question about a Johnson & Johnson product, you'd be directed to its consumer business customer division.

Some companies prefer a **customer division** structure because it enables them to better serve their various categories of customers. Thus, Johnson & Johnson's two hundred or so operating companies are grouped into three customer-based business segments: consumer business (personal-care and hygiene products sold to the general public), pharmaceuticals (prescription drugs sold to pharmacists), and professional business (medical devices and diagnostics products used by physicians, optometrists, hospitals, laboratories, and clinics).[13]

Process Division

If goods move through several steps during production, a company might opt for a **process division** structure. This form works well at Bowater Thunder Bay, a Canadian company that harvests trees and processes wood into newsprint and pulp. The first step in the production process is harvesting and stripping trees. Then, large logs are sold to lumber mills and smaller logs chopped up and sent to Bowater's mills. At the mill, wood chips are chemically converted into pulp. About 90 percent is sold to other manufacturers (as raw material for home and office products), and the remaining 10 percent is further processed into newspaper print. Bowater, then, has three divisions: tree cutting, chemical processing, and finishing (which makes newsprint).[14]

Geographical Division

Geographical division enables companies that operate in several locations to be responsive to customers at a local level. McDonald's, for example, is organized according to the regions of the world in which it operates. In the United States, the national unit is further subdivided into three geographic operating divisions: east, west and central.[15] (This approach might be appealing to Notes-4-You if it expands to serve schools around the country.)

There are pluses and minuses associated with divisional organization. On the one hand, divisional structure usually enhances the ability to respond to changes in a firm's environment. If, on the other hand, services must be duplicated across units, costs will be higher. In addition, some companies have found that units tend to focus on their own needs and goals at the expense of the organization as a whole.

3.3   The Organization Chart

Once an organization has set its structure, it can represent that structure in an **organization chart**: a diagram delineating the interrelationships of positions within the organization. Having decided that Notes-4-You will adopt a functional structure, you might create the organization chart shown in Figure 6.5.

FIGURE 6.5   Organization Chart for Notes-4-You

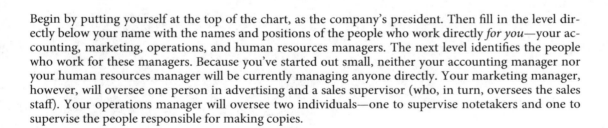

Begin by putting yourself at the top of the chart, as the company's president. Then fill in the level directly below your name with the names and positions of the people who work directly *for you*—your accounting, marketing, operations, and human resources managers. The next level identifies the people who work for these managers. Because you've started out small, neither your accounting manager nor your human resources manager will be currently managing anyone directly. Your marketing manager, however, will oversee one person in advertising and a sales supervisor (who, in turn, oversees the sales staff). Your operations manager will oversee two individuals—one to supervise notetakers and one to supervise the people responsible for making copies.

Reporting Relationships

With these relationships in mind, you can now draw lines to denote **reporting relationships**, or patterns of formal communication. Because four managers report to you, you'll be connected to four positions; that is, you'll have four direct "reports." Your marketing and operations managers will each be connected to two positions and their supervisors to one position each. The organization chart shows that if a member of the sales staff has a problem, he or she will report it to the sales supervisor. If the sales supervisor believes that the problem should be addressed at a higher level, then he or she will report it to the marketing manager.

Theoretically, you will communicate only with your four direct reports, but this isn't the way things normally work. Behind every formal communication network there lies a network of informal communications—unofficial relationships among members of an organization. You might find that over time, you receive communications directly from members of the sales staff; in fact, you might encourage this line of communication.

Now let's look at the chart of an organization that relies on a divisional structure based on goods or services produced—say, a theme park. The top layers of this company's organization chart might look like the one in Figure 6.6(a). We see that the president has two direct reports—a vice president in charge of rides and a vice president in charge of concessions. What about a bank that's structured according to its customer base? The bank's organization chart would begin like the one in Figure 6.6(b). Once again, the company's top manager has two direct reports, in this case a VP of retail-customer accounts and a VP of commercial-customer accounts.

FIGURE 6.6 Organization Charts for Divisional Structures

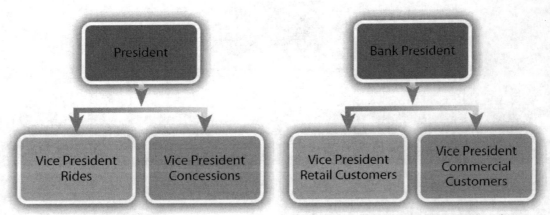

(a) Divisional structure by product   **(b)** Divisional structure by customer base

Over time, companies revise their organizational structures to accommodate growth and changes in the external environment. It's not uncommon, for example, for a firm to adopt a functional structure in its early years. Then, as it becomes bigger and more complex, it might move to a divisional structure—perhaps to accommodate new products or to become more responsive to certain customers or geographical areas. Some companies might ultimately rely on a combination of functional and divisional structures. This could be a good approach for a credit card company that issues cards in both the United States and Europe. A skeleton of this firm's organization chart might look like the one in Figure 6.7.

FIGURE 6.7 Organization Chart: Combination Divisional and Functional Structures

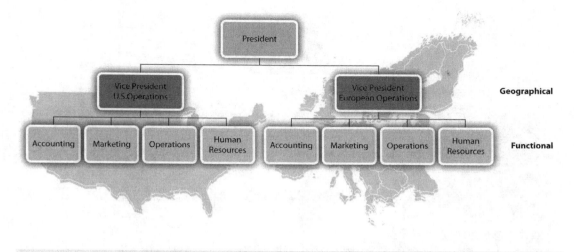

Organization Chart: Combination Divisional and Functional Structures

Click on this link to experience an active version of this figure.

Lines of Authority

You can learn a lot about a firm's reporting and authority relationships by looking at its organization chart. To whom does a particular person report? Does each person report to one or more supervisors? How many people does a manager supervise? How many layers are there, for example, between the top managerial position and the lowest managerial level?

Chain of Command

The vertical connecting lines in the organization chart show the firm's **chain of command**: the authority relationships among people working at different levels of the organization. That is to say, they show *who reports to whom*. When you're examining an organization chart, you'll probably want to know whether each person reports to one or more supervisors: to what extent, in other words, is there *unity of command*? To understand why unity of command is an important organizational feature, think about it from a personal standpoint. Would you want to report to more than one boss? What happens if you get conflicting directions? Whose directions would you follow?

There are, however, conditions under which an organization and its employees can benefit by violating the unity-of-command principle. Under a **matrix structure**, for example, employees from various functional areas (product design, manufacturing, finance, marketing, human resources, etc.) form teams to combine their skills in working on a specific project or product. This matrix organization chart might look like the one in the following figure.

chain of command

Authority and reporting relationships among people working at different levels of an organization.

matrix structure

Structure in which employees from various functional areas form teams to combine their skills in working on a specific project.

FIGURE 6.8 Organization Chart: Matrix Structure

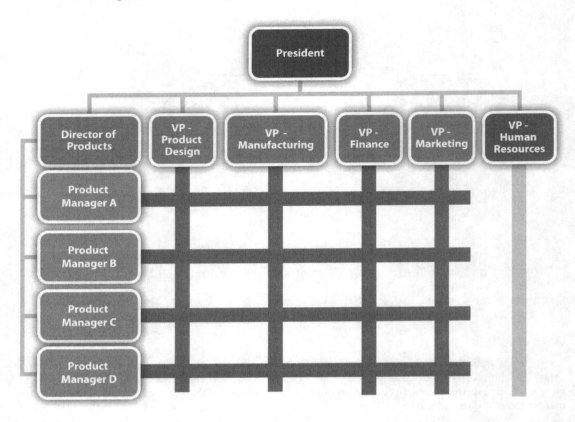

Nike sometimes uses this type of arrangement. To design new products, the company may create product teams made up of designers, marketers, and other specialists with expertise in particular sports categories—say, running shoes or basketball shoes. Each team member would be evaluated by both the team manager and the head of his or her functional department.

Span of Control

Another thing to notice about a firm's chain of command is the number of layers between the top managerial position and the lowest managerial level. As a rule, new organizations (such as Notes-4-You) have only a few layers of management—an organizational structure that's often called *flat*. Let's say, for instance, that a member of the Notes-4-You sales staff wanted to express concern about slow sales among a certain group of students. That person's message would have to filter upward through only two management layers—the sales supervisor and the marketing manager—before reaching the president.

As a company grows, however, it tends to add more layers between the top and the bottom; that is, it gets *taller*. Added layers of management can slow down communication and decision making, causing the organization to become less efficient and productive. That's one reason why many of today's organizations are restructuring to become flatter.

span of control

Number of people reporting to a particular manager.

There are trade-offs between the advantages and disadvantages of flat and tall organizations. Companies determine which trade-offs to make according to a principle called **span of control**, which measures the number of people reporting to a particular manager. If, for example, you remove layers of management to make your organization flatter, you end up increasing the number of positions reporting to a particular supervisor. If you refer back to the organization chart in Figure 6.5, you'll recall that, under your present structure, four managers report to you as the president of Notes-4-You: the heads of accounting, marketing, operations, and human resources. In turn, two of these managers have positions reporting to them: the advertising manager and sales supervisor report to the marketing manager, while the notetaker's supervisor and the copier's supervisor report to the operations manager. Let's say that you remove a layer of management by getting rid of the marketing and operations managers. Your organization would be flatter, but what would happen to your workload? As president, you'd now have six direct reports rather than four: accounting manager, advertising manager, sales manager, notetaker supervisor, copier supervisor, and human resources manager.

What's better—a *narrow* span of control (with few direct reports) or a *wide* span of control (with many direct reports)? The answer to this question depends on a number of factors, including frequency and type of interaction, proximity of subordinates, competence of both supervisor and subordinates, and the nature of the work being supervised. For example, you'd expect a much wider span of control at a nonprofit call center than in a hospital emergency room.

Delegating Authority

Given the tendency toward flatter organizations and wider spans of control, how do managers handle increased workloads? They must learn how to handle **delegation**—the process of entrusting work to subordinates. Unfortunately, many managers are reluctant to delegate. As a result, they not only over-burden themselves with tasks that could be handled by others, but they also deny subordinates the opportunity to learn and develop new skills.

Responsibility and Authority

As owner of Notes-4-You, you'll probably want to control every aspect of your business, especially during the start-up stage. But as the organization grows, you'll have to assign responsibility for performing certain tasks to other people. You'll also have to accept the fact that *responsibility* alone—the duty to perform a task—won't be enough to get the job done. You'll need to grant subordinates the *authority* they require to complete a task—that is, the power to make the necessary decisions. (And they'll also need sufficient resources.) Ultimately, you'll also hold your subordinates accountable for their performance.

Centralization and Decentralization

If and when your company expands (say, by offering note-taking services at other schools), you'll have to decide whether most decisions should still be made by individuals at the top or delegated to lower-level employees. The first option, in which most decision making is concentrated at the top, is called **centralization**. The second option, which spreads decision making throughout the organization, is called **decentralization**.

Let's say that you favor decentralizing Notes-4-You some four or five years down the road, when the company has expanded. Naturally, there are some decisions—such as strategic planning—that you won't delegate to lower-level employees, but you could certainly delegate the management of copy-center operations. In fact, putting someone in charge of this function would probably improve customer satisfaction, because copy-center customers would be dealing directly with the manager. It would also give the manager valuable decision-making experience, and while he or she is busy making daily decisions about the copy center, you'll have more time to work on higher-level tasks. The more you think about the possibility of decentralizing your company, the more you like the idea. First, though, you have to see it through its difficult start-up years.

delegation

Process of entrusting work to subordinates.

centralization

Decision-making process in which most decision making is concentrated at the top.

decentralization

Decision-making process in which most decision making is spread throughout the organization.

KEY TAKEAWAYS

- Managers coordinate the activities identified in the planning process among individuals, departments, or other units and allocate the resources needed to perform them.
- Typically, there are three levels of management: **top managers**, who are responsible for overall performance; **middle managers**, who report to top managers and oversee lower-level managers; and **first-line managers**, who supervise employees to make sure that work is performed correctly and on time.
- Management must develop an **organizational structure**, or arrangement of people within the organization, that will best achieve company goals.
- The process begins with **specialization**—dividing necessary tasks into jobs; the principle of grouping jobs into units is called **departmentalization**.
- Units are then grouped into an appropriate organizational structure. **Functional organization** groups people with comparable skills and tasks; **divisional organization** creates a structure composed of self-contained units based on **product**, **customer**, **process**, or **geographical division**. Forms of organizational division are often combined.
- An organization's structure is represented in an **organization chart**—a diagram showing the interrelationships of its positions.
- This chart highlights the **chain of command**, or authority relationships among people working at different levels.
- It also shows the number of layers between the top and lowest managerial levels. An organization with few layers has a wide **span of control**, with each manager overseeing a large number of subordinates; with a narrow span of control, only a limited number of subordinates reports to each manager.

Before going to the next section of this chapter, take a few minutes to test your knowledge of the material covered in this section. Quizzes can be found under the "Resources" tab, "Study Aids: Quizzes."

EXERCISES

1. Define *organizational structure* and identify five different forms that it can take. For each form, identify a type of company that might use it and explain why it would be appropriate for the company. Use examples other than those mentioned in the chapter.

2. How would you like to work at the "Sweetest Place on Earth"? Then, consider a career at Hershey Foods, the chocolate and candy maker. Your career path at Hershey Foods might follow a typical path: When you finish college, you may enter the business world as a first-line manager. After about ten years, you will probably have advanced to the middle-management level. Perhaps you'll keep moving up and eventually find yourself in a top-level management position with a big salary. Examining job opportunities may be an opportunity to start identifying the kinds of positions that interest you. Go to http://www.hersheys.com to link to the Hershey Foods Web site, click on "Careers" at the bottom of the home page, and check out available positions. Then, take the following steps:

   - Find an interesting entry-level management position. Describe the duties of the job and explain why you'd classify it as a first-line management position.

   - Pick a middle-level position to which you might advance after ten years with the company. Describe the duties of the job and explain why you'd classify it as a middle-level management position.

   - Finally, identify a top-level management position that you'd like to attain later in your career. To find these positions, you'll have to click on "Investors," "Corporate Governance," and "Management Team." Because Hershey Foods doesn't describe its management-team positions, you'll have to fill in a few blanks. Start by listing what you imagine to be the duties of a given position; then, explain why these duties qualify it as a top-level management position.

---

4. DIRECTING

LEARNING OBJECTIVES

1. **Explain how managers direct others and motivate them to achieve company goals.**
2. **Compare and contrast three forms of leadership: democratic, autocratic, and laissez-faire.**

directing

Management process that provides focus and direction to others and motivates them to achieve organizational goals.

The third management function is **directing**—providing focus and direction to others and motivating them to achieve organizational goals. As owner and president of Notes-4-You, you might think of yourself as an orchestra leader. You have given your musicians (employees) their sheet music (plans). You've placed them in sections (departments) and arranged the sections (organizational structure) so the music will sound as good as possible. Now your job is to tap your baton and lead the orchestra so that its members make beautiful music together.[16]

4.1 Leadership Styles

Actually, it's fairly easy to pick up a baton, cue each section, and strike up the band. But it doesn't follow that the music will sound good. What if your cues are ignored or misinterpreted or ambiguous? Maybe your musicians don't like your approach to making music and will just walk away. On top of everything else, you don't simply want to make music: you want to inspire your musicians to make *great* music. How do you accomplish this goal? How do you become an effective leader? What style, or approach, should you use to motivate others to achieve organizational goals?

leadership style

Particular approach used by a manager to interact with and influence others.

Unfortunately, there are no definitive answers to questions like these. Over time, every manager refines his or her own **leadership style**, or way of interacting with and influencing others. Despite a vast range of personal differences, leadership styles tend to reflect one of the following approaches to directing and motivating people: the *autocratic*, the *democratic*, or the *laissez-faire*. Let's see how managerial styles reflect each of them in a work situation.

■ *Autocratic style.* Managers who have developed an **autocratic leadership style** tend to make decisions without soliciting input from subordinates. They exercise authority and expect subordinates to take responsibility for performing the required tasks without undue explanation.

■ *Democratic style.* Managers who favor a **democratic leadership style** generally seek input from subordinates while retaining the authority to make the final decisions. They're also more likely to keep subordinates informed about things that affect their work.

■ *Laissez-faire style.* In practicing a **laissez-faire leadership style**, managers adopt a "hands-off" approach and provide relatively little direction to subordinates. They may advise employees but usually give them considerable freedom to solve problems and make decisions on their own.

At first glance, you'd probably not want to work for an autocratic leader. After all, you certainly don't want to be told what to do without having any input. You probably like the idea of working for a democratic leader; it's flattering to be asked for your input. Though working in a laissez-faire environment might seem a little unsettling at first, the opportunity to make your own decisions is appealing.

In general, your assessments of the three leadership styles would be accurate. Employees generally dislike working for autocratic leaders; they like working for democratic leaders, and they find working for laissez-faire leaders rewarding (as long as they feel they can handle the job). But there are situations when these generalities don't hold.

To learn what these situations are, let's turn things around and pretend you're the leader. To make it applicable to your current life, we'll say that you're leading a group of fellow students in a team project for your class. Are there times when it would be best for you to use an autocratic leadership style? What if your team was newly formed, unfamiliar with what needs to be done, under a tight deadline, and looking to you for direction? In this situation, you might find it appropriate to follow an autocratic leadership style (on a temporary basis) and assign tasks to each member of the group.

Now let's look at the leadership style you probably prefer—the democratic leadership style. Can you think of a situation where this style would *not* work for your team? What if the members of your team are unmotivated, don't seem interested in providing input, and aren't getting along? It might make sense to move away from a democratic style of leadership (temporarily) and delegate specific tasks to each member of the group that they can do on their own.

How about laissez-faire leadership? Will this always work with your group? Not always. It will work if your team members are willing and able to work independently and welcome the chance to make decisions. Otherwise, it could cause the team to miss deadlines or do poorly on the project.

The point being made here is that no one leadership style is effective all the time for all people. While the democratic style is viewed as the most appropriate (as is the laissez-faire style, to a lesser extent), there are times when following an autocratic style is better. Good leaders learn how to adjust their styles to fit both the situation and the individuals being directed.

Transformational Leadership

Theories on what constitutes effective leadership evolve over time. One theory that has received a lot of attention in the last decade contrasts two leadership styles: *transactional* and *transformational*. So-called **transactional leaders** exercise authority based on their rank in the organization. They let subordinates know what's expected of them and what they will receive if they meet stated objectives. They focus their attention on identifying mistakes and disciplining employees for poor performance. By contrast, **transformational leaders** mentor and develop subordinates, providing them with challenging opportunities, working one-on-one to help them meet their professional and personal needs, and encouraging people to approach problems from new perspectives. They stimulate employees to look beyond personal interests to those of the group.

autocratic leadership style

Management style identified with managers who tend to make decisions without soliciting input from subordinates.

democratic leadership style

Management style used by managers who generally seek input from subordinates while retaining the authority to make the final decision.

laissez-faire leadership style

Management style used by those who follow a "hands-off" approach and provide relatively little direction to subordinates.

transactional leaders

Managers who exercise authority based on their rank in the organization and focus their attention on identifying mistakes.

transformational leaders

Managers who mentor and develop subordinates and stimulate them to look beyond personal interests to those of the group.

FIGURE 6.9

Transformational leaders work one-on-one with subordinates to encourage and motivate them.

So, which leadership style is more effective? You probably won't be surprised by the opinion of most experts. In today's organizations, in which team building and information sharing are important and projects are often collaborative in nature, transformational leadership has proven to be more effective. Modern organizations look for managers who can develop positive relationships with subordinates and motivate employees to focus on the interests of the organization.[17]

© 2010 Jupiterimages Corporation

KEY TAKEAWAYS

- A manager's **leadership style** varies depending on the manager, the situation, and the people being directed. There are three common styles.
- Using an **autocratic style**, a manager tends to make decisions without soliciting input and expects subordinates to follow instructions without undue explanation.
- Managers who prefer a **democratic style** seek input into decisions.
- Exercising a **laissez-faire style**, the manager provides no more guidance than necessary and lets subordinates make decisions and solve problems.
- One current leadership theory focuses on two contrasting leadership styles: transactional and transformational.
- Managers adopting a **transactional style** exercise authority according to their rank in the organization, let subordinates know what's expected of them, and step in when mistakes are made.
- Practicing a **transformational style**, managers mentor and develop subordinates and motivate them to achieve organizational rather than merely personal goals. Transformational leadership is effective in organizations that value team building and information sharing.

Before going to the next section of this chapter, take a few minutes to test your knowledge of the material covered in this section. Quizzes can be found under the "Resources" tab, "Study Aids: Quizzes."

EXERCISE

Compare and contrast three forms of leadership—democratic, autocratic, and laissez-faire. Which style would you prefer to use yourself? Which would you prefer your boss to use? Explain your answers in both cases. Next, compare and contrast the transactional-leadership style with the transformational-leadership style? Which style would you adopt as a manager, and why?

5. CONTROLLING

LEARNING OBJECTIVE

1. Describe the five-step control process by which a manager monitors operations and assesses performance: (1) establish standards; (2) measure performance; (3) compare actual performance with standards, and identify any deviations; (4) determine the reason for deviations; and (5) take corrective action if needed.

Let's pause for a minute and reflect on the management functions that we've discussed so far—planning, organizing, and directing. As founder of Notes-4-You, you began by establishing plans for your new company. You defined its mission and set objectives, or performance targets, which you needed to meet in order to achieve your mission. Then, you organized your company by allocating the people and resources required to carry out your plans. Finally, you provided focus and direction to your employees and motivated them to achieve organizational objectives. Is your job finished? Can you take a well-earned vacation? Unfortunately, the answer is no: your work has just begun. Now that things are rolling along, you need to monitor your operations to see whether everything is going according to plan. If it's not, you'll need to take corrective action. This process of comparing actual to planned performance and taking necessary corrective action is called **controlling**.

controlling

Management process of comparing actual to planned performance and taking corrective actions when necessary.

5.1 A Five-Step Control Process

You can think of the control function as the five-step process outlined in Figure 6.10.

FIGURE 6.10 Five-Step Control Process

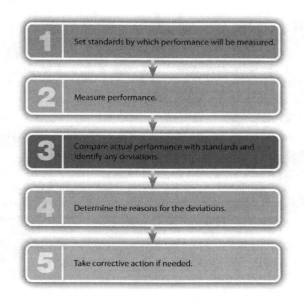

1 Set standards by which performance will be measured.

2 Measure performance.

3 Compare actual performance with standards and identify any deviations.

4 Determine the reasons for the deviations.

5 Take corrective action if needed.

Let's see how this process might work at Notes-4-You. Let's assume that, after evaluating class enrollments, you estimate that you can sell one hundred notes packages per month to students taking the sophomore-level geology course popularly known as "Rocks for Jocks." So you set your standard at a hundred units. At the end of the month, however, you look over your records and find that you sold only eighty. Comparing your actual performance with your planned performance, you realize that you came up twenty packages short. In talking with your salespeople, you learn why: it turns out that the copy machine broke down so often that packages frequently weren't ready on time. You immediately take corrective action by increasing maintenance on the copy machine.

Now, let's try a slightly different scenario. Let's say that you still have the same standard (one hundred packages) and that actual sales are still eighty packages. In investigating the reason for the shortfall, you find that you overestimated the number of students taking "Rocks for Jocks." Calculating a more accurate number of students, you see that your original standard—estimated sales—was too high by twenty packages. In this case, you should adjust your standards to reflect expected sales of eighty packages.

In both situations, your control process has been helpful. In the first instance, you were alerted to a problem that cut into your sales. Correcting this problem would undoubtedly increase sales and, therefore, profits. In the second case, you encountered a defect in your planning and learned a good managerial lesson: plan more carefully.

KEY TAKEAWAY

The process of comparing actual to planned performance and taking corrective action is called **controlling**. The control function can be viewed as a five-step process: (1) establish standards, (2) measure performance, (3) compare actual performance with standards and identify any deviations, (4) determine the reason for deviations, and (5) take corrective action if needed.

Before going to the next section of this chapter, take a few minutes to test your knowledge of the material covered in this section. Quizzes can be found under the "Resources" tab, "Study Aids: Quizzes."

EXERCISE

Have you ever gone to an ice cream stand and noticed that the "double dipper" ice cream cone the customer beside you bought has a lot more ice cream than your "double dipper" does? If you were the supervisor of the ice cream stand, how would you ensure that all cones received the same amount of ice cream? What if, instead of being the supervisor of the ice cream stand, you are the manager of a professional baseball team? How would you apply the five-step control process to your job as manager?

---

6. MANAGERIAL SKILLS

LEARNING OBJECTIVES

1. **Describe the skills needed to be a successful manager.**
2. **Explain why the skills needed by managers vary according to their level within an organization.**
3. **Identify the skills needed by top-level managers, midlevel managers, and lower-level managers.**

To be a successful manager, you'll have to master a number of skills. To get an entry-level position, you'll have to be technically competent at the tasks you're asked to perform. To advance, you'll need to develop strong interpersonal and conceptual skills. The relative importance of different skills varies from job to job and organization to organization, but to some extent, you'll need them all to forge a managerial career. Throughout your career, you'll also be expected to communicate ideas clearly, use your time efficiently, and reach sound decisions.

6.1 Technical Skills

technical skills

Skills needed to perform specific tasks.

You'll probably be hired for your first job based on your **technical skills**—the ones you need to perform specific tasks—and you'll use them extensively during your early career. If your college major is accounting, you'll use what you've learned to prepare financial statements. If you have a marketing degree and you join an ad agency, you'll use what you know about promotion to prepare ad campaigns. Technical skills will come in handy when you move up to a first-line managerial job and oversee the task performance of subordinates. Technical skills, though developed through job training and work experience, are generally acquired during the course of your formal education.

6.2 Interpersonal Skills

As you move up the corporate ladder, you'll find that you can't do everything yourself: you'll have to rely on other people to help you achieve the goals for which you're responsible. That's why **interpersonal skills**—the ability to get along with and motivate other people—are critical for managers in midlevel positions. These managers play a pivotal role because they report to top-level managers while overseeing the activities of first-line managers. Thus, they need strong working relationships with individuals at all levels and in all areas. More than most other managers, they must use "people skills" to foster teamwork, build trust, manage conflict, and encourage improvement.[18]

interpersonal skills

Skills used to get along with and motivate other people.

6.3 Conceptual Skills

Managers at the top, who are responsible for deciding what's good for the organization from the broadest perspective, rely on **conceptual skills**—the ability to reason abstractly and analyze complex situations. Senior executives are often called on to "think outside the box"—to arrive at creative solutions to complex, sometimes ambiguous problems. They need both strong analytical abilities and strong creative talents.

conceptual skills

Skills used to reason abstractly and analyze complex situations.

6.4 Communication Skills

Effective communication skills are crucial to just about everyone. At all levels of an organization, you'll often be judged on your ability to communicate, both orally and in writing. Whether you're talking informally or making a formal presentation, you must express yourself clearly and concisely. Talking too loudly, rambling, and using poor grammar reduce your ability to influence others, as does poor written communication. Confusing and error-riddled documents (including e-mails) don't do your message any good, and they will reflect poorly on you.[19]

6.5 Time-Management Skills

Managers face multiple demands on their time, and their days are usually filled with interruptions. Ironically, some technologies that were supposed to save time, such as voicemail and e-mail, have actually increased workloads. Unless you develop certain **time-management skills**, you risk reaching the end of the day feeling that you've worked a lot but accomplished little. What can managers do to ease the burden? Here are a few common-sense suggestions:

time-management skills

Skills used to manage time effectively.

- Prioritize tasks, focusing on the most important things first.
- Set aside a certain time each day to return phone calls and answer e-mail.
- Delegate routine tasks.
- Don't procrastinate.
- Insist that meetings start and end on time, and stick to an agenda.
- Eliminate unnecessary paperwork.[20]

FIGURE 6.11

Developing good time management skills is essential to being a successful manager.

6.6 Decision-Making Skills

Every manager is expected to make decisions, whether alone or as part of a team. Drawing on your **decision-making skills** is often a process in which you must define a problem, analyze possible solutions, and select the best outcome. As luck would have it, because the same process is good for making personal decisions, we'll use a personal example to demonstrate the process approach to decision making. Consider the following scenario: You're upset because your midterm grades are much lower than you'd hoped. To make matters worse, not only are you in trouble academically, but also the other members of your business-project team are annoyed because you're not pulling your weight. Your lacrosse coach is very upset because you've missed too many practices, and members of the mountain-biking club of which you're supposed to be president are talking about impeaching you if you don't show up at the next meeting. And your girlfriend says you're ignoring her. (You can substitute "boyfriend" here, of course; we're just trying to keep our exposition as simple as possible.)

© 2010 Jupiterimages Corporation

decision-making skills

Skills used in defining a problem, analyzing possible solutions, and selecting the best outcome.

6.7   A Six-Step Approach to Problem Solving

Assuming that your top priority is salvaging your GPA, let's tackle your problem by using a six-step approach to solving problems that don't have simple solutions. We've summarized this model in Figure 6.12.[21]

FIGURE 6.12   How to Solve a Problem

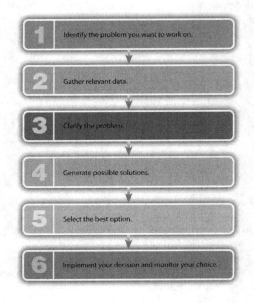

1. *Identify the problem you want to work on.* Step one is getting to know your problem, which you can formulate by asking yourself a basic question: How can I improve my grades?

2. *Gather relevant data.* Step two is gathering information that will shed light on the problem. Let's rehash some of the relevant information that you've already identified: (a) you did poorly on your finals because you didn't spend enough time studying; (b) you didn't study because you went to see your girlfriend (who lives about three hours from campus) over the weekend before your exams (and on most other weekends, as a matter of fact), (c) what little studying you got in came at the expense of your team project and lacrosse practice; and (d) while you were away for the weekend, you forgot to tell members of the mountain-biking club that you had to cancel the planned meeting.

3. *Clarify the problem.* Once you review all the given facts, you should see that your problem is bigger than simply getting your grades up; your life is pretty much out of control. You can't handle everything to which you've committed yourself. Something has to give. You clarify the problem by summing it up with another basic question: What can I do to get my life back in order?

4. *Generate possible solutions.* If you thought defining the problem was tough, wait until you've moved on to this stage. Let's say that you've come up with the following possible solutions to your problem: (a) quit the lacrosse team, (b) step down as president of the mountain-biking club, (c) let team members do your share of work on the business project, and (d) stop visiting your girlfriend so frequently. The solution to your main problem—how to get your life back in order—will probably require multiple actions.

5. *Select the best option.* This is clearly the toughest part of the process. Working your way through your various options, you arrive at the following conclusions: (a) you can't quit the lacrosse team because you'd lose your scholarship; (b) you can resign your post in the mountain-biking club, but that won't free up much time; (c) you can't let your business-project team down (and besides, you'd just get a low grade); and (d) she wouldn't like the idea, but you could visit your girlfriend, say, once a month rather than once a week. So what's the most feasible (if not necessarily perfect) solution? Probably visiting your girlfriend once a month and giving up the presidency of the mountain-biking club.

6. *Implement your decision and monitor your choice.* When you call your girlfriend, you're pleasantly surprised to find that she understands. The vice president is happy to take over the mountain-biking club. After the first week, you're able to attend lacrosse practice, get caught up

on your team business project, and catch up in all your other classes. The real test of your solution will be the results of the semester's finals.

6.8 Applying Your Skills at Notes-4-You

So, what types of skills will managers at Notes-4-You need? To oversee note-taking and copying operations, first-line managers will require technical skills, probably in operations and perhaps in accounting. Middle managers will need strong interpersonal skills to maintain positive working relationships with subordinates and to motivate them. As president, because you have to solve problems and come up with creative ways to keep the business growing, you'll need conceptual skills. And everyone will have to communicate effectively: after all, because you're in the business of selling written notes, it would look pretty bad if your employees wrote poorly. Finally, everyone will have to use time efficiently and call on problem-solving skills to handle the day-to-day crises that seem to plague every new company.

KEY TAKEAWAYS

- The skills needed by managers vary according to level.
- Top managers need strong **conceptual skills**, while those at midlevels need good **interpersonal skills** and those at lower levels need **technical skills**.
- All managers need strong **communication**, **decision-making**, and **time-management skills**.

Before going to the next chapter, take a few minutes to test your knowledge of the material covered in this section. Quizzes can be found under the "Resources" tab, "Study Aids: Quizzes."

EXERCISES

1. If you were to ask a job recruiter what skills he or she looks for in a candidate, one of the first things you'll hear is "communication skills." Strong communication skills will help you not only get a good job but also move up the ladder. How can you strengthen your written and oral communication skills while you're still a college student? Here are a few steps you can take:

   - Look for courses (or course components) designed to strengthen communication skills, such as writing (or composition) or speech classes.
   - Find out whether your college has a writing program.
   - Check into nonacademic programs designed to strengthen communication skills, such as courses on interview techniques offered by the career services office.
   - Find out how you can do some writing for the school newspaper or, if you're a little more outgoing, how you can appear in theatrical productions.

   By following these suggestions, you should get a very good idea of what your college can do to help you develop both written and oral communication skills. Write a brief report detailing your findings.

2. Do you ever reach the end of the day and wonder what you've accomplished? To succeed in management, you need to learn how to manage your time. The Internet is an interesting place to start. For many college students, surfing the Web takes up a lot of time that could be put to better use. How much time do you spend online, instant messaging, shopping, playing games, blogging, or indulging in some other enjoyable but time-consuming activity? One approach to solving the problem of wasted online time is to apply the six-step problem-solving procedure that we outlined in the chapter. Write a brief report detailing each of the steps that you take to solve the problem and implement a solution.

7. CASES AND PROBLEMS

Mission "Improvisable"

A mission statement tells customers, employees, and stakeholders why the organization exists—its purpose. It can be concise, like the one from Mary Kay Cosmetics—"To enrich the lives of women around the world"—or it can be more detailed, such as the following from FedEx:

FedEx Corporation will produce superior financial returns for its shareowners by providing high value-added logistics, transportation and related business services through focused operating companies. Customer requirements will be met in the highest quality manner appropriate to each market segment served. FedEx will strive to develop mutually rewarding relationships with its employees, partners and suppliers. Safety will be the first consideration in all operations. Corporate activities will be conducted to the highest ethical and professional standards.

Mission statements are typically constructed to communicate several pieces of information: what the company strives to accomplish, what it's known for, and how it serves its customers. Here are a few examples:

- Facebook: Facebook's mission is to give people the power to share and make the world more open and connected.[22]
- Microsoft: "Our mission is to create a family of devices and services for individuals and businesses that empower people around the globe at home, at work, and on the go for the activities they value most."[23]
- Google: Google's mission is to organize the world's information and make it universally accessible and useful.[24]

Assignment

Create hypothetical mission statements for each of these four companies: Outback Steakhouse, Tesoro, 1-800-GOT-JUNK, and Staples. To find descriptions of all four, go to the Web site for each of the companies: http://www.outbacksteakhouse.com, http://www.tesorocorp.com, http://www.1800gotjunk.com/us_en, and http://www.staples.com.

In composing your four mission statements, follow the format suggested previously: each statement should be about two or three sentences long and should provide several pieces of information—what the company strives to accomplish, what it's known for, and how it serves its customers (and perhaps its employees and shareholders, too).

One last thing: *your statements should be originals, not duplicates of the companies' official statements.*

To Manage or Not to Manage?

Are you interested in a career that pays well and offers power, prestige, and a feeling of accomplishment? A career in management may be for you, but be forewarned that there's a downside: you have to make tough decisions, other people will be after your job, and it can be lonely at the top. To find out more about the pros and cons of a management career, go to http://management.about.com/cs/yourself/a/ManagementForMe.htm to link to the About.com Web site and read the article "Is Management for Me?" Then, answer the following questions, being sure to provide an explanation for each of your answers:

- Which of the pros of being a manager are important to you? Which are not?
- Which of the cons might discourage you from pursuing a management career? Which might not?
- Considering balance, does a career in management appeal to you? Why, or why not?

ETHICS ANGLE

Sugarcoating the News at Krispy Kreme

According to Krispy Kreme's "Code of Ethics for Chief Executive and Senior Financial Officers," the company's top executives are expected to practice and promote honest, ethical conduct. They're also responsible for the health and overall performance of the company. Recently, however, things have gone wrong in the top echelons of the doughnut-shop chain.

First, a little background. Founded as one small doughnut shop in Winston-Salem, North Carolina, in 1937, the brand became increasingly popular over the next six decades, taking off in the 1980s and 1990s. By 2003, Krispy Kreme (which went public in 2000) was selling more than a billion doughnuts a year. That's when things started to go stale. (For more details on the company's ups and downs, go to http://jacksonville.com/tu-online/apnews/stories/012205/D87OTSIG0.shtml, and read the article "Krispy Kreme: The Rise, Fall, Rise and Fall of a Southern Icon.")

When sales first started to decline in the fall of 2003, CEO Scott Livengood offered a variety of creative explanations, mostly for the benefit of anxious investors: high gas prices discouraged people from driving to doughnut shops, supermarket sales were down because grocery stores were losing business to Wal-Mart, and people were cutting back on carbohydrates because of the popular Atkins diet. Unfortunately, other (more plausible) explanations were beginning to surface. To complete this exercise, you'll need to find out what they were. Go to both http://www.marketwatch.com/story/worst-ceo-krispy-kremes-scott-livengood and http://usatoday30.usatoday.com/money/industries/food/2005-08-10-krispy-kreme_x.htm?csp=34 to read these articles: "Worst CEO: Krispy Kreme's Scott Livengood" and "Krispy Kreme Must Restate Earnings by $25.6M." Once you have a good grasp of the company's problems and you've read about the people who are responsible, answer the following questions, being sure to provide explanations for your responses:

1. What factors contributed to the problems at Krispy Kreme? What happened to the company? Who was hurt?
2. Should the firm's problems be attributed to poor management, unethical behavior on the part of the executive team, or both?
3. Judging from the lessons of the Krispy Kreme case, how important do you think it is for a firm to have strong top-down leadership?
4. If you'd been the CEO of Krispy Kreme, what things would you have done differently?

TEAM-BUILDING SKILLS

Assessing Your School's Strengths, Weaknesses, Opportunities, and Threats

How can you and other members of your team help your college or university assess its fit with its environment? For one thing, you could apply SWOT analysis.

Begin by picking a member of the team to write down ideas generated by the group using brainstorming (a technique used to generate ideas that have no right or wrong answers and are accepted by the group without criticism). Pick a different member of the team to complete the SWOT analysis in the format listed subsequently. Then follow these steps:

1. Using brainstorming, identify *internal* factors, either positive or negative, that are unique to your school. List all items suggested by group members on a large sheet of paper or a blackboard.
2. Based on your analysis of the items listed (in step 1), the team should select at least five factors that are *strengths* and five that are *weaknesses*.
3. List the selected strengths and weaknesses in the SWOT analysis form.
4. Using brainstorming, identify *external* factors that could influence your school in either a positive or a negative way. Include all items suggested by group members. List the ideas on a large sheet of paper or a blackboard.
5. Based on your analysis of the items listed (in step 4), select at least five *opportunities* that could benefit your school and five *threats* to its success.
6. List the selected opportunities and threats in the SWOT analysis form.
7. Analyze the selected opportunities and strengths (which have been listed on the SWOT analysis form) and identify several ways in which your school can take advantage of opportunities by making the most of its strengths. Record your suggestions on the SWOT analysis form.
8. Analyze the selected threats and weaknesses (which have been listed on the SWOT analysis form) and identify several ways in which your school can protect itself from threats and overcome its weaknesses. Record your suggestions on the SWOT analysis form.

Team Members	
STRENGTHS	WEAKNESSES
OPPORTUNITIES	THREATS

- Ways in which your school can take advantage of opportunities by making the most of its strengths
- Ways in which your school can protect itself from threats and overcome its weaknesses

The Art and Science of Organizational Evolution

A company's organizational structure defines the formal relationships among the people in it. It also reflects an arrangement of positions that's most appropriate for the company at a specific point in time. As the business expands or changes directions, its organizational structure should also change.

With these principles in mind, let's trace the evolution of a hypothetical company called High-Tech Cases, which manufactures and sells DVD cases made out of a special high-tech material.

Stage 1

When the company was founded, it operated under a functional organizational structure, with the following key positions and reporting relationships:

Position	Reports to
CEO	No one
VP of Sales and Marketing	CEO
VP of Production	CEO
VP of Finance	CEO
Director of Sales	VP Sales/Marketing
Director of Advertising	VP Sales/Marketing
Director of Operations	VP Production
Director of Engineering	VP Production
Treasurer	VP Finance
Controller	VP Finance

In addition, two salespeople reported to the director of sales. The directors of advertising, operations, and engineering each had two assistants, as did the treasurer and the controller.

Stage 2

About three years after the company's founding, the management team decided to expand sales into Asia. The director of sales retained responsibility for the United States, while a new director was added for Asia. The two salespeople who had been with the company since its beginning focused on U.S. sales, and two new salespeople were hired to handle Asia. No other position changed, and for the next two years, all personnel worked out of the U.S. headquarters.

Stage 3

By the beginning of the fifth year of operations, Asian and U.S. sales were about the same. At this point, management decided to set up two separate operations—one in the United States and the other in China. A senior VP was hired to head each operation—senior VP of U.S. operations and senior VP of Asian operations. Both would report to the CEO. Each operational unit would run its own production facilities, arrange its own financing, and be in charge of its sales and marketing activities. As a result, High-Tech Cases almost doubled in size, but management believed that the restructuring was appropriate and would increase profits in the long run.

Assignment

Create three organization charts—one for each stage in High-Tech's development. Ideally, you should make your charts with some type of organization-chart software. To use the tool available in Microsoft Word, go to the *Standard Toolbar* in Microsoft Word, click on "Help," and type in *organization chart*. Then select "create a chart."

ENDNOTES

1. Lee Scott, "Three Basic Beliefs," *About Wal-Mart*, http://corporate.walmart.com/our-story (accessed March 30, 2014).

2. Mary Kay Inc., "Employment at Mary Kay," http://www.marykay.com/en-US/About-Mary-Kay/EmploymentMaryKay (accessed March 30, 2014).

3. Harley-Davidson Web site, Company/Student Center section, http://www.harley-davidson.com/en_GB/Content/Pages/Company/company.html?locale=en_GB&bmLocale=enGB (accessed March 30, 2014).

4. Volvo Group Global, http://www.volvogroup.com/group/global/en-gb/volvo%20group/our_brand/pages/ourbrands.aspx (accessed March 31, 2014).

5. The Coca-Cola Company, "Code of Business Conduct," http://www.thecoca-colacompany.com/ourcompany/mission_vision_values.html (accessed March 31, 2014).

6. "Most Executives Say Ethics, Integrity Are Among Core Corporate Values," *The Enterprise*, http://www.highbeam.com/doc/1P3-134301331.html (accessed March 31, 2014).

7. Scott Safranski and Ik-Whan Kwon, "Strategic Planning for the Growing Business" (1991), U.S. Small Business Administration, http://www.sbaonline.sba.gov/idc/groups/public/documents/sba_homepage/serv_pubs_eb_pdf_eb6.pdf (accessed March 31, 2014).

8. McDonald's Corp., "McDonald's Announces Plans to Revitalize Its Worldwide Business and Sets New Financial Targets," *Franchise Bison*, http://www.bison.com/press_mcdonalds_04072003 (accessed March 31, 2014).

9. Brian Perkins, "Defining Crisis Management," *Wharton Alumni Magazine*, Summer 2000, http://whartonmagazine.com/issues/summer-2000/reunion-2000 (accessed March 31, 2014).

10. Stewart Elliott, "Wendy's Gets a Break, but Still Has Work Ahead of It," *The New York Times*, April 29, 2005, http://www.nytimes.com/2005/04/29/business/media/29adco.html?ei=5088&en=bb0e017145269f5e& (accessed March 31, 2014).

11. "Embattled BP Chief: I Want My Life Back," *The Times of London*, May 31, 2010.

12. Associated Press, "General Motors Rebuilds with 4 Divisions," *The Augusta Chronicle*, October 7, 2010, http://chronicle.augusta.com/life/autos/2010-10-07/general-motors-rebuilds-4-divisions (accessed March 31, 2014).

13. Johnson & Johnson Services, "Business Segments," http://www.jnj.com/connect/about-jnj/company-structure (accessed March 31, 2014).

14. Northwest Forest Industry, Pulp and Paper Manufacturing, "From the Forest to the Office and Home: Bowater—A Case Study in Newsprint and Kraft Pulp Production," *Borealforest.org*, http://www.borealforest.org/paper/index.htm (accessed March 31, 2014).

15. McDonald's Corp., "Franchising," http://www.aboutmcdonalds.com/mcd/franchising/us_franchising.html (accessed March 31, 2014).

16. F. John Reh, "Management 101," *About Management*, http://management.about.com/cs/generalmanagement/a/Management101.htm (accessed March 31, 2014).

17. See Karen Collins, *Accountants' Management Styles and Effectiveness* (American Woman's Society of Certified Public Accountants, 1997).

18. Brian Perkins, "Defining Crisis Management," *Wharton Alumni Magazine*, Summer 2000, http://whartonmagazine.com/issues/summer-2000/reunion-2000 (accessed March 31, 2014).

19. Brian L. Davis et al., *Successful Manager's Handbook: Development Suggestions for Today's Managers* (Minneapolis: Personnel Decisions Inc., 1992), 189.

20. Brian L. Davis et al., *Successful Manager's Handbook: Development Suggestions for Today's Managers* (Minneapolis: Personnel Decisions Inc., 1992), 189.

21. Shari Caudron, "Six Steps in Creative Problem Solving," *Controller Magazine*, April 1998, 38. Caudron describes a systematic approach developed by Roger L. Firestien, president of Innovation Systems Group, Williamsville, NY.

22. Facebook, "Facebook," https://www.facebook.com/facebook?v=info.

23. Mary Jo Foley, "Microsoft's new mission statement: No more computer on every desk," *ZDNet*, http://www.zdnet.com/microsofts-new-mission-statement-no-more-computer-on-every-desk-7000021658/.

24. Google, "Company overview," http://www.google.com/about/company/.

CHAPTER 7

Recruiting, Motivating, and Keeping Quality Employees

THE GROUNDS OF A GREAT WORK ENVIRONMENT

Howard Schultz has vivid memories of his father slumped on the couch with his leg in a cast.[1] The ankle would heal, but his father had lost another job—this time as a driver for a diaper service. It was a crummy job; still, it put food on the table, and if his father couldn't work, there wouldn't be any money. Howard was seven, but he understood the gravity of the situation, particularly because his mother was seven months pregnant, and the family had no insurance.

This was just one of the many setbacks that plagued Schultz's father throughout his life—an honest, hardworking man frustrated by a system that wasn't designed to cater to the needs of common workers. He'd held a series of blue-collar jobs (cab driver, truck driver, factory worker), sometimes holding two or three at a time. Despite his willingness to work, he never earned enough money to move his family out of Brooklyn's federally subsidized housing projects. Schultz's father died never having found fulfillment in his work life—or even a meaningful job. It was the saddest day of Howard's life.

As a kid, did Schultz ever imagine that one day he'd be the founder and chairman of Starbucks Coffee Company? Of course not. But he did decide that if he was ever in a position to make a difference in the lives of people like his father, he'd do what he could. Remembering his father's struggles and disappointments, Schultz has tried to make Starbucks the kind of company where he wished his father had worked. "Without even a high school diploma," Schultz admits, "my father probably could never have been an executive. But if he had landed a job in one of our stores or roasting plants, he wouldn't have quit in frustration because the company didn't value him. He would have had good health benefits, stock options, and an atmosphere in which his suggestions or complaints would receive a prompt, respectful response."[2]

Schultz is motivated by both personal and business considerations: "When employees have self-esteem and self-respect," he argues, "they can contribute so much more: to their company, to their family, to the world."[3] His commitment to his employees is embedded in Starbuck's mission statement, which lists as one of its principles, "We always treat each other with respect and dignity."[4] Those working at Starbucks are called partners because Schultz believes working for his company is not just a job, it's a passion.[5]

Howard Schultz toasts at the launch of their new "everyday" brew, Pike Place Roast, April 8, 2008, in Bryant Park in New York City.

Photo by Mario Tama/Getty Images

Video Clip

A major piece of the Starbucks success story has been the superior service provided by its motivated employees.

View the video online at: http://www.youtube.com/embed/vizOXrc8fso

1. HUMAN RESOURCE MANAGEMENT

LEARNING OBJECTIVES

1. Define "human resource management" and explain how managers develop and implement a human resource plan.
2. Explain how managers conduct a job analysis and prepare a job description and job specifications.
3. Describe how a human resources manager forecasts future hiring needs.
4. Understand the importance of complying with antidiscrimination laws enforced by the Equal Employment Opportunity Commission (EEOC).
5. Explain when discrimination occurs, according to federal law.
6. Describe the steps taken in the selection process.

human resource management (HRM)

All actions that an organization takes to attract, develop, and retain quality employees.

Employees at Starbucks are vital to the company's success. They are its public face, and every dollar of sales passes through their hands.[6] According to Howard Schultz, they can make or break the company. If a customer has a positive interaction with an employee, the customer will come back. If an encounter is negative, the customer is probably gone for good. That's why it's crucial for Starbucks to recruit and hire the right people, train them properly, motivate them to do their best, and encourage them to stay with the company. Thus, the company works to provide satisfying jobs, a positive work environment, appropriate work schedules, and fair compensation and benefits. These activities are part of Starbucks's strategy to deploy human resources in order to gain competitive advantage. The process is called **human resource management (HRM)**, which consists of all actions that an organization takes to attract, develop, and retain quality employees. Each of these activities is complex. Attracting talented employees involves the recruitment of qualified candidates and the selection of those who best fit the organization's needs. Development encompasses both new-employee orientation and the training and development of current workers. Retaining good employees means motivating them to excel, appraising their performance, compensating them appropriately, and doing what's possible to retain them.

1.1 Human Resource Planning

How does Starbucks make sure that its worldwide retail locations are staffed with just the right number of committed employees? How does Walt Disney World ensure that it has enough qualified "cast members" to provide visitors with a "magical" experience? How does Norwegian Cruise Lines make certain that when the *Norwegian Dawn* pulls out of Boston harbor, it has a complete, fully trained crew on board to feed, entertain, and care for its passengers? Managing these tasks is a matter of **strategic human resource planning**—the process of developing a plan for satisfying an organization's human resources (HR) needs.

A strategic HR plan lays out the steps that an organization will take to ensure that it has the right number of employees with the right skills in the right places at the right times. HR managers begin by analyzing the company's mission, principles, or objectives, and strategies. One of Starbucks's principles is, for example, the commitment to "connect with, laugh with, and uplift the lives of [their] customers—even if just for a few moments,"[7] as well as to foster an environment in which employees treat both customers and each other with respect. Thus, the firm's HR managers look for people who are "adaptable, self-motivated, passionate, creative team members."[8] Likewise, Disney's overall objectives include not only making all visitors feel as if they're special in a special place but also ensuring that employees' appearance reflects a special image.[9] Disney hires people who best fulfill these job requirements.[10] The main goal of Norwegian Cruise Lines—to lavish passengers with personal attention—determines not only the type of employee desired (dynamic hospitality professionals)[11] but also the number needed (one for every two passengers).[12]

Job Analysis

To develop an HR plan, HR managers must obviously be knowledgeable about the jobs that the organization needs performed. They organize information about a given job by performing a **job analysis** to identify the tasks, responsibilities, and skills that it entails, as well as the knowledge and abilities needed to perform it. Managers also use the information collected for the job analysis to prepare two documents:

- A **job description**, which lists the duties and responsibilities of a position
- A **job specification**, which lists the qualifications—skills, knowledge, and abilities—needed to perform the job

HR Supply and Demand Forecasting

Once they've analyzed the jobs within the organization, HR managers must forecast future hiring (or firing) needs. This is the three-step process summarized in Figure 7.1.

FIGURE 7.1 How to Forecast Hiring (and Firing) Needs

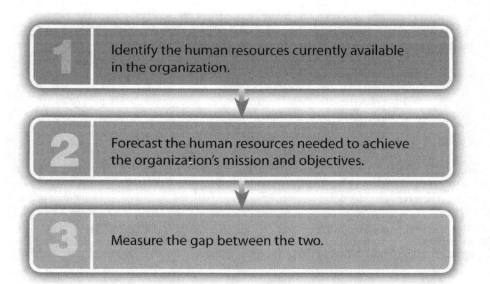

1 Identify the human resources currently available in the organization.

2 Forecast the human resources needed to achieve the organization's mission and objectives.

3 Measure the gap between the two.

Starbucks, for instance, might find that it needs three hundred new employees to work at stores scheduled to open in the next few months. Disney might determine that it needs two thousand new cast

strategic human resource planning

Process of developing a plan for satisfying an organization's human resource needs.

job analysis

Identification of the tasks, responsibilities, and skills of a job, as well as the knowledge and abilities needed to perform it.

job description

Outline of the duties and responsibilities of a position.

job specification

Detailed list of the qualifications needed to perform a job, including required skills, knowledge, and abilities.

members to handle an anticipated surge in visitors. The *Norwegian Dawn* might be short two dozen restaurant workers because of an unexpected increase in the number of passengers.

After calculating the disparity between supply and future demand, HR managers must draw up plans for bringing the two numbers into balance. If the demand for labor is going to outstrip the supply, they may hire more workers, encourage current workers to put in extra hours, subcontract work to other suppliers, or introduce labor-saving initiatives. If the supply is greater than the demand, they may deal with overstaffing by not replacing workers who leave, encouraging early retirements, laying off workers, or (as a last resort) firing workers.

1.2   Recruiting Qualified Employees

recruiting

Process of identifying suitable candidates and encouraging them to apply for openings in the organization.

Discrimination

Practice of treating a person unfairly on the basis of a characteristic unrelated to ability.

Equal Employment Opportunity Commission (EEOC)

Federal agency in charge of enforcing federal laws on employment discrimination.

Armed with information on the number of new employees to be hired and the types of positions to be filled, the HR manager then develops a strategy for recruiting potential employees. **Recruiting** is the process of identifying suitable candidates and encouraging them to apply for openings in the organization.

Before going any further, we should point out that, in recruiting and hiring, managers must comply with antidiscrimination laws; violations can have legal consequences. **Discrimination** occurs when a person is treated unfairly on the basis of a characteristic unrelated to ability. Under federal law, it's illegal to discriminate in recruiting and hiring on the basis of race, color, religion, sex, national origin, age, or disability. (The same rules apply to other employment activities, such as promoting, compensating, and firing.)[13] The **Equal Employment Opportunity Commission (EEOC)** enforces a number of federal employment laws, including the following:

- Title VII of the Civil Rights Act of 1964, which prohibits employment discrimination based on race, color, religion, sex, or national origin. Sexual harassment is also a violation of Title VII.
- The Equal Pay Act of 1963, which protects both women and men who do substantially equal work from sex-based pay discrimination.
- The Age Discrimination in Employment Act of 1964, which protects individuals who are forty or older.
- Title I and Title V of the Americans with Disabilities Act of 1990, which prohibits employment discrimination against individuals with disabilities.[14]

1.3   Where to Find Candidates

The first step in recruiting is to find qualified candidates. Where do you look for them, and how do you decide whether they're qualified? Let's start with the second part of the question first. A qualified person must be able to perform the duties listed in the job description and must possess the skills, knowledge, and abilities detailed in the job specification. In addition, he or she must be a good "fit" for the company. A Disney recruiter, for example, wants a candidate who fits a certain image—someone who's clean-cut and "wholesome" looking. The same recruiter might also favor candidates with certain qualities—someone who has a "good attitude," who's a "go-getter" and a "team player," and who's smart, responsible, and stable.[15]

Internal versus External Recruiting

Where do you find people who satisfy so many criteria? Basically, you can look in two places: inside and outside your own organization. Both options have pluses and minuses. Hiring internally sends a positive signal to employees that they can move up in the company—a strong motivation tool and a reward for good performance. In addition, because an internal candidate is a known quantity, it's easier to predict his or her success in a new position. Finally, it's cheaper to recruit internally. According to the Saratoga Institute, the average cost of hiring an external candidate is 1.7 times greater than the cost of promoting someone from inside the company. In addition, between 40 and 60 percent of those hired from outside the company are unsuccessful compared with only 25 percent of those promoted from within.[16]

On the other hand, entry-level jobs usually have to be filled from outside the company. Even when you hire internally, you'll probably have to fill the promoted employee's position. Going outside gives you an opportunity to bring fresh ideas and skills into the company. In any case, it's often the only alternative, especially if no one inside the company has just the right combination of skills and experiences.

1.4   How to Find Candidates

Whether you search inside or outside the organization, you need to publicize the opening. If you're looking internally in a small organization, you can alert employees informally. In larger organizations, HR managers generally post openings internally on electronic job boards or announce them in newsletters or e-mails.[17]

Companies with a strong interest in promoting from within are installing new career sites to facilitate the internal recruiting process.[18] Cisco, for example, uses a software system called Talent Connection to identify qualified employees who might be enticed to apply for a new position within the company. About half of its 65,000 employees have posted profiles on the site and more have used it to search job openings. The company brags that "Talent Connection has saved several million dollars in search-firm fees and other recruiting costs, while employee surveys show workers' satisfaction with career development has risen by 20 percentage points."

Another company using an internal recruiting system is the consulting firm Booz Allen Hamilton. Employees visiting the site, which is called Inside First, have access to a listing of job openings, while their managers have access to staff profiles. The site helped to increase the percentage of positions filled from inside from 10 percent to 30 percent. Lucy Sorrentini, a principle at Booz, admits that "we overlooked our own people. It was easier to go to the outside." But she now says that "the company has since found it is more efficient to bring insiders up to speed. They know our firm and in some cases they already know the client."[19]

Recruiting people from outside the company is a lot like marketing a product to buyers: in effect, you're marketing the virtues of working for your company. Recruiting talented future employees has changed over the years due to advances in technology. In the "old days," a company attracted job candidates by placing an ad in the local newspaper or putting a "help wanted" sign on its front door. This approach to recruiting is still followed by some small businesses, but most companies utilize technology in their recruiting efforts.

There are a variety of technology-based recruiting techniques available to companies today. Some companies, such as Google, merely post openings on their company Web site and wait for the résumés to appear (which for Google is about one million résumés a year). In addition to posting job openings on their company Web sites, businesses often post openings on job boards such as Monster.com and CareerBuilder.com, as well as job search engines such as US.jobs and DirectEmployers. But the real superstars in the recruiting world are LinkedIn, Facebook, and Twitter. For professional positions, LinkedIn is on top with 93 percent of employers stating they are using or plan to use the site. For social network recruiting, Facebook and Twitter take the lead with 66 percent of recruiters advertising positions on Facebook and 54 percent advertising on Twitter.[20]

We don't want to leave you with the impression that all recruiting takes place electronically. Companies utilize a number of in-person approaches to identifying talent, including college campus recruiting, job fairs, referrals, internships, and co-op programs.

1.5   The Selection Process

Recruiting gets people to apply for positions, but once you've received applications, you still have to select the best candidate—another complicated process. The **selection** process entails gathering information on candidates, evaluating their qualifications, and choosing the right one. At the very least, the process can be time-consuming—particularly when you're filling a high-level position—and often involves several members of an organization.

> **selection**
>
> Process of gathering information on candidates, evaluating their qualifications, and choosing the right one.

Let's examine the selection process more closely by describing the steps that you'd take to become a special agent for the Federal Bureau of Investigation (FBI).[21] Most business students don't generally aspire to become FBI agents, but the FBI is quite interested in business graduates—especially if you have a major in accounting or finance. With one of these backgrounds, you'll be given priority in hiring. Why? Unfortunately, there's a lot of white-collar crime that needs to be investigated, and people who know how to follow the money are well suited for the task.

Application

The first step in becoming a gun-toting accountant is, obviously, applying for the job. Don't bother unless you meet the minimum qualifications: you must be a U.S. citizen, be age twenty-three to thirty-seven, be physically fit, and have a bachelor's degree. To provide factual information on your education and work background, you'll submit an **application**, which the FBI will use as an initial screening tool.

> **application**
>
> Document completed by a job applicant that provides factual information on the person's education and work background.

Employment Tests

Next comes a battery of tests (a lot more than you'd take in applying for an everyday business position). Like most organizations, the FBI tests candidates on the skills and knowledge entailed by the job. Unlike most businesses, however, the FBI will also measure your aptitude, evaluate your personality, and assess your writing ability. You'll have to take a polygraph (lie-detector) test to determine the truthfulness of the information you've provided, uncover the extent of any drug use, and disclose potential security problems.

Interview

interview

Formal meeting during which the employer learns more about an applicant and the applicant learns more about the prospective employer.

If you pass all these tests (with sufficiently high marks), you'll be granted an **interview**. It serves the same purpose as it does for business recruiters: it allows the FBI to learn more about you and gives you a chance to learn more about your prospective employer and your possible future in the organization. The FBI conducts *structured interviews*—a series of standard questions. You're judged on both your answers and your ability to communicate orally.

Physical Exam and Reference Checks

Let's be positive and say you passed the interview. What's next? You still have to pass a rigorous physical examination (including a drug test), as well as background and reference checks. Given its mission, the FBI sets all these hurdles a little higher than the average retail clothing chain. Most businesses will ask you to take a physical exam, but you probably won't have to meet the fitness standards set by the FBI. Likewise, many businesses check references to verify that applicants haven't lied about (or exaggerated) their education and work experience. The FBI goes to great lengths to ensure that candidates are suitable for law-enforcement work.

Final Decision

The last stage in the process is out of your control. Will you be hired or rejected? This decision is made by one or more people who work for the prospective employer. For a business, the decision maker is generally the line manager who oversees the position being filled. At the FBI, the decision is made by a team at FBI headquarters. If you're hired as a special agent, you'll spend twenty-one weeks of intensive training at the FBI Academy in Quantico, Virginia.

1.6   Contingent Workers

contingent worker

Temporary or part-time worker hired to supplement a company's permanent workforce.

Though most people hold permanent, full-time positions, there's a growing number of individuals who work at temporary or part-time jobs. Many of these are **contingent workers** hired to supplement a company's permanent workforce. Most of them are independent contractors, consultants, or freelancers who are paid by the firms that hire them. Others are *on-call workers* who work only when needed, such as substitute teachers. Still others are *temporary workers* (or "temps") who are employed and paid by outside agencies or contract firms that charge fees to client companies.

The Positives and Negatives of Temp Work

The use of contingent workers provides companies with a number of benefits. Because they can be hired and fired easily, employers can better control labor costs. When things are busy, they can add temps, and when business is slow, they can release unneeded workers. Temps are often cheaper than permanent workers, particularly because they rarely receive costly benefits. Employers can also bring in people with specialized skills and talents to work on special projects without entering into long-term employment relationships. Finally, companies can "try out" temps: if someone does well, the company can offer permanent employment; if the fit is less than perfect, the employer can easily terminate the relationship. There are downsides to the use of contingent workers, including increased training costs and decreased loyalty to the company. Also, many employers believe that because temps are usually less committed to company goals than permanent workers, productivity suffers.

What about you? Does temporary work appeal to you? On the plus side, you can move around to various companies and gain a variety of skills. You can see a company from the inside and decide up front whether it's the kind of place you'd like to work at permanently. If it is, your temporary position lets you showcase your skills and talents and grab the attention of management, which could increase the likelihood you'll be offered a permanent position. There are also some attractive lifestyle benefits. You might, for example, work at a job or series of jobs for, say, ten months and head for the beach for the other two. On the other hand, you'll probably get paid less, receive no benefits, and have no job security. For most people, the idea of spending two months a year on the beach isn't *that* appealing.

KEY TAKEAWAYS

- The process of **human resource management** consists of all the actions that an organization takes to attract, develop, and retain quality employees.
- To ensure that the organization is properly staffed, managers engage in **strategic human resource planning**—the process of developing a plan for satisfying the organization's human resource needs.
- Managers organize information about a given job by performing a **job analysis**, which they use to prepare two documents: a **job description** listing the duties and responsibilities of a position and a **job specification**, which lists the qualifications—skills, knowledge, and abilities—needed to perform the job.
- After analyzing the jobs that must be performed, the HR manager forecasts future hiring needs and begins the **recruiting** process to identify suitable candidates and encourage them to apply.
- In recruiting and hiring, managers must comply with antidiscrimination laws enforced by the **Equal Employment Opportunity Commission (EEOC)**.
- **Discrimination** occurs when a person is treated unfairly on the basis of a characteristic unrelated to ability, such as race, color, religion, sex, national origin, age, or disability.
- Once a pool of suitable candidates has been identified, managers begin the **selection** process, reviewing information provided by candidates on employment **applications** and administering tests to assess candidates' skills and knowledge.
- Candidates who pass this stage may be granted an **interview** and, perhaps, offered a job.

Before going to the next section of this chapter, take a few minutes to test your knowledge of the material covered in this section. Quizzes can be found under the "Resources" tab, "Study Aids: Quizzes."

EXERCISE

You're the chairperson of the management department at your college. Describe the steps you'd take to ensure that your department has enough qualified faculty to meet its needs.

---

2. DEVELOPING EMPLOYEES

LEARNING OBJECTIVES

1. Define "orientation," and identify things you should do and should not do as part of new-employee orientation.
2. Explain how companies train and develop employees.
3. Compare and contrast off-the-job training and on-the-job training.
4. Discuss the importance of a diverse workforce.

Because companies can't survive unless employees do their jobs well, it makes economic sense to train them and develop their skills. This type of support begins when an individual enters the organization and continues as long as he or she stays there.

2.1 New-Employee Orientation

Have you ever started your first day at a new job feeling upbeat and optimistic only to walk out at the end of the day thinking that maybe you've taken the wrong job? If this happens too often, your employer may need to revise its approach to **orientation**—the way it introduces new employees to the organization and their jobs. Starting a new job is a little like beginning college; at the outset, you may be experiencing any of the following feelings:

- Somewhat nervous but enthusiastic
- Eager to impress but not wanting to attract too much attention

orientation

Activities involved in introducing new employees to the organization and their jobs.

- Interested in learning but fearful of being overwhelmed with information
- Hoping to fit in and worried about looking new or inexperienced[22]

The employer who understands how common such feelings are is more likely not only to help new-comers get over them but also to avoid the pitfalls often associated with new-employee orientation:

- Failing to have a workspace set up for you
- Ignoring you or failing to supervise you
- Neglecting to introduce you to coworkers (or introducing you to so many people that you have no chance of remembering anybody's name)
- Assigning you no work or giving you busywork unrelated to your actual job
- Swamping you with facts about the company[23]

A good employer will take things slowly, providing you with information about the company and your job on a need-to-know basis while making you feel as comfortable as possible. You'll get to know the company's history, traditions, policies, and culture over time. You'll learn more about salary and benefits and how your performance will be evaluated. Most importantly, you'll find out how your job fits into overall operations and what's expected of you.

2.2   Training and Development

It would be nice if employees came preprogrammed with all the skills they need to do their jobs. It would also be nice if job requirements stayed the same: once you've learned how to do a job (or been preprogrammed), you'd know how to do it forever. In reality, new employees must be trained; moreover, as they grow in their jobs or as their jobs change, they'll need additional training. Unfortunately, training is costly and time-consuming.

How costly? On average, companies spent $811 per learner in employee training and development in 2013.[24] For every $1 in payroll that it spends, the consulting firm Booz Allen Hamilton invests about $0.08 in employee training and development. Verizon, ranked as a Top 10 Training organization by Training Magazine for the past four years, invested almost $300 million in training and development during 2013. Its employees completed 8 million hours of training during the year, an average of 45 hours per individual.[25] What's the payoff? Why are such companies willing to spend so much money on their employees? Pfizer, whose motto is "every colleague, every country, every day," regards employee growth and development as its top priority. At Booz Allen Hamilton, consultants specialize in finding innovative solutions to client problems, and their employer makes sure that they're up-to-date on all the new technologies by maintaining a "technology petting zoo" at its training headquarters. It's called a "petting zoo" because employees get to see, touch, and interact with new and emerging technologies.[26]

At Booz Allen Hamilton's technology "petting zoo," employees are receiving **off-the-job training**. This approach allows them to focus on learning without the distractions that would occur in the office. More common, however, is informal **on-the-job training**, which may be supplemented with formal training programs. This is the method, for example, by which you'd move up from mere coffee maker to a full-fledged "barista" if you worked at Starbucks.[27] You'd begin by reading a large spiral book (titled *Starbucks University*) on the responsibilities of the barista. After you've passed a series of tests on the reading material, you'll move behind the coffee bar, where a manager or assistant manager will give you hands-on experience in making drinks. According to the rules, you can't advance to a new drink until you've mastered the one you're working on; the process, therefore, may take a few days (or even weeks). Next, you have to learn enough about different types of coffee to be able to describe them to customers. (Because this course involves drinking a lot of coffee, you don't have to worry about staying awake.) Eventually, you'll be declared a coffee connoisseur, but there's still one more set of skills to master: you must complete a customer-service course, which trains you in making eye contact with customers, anticipating their needs, and making them feel welcome.[28]

2.3   Diversity in the Workplace

The makeup of the U.S. workforce has changed dramatically over the past 50 years. In the 1950s, more than 60 percent was composed of white males.[29] Today's workforce, however, reflects the broad range of differences in the population—differences in gender, race, ethnicity, age, physical ability, religion, education, and lifestyle. As you can see in Table 7.1, more women and minorities have entered the workforce, and white males now make up only 36 percent of the workforce.[30] Their percentage representation diminished as more women and minorities entered the workforce.

off-the-job training

Formal employee training that occurs in a location away from the office.

on-the-job training

Employee training (often informal) that occurs while the employee is on the job.

Most companies today strive for diverse workforces. HR managers work hard to recruit, hire, develop, and retain a workforce that's representative of the general population. In part, these efforts are motivated by legal concerns: discrimination in recruiting, hiring, advancement, and firing is illegal under federal law and is prosecuted by the EEOC.[31] Companies that violate antidiscrimination laws not only are subject to severe financial penalties but also risk damage to their reputations. In November 2004, for example, the EEOC charged that recruiting policies at Abercrombie & Fitch, a national chain of retail clothing stores, had discriminated against minority and female job applicants between 1999 and 2004. The employer, charged the EEOC, had hired a disproportionate number of white salespeople, placed minorities and women in less visible positions, and promoted a virtually all-white image in its marketing efforts. Six days after the EEOC filed a lawsuit, the company settled the case at a cost of $50 million, but the negative publicity will hamper both recruitment and sales for some time to come.[32]

TABLE 7.1 Employment by Gender and Ethnic Group

Group	Total (%)	Males (%)	Females (%)
All employees	100	52	48
White	68	36	32
African American	14	6	8
Hispanic or Latino	13	7	5
Asian/Pacific Islander/Other	5	3	3

There's good reason for building a diverse workforce that goes well beyond mere compliance with legal standards. It even goes beyond commitment to ethical standards. It's good business. People with diverse backgrounds bring fresh points of view that can be invaluable in generating ideas and solving problems. In addition, they can be the key to connecting with an ethnically diverse customer base. If a large percentage of your customers are Hispanic or Latino, it might make sense to have a Hispanic or Latino marketing manager. In short, capitalizing on the benefits of a diverse workforce means that employers should view differences as assets rather than liabilities.

KEY TAKEAWAYS

- The process of introducing new employees to their jobs and to the company is called **orientation**.
- An effective approach is to take things slowly, providing new employees with information on a need-to-know basis while making them feel as comfortable as possible.
- New employees will need initial training to start their jobs, and they'll need additional training as they grow in or change their jobs.
- **Off-the-job training** allows them to focus on learning without the distractions that would occur in the office, but **on-the-job training** is more common.
- In addition to having well-trained employees, it's important that a workforce reflects the broad range of differences in the population.
- The efforts of HR managers to build a workforce that's representative of the general population are driven in part by legal concerns: discrimination is illegal, and companies that violate antidiscrimination laws are subject to prosecution.
- But ensuring a diverse workforce goes well beyond both legal compliance and ethical commitment. It's good business, because a diverse group of employees can bring fresh points of view that may be valuable in generating ideas and solving problems.
- Additionally, people from varied backgrounds can help an organization connect with an ethnically diverse customer base.

Before going to the next section of this chapter, take a few minutes to test your knowledge of the material covered in this section. Quizzes can be found under the "Resources" tab, "Study Aids: Quizzes."

1. Think about a full-time or part-time job that you've held. Was your orientation to the job satisfactory? If not, how would you have improved the process? Did you receive any training? Was it useful? What additional training would have helped you do a better job? How would it have benefited the company?

2. While visiting a mall in Los Angeles, you noticed two stores located side by side selling electronic-entertainment products—CDs, DVDs, and so on. All the employees in one store were white males. The mix of workers in the other store—which happened to be more profitable—was more diverse. Why do you think the store with the diverse workforce did more business? In terms of diversity, what would be your ideal workforce in a store similar to these in Los Angeles?

3. MOTIVATING EMPLOYEES

LEARNING OBJECTIVES

1. Define "motivation," and identify several theories of motivation.
2. Explain the hierarchy-of-needs theory, and indicate whether you believe it makes intuitive sense.
3. Describe the two-factor theory, and indicate what it means for managers.
4. Explain expectancy theory, and indicate how managers can use the theory to offer rewards to employees, set performance levels, and ensure a strong link between performance and reward.
5. Describe equity theory, and explain whether you find it appealing.

motivation

Internally generated drive to achieve a goal or follow a particular course of action.

Motivation refers to an internally generated drive to achieve a goal or follow a particular course of action. Highly motivated employees focus their efforts on achieving specific goals; those who are unmotivated don't. It's the manager's job, therefore, to motivate employees—to get them to try to do the best job they can. But what motivates employees to do well? How does a manager encourage employees to show up for work each day and do a good job? Paying them helps, but many other factors influence a person's desire (or lack of it) to excel in the workplace. What are these factors? Are they the same for everybody? Do they change over time? To address these questions, we'll examine four of the most influential theories of motivation: *hierarchy-of-needs theory*, *two-factor theory*, *expectancy theory*, and *equity theory*.

3.1 Hierarchy-of-Needs Theory

hierarchy-of-needs theory

Theory of motivation that holds that people are motivated by a hierarchical series of unmet needs.

Psychologist Abraham Maslow's **hierarchy-of-needs theory** proposed that we are motivated by the five unmet needs, arranged in the hierarchical order shown in Figure 7.3, which also lists examples of each type of need in both the personal and work spheres of life. Look, for instance, at the list of personal needs in the left-hand column. At the bottom are *physiological* needs (such life-sustaining needs as food and shelter). Working up the hierarchy we experience *safety* needs (financial stability, freedom from physical harm), *social* needs (the need to belong and have friends), *esteem* needs (the need for self-respect and status), and *self-actualization* needs (the need to reach one's full potential or achieve some creative success).

FIGURE 7.3 Maslow's Hierarchy-of-Needs Theory

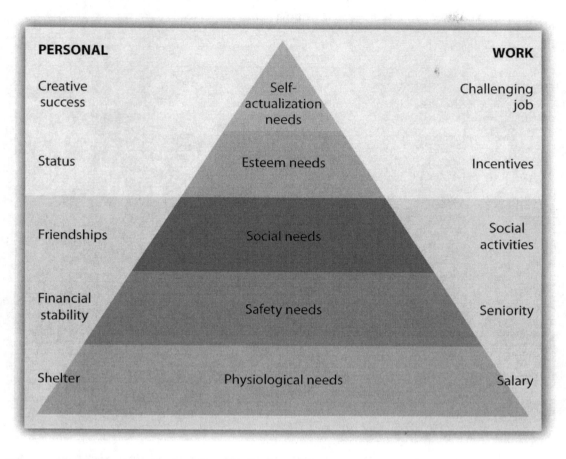

There are two things to remember about Maslow's model:

1. We must satisfy lower-level needs before we seek to satisfy higher-level needs.
2. Once we've satisfied a need, it no longer motivates us; the next higher need takes its place.

Let's say, for example, that you've just returned to college and that for a variety of reasons that aren't your fault, you're broke, hungry, and homeless. Because you'll probably take almost any job that will pay for food and housing (*physiological* needs), you go to work repossessing cars. Fortunately, your student loan finally comes through, and with enough money to feed yourself, you can look for a job that's not so risky (a *safety* need). You find a job as a night janitor in the library, and though you feel secure, you start to feel cut off from your friends, who are active during daylight hours. You want to work among people, not books (a *social* need). So now you join several of your friends selling pizza in the student center. This job improves your social life, but even though you're very good at making pizzas, it's not terribly satisfying. You'd like something that will let you display your intellectual talents (an *esteem* need). So you study hard and land a job as an intern in the governor's office. On graduation, you move up through a series of government appointments and eventually run for state senator. As you're sworn into office, you realize that you've reached your full potential (a *self-actualization* need) and you comment to yourself, "It doesn't get any better than this."

Needs Theory and the Workplace

FIGURE 7.4

Employees are motivated by different factors. For some, the ability to have fun at work is a priority.

© *Thinkstock Corporation*

What implications does Maslow's theory have for business managers? There are two key points: (1) not all employees are driven by the same needs, and (2) the needs that motivate individuals can change over time. Managers should consider which needs different employees are trying to satisfy and should structure rewards and other forms of recognition accordingly. For example, when you got your first job repossessing cars, you were motivated by the need for money to buy food. If you'd been given a choice between a raise and a plaque recognizing your accomplishments, you'd undoubtedly have opted for the money. As a state senator, by contrast, you may prefer public recognition of work well done (say, election to higher office) to a pay raise.

3.2 Two-Factor Theory

Another psychologist, Frederick Herzberg, set out to determine which work factors (such as wages, job security, or advancement) made people feel good about their jobs and which factors made them feel bad about their jobs. He surveyed workers, analyzed the results, and concluded that to understand employee *satisfaction* (or *dissatisfaction*), he had to divide work factors into two categories:

- *Motivation factors.* Those factors that are strong contributors to job satisfaction
- *Hygiene factors.* Those factors that are *not* strong contributors to satisfaction but that must be present to meet a worker's expectations and prevent job dissatisfaction

Figure 7.5 illustrates Herzberg's **two-factor theory**. Note that motivation factors (such as promotion opportunities) relate to *the nature of the work itself and the way the employee performs it.* Hygiene factors (such as physical working conditions) relate to *the environment in which it's performed.* (Note, too, the similarity between Herzberg's motivation factors and Maslow's esteem and self-actualization needs.)

two-factor theory

Theory that holds that motivation involves both motivation factors (which contribute to job satisfaction) and hygiene factors (which help to prevent job dissatisfaction).

FIGURE 7.5 Herzberg's Two-Factor Theory

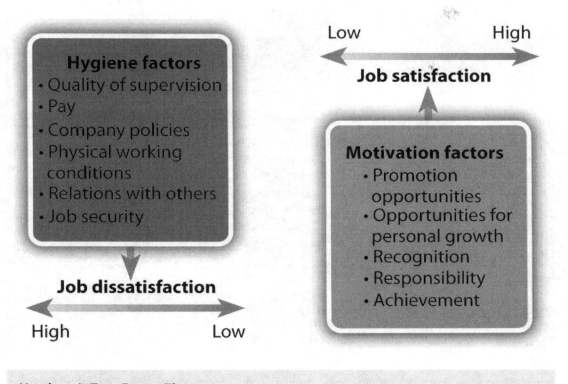

Herzberg's Two-Factor Theory

Click on this link to experience an active version of this figure.

Two-Factor Theory and the Workplace

We'll ask the same question about Herzberg's model as we did about Maslow's: What does it mean for managers? Suppose you're a senior manager in an accounting firm, where you supervise a team of accountants, each of whom has been with the firm for five years. How would you use Herzberg's model to motivate the employees who report to you? Let's start with hygiene factors. Are salaries reasonable? What about working conditions? Does each accountant have his or her own workspace, or are they crammed into tiny workrooms? Are they being properly supervised or are they left on their own to sink or swim? If hygiene factors like these don't meet employees' expectations, they may be dissatisfied with their jobs.

As you can see in Figure 7.5, fixing problems related to hygiene factors may alleviate job *dissatisfaction*, but it won't necessarily improve anyone's job *satisfaction*. To increase satisfaction (and motivate someone to perform better), you must address motivation factors. Is the work itself challenging and stimulating? Do employees receive recognition for jobs well done? Will the work that an accountant has been assigned help him or her to advance in the firm? According to Herzberg, motivation requires a twofold approach: eliminating dissatisfiers and enhancing satisfiers.

3.3   Expectancy Theory

If you were a manager, wouldn't you like to know how your employees decide to work hard or goof off? Wouldn't it be nice to know whether a planned rewards program will have the desired effect—namely, motivating them to perform better in their jobs? Wouldn't it be helpful if you could measure the effect of bonuses on employee productivity? These are the issues considered by psychologist Victor Vroom in his **expectancy theory**, which proposes that employees will work hard to earn rewards that they value and that they consider obtainable.

As you can see from Figure 7.6, Vroom argues that an employee will be motivated to exert a high level of effort to obtain a reward under three conditions:

1. The employee believes that his or her efforts will result in acceptable performance.

2. The employee believes that acceptable performance will lead to the desired outcome or reward.

3. The employee values the reward.

expectancy theory

Theory of motivation that proposes that employees will work hard to earn rewards they value and consider obtainable.

FIGURE 7.6 Vroom's Expectancy Theory

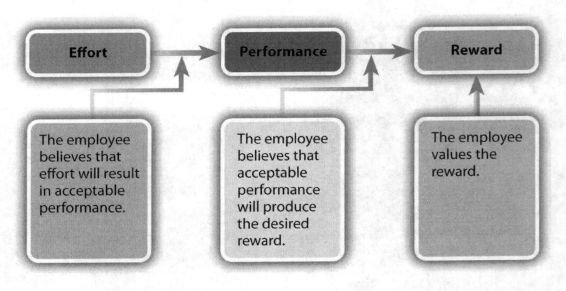

Vroom's Expectancy Theory

Click on this link to experience an active version of this figure.

Expectancy Theory and the Workplace

To apply expectancy theory to a real-world situation, let's analyze an automobile-insurance company with one hundred agents who work from a call center. Assume that the firm pays a base salary of $2,000 a month, plus a $200 commission on each policy sold above ten policies a month. In terms of expectancy theory, under what conditions would an agent be motivated to sell more than ten policies a month?

1. The agent would have to believe that his or her efforts would result in policy sales (that, in other words, there's a positive link between effort and performance).
2. The agent would have to be confident that if he or she sold more than ten policies in a given month, there would indeed be a bonus (a positive link between performance and reward).
3. The bonus per policy—$200—would have to be of value to the agent.

Now let's alter the scenario slightly. Say that the company raises prices, thus making it harder to sell the policies. How will agents' motivation be affected? According to expectancy theory, motivation will suffer. Why? Because agents may be less confident that their efforts will lead to satisfactory performance. What if the company introduces a policy whereby agents get bonuses only if buyers don't cancel policies within ninety days? How will this policy affect motivation? Now agents may be less confident that they'll get bonuses even if they do sell more than ten policies. Motivation will decrease because the link between performance and reward has been weakened. Finally, what will happen if bonuses are cut from $200 to $25? Obviously, the reward would be of less value to agents, and, again, motivation will suffer. The message of expectancy theory, then, is fairly clear: managers should offer rewards that employees value, set performance levels that they can reach, and ensure a strong link between performance and reward.

3.4 Equity Theory

What if you spent thirty hours working on a class report, did everything you were supposed to do, and handed in an excellent assignment (in your opinion). Your roommate, on the other hand, spent about five hours and put everything together at the last minute. You know, moreover, that he ignored half the requirements and never even ran his assignment through a spell-checker. A week later, your teacher returns the reports. You get a C and your roommate gets a B+. In all likelihood, you'll feel that you've been treated unfairly relative to your roommate.

Your reaction makes sense according to the **equity theory** of motivation, which focuses on our perceptions of how fairly we're treated *relative to others*. Applied to the work environment, this theory proposes that employees analyze their contributions or job inputs (hours worked, education, experience, work performance) and their rewards or job outcomes (salary, benefits, recognition). Then they create a contributions/rewards ratio and compare it to those of other people. The basis of comparison can be any one of the following:

- Someone in a similar *position*
- Someone holding a different position in the same *organization*
- Someone with a similar *occupation*
- Someone who shares certain *characteristics* (such as age, education, or level of experience)
- Oneself at another point in time

When individuals perceive that the ratio of their contributions to rewards is comparable to that of others, they perceive that they're being treated equitably; when they perceive that the ratio is out of balance, they perceive inequity. Occasionally, people will perceive that they're being treated better than others. More often, however, they conclude that others are being treated better (and that they themselves are being treated worse). This is what you concluded when you saw your grade. You've calculated your ratio of contributions (hours worked, research and writing skills) to rewards (project grade), compared it to your roommate's ratio, and concluded that the two ratios are out of balance.

What will an employee do if he or she perceives an inequity? The individual might try to bring the ratio into balance, either by decreasing inputs (working fewer hours, refusing to take on additional tasks) or by increasing outputs (asking for a raise). If this strategy fails, an employee might complain to a supervisor, transfer to another job, leave the organization, or rationalize the situation (perhaps deciding that the situation isn't so bad after all). Equity theory advises managers to focus on treating workers fairly, especially in determining compensation, which is, naturally, a common basis of comparison.

equity theory

Theory of motivation that focuses on our perceptions of how fairly we're treated relative to others.

KEY TAKEAWAYS

- **Motivation** describes an internally generated drive that propels people to achieve goals or pursue particular courses of action.
- There are four influential theories of motivation: hierarchy-of-needs theory, two-factor theory, expectancy theory, and equity theory.
- **Hierarchy-of-needs theory** proposes that we're motivated by five unmet needs—physiological, safety, social, esteem, and self-actualization— and must satisfy lower-level needs before we seek to satisfy higher-level needs.
- **Two-factor theory** divides work factors into motivation factors (those that are strong contributors to job satisfaction) and hygiene factors (those that, though not strong contributors to satisfaction, must be present to prevent job dissatisfaction). To increase satisfaction (and motivate someone to perform better), managers must address motivation factors.
- **Expectancy theory** proposes that employees work hard to obtain a reward when they value the reward, believe that their efforts will result in acceptable performance, and believe that acceptable performance will lead to a desired outcome or reward.
- **Equity theory** focuses on our perceptions of how fairly we're treated relative to others. This theory proposes that employees create contributions/rewards ratios that they compare to those of others. If they feel that their ratios are comparable to those of others, they'll perceive that they're being treated equitably.

Before going to the next section of this chapter, take a few minutes to test your knowledge of the material covered in this section. Quizzes can be found under the "Resources" tab, "Study Aids: Quizzes."

EXERCISE

This chapter describes four theories of motivation: hierarchy-of-needs theory, two-factor theory, expectancy theory, and equity theory. Briefly describe each theory. Which one makes the most intuitive sense to you? Why do you find it appealing?

4. WHAT MAKES A GREAT PLACE TO WORK?

L E A R N I N G   O B J E C T I V E S

1. Describe the following three types of job redesign: job rotation, job enlargement, and job enrichment.
2. Discuss the following company benefits designed to help employees strike a balance between their work and home lives: flextime, job sharing, telecommuting, dependent care, paid leave for new parents, employee-assistance programs, and on-site fitness centers.
3. Identify factors that make an organization a good place to work.
4. Compare wages with salaries.
5. Explain the following forms of compensation: commissions based on sales, commissions based on a piecework approach, bonuses, participation in profit-sharing plans, and stock options.
6. Identify the more common forms of employee benefits.

Every year, the Great Places to Work Institute analyzes comments from thousands of employees and compiles a list of "The 100 Best Companies to Work for in America," which is published in *Fortune* magazine. Having compiled its list for more than twenty years, the institute concludes that the defining characteristic of a great company to work for is trust between managers and employees. Employees overwhelmingly say that they want to work at a place where employees "trust the people they work for, have pride in what they do, and enjoy the people they work with."[33] They report that they're motivated to perform well because they're challenged, respected, treated fairly, and appreciated. They take pride in what they do, are made to feel that they make a difference, and are given opportunities for advancement.[34] The most effective motivators, it would seem, are closely aligned with Maslow's higher-level needs and Herzberg's motivating factors.

4.1 Job Redesign

job redesign

Management strategy used to increase job satisfaction by making jobs more interesting and challenging.

The average employee spends more than two thousand hours a year at work. If the job is tedious, unpleasant, or otherwise unfulfilling, the employee probably won't be motivated to perform at a very high level. Many companies practice a policy of **job redesign** to make jobs more interesting and challenging. Common strategies include *job rotation*, *job enlargement*, and *job enrichment*.

Job Rotation

job rotation

Job redesign strategy that allows employees to rotate from one job to another on a systematic basis.

Specialization promotes efficiency because workers get very good at doing particular tasks. The drawback is the tedium of repeating the same task day in and day out. The practice of **job rotation** allows employees to rotate from one job to another on a systematic basis, eventually cycling back to their original tasks. A computer maker, for example, might rotate a technician into the sales department to increase the employee's awareness of customer needs and to give the employee a broader understanding of the company's goals and operations. A hotel might rotate an accounting clerk to the check-in desk for a few hours each day to add variety to the daily workload. Rotated employees develop new skills and gain experience that increases their value to the company, which benefits management because cross-trained employees can fill in for absentees, thus providing greater flexibility in scheduling.

Job Enlargement

job enlargement

Job redesign strategy in which management enhances a job by adding tasks at similar skill levels.

Instead of a job in which you performed just one or two tasks, wouldn't you prefer a job that gave you many different tasks? In theory, you'd be less bored and more highly motivated if you had a chance at **job enlargement**—the policy of enhancing a job by adding tasks at similar skill levels (see Figure 7.7). The job of sales clerk, for example, might be expanded to include gift-wrapping and packaging items for shipment. The additional duties would add variety without entailing higher skill levels.

FIGURE 7.7 Job Enlargement versus Job Enrichment

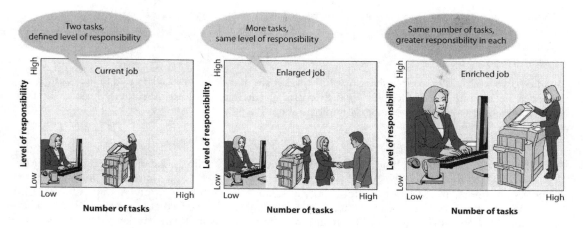

Job Enrichment

As you can see from Figure 7.7, merely expanding a job by adding similar tasks won't necessarily "enrich" it by making it more challenging and rewarding. **Job enrichment** is the practice of adding tasks that increase both responsibility and opportunity for growth. It provides the kinds of benefits that, according to Maslow and Herzberg, contribute to job satisfaction: stimulating work, sense of personal achievement, self-esteem, recognition, and a chance to reach your potential.

Consider, for example, the evolving role of support staff in the contemporary office. Today, employees who used to be called "secretaries" assume many duties previously in the domain of management, such as project coordination and public relations. Information technology has enriched their jobs because they can now apply such skills as word processing, desktop publishing, creating spreadsheets, and managing databases. That's why we now hear such a term as *administrative assistant* instead of *secretary*.[35]

> **job enrichment**
>
> Job redesign strategy in which management enriches a job by adding tasks that increase both responsibility and opportunity for growth.

4.2 Work/Life Quality

Building a career requires a substantial commitment in time and energy, and most people find that they aren't left with much time for nonwork activities. Fortunately, many organizations recognize the need to help employees strike a balance between their work and home lives.[36] By helping employees combine satisfying careers and fulfilling personal lives, companies tend to end up with a happier, less-stressed, and more productive workforce. The financial benefits include lower absenteeism, turnover, and health care costs.

Alternative Work Arrangements

The accounting firm KPMG, which has made the list of the "100 Best Companies for Working Mothers" for twelve years and "100 Best Companies to Work For" for seven years,[37] is committed to promoting a balance between its employees' work and personal lives. KPMG offers a variety of work arrangements designed to accommodate different employee needs and provide scheduling flexibility.[38]

Flextime

Employers who provide for **flextime** set guidelines that allow employees to designate starting and quitting times. Guidelines, for example, might specify that all employees must work eight hours a day (with an hour for lunch) and that four of those hours must be between 10 a.m. and 3 p.m. Thus, you could come in at 7 a.m. and leave at 4 p.m., while coworkers arrive at 10 a.m. and leave at 7 p.m. With permission, you could even choose to work from 8 a.m to 2 p.m., take two hours for lunch, and then work from 4 p.m. to 6 p.m.

> **flextime**
>
> Alternative work arrangement that allows employees to designate starting and quitting times.

Compressed Workweeks

Rather than work eight hours a day for five days a week, you might elect to earn a three-day weekend by working ten hours a day for four days a week.

Part-Time Work

If you're willing to have your pay and benefits adjusted accordingly, you can work fewer than forty hours a week.

Job Sharing

Under **job sharing**, two people share one full-time position, splitting the salary and benefits of the position as each handles half the job. Often they arrange their schedules to include at least an hour of shared time during which they can communicate about the job.

Telecommuting

Telecommuting means that you regularly work from home (or from some other nonwork location). You're connected to the office by computer, fax, and phone. You save on commuting time, enjoy more flexible work hours, and have more opportunity to spend time with your family. A study of 5,500 IBM employees (one-fifth of whom telecommute) found that those who worked at home not only had a better balance between work and home life but also were more highly motivated and less likely to leave the organization.[39]

Though it's hard to count telecommuters accurately, some estimates put the number of people who work at home at least one day a week at 20 percent. This estimate includes 2 percent of workers who run home-based businesses and 2 percent who work exclusively at home for other companies.[40] Telecommuting isn't for everyone. Working at home means that you have to discipline yourself to avoid distractions, such as TV, personal phone calls, home chores, or pets, and some people feel isolated from social interaction in the workplace.

4.3 Family-Friendly Programs

In addition to alternative work arrangements, many employers, including KPMG, offer programs and benefits designed to help employees meet family and home obligations while maintaining busy careers. KPMG offers each of the following benefits.[41]

Dependent Care

Caring for dependents—young children and elderly parents—is of utmost importance to some employees, but combining dependent-care responsibilities with a busy job can be particularly difficult. KPMG provides on-site child care during tax season (when employees are especially busy) and offers emergency backup dependent care all year round, either at a provider's facility or in the employee's home. To get referrals or information, employees can call KPMG's LifeWorks Resource and Referral Service. KPMG is by no means unique in this respect: more than eight thousand companies maintain on-site day care,[42] 9 percent of employers offer company-supported child care,[43] 4 percent offer back-up emergency child care, and 2 percent offer backup elder care.[44]

Paid Parental Leave

Any employee (whether male or female) who becomes a parent can take two weeks of paid leave. New mothers also get time off through short-term disability benefits.

Caring for Yourself

Like many companies, KPMG allows employees to aggregate all paid days off and use them in any way they want. In other words, instead of getting, say, ten sick days, five personal days, and fifteen vacation days, you get a total of thirty days to use for anything. If you're having personal problems, you can contact the Employee Assistance Program. If staying fit makes you happier and more productive, you can take out a discount membership at one of more than nine thousand health clubs.

4.4 Unmarried without Children

You've undoubtedly noticed by now that many programs for balancing work and personal lives target married people, particularly those with children. Single individuals also have trouble striking a satisfactory balance between work and nonwork activities, but many single workers feel that they aren't getting equal consideration from employers.[45] They report that they're often expected to work longer hours, travel more, and take on difficult assignments to compensate for married employees with family commitments.

Needless to say, requiring singles to take on additional responsibilities can make it harder for them to balance their work and personal lives. It's harder to plan and keep personal commitments while meeting heavy work responsibilities, and establishing and maintaining social relations is difficult if work schedules are unpredictable or too demanding. Frustration can lead to increased stress and job dissatisfaction. In several studies of stress in the accounting profession, unmarried workers reported higher levels of stress than any other group, including married people with children.[46]

With singles, as with married people, companies can reap substantial benefits from programs that help employees balance their work and nonwork lives: they can increase job satisfaction and employee productivity and reduce turnover. PepsiCo, for example, offers a "concierge service," which maintains a dry cleaner, travel agency, convenience store, and fitness center on the premises of its national office in Somers, New York.[47] Single employees seem to find these services helpful, but what they value most of all is control over their time. In particular, they want predictable schedules that allow them to plan social and personal activities. They don't want employers assuming that being single means that they can change plans at the last minute. It's often more difficult for singles to deal with last-minute changes because, unlike married coworkers, they don't have the at-home support structure to handle such tasks as tending to elderly parents or caring for pets.

4.5   Compensation and Benefits

Though paychecks and benefits packages aren't the only reasons why people work, they do matter. Competitive pay and benefits also help organizations attract and retain qualified employees. Companies that pay their employees more than their competitors generally have lower turnover. Consider, for example, The Container Store, which regularly appears on *Fortune* magazine's list of "The 100 Best Companies to Work For."[48] The retail chain staffs its stores with fewer employees than its competitors but pays them more—in some cases, three times the industry average for retail workers. This strategy allows the company to attract extremely talented workers who, moreover, aren't likely to leave the company. Low turnover is particularly valuable in the retail industry because it depends on service-oriented personnel to generate repeat business.

In addition to salary and wages, compensation packages often include other financial incentives, such as bonuses and profit-sharing plans, as well as benefits, such as medical insurance, vacation time, sick leave, and retirement accounts.

4.6   Wages and Salaries

The largest, and most important, component of a compensation package is the payment of wages or salary. If you're paid according to the number of hours you work, you're earning **wages**. Counter personnel at McDonald's, for instance, get wages, which are determined by multiplying an employee's hourly wage rate by the number of hours worked during the pay period. On the other hand, if you're paid for fulfilling the responsibilities of a position—regardless of the number of hours required to do it—you're earning a **salary**. The McDonald's manager gets a salary for overseeing the operations of the restaurant. He or she is expected to work as long as it takes to get the job done, without any adjustment in compensation.

Piecework and Commissions

Sometimes it makes more sense to pay workers according to the quantity of product that they produce or sell. Byrd's Seafood, a crab-processing plant in Crisfield, Maryland, pays workers on **piecework**: workers' pay is based on the amount of crabmeat that's picked from recently cooked crabs. (A good picker can produce fifteen pounds of crabmeat an hour and earn about $100 a day.)[49] If you're working on **commission**, you're probably getting paid for quantity of sales. If you were a sales representative for an insurance company, like The Hartford, you'd get a certain amount of money for each automobile or homeowner policy that you sell.

4.7   Incentive Programs

In addition to regular paychecks, many people receive financial rewards based on performance, whether their own, their employer's, or both. At computer-chip maker Texas Instruments (TI), for example, employees may be eligible for bonuses, profit sharing, and stock options. All three plans are **incentive programs**: programs designed to reward employees for good performance.[50]

wages

Compensation paid to employees based on the number of hours worked.

salary

Compensation paid for fulfilling the responsibilities of a position regardless of the number of hours required to do it.

piecework

Compensation paid to workers according to the quantity of a product that they produce or sell.

commission

Compensation paid to employees based on the dollar amount of sales that they make.

incentive programs

Program designed to financially reward employees for good performance.

Bonus Plans

bonuses

Annual income given to employees (in addition to salary) based on company-wide performance.

TI's year-end **bonuses**—annual income given in addition to salary—are based on company-wide performance. If the company has a profitable year, and if you contributed to that success, you'll get a bonus. If the company doesn't do well, you're out of luck, regardless of what you contributed.

Bonus plans have become quite common, and the range of employees eligible for bonuses has widened in recent years. In the past, bonus plans were usually reserved for managers above a certain level. Today, however, companies have realized the value of extending plans to include employees at virtually every level. The magnitude of bonuses still favors those at the top. High-ranking officers (such as CEOs and CFOs) often get bonuses ranging from 30 percent to 50 percent of their salaries. Upper-level managers may get from 15 percent to 25 percent and middle managers from 10 percent to 15 percent. At lower levels, employees may expect bonuses from 3 percent to 5 percent of their annual compensation.[51]

Profit-Sharing Plans

profit-sharing plan

Incentive program that uses a predetermined formula to distribute a share of company profits to eligible employees.

TI also maintains a **profit-sharing plan**, which relies on a predetermined formula to distribute a share of the company's profits to eligible employees. Today, about 40 percent of all U.S. companies offer some type of profit-sharing program.[52] TI's plan, however, is a little unusual: while most plans don't allow employees to access profit-sharing funds until retirement or termination, TI employees get their shares immediately—in cash.

TI's plan is also pretty generous—as long as the company has a good year. Here's how it works. An employee's profit share depends on the company's operating profit for the year. If profits from operations reach 10 percent of sales, the employee gets a bonus worth 4 percent of his or her salary. If operating profit soars to 20 percent, the employee bonuses go up to 26 percent of salary. But if operating profits fall short of a certain threshold, nobody gets anything.[53]

Stock-Option Plans

stock-option plans

Incentive program that allows eligible employees to buy a specific number of shares of company stock at a set price on a specified date.

Like most **stock-option plans**, the TI plan gives employees the right to buy a specific number of shares of company stock at a set price on a specified date. At TI, an employee may buy stock at its selling price at the time when he or she was given the option. So, if the price of the stock goes up, the employee benefits. Say, for example, that the stock was selling for $30 a share when the option was granted in 2007. In 2011, it was selling for $40 a share. Exercising his or her option, the employee could buy TI stock at the 2007 price of $30 a share—a bargain price.[54]

At TI, stock options are used as an incentive to attract and retain top people. Starbucks, by contrast, isn't nearly as selective in awarding stock options. At Starbucks, all employees can earn "Bean Stock"—the Starbucks employee stock-option plan. Both full- and part-time employees get options to buy Starbucks shares at a set price. If the company does well and its stock goes up, employees make a profit. CEO Howard Schultz believes that Bean Stock pays off: because employees are rewarded when the company does well, they have a stronger incentive to add value to the company (and so drive up its stock price). Shortly after the program was begun, the phrase "bean-stocking" became workplace lingo for figuring out how to save the company money.

4.8 Benefits

benefits

Compensation other than salaries, hourly wages, or financial incentives.

Another major component of an employee's compensation package is **benefits**—compensation other than salaries, hourly wages, or financial incentives. Types of benefits include the following:

- Legally required benefits (Social Security and Medicare, unemployment insurance, workers' compensation)
- Paid time off (vacations, holidays, sick leave)
- Insurance (health benefits, life insurance, disability insurance)
- Retirement benefits

Unfortunately, the cost of providing benefits is staggering. According to the Employee Benefit Research Institute, it costs an employer 30 percent of a worker's salary to provide the same worker with benefits. If you include pay for time not worked (while on vacation or sick and so on), the percentage increases to 41 percent. So if you're a manager making $100,000 a year, your employer is also paying out another $41,000 for your benefits. The most money goes for health care (8 percent of salary costs), paid time off (11 percent), and retirement benefits (5 percent).[55]

Some workers receive only benefits required by law, including Social Security, unemployment, and workers' compensation. Low-wage workers generally get only limited benefits and part-timers often nothing at all.[56] Again, Starbucks is generous in offering benefits. The company provides benefits even to the part-timers who make up two-thirds of the company's workforce; anyone working at least twenty hours a week gets medical coverage.

Let Me See the Noncash Incentive

Take a moment to pick the non-cash incentives you'd like from your employer. Click here to complete the exercise.

KEY TAKEAWAYS

- Employees report that they're motivated to perform well when they're challenged, respected, treated fairly, and appreciated.
- Other factors may contribute to employee satisfaction. Some companies use **job redesign** to make jobs more interesting and challenging.
    - **Job rotation** allows employees to rotate from one job to another on a systematic basis.
    - **Job enlargement** enhances a job by adding tasks at similar skill levels.
    - **Job enrichment** adds tasks that increase both responsibility and opportunity for growth.
- Many organizations recognize the need to help employees strike a balance between their work and home lives and offer a variety of work arrangements to accommodate different employee needs.
- **Flextime** allows employees to designate starting and quitting times, compress workweeks, or perform part-time work.
- With **job sharing**, two people share one full-time position.
- **Telecommuting** means working from home. Many employers also offer dependent care, paid leave for new parents, employee-assistance programs, and on-site fitness centers.
- Competitive compensation also helps.
- Workers who are paid by the hour earn **wages**, while those who are paid to fulfill the responsibilities of the job earn **salaries**.
- Some people receive **commissions** based on sales or are paid for output, based on a **piecework** approach.
- In addition to pay, many employees can earn financial rewards based on their own and/or their employer's performance.
- They may receive year-end **bonuses**, participate in **profit-sharing plans** (which use predetermined formulas to distribute a share of company profits among employees), or receive **stock options** (which let them buy shares of company stock at set prices).
- Another component of many compensation packages is **benefits**—compensation other than salaries, wages, or financial incentives. Benefits may include paid time off, insurance, and retirement benefits.

Before going to the next section of this chapter, take a few minutes to test your knowledge of the material covered in this section. Quizzes can be found under the "Resources" tab, "Study Aids: Quizzes."

EXERCISES

1. Describe the ideal job that you'd like to have once you've finished college. Be sure to explain the type of work schedule that you'd find most satisfactory, and why. Identify family-friendly programs that you'd find desirable and explain why these appeal to you.
2. Describe a typical compensation package for a sales manager in a large organization. If you could design your own compensation package, what would it include?

5. PERFORMANCE APPRAISAL

LEARNING OBJECTIVES

1. Explain how managers evaluate work performance.
2. Identify a variety of steps managers can take to retain qualified employees.
3. Identify potential reasons why employers may have to terminate some workers.
4. Explain the employment relationship classified as employment-at-will.

performance appraisals

Formal process in which a manager evaluates an employee's work performance.

Employees generally want their managers to tell them three things: what they should be doing, how well they're doing it, and how they can improve their performance. Good managers address these issues on an ongoing basis. On a semiannual or annual basis, they also conduct formal **performance appraisals** to discuss and evaluate employees' work performance.

5.1 The Basic Three-Step Process

Appraisal systems vary both by organization and by the level of the employee being evaluated, but as you can see in Figure 7.8, it's generally a three-step process:

1. Before managers can measure performance, they must set goals and performance expectations and specify the criteria (such as quality of work, quantity of work, dependability, initiative) that they'll use to measure performance.

2. At the end of a specified time period, managers complete written evaluations that rate employee performance according to the predetermined criteria.

3. Managers then meet with each employee to discuss the evaluation. Jointly, they suggest ways in which the employee can improve performance, which might include further training and development.

FIGURE 7.8 How to Do a Performance Appraisal

1 Set goals and performance expectations and specify the criteria that will be used to measure performance.

2 Complete a written evaluation that rates performance according to the stipulated criteria.

3 Meet with the employee to discuss the evaluation and suggest means of improving performance.

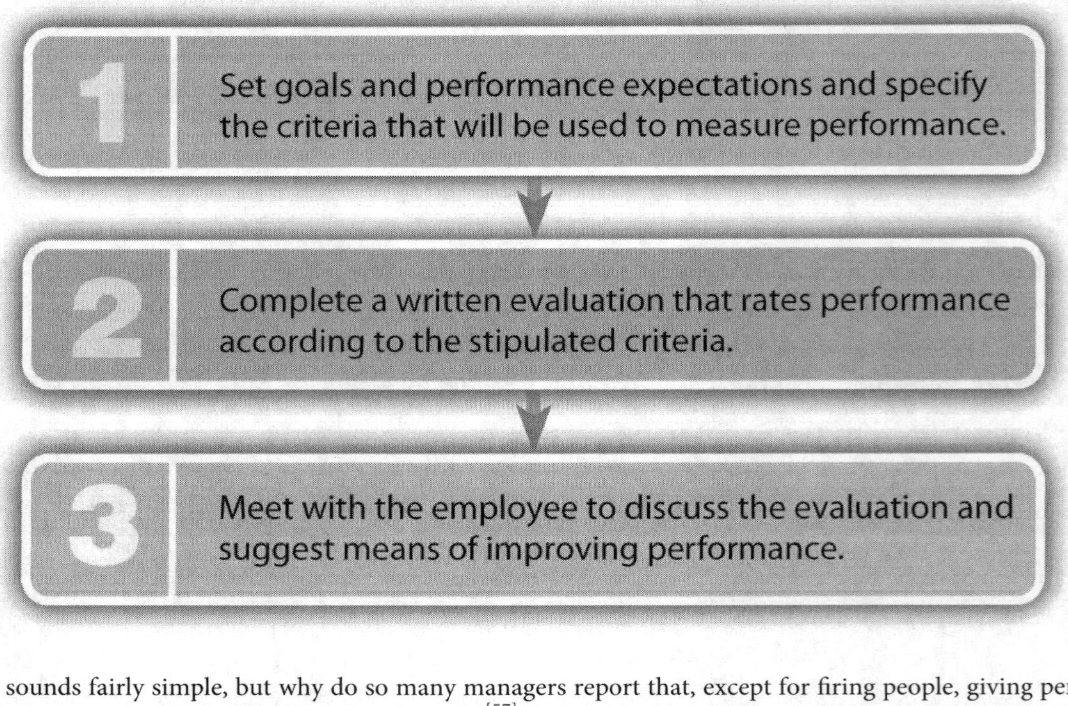

It sounds fairly simple, but why do so many managers report that, except for firing people, giving performance appraisals is their least favorite task?[57] To get some perspective on this question, we'll look at performance appraisals from both sides, explaining the benefits and identifying potential problems with some of the most common practices.

Among other benefits, formal appraisals provide the following:

- An opportunity for managers and employees to discuss an employee's performance and to set future goals and performance expectations
- A chance to identify and discuss appropriate training and career-development opportunities for an employee
- Formal documentation of the evaluation that can be used for salary, promotion, demotion, or dismissal purposes[58]

As for disadvantages, most stem from the fact that appraisals are often used to determine salaries for the upcoming year. Consequently, meetings to discuss performance tend to take on an entirely different dimension: the manager appears judgmental (rather than supportive), and the employee gets defensive. It's the adversarial atmosphere that makes many managers not only uncomfortable with the task but also unlikely to give honest feedback. (They tend to give higher marks in order to avoid delving into critical evaluations.) HR professionals disagree about whether performance appraisals should be linked to pay increases. Some experts argue that the connection eliminates the manager's opportunity to use the appraisal to improve an employee's performance. Others maintain that it increases employee satisfaction with the process and distributes raises on the basis of effort and results.[59]

5.2   360-Degree and Upward Feedback

Instead of being evaluated by one person, how would you like to be evaluated by several people—not only those above you in the organization but those below and beside you? The approach is called *360-degree feedback*, and the purpose is to ensure that employees (mostly managers) get feedback from all directions—from supervisors, reporting subordinates, coworkers, and even customers. If it's conducted correctly, this technique furnishes managers with a range of insights into their performance in a number of roles.

Some experts, however, regard the 360-degree approach as too cumbersome. An alternative technique, called *upward feedback*, requires only the manager's subordinates to provide feedback. Computer maker Dell uses this approach as part of its manager-development plan. Every six months, forty thousand Dell employees complete a survey in which they rate their supervisors on a number of dimensions, such as practicing ethical business principles and providing support in balancing work and personal life. Like most companies using this technique, Dell uses survey results for development purposes only, not as direct input into decisions on pay increases or promotions.[60]

5.3   Retaining Valuable Employees

When a valued employee quits, the loss to the employer can be serious. Not only will the firm incur substantial costs to recruit and train a replacement, but it also may suffer temporary declines in productivity and lower morale among remaining employees who have to take on heavier workloads. Given the negative impact of **turnover**—the permanent separation of an employee from a company—most organizations do whatever they can to retain qualified employees. Compensation plays a key role in this effort: companies that don't offer competitive compensation packages (including benefits) tend to lose employees. But other factors come into play, some of which we discussed earlier, such as training and development, as well as helping employees achieve a satisfying work/nonwork balance. In the following sections, we'll look at a few other strategies for reducing turnover and increasing productivity.[61]

turnover

Permanent separation of an employee from a company.

Creating a Positive Work Environment

Employees who are happy at work are more productive, provide better customer service, and are more likely to stay with the company. A study conducted by Sears, for instance, found a positive relationship between customer satisfaction and employee attitudes on ten different issues: a 5 percent improvement in employee attitudes results in a 1.3 percent increase in customer satisfaction and a 0.5 percent increase in revenue.[62]

The Employee-Friendly Workplace

What sort of things improve employee attitudes? The twelve thousand employees of software maker SAS Institute fall into the category of "happy workers." They choose the furniture and equipment in their own (private) offices; eat subsidized meals at one of three on-site restaurants; enjoy free soft drinks, fresh fruit on Mondays, M&M's on Wednesdays, and a healthy breakfast snack on Fridays in convenient break rooms; and swim and work out at a seventy-seven-thousand-square-foot fitness center. They set their own work hours, and they're encouraged to stay home with sick children. They also have job security: no one's ever been laid off because of an economic downturn. The employee-friendly work environment helps SAS employees focus on their jobs and contribute to the attainment of company goals.[63] Not surprisingly, it also results in very low 3 percent turnover.

Recognizing Employee Contributions

Thanking people for work done well is a powerful motivator. People who feel appreciated are more likely to stay with a company than those who don't.[64] While personal thank-yous are always helpful, many companies also have formal programs for identifying and rewarding good performers. The Container Store, a national storage and container retailer, rewards employee accomplishments in a variety of ways. Recently, for example, twelve employees chosen by coworkers were rewarded with a Colorado vacation with the company's owners, and the seven winners of a sales contest got a trip to visit an important supplier—in Sweden.[65] The company is known for its supportive environment and has frequently been selected as one of the top U.S. companies to work for.

Involving Employees in Decision Making

Companies have found that involving employees in decisions saves money, makes workers feel better about their jobs, and reduces turnover. Some have found that it pays to take their advice. When General Motors asked workers for ideas on improving manufacturing operations, management was deluged with more than forty-four thousand suggestions during one quarter. Implementing a few of them cut production time on certain vehicles by 15 percent and resulted in sizable savings.[66]

Similarly, in 2001, Edward Jones, a personal investment company, faced a difficult situation during the stock-market downturn. Costs had to be cut, and laying off employees was one option. Instead, however, the company turned to its workforce for solutions. As a group, employees identified cost savings of more than $38 million. At the same time, the company convinced experienced employees to stay with it by assuring them that they'd have a role in managing it.[67]

5.4 Why People Quit

As important as such initiatives can be, one bad boss can spoil everything. The way a person is treated by his or her boss may be the primary factor in determining whether an employee stays or goes. People who have quit their jobs cite the following behavior by superiors:

- Making unreasonable work demands
- Refusing to value their opinions
- Failing to be clear about what's expected of subordinates
- Rejecting work unnecessarily
- Showing favoritism in compensation, rewards, or promotions[68]

Holding managers accountable for excessive turnover can help alleviate the "bad-boss" problem, at least in the long run. In any case, whenever an employee quits, it's a good idea for someone—someone other than the individual's immediate supervisor—to conduct an exit interview to find out why. Knowing why people are quitting gives an organization the opportunity to correct problems that are causing high turnover rates.

5.5   Involuntary Termination

Before we leave this section, we should say a word or two about *termination*—getting fired. Though turnover—voluntary separations—can create problems for employers, they're not nearly as devastating as the effects of involuntary termination on employees. Losing your job is what psychologists call a "significant life change," and it's high on the list of "stressful life events" regardless of the circumstances. Sometimes, employers lay off workers because revenues are down and they must resort to **downsizing**—to cutting costs by eliminating jobs. Sometimes a particular job is being phased out, and sometimes an employee has simply failed to meet performance requirements.

Employment at Will

Is it possible for you to get fired even if you're doing a good job and there's no economic justification for your being laid off? In some cases, yes—especially if you're not working under a contract. Without a formal contract, you're considered to be *employed at will*, which means that both you and your employer have the right to terminate the employment relationship at any time. *You* can quit whenever you want (which is good for you), but your *employer* can fire you whenever it wants (which is obviously bad for you).

Fortunately for you, over the past several decades, the courts have undercut employers' rights under the **employment-at-will** doctrine.[69] By and large, management can no longer fire employees at will: usually, employers must show just cause for termination, and in some cases, they must furnish written documentation to substantiate the reasons for terminating an employee. If it's a case of poor performance, the employee is generally warned in advance that his or her current level of performance could result in termination. As a rule, managers give employees who have been warned a reasonable opportunity to improve performance. When termination is unavoidable, it should be handled in a private conversation, with the manager explaining precisely why the action is being taken.

FIGURE 7.9

Trying to meet unreasonable work demands can be extremely stressful and is a major reason people quit their jobs.

© 2010 Jupiterimages Corporation

downsizing

Practice of eliminating jobs to cut costs.

employment-at-will

Legal doctrine that allows an employer to fire an employee at will.

KEY TAKEAWAYS

- Managers conduct **performance appraisals** to evaluate work performance, usually following a three-step process:
    1. Setting goals and performance expectations and specifying the criteria for measuring performance
    2. Completing written evaluations to rate performance according to predetermined criteria
    3. Meeting with employees to discuss evaluations and ways to improve performance
- **Turnover**—the permanent separation of an employee from a company—has a negative effect on an organization.
- In addition to offering competitive compensation, companies may take a variety of steps to retain qualified employees:
    1. Providing appropriate training and development
    2. Helping employees achieve a satisfying work/nonwork balance in their lives
    3. Creating a positive work environment
    4. Recognizing employee efforts
    5. Involving employees in decision making
- On the other hand, employers may have to terminate the employment of (that is, fire) some workers.
    1. They may lay off workers because revenues are down and they have to **downsize**—to cut costs by eliminating jobs.
    2. Sometimes a job is phased out, and sometimes an employee simply fails to meet performance requirements.
- If there's no written employment contract, the employment relationship falls under the principle of **employment-at-will**, by which an employer can end it at any time. Usually, however, the employer must show just cause.

Before going to the next section of this chapter, take a few minutes to test your knowledge of the material covered in this section. Quizzes can be found under the "Resources" tab, "Study Aids: Quizzes."

EXERCISES

1. What steps does a manager take in evaluating an employee's performance? Explain the benefits of performance appraisals, and identify some of the potential problems entailed by the performance-evaluation process.
2. As an HR manager, what steps would you take to retain valuable employees? Under what circumstances would you fire an employee? Can you fire someone without giving that person a warning?

6. LABOR UNIONS

LEARNING OBJECTIVES

1. Explain why workers unionize.
2. Describe how unions are structured.
3. Explain what happens when there's a discrepancy between what workers want and what management is willing to give.
4. Indicate what union workers can do when they feel they've been treated unfairly.
5. Explain the tactics a union can take if labor differences can't be resolved through collective bargaining or formal grievance procedures.
6. Describe the tactics management may take if labor differences can't be resolved through collective bargaining or formal grievance procedures.

As we saw earlier, Maslow believed that individuals are motivated to satisfy five levels of unmet needs (physiological, safety, social, esteem, and self-actualization). From this perspective, employees should expect that full-time work will satisfy at least the two lowest-level needs: they should be paid wages that are sufficient for them to feed, house, and clothe themselves and their families, and they should have safe working conditions and some degree of job security. Organizations also have needs: they need to earn profits that will satisfy their owners. Sometimes, the needs of employees and employers are consistent: the organization can pay decent wages and provide workers with safe working conditions and job security while still making a satisfactory profit. At other times, there is a conflict—real, perceived, or a little bit of both—between the needs of employees and those of employers. In such cases, workers may be motivated to join a **labor union**—an organized group of workers that bargains with employers to improve its members' pay, job security, and working conditions.

Figure 7.10 charts *labor-union density*—union membership as a percentage of payrolls—in the United States from 1930 to 2013. As you can see, there's been a steady decline since the mid-1950s, and, today, only about 11 percent of U.S. workers belong to unions.[70] Only membership among public workers (those employed by federal, state, and local governments, such as teachers, police, and firefighters) has grown. In the 1940s, 10 percent of public workers and 34 percent of those in the private sector belonged to unions. Today, this has reversed: 35 percent of public workers and 7 percent of those in the private sector are union members.[71]

labor union

Organized group of workers that bargains with employers to improve its members' pay, job security, and working conditions.

FIGURE 7.10 Labor Union Density, 1930–2013

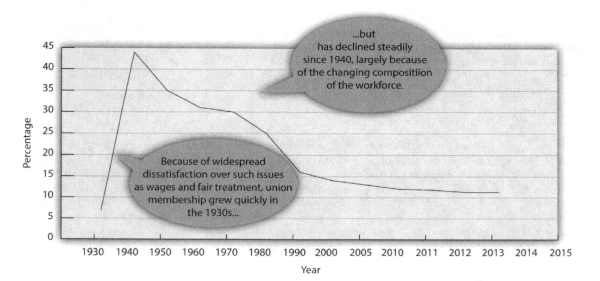

Why the decline in private sector unionization? Many factors come into play. The poor economy has reduced the number of workers who can become union members. In addition, we've shifted from a manufacturing-based economy characterized by large, historically unionized companies to a service-based economy made up of many small firms that are hard to unionize. Finally, there are more women in the workforce, and they're more likely to work part-time or intermittently.[72]

6.1   Union Structure

Unions have a pyramidal structure much like that of large corporations. At the bottom are *locals* that serve workers in a particular geographical area. Certain members are designated as *shop stewards* to serve as go-betweens in disputes between workers and supervisors. Locals are usually organized into *national unions* that assist with local contract negotiations, organize new locals, negotiate contracts for entire industries, and lobby government bodies on issues of importance to organized labor. In turn, national unions may be linked by a *labor federation*, such as the American Federation of Labor and Congress of Industrial Organizations (AFL-CIO), which provides assistance to member unions and serves as the principal political organ for organized labor.

6.2   Collective Bargaining

In a nonunion environment, the employer makes largely unilateral decisions on issues affecting its labor force, such as salary and benefits. Management, for example, may simply set an average salary increase of 3 percent and require employees to pay an additional $50 a month for medical insurance. Typically, employees are in no position to bargain for better deals. (At the same time, however, for reasons that we've discussed earlier in this chapter, employers have a vested interest in treating workers fairly. A reputation for treating employees well, for example, is a key factor in attracting talented people.)

collective bargaining

Process by which management and union-represented workers settle differences.

The process is a lot different in a union environment. Basically, union representatives determine with members what they want in terms of salary increases, benefits, working conditions, and job security. Union officials then tell the employer what its workers want and ask what they're willing to offer. When there's a discrepancy between what workers want and what management is willing to give—as there usually is—union officials serve as *negotiators* to bring the two sides together. The process of settling differences and establishing mutually agreeable conditions under which employees will work is called **collective bargaining**.

The Negotiation Process

Negotiations start when each side states its position and presents its demands. As in most negotiations, these opening demands simply stake out starting positions. Both parties expect some give-and-take and realize that the final agreement will fall somewhere between the two positions. If everything goes smoothly, a tentative agreement is reached and then voted on by union members. If they accept the agreement, the process is complete and a contract is put into place to govern labor-management relations for a stated period. If workers reject the agreement, negotiators go back to the bargaining table.

Mediation and Arbitration

mediation

Approach used to resolve a labor-contract dispute by following the recommendation of an impartial third party.

arbitration

Process of resolving a labor-contract dispute by having a third party study the situation and arrive at a *binding* agreement.

grievances

Union worker complaints on contract-related matters.

If negotiations stall, the sides may call in outsiders. One option is **mediation**, under which an impartial third party assesses the situation and makes recommendations for reaching an agreement. A mediator's advice can be accepted or rejected. If the two sides are willing to accept the decision of a third party, they may opt instead for **arbitration**, under which the third party studies the situation and arrives at a binding agreement.

Grievance Procedures

Another difference between union and nonunion environments is the handling of **grievances**—worker complaints on contract-related matters. When nonunion workers feel that they've been treated unfairly, they can take up the matter with supervisors, who may or may not satisfy their complaints. When unionized workers have complaints (such as being asked to work more hours than stipulated under their contract), they can call on union representatives to resolve the problem, in conjunction with supervisory personnel. If the outcome isn't satisfactory, the union can take the problem to higher-level management. If there's still no resolution, the union may submit the grievance to an arbitrator.

6.3   When Negotiations Break Down

At times, labor and management can't resolve their differences through collective bargaining or formal grievance procedures. When this happens, each side may resort to a variety of tactics to win support for its positions and force the opposition to agree to its demands.

Union Tactics

The tactics available to the union include *striking*, *picketing*, and *boycotting*. When they go on **strike**, workers walk away from their jobs and refuse to return until the issue at hand has been resolved. As undergraduates at Yale discovered when they arrived on campus in fall 2003, the effects of a strike can engulf parties other than employers and strikers: with four thousand dining room workers on strike, students had to scramble to find food at local minimarkets. The strike—the ninth at the school since 1968—lasted twenty-three days, and in the end, the workers got what they wanted: better pension plans.

Though a strike sends a strong message to management, it also has consequences for workers, who don't get paid when they're on strike. Unions often ease the financial pressure on strikers by providing cash payments. (Some unionized workers, by the way, don't have the right to strike. Strikes by federal employees, such as air-traffic controllers, are illegal because they jeopardize the public interest.)

When you see workers parading with signs outside a factory or an office building (or even a school), they're probably **picketing**. The purpose of picketing is informative—to tell people that a workforce is on strike or to publicize some management practice that's unacceptable to the union. In addition, because other union workers typically won't cross picket lines, marchers can interrupt the daily activities of the targeted organization. How would you like to show up for classes to find faculty picketing outside the classroom building? In April 2001, faculty at the University of Hawaii, unhappy about salaries, went on strike for thirteen days. Initially, many students cheerfully headed for the beach to work on their tans, but before long, many more—particularly graduating seniors—began to worry about finishing the semester with the credits they needed to keep their lives on schedule.[73]

The final tactic available to unions is **boycotting**, in which union workers refuse to buy a company's products and try to get other people to follow suit. The tactic is often used by the AFL-CIO, which maintains a national "Don't Buy or Patronize" boycott list. In 2003, for example, at the request of two affiliates, the Actor's Equity Association and the American Federation of Musicians, the AFL-CIO added the road show of the Broadway musical *Miss Saigon* to the list. Why? The unions objected to the use of nonunion performers who worked for particularly low wages and to the use of a "virtual orchestra," an electronic apparatus that can replace a live orchestra with software-generated orchestral accompaniment.[74]

Management Tactics

Management doesn't sit by passively, especially if the company has a position to defend or a message to get out. One available tactic is the **lockout**—closing the workplace to workers—though it's rarely used because it's legal only when unionized workers pose a credible threat to the employer's financial viability. Another tactic is replacing striking workers with **strikebreakers**—nonunion workers who are willing to cross picket lines to replace strikers. Though the law prohibits companies from permanently replacing striking workers, it's often possible for a company to get a court injunction that allows it to bring in replacement workers.

Lockout tactics were used in the 2011 labor dispute between the National Football League (NFL) and the National Football League Players Association when club owners and players failed to reach an agreement on a new contract. Prior to the 2011 season, the owners imposed a lockout, which prevented the players from practicing in team training facilities. Both sides had their demands: The players wanted a greater percentage of the revenues, which the owners were against. The owners wanted the players to play two additional season games, which the players were against. With the season drawing closer, an agreement was finally reached in July 2011 bringing the 130-day lockout to an end and ensuring that the 2011 football season would begin on time.[75]

6.4 The Future of Unions

As we noted earlier, union membership in the United States is declining. So, what's the future of organized labor? Will membership continue to decline and unions lose even more power? The AFL-CIO is optimistic about union membership, pointing out recent gains in membership among women and immigrants, as well as health care workers, graduate students, and professionals.[76]

But convincing workers to unionize is still more difficult than it used to be and could become even harder in the future. For one thing, employers have developed strategies for dissuading workers from unionizing—in particular, tactics for withholding job security. If unionization threatens higher costs for wages and benefits, they can resort to part-time or contract workers. They can also outsource work, eliminating jobs entirely, and more employers are now investing in technology designed to reduce the amount of human labor needed to produce goods or offer services.

strike

Union tactic by which workers walk away from their jobs and refuse to return until a labor-management dispute has been resolved.

FIGURE 7.11

The adverse effects of a strike can impact management and workers alike.

© 2010 Jupiterimages Corporation

picketing

Union tactic of parading with signs outside a factory or other facility to publicize a strike.

boycotting

Method used by union members to voice displeasure with certain organizations by refusing to buy the company's products and encouraging others to follow suit.

lockout

Management tactic of closing the workplace to union workers.

strikebreakers

Nonunion workers who are willing to cross picket lines to replace strikers.

KEY TAKEAWAYS

- Some workers belong to **labor unions**—organized groups of workers that bargain with employers to improve members' pay, job security, and working conditions.
- Unions have a pyramidal structure. At the bottom are *locals*, who serve workers in a particular geographical area.

    1. Locals are usually organized into *national unions* that assist with local contract negotiations and negotiate industry-wide contracts.
    2. Nationals may be linked by a *labor federation*, such as the AFL-CIO, which provides assistance to member unions and serves as the principal political organ for organized labor.

- When there's a discrepancy between what workers want in terms of salary increases, benefits, working conditions, and job security and what management is willing to give, the two sides engage in a process called **collective bargaining**.

    1. If everything goes smoothly, a contract is soon put into place.
    2. If negotiations break down, the sides may resort to **mediation** (in which an impartial third party makes recommendations for reaching an agreement) or **arbitration** (in which the third party imposes a binding agreement).

- When unionized workers feel that they've been treated unfairly, they can file **grievances**—complaints over contract-related matters that are resolved by union representatives and employee supervisors.
- If labor differences can't be resolved through collective bargaining or formal grievance procedures, each side may resort to a variety of tactics. The union can do the following:

    1. Call a **strike** (in which workers leave their jobs until the issue is settled)
    2. Organize **picketing** (in which workers congregate outside the workplace to publicize their position)
    3. Arrange for **boycotting** (in which workers and other consumers are urged to refrain from buying an employer's products)

- Management may resort to a **lockout**—closing the workplace to workers—or call in **strikebreakers** (nonunion workers who are willing to cross picket lines to replace strikers).

Before going to the next chapter, take a few minutes to test your knowledge of the material covered in this section. Quizzes can be found under the "Resources" tab, "Study Aids: Quizzes."

EXERCISES

1. You've just gotten a job as an autoworker. Would you prefer to work in a unionized or nonunionized plant? Why? If you were hired as a high-level manager in the company, would you want your workers to be unionized? Why, or why not? What's your opinion on the future of organized labor? Will union membership grow or decline in the next decade? Why, or why not?

2. What happens in a unionized company when negotiations between labor and management break down? Identify and describe the tactics that unions can use against management and those that management can use against unions.

7. CASES AND PROBLEMS

What's Your (Emotional) IQ?

If you were an HR manager, on what criteria would you base a hiring decision—intelligence (IQ), education, technical skills, experience, references, or performance on the interview? All these can be important determinants of a person's success, but some experts believe that there's an even better predictor of success. It's called *emotional intelligence* (or EI), and it gained some currency in the mid-1990s thanks to Daniel Goleman's book *Emotional Intelligence: Why It Can Matter More Than IQ*. EI is the ability to understand both our own emotions and those of others, as well as the ability to use that understanding in managing our behavior, motivating ourselves, and encouraging others to achieve goals.

An attractive aspect of EI is that, unlike IQ, it's not fixed at an early age. Rather, its vital components—self-awareness, self-management, social awareness, and relationship management—can be strengthened over time. To assess your level of EI, go to the Web site maintained by the Hay Group, a management-consulting firm, and take the ten-item test that's posted there (http://psychology.about.com/library/quiz/bl_eq_quiz.htm?questnum=6&cor=2399). After completing the test, you'll get your EI score, some instructions for interpreting it, and an answer key.

When you've finished with the test, rank the following items according to the importance that you'd give them in making a hiring decision: intelligence, education, technical skills, experience, references, interview skills, and emotional intelligence. Explain your ranking.

Are You a People Person?

You might not like the idea of sitting across the desk from a corporate college recruiter and asking for a job, but what if you were on the other side of the desk? As a recruiter, you'd get to return to campus each year to encourage students to join your company. Or, maybe you'd like to help your company develop a new compensation and benefits program, implement a performance-evaluation system, or create a new training program. All these activities fall under the umbrella of HR.

To learn more about the field of HR, go to the WetFeet Web site (https://www.wetfeet.com/articles/careers-and-industries-overview) and read the page "Human Resources Overview." Then answer the following questions:

1. What is the human resources field like?
2. What do HR professionals like about their jobs? What do they dislike?
3. Are job prospects in the HR field positive or negative? Which HR areas will experience the fastest growth?
4. Based on the job descriptions posted, which specific HR job would you want?

Finally, write a paragraph responding to this question: Do you find the HR field interesting? Why, or why not?

ETHICS ANGLE

Misstating the Facts

Life couldn't get much better for George O'Leary when he was named the head football coach at Notre Dame. Unfortunately, he barely had time to celebrate his new job before he was ruled ineligible: after just a week on the job, he was forced to resign, embarrassing himself, his family, his friends, and Notre Dame itself. Why? Because of a few lies that he'd put on his résumé twenty years earlier. To get the facts behind this story, go to the *Sports Illustrated* Web site (http://sportsillustrated.cnn.com/football/college/news/2001/12/14/oleary_notredame/) and read the article "Short Tenure: O'Leary Out at Notre Dame After One Week." Then, answer the following questions:

1. Was O'Leary's punishment appropriate? If you were the athletic director at Notre Dame, would you have meted out the same punishment? Why, or why not?

2. False information on his résumé came back to haunt O'Leary after twenty years. Once he'd falsified his résumé, was there any corrective action that he could have taken? If so, what?

3. If O'Leary had told Notre Dame about the falsifications before they came to light, would they have hired him?

4. Would his previous employer take him back?

5. O'Leary was later hired as a head coach by the University of Central Florida. Will the episode involving his résumé undermine his ability to encourage players to act with integrity? Will it affect his ability to recruit players?

6. What's the lesson to be learned from O'Leary's experience? In what ways might a few (theoretical) misstatements on your résumé come back to haunt you?

TEAM-BUILDING SKILLS

Dorm Room Rescue

Any night of the week (at least as of this writing), you can relax in front of the TV and watch a steady stream of shows about how to improve your living space—such as *New Spaces*. You like the concept of these programs well enough, but you're tired of watching them in a tiny, cluttered dorm room that's decorated in early barracks style. Out of these cramped conditions, however, you and a team of friends come up with an idea. On graduation, you'll start a business called Dorm Room Rescue to provide decorating services to the dorm dwellers who come after you. You'll help college students pick colors and themes for their rooms and select space-saving furniture, storage materials, area rugs, and wall decorations. Your goal will be to create attractive dorm rooms that provide comfort, functionality, and privacy, as well as pleasant spaces in which students can relax and even entertain.

The team decides to develop a plan for the HR needs of your future company. You'll need to address the following issues:

1. HR plan

    - Number of employees
    - Job descriptions: duties and responsibilities for each type of employee
    - Job specifications: needed skills, knowledge, and abilities

2. Recruitment of qualified employees

    - Recruitment plan: how and where to find candidates
    - Selection process: steps taken to select employees

3. Developing employees

    - New-employee orientation
    - Training and development

4. Compensation and benefits

    - Wages, salaries, and incentive programs
    - Benefits

5. Work/Life quality

    - Work schedules and alternative work arrangements
    - Family-friendly programs

6. Performance appraisal

    - Appraisal process
    - Retaining valuable employees

You might want to divide up the initial work, but you'll need to regroup as a team to make your final decisions on these issues and to create a team-prepared report.

THE GLOBAL VIEW

Sending Ed to China

You're the HR manager for a large environmental consulting firm that just started doing business in China. You've asked your top engineer, Ed Deardon, to relocate to Shanghai for a year. Though China will be new to Deardon, working overseas won't be; he's already completed assignments in the Philippines and Thailand; as before, his wife and three children will be going with him.

You've promised Deardon some advice on adapting to living and working conditions in Shanghai, and you intend to focus on the kinds of cultural differences that tend to create problems in international business dealings. Unfortunately, you personally know absolutely nothing about living in China and so must do some online research. Here are some promising sites:

- Executive Planet (http://www.executiveplanet.com/index.php?title=China)
- China Window (http://china-window.com)
- Kwintessential (http://www.kwintessential.co.uk/etiquette/doing-business-china.html)

Instructions

Prepare a written report to Deardon in which you identify and explain five or six cultural differences between business behavior in the United States and China, and offer some advice on how to deal with them.

ENDNOTES

1. Introductory material on Howard Schultz and Starbucks comes from Howard Schultz and Dori Jones Yang, *Pour Your Heart into It: How Starbucks Built a Company One Cup at a Time* (New York: Hyperion, 1997), 3–8.

2. Howard Schultz and Dori Jones Yang, *Pour Your Heart into It: How Starbucks Built a Company One Cup at a Time* (New York: Hyperion, 1997), 138.

3. Howard Schultz and Dori Jones Yang, Pour Your Heart into It: How Starbucks Built a Company One Cup at a Time (New York: Hyperion, 1997), 6–7.

4. Starbucks, "Our Starbucks Mission Statement," http://www.starbucks.com/about-us/company-information/mission-statement (accessed April 1, 2014).

5. Starbucks, "Our Starbucks Mission Statement," http://www.starbucks.com/about-us/company-information/mission-statement (accessed April 1, 2014).

6. Howard Schultz and Dori Jones Yang, *Pour Your Heart into It: How Starbucks Built a Company One Cup at a Time* (New York: Hyperion, 1997), 125.

7. Starbucks, "Our Starbucks Mission Statement," http://www.starbucks.com/about-us/company-information/mission-statement (accessed April 1, 2014).

8. "25 Top MBA Employers," *CNNMoney*, http://money.cnn.com/galleries/2007/fortune/0704/gallery.MBA_employers.fortune/index.html?utm_source=feedburner&utm_medium=feed&utm_campaign=Feed:+rss/cnn_education+(RSS:+Education) (accessed April 1, 2014).

9. Disney, "The Disney Look," http://cp.disneycareers.com/en/about-disney-college-program/disney-look (accessed April 1, 2014).

10. Janna Oberdorf, "The Secret behind the Magic of Disney," *NYU Livewire*, http://journalism.nyu.edu/publishing/archives/livewire/archived/the_secret_behind_the_magic_of (accessed April 1, 2014).

11. Norwegian Cruise Line, "Shipboard Employment," http://www.ncl.com/about/careers/shipboard-employment (accessed April 1, 2014).

12. Expedia Cruise Ship Centers, "Luxury Cruises," http://www.cruiseshipcenters.com/en-us/canada/cruise-lines/Luxury (accessed April 1, 2014).

13. The U.S. Equal Employment Opportunity Commission, "Discriminatory Practices," http://www.eeoc.gov/laws/practices/index.cfm (accessed April 1, 2014).

14. The U.S. Equal Employment Opportunity Commission, "Federal Equal Employment Opportunity (EEO) Laws," http://www.eeoc.gov/laws/statutes/index.cfm (accessed October 8, 2011).

15. Bob Nelson and Peter Economy, *Managing for Dummies*, 2nd ed. (New York: Wiley, 2003), 60.

16. Dan Schawbel, "The Power Within: Why Internal Recruiting and Hiring Are on the Rise," *Time*, August 15, 2012, http://business.time.com/2012/08/15/the-power-within-why-internal-recruiting-hiring-are-on-the-rise (accessed April 1, 2014).

17. Dan Schawbel, "The Power Within: Why Internal Recruiting and Hiring Are on the Rise," *Time*, August 15, 2012, http://business.time.com/2012/08/15/the-power-within-why-internal-recruiting-hiring-are-on-the-rise (accessed April 1, 2014).

18. Rachel Emma Silverman and Lauren Weber, "An Inside Job: More Firms Opt to Recruit from Within," *Wall Street Journal*, May 29, 2012, http://online.wsj.com/news/articles/SB10001424052702303395604577434563715828218 (accessed April 1, 2014).

19. Rachel Emma Silverman and Lauren Weber, "An Inside Job: More Firms Opt to Recruit from Within," *Wall Street Journal*, May 29, 2012, http://online.wsj.com/news/articles/SB10001424052702303395604577434563715828218 (accessed April 1, 2014).

20. The information in this section was taken from the following article by Alison Doyle, "How Companies Recruit—Multi-Pronged Recruitment Strategies," *About.com*, http://jobsearch.about.com/od/recruiting/a/how-companies-recruit.htm (accessed April 1, 2014).

21. The information in this section comes from two sources: Federal Bureau of Investigation, "Jobs: Special Agents," http://www.fbijobs.gov (accessed April 2, 2014); Federal Bureau of Investigation, "Special Agent Application and Hiring Process," http://www.fbijobs.gov/112.asp (accessed April 2, 2014).

22. "Induction: Orienting the New Employee," *HRM Guide Network*, http://www.bestbooks.biz/learning/induction.html (accessed April 2, 2014).

23. Susan Heathfield, "Top Ten Ways to Turn Off a New Employee," *About, Inc.*, http://humanresources.about.com/library/weekly/aa022601a.htm (accessed April 2, 2014).

24. "2013 Training Industry Report," *Training*, http://www.trainingmag.com/2013-training-industry-report (accessed April 2, 2014).

25. Ray McConville, "Verizon Inducted into Training Magazine's Top 10 Hall of Fame," http://newscenter.verizon.com/corporate/news-articles/2014/02-05-training-magazine-hall-of-fame/ (accessed August 16, 2014).

26. "For IT, Booz Allen is One of the Best," June 21, 2010, http://www.boozallen.com/about/awards-recognition/2010/06/43140922 (accessed August 16, 2014).

27. Brooke Locascio, "Working at Starbucks: More Than Just Pouring Coffee," *Tea and Coffee*, January/February 2004, http://www.teaandcoffee.net/0104/coffee.htm (accessed April 2, 2014).

28. Howard Schultz and Dori Jones Yang, *Pour Your Heart into It: How Starbucks Built a Company One Cup at a Time* (New York: Hyperion, 1997), 250–51.

29. Judith Lindenberger and Marian Stoltz-Loike, "Diversity in the Workplace," *The Economics and Policy Resource Center*, http://www.zeromillion.com/econ (accessed April 2, 2014).

30. U.S. Equal Employment Opportunity Commission, "Occupational Employment in Private Industry by Race/Ethnic Group/Sex, and by Industry, United States, 2006," http://www.eeoc.gov/eeoc/statistics/employment/jobpat-eeo1/2006/national.html (accessed April 2, 2014).

31. U.S. Equal Employment Opportunity Commission, "Federal Laws Prohibiting Job Discrimination: Questions and Answers," *Federal Equal Employment Opportunity (EEO) Laws*, http://www.eeoc.gov/facts/qanda.html (accessed April 2, 2014).

32. U.S. Equal Employment Opportunity Commission, "EEOC Agrees to Landmark Resolution of Discrimination Case Against Abercrombie & Fitch," http://www.eeoc.gov/press/11-18-04.html (accessed April 2, 2014).

33. Great Place to Work Institute, "What Is a Great Workplace?" http://www.greatplacetowork.com/our-approach/what-is-a-great-workplace (accessed April 2, 2014).

34. Great Place to Work Institute, "What do Employees Say?" http://www.greatplacetowork.com/great/employees.php (accessed May 6, 2006). http://us.greatrated.com/review/great-place-to-work-institute-inc/what-employees-say (accessed April 2, 2014).

35. Sandra Kerka, "The Changing Role of Support Staff," http://files.eric.ed.gov/fulltext/ED378351.pdf (accessed April 2, 2014).

36. Jeffrey Greenhaus, Karen Collins, and Jason Shaw, "The Relationship between Work-Family Balance and Quality of Life," *Journal of Vocational Behavior* 63, 2003, 510–31.

37. KPMG, "Awards," http://www.kpmg.com/us/en/about/csr/diversity-inclusion/pages/awards.aspx (accessed April 2, 2014).

38. For information on KPMG's programs and benefits, see KPMG, "KPMG Careers," http://www.kpmgcareers.com/index.shtml (accessed April 2, 2014).

39. Reported in *Work-Life and Human Capital Solutions, The Business Case for Telecommuting* (Minnetonka, MN: WFC Resources), http://worklifeexpo.com/EXPO/docs/The_Business_Case_for_Telecommuting-WFCResources.pdf (accessed April 2, 2014).

40. Telework Research Network, "How Many People Telecommute?," http://www.teleworkresearchnetwork.com/research/people-telecommute (accessed April 2, 2014).

41. KPMG, "KPMG Named One of the Top Ten Best Companies for Working Mothers by Working Mother Magazine," news release, September 25, 2007, http://www.prnewswire.com/news-releases/kpmg-named-one-of-top-ten-bestcompanies-for-working-mothers-by-working-mother-magazine (accessed April 2, 2014).

42. Bonnie Harris, "Child Care Comes to Work," *Los Angeles Times*, November 19, 2000, http://articles.latimes.com/2000/nov/19/news/wp-54138 (accessed April 2, 2014).

43. Henry Unger, "Should More Employers Offer Help with Child and Elder Care?" *AJC.com*, June 2, 2011, http://blogs.ajc.com/business-beat/2011/06/02/should-more-employers-offer-help-with-child-and-elder-care/ (accessed April 2, 2104).

44. Henry Unger, "Should More Employers Offer Help with Child and Elder Care?" *AJC.com*, June 2, 2011, http://blogs.ajc.com/business-beat/2011/06/02/should-more-employers-offerhelp-with-child-and-elder-care (accessed April 2, 2104).

45. See Karen Collins and Elizabeth Hoover, "Addressing the Needs of the Single Person in Public Accounting," *Pennsylvania CPA Journal*, June 1995, 16.

46. Data was obtained from 1988 and 1991 studies of stress in public accounting by Karen Collins and from a 1995 study on quality of life in the accounting profession by Collins and Jeffrey Greenhaus. Analysis of the data on single individuals was not separately published.

47. Lifestyle Concierge Services, "Concierge Service Is a Surprisingly Low Cost Solution that Can Meet a Variety of Needs with a Single Provider," http://www.lifestyleconciergeservices.com/Corporate-Concierge-Service-for-businesses.html (accessed April 2, 2014).

48. "The 100 Best Companies to Work For," *Fortune*, http://archive.fortune.com/magazines/fortune/best-companies/2013/snapshots/16.html (accessed April 2, 2014).

49. See "Crisfield off the Beaten Path," VirtualTourist, http://www.virtualtourist.com/travel/North_America/United_States_of_America/Maryland/Crisfield-798585/Off_the_Beaten_Path-Crisfield-TG-C-1.html (April 2, 2014); Neil Learner, "Ashore, A Way of Life Built around the Crab," *Christian Science Monitor*, June 26, 2000, http://www.csmonitor.com/2000/0626/p15s1.html (accessed April 2, 2014).

50. Texas Instruments, "Benefits," http://www.ti.com/corp/docs/investor/proxy12/compensation_discussion_and_analysis.htm (accessed April 2, 2014).

51. Jeff D. Opdyke, "Getting a Bonus Instead of a Raise," *Wall Street Journal*, December 29, 2004, http://online.wsj.com/article/SB110427526449111461.html, (accessed April 2, 2014).

52. Lee Ann Obringer, "How Employee Compensation Works—Stock Options/Profit Sharing," *HowStuffWorks*, http://money.howstuffworks.com/benefits.htm (accessed April 2, 2014).

53. Texas Instruments, "Benefits," http://careers.ti.com/content/benefits-0 (accessed April 2, 2014).

54. Texas Instruments, "Benefits," http://careers.ti.com/content/benefits-0 (accessed April 2, 2014).

55. Employee Benefit Research Institute, "FAQs About Benefits—General Overview," http://www.ebri.org/publications/benfaq/?fa=fullfaq (accessed April 2, 2014).

56. *National Compensation Survey: Employee Benefits in Private Industry, 2003*, U.S. Department of Labor, Bureau of Labor Statistics, March 2003, 2, http://www.bls.gov/ncs/ebs/home.htm (accessed April 2, 2014).

57. Susan Heathfield, "Performance Appraisals Don't Work," *About*, http://humanresources.about.com/cs/perfmeasurement/l/aa061100a.htm (accessed April 3, 2014).

58. Bob Nelson and Peter Economy, *Managing for Dummies*, 2nd ed. (New York: Wiley, 2003), 140.

59. Archer North & Associates, "Reward Issues," *Performance Appraisal*, http://www.performance-appraisal.com/rewards.htm (accessed April 3, 2014).

60. Dell, Inc., "Tell Dell Survey," *2011 Dell Corporate Responsibility Report*, http://i.dell.com/sites/content/corporate/corp-comm/en/Documents/dell-fy11-cr-report.pdf (accessed April 3, 2014).

61. Gregory P. Smith, "How to Attract, Keep and Motivate Your Workforce," *Business Know-How*, http://www.businessknowhow.com/manage/attractworkforce.htm (accessed April 3, 2014).

62. Sue Shellenbarger, "Companies Are Finding It Pays to Be Nice to Employees," *Wall Street Journal*, July 22, 1998, http://online.wsj.com/news/articles/SB901063646490891000 (accessed April 4, 2014).

63. Morley Safer, "Working the Good Life," *CBS 60 Minutes*, interview with Jim Goodnight, president and founder of SAS Institute, April 20, 2003, http://www.cbsnews.com/stories/2003/04/18/60minutes/main550102.shtml (accessed April 3, 2014); "2011—100 Best Companies to Work For," *Fortune*, http://money.cnn.com/magazines/fortune/bestcompanies/2011/snapshots/1.html (accessed April 3, 2014). For a description of the company's work/life initiatives, visit its Web site at http://www.sas.com/en_us/company-information/great-workplace.html (accessed April 3, 2014).

64. Robert McGarvey, "A Tidal Wave of Turnover," *American Way*, December 15, 2004, 32–36.

65. The Container Store, "Careers," http://www.containerstore.com/careers/index.jhtml;jsessionid=0C2Q2LP3RTG0XQFIAIMCM44AVABBMJVC (accessed April 3, 2014).

66. Freda Turner, "An Effective Employee Suggestion Program Has a Multiplier Effect," *WebPro News*, March 4, 2003, http://www.webpronews.com/an-effective-employee-suggestion-program-has-a-multiplier-effect-2003-03 (accessed April 3, 2014).

67. Richard L. Daft and Dorothy Marcic, *Understanding Management* (Florence, KY: Cengage Learning, 2006), 219, http://books.google.com/books?id=xWxmFNMKXhEC&dq=isbn:9781439042328 (accessed April 4, 2014).

68. Gregory P. Smith, "Top Ten Reasons Why People Quit Their Jobs," *Business Know-How*, http://www.businessknowhow.com/manage/whyquit.htm (accessed April 4, 2014).

69. Charles J. Muhl, "The Employment-at-Will Doctrine: Three Major Exceptions," *Monthly Labor Review*, January 2001, 1–11, http://www.bls.gov/opub/mlr/2001/01/art1full.pdf (accessed April 3, 2014).

70. Bureau of Labor Statistics, U.S. Department of Labor, "Union Members 2013," January 24, 2014, http://www.bls.gov/news.release/pdf/union2.pdf (accessed April 3, 2014).

71. "Labor Unions in the United States," *Wikipedia*, April 1, 2014, http://en.wikipedia.org/wiki/Labor_unions_in_the_United_States#Membership (accessed April 3, 2014).

72. Kris Maher, "Union Membership Drops 10%," *Wall Street Journal*, January 10, 2010, http://online.wsj.com/article/SB10001424052748703822404575019350727544666.html (accessed April 3, 2014); Steven Greenhouse, "Union Membership in U.S. Fell to a 70-Year Low Last Year," *The New York Times*, January 21, 2011, http://www.nytimes.com/2011/01/22/business/22union.html?_r=0 (accessed April 3, 2014).

73. "Hawaii Professors End Strike," *USA Today*, June 19, 2001, http://www.usatoday.com/news/nation/2001-04-18-hawaii.htm (accessed April 3, 2014).

74. Union Label and Service Department, AFL-CIO, "AFL-CIO National Boycott List," http://members.csea.com/memberhome/Issues/BoycottList/tabid/325/Default.aspx (accessed April 3, 2014).

75. Vinnie Iyer and Clifton Brown, "NFL Lockout Ends as Owners, Player Reps Agree to 10-Year CBA," *Sporting News*, http://www.sportingnews.com/nfl/feed/2010-09/nfl-labor-talks/story/nfl-lockout-ends-owners-nflpa-10-year-deal-2011-season-cba-labor-agreement (accessed April 3, 2014).

76. Bureau of Labor Statistics, Economic News Release, "Union Members Summary," news release, January 27, 2012, http://www.bls.gov/news.release/union2.nr0.htm (accessed April 3, 2014); University Professional and Technical Employees—University of California, Davis, "Unions 101, A Quick Study of How Unions Help workers Win a Voice at Work," http://upteucdavis.org/wp-content/uploads/2010/08/union101.pdf (accessed April 3, 2014).

CHAPTER 8

Teamwork and Communications

THE TEAM WITH THE RAZR'S EDGE

In the fall of 2011, Motorola spun off its Mobile Devices division creating a new publically traded company, Motorola Mobility. The newly formed company's executive team was under intense pressure to come out with a winner: a smartphone that could grab substantial market share from Apple's iPhone 4S and Samsung's Galaxy Nexus. To do this, the team oversaw the design of an Android version of the Motorola RAZR, which used to be the best-selling phone in the world. The hope of the executive team is that past customers who loved the RAZR will really love the new ultra-thin smartphone—the Droid RAZR. As with other products produced by Motorola, the Droid RAZR was designed by a team of individuals. To understand how this team approach is implemented at Motorola, let's review the process used to design the original RAZR.

The mood was grim at Motorola in winter 2003, especially in the cell phone division: The company that for years had run ringtones around the competition had been bumped from the top spot in worldwide sales.[1] Sporting a popular line of "candy bar" phones (the ones without the flip-top lids), the Finnish company Nokia had grabbed the lead in global market share, and Motorola found itself stuck in the number-three slot (Samsung had slipped into second place). Why had sales at Motorola been put on hold? Among other things, consumers were less than enthusiastic about the uninspired *style* of Motorola phones, and make no mistake about it—for a lot of people, style is just as important in picking a cell phone as its features list. As a reviewer for one industry publication puts it, "With some phones, we just want to see the look on people's faces when we slide it out of our pockets to take a call."

And yet, there was a glimmer of hope at Motorola. Despite its recent lapse in cell phone fashion sense, Motorola (like just about every other maker of wireless hardware) still maintained a *concept-phone* unit—a group responsible for designing futuristic new product features such as speech-recognition capability, liquid batteries, flexible touchscreens, and touch-sensitive body covers. Now, in every concept-phone unit, developers are engaged in an ongoing struggle to balance the two often-opposing demands of cell phone design: how to build the smallest possible phone with the largest possible screen. The previous year, designers in the Motorola concept-phone unit had unveiled the rough model of an ultratrim phone—at 10 millimeters, about half the width of the average flip-top or "clamshell" design. It was on this concept that Motorola decided to stake the revival of its reputation as a cell phone maker who knew how to package functionality with a wow factor.

The next step in developing a concept phone, of course, is actually *building* it. And this is where teamwork comes in. For one thing, you need a little diversity in your expertise. An *electronic engineer*, for example, knows how to apply energy to transmit information through a system but not how to apply physics to the design and

The Motorola RAZR: Thin is in, according to Motorola.

manufacture of the system; that's the specialty of a *mechanical engineer*. And engineers aren't *designers*—the specialists who know how to enhance the marketability of a product by adding aesthetic value.

In addition, when you set out to build any kind of innovative high-tech product, you need to become a master of *trade-offs*—in Motorola's case, the compromises resulting from the demands of state-of-the-art functionality on the one hand and fashionable design on the other. *Negotiating trade-offs is a team sport*: it takes at least two people, for example, to resolve such disputes as whether you can put the antenna of a cell phone inside its mouthpiece or whether you should put the caller-ID display inside or outside the flip-top.

The responsibility for assembling and managing the Motorola "thin-clam" team fell to veteran electronic engineer Roger Jellicoe. His mission: create the world's thinnest phone, do it in one year, and try to keep it a secret. Before the project was completed, the team had grown to more than twenty members, and with increased creative input and enthusiasm came increased confidence and clout. Jellicoe, for instance, had been warned by company specialists in such matters that no phone wider than 49 millimeters could be held comfortably in the human hand. When the team had finally arrived at a satisfactory design that couldn't work at less than 53 millimeters, they ignored the "49 millimeters warning," built a model, handed it around, and came to a consensus: As one team member put it, "People could hold it in their hands and say, 'Yeah, it doesn't feel like a brick.'" Four millimeters, they decided, was an acceptable trade-off, and the new phone went to market at 53 millimeters.

Team members liked to call this process the "dance." Sometimes it flowed smoothly and sometimes people stepped on one another's toes, but for the most part, the team moved in lockstep toward its goal. After a series of trade-offs about what to call the final product (suggestions ranged from *Razor Clam* to *V3*), Motorola's new RAZR was introduced in July 2004. Recall that the product was originally conceived as a high-tech toy—something to restore the luster to Motorola's tarnished image. It wasn't supposed to set sales records, and sales in the fourth quarter of 2004, though promising, were in fact fairly modest. Back in September, however, a new executive named Ron Garriques had taken over Motorola's cell phone division, and one of his first decisions was to raise the bar for RAZR. Disregarding a 2005 budget that called for sales of two million units, Garriques pushed expected sales for the RAZR up to twenty million. The RAZR topped that target, shipped ten million in the first quarter of 2006, and hit the fifty-million mark at midyear. Talking on a RAZR, declared hip-hop luminary Sean "P. Diddy" Combs, "is like driving a Mercedes versus a regular ol' ride."

As for Jellicoe and his team, they were invited to attend an event hosted by top executives. As they walked into the room, they received a standing ovation—along with a cartload of stock options—and outside observers applauded them for revitalizing "the stodgy, engineering-driven, Midwestern company that was Motorola." One of the reasons for the RAZR's success, admits Jellicoe, "was that it took the world by surprise. Very few Motorola products do that." After the introduction of the RAZR, perceptions of the company's flair for fashion and innovation underwent a critical change: "Now," reports Jellicoe, "whenever we say we have this secret program we're working on, nobody wants to be left out….It's kicked down some doors…and gets us noticed. It really is a tremendous brand builder. As for credibility in the marketplace, it's been a very big win." In fact, for a while it was the best selling phone in the world.

Will the Droid RAZR be as successful as the original RAZR? Only time will tell, but many are optimistic about its chances. In a November 2011 *New York Times* article, "Motorola's Droid Razr Still Has It," Roy Furchgott conveys the opinions of many in the tech field:

> *The new Droid RAZR has a lot to live up to. The original RAZR was a flip-phone marvel of sleek design. It became the best-selling phone in the United States until the iPhone knocked it from its perch. The new RAZR, while lacking the wow factor of the original, is still a credible heir to the name. Two things—speed and battery life—set the phone apart.[2]*

And, if an incredibly fast download speed and approximately 12 hours of talk time and 250 hours of standby time are not enough to get customers onboard, they might be won over by the purple version.

1. THE TEAM AND THE ORGANIZATION

LEARNING OBJECTIVES

1. Define a "team."
2. Describe the key characteristics of a team.
3. Explain why organizations use teams.
4. Describe different types of teams.

1.1 What Is a Team? How Does Teamwork Work?

A **team** (or a *work team*) is a group of people with complementary skills who work together to achieve a specific goal.[3] In the case of Motorola's RAZR team, the specific goal was to develop (and ultimately bring to market) an ultrathin cell phone that would help restore the company's reputation as a designer of stylistically appealing, high-function phones. The team achieved its goal by integrating specialized but complementary skills in engineering and design and by making the most of its authority to make its own decisions and manage its own operations.

team

Group of people with complementary skills who work together to achieve a specific goal.

Teams versus Groups

"A group," suggests Bonnie Edelstein, a consultant in organizational development, "is a bunch of people in an elevator. A team is also a bunch of people in an elevator, but the elevator is broken." This distinction may be a little oversimplified, but as our tale of teamwork at Motorola reminds us, a *team* is clearly something more than a mere *group* of individuals. In particular, members of a group—or, more accurately, a *working group*—go about their jobs independently and meet primarily to share information. A group of department-store managers, for example, might meet monthly to discuss their progress in cutting plant costs, but each manager is focused on the goals of his or her department because each is held accountable for meeting only those goals. Teams, by contrast, are responsible for achieving specific common goals, and they're generally empowered to make the decisions needed to complete their authorized tasks.

Some Key Characteristics of Teams

To keep matters in perspective, let's identify five key characteristics of work teams:[4]

1. *Teams are accountable for achieving specific common goals.* Members are collectively responsible for achieving team goals, and if they succeed, they're rewarded collectively.
2. *Teams function interdependently.* Members cannot achieve goals independently and must rely on each other for information, input, and expertise.
3. *Teams are stable.* Teams remain intact long enough to finish their assigned tasks, and each member remains on board long enough to get to know every other member.
4. *Teams have authority.* Teams possess the decision-making power to pursue their goals and to manage the activities through which they complete their assignments.
5. *Teams operate in a social context.* Teams are assembled to do specific work for larger organizations and have the advantage of access to resources available from other areas of their organizations.

1.2 Why Organizations Build Teams

Why do major organizations now rely more and more on teams to improve operations? Executives at Xerox have reported that team-based operations are 30 percent more productive than conventional operations. General Mills says that factories organized around team activities are 40 percent more productive than traditionally organized factories. According to in-house studies at Shenandoah Life Insurance, teams have cut case-handling time from twenty-seven to two days and virtually eliminated service complaints. FedEx says that teams reduced service errors (lost packages, incorrect bills) by 13 percent in the first year.[5]

Today it seems obvious that teams can address a variety of challenges in the world of corporate activity. Before we go any further, however, we should remind ourselves that data like those we've just cited aren't necessarily definitive. For one thing, they may not be objective—companies are more likely to report successes than failures. As a matter of fact, teams *don't* always work. Indeed, according to one study, team-based projects fail 50 to 70 percent of the time.[6]

The Effect of Teams on Performance

Research shows that companies build and support teams because of their effect on overall workplace performance, both organizational and individual. If we examine the impact of team-based operations according to a wide range of relevant criteria—including product quality, worker satisfaction, and quality of work life, among others—we find that overall organizational performance improves. Table 8.1 lists several areas in which we can analyze workplace performance and indicates the percentage of companies that have reported improvements in each area.

TABLE 8.1   Effect of Teams on Workplace Performance

Area of Performance	Percent of Firms Reporting Improvement
Product and service quality	70
Customer service	67
Worker satisfaction	66
Quality of work life	63
Productivity	61
Competitiveness	50
Profitability	45
Absenteeism/turnover	23

Source: Adapted from Edward E. Lawler, S. A. Mohman, and G. E. Ledford, Creating High Performance Organizations: Practices and Results of Employee Involvement and Total Quality in Fortune 1000 Companies (San Francisco: Wiley, 1992). Reprinted with permission of John Wiley & Sons Inc.

1.3 Types of Teams

Teams, then, can improve company and individual performance in a number of areas. Not all teams, however, are formed to achieve the same goals or charged with the same responsibilities. Nor are they organized in the same way. Some, for instance, are more *autonomous* than others—less accountable to those higher up in the organization. Some depend on a team leader who's responsible for defining the team's goals and making sure that its activities are performed effectively. Others are more or less self-governing: though a leader lays out overall goals and strategies, the team itself chooses and manages the methods by which it pursues its goals and implements its strategies.[7] Teams also vary according to their membership. Let's look at several categories of teams.

Manager-Led Teams

manager-led team

Team on which a manager defines goals and methods and is solely responsible for interactions with higher-level management.

As its name implies, in the **manager-led team** the manager is the team leader and is in charge of setting team goals, assigning tasks, and monitoring the team's performance. The individual team members have relatively little autonomy. For example, the key employees of a professional football team (a manager-led team) are highly trained (and highly paid) athletes, but their activities on the field are tightly controlled by a head coach. As team manager, the coach is responsible both for developing the strategies by which the team pursues its goal of winning games and for the final outcome of each game (not to mention the season). He's also solely responsible for interacting with managers above him in the organization. The players are responsible only for executing plays.[8]

Self-Managing Teams

Self-managing teams (also known as *self-directed* or *self-regulating teams*) have considerable autonomy. They are usually small and often absorb activities that were once performed by traditional supervisors. A manager or team leader may determine overall goals, but the members of the self-managing team control the activities needed to achieve the goals, such as planning and scheduling work, sharing tasks, meeting quality standards, and handling day-to-day operations.

Self-managing teams are the organizational hallmark of Whole Foods Market, the largest natural-foods grocer in the United States. Each store is run by ten teams (produce, prepared foods, and so forth), and virtually every store employee is a member of a team. Each team has a designated leader and its own performance targets. (Team leaders also belong to a store team, and store-team leaders belong to a regional team.) To do its job, every team has access to the kind of information—including sales and even salary figures—that most companies reserve for the eyes of traditional managers.[9]

Needless to say, not every self-managed team enjoys the same degree of autonomy. Companies vary widely in choosing which tasks teams are allowed to manage and which ones are best left to upper-level management only. As you can see in Figure 8.1, for example, self-managing teams are often allowed to schedule assignments, but they are rarely allowed to fire coworkers.

FIGURE 8.1 What Teams Do (and Don't) Manage

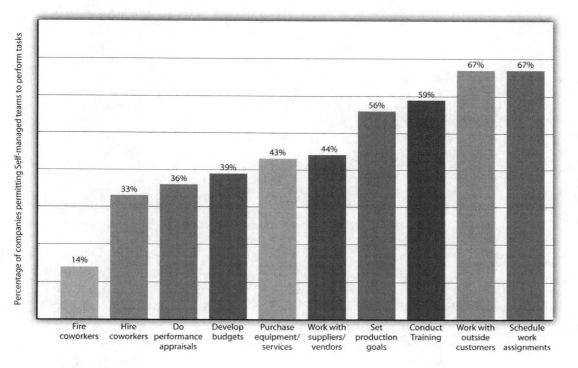

Cross-Functional Teams

Many companies use **cross-functional teams**—teams that, as the name suggests, cut across an organization's *functional areas* (operations, marketing, finance, and so on). A cross-functional team is designed to take advantage of the special expertise of members drawn from different functional areas of the company. When the Internal Revenue Service, for example, wanted to study the effects on employees of a major change in information systems, it created a cross-functional team composed of people from a wide range of departments. The final study reflected expertise in such areas as job analysis, training, change management, industrial psychology, and even ergonomics.[10]

Cross-functional teams figure prominently in the product-development process at Nike, where they take advantage of expertise from both inside and outside the company. Typically, team members include not only product designers, marketing specialists, and accountants but also sports-research experts, coaches, athletes, and even consumers. Likewise, Motorola's RAZR team was a cross-functional team: Responsibility for developing the new product wasn't passed along from the design team to the engineering team but rather was entrusted to a special team composed of both designers and engineers.

We can also classify the RAZR team as a *product-development* or *project team* (a topic we'll discuss in more detail in Chapter 10). *Committees* and *task forces*, both of which are dedicated to specific issues or tasks, are often cross-functional teams. *Problem-solving teams*, which are created to study such issues as improving quality or reducing waste, may be either intradepartmental or cross-functional.[11]

self-managing team (or self-directed or self-regulating team)

Team on which employees control the activities needed to meet overall goals.

cross-functional teams

Team designed to take advantage of the special expertise of members drawn from different functional areas of the organization.

Virtual Teams

"Teamwork," said someone (we're not sure who), "doesn't tolerate the inconvenience of distance." Indeed, technology now makes it possible for teams to function not only across such organizational boundaries as functional areas, departments, and divisions but also across time and space, as well. Working in **virtual teams**, geographically dispersed members interact electronically in the process of pursuing a common goal. Such technologies as videoconferencing, instant messaging, and electronic meetings, which allow people to interact simultaneously and in real time, offer a number of advantages in conducting the business of a virtual team.[12] Among other things, members can participate from any location or at any time of day, and teams can "meet" for as long as it takes to achieve a goal or solve a problem—a few days, a few weeks, or a few months.

Nor does team size seem to be an obstacle when it comes to calling virtual-team meetings: In building the F-35 Strike Fighter, U.S. defense contractor Lockheed Martin staked the $225 billion project on a virtual product-team of unprecedented global dimension, drawing on designers and engineers from the ranks of eight international partners ranging from Canada and the United Kingdom to Norway and Turkey.[13]

KEY TAKEAWAYS

- Teamwork brings diverse areas of expertise to bear on organizational problems and projects.
- Reaching teamwork goals requires skills in negotiating trade-offs, and teamwork brings these skills into play at almost every step in the process.
- To be successful, teams need a certain amount of autonomy and authority in making and implementing their decisions.
- A **team** (or a *work team*) is a group of people with complementary skills who work together to achieve a specific goal. Members of a *working group* work independently and meet primarily to share information.
- Work teams have five key characteristics:
    1. They are accountable for achieving specific common goals.
    2. They function interdependently.
    3. They are stable.
    4. They have authority.
    5. They operate in a social context.
- Companies build and support teams because of their effect on overall workplace performance, both organizational and individual.
- Work teams may be of several types:
    1. In the traditional **manager-led team**, the leader defines the team's goals and activities and is responsible for its achieving its assigned goals.
    2. The leader of a **self-managing team** may determine overall goals, but employees control the activities needed to meet them.
    3. A **cross-functional team** is designed to take advantage of the special expertise of members drawn from different functional areas of the company.
    4. On **virtual teams**, geographically dispersed members interact electronically in the process of pursuing a common goal.

Before going to the next section of this chapter, take a few minutes to test your knowledge of the material covered in this section. Quizzes can be found under the "Resources" tab, "Study Aids: Quizzes."

EXERCISE

You're a marketing researcher for a multinational food-products corporation, and for the past two years, you've been able to work at home. The international division of the company has asked you to join a virtual team assigned to assess the prospects for a new sandwich planned for the Indian market.

List a few of the challenges that you're likely to encounter as a member of the virtual team. Explain the steps you'd take to deal with each of the challenges that you've listed.

2. WHY TEAMWORK WORKS

LEARNING OBJECTIVES

1. Explain why teams may be effective or ineffective.
2. Identify factors that contribute to team cohesiveness.
3. Discuss common obstacles to team success.

Now that we know a little bit about *how* teams work, we need to ask ourselves *why* they work. Not surprisingly, this is a fairly complex issue. In this section, we'll answer these closely related questions: Why are teams often effective? Why are they sometimes *ineffective*?

2.1 Factors in Effective Teamwork

First, let's begin by identifying several factors that, in practice, tend to contribute to effective teamwork. Generally speaking, teams are effective when the following factors are met:[14]

- *Members depend on each other*. When team members rely on each other to get the job done, team productivity and efficiency are high.
- *Members trust one another*. Teamwork is more effective when members trust each other.
- *Members work better together than individually*. When team members perform better as a group than alone, collective performance exceeds individual performance.
- *Members become boosters*. When each member is encouraged by other team members to do his or her best, collective results improve.
- *Team members enjoy being on the team*. The more that team members derive satisfaction from being on the team, the more committed they become.
- *Leadership rotates*. Teams function effectively when leadership responsibility is shared over time.

Most of these explanations probably make pretty clear intuitive sense. Unfortunately, because such issues are rarely as clear-cut as they may seem at first glance, we need to examine the issue of group effectiveness from another perspective—one that considers the effects of factors that aren't quite so straightforward.

Group Cohesiveness

The idea of **group cohesiveness** refers to the *attractiveness* of a team to its members. If a group is high in cohesiveness, membership is quite satisfying to its members; if it's low in cohesiveness, members are unhappy with it and may even try to leave it. The principle of group cohesiveness, in other words, is based on the simple idea that groups are most effective when their members like being members of the group.[15]

group cohesiveness

Principle that groups are most effective when members like being members.

What Makes a Team Cohesive?

Numerous factors may contribute to team cohesiveness, but in this section, we'll focus on five of the most important:

1. *Size*. The bigger the team, the less satisfied members tend to be. When teams get too large, members find it harder to interact closely with other members; a few members tend to dominate team activities, and conflict becomes more likely.
2. *Similarity*. People usually get along better with people like themselves, and teams are generally more cohesive when members perceive fellow members as people who share their own attitudes and experience.
3. *Success*. When teams are successful, members are satisfied, and other people are more likely to be attracted to their teams.
4. *Exclusiveness*. The harder it is to get into a group, the happier the people who are already in it. Status (the extent to which outsiders look up to a team, as well as the perks that come with membership) also increases members' satisfaction.
5. *Competition*. Members value membership more highly when they're motivated to achieve common goals—especially when those goals mean outperforming other teams.

There's such a thing as too much cohesiveness. When, for instance, members are highly motivated to collaborate in performing the team's activities, the team is more likely to be effective in achieving its goals. Clearly, when those goals are aligned with the goals of the larger organization, the organization, too, will be happy. If, however, its members get too wrapped up in more immediate team goals, the whole team may lose sight of the larger organizational goals toward which it's supposed to be working.

Groupthink

Likewise, it's easier for leaders to direct members toward team goals when members are all on the same page—when there's a basic willingness to conform to the team's rules and guidelines. When there's too much conformity, however, the group can become ineffective: It may resist change and fresh ideas and, what's worse, may end up adopting its own dysfunctional tendencies as its way of doing things. Such tendencies may also encourage a phenomenon known as **groupthink**—the tendency to conform to group pressure in making decisions, while failing to think critically or to consider outside influences.

Groupthink is often cited as a factor in the explosion of the space shuttle *Challenger* in January 1986: Engineers from a supplier of components for the rocket booster warned that the launch might be risky because of the weather but were persuaded to reverse their recommendation by NASA officials who wanted the launch to proceed as scheduled.[16]

2.2 Why Teams Fail

Teams don't always work. To learn why, let's take a quick look at four common obstacles to success in introducing teams into an organization:[17]

- *Unwillingness to cooperate.* Failure to cooperate can occur when members don't or won't commit to a common goal or set of activities. What if, for example, half the members of a product-development team want to create a brand-new product and half want to improve an existing product? The entire team may get stuck on this point of contention for weeks or even months.
- *Lack of managerial support.* Every team requires organizational resources to achieve its goals, and if management isn't willing to commit the needed resources—say, funding or key personnel—a team will probably fall short of those goals.
- *Failure of managers to delegate authority.* Team leaders are often chosen from the ranks of successful supervisors—first-line managers who, as we saw in Chapter 6, give instructions on a day-to-day basis and expect to have them carried out. This approach to workplace activities may not work very well in leading a team—a position in which success depends on building a consensus and letting people make their own decisions.
- *Failure of teams to cooperate.* If you're on a workplace team, your employer probably depends on teams to perform much of the organization's work and meet many of its goals. In other words, it is, to some extent, a team-based organization, and as such, reaching its overall goals requires a high level of cooperation *among teams.*[18] When teams can't agree on mutual goals (or when they duplicate efforts), neither the teams nor the organization is likely to meet with much success.

Motivation and Frustration

Finally, remember that teams are composed of people, and whatever the roles they happen to be playing at a given time, people are subject to psychological ups and downs. As members of workplace teams, they need motivation, and as we observed in Chapter 7, when motivation is down, so are effectiveness and productivity. As you can see in Figure 8.3, the difficulty of maintaining a high level of motivation is the chief cause of frustration among members of teams. As such, it's also a chief cause of ineffective teamwork, and that's one reason why more employers now look for the ability to develop and sustain motivation when they're hiring new managers.[19]

FIGURE 8.3 Sources of Frustration

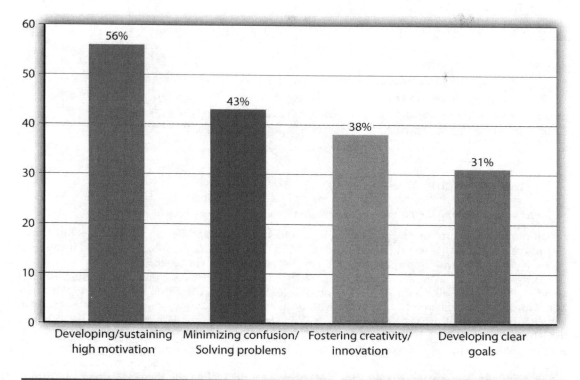

- Generally speaking, teams are effective when the following are true:
    1. Members are interdependent.
    2. Members work better together than individually.
    3. Teams work well enough to satisfy members.
    4. Leadership rotates.
    5. Members help one another.
    6. Members become boosters.
    7. Members trust one another.

- **Group cohesiveness** refers to the *attractiveness* of a team to its members. If a group is high in cohesiveness, membership is quite satisfying to its members; if it's low in cohesiveness, members are unhappy with it and may even try to leave it.

- Common obstacles to team success include the following:
    1. Unwillingness to cooperate
    2. Lack of managerial support
    3. Failure of managers to delegate authority
    4. Failure of teams to cooperate

Before going to the next section of this chapter, take a few minutes to test your knowledge of the material covered in this section. Quizzes can be found under the "Resources" tab, "Study Aids: Quizzes."

EXERCISE

At some point in the coming week, while you're working on an assignment for any one of your classes, ask at least one other member of the class to help you with it or to collaborate with you in studying for it. After you've completed your assignment, make a list of the advantages and disadvantages of working on the assignment with another person.

3. THE TEAM AND ITS MEMBERS

LEARNING OBJECTIVES

1. Understand the importance of learning to participate in team-based activities.
2. Identify the skills needed by team members and the roles that members of a team might play.
3. Learn how to survive team projects in college (and actually enjoy yourself).
4. Explain the skills and behaviors that foster effective team leadership.

3.1 "Life Is All about Group Work"

"I'll work extra hard and do it myself, but please don't make me have to work in a group."

Like it or not, you'll probably be given some teamwork assignments while you're in college. More than two-thirds of all students report having participated in the work of an organized team, and if you're in business school, you will almost certainly find yourself engaged in team-based activities.[20]

Why do we put so much emphasis on something that, reportedly, makes many students feel anxious and academically drained? Here's one college student's practical-minded answer to this question: "In the real world, you have to work with people. You don't always know the people you work with, and you don't always get along with them. Your boss won't particularly care, and if you can't get the job done, your job may end up on the line. Life is all about group work, whether we like it or not. And school, in many ways, prepares us for life, including working with others."[21] She's right. In placing so much emphasis on teamwork skills and experience, college business departments are doing the responsible thing—preparing students for the business world that awaits them. A survey of Fortune 1000 companies reveals that 79 percent already rely on self-managing teams and 91 percent on various forms of employee work groups. Another survey found that the skill that most employers value in new employees is the ability to work in teams.[22] The importance of the ability to work in teams was confirmed in a survey of leadership practices of more than sixty of the world's top organizations.[23] When top executives in these organizations were asked, "What causes high-potential leadership candidates to derail? (stop moving up in the organization)," 60 percent of the organizations cited "inability to work in teams." Interestingly, only 9 percent attributed the failure of these executives to advance to "lack of technical ability." While technical skills will be essential in your getting hired into an organization, your team skills will play a significant role in your ability to advance.

To be team-ready or not to be team-ready—that is the question. Or, to put it in plainer terms, the question is not whether you'll find yourself working as part of a team. You will. The question is whether you'll know how to participate successfully in team-based activities.

3.2 Will *You* Make a Good Team Member?

What if your instructor in this course decides to divide the class into several three-, four-, or five-member teams and assigns each team to develop a new product plus a business plan to get it into production and out on the market? What teamwork skills could you bring to the table? What teamwork skills do you need to work on? What qualities do you possess that might make you a good team leader?

What Skills Does the Team Need?

Sometimes we hear about a sports team made up of mostly average players who win a championship because of coaching genius, flawless teamwork, and superhuman determination.[24] But not terribly often. In fact, we usually hear about such teams simply because they're newsworthy—exceptions to the rule. Typically a team performs well because its members possess some level of talent. This doesn't mean, however, that we should reduce team performance to the mere sum of its individual contributions: Members' talents aren't very useful if they're not managed in a collective effort to achieve a common goal.

In the final analysis, of course, a team can succeed only if its members provide the skills that need managing. In particular, every team requires some mixture of three sets of skills:

- *Technical skills.* Because teams must perform certain tasks, they need people with the skills to perform them. For example, if your project calls for a lot of math work, it's good to have someone with the necessary quantitative skills.

- *Decision-making and problem-solving skills*. Because every task is subject to problems, and because handling every problem means deciding on the best solution, it's good to have members who are skilled in identifying problems, evaluating alternative solutions, and deciding on the best options.

- *Interpersonal skills*. Because teams are composed of people, and because people need direction and motivation and depend on communication, every group benefits from members who know how to listen, provide feedback, and smooth ruffled feathers. The same people are usually good at communicating the team's goals and needs to outsiders.

The key to success is ultimately the right mix of these skills. Remember, too, that no team needs to possess all these skills—never mind the right balance of them—from day one. In many cases, a team gains certain skills only when members volunteer for certain tasks and perfect their skills in the process of performing them. For the same reason, effective teamwork develops over time as team members learn how to handle various team-based tasks. In a sense, teamwork is always work in progress.

What Roles Do Team Members Play?

Like your teamwork skills, expect your role on a team to develop over time. Also remember that, both as a student and as a member of the workforce, you'll be a *member* of a team more often than a *leader* (a subject that we'll take up in the next section). Team members, however, can have as much impact on a team's success as its leaders. The key is the quality of the contributions they make in performing non-leadership roles.[25]

What, exactly, are those roles? At this point, you've probably concluded that every team faces two basic challenges:

1. Accomplishing its assigned task
2. Maintaining or improving group cohesiveness

Whether you affect the team's work positively or negatively depends on the extent to which you help it or hinder it in meeting these two challenges.[26] We can thus divide teamwork roles into two categories, depending on which of these two challenges each role addresses. These two categories (task-facilitating roles and relationship-building roles) are summarized in Table 8.2.

TABLE 8.2 Roles that Team Members Play

Task-facilitating Roles	Example	Relationship-building Roles	Example
Direction giving	"Jot down a few ideas and we'll see what everyone has come up with."	Supporting	"Now, that's what I mean by a practical application."
Information seeking	"Does anyone know if this is the latest data we have?"	Harmonizing	"Actually, I think you're both saying pretty much the same thing."
Information giving	"Here are latest numbers from…."	Tension relieving	"Before we go on to the next section, how many people would like a pillow?"
Elaborating	"I think a good example of what you're talking about is…."	Confronting	"How does that suggestion relate to the topic that we're discussing?"
Urging	"Let's try to finish this proposal before we adjourn."	Energizing	"It's been a long time since I've had this many laughs at a meeting in *this* department."
Monitoring	"If you'll take care of the first section, I'll make sure that we have the second by next week."	Developing	"If you need some help pulling the data together, let me know."
Process analyzing	"What happened to the energy level in this room?"	Consensus building	"Do we agree on the first four points even if number five needs a little more work?"
Reality testing	"Can we make this work and stay within budget?"	Empathizing	"It's not you. The numbers *are* confusing."
Enforcing	"We're getting off track. Let's try to stay on topic."		
Summarizing	"Before we jump ahead, here's what we've decided so far."		

Source: Adapted from David A. Whetten and Kim S. Cameron, Developing Management Skills, 7th ed. (Upper Saddle River, NJ: Pearson Education, 2007), 517, 519.

Task-Facilitating Roles

Task-facilitating roles address challenge number one—accomplishing the team goals. As you can see from Table 8.2, such roles include not only providing information when someone else needs it but also asking for it when you need it. In addition, it includes *monitoring* (checking on progress) and *enforcing* (making sure that team decisions are carried out). Task facilitators are especially valuable when assignments aren't clear or when progress is too slow. Moreover, every team needs people who recognize when a little task facilitation is called for.

Relationship-Building Roles

When you challenge unmotivated behavior or help other team members understand their roles, you're performing a **relationship-building role** and addressing challenge number two—maintaining or improving group cohesiveness. This type of role includes just about every activity that improves team "chemistry," from *confronting* to *empathizing*.

Bear in mind three points about this model of team-membership roles: (1) Teams are most effective when there's a good balance between task facilitation and relationship building; (2) it's hard for any given member to perform both types of roles, as some people are better at focusing on tasks and others on relationships; and (3) overplaying any facet of any role can easily become counterproductive. For example, *elaborating* on something may not be the best strategy when the team needs to make a quick decision; and *consensus building* may cause the team to overlook an important difference of opinion.

Blocking Roles

Finally, review Table 8.3, which summarizes a few characteristics of another kind of team-membership role. So-called **blocking roles** consist of behavior that inhibits either team performance or that of individual members. Every member of the team should know how to recognize blocking behavior. If teams don't confront dysfunctional members, they can destroy morale, hamper consensus building, create conflict, and hinder progress.

TABLE 8.3 How to Block Teamwork

Blocking Strategy	Tactics
Dominate	Talk as much as possible; interrupt and interject
Overanalyze	Split hairs and belabor every detail
Stall	Frustrate efforts to come to conclusions: decline to agree, sidetrack the discussion, rehash old ideas
Remain passive	Stay on the fringe; keep interaction to a minimum; wait for others to take on work
Overgeneralize	Blow things out of proportion; float unfounded conclusions
Find fault	Criticize and withhold credit whenever possible
Make premature decisions	Rush to conclusions before goals are set, information is shared, or problems are clarified
Present opinions as facts	Refuse to seek factual support for ideas that you personally favor
Reject	Object to ideas offered by people who tend to disagree with you
Pull rank	Use status or title to push through ideas, rather than seek consensus on their value
Resist	Throw up roadblocks to progress; look on the negative side
Deflect	Refuse to stay on topic; focus on minor points rather than main points

Source: Adapted from David A. Whetten and Kim S. Cameron, Developing Management Skills, 7th ed. (Upper Saddle River, NJ: Pearson Education, 2007), 519–20.

3.3 Class Team Projects

As we highlighted earlier, throughout your academic career you'll likely participate in a number of team projects. Not only will you make lasting friends by being a member of a team, but in addition, you'll produce a better product. To get insider advice on how to survive team projects in college (and perhaps really enjoy yourself in the process), let's look at some suggestions offered by two students who have gone through this experience.[27]

- *Draw up a team charter.* At the beginning of the project, draw up a team charter (or contract) that includes the goals of the group; ways to ensure that each team member's ideas are considered and respected; when and where your group will meet; what happens if a team member skips meetings or doesn't do his or her share of the work; how conflicts will be resolved.

- *Contribute your ideas.* Share your ideas with your group; they might be valuable to the group. The worst that could happen is that they won't be used (which is what would happen if you kept quiet).

- *Never miss a meeting.* Pick a weekly meeting time and write it into your schedule as if it were a class. Never skip it. And make your meetings productive.

- *Be considerate of each other.* Be patient, listen to everyone, communicate frequently, involve everyone in decision making, don't think you're always right, be positive, avoid infighting, and build trust.

- *Create a process for resolving conflict.* Do this before conflict arises. Set up rules to help the group decide whether the conflict is constructive, whether it's personal, or whether it arises because someone won't pull his or her weight. Decide, as a group, how conflict will be handled.

- *Use the strengths of each team member.* Some students are good researchers, others are good writers, others have strong problem-solving or computer skills, while others are good at generating ideas. Don't have your writer do the research and your researcher do the writing. Not only would the team not be using its resources wisely, but two team members will be frustrated because they're not using their strengths.

- *Don't do all the work yourself.* Work with your team to get the work done. The project output is not as important as the experience of working in a team.

- *Set deadlines.* Don't leave everything to the end; divide up tasks, hold team members accountable, and set intermediary deadlines for each team member to get his or her work done. Work together to be sure the project is in on time and in good shape.

3.4 What Does It Take to Lead a Team?

"Some people are born leaders, some achieve leadership, and some have leadership thrust upon them." Or so Shakespeare might have said if he were managing a twenty-first-century work team instead of a sixteenth-century theater troupe. At some point in a successful career, whether in business, school, or any other form of organizational work, you may be asked (or assigned) to lead a team. The more successful you are, the more likely you are to receive such an invitation. So, what will you have to do as a leader? What skills will you need?

Like so many of the questions that we ask in this book, these questions don't have any simple answers. As for the first question—what does a leader have to do?—we can provide one broad answer: A leader must help members develop the attitudes and behavior that contribute to team success: interdependence, collective responsibility, shared commitment, and so forth.

Influence Team Members and Gain their Trust

Team leaders must be able to influence their team members. And notice that we say *influence*: except in unusual circumstances, giving commands and controlling everything directly doesn't work very well.[28] As one team of researchers puts it, team leaders are more effective when they work *with* members rather than *on* them.[29] Hand in hand with the ability to influence is the ability to gain and keep the *trust* of team members. People aren't likely to be influenced by a leader whom they perceive as dishonest or selfishly motivated.

Assuming you were asked to lead a team, there are certain leadership skills and behaviors that would help you influence your team members and build trust. Let's look at seven of these:

- *Demonstrate integrity.* Do what you say you'll do, and act in accordance with your stated values. Be honest in communicating with members, and follow through on promises.

- *Be clear and consistent.* Let members know that you're certain about what you want, and remember that being clear and consistent reinforces your credibility.

- *Generate positive energy.* Be optimistic and compliment team members. Recognize their progress and success.

- *Acknowledge common points of view.* Even if you're about to propose some kind of change, before embarking on a new stage of a project recognize the value of the views that members already hold in common.

- *Manage agreement and disagreement.* When members agree with you, focus on your point of view and present it reasonably. When they disagree with you, acknowledge both sides of the issue and support your own with strong, clearly presented evidence.

FIGURE 8.4

Team leaders are most effective when they can not only influence members but also gain their trust.

© *2010 Jupiterimages Corporation*

- *Encourage and coach.* Buoy up members when they run into new and uncertain situations and when success depends on their performing at a high level. Give them the information they need and otherwise help them to perform tasks.

- *Share information.* Let members know that you're knowledgeable about team tasks and individual talents. Check with team members regularly to find out what they're doing and how the job is progressing. Collect information from outside sources, and make sure that it gets to the team members who need it.

KEY TAKEAWAYS

- As the business world depends more and more on teamwork, it's increasingly important for incoming members of the workforce to develop skills and experience in team-based activities.

- Every team requires some mixture of three skill sets:

    1. *Technical skills*: skills needed to perform specific tasks
    2. *Decision-making and problem-solving skills*: skills needed to identify problems, evaluate alternative solutions, and decide on the best options
    3. *Interpersonal skills*: skills in listening, providing feedback, and resolving conflict

- Team members deal with two basic challenges: (1) accomplishing the team's assigned task and (2) maintaining or improving group cohesiveness.

- **Task-facilitating roles** address challenge number one—accomplishing team tasks. **Relationship-building roles** address challenge number two—maintaining or improving group cohesiveness. **Blocking roles** consist of behavior that inhibits either team performance or that of individual members.

- The following are eight ways to add value to and survive team projects in college:

    1. Draw up a team charter.
    2. Contribute your ideas.
    3. Never miss a meeting.
    4. Be considerate of each other.
    5. Create a process for resolving conflict.
    6. Use the strengths of each team member.
    7. Don't do all the work yourself.
    8. Set deadlines.

- The following are seven types of skills and behaviors that help team leaders influence their members and gain their trust:

    1. Demonstrating integrity
    2. Being clear and consistent
    3. Generating positive energy
    4. Acknowledging common points of view
    5. Managing agreement and disagreement
    6. Encouraging and coaching
    7. Sharing information

Before going to the next section of this chapter, take a few minutes to test your knowledge of the material covered in this section. Quizzes can be found under the "Resources" tab, "Study Aids: Quizzes."

EXERCISE

One student, a veteran of team-based assignments, has some good advice to offer students who are following in her footsteps. Don't start, she advises, until you've drawn up a *team charter*. This charter (or contract) should include the following: the goals of the group, information on meeting times and places, ways to ensure that each member's ideas are considered and respected, methods for resolving conflicts, and a "kick-out" clause—a statement of what will happen if a team member skips meetings or fails to do his or her share of the work.

Now assume that you've just been assigned to a team in one of your classes. Prepare a first-draft charter in which you spell out rules of conduct for the team and its members.

---

4.   THE BUSINESS OF COMMUNICATION

LEARNING OBJECTIVES

1. **Discuss the role of communication in the design of the RAZR cell phone.**
2. **Define "communication," and discuss the ways in which organizations benefit from effective communication.**

4.1   Communication by Design

As the chief designer assigned to the "thin-clam" team at Motorola, Chris Arnholt was responsible for some of the phone's distinctive physical features, including its sleek aluminum finish and backlit keyboard. In fact, it was he who pushed the company's engineers and marketers to buck an industry trend toward phones that were getting fatter because of many add-ons such as cameras and stereo speakers. For Arnholt had a vision. He called it "rich minimalism," and his goal was to help the Motorola cell phone team realize a product that embodied that profile.

But what exactly did Arnholt mean by rich minimalism? "Sometimes," he admits, "my ideas are tough to communicate," but as a veteran in his field, he also understands that "design is really about communication."[30] His chief (and ongoing) task, then, was communicating to the cell phone team what he meant by rich minimalism. Ultimately, of course, he had to show them what rich minimalism looked like when it appeared in tangible form in a fashionable new cell phone. In the process, he also had to be sure that the cell phone included certain key benefits that prospective consumers would want. As always, the physical design of the finished product had to be right for its intended market.

We'll have much more to say about the process of developing new products in Chapter 10. Here, however, let's simply highlight two points about the way successful companies approach the challenges of new-product design and development (which you will likely recognize from reading the first part of this chapter):

1. In contributing to the new-product design and development process, industrial designers like Chris Arnholt must effectively communicate both ideas and practical specifications.
2. The design and development process usually succeeds only when the assigned team integrates input from every relevant area of the organization.[31]

The common denominator in both facets of the process is effective communication. The designer, for example, must communicate not only his vision of the product but also certain specifications for turning it into something concrete. Chris Arnholt sculpted models out of cornstarch and then took them home at night to refashion them according to suggestions made by the product team. Then he'd put his newest ideas on paper and hand the drawings over to another member of his design team, who'd turn them into 3D computer graphics from which other specialists would build plastic models. Without effective communication at every step in this process, it isn't likely that a group of people with different skills would produce plastic models bearing a practical resemblance to Arnholt's original drawings. On top of everything else, Arnholt's responsibility as chief designer required him to communicate his ideas not only about the product's visual and physical features but also about the production processes and manufacturing requirements for building it.[32]

Thus Arnholt's job—which is to say, his responsibility on the cell phone team—meant that he had to do a lot more than merely design the product. Strictly speaking, the designer's function is to understand a product from the consumer's point of view; develop this understanding into a set of ideas and specifications that will satisfy not only consumer needs but producer requirements; and make recommendations through drawings, models, and verbal communications.[33] Even our condensed version of the RAZR story, however, indicates that Arnholt's job was far broader. Why? Because new-product design is an integrative process: contributions must come from all functions within an organization, including *operations* (which includes research and development, engineering and manufacturing), *marketing, management, finance,* and *accounting.*[34]

Our version of the RAZR story has emphasized operations (which includes research and development, engineering, and manufacturing) and touched on the role of marketing (which collects data about consumer needs). Remember, though, that members from several areas of management were recruited for the team. Because the project required considerable investment of Motorola's capital, finance was certainly involved, and the decision to increase production in late 2004 was based on numbers crunched by the accounting department. At every step, Arnholt's drawings, specs, and recommendations reflected his collaboration with people from all these functional areas.

As we'll see in Section 4, what all this interactivity amounts to is *communication.*[35] As for what Arnholt meant by rich minimalism, you'll need to take a look at the picture of the RAZR at the beginning of the chapter. Among other things, it means a blue electroluminescent panel and a 22 kHz polyphonic speaker.

4.2 What Is Communication?

Let's start with a basic (and quite practical) definition of **communication** as the process of transferring information from a sender to a receiver. When you call up a classmate to inform him that your Introduction to Financial Accounting class has been canceled, you're sending information and your classmate is receiving it. When you go to your professor's Web site to find out the assignment for the next class, your professor is sending information and you're receiving it. When your boss e-mails you the data you need to complete a sales report and tells you to e-mail the report back to her by 4 o'clock, your boss is sending information and, once again, you're receiving it; later in the day, the situation will be reversed.

4.3 Your Ticket In (or Out)

Obviously, you participate in dozens of "informational transfers" every day. (In fact, they take up about 70 percent of your waking hours—80 percent if you have some sort of managerial position.)[36] In any case, it wouldn't make much sense for us to pursue the topic much further without assuming that you've gained *some* experience and mastered *some* skills in the task of communicating. At the same time, though, we'll also venture to guess that you're much more comfortable having casual conversations with friends than writing class assignments or giving speeches in front of classmates. That's why we're going to resort to the same plain terms that we used when we discussed the likelihood of your needing teamwork skills in an organizational setting: The question is not whether you'll need communication skills (both written and verbal). You will. The question is whether you'll develop the skills to communicate effectively in a variety of organizational situations.

When it comes to the importance of candidate skills and qualities, employers are looking for team players who can solve problems, organize their work, and communicate effectively, according to the results of a new survey by the National Association of Colleges and Employers (NACE).

Once again, the numbers back us up. In a recent survey by the Association of Colleges and Employers, the ability to communicate well was one of the top skills that business recruiters want in potential hires (in addition to the ability to work in a team).[37] A College Board survey of 120 major U.S. companies concludes that writing is a "threshold skill" for both employment and promotion. "In most cases," volunteered one human resources director, "writing ability could be your ticket in—or your ticket out." Applicants and employees who can't write and communicate clearly, says the final report, "will not be hired and are unlikely to last long enough to be considered for promotion."[38]

Why Are Communication Skills Important?

They're important to you because they're important to prospective employers. And why do employers consider communication skills so important? Because they're good for business. Research shows that businesses benefit in several ways when they're able to foster effective communication among employees:[39]

- Decisions are more convincing and certain, and problem solving is faster.

FIGURE 8.5

The explosion of text messaging has changed the way people use their cell phones and created new design needs for manufacturers like Motorola.

© 2010 Jupiterimages Corporation

communication

Process of transferring information from a sender to a receiver.

- Warning signs of potential problems appear earlier.
- Workflow moves more smoothly and productivity increases.
- Business relationships are stronger.
- Marketing messages are more persuasive.
- The company's professional image is enhanced.
- Employee satisfaction goes up and turnover goes down.
- The firm and its investors enjoy better financial results.

What Skills Are Important?

Figure 8.6 reveals some further findings of a College Board survey—namely, the percentage of companies that identified certain communication skills as being "frequently" or "almost always" necessary in their workplaces. As you can see, ability in using e-mail is a nearly universal requirement (and in many cases this includes the ability to adapt messages to different receivers or compose persuasive messages when necessary). The ability to make presentations (with visuals) also ranks highly.[40]

FIGURE 8.6 Required Skills

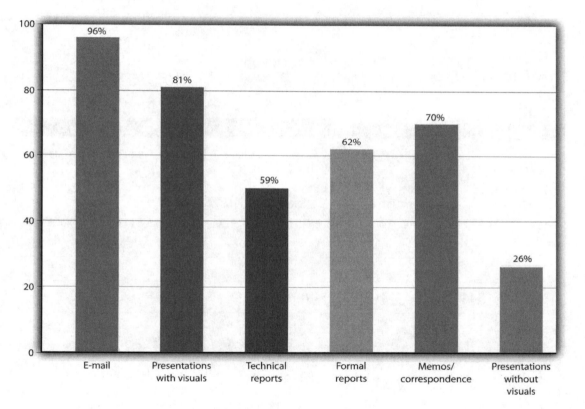

- Effective communication is needed in several facets of the new-product design and development process:
    1. Designers must effectively communicate both ideas and practical specifications.
    2. The process usually succeeds only when the assigned team integrates input from every relevant area of the organization.
- **Communication** is the process of transferring information from a sender to a receiver.
- Businesses benefit in several ways when they're able to foster effective communication among employees:
    1. Decisions are more assured and cogent, and problem solving is faster.
    2. Warning signs of potential problems appear earlier.
    3. Workflow moves more smoothly and productivity increases.
    4. Business relationships are stronger.
    5. Marketing messages are more persuasive.
    6. The company's professional image is enhanced.
    7. Employee satisfaction goes up and turnover goes down.
    8. The firm and its investors enjoy better financial results.

Before going to the next section of this chapter, take a few minutes to test your knowledge of the material covered in this section. Quizzes can be found under the "Resources" tab, "Study Aids: Quizzes."

Pick a company you're interested in working for when you graduate from college. For this company, identify the following:

1. A starting position you'd like to obtain on graduation
2. A higher-level position you'd like to be promoted to in five years.

For each of these positions, describe the skills needed to get the job and those needed to be successful in the position.

5. COMMUNICATION CHANNELS

1. **Discuss the nature of communications in an organizational setting, including communication flows, channels, and networks.**
2. **Explain barriers to communication, and discuss the most common types of barriers to group communication.**

5.1 What Is *Organizational* Communication?

Clearly, the task of preparing and submitting a finished sales report doesn't require the same kinds of communication skills as talking on the phone with a classmate. No matter what your "workstation" happens to be—whether your workplace office or your kitchen table—you're performing the task of preparing that sales report in an *organizational setting*. You're still a sender transferring information to a receiver, but the organizational context of the task requires you to consider different factors for success in communicating effectively (including barriers to success). A report, for example, must be targeted for someone in a specific position and must contain the information necessary to make a specific set of decisions.[41]

5.2   Communication Flows

Here's another way of thinking about communication in an organizational setting. Let's assume that you and the classmate you called on the phone are on roughly equal footing—you're both juniors, your grades in the class are about the same, and so forth. Your phone conversation, therefore, is "lateral": You belong to the same group (your accounting class), and your group activities take place on the same level.

Communication may also flow laterally in organizational settings (as it does between you and your classmate), but more often it flows up or down. Take a look at Figure 8.7. If it looks familiar, that's because we've borrowed it from Chapter 6, where it appeared as the *organization chart* for the fictional company Notes-4-You. As you can see, we've added a few lines to show the three directions in which communications can flow in a typical organization:[42]

- As the term suggests, **downward communication** flows from higher organizational levels (supervisors) to lower organizational levels (subordinates).
- **Upward communication** flows from lower to higher organizational levels.
- **Lateral (or horizontal) communication** flows across the organization, among personnel on the same level.

Your boss's request for a sales report is an instance of downward communication, and when you've finished and submitted it, you will have completed a task of upward communication.

downward communication

Communication flow from higher to lower organizational levels.

upward communication

Communication flow from lower to higher organizational levels.

lateral (or horizontal) communication

Communication flow across the organization, among personnel on the same level.

FIGURE 8.7   Formal Communication Flows

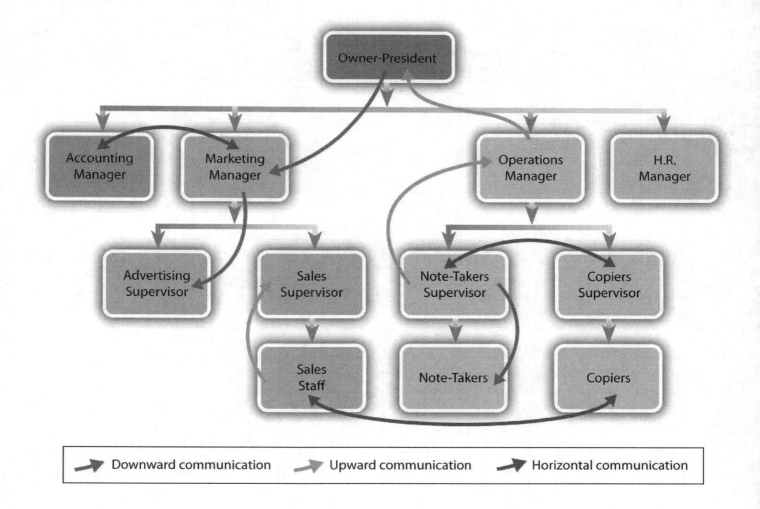

Advantages of Communication Flows

Naturally, each of these different directional flows has its functions and advantages. Downward communication, for example, is appropriate for giving instructions or directions—telling people what to do. (As a goal of communication, by the way, giving orders isn't as one-sided as it may seem. One of the things that employees—the receivers—most want to know is "What, exactly, does my job entail?")[43] Like a sales report, upward communication usually provides managers with information that they need for making decisions, but it's also the vehicle for new ideas, suggestions, and complaints. Horizontal communication supports efforts to coordinate tasks and otherwise help people work together.

Disadvantages of Communication Flows

And, of course, each type of flow has its disadvantages. As information seeps downward, for instance, it tends to lose some of its original clarity and often becomes distorted or downright wrong. (This is especially true when it's delivered orally.) In addition, unlike Donald Trump, most people who are responsible for using downward communication don't like delivering bad news (such as "You're fired" or, more commonly, "Your job is being phased out"); as a result, bad news—including bad news that happens to be important news—is often ignored or disguised. The same thing may happen when bad news—say, a negative status report—must be sent upward.

Finally, while horizontal flows are valuable for promoting cooperation, they can also be used to engage in conflict—for instance, between two departments competing for the same organizational resources. The problem is especially bad when such horizontal communications breach official upward or downward lines of communication, thus bypassing managers who might be able to resolve the conflict.

5.3   Channels of Communication

Internal communication

Channel by which communication is shared by people at all levels within a company.

External communication

Channel through which communication occurs between parties inside a company and parties outside it.

Figure 8.8 summarizes two additional sets of characteristics of organizational communication—*internal and external channels* and *formal and informal channels*.[44] **Internal communication** is shared by people at all levels within a company. **External communication** occurs between parties inside a company and parties outside the company, such as suppliers, customers, and investors. Both internal and external forms of communication include everything from formal e-mail and official reports to face-to-face conversations and casual phone calls. External communication also takes such forms as customer and supplier Web sites, news releases, and advertising.

FIGURE 8.8 Channels of Communication

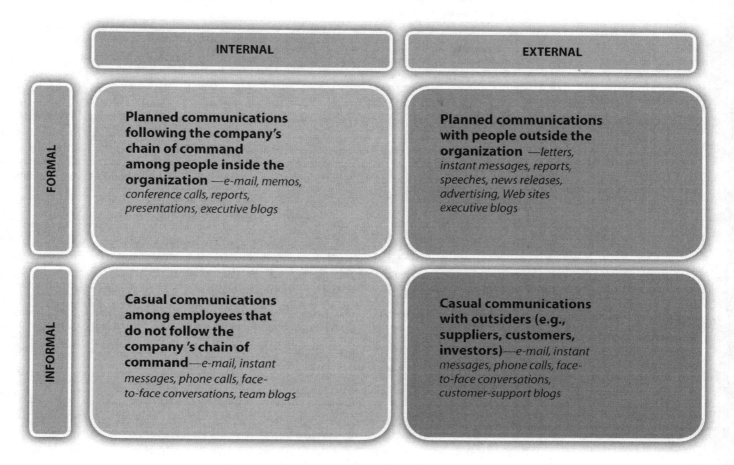

Note that Figure 8.8 takes the form of a grid, thus creating four dimensions in which communication can take place. Informal communication, for example, can take place either among people within the company (internally) or between insiders and outsiders (externally). By and large, though you can use the same set of tools (memos, reports, phone calls) to communicate in any of these four situations, some tools (team blogs, news releases, supplier Web sites) are useful only in one or two.

The Formal Communication Network

An organization's **formal communication network** consists of all communications that flow along its official lines of authority. Look again at Figure 8.7. Because it incorporates the *organization chart* for Notes-4-You, it shows the company's lines of authority—what, in Chapter 6, we called its *reporting relationships*. Here we can see that the reporting relationships in question consist of *upward communication* from subordinates to superiors. In reporting to the operations manager, for example, the notetakers' supervisor communicates upward. Conversely, when the notetakers' manager needs to give direction to notetakers, she will use *downward communication*. If the notetakers' manager and the copiers' manager must get together to prepare a joint report for the operations manager, they'll engage in *lateral communication*. In short, an organization's formal communication network is basically the same thing as its network of reporting relationships and lines of authority.[45]

formal communication network

Network consisting of all communications that flow along an organization's official lines of authority.

The Informal Communication Network

Every company also has an **informal communication network (or grapevine)**, which goes to work whenever two or more employees get together and start talking about the company and their jobs. Informal communication can take place just about anywhere (in one person's cubicle, in the cafeteria, on the golf course) and by just about any means (phone, e-mail, instant messaging, face-to-face conversation).

   Though it's sometimes called the *grapevine*, an informal network is an extremely important communication channel. Why? For the simple reason that it's typically widespread and can rarely be prevented, even if it's not officially sanctioned by the company—indeed, even when the company tries to discourage or bypass it. Unofficial information crosses virtually every boundary drawn by a firm's

informal communication network (or grapevine)

Network that carries information whenever two or more employees get together and start talking about the company and their jobs.

organization chart, reaching out and touching everyone in the organization, and what's more, it travels a lot faster than official information.

Problems with the Flow of Information through Informal Channels

The downside of "unofficial" information should be obvious. Because much of it is communicated orally, it's likely to get distorted and often degenerates into outright misinformation. Say, for example, that a rumor about layoffs gets started in your workplace. As more than one manager will verify, such rumors can do more damage than the reality. Morale may plummet and productivity won't be far behind. Valuable employees may abandon ship (needlessly, if the rumors are false).[46]

And imagine what can happen if informal information gets outside the organization. In the 1970s, Chicago-area McDonald's outlets found themselves fighting rumors about worms in their hamburgers. Over the years, Coca-Cola has had to fight rumors about terrorists joining its organization, subversive messages concealed in its label, and hyperacidity (false rumors that Coke causes osteoporosis and makes a good pesticide and an equally good spermicide).[47]

What to Do about Informal Information Flows

On the upside, savvy managers can tap into the informal network, either to find out what sort of information is influencing employee activities or to circulate more meaningful information, including new ideas as well as corrective information. In any case, managers have to deal with the grapevine, and one manager has compiled a list of suggestions for doing so effectively:[48]

- *Learn to live with it.* It's here to stay.
- *Tune into it.* Pay attention to the information that's circulating and try to learn something from it. Remember: The more you know about grapevine information, the better you can interact with employees (who, in turn, will probably come to regard you as someone who keeps in touch with the things that concern them).
- *Don't participate in rumors.* Resist the temptation to add your two cents' worth, and don't make matters worse.
- *Check out what you hear.* Because it's your job to replace bad information with good information, you need to find out what's really going on.
- *Take advantage of the grapevine.* Its only function is to carry information, so there's no reason why you can't pump some useful information through it.

Perhaps most importantly, when alert managers notice that the grapevine is particularly active, they tend to reach a sensible twofold conclusion:

1. The organization's formal lines of communication aren't working as well as they should be.
2. The best way to minimize informal communication and its potential damage is to provide better formal communication from the outset—or, failing that, to provide whatever formal communication will counteract misinformation as thoroughly as possible.

Let's go back to our example of a workplace overwhelmed by layoff rumors. In a practical sense, what can a manager—say, the leader of a long-term product-development team—do to provide better communication? One manager suggests at least three specific responses:[49]

1. Go to your supervisor or another senior manager and try to find out as much as you can about the organization's real plans.
2. Ask a senior manager or a human resources representative to meet with your team and address members' concerns with accurate feedback.
3. Make it a priority to keep channels open—both between yourself and your team members and between team members and the human resources department.

Because actions of this sort send a message, they can legitimately be characterized as a form of formal communication. They also reflect good leadership: Even though the information in this case relates only indirectly to immediate team tasks, you're sharing information with people who need it, and you're demonstrating integrity (you're being honest, and you're following through on a commitment to the team).

5.4 Overcoming Barriers to Communication

What Are Barriers to Communication?

By *barriers* we mean anything that prevents people from communicating as effectively as possible. Noise, for example, can be a barrier to communication; if you and other team members are mumbling among yourselves while your team leader is trying to explain task assignments, you're putting up a barrier to group communication. As a matter of fact, you're putting up two barriers: In addition to *creating noise*, you're *failing to listen*. About 80 percent of top executives say that learning to listen is the most important skill in getting things done in the workplace,[50] and as President Calvin Coolidge once remarked, "No man ever listened himself out of a job." Business people who don't listen risk offending others or misinterpreting what they're saying.

5.5 Two Types of Barriers

As for creating unnecessary verbal noise and failing to listen, we can probably chalk them up to poor communication habits (or maybe the *same* habit, for as legendary management expert Peter Drucker argues, "Listening is not a skill; it is a discipline. All you have to do is keep your mouth shut"). In the rest of this section, we'll overlook personal barriers to communication and concentrate instead on two types of barriers that are encountered by groups of people, sometimes large and sometimes small, working toward organizational goals.

Cultural Barriers

Cultural barriers, which are sometimes called cultural filters, are the barriers that result from differences among people of different cultures.[51] As we point out in Chapter 7, experts and managers agree that cultural diversity in the workplace can and should be a significant asset: It broadens the perspectives from which groups approach problems, gives them fresh ideas, and sparks their creativity; it also gives organizations an advantage in connecting with diverse customer bases. None of these advantages, though, magically appears simply because workplace diversity increases. To the contrary: As diversity increases, so does the possibility that a group will be composed of people who have different attitudes and different ways of expressing them.

If it hasn't happened already, for example, one of these days you'll find yourself having a work-related conversation with a member of the opposite sex. If the conversation doesn't go as smoothly as you'd expected, there's a good reason: Men and women in the workplace don't communicate the same way. According to American linguist Deborah Tannen, men tend to assert their status, to exert confidence, and to regard asking questions as a sign of weakness. Women, in contrast, tend to foster positive interrelationships, to restrain expressions of confidence, and to ask questions with no trouble.[52]

It really doesn't matter which "style" (if either) is better suited to making a conversation more productive. Two points, however, are clear:

1. Even if two people of the opposite sex enter a conversation with virtually identical viewpoints, their different styles of expressing themselves might very well present a barrier to their reaching an agreement. Much the same can be said of differences in style arising from other cultural filters, such as ethnicity, education, age, and experience.

2. Workplace conversations can be tricky to negotiate, yet there's no escaping them. Like life in the outside world, observes Tannen, life in the workplace "is a matter of dealing with people…and that means a series of conversations." That's also why surveys continue to show that managers regard the ability to communicate face to face as a key factor in an employee's promotability.[53]

Functional Barriers

Let's return for a moment to Figure 8.7. Recall that when we introduced the organizational structure of Notes-4-You in Chapter 6, we characterized it as a *functional organization*—one that groups together people who have comparable skills and perform similar tasks. Note, however, that in setting up this form of organization for our hypothetical company, we found it necessary to insert two layers of management (four functional managers and two job supervisors) between our owner/president and our lowest-level employees. In this respect, our structure shares certain characteristics with another form of organization—*divisional*, which groups people into units that are more or less self-contained and that are largely accountable for their own performance.

FIGURE 8.9

Though developed to improve communication, in some cases cell phones can create a barrier.

© 2010 Jupiterimages Corporation

Cultural barriers

Barriers that result from differences among people of different cultures.

What does all this have to do with barriers to communication? Simply this: The more "divisionalized" an organization becomes, the more likely it will be to encounter communication barriers. Not surprisingly, communication gets more complicated, for the same reason that an organization comes to rely on more levels of management.[54] Notes-4-You, for instance, needs two supervisors because its notetakers don't do the same work as its copiers. In addition, because their groups don't perform the same work, the two supervisors don't call on the same resources from the company's four functional managers. (Likewise, Notes-4-You also has four functional-area managers because none of them does the same work as any of the others.)

Officially, then, the operations of the two work groups remain distinct or specialized. At the same time, each group must contribute to the company-wide effort to achieve common goals. Moreover, certain organizational projects, like Motorola's cell phone project, may require the two groups to work together more closely than usual. When that happens, employees from each of the two groups may find themselves working together on the same team, but even so, one crucial fact remains: Information that one group possesses and the other doesn't must still be exchanged among team members. It may not be quite as apparent as the *cultural diversity* among men and women in many workplace situations, but there is in fact a *functional diversity* at Notes-4-You among notetakers and copiers.[55]

Figure 8.10 illustrates the location of barriers that may be present when a team-based project must deal with a certain degree of functional diversity. As you can see, we've modeled our process on the process of the Motorola ultratrim phone project.[56] We don't need to describe the entire process in detail, but we will focus on two aspects of it that we've highlighted in the drawing:

1. The company has assigned team members from different functional areas, notably marketing and operations (which, as at Motorola, includes design, engineering, and production).

2. Information (which we've characterized as different types of "specs") must be transferred from function to function, and at the key points where this occurs, we've built in communication barriers (symbolized by brick walls).

If, for example, marketing specs called for the new Motorola phone to change colors with the user's mood, someone in engineering might have to explain the difficulties in designing the software. If design specs called for quadraphonic sound, production might have to explain the difficulties in procuring sufficiently lightweight speaker components.

FIGURE 8.10 Functional Barriers to Communication

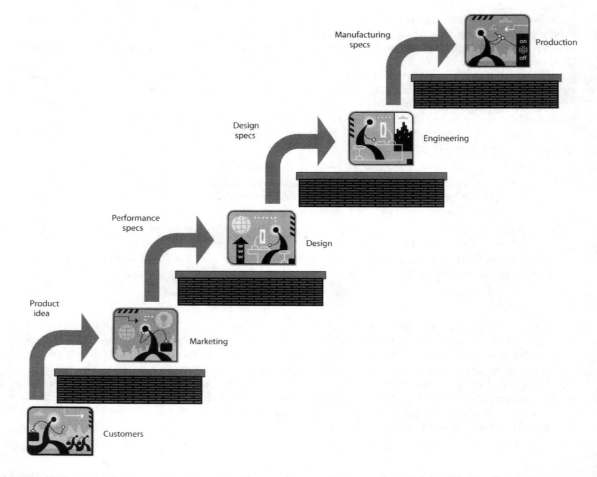

Each technical problem—each problem that arises because of differences in team members' knowledge and expertise—becomes a problem in communication. In addition, communicating as a member of a team obviously requires much more than explaining the limitations of someone else's professional expertise. Once they've surfaced, technical and other problems have to be resolved—a process that will inevitably require even more communication. As we've seen in this part of the chapter, improving communication is a top priority for most organizations (for one thing, developing a team-based environment is otherwise impossible), and the ongoing task of improving communication is pretty much the same thing as the ongoing task of overcoming barriers to it.

KEY TAKEAWAYS

- In a typical organizational setting, *communication flows* may take three directions:
    1. **Downward communication** flows from higher organizational levels (supervisors) to lower organizational levels (subordinates).
    2. **Upward communication** flows from lower to higher organizational levels.
    3. **Lateral** (or **horizontal**) **communication** flows across the organization, among personnel on the same level.
- Organizational communication flows through two different *channels*. **Internal communication** is shared by people at all levels within a company. **External communication** occurs between parties inside a company and parties outside the company, such as suppliers, customers, and investors.
- Organizational communication also flows through two different *networks*. Its **formal communication network** consists of all communications that flow along an organization's official lines of authority. The **informal communication network**, sometimes called the *grapevine*, goes to work whenever two or more employees get together and start talking about the company and their jobs.
- *Barriers to communication* include anything that prevents people from communicating as effectively as possible. Among groups, two types of barriers are common. *Cultural barriers*, sometimes called *cultural filters*, are the barriers that result from differences among people of different cultures. *Functional barriers* arise when communication must flow among individuals or groups who work in different functional areas of an organization.

Before going to the next section of this chapter, take a few minutes to test your knowledge of the material covered in this section. Quizzes can be found under the "Resources" tab, "Study Aids: Quizzes."

EXERCISE

Write three messages (you decide which communication channel to use):

1. To a coworker asking her for a report on this quarter's sales for your division
2. To your manager telling him what the sales were for the quarter and whether sales improved (or got worse), and why
3. To the vice president of the company recommending a new system for tracking sales in your division

---

6. FORMS OF COMMUNICATION

LEARNING OBJECTIVES

1. **Explain the dos and don'ts of business e-mails.**
2. **Describe the process followed to create and deliver successful presentations.**
3. **Learn how to write clear, concise memos.**

As mentioned previously, the College Board identified these communication skills as "frequently" or "almost always" necessary in the workplace:[57] e-mail, presentation with visuals, technical reports, formal reports, memos, and presentations without visuals. The skill ranked highest in importance was the use of e-mails, including the ability to adapt messages to different receivers or compose persuasive messages when necessary. The ability to make presentations (with visuals) ranked second in importance. Report writing came next. Given the complexity of report writing, we will not cover this topic here. Instead, we will look at the remaining three forms of communication: e-mail, presentations with visuals, and memos.

6.1   How to Write a Formal Business E-Mail

To be taken seriously in the business world, you need to know how to craft an e-mail that is succinct, appropriate, and informative. The following are guidelines to help you achieve effective communication using formal e-mails:

- Organization is key. You have three to five paragraphs to accomplish many things. Beware of redundancy, irrelevant information, and flowery or overly technical language.
- Salutation (greeting) and closing should use the same level of formality you would use when face-to-face with the person you are e-mailing.
- The introduction should state who you are and why you are writing. The conclusion should tie your points together without simply repeating yourself.
- Formatting should help to make the e-mail easy to read with a double space between paragraphs. Each paragraph should be no longer than eight sentences. Bullets should be used for lists.
- List attachments before the body of the e-mail, never as a postscript (people don't usually read below the signature line).
- Arguments and opinions must be supported. Use facts, not vague statements, and double-check your facts before sending the e-mail.
- Maintain an appropriate tone; an informal tone could be disrespectful, slang or jargon can be misunderstood, sarcasm or jokes can be offensive without meaning to be, and shortcuts (like "lol") could be signs of immaturity and a lack of professionalism.
- Do not use all capital letters or more than one exclamation point.
- Use gender-neutral language when possible. Be careful to observe subject-verb agreement.
- Your signature should contain your title, company name, phone number, mailing address, and a URL for your Web site.

Tips for Writing Business E-Mails

Dennis Jerz and Jessica Bauer created the following list of the top 10 tips for writing effective e-mail messages:[58]

1. *Write a meaningful subject line.* Recipients use the subject line to decide whether to open or delete a message and sometimes where to store it. Write a subject line that describes the content.
2. *Keep the message focused.* Avoid including multiple messages or requests in one e-mail. Try to focus on only one topic. Use standard capitalization and spelling; none of this "thx 4 ur help 2day ur gr8."
3. *Avoid attachments.* Extract the relevant text from a large file and ask the recipient if he or she wants to see the full document.
4. *Identify yourself clearly. Identify yourself in the first few lines*—otherwise your message might be deleted quickly.
5. *Be kind. Don't flame.* Avoid writing e-mails when you are upset. Always think before you hit the "send" button. Once it's gone, you can't get it back. If you're mad, write the e-mail, but don't send it. Keep it in your "save" or "draft" folder and reread it the next day.
6. *Proofread.* Use spell check and read the memo carefully before sending it.
7. *Don't assume privacy.* Don't send anything you wouldn't want posted on the office bulletin board (with your name on it). Remember, employers can read your e-mails!
8. *Distinguish between formal and informal situations.* When writing to a coworker with whom you are friends, you can be less formal than when you are writing to your manager or a client.
9. *Respond promptly.* Get back quickly to the person who sent you the e-mail. If you're too busy to answer, let the person know you got the message and will respond as soon as you can.
10. *Show respect and restraint.* Watch out: Don't use the "reply to all" button in error. Don't forward an e-mail before getting permission from the sender.

How to Write an Effective Memo

Memos are effective at conveying fairly detailed information. To help you understand how to write a memo, read the following sample memorandum.

Memorandum

To:
From:
Date:
Re:

As college students, you'll be expected to analyze real-world situations, research issues, form opinions, and provide support for the conclusions that you reach. In addition to engaging in classroom discussions of business issues, you'll be asked to complete a number of written assignments. For these assignments, we'll give you a business situation and ask you to analyze the issues, form conclusions, and provide support for your opinions.

In each assignment, you'll use the *memo format*, which is the typical form of written communication used in business. Writing in the memo format means providing a *complete but concise response* to the issues at hand. Good memo writing demands time and effort. Because the business world expects you to possess this skill, we want to give you an opportunity to learn it now.

Guidelines

Here are a few helpful hints to get you started on the right track:

1. **The format should follow the format of this memo.** Note the **guide headings**: "To," "From," "Date," and "Re" (which, by the way, stands for "regarding" or "reference"). We also include a line across the page to signal the beginning of the body of the memo.

2. Keep **paragraphs** short and to the point. The trick is being concise yet complete—summarizing effectively. Paragraphs should be single-spaced, flush against the left margin, and separated by a single blank line.

3. Accent or highlight **major points**. Use underlining, bullets, or bold type for desired effect (taking care not to overdo it).

4. Use *short* **headings** to distinguish and highlight vital information. Headings keep things organized, provide structure, and make for smooth reading. Headings (and, as appropriate, subheadings) are an absolute *must*.

5. Your **title** (the "Re" line) should reflect the contents of your memo: it should let the reader know why he or she should read it. Keep the title short—a phrase of a few words, not a sentence.

6. Be persuasive and convincing in your narrative. You have limited space in which to get your **key points** across. State your positions clearly. And again, be concise (a memo is not a term paper).

7. If you have any additional information in the form of **exhibits**—charts, tables, illustrations, and so forth—put them in an **attachment**. Label each item "Exhibit 1," "Exhibit 2," and the like. Give each one a title, and be sure to reference them in your narrative ("As shown in Exhibit 1, the annual growth rate in sales has dropped from double-digit to single-digit levels").

8. Finally, staple multiple pages for submission. Needless to say, be sure to proofread for correct spelling and punctuation. Don't scribble in changes by hand: they're sloppy and leave a bad impression.

Final Comment

Now that you've read our memo, we expect you to follow the simple guidelines presented in it. This form of communication is widely practiced in business, so take advantage of this opportunity to practice your memo-writing skills.

Planning, Preparing, Practicing, and Presenting

For some, the thought of making a presentation is traumatic. If you're one of those people, the best way to get over your fear is to get up and make a presentation. With time, it will get easier, and you might even start enjoying it. As you progress through college, you will have a number of opportunities to make presentations. This is good news—it gives you practice, lets you make your mistakes in a protected environment (before you hit the business world), and allows you to get fairly good at it. Your opportunities to talk in front of a group will multiply once you enter the business world. Throughout your business career, you'll likely be called on to present reports, address groups at all levels in the organization, represent your company at various events, run committee meetings, lead teams, or make a sales pitch.[59] In preparing and delivering your presentation, you can follow a four-step process (plan, prepare, practice, and present) designed by Dale Carnegie, a global training company named after its famed founder.[60]

Plan

Plan your presentation based on your purpose and the knowledge level and interest of your audience. Use words and concepts your audience can understand, and stay focused. If your audience is knowledgeable about your topic, you can skim over the generalities and delve into the details. On the other hand, if the topic is new to them, you need to move through it slowly. As you plan your presentation, ask yourself these questions: What am I trying to accomplish? Am I trying to educate, inform, motivate, or persuade my audience? What does my audience know about the topic? What do I want them to know? How can I best convey this information to them?

Prepare

Once you have planned your presentation, you're ready to prepare. It might be easier to write your presentation if you divide it into three sections: opening, body, close. Your opening should grab your audience's attention. You can do this by asking a question, telling a relevant story, or even announcing a surprising piece of information. About 5 to 10 percent of your time can be spent on the opening. The body covers the bulk of the material and consumes about 80 to 85 percent of your time. Cover your key points, stay focused, but do not overload your audience. It has been found that an audience can absorb only about four to six points. Your close, which uses about 5 to 10 percent of your time, should leave the audience with a positive impression of you and your presentation. You have lots of choices for your close: You can either summarize your message or relate your closing remarks to your opening remarks or do both.

Practice

This section should really be called "Practice, Practice, Practice" (and maybe another Practice for emphasis). The saying "practice makes perfect" is definitely true with presentations, especially for beginners. You might want to start off practicing your presentation by yourself, perhaps in front of a mirror. You could even videotape yourself and play it back (that should be fun). As you get the hang of it, ask a friend or a group of friends to listen to and critique your talk. When you rehearse, check your time to see whether it's what you want. Avoid memorizing your talk, but know it well.

Present

FIGURE 8.11

Preparation is key to a successful presentation.

Now you're ready for the big day—it's time to present. Dress for the part—if it's a professional talk, dress like a professional. Go early to the location where you'll present, check out the room, and be sure any equipment you'll need is there and works. Try to connect with your audience as soon as you start your presentation. Take your time delivering your opening. Act as natural as you can, and try to relax. Slow your speech down, as you'll likely have a tendency to speed up if you get nervous. Pause before and after your main point for emphasis. If you put brief notes on index cards, avoid reading from the cards. Glance down at them when needed, but then look up at your audience as you speak. Involve your audience in your presentation by asking them questions. Not only will they feel included, but it will help you relax. When you're close to finishing, let your audience know this (but don't announce it too early in the talk or your audience might start packing up prematurely). Remember to leave some time for questions and answers.

Visual Aids

It's very common to use visual aids (generally PowerPoint slides) in business presentations. The use of visual aids helps your audience remember your main points and keeps you focused. If you do use PowerPoint slides, follow some simple (but important) rules:[61]

- Avoid wordiness: use key words and phrases only.
- Don't crowd your slide: include at most four to five points per slide.
- Use at least an eighteen-point font (so that it can be seen from the back of the room).
- Use a color font that contrasts with the background (for example, blue font on white background).
- Use graphs rather than just words.
- Proof your slides and use spell check.

And most important: The PowerPoint slides are background, but you are the show. Avoid turning around and reading the slides. The audience wants to see *you* talk; they are not interested in seeing the back of your head.

Nonverbal Communication

Sometimes it's not what you say or how you say it that matters, but what your body language communicates about you and how you feel. When a good friend who's in a bad mood walks into a room, you don't need to hear a word from her to know she's having an awful day. You can read her expression. In doing this, you're picking up on her **nonverbal communication**—"nonword" messages communicated through facial expressions, posture, gestures, and tone of voice. People give off nonverbal cues all the time. So what effect do these cues have in the business setting? Quite a bit—these cues are often better at telling you what's on a person's mind than what the person actually says. If an employee is meeting with his supervisor and frowns when she makes a statement, the supervisor will conclude that he disapproved of the statement (regardless of what he claims). If two employees are discussing a work-related problem and one starts to fidget, the other will pick this up as disinterest.

Given the possible negative effect that nonverbal cues can have in business situations, how can you improve your body language? The best approach is to become aware of any nonverbal cues you give out, and then work to eliminate them. For example, if you have a habit of frowning when you disapprove of something, recognize this and stop doing it. If the tone of your voice changes when you are angry, try to maintain your voice at a lower pitch.

nonverbal communication

"Nonword" messages communicated through facial expressions, posture, gestures, and tone of voice.

KEY TAKEAWAY

- Here are ten tips for writing an e-mail:
    1. Write a meaningful subject line.
    2. Keep the message focused and readable.
    3. Avoid attachments.
    4. Identify yourself clearly in the first few lines.
    5. Be kind. Don't flame. Always think before hitting the "send" button.
    6. Proofread.
    7. Don't assume privacy.
    8. Distinguish between formal and informal situations.
    9. Respond promptly.
    10. Show respect and restraint.
- In preparing and delivering your presentation, you can follow a four-step process: plan, prepare, practice, and present.
- You should **plan** your presentation based on your purpose and the knowledge level and interest of your audience.
- In **preparing** your presentation, it helps to divide it into three sections: opening, body, and close.
    1. Your **opening**, which uses about 5–10 percent of your time, should grab your audience's attention.
    2. The **body** covers your main points and uses about 80 to 85 percent of your time.
    3. Your **close**, which uses about 5 to 10 percent of your time, should leave the audience with a positive impression of you and your presentation.
- The saying "**practice** makes perfect" is definitely true when giving presentations (especially for beginners).
- When you **present**, dress professionally, connect with your audience, try to relax and pause before and after your main points for emphasis.
    1. Visual aids, such as PowerPoint slides, can aid your presentation if they are used properly.
- Memos are effective at conveying fairly detailed information. Here are some tips:
    1. Keep paragraphs short and to the point.
    2. Accent or highlight **major points**.
    3. Use **short** headings.
    4. Your **title** should reflect the contents of your memo.
    5. Be persuasive and convincing in your narrative.

Before going to the next chapter, take a few minutes to test your knowledge of the material covered in this section. Quizzes can be found under the "Resources" tab, "Study Aids: Quizzes."

EXERCISES

1. Ask a friend or a family member to tell you which nonverbal cues you frequently transmit. Identify those that would be detrimental to you in a business situation. Indicate how you could eliminate or reduce the impact of these cues. Ask the same person (or someone else) whether you are a good listener. If the answer is no, indicate how you could improve your listening skills.
2. Prepare a presentation on "planning, preparing, practicing, and presenting." Divide your presentation into three parts: opening, body, and closing. Prepare visual aids. Pretend that your audience is made up of recent college graduates hired by Nike.

7.   CASES AND PROBLEMS

LEARNING ON THE WEB

Factors Contributing to Nike's Success

This writing assignment solicits your opinion on factors contributing to Nike's success. To complete it, you should go to http://www.nikebiz.com/company_overview/timeline to learn about Nike's history by reviewing the company's time line.

Memo Format

Use the memo format described in the chapter for this assignment. Your memo should not exceed two pages. It should be single spaced (with an extra space between paragraphs and bulleted items).

Scenario

You're one of the fortunate college students selected to participate in Nike's summer internship program. The program is quite competitive, and you still can't believe that you were chosen. You arrived in Beaverton, Oregon, yesterday morning and have been busy ever since. Last night, you attended a dinner for new interns where you were welcomed to Nike by CEO Mark Parker.

You were lucky to be sitting next to a personable, well-informed Nike veteran named Simon Pestridge. Pestridge joined Nike about twelve years ago. He was telling you about a past assignment he had as director of marketing for Australia. (You were impressed with his status at Nike, not just because he doesn't look much older than you, but also because you've always wanted to travel to Australia.) The dinner conversation turned to a discussion of the reasons for Nike's success. Others at the table were giving their opinions on the subject when Pestridge turned to you and said, "As a new intern, give us an outsider's point of view. Why do you think Nike's been so successful?" You were about to venture an opinion when Pestridge was called away for a phone call. As he got up, however, he quickly said, "Send me a memo telling me what factors you think have contributed to Nike's success. Keep it simple. Three factors are plenty." Though you were relieved to have a little time to think about your answer, you were also a bit nervous about the prospect of writing your first official memo.

As everyone else headed for the Bo Jackson gym, you went back to your room to think about Pestridge's question and to figure out how to go about writing your memo. You want to be sure to start by telling him that you enjoyed talking with him. You also need to remind him that you're responding to his question about three factors in Nike's success, and must be sure to explain why you believe they're important. You'll end by saying that you hope the information is helpful and that he can contact you if he has any further questions.

So far, so good, but you're still faced with the toughest part of your task—identifying the three factors that you deem important to Nike's success. Fortunately, even at Nike there's always tomorrow to get something done, so you decide to sleep on it and write your memo in the morning.

ETHICS ANGLE

The Goof-Off

You and three other students have been working on a group project all semester in your Introduction to Business class. One of the members of the team did very little work; he failed to attend almost all the meetings, took no responsibility for any of the tasks, didn't attend the practice session before your presentation, and in general was a real goof-off. But he happens to be friends with two of the team members. You and your other team members have been asked to complete the attached team member evaluation. You want to give the student what he deserves—almost no credit. But your other two team members don't agree. They argue that it is "unsocial and mean" to tell the truth about this student's lack of contribution. Instead, they want to report that everyone shared the work equally. The evaluation will be used in determining grades for each team member. Those who contributed more will get a higher grade than those who did not. Prepare an argument that you can advance to the other team members on the ethics of covering for this student. Assuming that your two teammates won't change their minds, what would you do?

Attachment to Ethics Angle Problem: Introduction to Business

Team Member Evaluation

(To be given to your faculty member during the last week of class)

TEAM _____

You have a total of $100,000. You can use this to reward your team members (including yourself) for their contributions to the team project.

Fill in each team member's name below (including your own), and show beside each name how much of the $100,000 you would give that member for his or her contributions to the preparation and presentation of the team project. Do not share your recommendations with your team members.

Your recommendations will be confidential.

Team Members (including yourself)	Amount to be given for efforts on team project
_____	$_____
_____	$_____
_____	$_____
_____	$_____
_____	$_____
_____	$_____
TOTAL (MUST EQUAL $100,000)	$_____

YOUR NAME _____

TEAM-BUILDING SKILLS

Team Skills and Talents

Team projects involve a number of tasks that are handled by individual team members. These tasks should be assigned to team members based on their particular skills and talents. The next time you work on a team project, you should use the following table to help your team organize its tasks and hold its members responsible for their completion.

Here is how you should use this document:

1. Identify all tasks to be completed.
2. Assign each task to a member (or members) of your team based on their skills, talents, and time available.
3. Determine a due date for each task.
4. As a task is completed, indicate its completion date and the team member (or members) who completed the task. If more than one team member works on the assignment, indicate the percentage of time each devoted to the task. You can add tasks that surface as your team works its way through the project.
5. If the assigned person fails to complete the task, or submits poor quality work, add a note to the report explaining what happened and how the situation was corrected (for example, another team member had to redo the task).
6. Submit the completed form (with all columns completed) to your faculty member at the class after your team project is due. Include a cover sheet with your team's name (or number) and the name of each team member.

Tasks to Be Completed	Initials of Team Member(s) Who Will Complete Task	Date to Be Completed	Date Completed	Initials of Team Member(s) Who Completed Task (Add a Note Below the Table Explaining Any Problems with Completion or Quality of Work)
_____	_____	_____	_____	_____
_____	_____	_____	_____	_____
_____	_____	_____	_____	_____
_____	_____	_____	_____	_____
_____	_____	_____	_____	_____

THE GLOBAL VIEW

A Multicultural Virtual Team

You work for Nike, a global company. You just learned that you were assigned to a virtual team whose mission is to assess the feasibility of Nike's making an inexpensive shoe that can be sold in Brazil. The team consists of twelve members. Three of the members work in the United States (two in Beaverton, Oregon, and one in New York City). Two work in England, two in China, two in India, and three in Brazil. All are Nike employees and all were born in the country in which they work. All speak English, though some speak it better than others. What challenges do you anticipate the team will face because of its multicultural makeup? How could these challenges be overcome?

ENDNOTES

1. This vignette is based on the following sources: Adam Lashinsky, "RAZR's Edge," *Fortune, CNNMoney.com*, June 1, 2006, http://money.cnn.com/magazines/fortune/fortune_archive/2006/06/12/8379239/index.htm (accessed April 16, 2014); Scott D. Anthony, "Motorola's Bet on the RAZR's Edge," *HBS Working Knowledge*, September 12, 2005, http://hbswk.hbs.edu/archive/4992.html (accessed April 16, 2014); "The Leading Edge Is RAZR-Thin," *BusinessWeek*, December 5, 2005, http://www.businessweek.com/magazine/content/05_49/b3962087.htm (accessed April 16, 2014); Arik Hessedahl, "Motorola vs. Nokia," *Forbes.com*, January 19, 2004, at http://www.forbes.com/2004/01/19/cx_ah_0119mondaymatchup.html (accessed April 16, 2014); "Talk Like a Supermodel: Sexy Fashion Phones," *CNET.co.au*, April 2008, http://www.cnet.com.au/talk-like-a-supermodel-sexy-fashion-phones-240058430.htm#image0 (accessed April 16, 2014); Vlad Balan, "10 Coolest Concept Phones Out There," *Cameraphones Plaza*, April 17, 2007, http://www.cameraphonesplaza.com/10-coolest-concept-phones-out-there (accessed April 16, 2014); Mike Elgan, "All-Screen Clamshell Concept Phone: A Glimpse of the Future," *Computerworld Blogs*, August 1, 2008, http://blogs.computerworld.com/all_screen_clamshell_concept_phone_a_glimpse_of_the_future (accessed April 16, 2014); "Motorola Gains on 10 Mn in RAZR Sales," *The Financial Express*, January 19, 2006, http://www.financialexpress.com/old/latest_full_story.php?content_id=115012 (accessed April 16, 2014).

2. Roy Furchgott, "Motorola's Droid Razr Still Has It," *New York Times*, November 28, 2011, http://gadgetwise.blogs.nytimes.com/2011/11/28/motorolas-droid-razr-still-has-it (accessed April 16, 2014).

3. This section is based in part on Leigh L. Thompson, *Making the Team: A Guide for Managers* (Upper Saddle River, NJ: Pearson Education, 2008), 4.

4. Adapted from Leigh L. Thompson, *Making the Team: A Guide for Managers* (Upper Saddle River, NJ: Pearson Education, 2008), 4–5. See C. P. Alderfer, "Group and Intergroup Relations," in *Improving Life at Work*, ed. J. R. Hackman and J. L. Suttle (Palisades, CA: Goodyear, 1977), 277–96.

5. Kimball Fisher, *Leading Self-Directed Work Teams: A Guide to Developing New Team Leadership Skills*, rev. ed. (New York: McGraw-Hill Professional, 1999). See Jerald Greenberg and Robert A. Baron, *Behavior in Organizations*, 9th ed. (Upper Saddle River, NJ: Pearson Education, 2008), 315–16.

6. Jerald Greenberg and Robert A. Baron, *Behavior in Organizations*, 9th ed. (Upper Saddle River, NJ: Pearson Education, 2008), 316; Leigh L. Thompson, *Making the Team: A Guide for Managers* (Upper Saddle River, NJ: Pearson Education, 2008), 5.

7. See Leigh L. Thompson, *Making the Team: A Guide for Managers* (Upper Saddle River, NJ: Pearson Education, 2008), 8–13.

8. Leigh L. Thompson, *Making the Team: A Guide for Managers* (Upper Saddle River, NJ: Pearson Education, 2008), 9.

9. Charles Fishman, "Whole Foods Is All Teams," *Fast Company*, December 18, 2007, http://www.fastcompany.com/node/26671/print (accessed October 11, 2011).

10. Human Technology Inc., "Organizational Learning Strategies: Cross-Functional Teams," *Getting Results through Learning*, http://www.humtech.com/opm/grtl/ols/ols3.cfm (accessed October 11, 2011).

11. See Stephen P. Robbins and Timothy A. Judge, *Organizational Behavior*, 13th ed. (Upper Saddle River, NJ: Pearson Education, 2009), 340–42.

12. See Jennifer M. George and Gareth R. Jones, *Understanding and Managing Organizational Behavior*, 5th ed. (Upper Saddle River, NJ: Pearson Education, 2008), 381–82.

13. "Lockheed Martin Chooses Mathcad as a Standard Design Package for F-35 Joint Strike Fighter Project," *Adept Science*, September 23, 2003, http://www.adeptscience.co.uk/pressroom/article/96 (accessed October 11, 2011).

14. This section is based on David A. Whetten and Kim S. Cameron, *Developing Management Skills*, 7th ed. (Upper Saddle River, NJ: Pearson Education, 2007), 497.

15. This section is based mostly on Jennifer M. George and Gareth R. Jones, *Understanding and Managing Organizational Behavior*, 5th ed. (Upper Saddle River, NJ: Pearson Education, 2008), 371–77. See Leon Festinger, "Informal Social Communication," *Psychological Review* 57 (1950): 271–82.

16. See Em Griffin, "Groupthink of Irving Janis," 1997, http://www.doh.state.fl.us/alternatesites/cms-kids/providers/early_steps/training/documents/groupthink_irving_janus.pdf (accessed April 14, 2014).

17. This section is based on Jerald Greenberg and Robert A. Baron, *Behavior in Organizations*, 9th ed. (Upper Saddle River, NJ: Pearson Education, 2008), 317–18.

18. See Leigh L. Thompson, *Making the Team: A Guide for Managers* (Upper Saddle River, NJ: Pearson Education, 2008), 323–24.

19. See Leigh L. Thompson, *Making the Team: A Guide for Managers* (Upper Saddle River, NJ: Pearson Education, 2008), 18–19.

20. David A. Whetten and Kim S. Cameron, *Developing Management Skills*, 7th ed. (Upper Saddle River, NJ: Pearson Education, 2007), 498–99. See Richard S. Wellins, William C. Byham, and Jeanne M. Wilson, *Empowered Teams* (San Francisco: Jossey-Bass, 1991).

21. Hannah Nichols, "Teamwork in School, Work, and Life," *iamnext.com*, 2003, http://www.iamnext.com/academics/groupwork.html (accessed September 1, 2008).

22. David A. Whetten and Kim S. Cameron, *Developing Management Skills*, 7th ed. (Upper Saddle River, NJ: Pearson Education, 2007), 498–99. See Edward E. Lawler, *Treat People Right* (San Francisco: Jossey-Bass, 2003).

23. "What Makes Great Leaders: Rethinking the Route to Effective Leadership," Findings from the Fortune Magazine/Hay Group 1999 Executive Survey of Leadership Effectiveness, http://www.haygroup.com/ww/downloads/details.aspx?id=921 (accessed April 16, 2014).

24. This section is based on Stephen P. Robbins and Timothy A. Judge, *Organizational Behavior*, 13th ed. (Upper Saddle River, NJ: Pearson Education, 2009), 346–47.

25. This section is based on David A. Whetten and Kim S. Cameron, *Developing Management Skills*, 7th ed. (Upper Saddle River, NJ: Pearson Education, 2007), 516–20.

26. David A. Whetten and Kim S. Cameron, *Developing Management Skills*, 7th ed. (Upper Saddle River, NJ: Pearson Education, 2007), 516–17.

27. Hannah Nichols, "Teamwork in School, Work and Life," *iamnext.com*, 2003, http://www.iamnext.com/academics/groupwork.html (accessed September 1, 2008); and Kristin Feenstra, "Study Skills: Team Work Skills for Group Projects," *iamnext.com*, 2002, http://www.iamnext.com/academics/groupproject.html (accessed October 11, 2011).

28. This section is based on David A. Whetten and Kim S. Cameron, *Developing Management Skills*, 7th ed. (Upper Saddle River, NJ: Pearson Education, 2007), 510–13.

29. David A. Whetten and Kim S. Cameron, *Developing Management Skills*, 7th ed. (Upper Saddle River, NJ: Pearson Education, 2007), 511.

30. See Adam Lashinsky, "RAZR's Edge," *Fortune, CNNMoney.com*, June 1, 2006, http://money.cnn.com/magazines/fortune/fortune_archive/2006/06/12/8379239/index.htm (accessed April 16, 2014); Scott D. Anthony, "Motorola's Bet on the RAZR's Edge," *HBS Working Knowledge*, September 12, 2005, http://hbswk.hbs.edu/archive/4992.html (accessed April 16, 2014).

31. See Glen L. Urban and John R. Hauser, *Design and Marketing of New Products*, 2nd ed. (Upper Saddle River, NJ: Prentice Hall, 1993), 173.

32. See Industrial Designers Society of America (IDSA), "About ID," *IDSA*, http://www.idsa.org/about (accessed April 16, 2014).

33. Industrial Designers Society of America (IDSA), "About ID," *IDSA*, http://www.idsa.org/about (accessed April 16, 2014).

34. See Glen L. Urban and John R. Hauser, *Design and Marketing of New Products*, 2nd ed. (Upper Saddle River, NJ: Prentice Hall, 1993), 173.

35. See Glen L. Urban and John R. Hauser, *Design and Marketing of New Products*, 2nd ed. (Upper Saddle River, NJ: Prentice Hall, 1993), 653.

36. Stephen P. Robbins and Timothy A. Judge, *Organizational Behavior*, 13th ed. (Upper Saddle River, NJ: Pearson Education, 2009), 368; David A. Whetten and Kim S. Cameron, *Developing Management Skills*, 7th ed. (Upper Saddle River, NJ: Pearson Education, 2007), 243.

37. National Association of Colleges and Employers, "2014 Job Outlook Survey—Job Outlook: The Candidate Skills/Qualities Employers Want," October 2, 2013, https://www.naceweb.org/s10022013/job-outlook-skills-quality.aspx (accessed April 16, 2014).

38. College Board, "Writing: A Ticket to Work…or a Ticket Out: A Survey of Business Leaders," *Report of the National Commission on Writing*, September 2004, http://www.collegeboard.com/prod_downloads/writingcom/writing-ticket-to-work.pdf (accessed April 16, 2014).

39. John V. Thill and Courtland L. Bovée, *Excellence in Business Communication*, 8th ed. (Upper Saddle River, NJ: Pearson Education, 2008), 4. See Nicholas Carr, "Lessons in Corporate Blogging," *Business Week*, July 18, 2006, 9.

40. National Association of Colleges and Employers, "2006 Job Outlook," http://www.naceweb.org (accessed October 11, 2011).

41. See Michael Netzley and Craig Snow, *Guide to Report Writing* (Upper Saddle River, NJ: Prentice Hall, 2002), 3–21.

42. This section is based on Jerald Greenberg and Robert A. Baron, *Behavior in Organizations*, 9th ed. (Upper Saddle River, NJ: Pearson Education, 2008), 351–53.

43. Jerald Greenberg and Robert A. Baron, *Behavior in Organizations*, 9th ed. (Upper Saddle River, NJ: Pearson Education, 2008), 350–51.

44. This section is based on John V. Thill and Courtland L. Bovée, *Excellence in Business Communication*, 8th ed. (Upper Saddle River, NJ: Pearson Education, 2008), 4–6.

45. See Jerald Greenberg and Robert A. Baron, Behavior in Organizations, 9th ed. (Upper Saddle River, NJ: Pearson Education, 2008), 349–50.

46. See Steven A. Watson, "Sharing Info and Defusing Rumors Helps Keep Staff Motivated During Layoffs," *TechRepublic*, June 17, 2003, http://www.techrepublic.com/article/sharing-info-and-defusing-rumors-helps-keep-staff-motivated-during-layoffs (accessed April 16, 2014).

47. Allan J. Kimmel, *Rumors and Rumor Control* (Mahwah, NJ: Erlbaum, 2004), http://books.google.com/books?id=a0FZz3Jq8llC&pg=PA64&lpg=PA64&dq=rumors+about+Coke&source=web&ots=wtBktafiKZ&sig=HbsDm2Byd0ZPkZH2YUWITwWTDac&hl=en&sa=X&oi=book_result&resnum=6&ct=result (accessed April 16, 2014). See also Jerald Greenberg and Robert A. Baron, *Behavior in Organizations*, 9th ed. (Upper Saddle River, NJ: Pearson Education, 2008), 359.

48. Charles R. McConnell, "Controlling the Grapevine," *Small Business Toolbox*, June 18, 2008, http://www.nfib.com/object/IO_37650?_templateId=315 (accessed September 6, 2008).

49. Steven A. Watson, "Sharing Info and Defusing Rumors Helps Keep Staff Motivated During Layoffs," *TechRepublic*, June 17, 2003, http://www.techrepublic.com/article/sharing-info-and-defusing-rumors-helps-keep-staff-motivated-during-layoffs (accessed April 16, 2014).

50. John V. Thill and Courtland L. Bovée, *Excellence in Business Communication*, 8th ed. (Upper Saddle River, NJ: Pearson Education, 2008), 53. See Judi Brownell, *Listening*, 2nd ed. (Boston: Allyn & Bacon, 2002), 9–10.

51. See Melinda G. Kramer, *Business Communication in Context: Principles and Practice* (Upper Saddle River, NJ: Prentice Hall, 2001), 87.

52. See Jerald Greenberg and Robert A. Baron, *Behavior in Organizations*, 9th ed. (Upper Saddle River, NJ: Pearson Education, 2008), 360–61. See Deborah Tannen, *Talking 9 to 5: Women and Men at Work* (New York: Avon, 1995).

53. David A. Whetten and Kim S. Cameron, *Developing Management Skills*, 7th ed. (Upper Saddle River, NJ: Pearson Education, 2007), 243.

54. See Jennifer M. George and Gareth R. Jones, *Understanding and Managing Organizational Behavior*, 5th ed. (Upper Saddle River, NJ: Pearson Education, 2008), 544.

55. See Anne S. Tsui and Barbara A. Gutek, *Demographic Differences in Organizations* (Lanham, MD: Lexington Books, 1999), 91–95, http://books.google.com/books?hl=en&id=Rr8jYPKF0hoC&dq=Tsui+Gutek&printsec=frontcover&source=web&ots=svMB027a6&sig=wpXFenfKbkpWrd/HbNBPrfg12iodDbsk/Reserhadiknrdsph&tenum=(accessed April 16, 2014).

56. See Roberta S. Russell and Bernard W. Taylor, *Operations Management*, 5th ed. (Hoboken, NJ: Wiley, 2005), 85.

57. College Board, "Writing: A Ticket to Work…or a Ticket Out: A Survey of Business Leaders," *Report of the National Commission on Writing*, September 2004, http://www.collegeboard.com/prod_downloads/writingcom/writing-ticket-to-work.pdf (accessed April 16, 2014).

58. Dennis G. Jerz and Jessica Bauer, "Writing Effective E-Mail: Top 10 Email Tips," *Jerz's Literacy Weblog*, March 8, 2011, http://jerz.setonhill.edu/writing/e-text/email (accessed October 19, 2011).

59. Paul W. Barada, "Confront Your Fears and Communicate," http://career-advice.monster.com/in-the-office/workplace-issues/confront-your-fears-and-communicate/article.aspx (accessed April 16, 2014).

60. Dale Carnegie, "Presentation Tips from Dale Carnegie Training," 6t&siz/wpoVerzifKbkpWrd/HbNBPrfg12iodDbsk/Reserbadiknrdsph&tenum=(accessed April 16, 2014).

61. "Making PowerPoint Slides—Avoiding the Pitfalls of Bad Slides," http://www.iasted.org/conferences/formatting/Presentations-Tips.ppt (accessed April 16, 2014).

CHAPTER 9
Marketing: Providing Value to Customers

A ROBOT WITH ATTITUDE

Mark Tilden used to build robots for NASA that were trashed on Mars, but after seven years of watching the results of his work meet violent ends thirty-six million miles from home, he decided to specialize in robots for earthlings. He left the space world for the toy world and teamed up with Wow Wee Toys Ltd. to create "Robosapien," an intelligent robot with an attitude.[1] The fourteen-inch-tall robot, which is operated by remote control, has great moves: In addition to the required maneuvers (walking forward and backward and turning), he dances, raps, and gives karate chops. He can pick up (fairly small) stuff and even fling it across the room, and he does everything while grunting, belching, and emitting other bodily sounds.

Robosapien gave Wow Wee Toys a good headstart in the toy robot market: in the first five months, more than 1.5 million Robosapiens were sold.[2] The company expanded the line to more than a dozen robotics and other interactive toys, including Roborover (an adventurous robot explorer), FlyTech Dragon Fly (a futuristic bug named as one of the inventions of the year by *Time* Magazine in 2007 and *Popular Mechanics* in 2008), FlyTech Bladestor (a revolutionary indoor flying machine that won an Editor's Choice Award in 2008 by *Popular Mechanics* magazine), Robome (a customizable robotic buddy that has been honored with multiple high-status awards), PaperJamz (paper technology–produced guitars, drums, and amps that received many prestigious awards), and RobosapienX (an updated Robosapien).[3]

What does Robosapien have to do with marketing? The answer is fairly simple: Though Mark Tilden is an accomplished inventor who has created a clever product, Robosapien wouldn't be going anywhere without the marketing expertise of Wow Wee (certainly not forward). In this chapter, we'll look at the ways in which marketing converts product ideas like Robosapien into commercial successes.

Robosapien is a robot with attitude.

Marketing

Marketing is the activity, set of institutions, and processes for creating, communicating, delivering, and exchanging offerings that have value for customers, clients, partners, and society at large.

1. WHAT IS MARKETING?

LEARNING OBJECTIVES

1. **Define the terms "marketing," "marketing concept," and "marketing strategy."**
2. **Outline the tasks involved in selecting a target market.**
3. **Identify variables that can be used to divide a market into market segments.**

When you consider the functional areas of business—accounting, finance, management, marketing, and operations—marketing is the one you probably know the most about. After all, as a consumer and target of all sorts of advertising messages, you've been on the receiving end of marketing initiatives for most of your life. What you probably don't appreciate, however, is the extent to which marketing focuses on providing value to the customer. According to the American Marketing Association, "**Marketing** is the activity, set of institutions, and processes for creating, communicating, delivering, and exchanging offerings that have value for customers, clients, partners, and society at large."[4]

In other words, marketing isn't just advertising and selling. It includes everything that organizations do to satisfy customer needs:

- Coming up with a product and defining its features and benefits
- Setting its price
- Identifying its target market
- Making potential customers aware of it
- Getting people to buy it

- Delivering it to people who buy it
- Managing relationships with customers after it has been delivered

Not surprisingly, marketing is a team effort involving everyone in the organization. Think about a typical business—a local movie theater, for example. It's easy to see how the person who decides what movies to show is involved in marketing: he or she selects the product to be sold. It's even easier to see how the person who puts ads in the newspaper works in marketing: he or she is in charge of advertising—making people aware of the product and getting them to buy it. But what about the ticket seller and the person behind the counter who gets the popcorn and soda? What about the projectionist? Are they marketing the business? Absolutely: the purpose of every job in the theater is satisfying customer needs, and as we've seen, identifying and satisfying customer needs is what marketing is all about.

If everyone is responsible for marketing, can the average organization do without an official marketing department? Not necessarily: most organizations have marketing departments in which individuals are actively involved in some marketing-related activity—product design and development, pricing, promotion, sales, and distribution. As specialists in identifying and satisfying customer needs, members of the marketing department manage—plan, organize, direct, and control—the organization's overall marketing efforts.

1.1 The Marketing Concept

Figure 9.1 is designed to remind you that to achieve business success you need to do three things:

1. Find out what customers or potential customers need.
2. Develop products to meet those needs.
3. Engage the entire organization in efforts to satisfy customers.

FIGURE 9.1 The Marketing Concept

At the same time, you need to achieve organizational goals, such as profitability and growth. This basic philosophy—satisfying customer needs while meeting organizational goals—is called the **marketing concept**, and when it's effectively applied, it guides all of an organization's marketing activities.

The marketing concept puts the customer first: as your most important goal, satisfying the customer must be the goal of everyone in the organization. But this doesn't mean that you ignore the bottom line; if you want to survive and grow, you need to make some profit. What you're looking for is the proper balance between the commitments to customer satisfaction and company survival. Consider the case of Medtronic, a manufacturer of medical devices, such as pacemakers and defibrillators. The company boasts more than 50 percent of the market in cardiac devices and is considered the industry standard setter.[5] Everyone in the organization understands that defects are intolerable in products that are designed to keep people alive. Thus, committing employees to the goal of zero defects is vital to both Medtronic's customer base and its bottom line. "A single quality issue," explains CEO Arthur D. Collins Jr., "can deep-six a business."[6]

1.2 Marketing Strategy

Declaring that you intend to develop products that satisfy customers and that everyone in your organization will focus on customers is easy. The challenge is doing it. As you can see in Figure 9.2, to put the marketing concept into practice, you need a **marketing strategy**—a plan for performing two tasks:

1. Selecting a target market
2. Developing your *marketing mix*—implementing strategies for creating, pricing, promoting, and distributing products that satisfy customers

We'll use Figure 9.2 as a blueprint for our discussion of target-market selection, and we'll analyze the concept of the marketing mix in more detail in Section 2.

marketing concept

Basic philosophy of satisfying customer needs while meeting organizational goals.

marketing strategy

Plan for selecting a target market and creating, pricing, promoting, and distributing products that satisfy customers.

FIGURE 9.2 Marketing Strategy

Marketing Strategy

Click on this link to experience an active version of this figure.

1.3 Selecting a Target Market

target market

Specific group of customers who should be interested in your product, have access to it, and have the means to buy it.

As we saw earlier, businesses earn profits by selling goods or providing services. It would be nice if everybody in the marketplace was interested in your product, but if you tried to sell it to everybody, you'd spread your resources too thin. You need to identify a specific group of consumers who should be particularly interested in your product, who would have access to it, and who have the means to buy it. This group is your **target market**, and you'll aim your marketing efforts at its members.

Identifying Your Market

How do marketers identify target markets? First, they usually identify the overall market for their product—the individuals or organizations that need a product and are able to buy it. As Figure 9.2 shows, this market can include either or both of two groups:

1. A **consumer market**—buyers who want the product for personal use
2. An **industrial market**—buyers who want the product for use in making other products

You might focus on only one market or both. A farmer, for example, might sell blueberries to individuals on the consumer market and, on the industrial market, to bakeries that will use them to make muffins and pies.

Segmenting the Market

The next step in identifying a target market is to divide the entire market into smaller portions, or **market segments**—groups of potential customers with common characteristics that influence their buying decisions. You can use a number of characteristics to narrow a market. Let's look at some of the most useful categories in detail.

Demographic Segmentation

Demographic segmentation divides the market into groups based on such variables as age, marital status, gender, ethnic background, income, occupation, and education. Age, for example, will be of interest to marketers who develop products for children, retailers who cater to teenagers, colleges that recruit students, and assisted-living facilities that promote services among the elderly. The wedding industry, which markets goods and services to singles who will probably get married in the near future, is interested in trends in marital status. Gender and ethnic background are important to TV networks in targeting different audiences. Lifetime Television for Women targets female viewers; Spike TV targets men; Telemundo networks target Hispanic viewers. If you're selling yachts, you'll want to find people with lots of money; so income is an important variable. If you're the publisher of *Nurses* magazine, you want to reach people in the nursing profession. When Hyundai offers recent (and upcoming) college graduates the opportunity to buy a new car with no money down, the company's marketers have segmented the market according to education level.[7]

Geographic Segmentation

Geographic segmentation—dividing a market according to such variables as climate, region, and population density (urban, suburban, small-town, or rural)—is also quite common. Climate is crucial for many products: try selling snow shovels in Hawaii or above-ground pools in Alaska. Consumer tastes also vary by region. That's why McDonald's caters to regional preferences, offering a breakfast of Spam and rice in Hawaii, tacos in Arizona, and lobster rolls in Massachusetts.[8] Outside the United States, menus diverge even more widely (you can get seaweed burgers or, if you prefer, seasoned seaweed fries in Japan).[9]

   Likewise, differences between urban and suburban life can influence product selection. As exhilarating as urban life can be, for example, it's a hassle to parallel park on crowded city streets. Thus, Toyota engineers have developed a product especially for city dwellers (at least in Japan). The Japanese version of the Prius, Toyota's hybrid gas-electric car, can automatically parallel park itself. Using computer software and a rear-mounted camera, the parking system measures the spot, turns the steering wheel, and swings the car into the space (making the driver—who just sits there—look like a master of urban survival skills).[10] After its success in the Japanese market, the self-parking feature was brought to the United States. So if you ever see a car doing a great job parallel parking without the driver touching the wheel, it is likely a self-parking Prius[11] (I wonder if you could use one of these cars in a driving test).

Behavioral Segmentation

Dividing consumers by such variables as attitude toward the product, user status, or usage rate is called **behavioral segmentation**. Companies selling technology-based products might segment the market according to different levels of receptiveness to technology. They could rely on a segmentation scale developed by Forrester Research that divides consumers into two camps: *technology optimists*, who embrace new technology, and *technology pessimists*, who are indifferent, anxious, or downright hostile when it comes to technology.[12]

   Some companies segment consumers according to *user status*, distinguishing among nonusers, potential users, first-time users, and regular users of a product. Depending on the product, they can then target specific groups, such as first-time users. credit card companies use this approach when they offer frequent flyer miles to potential customers in order to induce them to get their card. Once they start using it, they'll probably be segmented according to usage. "Heavy users" who pay their bills on time will likely get increased credit lines.

FIGURE 9.3

Maybelline and Cover Girl use segmentation strategies to target their predominant consumers: women.

© 2010 Jupiterimages Corporation

Psychographic Segmentation

Psychographic segmentation classifies consumers on the basis of individual lifestyles as they're reflected in people's interests, activities, attitudes, and values. If a marketer profiled you according to your lifestyle, what would the result be? Do you live an active life and love the outdoors? If so, you may be a potential buyer of athletic equipment and apparel. Maybe you'd be interested in an ecotour offered by a travel agency. If you prefer to sit on your couch and watch TV, you might show up on the radar screen of a TiVo provider. If you're compulsive or a risk taker, you might catch the attention of a gambling casino. If you're thrifty and uncomfortable with debt, Citibank might want to issue you a debit card.

Clustering Segments

Typically, marketers determine target markets by combining, or "clustering," segmenting criteria. What characteristics does Starbucks look for in marketing its products? Three demographic variables come to mind: age, geography, and income. Buyers are likely to be males and females ranging in age from about twenty-five to forty (although college students, aged eighteen to twenty-four, are moving up in importance). Geography is a factor as customers tend to live or work in cities or upscale suburban areas. Those with relatively high incomes are willing to pay a premium for Starbucks specialty coffee and so income—a socioeconomic factor—is also important.

KEY TAKEAWAYS

- **Marketing** is a set of processes for creating, communicating, and delivering value to customers and for improving customer relationships. It includes everything that organizations do to satisfy customers' needs.
- The philosophy of satisfying customers' needs while meeting organizational profit goals is called the **marketing concept** and guides all of an organization's marketing activities.
- To apply this approach, marketers need a **marketing strategy**—a plan for doing two things: selecting a target market and then implementing strategies for creating, pricing, promoting, and distributing products that satisfy customers' needs.
- A **target market** is a specific group of consumers who are particularly interested in a product, would have access to it, and are able to buy it.
- To identify this group, marketers first identify the overall market for the product (from the **consumer market**, the **industrial market**, or both).
- Then, they divide the market into **market segments**—groups of customers with common characteristics that influence their buying decisions.
- The market can be divided according to any of the following variables:
    1. **Demographics** (age, gender, income, and so on)
    2. **Geographics** (region, climate, population density)
    3. **Behavior** (receptiveness to technology, usage)
    4. **Psychographics** or lifestyle variables (interests, activities, attitudes, and values)

Before going to the next section of this chapter, take a few minutes to test your knowledge of the material covered in this section. Quizzes can be found under the "Resources" tab, "Study Aids: Quizzes."

EXERCISE

If you were developing a marketing campaign for the Harley-Davidson Motorcycle Company, what group of consumers would you target? What if you were marketing an iPod? What about time-shares (vacation-ownership opportunities) in Vail, Colorado? For each of these products, identify at least five segmentation characteristics that you'd use in developing a profile of your customers. Explain the segmentation category into which each characteristic falls—demographic, geographic, behavioral, or psychographic. Where it's appropriate, be sure to include at least one characteristic from each category.

2. THE MARKETING MIX

After identifying a target market, your next step is developing and implementing a marketing program designed to reach it. As Figure 9.4 shows, this program involves a combination of tools called the **marketing mix**, often referred to as the "four Ps" of marketing:

1. Developing a *product* that meets the needs of the target market
2. Setting a *price* for the product
3. Distributing the product—getting it to a *place* where customers can buy it
4. *Promoting* the product—informing potential buyers about it

marketing mix

Combination of product, price, place, and promotion (often called the four Ps) used to market products.

FIGURE 9.4 The Marketing Mix

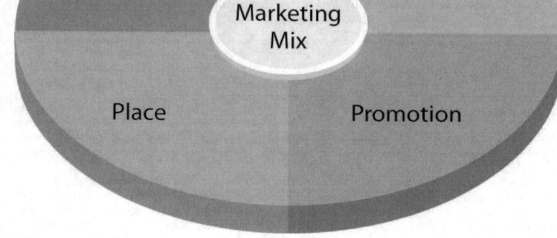

The goal is to develop and implement a marketing strategy that combines these four elements. To see how this process works, let's look at Wow Wee Toys's marketing program for Robosapien.[13]

2.1 Developing a Product

The development of Robosapien was a bit unusual for a company that was already active in its market. Generally, product ideas come from people within the company who understand its customers' needs. Internal engineers are then challenged to design the product. In the case of Robosapien, however, the creator, Mark Tilden, had conceived and designed the product before joining Wow Wee Toys. The company gave him the opportunity to develop the product for commercial purposes, and Tilden was brought on board to oversee the development of Robosapien into a product that satisfied Wow Wee's commercial needs.

Robosapien is not a "kid's toy," though kids certainly love its playful personality. It's a home-entertainment product that appeals to a broad audience—children, young adults, older adults, and even the elderly. It's a big gift item, and it has developed a following of techies and hackers who take it apart, tinker with it, and even retrofit it with such features as cameras and ice skates. In fact, Tilden wanted the robot to be customizable; that's why he insisted that its internal parts be screwed together rather than soldered.

2.2   Conducting Marketing Research

Before settling on a strategy for Robosapien, the marketers at Wow Wee did some homework. First, to zero in on their target market, they had to find out what various people thought of the product. More precisely, they needed answers to questions like the following:

- Who are our potential customers? What are they like?
- Do people like Robosapien? What gets them excited about it? What don't they like? What would they change?
- How much are they willing to pay for Robosapien?
- Where will they probably go to buy the product?
- How should it be promoted? How can we distinguish it from competing products?
- Will enough people buy Robosapien to return a reasonable profit?
- Should we go ahead and launch the product?

marketing research

Process of collecting and analyzing data that's relevant to a specific marketing situation.

secondary data

Information used in marketing decisions that has already been collected for other purposes.

primary data

Newly collected marketing information that addresses specific questions about the target market.

The last question would be left up to Wow Wee management, but, given the size of the investment needed to bring Robosapien to market, Wow Wee couldn't afford to make the wrong decision. Ultimately, the company was able to make an informed decision because its marketing team provided answers to all the other questions. They got these answers through **marketing research**—the process of collecting and analyzing the data that are relevant to a specific marketing situation.

This data had to be collected in a systematic way. Market research seeks two types of data:

1. Marketers generally begin by looking at **secondary data**—information already collected, whether by the company or by others, that pertains to the target market.

2. Then, with secondary data in hand, they're prepared to collect **primary data**—newly collected information that addresses specific questions.

You can get secondary data from inside or outside the organization. Internally available data includes sales reports and other information on customers. External data can come from a number of sources. The U.S. Census Bureau, for example, posts demographic information on American households (such as age, income, education, and number of members), both for the country as a whole and for specific geographic areas. You can also find out whether an area is growing or declining.

Population data helped Wow Wee estimate the size of its potential U.S. target market. Other secondary data helped the firm assess the size of foreign markets in regions around the world, such as Europe, the Middle East, Latin America, Asia, and the Pacific Rim. This data positioned the company to sell Robosapien in eighty-five countries, including Canada, England, France, Germany, South Africa, Australia, New Zealand, Hong Kong, and Japan.

Using secondary data that are already available (and free) is a lot easier than collecting your own information. Unfortunately, however, secondary data didn't answer all the questions that Wow Wee was asking in this particular situation. To get these answers, the marketing team had to conduct primary research: they had to work directly with members of their target market. It's a challenging process. First, they had to decide exactly *what* they wanted to know. Then they had to determine *whom* to ask. Finally, they had to pick the best *methods* for gathering information.

We know what they wanted to know—we've already listed the questions they asked themselves. As for whom to talk to, they randomly selected representatives from their target market. Now, they could have used a variety of tools for collecting information from these people, each of which has its advantages and disadvantages. To understand the marketing-research process fully, we need to describe the most common of these tools:

- *Surveys.* Sometimes marketers mail questionnaires to members of the target market. In Wow Wee's case, the questionnaire could have included photos of Robosapien. It's an effective way to reach people, but the process is time consuming and the response rate is generally low. Phoning people also takes a lot of time, but a good percentage of people tend to respond. Unfortunately, you can't show them the product. Online surveys are easier to answer and get better response rates, and the site can link to pictures or even videos of Robosapien.

- *Personal interviews.* Though time consuming, personal interviews not only let you talk with real people but also let you demonstrate Robosapien. You can also clarify answers and ask open-ended questions.

- *Focus groups.* With a **focus group**, you can bring together a group of individuals (perhaps six to ten) and ask them questions. A trained moderator can explain the purpose of the group and lead the discussion. If sessions are run effectively, you can come away with valuable information about customer responses to both your product and your marketing strategy.

focus group

Group of individuals brought together for the purpose of asking them questions about a product or marketing strategy.

Wow Wee used focus groups and personal interviews because both approaches had the advantage of allowing people to interact with Robosapien. In particular, focus-group sessions provided valuable opinions about the product, proposed pricing, distribution methods, and promotion strategies. Management was pleased with the feedback and confident that the product would succeed.

Researching your target market is necessary before you launch a new product. But the benefits of marketing research don't extend merely to brand-new products. Companies also use it when they're deciding whether or not to refine an existing product or develop a new marketing strategy for an existing product. Kellogg's, for example, conducted online surveys to get responses to a variation on its Pop-Tarts brand—namely, Pop-Tarts filled with a mixture of traditional fruit filling and yogurt. Marketers had picked out four possible names for the product and wanted to know which one kids and mothers liked best. They also wanted to know what they thought of the product and its packaging. Both mothers and kids liked the new Pop-Tarts (though for different reasons) and its packaging, and the winning name for the product launched in the spring of 2011 was "Pop-Tarts Yogurt Blasts." The online survey of 175 mothers and their children was conducted in one weekend by an outside marketing research group.[14]

2.3   Branding

Armed with positive feedback from their research efforts, the Wow Wee team was ready for the next step: informing buyers—both consumers and retailers—about their product. They needed a **brand**—some word, letter, sound, or symbol that would differentiate their product from similar products on the market. They chose the brand name *Robosapien*, hoping that people would get the connection between *homo sapiens* (the human species) and *Robosapien* (the company's coinage for its new robot "species"). To prevent other companies from coming out with their own "Robosapiens," they took out a **trademark** by registering the name with the U.S. Patent and Trademark Office.

Though this approach—giving a unique brand name to a particular product—is a bit unusual, it isn't unprecedented. Mattel, for example, established a separate brand for Barbie, and Anheuser-Busch sells beer under the brand name Budweiser. Note, however, that the more common approach, which is taken by such companies as Microsoft, Dell, and Apple, calls for marketing all the products made by a company under the company's brand name.

brand

Word, letter, sound, or symbol that differentiates a product from similar products on the market.

trademark

Word, symbol, or other mark used to identify and legally protect a product from being copied.

Branding Strategies

Companies can adopt one of three major strategies for branding a product:

1. With **private branding** (or *private labeling*), a company makes a product and sells it to a retailer who in turn resells it under its own name. A soft-drink maker, for example, might make cola for Wal-Mart to sell as its Sam's Choice Cola house brand.

2. With **generic branding**, the maker attaches no branding information to a product except a description of its contents. Customers are often given a choice between a brand-name prescription drug or a cheaper generic drug with a similar chemical makeup.

private branding

Product made by a manufacturer and sold to a retailer who in turn resells it under its own name.

generic branding

Product with no branding information attached to it except a description of its contents.

FIGURE 9.5

Though the generic brand Fluoxetine has the same chemical makeup as Prozac, it has a much lower price tag.

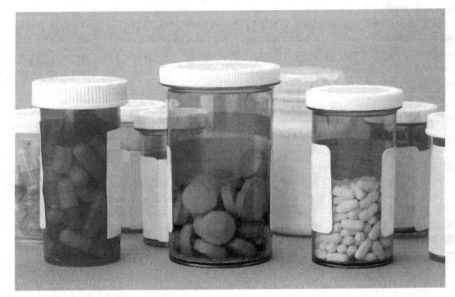

© 2010 Jupiterimages Corporation

manufacturer branding

Branding strategy in which a manufacturer sells one or more products under its own brand names.

3. With **manufacturer branding**, a company sells one or more products under its own brand names. Adopting a *multiproduct-branding* approach, it sells all its products under one brand name (generally the company name). Using a *multibranding* approach, it will assign different brand names to different products. Campbell's Soup, which markets all its soups under the company's name, uses the multiproduct-branding approach. Automakers generally use multibranding. Toyota, for example, markets to a wide range of potential customers by offering cars under various brand names (Toyota, Lexus, and Scion).

Building Brand Equity

brand equity

Value of a brand generated by a favorable consumer experience with a product.

brand loyalty

Consumer preference for a particular brand that develops over time based on satisfaction with a company's products.

Wow Wee went with the multibranding approach, deciding to market Robosapien under the robot's own brand name. Was this a good choice? The answer depends, at least in part, on how the product sells. If customers don't like Robosapien, its failure won't reflect badly on Wow Wee's other products. On the other hand, people might like Robosapien but have no reason to associate it with other Wow Wee products. In this case, Wow Wee wouldn't gain much from its **brand equity**—any added value generated by favorable consumer experiences with Robosapien. To get a better idea of how valuable brand equity is, think for a moment about the effect of the name "Apple" on a product. When you have a positive experience with an Apple product—say, a laptop or a cell phone—you come away with a positive opinion of the entire Apple product *line* and will probably buy more Apple products. Over time, you may even develop **brand loyalty**: you may prefer—or even insist on—Apple products. Not surprisingly, brand loyalty can be extremely valuable to a company. Because of customer loyalty, the value of the Apple brand is estimated at more than $98 billion, followed by Google at $93 billion, Coca-Cola and IBM at $79 billion each, and Microsoft at $59 billion.[15]

2.4 Packaging and Labeling

packaging

Container that holds a product and can influence a consumer's decision to buy or pass it up.

labeling

Information on the package of a product that identifies the product and provides details of the package contents.

Packaging—the container that holds your product—can influence a consumer's decision to buy a product or pass it up. Packaging gives customers a glimpse of the product, and it should be designed to attract their attention. **Labeling**—what you say about the product on your packaging—not only identifies the product but also provides information on the package contents: who made it and where or what risks are associated with it (such as being unsuitable for small children).

How has Wow Wee handled the packaging and labeling of Robosapien? The robot is fourteen inches tall, and it's almost as wide. It's also fairly heavy (about seven pounds), and because it's made out of plastic and has movable parts, it's breakable. The easiest, and least expensive, way of packaging it would be to put it in a square box of heavy cardboard and pad it with Styrofoam. This arrangement would not only protect the product from damage during shipping but also make the package easy to store. Unfortunately, it would also eliminate any customer contact with the product inside the box (such as seeing what it looks like and what it's made of). Wow Wee, therefore, packages Robosapien in a container that is curved to his shape and has a clear plastic front that allows people to see the whole robot. It's protected during shipping because it is wired to the box. Why did Wow Wee go to this much trouble and expense? Like so many makers of so many products, it has to market the product while it's still in the box. Because he's in a custom-shaped see-through package, you tend to notice Robosapien (who seems to be looking at you) while you are walking down the aisle of the store.

Meanwhile, the labeling on the package details some of the robot's attributes. The name is highlighted in big letters above the descriptive tagline "A fusion of technology and personality." On the sides and back of the package are pictures of the robot in action with such captions as "Dynamic Robotics with Attitude" and "Awesome Sounds, Robo-Speech & Lights." These colorful descriptions are conceived to entice the consumer to make a purchase because its product features will satisfy some need or want.

Packaging can serve many purposes. The purpose of the Robosapien package is to attract your attention to the product's features. For other products, packaging serves a more functional purpose. Nabisco, for example, packages some of its tastiest snacks—Oreos, Chips Ahoy, and Lorna Doone's—in "100 Calorie Packs" that deliver exactly one hundred calories per package.[16] Thus, the packaging itself makes life simpler for people who are keeping track of calories (and reminds them of how many cookies they can eat without exceeding one hundred calories).

KEY TAKEAWAYS

- Developing and implementing a marketing program involves a combination of tools called the marketing mix (often referred to as the "four Ps" of marketing): product, price, place, and promotion.
- Before settling on a marketing strategy, marketers often do **marketing research** to collect and analyze relevant data.
- First, they look at **secondary data** that have already been collected, and then they collect new data, called **primary data**.
- Methods for collecting primary data include surveys, personal interviews, and **focus groups**.
- A **brand** is a word, letter, sound, or symbol that differentiates a product from its competitors.
- To protect a brand name, the company takes out a **trademark** by registering it with the U.S. Patent and Trademark Office.
- There are three major branding strategies:

    1. With **private branding**, the maker sells a product to a retailer who resells it under its own name.
    2. Under **generic branding**, a no-brand product contains no identification except for a description of the contents.
    3. Using **manufacture branding**, a company sells products under its own brand names.

- When consumers have a favorable experience with a product, it builds **brand equity**. If consumers are loyal to it over time, it enjoys **brand loyalty**.
- **Packaging**—the container holding the product—can influence consumers' decisions to buy products or not buy them. It offers them a glimpse of the product and should be designed to attract their attention.
- **Labeling**—the information on the packaging—identifies the product. It provides information on the contents, the manufacturer, the place where it was made, and any risks associated with its use.

Before going to the next section of this chapter, take a few minutes to test your knowledge of the material covered in this section. Quizzes can be found under the "Resources" tab, "Study Aids: Quizzes."

3. PRICING A PRODUCT

LEARNING OBJECTIVE

1. Identify pricing strategies that are appropriate for new and existing products.

The second of the four Ps in the marketing mix is price. Pricing a product involves a certain amount of trial and error because there are so many factors to consider. If you price too high, a lot of people simply won't buy your product. Or you might find yourself facing competition from some other supplier that thinks it can beat your price. On the other hand, if you price too low, you might not make enough profit to stay in business. So how do you decide on a price? Let's look at several pricing options that were available to those marketers at Wow Wee who were responsible for pricing Robosapien. We'll begin by discussing two strategies that are particularly applicable to products that are being newly introduced.

3.1 New Product Pricing Strategies

When Robosapien was introduced into the market, it had little direct competition in its product category. True, there were some "toy" robots available, but they were not nearly as sophisticated. Sony offered a pet dog robot called Aibo, but its price tag of $1,800 was really high. Even higher up the price-point scale was the $3,600 iRobi robot made by the Korean company Yujin Robotics to entertain kids and even teach them foreign languages. Parents could also monitor kids' interactions with the robot through its own video-camera eyes; in fact, they could even use the robot itself to relay video messages telling kids to shut it off and go to sleep.[17]

Skimming and Penetration Pricing

Because Wow Wee was introducing an innovative product in an emerging market with few direct competitors, it considered one of two pricing strategies:

1. With **skimming pricing**, Wow Wee would start off with the highest price that keenly interested customers would pay. This approach would generate early profits, but when competition enters—and it will, because healthy profits can be made in the market—Wow Wee would have to lower its price.

2. Using **penetration pricing**, Wow Wee would initially charge a low price, both to discourage competition and to grab a sizable share of the market. This strategy might give the company some competitive breathing room (potential competitors won't be attracted to low prices and modest profits). Over time, as its growing market discourages competition, Wow Wee could push up its prices.

3.2   Other Pricing Strategies

In their search for the best price level, Wow Wee's marketing managers could consider a variety of other approaches, such as *cost-based pricing, demand-based pricing, target costing, odd-even pricing,* and *prestige pricing.* Any of these methods could be used not only to set an initial price but also to establish long-term pricing levels.

Before we examine these strategies, let's pause for a moment to think about the pricing decisions that you have to make if you're selling goods for resale by retailers. Most of us think of price as the amount that we—consumers—pay for a product. But when a manufacturer (such as Wow Wee) sells goods to retailers, the price it gets is *not* what we the consumers will pay for the product. In fact, it's a lot less.

Here's an example. Say you buy a shirt at a store in the mall for $40. The shirt was probably sold to the retailer by the manufacturer for $20. The retailer then marks up the shirt by 100 percent, or $20, to cover its costs and to make a profit. The $20 paid to the manufacturer plus the $20 markup results in a $40 sales price to the consumer.

Cost-Based Pricing

Using **cost-based pricing**, Wow Wee's accountants would figure out how much it costs to make Robosapien and then set a price by adding a profit to the cost. If, for example, it cost $40 to make the robot, Wow Wee could add on $10 for profit and charge retailers $50.

Demand-Based Pricing

Let's say that Wow Wee learns through market research how much people are willing to pay for Robosapien. Following a **demand-based pricing** approach, it will use this information to set the price that it charges retailers. If consumers are willing to pay $120 retail, Wow Wee will charge retailers a price that will allow retailers to sell the product for $120. What would that price be? Here's how we would arrive at it: $120 consumer selling price minus a $60 markup by retailers means that Wow Wee can charge retailers $60.

Target Costing

With **target costing**, you work backward. You figure out (again using research findings) how much consumers are willing to pay for a product. You then subtract the retailer's profit. From this price—the selling price to the retailer—you subtract an amount to cover your profit. This process should tell you how much you can spend to make the product. For example, Wow Wee determines that it can sell Robosapien to retailers for $70. The company decides that it wants to make $15 profit on each robot. Thus, Wow Wee can spend $55 on the product ($70 selling price to the retailer minus $15 profit means that the company can spend $55 to make each robot).

skimming pricing

Pricing strategy in which a seller generates early profits by starting off charging the highest price that customers will pay.

penetration pricing

Pricing strategy in which the seller charges a low price on a new product to discourage competition and gain market share.

cost-based pricing

Pricing strategy that bases the selling price of a product on its cost plus a reasonable profit.

demand-based pricing

Pricing strategy that bases the price of a product on how much people are willing to pay for it.

target costing

Pricing strategy that determines how much to invest in a product by figuring out how much customers will pay and subtracting an amount for profit.

FIGURE 9.6

Luxury goods, like jewelry and watches, are priced based on a prestige approach.

© 2010 Jupiterimages Corporation

prestige pricing

Practice of setting a price artificially high to foster the impression that it is a product of high quality.

odd-even pricing

Practice of pricing products a few cents (or dollars) under an even number.

Prestige Pricing

Some people associate a high price with high quality—and, in fact, there generally is a correlation. Thus, some companies adopt a **prestige-pricing** approach—setting prices artificially high to foster the impression that they're offering a high-quality product. Competitors are reluctant to lower their prices because it would suggest that they're lower-quality products. Let's say that Wow Wee finds some amazing production method that allows it to produce Robosapien at a fraction of its current cost. It could pass the savings on by cutting the price, but it might be reluctant to do so: What if consumers equate low cost with poor quality?

Odd-Even Pricing

Do you think $9.99 sounds cheaper than $10? If you do, you're part of the reason that companies sometimes use **odd-even pricing**—pricing products a few cents (or dollars) under an even number. Retailers, for example, might price Robosapien at $99 (or even $99.99) if they thought consumers would perceive it as less than $100.

Skimming and Penetration Pricing

Want to be a pricing guru? Take a moment to complete an exercise that tests your understanding of skimming and penetration pricing.

KEY TAKEAWAYS

- With a new product, a company might consider the **skimming approach**—starting off with the highest price that keenly interested customers are willing to pay. This approach yields early profits but invites competition.
- Using a **penetration approach**, marketers begin by charging a low price, both to keep out competition and to grab as much market share as possible.
- Several strategies work for existing as well as new products.
- With **cost-based pricing**, a company determines the cost of making a product and then sets a price by adding a profit to the cost.
- With **demand-based pricing**, marketers set the price that they think consumers will pay. Using **target costing**, they figure out how much consumers are willing to pay and then subtract a reasonable profit from this price to determine the amount that can be spent to make the product.
- Companies use **prestige pricing** to capitalize on the common association of high price and quality, setting an artificially high price to substantiate the impression of high quality.
- Finally, with **odd-even pricing**, companies set prices at such figures as $9.99 (an odd amount), counting on the common impression that it sounds cheaper than $10 (an even amount).

Before going to the next section of this chapter, take a few minutes to test your knowledge of the material covered in this section. Quizzes can be found under the "Resources" tab, "Study Aids: Quizzes."

EXERCISE

Most calculators come with a book of instructions. Unfortunately, if you misplace the book, you're left to your own devices in figuring out how to use the calculator. Wouldn't it be easier if the calculator had a built-in "help" function similar to the one on your computer? You could just punch the "Help" key on your keypad and call up the relevant instructions on your display screen. You just invented a calculator with this feature, and you're ready to roll it out. First, however, you have to make some pricing decisions:

- When you introduce the product, should you use skimming or penetration pricing?
- Which of the following pricing methods should you use in the long term: cost-based pricing, demand-based pricing, target costing, or prestige pricing?

Prepare a report describing both your introductory and your long-term alternatives. Then explain and justify your choice of the methods that you'll use.

---

4.   PLACING A PRODUCT

LEARNING   OBJECTIVES

1. Explore various product-distribution strategies.
2. Describe the interrelated activities required to get products from producers to customers.
3. Explain how companies create value through effective supply chain management.

The next element in the marketing mix is *place*, which refers to strategies for *distribution*. **Distribution** entails all activities involved in getting the right quantity of your product to your customers at the right time and at a reasonable cost. Thus, distribution involves selecting the most appropriate *distribution channels* and handling the *physical distribution* of products.

distribution

All activities involved in getting the right quantity of a product to the right customer at the right time and at a reasonable cost.

4.1   Distribution Channels

Companies must decide how they will distribute their products. Will they sell directly to customers (perhaps over the Internet)? Or will they sell through an **intermediary**—a wholesaler or retailer who helps move products from their original source to the end user? As you can see from Figure 9.7, various marketing channels are available to companies.

intermediary

Wholesaler or retailer who helps move products from their original source to the end user.

FIGURE 9.7   Distribution Channels

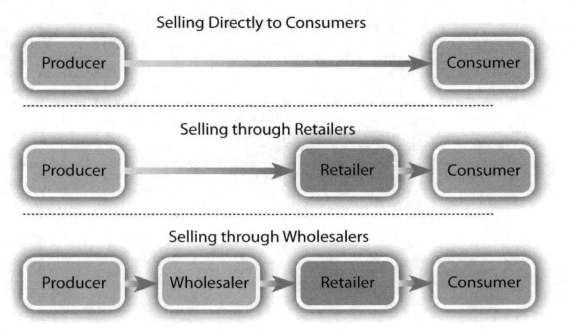

Selling Directly to Customers

Many businesses, especially small ones and those just starting up, sell directly to customers. Michael Dell, for example, started out selling computers from his dorm room. Tom First and Tom Story began operations at Nantucket Nectars by peddling home-brewed fruit drinks to boaters in Nantucket Harbor. Most service companies sell directly to their customers; it's impossible to give a haircut, fit contact lenses, mow a lawn, or repair a car through an intermediary. Many business-to-business sales take place through direct contact between producer and buyer. Toyota, for instance, buys components directly from suppliers.

The Internet has greatly expanded the number of companies using direct distribution, either as their only distribution channel or as an additional means of selling. Dell sells only online, while Adidas and Apple sell both on Web sites and in stores. The eBay online auction site has become the channel of choice for countless small businesses. Many of the companies selling over the Internet are enjoying tremendous sales growth. The largest of the online retailers—Amazon—was founded by Jeff Bezos in 1995 as an online bookstore. In its fifteen-plus years in business, the company has experienced tremendous success, generating more than $75 billion in revenues during 2013. With sales soaring by 23 percent, the future looks bright for the company.[18]

The advantage of this approach of selling direct to the customer is a certain degree of control over prices and selling activities: you don't have to depend on or pay an intermediary. On the other hand, you must commit your own resources to the selling process, and that strategy isn't appropriate for all businesses. It would hardly be practical for Wow Wee to sell directly to individual consumers scattered around the world.

Selling through Retailers

Retailers

Intermediaries who buy goods from producers and sell them to consumers.

Retailers buy goods from producers and sell them to consumers, whether in stores, by phone, through direct mailings, or over the Internet. Toys "R" Us, for example, buys Robosapiens from Wow Wee and sells them to customers in its stores. Moreover, it promotes Robosapiens to its customers and furnishes technical information and assistance. Without the willingness of stores such as Toys "R" Us to make Wow Wee products available to its customers, Wow Wee's revenues would be much lower. On the other hand, selling through retailers means giving up some control over pricing and promotion. The wholesale price you get from a retailer, who has to have room to mark up a retail price, is substantially lower than you'd get if you sold directly to consumers

Selling through Wholesalers

wholesalers (distributors)

Intermediaries who buy goods from suppliers and sell them to businesses that will either resell or use them.

Selling through retailers works fine if you're dealing with only a few stores (or chains). But what if you produce a product—bandages—that you need to sell through thousands of stores, including pharmacies, food stores, and discount stores. You'll also want to sell to hospitals, day-care centers, and even college health centers. In this case, you'd be committing an immense portion of your resources to the selling process. Besides, buyers like the ones you need don't want to deal directly with you. Imagine a chain like CVS Pharmacy negotiating sales transactions with the maker of every single product that it carries in its stores. CVS deals with **wholesalers** (sometimes called *distributors*): intermediaries who buy goods from suppliers and sell them to businesses that will either resell or use them. Likewise, you'd sell your bandages to a wholesaler of health care products, which would, in turn, sell them both to businesses like CVS, Kmart, and Giant Supermarkets and to institutions, such as hospitals and college health care centers.

profit margin

Amount that a company earns on each unit sold.

The wholesaler doesn't provide this service for free. Here's how it works. Let's say that CVS is willing to pay $2 a box for your bandages. If you go through a wholesaler, you'll probably get only $1.50 a box. In other words, you'd make $0.50 less on each box sold. Your **profit margin**—the amount you earn on each box—would therefore be less.

While selling through wholesalers will cut into your profit margins, the practice has several advantages. For one thing, wholesalers make it their business to find the best outlets for the goods in which they specialize. They're often equipped to warehouse goods for suppliers and to transport them from the suppliers' plants to the point of final sale. These advantages would appeal to Wow Wee. If it sold Robosapien's to just a few retailers, it wouldn't need to go through a distributor. However, the company needs wholesalers to supply an expanding base of retailers who want to carry the product.

Finally, intermediaries, such as wholesalers, can make the distribution channel more cost-effective. Look, for example, at Figure 9.8. Because every contact between a producer and a consumer incurs costs, the more contacts in the process (panel *a*), the higher the overall costs to consumers. The presence of an intermediary substantially reduces the total number of contacts (panel *b*).

FIGURE 9.8 What an Intermediary Can Do

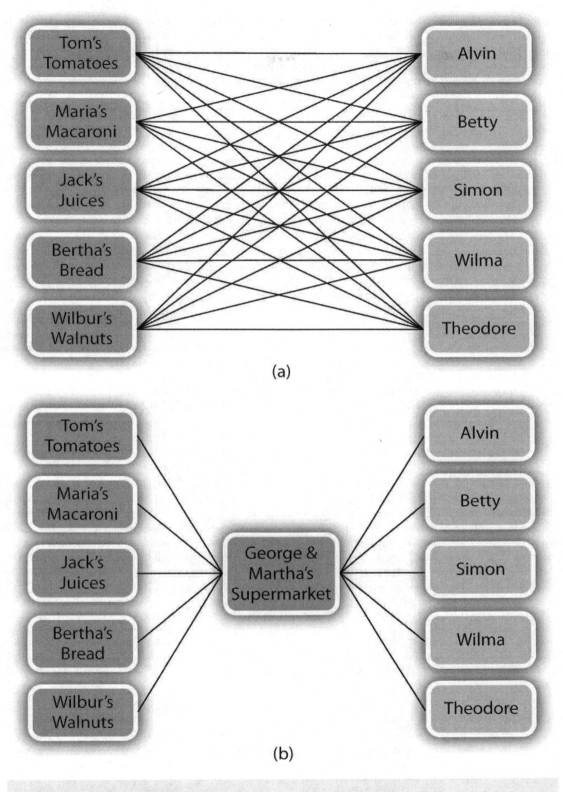

What an Intermediary Can Do

Click on this link to experience an active version of this figure.

4.2 Physical Distribution

Buyers from the stores that sell Robosapiens don't go to the Wow Wee factory (which happens to be in China) to pick up their orders. The responsibility for getting its products to customers, called **physical distribution**, belongs to Wow Wee itself. To keep its customers satisfied, Wow Wee must deliver robots on time, in good shape, and in the quantity ordered. To accomplish this, Wow Wee must manage several interrelated activities: *warehousing*, *materials handling*, and *transportation*.

Warehousing

After the robots have been packaged, they're ready for sale. It would be convenient if they've already been sold and only needed to be shipped to customers, but business-to-business (B2B) transactions don't always work out this way. More often, there's a time lag between manufacture and delivery. During this period, the robots must be stored somewhere. If Wow Wee has to store a large volume over an extended period (perhaps a month or two right before the holiday season), it will keep unsold robots in a **storage warehouse**. On the other hand, if Wow Wee has to hold them only temporarily while they're en route to their final destinations, they'll be kept in a **distribution center**.

Wal-Mart, for example, maintains 158 regional U.S. distribution centers[19] at which it receives goods purchased from suppliers, sorts them, and distributes them to 4,240 stores[20] around the country. Its efficiency in moving goods to its stores is a major factor in Wal-Mart's ability to satisfy customer needs. How major? "The misconception," says one senior executive "is that we're in the retail business, but in reality, we're in the distribution business."[21]

Materials Handling

Making, storing, and distributing Robosapien entails a good deal of **materials handling**—the process of physically moving or carrying goods during production, warehousing, and distribution. Someone (or some machine) needs to move both the parts that go into Robosapien and the partially finished robot through the production process. In addition, the finished robot must be moved into storage facilities and, after that, out of storage and onto a truck, plane, train, or ship. At the end of this leg of the trip, it must be moved into the store from which it will be sold.

Automation

All these activities draw on company resources, particularly labor, and there's always the risk of losing money because the robot's been damaged during the process. To sell goods at competitive prices, companies must handle materials as efficiently and inexpensively as possible. One way is by automating the process. For example, parts that go into the production of BMWs are stored and retrieved through automated sequencing centers.[22] Cars are built on moving assembly lines made of "skillets" large enough to hold workers who move along with the car while it's being assembled. Special assistors are used to help workers handle heavy parts. For hard-to-reach areas under the car, equipment rotates the car 90 degrees and sets the undercarriage at waist level. Records on each car's progress are updated by means of a bar code that's scanned at each stage of production.[23]

Just-in-Time Production

Another means of reducing materials-handling costs is called **just-in-time production**. Typically, companies require suppliers to deliver materials to their facilities *just in time* for them to go into the production process. This practice cuts the time and cost entailed by moving raw materials into and out of storage.

4.3 Transportation

There are several ways to transport goods from manufacturing facilities to resellers or customers—trucks, trains, planes, ships, and even pipelines. Companies select the best mode (or combination of modes) by considering several factors, including cost, speed, match of transport mode to type of good, dependability, and accessibility. The choice usually involves trade-offs. Planes, for example, are generally faster but cost more than other modes. Sending goods by cargo ship or barge is inexpensive but very slow (and out of the question if you want to send something from Massachusetts to Chicago). Railroads are moderately priced, generally accessible, and faster than ships but slower than planes. They're particularly appropriate for some types of goods, such as coal, grain, and bulky items (such as heavy equipment and cars). Pipelines are fine if your product happens to be petroleum or natural gas.

Trucks, though fairly expensive, work for most goods and can go just about anywhere in a reasonable amount of time.

According to the U.S. Department of Transportation,[24] trucks are the transportation of choice for most goods, accounting for 65 percent of U.S. transportation expenditures. Trucks also play an important role in the second highest category—multimodal combinations, which account for 11 percent of expenditures. *Multimodal combinations* include rail and truck and water and truck. New cars, for example, might travel from Michigan to California by rail and then be moved to tractor trailers to complete their journey to dealerships. Water accounts for 9 percent of expenditures, air for 8 percent. When used alone, rail accounts for only 4 percent but is commonly combined with other modes. Pipelines account for 3 percent of expenditures. Crowded highways notwithstanding, the economy would come to a standstill without the two million workers that make up the U.S. trucking industry.[25]

4.4   Creating an Effective Distribution Network: The Supply Chain

FIGURE 9.9

Trucks are the primary source of transportation in the lumber industry.

© 2010 Jupiterimages Corporation

Before we go on to the final component in the marketing mix—*promotion*—let's review the elements that we've discussed so far: product, price, and place. As we've seen, to be competitive, companies must produce quality products, sell them at reasonable prices, and make them available to customers at the right place at the right time. To accomplish these three tasks, they must work with a network of other firms, both those that supply them with materials and services and those that deliver and sell their products. To better understand the links that must be forged to create an effective network, let's look at the steps that the candy maker Just Born takes to produce and deliver more than one billion Marshmallow Peeps each year to customers throughout the world. Each day, the company engages in the following process:

- Purchasing managers buy raw materials from suppliers (sugar and other ingredients used to make marshmallow, food coloring, and so forth).
- Other operations managers transform these raw materials, or ingredients, into 4.2 million Marshmallow Peeps every day.
- Operations managers in shipping send completed packages to a warehouse where they're stored for later distribution.
- Operations managers at the warehouse forward packaged Marshmallow Peeps to dealers around the world.
- Retail dealers sell the Marshmallow Peeps to customers.

This process requires considerable cooperation not only among individuals in the organization but also between Just Born and its suppliers and dealers. Raw-materials suppliers, for instance, must work closely with Just Born purchasing managers, who must, in turn, work with operations managers in manufacturing at Just Born itself. People in manufacturing have to work with operations managers in the warehouse, who have to work with retail dealers, who have to work with their customers.

If all the people involved in each of these steps worked independently, the process of turning raw materials into finished Marshmallow Peeps and selling them to customers would be inefficient (to say the least). However, when everyone works in a coordinated manner, all parties benefit. Just Born can make a higher-quality product at a lower cost because it knows that it's going to get cooperation from suppliers whose livelihood, after all, depends on the success of customers like Just Born: suppliers can operate more efficiently because they can predict the demand for their products (such as sugar and food coloring). At the other end of the chain, dealers can operate efficiently because they can depend on Just Born to deliver a quality product on time. The real beneficiary is ultimately the end user, or customer: because the process that delivers the product is efficient, its costs are minimized and its quality is optimized. The customer, in other words, gets a higher-quality product at a lower price.

Supply Chain Management

As you can see in Figure 9.10, the flow that begins with the purchase of raw materials and culminates in the sale of the Marshmallow Peeps to end users is called the **supply chain**. The process of integrating all the activities in the supply chain is called **supply chain management (SCM)**. As you can see from our discussion so far, SCM requires a high level of cooperation among the members of the chain. All parties must be willing to share information and work together to maximize the final customer's satisfaction.[26]

FIGURE 9.10 A Simplified Supply Chain

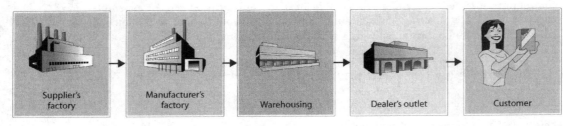

A Simplified Supply Chain

Click on this link to experience an active version of this figure.

Managing your supply chain can be difficult, particularly if your company has large seasonal fluctuations. This is certainly true at Just Born. Even though it has a Marshmallow Peep for every season (heart Peeps for Valentine's Day, spooky Peeps for Halloween, patriotic Peeps for the Fourth of July, and so on), the biggest problem rests with the standard yellow Marshmallow Peep that provides a major spike in sales each spring. Without careful supply chain management, there would be either too many or two few yellow Marshmallow Peeps—both big problems. To reduce the likelihood of either situation, the manager of the company's supply chain works to ensure that all members of the chain work together throughout the busy production season, which begins each fall. Suppliers promise to deliver large quantities of ingredients, workers recognize that they will be busy through February, and dealers get their orders in early. Each member of the chain depends on the others to meet a mutually shared goal: getting the right quantity of yellow Marshmallow Peeps to customers at the right time.

But what if a company has multiple sales spikes (and lulls)? What effect does this pattern have on its supply chain? Consider Domino's Pizza. Have you ever thought about what it takes to ensure that a piping-hot pizza will arrive at your door on Super Bowl Sunday (Domino's busiest day of the year)? What about on the average weekend? How about when the weather's bad and you just don't want to go out? Clearly, Domino needs a finely tuned supply chain to stay on top of demand. Each year, the company sells about four hundred million pizzas (more than one pizza for every man, woman, and child in the United States). Its suppliers help to make this volume possible by providing the company with about one hundred fifty million pounds of cheese and toppings. Drivers do their part by logging nine million miles a week (the equivalent of 37.5 round trips to the moon every week).

How are these activities managed? Dominos relies on a software system that uses historical data to forecast demand by store; determines, orders, and adjusts supplies; fills staffing needs according to expected sales levels; and facilitates the smooth flow of accurate information among members of the chain. All this coordination is directed at a single goal—satisfying the largest possible number of end users.[27]

The Value Chain

Supply chain management helps companies produce better products at lower costs and to distribute them more effectively. Remember, however, that effective supply chain management doesn't necessarily guarantee success. A company must also persuade consumers to buy its products, rather than those of its competitors, and the key to achieving this goal is delivering the most value.

The Customer Value Triad

Today's consumers can choose from a huge array of products offered at a range of prices through a variety of suppliers. So how do they decide which product to buy? Most people buy the product that gives them the highest value, and they usually determine value by considering the three factors that many marketers call the **customer value triad**: *quality, service,* and *price*.[28] In short, consumers tend to select the product that provides the best combination of these factors.

To deliver high customer value, a company must monitor and improve its **value chain**—the entire range of activities involved in delivering value to customers.[29] Some of these activities arise in the process of supply chain management—obtaining raw materials, manufacturing products, getting finished goods to customers. Others take place outside the supply chain, particularly those associated with marketing and selling products and with providing customer support. In addition, companies need to find ways of creating value by improving the internal operations—procurement, research and development, human resource management, and financial management—that support their primary value-chain activities.

The idea is fairly simple: by focusing on the interrelated links in its value chain, a company can increase product quality, provide better service, and cut prices. In other words, it can improve its quality-service-price mix, thereby making its products more competitive.

> **customer value triad**
>
> Three factors that customers consider in determining the value of a product: quality, service, and price.

> **value chain**
>
> Entire range of activities involved in delivering value to customers.

Driving a Better Bargain

Take a few minutes to complete an exercise that allows you to decide which well-known car brands are over-valued and which are undervalued.

KEY TAKEAWAYS

- **Distribution** entails all activities involved in getting the right quantity of a product to customers at the right time and at a reasonable cost.
- Companies can sell directly (from stores or over the Internet) or indirectly, through **intermediaries**—retailers or wholesalers who help move products from producers to end users.
- **Retailers** buy goods from producers and sell them to consumers, whether in stores, by phone, through direct mailings, or over the Internet.
- **Wholesalers** (or distributors) buy goods from suppliers and sell them to businesses that will resell or use them.
- **Physical distribution**—the process of getting products from producers to customers—entails several interrelated activities: *warehousing* in either a **storage warehouse** or a **distribution center**, **materials handling** (physically moving products or components), and *transportation* (shipping goods from manufacturing facilities to resellers or customers).
- A firm can produce better-quality products at lower cost and distribute them more effectively by successfully managing its **supply chain**—the entire range of activities involved in producing and distributing products, from purchasing raw materials, transforming raw materials into finished goods, storing finished goods, and distributing them to customers.
- Effective **supply chain management (SCM)** requires cooperation, not only among individuals within the organization but also among the company and its suppliers and dealers. In addition, a successful company provides customers with added value by focusing on and improving its **value chain**—the entire range of its value-creating activities.

Before going to the next section of this chapter, take a few minutes to test your knowledge of the material covered in this section. Quizzes can be found under the "Resources" tab, "Study Aids: Quizzes."

EXERCISES

1. Working in the school chemistry lab, you come up with a fantastic-tasting fruit drink. You're confident that it can be a big seller, and you've found a local company that will manufacture it. Unfortunately, you have to handle the distribution yourself—a complex task because your product is made from natural ingredients and can easily spoil. What distribution channels would you use, and why? How would you handle the physical distribution of your product?

2. Students at Penn State University can take a break from their studies to visit an on-campus ice cream stand called the Creamery. Milk for the ice cream comes from cows that graze on university land as part of a program run by the agriculture school. Other ingredients, including sugar and chocolate syrup, are purchased from outside vendors, as are paper products and other supplies. Using your personal knowledge of ice cream stand operations (which probably comes from your experience as a customer), diagram the Creamery's supply chain. How would the supply chain change if the company decided to close its retail outlet and sell directly to supermarkets?

---

5. PROMOTING A PRODUCT

LEARNING OBJECTIVE

1. **Describe the elements of the promotion mix.**

promotion mix

Various ways to communicate with customers, including advertising, personal selling, sales promotion, and publicity.

Your **promotion mix**—the means by which you communicate with customers—may include advertising, personal selling, sales promotion, and publicity. These are all tools for telling people about your product and persuading potential customers, whether consumers or organizational users, to buy it. Before deciding on an appropriate promotional strategy, you should consider a few questions:

- What's the main purpose of the promotion? Am I simply trying to make people aware of my product, or am I trying to get people to buy it right now? Am I trying to develop long-term customers? Am I trying to connect with my current customers? Am I trying to promote my company's image?

- What's my target market? What's the best way to reach it?

- Which product features (quality, price, service, availability, innovativeness) should I emphasize? How does my product differ from those of competitors?

- How much can I afford to invest in a promotion campaign?

- How do my competitors promote their products? Should I take a similar approach?

To promote a product, you need to imprint a clear image of it in the minds of your target audience. What do you think of, for instance, when you hear "Ritz-Carlton"? What about "Motel 6"? They're both hotel chains, but the names certainly conjure up different images. Both have been quite successful in the hospitality industry, but they project very different images to appeal to different clienteles. The differences are evident in their promotions. The Ritz-Carlton Web site describes "luxury hotels" and promises that the chain provides "the finest personal service and facilities throughout the world."[30] Motel 6, by contrast, characterizes its facilities as "discount hotels" and assures you that you'll pay "discount hotel rates."[31]

5.1 Promotional Tools

We'll now examine each of the elements that can go into the promotion mix—*advertising, personal selling, sales promotion*, and *publicity*. Then we'll see how Wow Wee incorporated them into a promotion mix to create a demand for Robosapien.

Advertising

Advertising

Paid, nonpersonal communication designed to create an awareness of a product or company.

Advertising is paid, nonpersonal communication designed to create an awareness of a product or company. Ads are everywhere—in print media (such as newspapers, magazines, the *Yellow Pages*), on billboards, in broadcast media (radio and TV), and on the Internet. It's hard to escape the constant barrage of advertising messages; indeed, it's estimated that the average consumer is confronted by about five thousand ad messages each day (compared with about five hundred ads a day in the 1970s).[32] For this very reason, ironically, ads aren't as effective as they used to be. Because we've learned to tune them out, companies now have to come up with innovative ways to get through to potential customers. A *New York Times* article[33] claims that "anywhere the eye can see, it's likely to see an ad." Subway turnstiles are plastered with ads for GEICO auto insurance, Chinese food containers are decorated with ads for Continental Airways, parking meters display ads for Campbell's Soup,[34] examining tables in pediatricians' offices are covered with ads for Disney's *Little Einsteins* DVDs, school buses play radio ads for children, "Got Milk" billboards at San Francisco bus stops give off the smell of chocolate chip cookies, and U.S. Airways is even selling ads on motion sickness bags (yuck!).[35] Even so, advertising is still the most prevalent form of promotion.

Your choice of advertising media depends on your product, your target audience, and your budget. A travel agency selling spring-break getaways to college students might post flyers on campus bulletin boards or run ads in campus newspapers. A pharmaceutical company trying to develop a market for a new allergy drug might focus on TV ads that reach a broad audience of allergy sufferers. A fitness center might purchase a Google ad that appears next to the search results when someone puts in a relevant keyword, such as fitness. A small hot dog and hamburger stand will probably spend its limited advertising budget on ads in the *Yellow Pages* and local newspapers (or pay a broke college student to stand by the side of the road dressed in a hot dog costume and hold a sign that entices potential customers to "come on in"). The cofounders of Nantucket Nectars found radio ads particularly effective. Rather than pay professionals, they produced their own ads themselves. (Actually, they just got on the radio and started rambling about their product or their lives or anything else that seemed interesting at the time.)[36] As unprofessional as they sounded, the ads worked, and the business grew.

Personal Selling

Personal selling refers to one-on-one communication with customers or potential customers. This type of interaction is necessary in selling large-ticket items, such as homes, and it's also effective in situations in which personal attention helps to close a sale, such as sales of cars and insurance policies.

> **personal selling**
>
> One-on-one communication with customers or potential customers.

Many retail stores depend on the expertise and enthusiasm of their salespeople to persuade customers to buy. Home Depot has grown into a home-goods giant in large part because it fosters one-on-one interactions between salespeople and customers. The real difference between Home Depot and everyone else, says one of its cofounders, isn't the merchandise; it's the friendly, easy-to-understand advice that salespeople give to novice homeowners. Customers who never thought they could fix anything suddenly feel empowered to install a carpet or hang wallpaper.[37]

"Congratulations! You can spend two free nights at any Hyatt Hotel in the world! All you have to do is sign up for a Hyatt-branded credit card."[38] This tactic is a form of **sales promotion** in which a company provides an incentive for a potential customer to buy something. Most sales promotions are more straightforward than our hotel stay/credit card offer. Promotional giveaways might feature free samples or money-off coupons. Promotions can involve in-store demonstrations or trade-show displays. They can be cheaper than advertising and can encourage customers to buy something quickly.

> **sales promotion**
>
> Sales approach in which a company provides an incentive for potential customers to buy something.

Apple Inc. and Starbucks partner to promote the iTunes experience by giving away free iTunes products, including a "Pick of the Week" music download, apps, book samples from the iBookstore, TV shows, and games. The current app giveaway is the Shazam Encore App, a music recognition service that allows users to immediately identify any song that's playing, see the lyrics, watch the music videos, purchase concert tickets, and buy the track and share it with friends on Facebook and Twitter. The joint promotion benefits both companies: Apple gets to plug its iTunes download and other products, and Starbucks entices customers to come into its stores, enjoy free Wi-Fi, and buy coffee.[39]

Publicity and Public Relations

Free **publicity**—say, getting your company or your product mentioned in a newspaper or on TV—can often generate more customer interest than a costly ad. You may remember the holiday season buying frenzy surrounding a fuzzy red doll named "Tickle Me Elmo." The big break for this product came when the marketing team sent a doll to the one-year-old son of talk-show host Rosie O'Donnell. Two months before Christmas, O'Donnell started tossing dolls into the audience every time a guest said the word *wall*. The product took off, and the campaign didn't cost marketers anything except a few hundred dolls.[40]

> **publicity**
>
> Form of promotion that focuses on getting a company or product mentioned in a newspaper, on TV, or in some other news media.

Consumer perception of a company is often important to a company's success. Many companies, therefore, manage their **public relations** in an effort to garner favorable publicity for themselves and their products. When the company does something negative, such as selling a prescription drug that has unexpected side effects, the public relations department will work to control the damage to the company. On the other hand, when the company does something noteworthy, such as sponsoring a fund-raising event, the public relations department may issue a press release to promote the event. Those firms on *Fortune*'s list of the World's Most Respected Companies enjoy special bragging rights. These companies were chosen by CEOs, other executives, and analysts for their industry based on

> **public relations**
>
> Communication activities undertaken by companies to garner favorable publicity for themselves and their products.

several criteria including investment value and social responsibility. The top ten companies on the 2013 list are Apple, Google, Amazon.com, Coca-Cola, Starbucks, IBM, Southwest Airlines, Berkshire Hathaway, Walt Disney, and FedEx.[41]

5.2 Marketing Robosapien

Now let's look more closely at the strategy that Wow Wee pursued in marketing Robosapien in the United States. The company's goal was ambitious: to promote the robot as a must-have item for kids of all ages. As we know, Wow Wee intended to position Robosapien as a home-entertainment product, not as a toy. The company rolled out the product at Best Buy, which sells consumer electronics, computers, entertainment software, and appliances. As marketers had hoped, the robot caught the attention of consumers shopping for TV sets, DVD players, home and car audio equipment, music, movies, and games. Its $99 price tag was also consistent with Best Buy's storewide pricing. Indeed, the retail price was a little lower than the prices of other merchandise, and that fact was an important asset: shoppers were willing to treat Robosapien as an *impulse item*—something extra to pick up as a gift or as a special present for children, as long as the price wasn't too high.

Meanwhile, Robosapien was also getting lots of free publicity. Stories appeared in newspapers and magazines around the world, including the *New York Times*, the *Times of London, Time* magazine, and *National Parenting* magazine. Commentators on *The Today Show, The Early Show*, CNN, ABC News, and FOX News remarked on it; it was even the talk of the prestigious New York Toys Fair. It garnered numerous awards, and experts predicted that it would be a hot item for the holidays.

At Wow Wee, Marketing Director Amy Weltman (who had already had a big hit with the Rubik's Cube) developed a gala New York event to showcase the product. From mid- to late August, actors dressed in six-foot robot costumes roamed the streets of Manhattan, while the fourteen-inch version of Robosapien performed in venues ranging from Grand Central Station to city bars. Everything was recorded, and film clips were sent to TV stations.

Then the stage was set for expansion into other stores. Macy's ran special promotions, floating a twenty-four-foot cold-air robot balloon from its rooftop and lining its windows with armies of Robosapien's. Wow Wee trained salespeople to operate the product so that they could help customers during in-store demonstrations. Other retailers, including The Sharper Image, Spencer's, and Toys "R" Us, carried Robosapien, as did e-retailers such as Amazon.com. The product was also rolled out (with the same marketing flair) in Europe and Asia.

When national advertising hit in September, all the pieces of the marketing campaign came together—publicity, sales promotion, personal selling, and advertising. Wow Wee ramped up production to meet anticipated fourth-quarter demand and waited to see whether Robosapien would live up to commercial expectations.

KEY TAKEAWAYS

- The **promotion mix**—the ways in which marketers communicate with customers—includes all the tools for telling people about a product and persuading potential customers to buy it.
- **Advertising** is paid, nonpersonal communication designed to create awareness of a product or company.
- **Personal selling** is one-on-one communication with existing and potential customers.
- **Sales promotions** provide potential customers with direct incentives to buy.
- **Publicity** involves getting the name of the company or its products mentioned in print or broadcast media.

EXERCISE

Companies encourage customers to buy their products by using a variety of promotion tools, including advertising, personal selling, sales promotion, and publicity. Your task is to develop a promotion strategy for two products—the Volkswagen Jetta and Red Bolt soda. For each product, answer the following questions:

- What's the purpose of the promotion?
- What's your target market?
- What's the best way to reach that target market?
- What product features should you emphasize?
- How does your product differ from competitors'?

Then describe the elements that go into your promotion mix, and explain why you chose the promotional tools that you did.

6. INTERACTING WITH YOUR CUSTOMERS

LEARNING OBJECTIVES

1. Compare and contrast permission marketing and interruption marketing.
2. Describe social media marketing and identify its advantages and disadvantages.

6.1 Customer-Relationship Management

Customers are the most important asset that any business has. Without enough good customers, no company can survive, and to survive, a firm must not only attract new customers but, perhaps more importantly, also hold on to its current customers. Why? Because repeat customers are more profitable. Studies show that it is more expensive to attract and sell to a new customer than to an existing one.[42] Repeat customers also tend to spend more, and they're much more likely to recommend you to other people.

Retaining customers is the purpose of **customer-relationship management**—a marketing strategy that focuses on using information about current customers to nurture and maintain strong relationships with them. The underlying theory is fairly basic: to keep customers happy, you treat them well, give them what they want, listen to them, reward them with discounts and other loyalty incentives, and deal effectively with their complaints.

Take Caesars Entertainment Corporation (formerly Harrah's Entertainment), which operates more than fifty casinos under several brands, including Caesars, Harrah's, Bally's, and Horseshoe. Each year, it sponsors the World Series of Poker with a top prize of $9 million. Caesars gains some brand recognition when the twenty-two-hour event is televised on ESPN, but the real benefit derives from the information cards filled out by the seven thousand entrants who put up $10,000 for a chance to walk away with $9 million. Data from these cards is fed into Caesars database, and almost immediately every entrant starts getting special attention, including party invitations, free entertainment tickets, and room discounts. The program is all part of Harrah's strategy for targeting serious gamers and recognizing them as its best customers.[43]

customer-relationship management

Strategy for retaining customers by gathering information about them, understanding them, and treating them well.

FIGURE 9.11

Customer-relationship management is especially important to businesses that provide services. A concierge ensures that hotel guests are treated well during their stay.

© 2010 Jupiterimages Corporation

permission marketing

Form of marketing in which companies ask customers or potential customers for permission to contact them or send them marketing materials.

mass marketing

The practice of sending out messages to a vast audience of anonymous people.

interruption marketing

Marketing that interrupts people to get their attention (with the hope they will listen to the ad), such as TV advertising.

social media marketing

The practice of including social media as part of a company's marketing program.

Sheraton Hotels uses a softer approach to entice return customers. Sensing that its resorts needed both a new look and a new strategy for attracting repeat customers, Sheraton launched its "Year of the Bed" campaign: in addition to replacing all its old beds with luxurious new mattresses and coverings, it issued a "service promise guarantee"—a policy that any guest who's dissatisfied with his or her Sheraton stay will be compensated. The program also calls for a customer-satisfaction survey and discount offers, both designed to keep the hotel chain in touch with its customers.[44]

Another advantage of keeping in touch with customers is the opportunity to offer them additional products. Amazon.com is a master at this strategy. When you make your first purchase at Amazon.com, you're also making a lifelong "friend"—one who will suggest (based on what you've bought before) other things that you might like to buy. Because Amazon.com continually updates its data on your preferences, the company gets better at making suggestions. Now that the Internet firm has expanded past books, Amazon.com can draw on its huge database to promote a vast range of products, and shopping for a variety of products at Amazon.com appeals to people who value time above all else.

Permission versus Interruption Marketing

Underlying Amazon.com's success in communicating with customers is the fact that customers have given the company permission to contact them. Companies that ask for customers' cooperation engage in **permission marketing**.[45] The big advantage is focusing on an audience of people who have already shown an interest in what they have to offer. Compare this approach with **mass marketing**—the practice of sending out messages to a vast audience of anonymous people. If you advertise on TV, you're hoping that people will listen, even though you're interrupting them; that's why some marketers call such standard approaches **interruption marketing**.[46] Remember, however, that permission marketing isn't free. Because winning and keeping customers means giving them incentives, Caesars lets high rollers sleep and eat free (or at a deep discount), Norwegian Cruise Line gives members of its past guest program, Latitudes, discounts on sailings, priority check-in, and members-only cocktail parties. Customer-relations management and permission marketing have actually been around for a long time. But recent advances in technology, especially the Internet, now allow companies to practice these approaches in more cost-effective ways.

6.2 Social Media Marketing

In the last five years, the popularity of **social media marketing** has exploded. Most likely you already know what social media is—you use it every day when you connect to Facebook, Twitter, LinkedIn, YouTube, or any number of other online sites that allow you to communicate with others, network, and bookmark and share your opinions, ideas, photos, and videos. So what is social media marketing? Quite simply social media marketing is the practice of including social media as part of a company's marketing program.

Why do businesses use social media marketing? Before responding, ask yourself these questions: How much time do I spend watching TV? When I watch TV, do I sit through the ads? Do I read the newspaper? What about magazines—when was the last time I sat for hours reading a magazine, including the ads? How do I spend my spare time? Now, put yourself in the place of Annie Young-Scrivner, global chief marketing officer of Starbucks. Does it make sense for her to spend millions of dollars to place an ad for Starbucks on TV or in a newspaper or magazine? Or should she instead spend the money on social media marketing initiatives that have a high probability of connecting to Starbucks's market?

For companies like Starbucks, the answer is clear. The days of trying to reach customers through ads on TV, in newspapers, or in magazines are over. Most television watchers skip over commercials (or avoid the ads by using TiVo), and few Starbucks's customers read newspapers or magazines, and even if they do, they don't focus on the ads. Social media marketing provides a number of advantages to companies, including enabling them to:[47]

- create brand awareness;
- connect with customers and potential customers by engaging them in two-way communication;
- build brand loyalty by providing opportunities for a targeted audience to participate in company-sponsored activities, such as a contest;
- offer and publicize incentives, such as special discounts or coupons, which increase sales;
- gather feedback and ideas on how to improve products and marketing initiatives;

- allow customers to interact with each other and spread the word about a company's products or marketing initiatives; and

- take advantage of low-cost marketing opportunities by being active on free social sites, such as Facebook.

To get a flavor of the power of social media marketing, let's look at social media campaigns of two leaders in this field: PepsiCo (Mountain Dew) and Starbucks.

Mountain Dew (PepsiCo)

When PepsiCo announced it wouldn't show a television commercial during the 2010 Super Bowl game, it came as a surprise (probably a pleasant one to its competitor, Coca-Cola, who had already signed on to show several Super Bowl commercials). What PepsiCo planned to do instead was invest $20 million into social media marketing campaigns. One of PepsiCo's most successful social media initiatives was to extend the DEWmocracy campaign, which two years earlier, resulted in the launch of product—Voltage—created by Mountain Dew fans. DEWmocracy 2 was a yearlong marketing campaign designed to create another Mountain Dew drink. The campaign was rolled out nationally in seven stages and engaged a number of social media outlets, including an online community of enthusiastic fans of Mountain Dew, Twitter, USTREAM (a live video streaming Web site), a 12secondTV.com video contest, and a dedicated YouTube channel.[48] According to Mountain Dew's director of marketing, the goal of the campaign was "to engage in a direct dialogue with our consumers. And through this dialogue really start what we like to call a social movement in order to create this innovation."[49] The flavors created through fan input are Whiteout (a citrus flavor that is white), Typhoon (a punch flavor), and Distortion (a hint of lime). All three flavors were launched in the spring of 2010, and it was up to the fans to select the best flavor, which would become a permanent member of Mountain Dew's offerings. And the winner was Whiteout.[50] In addition to using fans to select the best flavors, the campaign used forums and live chats to allow fans to create the packaging, graphics, and social marketing for the products using viral videos, Twitter, and professional commercials.[51]

Speaking of professional commercials, all you Super Bowl fans and followers of Super Bowl ads will be glad to hear that PepsiCo reversed its position, and its ads were showcased in the 2011 Super Bowl. It was likely a little jealous of its competitor, Coca-Cola, who was very effective at combining its Super Bowl ads with a social media campaign. Facebook fans who went online and donated $1 to the Boys & Girls Club of America received an image of a Coca-Cola bottle to post on their Facebook page and a twenty-second sneak preview of one of Coca-Cola's Super Bowl ads.[52]

Starbucks

One of most enthusiastic users of social media marketing is Starbucks. Let's looks at a few of their recent promotions: discount for Foursquare "mayors," free coffee on Tax Day via Twitter's promoted tweets, and a free pastry day promoted through Twitter.

Discount for "Foursquare" Mayors of Starbucks

This promotion was a joint effort of Foursquare and Starbucks. Foursquare is a mobile social network, and in addition to the handy "friend finder" feature, you can use it to find new and interesting places around your neighborhood to do whatever you and your friends like to do. It even rewards you for doing business with sponsor companies, such as Starbucks. The individual with the most "check in's" at a particular Starbucks holds the title of mayor. For a period of time, the mayor of each store got $1 off a Frappuccino. Those who used Foursquare were particularly excited about Starbucks's nationwide mayor rewards program because it brought attention to the marketing possibilities of the location-sharing app.[53]

Free Coffee on Tax Day (via Twitter's Promoted Tweets)

Starbucks was not the only company to give away freebies on Tax Day, April 15, 2010. Lots of others did.[54] For example, Cinnabon gave away free cupcake bites, Dairy Queen gave free mini blizzards, and Maggie Moo's offered a free slice of their new Maggie Moo ice cream pizza. But it was the only company to spread the message of their giveaway on the then-new Twitter's Promoted Tweets platform (which went into operation on April 13, 2010). Promoted Tweets are Twitter's means of making money by selling sponsored links to companies.[55] Keeping with Twitter's 140 characters per tweet rule, Starbucks's Promoted Tweet read, "On 4/15 bring a reusable tumbler and we'll fill it with brewed coffee for free. Let's all switch from paper cups." The tweet also linked to a page that detailed Starbucks's environmental initiatives.[56]

Free Pastry Day (Promoted through Twitter and Facebook)

Starbucks's "free pastry day" was promoted on Facebook and Twitter.[57] As the word spread from person to person in digital form, the wave of social media activity drove more than a million people to Starbucks's stores around the country in search of free food.[58]

As word of the freebie offering spread, Starbucks became the star of Twitter, with about 1 percent of total tweets commenting on the brand. That's almost ten times the number of mentions on an average day. It performed equally well on Facebook's event page where almost 600,000 people joined their friends and signed up as "attendees." This is not surprising given that Starbucks is the most popular brand on Facebook and the first to reach the 10-million fan mark.[59]

How did Starbucks achieve this notoriety on Facebook? According to social media marketing experts, Starbucks earned this notoriety by making social media a central part of its marketing mix, distributing special offers, discounts, and coupons to Facebook users and placing ads on Facebook to drive traffic to its page. As explained by the CEO of Buddy Media, which oversees the brand's social media efforts, "Starbucks has provided Facebook users a reason to become a fan."[60]

Social Media Marketing Challenges

The main challenge of social media marketing is that it can be very time consuming. It takes determination and resources to succeed. Small companies often lack the staff to initiate and manage social media marketing campaigns.[61] Even large companies can find the management of media marketing initiates overwhelming. A recent study of 1,700 chief marketing officers indicates that many are overwhelmed by the sheer volume of customer data available on social sites, such as Facebook and Twitter.[62] This is not surprising given that Facebook has more than eight hundred million active users, and two hundred million tweets are sent each day. The marketing officers recognize the potential value of this data but are not capable of using it. A chief marketing officer in the survey described the situation as follows: "The perfect solution is to serve each consumer individually. The problem? There are 7 billion of them."[63] In spite of these limitations, 82 percent of those surveyed plan to increase their use of social media marketing over the next 3 to 5 years. To understand what real-time information is telling them, companies will use analytics software, which is capable of analyzing unstructured data. This software is being developed by technology companies, such as IBM, and advertising agencies.

The bottom line: what is clear is that marketing, and particularly advertising, has changed forever. As Simon Pestridge, Nike's global director of marketing for Greater China, said about Nike's marketing strategy,[64] "We don't do advertising any more. We just do cool stuff…but that's just the way it is. Advertising is all about achieving awareness, and we no longer need awareness. We need to become part of people's lives and digital allows us to do that."

KEY TAKEAWAYS

- Because customers are vital to a business, successful companies practice **customer-relationship management**—retaining good customers by keeping information on current customers, to foster and maintain strong ongoing relationships.
- Companies that ask customers if they can contact them are engaged in **permission marketing**.
- **Mass marketing** is the practice of sending out messages to a vast audience of anonymous people.
- TV advertising is a form of **interruption marketing** that interrupts people to get their attention (with the hope they will listen to the ad).
- **Social media marketing** is the practice of including social media as part of a company's marketing program.
- Advantages of social media marketing include the following:
  - Create brand awareness
  - Engage customers and potential customers in two-way conversations
  - Build brand loyalty
  - Offer and publicize incentives
  - Gather feedback on products and marketing initiatives
  - Have customers spread the word about products and marketing initiatives
  - Use low-cost marketing opportunities
- A challenge of social media marketing is that it can be very time consuming to stay in touch with your customers and potential customers.

Before going to the next section of this chapter, take a few minutes to test your knowledge of the material covered in this section. Quizzes can be found under the "Resources" tab, "Study Aids: Quizzes."

EXERCISES

1. If you ran an airline, how would you practice customer-relationship management (CRM)? How would you get permission to market your product to customers? What information would you collect on them? What incentives would you offer them to continue flying with you? What advantages can you gain through effective CRM?

2. One of the most successful social media marketing campaigns was for Old Spice. Procter & Gamble enlisted former NFL wide receiver Isaiah Mustafa to star in a number of videos pointing out to women that their men could be as fantastic as he is if only they wore Old Spice aftershave. Review the following articles, watch the videos embedded in the articles, and answer the listed questions.

   - Brenna Ehrlich, "The Old Spice Social Media Campaign by the Numbers, Mashable Business," *Mashable*, July 15, 2010, http://mashable.com/2010/07/15/old-spice-stats/
   - Samuel Axon, "Top 10 Funniest Old Spice Guy Videos," *Mashable Business*, http://mashable.com/2010/07/18/old-spice-guy-videos (accessed April 29, 2014).
   - Describe the campaign and identify the goal of the campaign.
   - How was this campaign different from anything done in the past?
   - Did you like the videos? Why, or why not?
   - Would you buy Old Spice products? Why, or why not?

---

7.   THE PRODUCT LIFE CYCLE

LEARNING OBJECTIVE

1. **Explain how a product moves through its life cycle and how this brings about shifts in marketing-mix strategies.**

Did you play with LEGO blocks when you were a kid? Almost everyone did. They were a big deal. Store shelves were stacked with boxes of plastic bricks, wheels, and windows, plus packages containing just the pieces you needed to make something special, like a LEGO helicopter. McDonald's put LEGO sets in Happy Meals. If you walk down a toy-store aisle today, you'll still find LEGOs. They're shelved alongside the XBOX Kinect, Buzz Lightyear, and other playthings that appeal to contemporary kids. Like these products, they're more sophisticated. They're often tied in with movies, such as *Toy Story*, *Cars*, *Star Wars*, super hero movies, *Harry Potter*, and *The LEGO Movie* figures.

Nowadays, the eighty-two-year-old Denmark company is doing very well: in fewer than ten years, the company quadrupled its sales.[65] The LEGO Group has moved its way up to become the second largest toy company in the world based on sales.[66] Things were very different ten years earlier—LEGO sales had declined drastically in the early 2000s. In its 2003 annual report, its CEO admitted that "2003 was a very disappointing year for LEGO Company." Net sales fell by 26 percent, resulting in a loss in earnings for the year and a significant decline in market share. LEGO planned to drop many of its recent initiatives and focus on its classic LEGO brick products.[67]

Let's look closer and find out what happened to the LEGO brand prior to its turnaround ten years ago. It was moving through stages of development and decline.[68] Marketers call this process the **product life cycle**, which is illustrated in Figure 9.13. In theory, it's a lot like the life cycle that people go through. Once it's developed, a new product is *introduced* to the market. With any success at all, it begins to *grow*, attracting more buyers. At some point, the market stabilizes, and the product becomes *mature*. Eventually, however, its appeal diminishes, and it's overtaken by competing brands or substitute products. Sales *decline*, and it's ultimately taken off the market.

FIGURE 9.12

LEGO has decided to go back to basics and focus on the classic bricks rather than complicated kits.

product life cycle

Four stages that a product goes through over its life: introduction, growth, maturity, and decline.

FIGURE 9.13 The Product Life Cycle

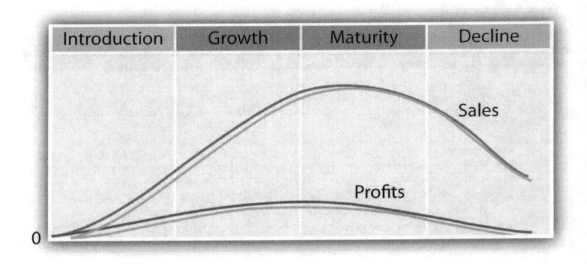

This is a simplified version of the cycle. There are lots of exceptions to the product life-cycle rules. For one thing, most products never make it past the introduction stage; they die an early death. Second, some products (like some people) avoid premature demise by reinventing themselves. This is what the LEGO Group did. The company had been reinventing itself during the fifteen-year period of 1990 to 2005, launching new products in an effort to recover its customer base and overcome a series of financial crises. Unfortunately, this strategy was unsuccessful. As pointed out by its CEO, the introduction of new products and the resulting costs "have not produced the desired results. In some cases," admits the company, "new products have even cannibalized on the sales of LEGO Company's core products and thus eroded earnings."[69]

A take-over threat by Mattel Toy Company forced its CEO into action.[70] His first stop in formulating a resurrection plan was to fly to Virginia and attend a convention for adult fans of LEGO's. The attendees' stories of how LEGOs helped shape their minds gave him hope that the family-owned company could be saved. He returned to Denmark and put into place a plan that included downsizing the number of employees, selling its LEGOLAND theme parks, simplifying product designs, cutting unprofitable product lines, and focusing on what made the company great: LEGO building blocks.

7.1 Life Cycle and the Changing Marketing Mix

As a product or brand moves through its life cycle, the company that markets it will shift its marketing-mix strategies. Let's see how the mix might be changed at each stage.

Introduction

At this stage, most companies invest in advertising to make consumers aware of a product. If it faces only limited competition, it might use a skimming-pricing approach. Typically, because it will sell only a relatively small quantity of the product, it will distribute through just a few channels. Because sales are low while advertising and other costs are high, the company tends to lose money during this stage.

Growth

As the company focuses on building sales, which are increasing rapidly at this stage, its advertising costs will go up. If competition appears, it may respond by lowering prices and distributing through multiple distribution channels. With sales going up and costs going down, the product becomes more profitable.

Maturity

If a product survives the growth stage, it will probably remain in the maturity stage for a long time. Sales still grow, though at a decreasing rate, and will eventually stabilize. Advertising will be used to differentiate the product from competition. Price wars may occur, but profits will be good because sales volume will remain high. As the product becomes outdated, the company may make changes in keeping with changing consumer preferences.

Decline

In 2004, LEGO was in this stage: demand had declined as more innovative products absorbed the attention of kids. Price competition had become more intense, and profits were harder to come by; in fact, in some years, they had turned into losses. But, unlike most products that enter the decline stage, LEGO avoided its likely demise by reinventing itself. Now, as the Danish phrase *leg godt*, from which the name LEGO was coined, suggests, children all over the world can take out their LEGOs and "play-well."

The Product Life Cycle

Here is your chance to reinforce your understanding of the product life cycle. Complete the exercise and see how well you do.

KEY TAKEAWAYS

- The stages of development and decline that products go through over their lives is called the **product life cycle**.
- The stages a product goes through are introduction, growth, maturity, and decline.
    1. Once it's developed, a new product is *introduced* to the market.
    2. With any success at all, it begins to *grow*, attracting more buyers.
    3. At some point the market stabilizes, and the product becomes *mature*.
    4. Eventually, its appeal diminishes, and it's overtaken by competing brands or substitute products. Sales *decline* and it's ultimately taken off the market.
- As a product moves through its life cycle, the company that markets it will shift its marketing-mix strategies.

Before going to the next section of this chapter, take a few minutes to test your knowledge of the material covered in this section. Quizzes can be found under the "Resources" tab, "Study Aids: Quizzes."

EXERCISE

Did you ever have a Nintendo Game Boy? Is the product still popular? Like all products, Game Boy has a product life cycle. Your job is to describe that product life cycle. To learn something about the product, go to the Web, log on to your favorite search engine (Google, Yahoo!), and enter the phrase "Game Boy history." Identify each of the product life stages that Game Boy has gone through, and speculate on the marketing actions that Nintendo would have taken during each stage. Where do you think Game Boy is now in its product life cycle? Where do you think it will be in five years? Justify your answers.

8.   THE MARKETING ENVIRONMENT

LEARNING OBJECTIVES

1. Describe the external marketing environment in which businesses operate.
2. Compare and contrast the characteristics attributed to the following groups: the *baby-boom generation*, *Generation* X, and *Generation* Y.
3. Discuss the factors that influence consumer behavior.
4. Examine the psychological and social variables that influence buyers' decisions, and identify the steps a consumer goes through in reaching the decision to buy a product.

external marketing environment

Factors external to the firm that present threats and opportunities and that require shifts in marketing plans.

By and large, managers can control the four Ps of the marketing mix: they can decide which products to offer, what prices to charge for them, how to distribute them, and how to reach target audiences. Unfortunately, there are other forces at work in the marketing world—forces over which marketers have much less control. These forces make up a company's **external marketing environment**, which, as you can see in Figure 9.14, we can divide into five sets of factors:

1. Political and regulatory
2. Economic
3. Competitive
4. Technological
5. Social and cultural

FIGURE 9.14   The Marketing Environment

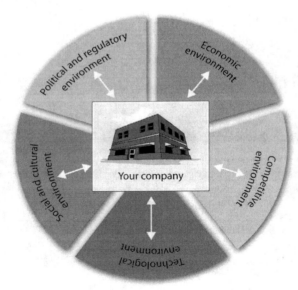

These factors—and changes in them—present both threats and opportunities that require shifts in marketing plans. To spot trends and other signals that conditions may be in flux, marketers must continually monitor the environment in which their companies operate. To get a better idea of how they affect a firm's marketing activities, let's look at each of the five areas of the external environment.

8.1   The Political and Regulatory Environment

Federal, state, and local bodies can set rules or restrictions on the conduct of businesses. The purpose of regulation is to protect both consumers and businesses. Businesses favor some regulations (such as patent laws) while chafing under others (such as restrictions on advertising). The tobacco industry, for example, has had to learn to live with a federal ban on TV and radio advertising. More recently, many companies in the food industry have expressed unhappiness over regulations requiring the labeling of trans-fat content. The broadcasting industry is increasingly concerned about fines being imposed by the Federal Communications Commission for offenses against "standards of decency." The loudest outcry probably came from telemarketers in response to the establishment of "do-not-call" registries.

All these actions occasioned changes in the marketing strategies of affected companies. Tobacco companies rerouted advertising dollars from TV to print media. Food companies reduced trans-fat levels and began targeting health-conscious consumers. Talent coordinators posted red flags next to the names of Janet Jackson (of the now-famous malfunctioning costume) and other performers. The telemarketing industry fired workers and scrambled to reinvent its entire business model.

8.2   The Economic Environment

Every day, marketing managers face a barrage of economic news. They must digest it, assess its impact, and alter marketing plans accordingly. Sometimes (but not recently), the news is cause for optimism—the economy's improving, unemployment's declining, consumer confidence is up. At other times (like today), the news makes them nervous—our economy is slow to recover, the labor force participation rate is declining, the jobs that are being added are mainly low-wage jobs, home prices (which had been creeping up) have flattened, and consumer debt is growing rapidly (again). Naturally, business thrives when the economy is growing, employment is full, and prices are stable. Marketing products is easier because consumers are willing to buy. On the other hand, when the economy is slowing (or stalled) and unemployment is rising, people have less money to spend, and the marketer's job is harder.

Then there's inflation, which pushes interest rates upward. If you're trying to sell cars, you know that people facing higher interest rates aren't so anxious to take out car loans. Sales will slip, and to counteract the anticipated slowdown, you might have to add generous rebates to your promotional plans.

Moreover, if you operate in foreign markets, you can't focus on solely domestic economic conditions: you have to monitor the economy in every region where you do business. For example, if you're the marketing director for a U.S. company whose goods are manufactured in China and sold in Brazil, you'll need to know as much as you can about the economies in three countries: the United States, China, and Brazil. For one thing, you'll have to pay particular attention to fluctuations in exchange rates, because changes will affect both your sales and your profits.

8.3   The Competitive Environment

Imagine playing tennis without watching what your opponent was doing. Marketers who don't pay attention to their competitors are playing a losing game. In particular, they need to monitor the activities of two groups of competitors: the makers of competing brands and the makers of substitute products. Coke and Pepsi, for instance, are brand competitors who have engaged in the so-called cola wars for decades. Each tries to capture market share by convincing people that its soft drinks are better. Because neither wants to lose share to the other, they tend to resort to similar tactics. In summer 2004, both companies came out with nearly identical new colas boasting half the sugar, half the calories, and half the carbohydrates of regular colas. Coke called its product Coke C2, while Pepsi named its competing brand PepsiEdge. Both companies targeted cola drinkers who want the flavor of a regular soda but fewer calories. (By the way, both products failed and were taken off the market.)

Meanwhile, Coke and Pepsi have to watch Nantucket Nectars, whose fruit drinks are substitute products. What if Nantucket Nectars managed to get its drinks into the soda machines at more fast-food restaurants? How would Coke and Pepsi respond? What if Nantucket Nectars, which markets an ice tea with caffeine, introduced an ice tea drink with mega amounts of caffeine? Would marketers at Coke and Pepsi take action? What if Nantucket Nectars launched a marketing campaign promoting the health benefits of fruit drinks over soda? Would Coke and Pepsi reply with campaigns of their own? Would they respond by introducing new non-cola products?

8.4   The Technological Environment

When's the last time you rented a VHS tape of a new movie? If you had trouble finding it, that's because DVDs are in and videotapes are out. Videotape makers who were monitoring technological trends in the industry would probably have taken steps to keep up (go into DVDs) or otherwise protect themselves from losses (maybe even getting out of the market). In addition to making old products obsolete, technological advances create new products. Where would we be without the cell phone, digital cameras, text messaging, LASIK surgery, and global positioning systems?

FIGURE 9.15

Web sites like iTunes and Amazon.com are now offering customers the option of downloading movies. Do you think DVDs will suffer the same fate as videocassettes?

© 2010 Jupiterimages Corporation

New technologies also transform the marketing mix in another important way: they alter the way companies market their products. Consider the revolutionary changes brought about by the Internet, which offers marketers a new medium for promoting and selling a vast range of goods and services. Marketers must keep abreast of technological advances and adapt their strategies, both to take advantage of the opportunities and to ward off threats.

8.5 The Social and Cultural Environment

Marketers also have to stay tuned to social and cultural factors that can affect sales. The values and attitudes of American consumers are in a state of almost constant flux; what's cool one year is out of style the next. Think about the clothes you wore five years ago: would you wear them today? A lot of people wouldn't—they're the wrong style, the wrong fit, the wrong material, the wrong color, or just plain wrong. Now put yourself in the place of a marketer for a clothing company that targets teenagers and young adults. You wouldn't survive if you tried to sell the same styles every year. As we said at the outset of this chapter, the key to successful marketing is meeting the needs of customers. This means knowing what they want right now, not last year.

Here's another illustration. The last few decades have witnessed monumental shifts in the makeup of the American workforce. The number of women at all levels has increased significantly, the workforce has become more diverse, and telecommuting is more common. More people place more importance on balancing their work lives with the rest of their lives, and fewer people are willing to sacrifice their health to the demands of hectic work schedules. With these changes have come new marketing opportunities. As women spend more time at work, the traditional duties of the "homemaker" have shifted to day-care centers, nannies, house-cleaning services, and (for those who can afford them) child chauffeurs, birthday-party coordinators, and even family-photo assemblers.[71] The number of gyms has mushroomed, the selection of home office furniture has expanded, and McDonald's has bowed to the wishes of the health-conscious by eliminating its "super-size" option.

Generation Gaps

Clothiers who target teens and young adults (such as Gap and Abercrombie & Fitch) must estimate the size of both current and future audiences. So must companies that specialize in products aimed at customers in other age brackets—say, young children or retirees. Marketers pay particular attention to population shifts because they can have dramatic effects on a consumer base, either increasing or decreasing the number of potential customers.

Marketers tend to assign most Americans born in the last sixty-eight years to one of three groups: the *baby-boom generation* (those born between 1946 and 1964), *Generation* X (1965 to 1975), and *Generation* Y—also known as "echo baby boomers" or "millenniums" (1976 to 2001).[72] In addition to age, members of each group tend to share common experiences, values, and attitudes that stay with them as they mature. These values and attitudes have a profound effect on both the products they want and the marketing efforts designed to sell products to them. Let's look a little more closely at some of the defining characteristics of each group.

Baby Boomers

The huge wave of baby boomers began arriving in 1946, following World War II, and marketers have been catering to them ever since. What are they like? Sociologists have attributed to them such characteristics as individuality, tolerance, and self-absorption.[73] There are seventy-seven million of them,[74] and as they marched through life over the course of five decades, marketers crowded the roadside to supply them with toys, clothes, cars, homes, and appliances—whatever they needed at the time. They're still a major marketing force, but their needs have changed: they're now the target market for Botox, pharmaceutical products, knee surgery, cataract surgery, financial investments, cruises, vacation homes, and retirement communities.

Generation X

Because birth rates had declined by the time the "Gen X" babies first arrived in 1965, this group had just one decade to grow its numbers. Thus, it's considerably smaller (forty-six million)[75] than the baby-boomer group, and it has also borne the brunt of rising divorce rates and the arrival of AIDS. Experts say, however, that they're adaptive and independent[76] and point out that even though they were once thought of as "slackers," they actually tend to be self-reliant and successful. At this point in their lives, most are at their peak earning power and affluent enough to make marketers stand up and take notice.

Generation Y

When they became parents, baby boomers delivered a group to rival their own. Born between 1976 and 2001, their sixty million[77] children are sometimes called "echo boomers" (because their population boom is a reverberation of the baby boom). They're still evolving, but they've already been assigned some attributes: they're committed to integrity and honesty, family oriented and close to parents, ethnically diverse and accepting of differences, upbeat and optimistic about the future (although the troubled economy is lessening their optimism), education focused, independent, and goal oriented.[78] They also seem to be coping fairly well: among today's teens, arrests, drug use, drunk driving, and school dropout rates are all down.[79]

Generation Ys are being courted by carmakers. Global car manufacturers have launched a number of 2014 cars designed to cater to the members of Generation Y.[80] Advertisers are also busy trying to find innovative ways to reach this group, but they're finding that it's not easy. Generation Ys grew up with computers and other modes of high technology, and they're used to doing several things at once—simultaneously watching TV, texting, and playing games on the computer. As a result, they're quite adept at tuning out ads. Try to reach them through TV ads, and they'll channel-surf right past them or click their TiVo remotes.[81] You can't get to them over the Internet because they know all about pop-up blockers. In one desperate attempt to get their attention, an advertiser paid college students fifty cents to view thirty-second ads on their computers.[82] Advertisers keep trying, because Generation Y is big enough to wreck a brand by giving it a cold shoulder.

8.6   Consumer Behavior

Why did you buy an Apple computer when your friend bought a Dell PC? What information did you collect before making the decision? What factors did you consider when evaluating alternatives? How did you make your final choice? Were you happy with your decision? To design effective strategies, marketers need to find the answers that consumers give to questions such as these. In other words, they try to improve their understanding of **consumer behavior**—the decision process that individuals go through when purchasing or using products. In Section 8, we'll look at the process that buyers go through in choosing one product over another. Then, we'll explore some factors that influence consumers' behavior.

> **consumer behavior**
>
> Decision process that individuals go through when purchasing or using products.

8.7   The Buying Process

Generally speaking, buyers run through a series of steps in deciding whether to purchase a particular product. Some purchases are made without much thought. You probably don't think much, for example, about the brand of gasoline you put in your car; you just stop at the most convenient place. Other purchases, however, require considerable thought. For example, you probably spent a lot of time deciding which college to attend. Let's revisit that decision as a means of examining the five steps that are involved in the consumer buying process and that are summarized in Figure 9.16: *need recognition, information search, evaluation, purchase,* and *postpurchase evaluation.*

FIGURE 9.16 The Buying Process

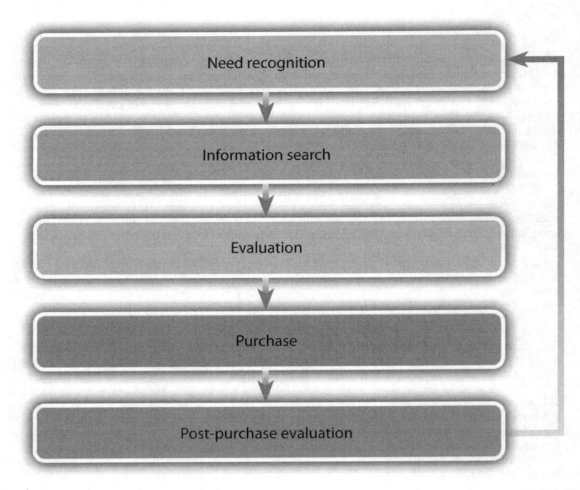

1. *Need recognition.* The process began when you recognized a need to go to college. Perhaps you wanted to prepare for a particular career, to become better educated, or to postpone going to work full time. Maybe your parents insisted.

2. *Information search.* Once you recognized the need to go to college, you probably started gathering information about colleges. You may have gone online and studied the Web sites posted by a few schools. Perhaps you attended college fairs or spoke with your high school guidance counselor. You probably talked with friends about your options. Once you let colleges know that you were interested, admissions departments likely sent you tons of information.

3. *Evaluation.* At this point, you studied the information you'd gathered. First, you probably decided what you wanted from a college. Perhaps price was your number-one criterion, or maybe distance from home. Maybe size was important, or reputation or available majors. Maybe it was the quality of the football team or the male-to-female ratio.

4. *Purchase.* Ultimately you made a "purchase" decision. In so doing, you focused on what was most important to you. Naturally, you could choose only among schools that had accepted you.

5. *Postpurchase evaluation.* The buying process didn't end when you selected a school. It continues today, while you're using the "product" you purchased. How many times have you rethought your decision? Are you happy with it? Would you make the same choice again?

Understanding the buying process of potential students is crucial to college administrators in developing marketing strategies to attract qualified "buyers." They'd certainly like to know what information you found useful, which factors most influenced your decision, and how you made your final choice. They'll also want to know whether you're happy with your choice. This is the kind of information that colleges are seeking when they solicit feedback, both from students who chose their schools and from those who didn't.

8.8   Influences on Buying Behavior

Did you ever buy something you knew you shouldn't buy but just couldn't help yourself—something you simply wanted? Maybe it was a spring-break trip to the Bahamas that you really couldn't afford. Objectively, you may have made a bad decision, but not all decisions are made on a purely objective basis. *Psychological* and *social influences* come into play. Let's take a closer look at each of these factors.

Psychological Influences

Under this category, we can identify at least five variables:

1. *Motivation.* The internal process that causes you to seek certain goals.
2. *Perception.* The way you select, organize, and interpret information.
3. *Learning.* Knowledge gained through experience and study.
4. *Attitudes.* Your predisposition to respond in particular ways because of learned values and beliefs.
5. *Personality.* The collection of attributes that characterize an individual.

Social Influences

Here, we find four factors:

1. *Family.*
2. *Reference groups.* Friends or other people with whom you identify.
3. *Economic or social status.*
4. *Culture.* Your set of accepted values.

It shouldn't be surprising that marketers are keenly interested in the effect of all these influences on your buying decisions. For instance, suppose the travel agency that sold you your spring-break getaway found that you bought the package because you viewed it as a reward for studying hard and doing well academically. In that case, it might promote student summer-travel programs as rewards for a hard year's work at school.

KEY TAKEAWAYS

- A number of forces over which it has little or no control affect a company's marketing activities.
- Taken together, they make up its **external marketing environment**, which includes regulatory and political activity, economic conditions, competitive forces, changes in technology, and social and cultural influences.
- Successful marketing often hinges on understanding **consumer behavior**—the decision process that individuals go through when purchasing or using products.
- Several psychological and social variables influence buyers' decisions. They go through a series of steps in reaching the decision to buy a product: *need recognition, information search, evaluation, purchase,* and *postpurchase evaluation.*

Before going to the next section of this chapter, take a few minutes to test your knowledge of the material covered in this section. Quizzes can be found under the "Resources" tab, "Study Aids: Quizzes."

1. Shifts in the external marketing environment often necessitate changes in a company's marketing plans. All companies are affected by external factors, but certain factors can have a stronger influence on particular products. Which of these five types of external factors—political/regulatory, economic, competitive, technological, or social/cultural—would have the greatest impact on each of the following products: a Toll Brothers home, P&G Tide laundry detergent, Apple iPod, Pfizer heart medicine, and Gap jeans. In matching products with external factors, apply each factor only once. Be sure to explain exactly how a given factor might affect product sales.

2. Experts have ascribed a number of attributes to Generation Y—people born between 1976 and 2001. On a scale of 1 to 10 (with 10 being the highest), indicate the extent to which each of the following attributes applies to you:

Attribute	To No Extent					To a Great Extent				
You're committed to integrity and honesty	1	2	3	4	5	6	7	8	9	10
You're family oriented and close to your parents	1	2	3	4	5	6	7	8	9	10
You're accepting of differences among people	1	2	3	4	5	6	7	8	9	10
You're upbeat and optimistic about the future	1	2	3	4	5	6	7	8	9	10
You're education focused	1	2	3	4	5	6	7	8	9	10
You're independent	1	2	3	4	5	6	7	8	9	10
You're goal oriented	1	2	3	4	5	6	7	8	9	10
You're fairly good at coping	1	2	3	4	5	6	7	8	9	10

9. CAREERS IN MARKETING

LEARNING OBJECTIVE

1. Describe opportunities in the field of marketing.

The field of marketing is extensive, and so are the opportunities for someone graduating with a marketing degree. While one person may seek out the excitement of an advertising agency that serves multiple clients, another might prefer to focus on brand management at a single organization. For someone else, working as a buyer for a retail chain is appealing. A few people might want to get into marketing research. Others might have an aptitude for supply chain management or *logistics management*, the aspect of supply chain management that focuses on the flow of products between suppliers and customers. Many people are attracted to sales positions because of the potential financial rewards. Let's look more closely at a few of your options.

9.1 Advertising

advertising agency

Marketing consulting firm that develops and executes promotional campaigns for clients.

If you're interested in advertising, you'll probably start out at an **advertising agency**—a marketing consulting firm that develops and executes promotional campaigns for clients. Professionals work on either the "creative" side (developing ads and other campaign materials) or the business side (acting as liaisons between the firm and its clients). If you're new, you'll probably begin as an assistant and work your way up. You might, for example, start as an assistant copywriter, helping to develop advertising messages. Or you could assist an account coordinator, helping in the management of accounts, including the planning and implementation of marketing campaigns.

9.2 Brand and Product Management

Brand and product managers are responsible for all aspects of the development and marketing of assigned products. They oversee the marketing program, including marketing research, pricing, distribution, and promotion. They track and analyze sales, gather feedback from customers, and assess the competition. You'd probably join the company as a brand assistant assigned to a more senior-level manager. After a few years, you may be promoted to assistant brand manager and, eventually, to brand manager. At this point, you'd be given responsibility for your own brand or product.

9.3   Marketing Research

Marketing researchers meet with company managers to determine their information needs. Then they gather and analyze relevant data, write reports, and present their findings and recommendations. If you want to get into this field, you'll need to acquire some skills in disciplines outside marketing, including statistics, research methods, and psychology. You'll start out as an assistant, but you may advance comparatively quickly.

9.4   Supply Chain and Logistics Management

Effective supply chain management is vital to success in today's business environment. Those who start their careers in supply chain management typically work in one of the following areas: purchasing and supply management, transportation and logistics, operations management, or inventory management and control. If this field appeals to you, you'll need to take courses in several disciplines: management, marketing, operations management, and accounting. If you want to specialize in logistics management, you'll be happy to know that many organizations—manufacturers, wholesalers, retailers, service providers, and transportation carriers—are looking for people interested in physical distribution. If you want to go into this field, you'll need strong quantitative skills in addition to a background in business with a specialization in marketing.

9.5   Retailing

Retailing offers all sorts of options, such as merchandise buying and store management. As a buyer, you'd select and buy merchandise for a department, a store, or maybe even an entire chain. Store managers display merchandise, supervise personnel, and handle day-to-day operations. Graduates looking for jobs in both areas generally start as trainees and work their way up.

9.6   Sales

Many marketing graduates begin their careers in sales positions, often for service organizations, such as insurance, real estate, and financial-services companies. Others are employed in the wholesale and retail trades or enter the manufacturing sector, selling anything from industrial goods to pharmaceuticals. To succeed in sales, you need a thorough understanding of customers' needs and an extensive knowledge of your product. You should also be able to communicate well, and you'll need strong interpersonal skills. Bear in mind that experience in sales is excellent preparation for almost any position in business.

KEY TAKEAWAYS

- The field of marketing is extensive, and so are the opportunities for someone graduating with a marketing degree.
- A few of the options available include advertising, brand and product management, marketing research, supply chain and logistics management, retailing, and sales.

Before going to the next chapter, take a few minutes to test your knowledge of the material covered in this section. Quizzes can be found under the "Resources" tab, "Study Aids: Quizzes."

EXERCISE

Do you find a career in marketing interesting? Why, or why not? Which of the following marketing career options are most appealing to you—advertising, brand and product management, marketing research, supply chain and logistics management, retailing, or sales? Why?

10. CASES AND PROBLEMS

LEARNING ON THE WEB

The Economics of Online Annoyance

You've just accessed a Web page and begun searching for the information you want to retrieve. Suddenly the page is plastered from top to bottom with *banner ads*. Some pop up, some float across the screen, and in some, animated figures dance and prance to inane music. As a user of the Internet, feel free to be annoyed. As a student of business, however, you should stop and ask yourself a few questions: Where do banner ads come from? Who stands to profit from them?

To get a handle on these questions, go to the How Stuff Works Web site (http://computer.howstuffworks.com/web-advertising.htm) and read the article "How Web Advertising Works," by Marshall Brain. When you've finished, answer the following questions *from the viewpoint of a company advertising on the Web*:

1. What are the advantages and disadvantages of banner ads? Why are they less popular with advertisers today than they were about ten years ago?
2. What alternative forms of Web advertising are more common today? (For each of these alternative forms, describe the type of ad, explain how it's more effective than banner advertising, and list any disadvantages.)
3. Why are there so many ads on the Web? Is it easy to make money selling ads on the Web? Why, or why not?
4. Assume that you're in charge of Web advertising for a company that sells cell-phone ring tones. On which sites would you place your ads and what type of ads would you use? Why?

CAREER OPPORTUNITIES

So Many Choices

How would you like to work for an advertising agency? How about promoting a new or top-selling brand? Want to try your hand at sales? Or does marketing research or logistics management sound more appealing? With a marketing degree, you can pursue any of these career options—and more. To learn more about these options, go to the WetFeet Web site (https://www.wetfeet.com/articles/careers-and-industries-overview). Scroll down to the "Careers" section and select **two** of the following career options that interest you: advertising, brand management, marketing, sales, or supply chain management. For each of the two selected, answer the following questions:

1. What would you do if you worked in this field?
2. Who does well?
3. What requirements are needed to be hired into this field?
4. Are job prospects in the field positive or negative?
5. What career track would you follow?

Finally, write a paragraph responding to these questions: Does a career in marketing appeal to you? Why, or why not? Which career option do you find most interesting? Why?

ETHICS ANGLE

Pushing Cigarettes Overseas

A senior official of the United Nation's World Health Organization (WHO) claims that the marketing campaigns of international tobacco companies are targeting half a billion young people in the Asia Pacific region by linking cigarette smoking to glamorous and attractive lifestyles. WHO accuses tobacco companies of "falsely associating use of their products with desirable qualities such as glamour, energy and sex appeal, as well as exciting outdoor activities and adventure."[83] WHO officials have expressed concern that young females are a major focus of these campaigns.

The organization called on policymakers to support a total ban on tobacco advertising saying that "the bombardment of messages through billboards, newspapers, magazines, radio and television ads, as well as sports and fashion sponsorships and other ploys, are meant to deceive young people into trying their first stick."[84] WHO stresses the need for a total ban on advertising as partial bans let tobacco companies switch from one marketing scheme to another.

WHO officials believe that extensive tobacco advertising gives young people the false impression that smoking is normal and diminishes their ability to comprehend that it can kill. Representatives of the organization assert that the tobacco industry is taking advantage of young people's vulnerability to advertising.

Instructions: Read the following articles and provide your opinion on the questions that follow:

- Agence France Presse (AFP), "WHO: Half a Billion Young Asians at Risk from Tobacco Addiction," May 31, 2008, http://womanat35.wordpress.com/2008/05/31/who-half-a-billion-young-asians-at-risk-from-tobacco-addiction.
- Associated Press, "WHO Criticizes Tobacco Industry Focus on Asian Young People," May 30, 2008, http://www.chinapost.com.tw/news/2008/05/30/158840/WHO-criticizes.htm.

Provide your opinion on the following questions:

- U.S. laws prohibit advertising by the tobacco companies. Should developing countries in which cigarette smoking is promoted by the international tobacco companies follow suit—should they also ban tobacco advertising?
- Are U.S. companies that engage in these advertising practices acting unethically? Why, or why not?
- Should international policymakers support a total ban on tobacco advertising? Why, or why not?
- If tobacco advertising was banned globally, what would be the response of the international tobacco companies?

TEAM-BUILDING SKILLS

Build a Better iPod and They Will Listen

Right now, Apple is leading the pack of consumer-electronics manufacturers with its successful iPod. But that doesn't mean that Apple's lead in the market can't be surmounted. Perhaps some enterprising college students will come up with an idea for a better iPod and put together a plan for bringing it to market. After all, Apple founders (the late Steve Jobs and Stephen Wozniak) were college students (actually, college dropouts) who found entrepreneurship more rewarding than scholarship. Here's your team assignment for this exercise:

1. Go to the *BusinessWeek* Web site (http://www.businessweek.com/technology/content/dec2004/tc2004127_7607_tc185.htm) and read the article "Could Apple Blow Its iPod Lead?"
2. Create a marketing strategy for your hypothetical iPod competitor. Be sure that you touch on all the following bases:

   - Select a target market for your product.
   - Develop your product so that it offers features that meet the needs of your target market.
   - Describe the industry in which you'll compete.
   - Set a price for your product and explain your pricing strategy.
   - Decide what distribution channels you'll use to get your product to market.
   - Develop a promotion mix to create demand for your product.

3. Write a report that details your marketing strategy.

Made in China—Why Not Sell in China?

One of Wow Wee's recent robots, Roboscooper, is manufactured in China. Why shouldn't it sell the product in China? In fact, the company has introduced its popular robot to the Chinese market through a Toys "R" Us store in Hong Kong. Expanding into other parts of China, however, will require a well-crafted, well-executed marketing plan. You're director of marketing for Wow Wee, and you've been asked to put together a plan to expand sales of Roboscooper in China. You can be introduced to Roboscooper by going to the product section of Wow Wee's site: http://www.wowwee.com/en/products/toys/robots/robotics/roboscooper. To get some background on selling toys in China, go to the Epoch Times Web site (http://www.theepochtimes.com/news/4-12-23/25184.html) and read the article "China Could Soon Become Booming Toy Market." Then, draw up a brief marketing plan for increasing sales in China, being sure to include all the following components:

- Profile of your target market (gender, age, income level, geographic location, interests, and so forth)
- Proposed changes to the company's current marketing mix: modifications to product design, pricing, distribution, and promotional strategies
- Estimated sales in units for each of the next five years, including a list of the factors that you considered in arriving at your projections
- Discussion of threats and opportunities posed by expansion in the Chinese market

ENDNOTES

1. To see the robot in action, go to Wow Wee Toys, "Robosapien: A Fusion of Technology and Personality," http://www.wowwee.com/en/products/toys/robots/robotics/robosapiens/robosapien, and click on "Robosapien." Then click on the video under "Watch."

2. Michael Taylor, "Innovative Toy Packs a Punch: The Popular Robosapien Has Been Flying Off the Shelves, with 1.5 Million Toys Already," *Access My Library*, http://www.accessmylibrary.com/coms2/summary_0286-14477835_ITM (accessed October 12, 2011).

3. Wow Wee Toys, "Awards and Archives," http://www.wowwee.com/en/company/awards-archives (accessed April 27, 2014).

4. American Marketing Association, "The American Marketing Association Definition for Marketing," https://www.ama.org/AboutAMA/Pages/Definition-of-Marketing.aspx (accessed April 27, 2014).

5. Medtronics, "Company History," http://www.fundinguniverse.com/company-histories/Medtronic-Inc-Company-History.html (accessed April 27, 2014).

6. Michael Arndt, "High Tech—and Handcrafted," *BusinessWeek Online*, July 5, 2004, http://www.businessweek.com/magazine/content/04_27/b3890113_mz018.htm (accessed April 27, 2014).

7. Hyundai Motor America, "Special Programs: College Graduate Program," http://www.hyundaiusa.com/financing/specialoffers/collegegraduate.aspx (accessed April 27, 2014).

8. "McDonald's Test Markets Spam," *Pacific Business News*, June 11, 2002, http://www.bizjournals.com/pacific/stories/2002/06/10/daily22.html (accessed April 27, 2014).

9. "The Super McDonalds," *Halfbakery*, http://www.halfbakery.com/idea/The_20Super_20McDonalds (accessed April 27, 2014); "Interesting Menu Items from McDonalds in Asia," *Weird Asia News*, http://www.weirdasianews.com/2010/03/23/blank-interesting-menu-items-mcdonalds-asia (accessed April 27, 2014).

10. "Coolest Inventions 2003: Parking-Space Invader," *Time* (Online Edition), http://www.time.com/time/2003/inventions/invprius.html (accessed April 27, 2014).

11. "2010 Toyota Prius Self Park In-car Demo," YouTube video, 2:41, posted by "htmlspinnr," March 4, 2009, http://www.youtube.com/watch?v=kxTAYqs5bTY (accessed April 27, 2014).

12. Rob Rubin and William Bluestein, "Applying Technographics," *Forrester Research*, http://www.kaschassociates.com/417web/417modahlmaster.htm (accessed October 13, 2011).

13. Information in this section was obtained through an interview with the director of marketing at Wow Wee Toys Ltd. conducted on July 15, 2004.

14. Brandan Light, "Kellogg's Goes Online for Consumer Research," *Packaging Digest*, July 1, 2004, http://www.packagingdigest.com/article/345315-Kellogg_s_goes_online_for_consumer_research.php (accessed April 28, 2014).

15. "Best Global Brands 2013," Interbrand, http://www.interbrand.com/en/best-global-brands/2013/Best-Global-Brands-2013-Brand-View.aspx (accessed April 28, 2014).

16. Nabisco, "So Many Delicious Ways to Enjoy Nabisco 100 Calorie Packs," http://www.nabiscoworld.com/100caloriepacks (accessed April 28, 2014).

17. Cliff Edwards, "Ready to Buy a Home Robot?" *Business Week*, July 19, 2004, 84–90.

18. "Finance," Yahoo!, http://finance.yahoo.com/q?s=AMZN&ql=1 (accessed April 28, 2014).

19. Wal-Mart, "Logistics," http://corporate.walmart.com/our-story/our-business/logistics (accessed April 28, 2014).

20. Wal-Mart, "Our Locations," http://corporate.walmart.com/our-story/our-business/locations (accessed April 28, 2014).

21. Andres Lillo, "Wal-Mart Gains Strength from Distribution Chain," *Home Textiles Today*, March 24, 2003, http://www.hometextilestoday.com/article/495437-Wal_Mart_gains_strength_from_distribution_chain.php (accessed April 28, 2014).

22. David Maloney, "Warehouse of the Month / Destination: Production," *WITRON*, August 1, 2003.

23. "BMW Oxford Plant: The MINI Plant," *Automotive Intelligence*, July 10, 2001, http://www.autointell.com/european_companies/BMW/mini/oxford-plant/bmw-oxford-plant-01.htm (accessed April 28, 2014). Also see BMW, "BMW Dingolfing (Germany) Virtual Plant Tour," http://www.bmw-plant-dingolfing.com (accessed April 28, 2014).

24. U.S. Department of Transportation, Bureau of Transportation Statistics, *Commercial Freight Activities in the U.S.by Mode of Transportation (1993, 1997, and 2002)*, http://www.bts.gov/publications/freight_shipments_in_america/html/table_01.html (accessed April 28, 2014).

25. U.S. Department of Labor, Bureau of Labor Statistics, *Truck, Transportation and Warehousing*, Career Guide to Industry, http://bls.gov/oco/cg/cgs021.htm (accessed October 17, 2011).

26. Lawrence D. Fredendall and Ed Hill, *Basics of Supply Chain Management* (Boca Raton, FL: St. Lucie Press, 2001), 8.

27. "Supply Chain Management Helps Domino's Deliver," *Retail Solutions Online*, October 1, 2000, http://www.retailsolutionsonline.com/article.mvc/Supply-Chain-Management-Helps-Dominos-Deliver-0002 (accessed April 28, 2014).

28. Philip Kotler, *Marketing Management*, 11th ed. (Upper Saddle River, NJ: Prentice Hall, 2003), 11.

29. The concept of the value chain was first analyzed by Michael Porter in *Competitive Advantage: Creating and Sustaining Superior Performance* (New York: The Free Press, 1985).

30. Ritz-Carlton, "About Us," http://corporate.ritzcarlton.com/en/about/goldstandards.htm (accessed April 28, 2014).

31. Motel 6, "Motel 6 Corporate Profile," http://www.motel6.com/about/corpprofile.aspx (accessed April 28, 2014).

32. Caitlin A. Johnson, "Cutting Through Advertising Clutter," *CBSNews*, February 11, 2009, http://www.cbsnews.com/stories/2006/09/17/sunday/main2015684.shtml (accessed April 28, 2014).

33. Louise Story, "Anywhere the Eye Can See, It's Likely to See an Ad," *The New York Times*, January 15, 2007, http://www.nytimes.com/2007/01/15/business/media/15everywhere.html?pagewanted=all (accessed April 28, 2014).

34. Seth Godin, *Permission Marketing: Turning Strangers into Friends, and Friends into Customers* (New York: Simon & Schuster, 1999), 31.

35. Louise Story, "Anywhere the Eye Can See, It's Likely to See an Ad," *The New York Times*, January 15, 2007, http://www.nytimes.com/2007/01/15/business/media/15everywhere.html?pagewanted=all (accessed April 28, 2014).

36. Nantucket Allserve, Inc., "Nantucket Nectars from the Beginning," http://www.drpeppersnapplegroup.com/brands/nantucket-nectars (accessed April 28, 2014).

37. Kevin J. Clancy, "Sleuthing for New Products, Not Slashing for Growth," *Across the Board*, September–October 2001, http://www.copernicusmarketing.com/about/docs/new_products.htm (accessed May 21, 2006).

38. Hyatt Hotels and Resorts, "Hyatt and Chase Launch First Ever Hyatt-Branded Credit Card," http://www.hyattpressroom.com/content/hyatt/en/news_releases0/2010/Hyatt-And-Chase-Launch-First-Ever-Hyatt-Branded-Credit-Card.html (accessed April 28, 2014).

39. Kelly B., "Pick of the Week: Apps, Books, TV, Music and More!" *Starbucks Blog*, August 22, 2011, http://www.starbucks.com/blog/pick-of-the-week-apps-books-tv-music-and-more-/1064 (accessed April 28, 2014).

40. "Tickle Me Elmo: Using the Media to Create a Marketing Sensation," *MediaSmarts*, http://mediasmarts.ca/sites/default/files/pdfs/lesson-plan/Lesson_Creating_Marketing_Frenzy.pdf (accessed April 28, 2014).

41. "Fortune's Most Admired Companies, 2014," *Fortune*, http://money.cnn.com/magazines/fortune/most-admired (accessed April 29, 2014).

42. Microsoft Corporation, "How to Get Repeat Customers—7 Steps," http://www.microsoft.com/business/en-us/resources/management/customer-relations/how-to-get-repeat-customers-7-steps.aspx?fbid=SKGjR9kqr8V (accessed April 29, 2014).

43. "Two Remain at World Series of Poker," *ESPN Poker*, November 7, 2010, http://sports.espn.go.com/espn/poker/news/story?id=5776591&source=ESPNHeadlines (accessed April 29, 2014); Stephane Fitch, "Stacking the Deck: Harrah's Wants Your Money," *Forbes*, July 5, 2004, http://www.forbes.com/forbes/2004/0705/132.html (accessed April 29, 2014).

44. "Sheraton Hotels Lure Travelers with the Promise of a Good Night's Sleep in New $12 Million Television and Print Ad Campaign," *Hotel News Resource*, http://www.hotelnewsresource.com/article10706Sheraton_Hotels_Lure_Travelers_with_the_Promise_of_a_Good_Night_s_Sleep_in_New_____Million_Television_and_Print_Ad_Campaign.html (accessed April 29, 2014).

45. Seth Godin, *Permission Marketing: Turning Strangers into Friends, and Friends into Customers* (New York: Simon & Schuster, 1999), 40–52.

46. Anthony Bianco, "The Vanishing Mass Market," *Business Week*, July 12, 2004, 61–68.

47. Devon G. Artis, "Advantages of Social Media Marketing," *Ezine Articles*, http://ezinearticles.com/?Advantages-of-Social-Media-Marketing&id=6111206 (accessed April 29, 2014); Susan Ward, "Social Media Marketing," *About.com*, http://sbinfocanada.about.com/od/socialmedia/g/socmedmarketing.htm (accessed April 29, 2014); Laura Lake, "Social Media Marketing—Is It Right for your Business?" *About.com*, http://marketing.about.com/od/internetmarketing/a/socialmediaforyourbiz.htm (accessed April 29, 2014).

48. Matthew Yeomans, "Mountain Dew's Ongoing Dewmocracy—Ripping Up the Book on Campaigns," *SMI*, January 29, 2010, http://socialmediainfluence.com/2010/01/29/mountain-dews-ongoing-dewmocracy-ripping-up-the-book-on-campaigns (accessed April 29, 2014); Jennifer Cirillo, "DEWmocracy 2 Continues to Buzz," *Beverage World*, http://www.beverageworld.com/index.php?option=com_content&view=article&id=37525&catid=34 (accessed April 29, 2014).

49. Jennifer Cirillo, "DEWmocracy 2 Continues to Buzz," *Beverage World*, http://www.google.com/url?sa=t&rct=j&q=&esrc=s&source=web&cd=2&ved=0CDMQFjAB&url=http://jordanschole2012/04/dewmocracy-21.doc&ei=5IRgU_H7Oca_sQT9mIGgDg&usg=AFQjCNFvDMlyvbWo52kQqQ (accessed April 29, 2014).

50. "Five Game-Changing Social Media Marketing Campaigns," *Mashable Social Media*, http://mashable.com/2010/10/08/creative-social-media-campaigns (accessed April 29, 2014).

51. Jennifer Cirillo, "DEWmocracy 2 Continues to Buzz," *Beverage World*, http://www.google.com/url?sa=t&rct=j&q=&esrc=s&source=web&cd=2&ved=0CDMQFjAB&url=http://jordanschole2012/04/dewmocracy-21.doc&ei=5IRgU_H7Oca_sQT9mIGgDg&usg=AFQjCNFvDMlyvbWo52kQqQ (accessed April 29, 2014).

52. "Coca-Cola Virtual Gifts Trigger Peek at Super Bowl Ads," *Chief Marketer*, February 4, 2010, http://www.chiefmarketer.com/news/coca-cola-virtual-gifts-trigger-peek-at-super-bowl-ads-04022010 (accessed April 29, 2014).

53. Jennifer Van Grove, "Mayors of Starbucks Now Get Discounts Nationwide with Foursquare," *Mashable Business*, May 17, 2010, http://mashable.com/2010/05/17/starbucks-foursquare-mayor-specials (accessed April 29, 2014).

54. Jennifer Van Grove, "Celebrate Tax Day with Free Stuff," *Mashable Business*, April 15, 2010, http://mashable.com/2010/04/15/tax-day-2010-freebies (accessed April 29, 2014).

55. Amir Efrati, "How Twitter's Ads Work," *Wall Street Journal*, July 28, 2011, http://blogs.wsj.com/digits/2011/07/28/how-twitters-ads-work (accessed April 29, 2014).

56. Dianna Dilworth, "Twitter Debuts Promoted Tweets; Virgin America, Starbucks among First To Use Service," *Direct Marketing News*, April 13, 2010, http://www.dmnews.com/twitter-debuts-promoted-tweets-virgin-america-starbucks-among-first-to-use-service/article/167885 (accessed April 29, 2014).

57. "Starbucks Free Pastry Day: July 21, 2009," *Starbucks's Facebook Event Page*, http://www.facebook.com/event.php?eid=111190617889 (accessed April 29, 2014).

58. Jennifer Van Grove, "Starbucks Used Social Media to Get One Million to Stores in One Day," *Mashable*, June 08, 2010, http://mashable.com/author/jennifer-van-grove (accessed April 29, 2014).

59. Mark Walsh, "Starbucks Tops 10 Million Facebook Fans," *Marketing Daily*, Jul 14, 2010, http://www.mediapost.com/publications/article/132008 (accessed April 29, 2014).

60. Adam Ostrow, "Starbucks Free Pastry Day: A Social Media Triple Shot," *Mashable Social Media*, July 21, 2009, http://mashable.com/2009/07/21/starbucks-free-pastry-day (accessed April 29, 2014).

61. Susan Ward, "Social Media Marketing," *About.com*, http://sbinfocanada.about.com/od/socialmedia/g/socmedmarketing.htm (accessed April 29, 2014).

62. Georgina Prodhan, "Marketers Struggle to Harness Social Media—Survey," *Reuters*, October 11, 2011, http://www.reuters.com/article/2011/10/11/socialmedia-ibm-idUSL5E7LA3JO20111011 (accessed April 29, 2014).

63. Georgina Prodhan, "Marketers Struggle to Harness Social Media—Survey," *Reuters*, October 11, 2011, http://www.reuters.com/article/2011/10/11/socialmedia-ibm-idUSL5E7LA3JO20111011 (accessed April 29, 2014).

64. "Simon Pestridge From Nike Makes Future Advertising Sound Simple," *Ronnestam.com*, March 19, 2010, http://www.ronnestam.com/simon-pestridge-from-nike-make-future-advertising-sound-simple (accessed April 29, 2014).

65. Katarina Gustafsson, "Lego Tops U.S. Toymaker Rivals as Full-Year Sales Jump 10 Percent," *Bloomberg News*, http://www.bloomberg.com/news/2014-02-27/lego-beats-u-s-toymaker-rivals-as-full-year-revenue-jumps-10-.html (accessed April 29, 2014).

66. Katarina Gustafsson, "Lego Tops U.S. Toymaker Rivals as Full-Year Sales Jump 10 Percent," *Bloomberg News*, http://www.bloomberg.com/news/2014-02-27/lego-beats-u-s-toymaker-rivals-as-full-year-revenue-jumps-10-.html (accessed April 29, 2014).

67. LEGO Group, *Annual Report 2003*, http://cache.LEGO.com/upload/contentTemplating/AboutUsFactsAndFiguresContent/otherfiles/download049677E7DF3EF6655CF3EE4ADF8DF598.pdf (accessed April 29, 2014).

68. See Charles Fishman, "Why Can't LEGO Click," *Fast Company*, September 1, 2001, http://www.fastcompany.com/43497/why-cant-lego-click (accessed April 29, 2014).

69. LEGO Group, *Annual Report 2003*, http://cache.LEGO.com/upload/contentTemplating/AboutUsFactsAndFiguresContent/otherfiles/download049677E7DF3EF6655CF3EE4ADF8DF598.pdf (accessed April 29, 2014).

70. For an excellent history of the life of LEGO, see Kartikeya Batra, "The Life of LEGO," *Bizwatch*, October 17, 2010, http://bizwatchkartikeyabatra.blogspot.com/2010/10/life-of-lego.html (accessed April 29, 2014). Much of the material covered in this section was derived from this article.

71. Sandra Tsing Loh, "Nannyhood and Apple Pie," *The Atlantic*, October 1, 2003, 122–23.

72. Jessica R. Sincavage, "The Labor Force and Unemployment: Three Generations of Change," *Monthly Labor Review*, June 2004, 34.

73. "Valuing Generational Differences," https://www.google.com/url?sa=t&rct=j&q=&esrc=s&source=web&cd=1&ved=0CCAQFjAA&url=http%3A%2F%2Fneashrm.s (accessed April 29, 2014).

74. "Baby Boomer Generation Fast Facts," *CNN.com*, http://www.cnn.com/2013/11/06/us/baby-boomer-generation-fast-facts (accessed April 29, 2014).

75. "Who Is Generation X?" *Generations (blog)*, http://www.jenx67.com/who-is-generation-x (accessed April 29, 2014).

76. "Generation X," *ValueOptions*, http://www.valueoptions.com/spotlight_YIW/gen_x.htm (accessed April 29, 2014).

77. Ellen Neuborne and Kathleen Kerwin, "Generation Y," *BusinessWeek Online*, February 15, 1999, http://www.businessweek.com/stories/1999-02-14/generation-y (accessed April 29, 2014).

78. Ellen Neuborne and Kathleen Kerwin, "Generation Y," *BusinessWeek Online*, February 15, 1999, http://www.businessweek.com/stories/1999-02-14/generation-y (accessed April 29, 2014); Kari Richardson, "Zell Conference Reveals Next Marketing Wave," *Kellogg World* (Kellogg School of Management, Northwestern University, Winter 2002), http://www.kellogg.northwestern.edu/kwo/win02/inbrief/zell.htm (accessed April 29, 2014).

79. Bruce Tulgan and Carolyn A. Martin, "Book Excerpt: Managing Generation Y—Part I," *BusinessWeek Online*, September 28, 2001, http://www.businessweek.com/smallbiz/content/sep2001/sb20010928_113.htm (accessed April 29, 2014).

80. Jason Siu, "Top 10 Cars Favored by Gen Y," Autoguide.com, February 21, 2013, http://www.autoguide.com/auto-news/2013/02/top-10-cars-favored-by-gen-y.html (accessed April 29, 2014).

81. Anthony Bianco, "The Vanishing Mass Market," *Business Week*, July 12, 2004, 61–68.

82. Stephen Baker, "Channeling the Future," *BusinessWeek Online*, July 12, 2004, http://www.businessweek.com/magazine/content/04_28/b3891013_mz001.htm (accessed October 21, 2011).

83. Agence France Presse, "WHO: Half a Billion Young Asians at Risk from Tobacco Addiction," *This Woman's Views* (blog), May 31, 2008, http://womanat35.wordpress.com/2008/05/31/who-half-a-billion-young-asians-at-risk-from-tobacco-addiction (accessed April 29, 2014).

84. "WHO Criticizes Tobacco Industry Focus on Asian Young People," *The China Post*, May 30, 2008, http://www.chinapost.com.tw/news/2008/05/30/158840/WHO-criticizes.htm (accessed April 30, 2014).

CHAPTER 10

Product Design and Development

RIDING THE CREST OF INNOVATION

Video Clip

View the video online at: http://www.youtube.com/v/fLzcsJtFZrs

Have you ever wanted to go surfing but couldn't find a body of water with decent waves? You no longer have a problem: the PowerSki Jetboard makes its own waves. This innovative product combines the ease of waterskiing with the excitement of surfing. A high-tech surfboard with a forty-five-horsepower, forty-five-pound watercraft engine, the PowerSki Jetboard has the power of a small motorcycle. Experienced surfers use it to get to the top of rising ocean waves, but if you're just a weekend water-sports enthusiast, you can get your adrenaline going by skimming across the surface of a local lake at forty miles an hour. All you have to do is submerge the tail of the board, slide across on your belly, and stand up (with the help of a flexible pole). To innocent bystanders, you'll look like a very fast water-skier without a boat.

Where do product ideas like the PowerSki Jetboard come from? How do people create products that meet customer needs? How are *ideas* developed and turned into actual *products*? How do you forecast demand for a product? How do you protect your product ideas? These are some of the questions that we'll address in this chapter.

1. WHAT IS A PRODUCT?

product

Something that can be marketed to customers because it provides a benefit and satisfies a need.

Basically, a **product** is something that can be marketed to customers because it provides them with a benefit and satisfies a need. It can be a physical *good*, such as the PowerSki Jetboard, or a *service*, such as a haircut or a taxi ride. The distinction between goods and services isn't always clear-cut. Say, for example, that a company hires a professional to provide an in-house executive training program on "netiquette" (e-mail etiquette). Off the top of our heads, most of us would say that the company is buying a service. What if the program is offered online? We'd probably still argue that the product is a service. But what if the company buys training materials that the trainer furnishes on DVD? Is the customer still buying a service? Probably not: we'd have to say that when it buys the DVD, the company is buying a tangible good.

In this case, the product that satisfies the customer's need has both a tangible component (the training materials on DVD) and an intangible component (the educational activities performed by the seller). Not surprisingly, many products have both tangible and intangible components. If, for example, you buy a Hewlett-Packard computer, you get not only the computer (a tangible good) but certain promises to answer any technical questions that you might have and certain guarantees to fix your computer if it breaks within a specified time period (intangible services).

1.1 Types of Product Developments

New product developments can be grouped into four major categories: new-to-the-company, improvement of existing product, extension of product line, and new-to-the-market.

FIGURE 10.1

Holiday decorating kits have extended Just Born's product line beyond Peeps.

© 2010 Jupiterimages Corporation

For examples of the first three types of new product developments, we'll take a look at Just Born. The company is known for its famous "Marshmallow Peeps," and consequently its management is very interested in marshmallows. It conducted research that revealed that families use marshmallows in lots of ways, including crafts and decorating. This led Just Born to develop an Easter decorating kit that used Peeps marshmallows. It was such a hit that the company followed by creating decorating kits for Halloween and the Christmas season. Because similar products are made by other companies, the decorating kits are not "new to the market" but are "new to the company." Now, let's look at another product development involving Just Born's also famous Mike & Ike's. The marketing people at Just Born discovered that teenagers prefer to buy candies that come in pouches (which fit into their pants pockets) rather than in small boxes. In response, the company reduced the piece size, added some new ingredients, and put the Mike & Ike's in pouches. This "improvement in an existing product" resulted in a 20 percent annual sales jump for Mike & Ike's. Our last look at Just Born demonstrates an approach used by the company to "extend its existing product line." Most of us like chocolate and most of us also like marshmallow, so how about putting them together? This is just what Just Born did—the company extended its Peeps product line to include "Peeps in a chocolate egg." Consumers loved the combination, and its success prompted the company to extend its product line again and launch a chocolate crispy version for Easter.

New-to-the-Market Products

The PowerSki Jetboard is a "new-to-the-market product." Before it was invented, no comparable product existed. Launching a new-to-the-market product is very risky, and only about 10 percent of products created fall into this category. On a positive note, introducing a new product to the market can be very profitable, because the product often enjoys a temporary monopolistic position.

Entrepreneurial Start-Ups

Inventors of new-to-the-market products often form entrepreneurial start-ups to refine their product idea and bring it to market. This was the path taken by Bob Montgomery, inventor of the PowerSki Jetboard. As is typical of entrepreneurial start-ups, the company that Montgomery founded has these characteristics:[1]

- *It's characterized by innovative products and/or practices.* Before the PowerSki Jetboard was invented, no comparable product existed.

- *Its goals include profitability and growth.* Because the patented Jetboard enjoys a temporary monopolistic position, PowerSki potentially could be very profitable.

- *It focuses on new opportunities.* Bob Montgomery dreamed of creating the first motorized surfboard. This dream began when he and a few of his surfer friends (all around age twelve) missed a wave because it was too far down the beach for them to catch. He imagined that if he was on a motorized surfboard (instead of an ordinary one that you had to paddle), he would have been able to catch that wave. His dream became the mission of his company: "PowerSki International Corp. was founded to deliver the patented PowerSki Jetboard, the world's only motorized surfboard, and its engine technology to the world market. It's PowerSki's goal to bring the experience of surfing to everyone on lakes, rivers, seas, and the ocean. 'Now everybody has an ocean, and can ride an endless wave.'"[2]

- *Its owners are willing to take risks.* Anybody who starts *any* business is taking a risk of some kind. The key to *entrepreneurial* risk is related to the idea of innovation: as Woody Allen once put it, "If you're not failing every now and again, it's a sign you're not doing anything very innovative."[3]

How to Take a Calculated Risk

As Montgomery learned, the introduction of an *innovative* product to the market is more unpredictable, and thus more risky, than the introduction of a market-tested product. Starting up a store to sell an improved version of an existing surfboard entails one level of risk; starting up a business to market the first motorized surfboard entails quite another. Even though the introduction of new-to-the-market products are more risky, some of this risk can be avoided. What if, for example, Montgomery had brought the Jetboard to market only to discover that many of the buyers in his target market—watersports enthusiasts—couldn't easily maneuver the Jetboard? We could then say that he took an unnecessarily risky step in bringing his product to market, but we could also say that he simply attempted to market his product without adequate information. Surely a little research would have alerted Montgomery to the probable consequences of his decision to go to market when he did and with his product in its current state of development.

A couple of final words, therefore, about introducing an entirely new product to the market. First, this type of product introduction is about carefully *calculated* risks, not *unnecessary* risks. Second, though little is certain in the entrepreneurial world, most decision making can be improved with input from one or both of two sources:

1. Information gathered from research
2. Knowledge gained from personal experience

Again, you can't be *certain* about any results, but remember that *uncertainty* reflects merely the lack of complete knowledge or information; thus, the more knowledge and information that you can bring to bear on a situation, the less uncertain—and the less risky—the decision becomes.[4] In short, always do your homework, and if you're new to entrepreneurship or to your market, make it a point to work with people who know from experience what they're talking about.

- A **product** is something that can be marketed to customers because it provides them with a benefit and satisfies a need. Products can be goods or services or a combination of both.
- A "new-to-the-company product" is a good or a service that is new to the company but has been sold by a competitor in the past—for example, Peeps marshmallow Easter decorating kits.
- An "improvement in an existing product" is an enhancement of a product already on the market—for example, a change of ingredients and packaging for Mike & Ike's.
- An "extension to an existing product line" is a new product developed as a variation of an already existing product—for example, Peeps chocolate eggs.
- A "new-to-the-market product" is a good or a service that has not been available to consumers or manufacturers in the past—for example, the PowerSki Jetboard.
- Four characteristics of the entrepreneurial start-up are:
    1. It's characterized by innovative products and/or practices.
    2. Its goals include profitability and growth.
    3. It focuses on new opportunities.
    4. Its owners are willing to take risks.
- Entrepreneurship is about carefully *calculated* risks, not *unnecessary* risks. Most entrepreneurial decision making can be improved with input from one or both of two sources:
    1. Information gathered from research
    2. Knowledge gained from personal experience

Before going to the next section of this chapter, take a few minutes to test your knowledge of the material covered in this section. Quizzes can be found under the "Resources" tab, "Study Aids: Quizzes."

Identify a good or a service for each of the following product development categories: new-to-the-market, new-to-the-company, improvement of existing product, and extension of product line. To come up with the products, you might visit a grocery store or a mall. Don't use the Just Born examples presented in the chapter.

2. WHERE DO PRODUCT IDEAS COME FROM?

1. **Explain where product ideas come from.**
2. **Identify the approaches used by firms to seek product ideas.**

For some people, coming up with a great product idea is a gratifying adventure. For most, however, it's a daunting task. The key to coming up with a product idea is identifying something that customers want—or, perhaps more important, filling an unmet customer need. In coming up with a product idea, ask not "what do I want to sell?" but rather "what does the customer want to buy?"[5] With this piece of advice in mind, let's get back to the task of coming up with a product idea. Nobel Prize–winning chemist Linus Pauling suggested that "the best way to have a good idea is to have lots of ideas," and though this notion might seem a little whimsical at first, it actually makes a lot of sense, especially if you're trying to be innovative in the entrepreneurial sense. Every year, for example, companies launch about thirty thousand new food, beverage, and beauty products, and up to 90 percent fail within a year.[6] You might need ten good ideas just to have one that stands a chance.

2.1 Purple Cow Ideas

So where do these ideas come from? Product ideas can originate from almost anywhere. How many times have you looked at a product that just hit the market and said, "I could have thought of that"? Just about anybody can come up with a product *idea*; basically, you just need a little imagination. Success is more likely to result from a truly remarkable product—something that grabs the attention of consumers. Entrepreneur and marketing consultant Seth Godin refers to truly remarkable products as "purple cows."[7] He came up with the term while driving through the countryside one day. As he drove along, his interest was attracted by the hundreds of cows dotting the countryside. After a while, however, he started to ignore the cows because looking at them had become tedious. For one thing, they were all brown, and it occurred to him that a glimpse of a *purple* cow would be worth writing home about. People would tend to remember a purple cow; in fact, they might even want one.

Who thinks up "purple cow" ideas? Where do the truly remarkable business ideas come from? As we pointed out in an earlier chapter, entrepreneurs and small business owners are a rich source of new product ideas (according to the Small Business Administration, 55 percent of all new product innovations come from small businesses). Take Dean Kamen, inventor of the Segway Human Transporter, a battery-operated vehicle that responds to the rider's movements: lean forward and you can go straight ahead at 12.5 miles per hour; to stop, just tilt backward. This revolutionary product is only one of Kamen's many remarkable business ideas. He invented his first product—a wearable infusion pump for administering chemotherapy and other drugs—while he was still a college undergraduate.[8] Jacob Dunnack is also getting an early entrepreneurial start. At *age six*, Jacob became frustrated one day when he took his baseball bat to his grandmother's house but forgot to take some baseballs as well. His solution? A hollow baseball bat that holds baseballs. Dunnack's invention, now called the JD Batball, was quickly developed and sold in stores such as Toys "R" Us.[9]

Why do so many entrepreneurs and small businesspeople come up with so many purple cows? For one thing, entrepreneurs are often creative people; moreover, they're often willing to take risks. This is certainly true of Bob Montgomery, inventor of the PowerSki Jetboard (which undoubtedly qualifies as a purple cow). With more than twenty years' experience in the water-sports industry and considerable knowledge of the personal-watercraft market, Montgomery finally decided to follow his long-cherished dream of creating an entirely new and conceptually different product—one that would offer users ease of operations, high performance, speed, and quality. His creative efforts have earned him the prestigious *Popular Science* "Best of What's New" award.[10]

To remain competitive, medium and large organizations alike must also identify product development opportunities. Many companies actively solicit product ideas from people inside the organization, including marketing, sales, research, and manufacturing personnel, and some even establish internal "entrepreneurial" units. Others seek product ideas from outside the organization by talking to customers and paying attention to what the competition is doing. In addition to looking out for new product ideas, most companies constantly seek out ways to make incremental improvements in existing products by adding features that will broaden their consumer appeal. As you can see from Figure 10.2, the market leaders in most industries are the firms that are most successful at developing new products.

FIGURE 10.2 Sales from New Products

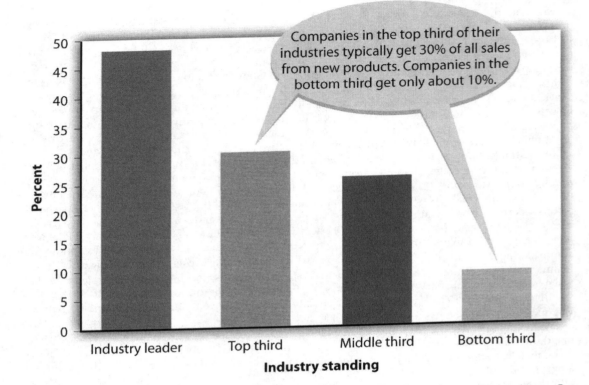

A novel approach to generating new-to-the-world product ideas is hiring "creativity" consultants. One of the best is Doug Hall, who's been called "America's Number 1 Idea Guru." At a Cincinnati idea factory called Eureka!Ranch, Hall and other members of his consulting firm specialize in helping corporate executives get their creative juices flowing.[11] Hall's job is getting people to invent products that make a real difference to consumers, and his strategies are designed to help corporate clients become more innovative—to jump-start their brains. As Hall puts it, "You have to swing to hit home runs."[12] Eureka!Ranch's client list includes Disney, Kellogg, Johnson & Johnson, and Procter & Gamble, as well as a number of budding entrepreneurs. Hall boasts that the average home uses eighteen goods or services that the Ranch helped shape, and if he's right, you yourself have probably benefited from one of the company's idea-generating sessions.[13]

KEY TAKEAWAYS

- The majority of product ideas come from entrepreneurs and small business owners, though medium and large organizations also must identify product-development opportunities in order to remain competitive.
- Firms seek product ideas from people inside the organization, including those in marketing, sales, research, and manufacturing, as well as from customers and others outside the organization.

Before going to the next section of this chapter, take a few minutes to test your knowledge of the material covered in this section. Quizzes can be found under the "Resources" tab, "Study Aids: Quizzes."

---

3. IDENTIFYING BUSINESS OPPORTUNITIES

LEARNING OBJECTIVES

1. Explain how an idea turns into a business opportunity.
2. Describe the four types of utility provided by a product: time, place, ownership, and form.

An idea turns into a business opportunity when it has commercial potential—when you can make money by selling the product. But needless to say, not all ideas generate business opportunities. Consider these products that made the list of the "Top 25 Biggest Product Flops of All Time":[14]

- *Bic underwear.* When you think of Bic, you think of inexpensive pens, disposable razors, and lighters. But disposable underwear? Women didn't find the idea of buying intimate attire from a pen manufacturer appealing, and the disposability factor was just plain weird.

- *Harley Davidson perfume.* Even its loyal fans found the idea of Harley-Davidson perfume peculiar (and they weren't terribly fond of the Harley-Davidson aftershave, either). Perhaps they were afraid they would end up smelling like a motorcycle.

- *Bottled water for pets.* OK, so people love their pets and cater to them, but does it really make sense to serve Thirsty Cat! and Thirsty Dog! bottled water to your four-legged friends? Even though the water came in tantalizing flavors such as Crispy Beef and Tangy Fish, it never caught on. Do you wonder why?

- *Colgate kitchen entrees.* Colgate's entrance into food products wasn't well received. Maybe the company believed customers would buy into the idea of eating one of its prepared meals and then brushing their teeth with Colgate toothpaste. For most of us, the name Colgate doesn't get our taste buds tingling.

FIGURE 10.3

There might be many creative ways for Bic to extend its product lines, aside from the disposable underwear idea. Can you think of a product idea that might be more successful for Bic?

© 2010 Jupiterimages Corporation

3.1 Utility

Remember: being in business is not about you—it's about the customer. Successful businesspeople don't ask themselves "What do I want to sell?" but rather "What does the customer want to buy?" *Customers buy products to fill unmet needs and because they expect to derive some value or utility from them.* People don't buy Alka-Seltzer because they like the taste or even because the price is right: they buy it because it makes their indigestion go away. They don't shop at Amazon.com because the Web site is entertaining: they shop there because they want their purchases delivered quickly. The realization that this kind of service would meet customer needs made Amazon.com a genuine business opportunity.

Products provide customers with four types of utility or benefit:

1. *Time utility.* The value to a consumer of having a good or a service available at a convenient time. A concessionaire selling bottled water at a summer concert is making liquid refreshment available when it's needed.

2. *Place utility.* The value to a consumer of having a product available in a convenient location. A street vendor selling hotdogs outside an office building is making fast food available where it's needed.

3. *Ownership utility*. Value created by transferring a product's ownership. A real estate agent helping a young couple buy a home is transferring ownership from someone who doesn't need it to someone who does.

4. *Form utility*. The value to consumers from changing the composition of a product. A company that makes apparel is turning raw material (fabric) into a form (clothing) that people need. A company that produces liquid detergent, rather than powdered detergent, is adding form utility for some consumers.

How can you decide whether an idea provides utility and has the potential to become a business opportunity? You should start by asking yourself the questions in Figure 10.4: if you can't come up with good answers to these questions, you probably don't have a highly promising product. On the other hand, if you conclude that you have a potential product for which people would pay money, you're ready to take the next step: analyze the market to see whether you should go forward with the development of the product.

FIGURE 10.4 When Is an Idea a Business Opportunity?

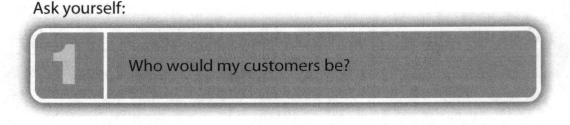

Ask yourself:

1 Who would my customers be?

2 Why will customers buy the product from me?

3 How will customers benefit from my product?

KEY TAKEAWAYS

- An idea turns into a business opportunity when it has commercial potential—when you can make money by selling the product.
- Time utility provides value by having a product available at a convenient time.
- Place utility provides value by having a product available in a convenient location.
- Ownership utility provides value by transferring a product's ownership.
- Form utility provides value by changing the composition of a product.

Before going to the next section of this chapter, take a few minutes to test your knowledge of the material covered in this section. Quizzes can be found under the "Resources" tab, "Study Aids: Quizzes."

4.   UNDERSTAND YOUR INDUSTRY

LEARNING OBJECTIVES

1. Define an "industry."
2. Explain how to research an industry.
3. Define and give an example of a "niche market."

Before you invest a lot of time and money to develop a new product, you need to understand the industry in which it's going to be sold. As inventor of the PowerSki Jetboard, Bob Montgomery had the advantage of being quite familiar with the industry that he proposed to enter. With more than twenty years' experience in the water-sports and personal-watercraft industry, he felt at home in this business environment. He knew who his potential customers were, and he knew who his competitors were. He had experience in marketing similar products, and he was familiar with industry regulations.

Most people don't have the same head start as Montgomery. So, how does the average would-be businessperson learn about an industry? What should you want to know about it? Let's tackle the first question first.

4.1   Evaluating Your Industry

Before you can study an industry, you need to know what industry to study. An **industry** is a group of related businesses: they do similar things and they compete with each other. In the footwear industry, for example, firms make footwear, sell it, or both. Players in the industry include Nike and Adidas, both of which specialize in athletic footwear; but the industry is also sprinkled with companies like Candies (which sells young women's fashion footwear) and Florsheim (quality men's dress shoes).

Let's say that you want to know something about the footwear industry because your potential purple cow is a line of jogging shoes designed specifically for older people (those over sixty-five) who live in the Southeast. You'd certainly need a broad understanding of the footwear industry, but would general knowledge be enough? Wouldn't you feel more comfortable about pursuing your idea if you could focus on a smaller segment of the industry—namely, the segment that specializes in products similar to the one you plan to sell? Here's a method that will help you narrow your focus.[15]

> **industry**
>
> Group of businesses that compete with one another to market products that are the same or similar.

4.2   Segmenting Your Market

Begin with the overall industry—in this case, the footwear industry. Within this industry, there are several groups of customers, each of which is a **market**. You're interested in the *consumer market*—retail customers. But this, too, is a fairly broad market; it includes everybody who buys shoes at retail. Your next step, then, is to subdivide this market into smaller **market segments**—groups of potential customers with common characteristics that influence their buying decisions. You can use a variety of standard characteristics, including *demographics* (age, sex, income), *geography* (region, climate, city size), and *psychographics* (lifestyle, activities, interests). The segment you're interested in consists of older people (a demographic variable) living in the Southeast (a geographic variable) who jog (a psychographic variable). Within this market segment, you might want to subdivide further and find a **niche**—an unmet need. Your niche might turn out to be providing high-quality jogging shoes to active adults living in retirement communities in Florida.

The goal of this process is to identify progressively narrower sectors of a given industry. You need to become familiar with the whole industry—not only with the footwear industry but also with the retail market for jogging shoes designed for older people. You also need to understand your niche market, which consists of older people who live active lives in Florida.

Now that we know something about the process of focusing in on an industry, let's look at another example. Suppose that your product idea is offering dedicated cruises for college students. You'd begin by looking at the recreational-activities *industry*. Your *market* would be people who travel for leisure,

> **market**
>
> Group of buyers or potential buyers who share a common need that can be met by a certain product.
>
> **market segment**
>
> Group of potential customers with common characteristics that influence their buying decisions.
>
> **niche**
>
> Narrowly defined group of potential customers with a fairly specific set of needs.

and within that market, you'd focus on the *market segment* consisting of people who take cruises. Your *niche* would be college students who want to take cruises.

Market Segmentation and Selected Variables

Take a moment to complete an exercise that reinforces your understanding of segmentation variables.

4.3 Assessing Your Competition

Now that you've identified your industry and its various sectors, you're ready to consider such questions as the following:[16]

- Is the industry growing or contracting? Are sales revenues increasing or decreasing?
- Who are your major competitors? How does your product differ from those of your competitors?
- What opportunities exist in the industry? What threats?
- Has the industry undergone recent changes? Where is it headed?
- How important is technology to the industry? Has it brought about changes?
- Is the industry mature, or are new companies successfully entering it?
- Do companies in the industry make reasonable profits?

Where do you find answers to questions such as these? A good place to start is by studying your competitors: Who are their customers? What products do they sell? How do they price their products? How do they market them? How do they treat their customers? Do they seem to be operating successfully? Observe their operations and buy their goods and services. Search for published information on your competitors and the industry. For example, there's a great deal of information about companies on the Internet, particularly in company Web sites. The Internet is also a good source of industry information. Look for the site posted by the industry trade association. Find out whether it publishes a magazine or other materials. Talk with people in the industry—business owners, managers, suppliers; these people are usually experts. And talk with customers. What do they like or dislike about the products that are currently available? What benefits are they looking for? What benefits are they getting?

KEY TAKEAWAYS

- Before developing a new product, you need to understand the industry in which it will be sold.
- An **industry** is a group of related businesses that do similar things and compete with each other.
- To research an industry, you begin by studying the overall industry and then progressively narrow your search by looking at smaller sectors of the industry, including **markets** (or groups of customers) and **market segments** (smaller groups of customers with common characteristics that influence their buying decisions).
- Within a market segment, you might want to subdivide further to isolate a **niche**, or unmet need.

Before going to the next section of this chapter, take a few minutes to test your knowledge of the material covered in this section. Quizzes can be found under the "Resources" tab, "Study Aids: Quizzes."

EXERCISE

To introduce a successful new service, you should understand the industry in which you'll be offering the service. Select a service business that you'd like to run and explain what information you'd collect on its industry. How would you find it?

5. FORECASTING DEMAND

It goes without saying, but we'll say it anyway: without enough customers, your business will go nowhere. So, before you delve into the complex, expensive world of developing and marketing a new product, ask yourself questions like those in Figure 10.5. When Bob Montgomery asked himself these questions, he concluded that he had two groups of customers for the PowerSki Jetboard: (1) the dealerships that would sell the product and (2) the water-sports enthusiasts who would buy and use it. His job, therefore, was to design a product that dealers would want to sell and enthusiasts would buy. When he was confident that he could satisfy these criteria, he moved forward with his plans to develop the PowerSki Jetboard.

FIGURE 10.5 When to Develop and Market a New Product

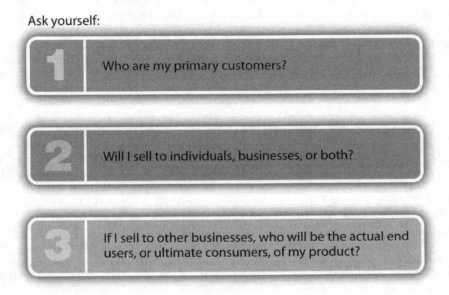

Ask yourself:

1. Who are my primary customers?

2. Will I sell to individuals, businesses, or both?

3. If I sell to other businesses, who will be the actual end users, or ultimate consumers, of my product?

After you've identified a group of potential customers, your next step is finding out as much as you can about what they think of your product idea. Remember: because your ultimate goal is to roll out a product that satisfies customer needs, you need to know ahead of time what your potential customers want. Precisely what are their unmet needs? Ask them questions such as these:[17]

- What do you like about this product idea? What don't you like?
- What improvements would you make?
- What benefits would you get from it?
- Would you buy it? Why, or why not?
- What would it take for you to buy it?

Before making a substantial investment in the development of a product, you need to ask yourself yet another question: are there enough customers willing to buy my product at a price that will allow me to make a profit? Answering this question means performing one of the hardest tasks in business: forecasting demand for your proposed product. There are several possible approaches to this task that can be used alone or in combination.

5.1 People in Similar Businesses

Though some businesspeople are reluctant to share proprietary information, such as sales volume, others are willing to help out individuals starting new businesses or launching new products. Talking to people in your prospective industry (or one that's similar) can be especially helpful if your proposed product is a service. Say, for example, that you plan to open a pizza parlor with a soap opera theme: customers will be able to eat pizza while watching reruns of their favorite soap operas on personal TV/ DVD sets. If you visited a few local restaurants and asked owners how many customers they served every day, you'd probably learn enough to estimate the number of pizzas that you'd serve during your first year. If the owners weren't cooperative, you could just hang out and make an informal count of the customers.

5.2 Potential Customers

You can also learn a lot by talking with potential customers. Ask them how often they buy products similar to the one you want to launch. Where do they buy them and in what quantity? What factors affect demand for them? If you were contemplating a frozen yogurt store in Michigan, it wouldn't hurt to ask customers coming out of a bakery whether they'd buy frozen yogurt in the winter.

5.3 Published Industry Data

To get some idea of the total market for a particular product, you might begin by examining pertinent industry research. For example, to estimate the demand for jogging shoes among consumers ages sixty-five and older who live in retirement communities in Florida, you could look at data published by the National Sporting Goods Association (http://www.nsga.org). This organization collects extensive data annually, compiles the data, creates reports on various topics, and sells the reports on its Web site to its members and other interested buyers. You might be particularly interested in four of the organization's reports: (1) "Sports Participation in the U.S." (provides overall statistics on the current and future state of the sporting goods industry), (2) "Sports Participation State-by-State" (reports sports participation statistics for each state, including Florida), (3) "Sports Participation: Lifecycle Demographics" (details participation in sports by various demographic variables, including age and geographical location), and (4) "Sports Participation, Single Sport" (reports detailed participation figures for a variety of sports, including running and jogging).

market share

Company's portion of the market that it has targeted.

Now, let's say that your research turns up the fact that there are three million joggers older than sixty-five and that six hundred thousand of them live in Florida, which attracts 20 percent of all people who move when they retire. How do you use this information to estimate the number of jogging shoes that you'll be able to sell during your first year of business? First, you have to estimate your **market share**: your portion of total sales in the older-than-sixty-five jogging shoe market in Florida. Being realistic (but having faith in an excellent product), you estimate that you'll capture 2 percent of the market during your first year. So you do the math: 600,000 pairs of jogging shoes sold in Florida × 0.02 (a 2 percent share of the market) = 12,000, the estimated first-year demand for your proposed product.

Granted, this is just an estimate. But at least it's an educated guess rather than a wild one. You'll still want to talk with people in the industry, as well as potential customers, to hear their views on the demand for your product. Only then would you use your sales estimate to make financial projections and decide whether your proposed business is financially feasible. We'll discuss this process in a later chapter.

KEY TAKEAWAYS

- After you've identified a group of potential customers, your next step is finding out as much as you can about what they think of your product idea.
- Before making a substantial investment in the development of a product, you need to ask yourself: are there enough customers willing to buy my product at a price that will allow me to make a profit?
- Answering this question means performing one of the hardest tasks in business: forecasting demand for your proposed product.
- There are several possible approaches to this task that can be used alone or in combination.
- You can obtain helpful information about product demand by talking with people in similar businesses and potential customers.
- You can also examine published industry data to estimate the total market for products like yours and estimate your **market share**, or portion of the targeted market.

Before going to the next section of this chapter, take a few minutes to test your knowledge of the material covered in this section. Quizzes can be found under the "Resources" tab, "Study Aids: Quizzes."

EXERCISE

Your friends say you make the best pizzas they've ever eaten, and they're constantly encouraging you to set up a pizza business in your city. You have located a small storefront in a busy section of town. It doesn't have space for an eat-in restaurant, but it will allow customers to pick up their pizzas. You will also deliver pizzas. Before you sign a lease and start the business, you need to estimate the number of pizzas you will sell in your first year. At this point you plan to offer pizza in only one size.

Before arriving at an estimate, answer these questions:

1. What factors would you consider in estimating pizza sales?
2. What assumptions will you use in estimating sales (for example, the hours your pizza shop will be open)?
3. Where would you obtain needed information to calculate an estimate?

Then, estimate the number of pizzas you will sell in your first year of operations.

---

6. BREAKEVEN ANALYSIS

LEARNING OBJECTIVE

1. **Learn how to use breakeven analysis to estimate the number of sales units at which net income is zero.**

Forecasting sales of shoes has started you thinking. Selling twelve thousand pair of shoes the first year you run the business sounds great, but you still need to find an answer to the all-important question: are there enough customers willing to buy my jogging shoes at a price that will allow me to make a profit? Is there some way to figure out the level of sales I would need to avoid *losing* money—to "break even"? Fortunately, an accountant friend of yours informs you that there is. Not surprisingly, it's called **breakeven analysis**, and here's how it works: to break even (have no profit or loss), *total sales revenue must exactly equal all your expenses (both variable and fixed)*. To determine the level of sales at which this will occur, you need to do the following:

1. Determine your total **fixed costs**, which are so called because the total cost doesn't change as the quantity of goods sold changes:

   - Fixed costs = $210,000 salaries + $60,000 rent + $10,000 advertising + $8,000 insurance + 12,000 other fixed costs = $300,000

2. Identify your **variable costs.** These are costs that vary, in total, as the quantity of goods sold changes but that stay constant on a per-unit basis. State variable costs on a per-unit basis:

   - Variable cost per unit = $40 (cost of each pair of shoes) + $5 sales commission = $45

3. Determine your **contribution margin per unit**: selling price per unit less variable cost per unit:

   - Contribution margin per unit = $80 selling price minus $45 variable cost per unit = $35

4. Calculate your **breakeven point in units**: fixed costs ÷ contribution margin per unit:

   - Breakeven in units = $300,000 fixed costs ÷ $35 contribution margin per unit = 8,571 units

Your calculation means that if you sell 8,571 pairs of shoes, you will end up with zero profit (or loss) and will exactly break even.

   If your sales estimate is realistic (a big "if"), then you should be optimistic about starting the business. All your fixed costs will be covered once you sell 8,571 pairs of shoes. Any sales above that level will be pure profit. So, if you sell your expected level of twelve thousand pairs of shoes, you'll make a profit of $120,015 for the first year. Here's how we calculated that profit:

   - 12,000 expected sales level – 8,571 breakeven sales level = 3,429 units × $35 contribution margin per unit = $120,015 first-year profit

As you can see, breakeven analysis is pretty handy. It allows you to determine the level of sales that you must reach to avoid losing money and the profit you'll make if you reach a higher sales goal. Such information will help you plan for your business.

breakeven analysis

Method of determining the level of sales at which the company will break even (have no profit or loss).

fixed costs

Costs that don't change when the amount of goods sold changes.

variable costs

Costs that vary, in total, as the quantity of goods sold changes but stay constant on a per-unit basis.

contribution margin per unit

Excess of revenue per unit over variable cost per unit.

breakeven point in units

Number of sales units at which net income is zero.

KEY TAKEAWAYS

- Breakeven analysis is a method of determining the level of sales at which the company will break even (have no profit or loss).
- The following information is used in calculating the breakeven point: fixed costs, variable costs, and contribution margin per unit.
- Fixed costs are costs that don't change when the amount of goods sold changes. For example, rent is a fixed cost.
- Variable costs are costs that vary, in total, as the quantity of goods sold changes but stay constant on a per-unit basis. For example, sales commissions paid based on unit sales are a variable cost.
- Contribution margin per unit is the excess revenue per unit over the variable cost per unit.
- The breakeven point in units is calculated with this formula: fixed costs divided by contribution margin per unit (selling price per unit less variable cost per unit).

Before going to the next section of this chapter, take a few minutes to test your knowledge of the material covered in this section. Quizzes can be found under the "Resources" tab, "Study Aids: Quizzes."

EXERCISE

For the past ten years, you've worked at a PETCO Salon as a dog groomer. You're thinking of starting your own dog grooming business. You found a place you could rent that's right next to a popular shopping center, and two of your friends (who are also dog groomers) have agreed to work for you. The problem is that you need to borrow money to start the business and your banker has asked for a breakeven analysis. You have prepared the following cost estimates for your first year of operations:

Fixed Costs	
Salaries	$105,000
Rent and utilities	$36,000
Advertising	$2,000
Equipment	$3,000

Variable Cost per Dog	
Shampoo	$2.00
Coat conditioner	$1.50
Pet cologne	$0.75
Dog treats	$1.25
Hair ribbons	$0.50

You went online and researched grooming prices in your area. Based on your review, you have decided to charge $32 for each grooming.

- Part 1:
    - What's the breakeven point in units—how many dogs will you need to groom in the first year to break even?
    - If you and your two employees groomed dogs five days a week, seven hours a day, fifty weeks a year, how many dogs would each of you need to groom each day? Is this realistic given that it takes one hour to groom a dog?

- Part 2:
    - If you raised your grooming fee to $38, how many dogs would you need to groom to break even?
    - At this new price, how many dogs will each of you have to groom each day (assuming, again, that the three of you groom dogs fifty weeks a year, five days a week, seven hours a day)?

- Part 3:
    - Would you start this business?
    - What price would you charge to groom a dog?
    - How could you lower the breakeven point and make the business more profitable?

7.   PRODUCT DEVELOPMENT

project team

Individuals from different functional areas assigned to work together throughout the product development process.

Like PowerSki, every organization—whether it produces goods or provides services—sees Job 1 as furnishing customers with quality products. The success of a business depends on its ability to identify the unmet needs of consumers and to develop products that meet those needs at a low cost.[18] In other words, effective product development results in goods and services that can be sold at a profit. In addition, it results in high-quality products that not only satisfy consumer needs but also can be developed in a timely, cost-efficient manner. Accomplishing these goals entails a collaborative effort by individuals from all areas of an organization: operations management (including representatives from engineering, design, and manufacturing), marketing, accounting, and finance. In fact, companies increasingly assign representatives from various functional areas who work together as a **project team** throughout the product development processes. This approach allows individuals with varied backgrounds and experience to provide input as the product is being developed.

7.1   Product Development Is a Risky Proposition

Not surprisingly, developing profitable products is difficult, and the success rate is low. On average, for every successful product, a company has twelve failures. At this rate, the firms on the *Fortune* 1000 list waste over $60 billion a year in research and development.[19] There are several reasons why product development is such a risky proposition:

- *Trade-offs*. You might, for instance, be able to make your jogging shoes lighter than your competitors', but if you do, they probably won't wear as well. They could be of higher quality, but that will make them more costly (they might price themselves out of the market).
- *Time pressure*. Developing a product can require hundreds of decisions that must be made quickly and with imperfect information.
- *Economics*. Because developing a product requires a lot of time and money, there's always pressure to make sure that the project not only results in a successful product but also gets it to market at the most opportune time. Failure to be first to market with an otherwise desirable new product can cost a company a great deal of money.

Even so, organizations continue to dedicate immense resources to developing new products. Your supermarket, for example, can choose from about one hundred thousand items to carry on its shelves—including twenty thousand *new* products every year. Unfortunately, the typical supermarket can stock only thirty thousand products.[20]

Video Clip

Even the mighty Coca-Cola has had its share of failures—New Coke, anyone?

View the video online at: http://www.youtube.com/embed/o4YvmN1hvNA

7.2   The Product Development Process

The **product development process** is a series of activities by which a product idea is transformed into a final product. It can be broken down into the seven steps summarized in Figure 10.6.

product development process

Series of activities by which a product idea is transformed into a final product.

FIGURE 10.6 The Product Development Process

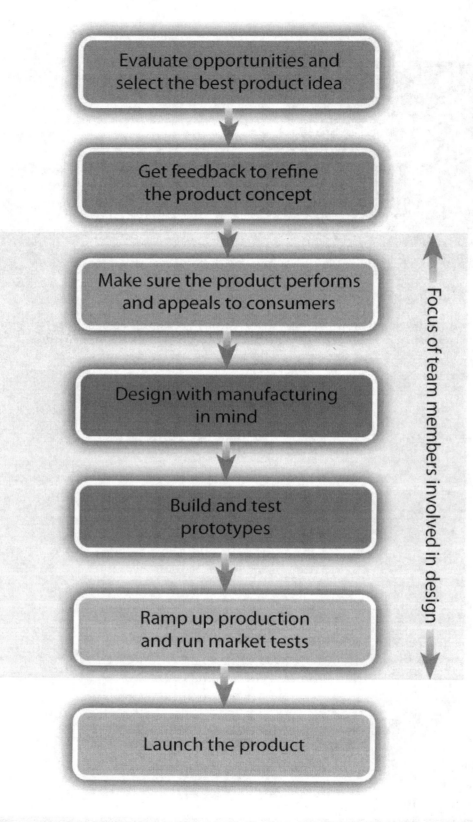

The Product Development Process

Click on this link to experience an active version of this figure.

Evaluate Opportunities and Select the Best Product Idea

If you're starting your first business, you might have only one product idea. But existing organizations often have several ideas for new products, as well as improvements to existing ones. Where do they come from? They can come from individuals within the organization or from outside sources, such as customers. Typically, various ideas are reviewed and evaluated by a team of individuals, who identify the most promising ideas for development. They may rely on a variety of criteria: Does the proposed product fill an unmet need of our customers? Will enough people buy our product to make it commercially successful? Do we have the resources and expertise to make it?

Get Feedback to Refine the Product Concept

From the selected product idea, the team generates an initial **product concept** that describes what the product might look like and how it might work. Members talk both with other people in the organization and with potential buyers to identify customer needs and the benefits that consumers will get from the product. They study the industry in which the product will be sold and investigate competing products. They brainstorm various *product designs*—that is, the specifications for how the product is to be made, what it's to look like, and what performance standards it's to meet.

Based on information gathered through this process, the team will revise the product concept, probably pinpointing several alternative models. Then they'll go back to potential customers and get their feedback on both the basic concept and the various alternatives. Based on this feedback, the team will decide what the product will look like, how it will work, and what features it will have.

product concept
Description of what a new product will look like and how it will work.

Make Sure the Product Performs and Appeals to Consumers

The team then decides how the product will be made, what components it will require, and how it will be assembled. It will decide whether the product should be made in-house or outsourced to other companies. For products to be made in-house, the team determines where parts will be obtained. During this phase, team members are involved in design work to ensure that the product will be appealing, safe, and easy to use and maintain.

Design with Manufacturing in Mind

As a rule, there's more than one way to make any product, and some methods are more expensive than others. During the next phase, therefore, the team focuses its attention on making a high-quality product at the lowest possible cost, working to minimize the number of parts and simplify the components. The goal is to build both quality and efficiency into the manufacturing process.

Build and Test Prototypes

A **prototype** is a physical model of the product. In the next phase, prototypes are produced and tested to make sure that the product meets the customer needs that it's supposed to. The team usually begins with a preliminary prototype from which, based on feedback from potential customers, a more sophisticated model will then be developed. The process of building and testing prototypes will continue until the team feels comfortable that it has fashioned the best possible product. The final prototype will be extensively tested by customers to identify any changes that need to be made before the finished product is introduced.

prototype
Physical model of a new product.

Ramp Up Production and Run Market Tests

During the production **ramp-up stage**, employees are trained in manufacturing and assembly processes. Products turned out during this phase are carefully inspected for residual flaws. Samples are often demonstrated or given to potential customers for testing and feedback.

ramp-up stage
Stage in the product development process during which employees are trained in necessary production processes and new products are tested.

Launch the Product

In the final stage, the firm starts ongoing production and makes the product available for widespread distribution.

KEY TAKEAWAYS

- The success of a business depends on its ability to identify the unmet needs of consumers and to develop products that meet those needs at a reasonable cost.
- Accomplishing these goals requires a collaborative effort by individuals from all areas of the organization: operations management (including representatives from engineering, design, and manufacturing), marketing, accounting, and finance.
- Representatives from these various functional areas often work together as **project teams** throughout the **product development process**, which consists of a series of activities that transform a product idea into a final product.
- This process can be broken down into seven steps:
    1. Evaluate opportunities and select the best product mix
    2. Get feedback to refine the **product concept** that describes what the product might look like and how it might work
    3. Make sure that the product performs and appeals to consumers
    4. Design with manufacturing in mind to build both quality and efficiency into the manufacturing process
    5. Build and test **prototypes**, or physical models of the product
    6. Run market tests and enter the **ramp-up stage** during which employees are trained in the production process
    7. Launch the product

Before going to the next section of this chapter, take a few minutes to test your knowledge of the material covered in this section. Quizzes can be found under the "Resources" tab, "Study Aids: Quizzes."

EXERCISE

Use your imagination to come up with a hypothetical product idea. Now, identify the steps you'd take to design, develop, and bring your product to market.

---

8. PROTECTING YOUR IDEA

LEARNING OBJECTIVE

1. **Learn how to protect your product idea by applying for a patent.**

patent

Grant of the exclusive right to produce or sell a product, process, or invention.

You can protect your rights to your idea with a **patent** from the U.S. Patent and Trademark Office, which grants you "the right to exclude others from making, using, offering for sale, or selling" the invention in the United States for twenty years.[21]

What do you need to know about applying for a patent? For one thing, document your idea as soon as you think of it. Simply fill out a form, stating the purpose of your invention and the current date. Then sign it and get someone to witness it. The procedure sounds fairly informal, but you may need this document to strengthen your claim that you came up with the idea before someone else who also claims it. Later, you'll apply formally for a patent by filling out an application (generally with the help of a lawyer), sending it to the U.S. Patent and Trademark Office, and waiting. Nothing moves quickly through the U.S. Patent and Trademark Office, and it takes a long time for any application to get through the process.

Will your application get through at all? There's a good chance if your invention meets all the following criteria:

- *It's new.* No one else can have known about it, used it, or written about it before you filed your patent application (so keep it to yourself until you've filed).

- *It's not obvious*. It has to be sufficiently different from everything that's been used for the purpose in the past (you can't patent a new color for a cell phone).

- *It has utility*. It can't be useless; it must have some value.

Applying for a U.S. patent is only the first step. If you plan to export your product outside the United States, you'll need patent protection in each country in which you plan to do business, and as you've no doubt guessed, getting a foreign patent isn't any easier than getting a U.S. patent. The process keeps lawyers busy: during a three-year period, PowerSki International had to take out more than eighty patents on the PowerSki Jetboard. It still has a long way to go to match the number of patents issued to some extremely large corporations. Microsoft, for example, recently obtained its ten thousandth patent.[22]

Clearly, the patent business is booming. The U.S. Patent and Trademark Office issued more than a half million patents in 2010.[23] One reason for the recent proliferation of patents is the high-tech boom: over the last decade, the number of patents granted has increased by more than 50 percent.

KEY TAKEAWAYS

- You can protect your rights to your idea with a **patent** from the U.S. Patent and Trademark Office.

- A patent grants you "the right to exclude others from making, using, offering for sale, or selling" the invention in the United States for twenty years.

- To be patentable, an invention must meet all the following criteria: it's new (no one else can have known about it, used it, or written about it before you filed your patent application); it's not obvious (it's sufficiently different from everything that's been used for the purpose in the past); and it has utility (it must have some value; it can't be useless).

Before going to the next chapter, take a few minutes to test your knowledge of the material covered in this section. Quizzes can be found under the "Resources" tab, "Study Aids: Quizzes."

EXERCISE

A friend of yours described a product idea she had been working on. It is a child's swing set with a sensor to stop the swing if anyone walks in front of it. She came to you for advice on protecting her product idea. What questions would you need to ask her to determine whether her product idea is patentable? How would she apply for a patent? What protection would the patent give her? How long would the patent apply?

9. CASES AND PROBLEMS

LEARNING ON THE WEB

Breaking Even on Burgers

You and your business partner plan to open a gourmet burger restaurant. Your partner estimated the new business will sell a hundred fifty thousand burgers during its first year and a half of operations. You want to determine the number of burgers you must sell to break even during this period.

Here are the figures you know so far:

- The variable cost for each burger is $0.97 each.
- The fixed cost of making burgers for eighteen months is $140,000 (this includes costs such as rent, utilities, insurance).
- You will sell your burgers for $1.99 each.
- At the $1.99 per-unit selling price, how many burgers will you have to sell to break even?

Part 1: Using the previous information, manually calculate the breakeven number of burgers. How close is the breakeven number of burgers to your partner's sales estimate of one hundred fifty thousand burgers? How confident are you that your restaurant will be profitable?

Part 2: Now, recalculate the breakeven number of burgers using a higher selling price. Pretend that your likely customers are burger fanatics and will pay $2.79 for a burger (rather than $1.99). Also pretend that the variable cost for each burger and your fixed costs won't change (variable cost per burger is still $0.97 and fixed costs are still $140,000). Manually calculate the number of burgers you must sell to break even at this higher selling price. Are you now more confident that the business will succeed?

Part 3: Without recalculating breakeven, answer these two questions:

1. If the variable cost for each burger went down from $0.97 to $0.80 per burger (and your selling price stayed at $1.99), would you need to sell more or fewer burgers to break even?
2. If fixed costs went down from $140,000 to $100,000 (and your selling price stayed at $1.99 and variable cost per burger returned to $0.97), would you need to sell more or fewer burgers to break even?

CAREER OPPORTUNITIES

Being a "Big Idea" Person

Imagine a career in which you design the products people use every day. If you're a "big idea" person, have an active imagination, have artistic flair, and possess the ability to understand how products function, then a career in product design and development might be for you. To learn what opportunities are available in this field, go to the Job Bank section of the Product Development and Management Association's Web site (http://www.pdma.org) and click on "Career Center" and then "Job Seekers." Explore the various job openings by clicking on a position (to highlight it), and then read the section titled "Job Description" at the bottom of the screen. Find a position that interests you and look for answers to these questions:

1. What's the job like?
2. What educational background, work experience, and skills are needed for the job?
3. What aspects of the job appeal to you? What aspects are unappealing?
4. Are you cut out for a career in product design and development? Why, or why not?

ETHICS ANGLE

Who's Getting Fat from Fast Food?

Product liability laws cover the responsibility of manufacturers, sellers, and others for injuries caused by defective products. Under product liability laws, a toy manufacturer can be held liable if a child is harmed by a toy that's been marketed with a design flaw. The manufacturer can also be held liable for defects in marketing the toy, such as giving improper instructions on its use or failing to warn consumers about potential dangers. But what if the product isn't a toy, but rather a fast-food kid's meal? And what if the harm isn't immediately obvious but emerges over time?

These questions are being debated in the legal and health professions (and the media). Some people believe that fast-food restaurants should be held responsible (at least in part) for childhood obesity. They argue that fast-food products—such as kids' meals made up of high-calorie burgers, fried chicken fingers, French fries, and sugary soft drinks—are helping to make U.S. children overweight. They point out that while restaurant chains spend billions each year to advertise fast food to children, they don't do nearly enough to warn parents of the dangers posed by such foods. On the other side of the debate are restaurant owners, who argue that they're not the culprits. They say that their food can be a part of a child's diet—if it's eaten in moderation.

There's no disputing that 15 percent of American children are obese and that fast-food consumption by children has increased by 500 percent since 1970. Most observers also accept the data furnished by the U.S. Surgeon General: that obesity in the United States claims some three hundred thousand lives a year and costs $117 billion in health care. The controversy centers on the following questions:

1. Who really is to blame for the increase in obesity among U.S. children?
2. Under current consumer-protection laws, is fast-food marketing aimed at children misleading?
3. Should fast-food restaurants be held legally liable for the health problems associated with their products?

What's your opinion? If you owned a fast-food restaurant, what action (if any) would you take in response to the charges leveled by critics of your industry?

TEAM-BUILDING SKILLS

The Great Idea

Get together with members of your team and brainstorm ideas for a new-to-the-market product. Begin the brainstorming session by asking each person to write an idea on a sticky note. Post the idea and repeat the process four times. After the team has evaluated and discussed the ideas, all members should vote. Each gets ten votes, which can be placed on one idea or spread over many. Once the voting ends, add up the votes received by each idea and declare one idea the winner.

Write a group report that answers the following questions:

1. Product Idea
   - What is the idea?
   - How would the idea work?
   - Who would our customers be?
   - What unmet need does it fill?

2. Industry
   - What is the product's industry, segment, and niche?
   - Is the industry growing or contracting?
   - Who are our major competitors?
   - How does our product differ from those of our competitors?
   - What opportunities exist in the industry? What threats?

3. Product
   - What will the product look like?
   - What features will it have?
   - How will customers benefit from our product?
   - Why will customers buy the product from us?
   - Why will our product be financially successful?

What to Do When the "False" Alarm Goes Off

If someone on the street tried to sell you a "Rolex" watch for $20, you'd probably suspect that it's a fake. But what about a pair of New Balance athletic shoes? How do you know they're authentic? How can you tell? Often you can't. Counterfeiters are getting so good at copying products that even experts have trouble telling a fake from the real thing. What if the counterfeit product in question was a prescription drug? Even worse, what if it had been counterfeited with unsterile equipment or contained no active ingredients?

How likely is it that you'll buy a counterfeit product in the next year? Unfortunately, it's very likely. To learn a little more about the global counterfeiting business, go to the *BusinessWeek* and *Washington Post* Web sites. Read the *BusinessWeek* article "Fakes!" (http://www.businessweek.com/magazine/content/05_06/b3919001_mz001.htm) and the *Washington Post* article "Counterfeit Goods That Trigger the 'False' Alarm" (http://www.highbeam.com/doc/1P2-4576.html). After you read these articles, answer the following questions:

1. How has the practice of counterfeiting changed over time? What factors have allowed it to escalate?
2. What types of products are commonly counterfeited, and why might they be unsafe? What counterfeit products are particularly dangerous?
3. How do the counterfeiters get goods onto the market? How can you reduce your chances of buying fake goods?
4. Why is counterfeiting so profitable? How can counterfeiters compete on price with those making the authentic goods? How do counterfeiters harm U.S. businesses?
5. What efforts are international companies and governments (including China) making to stop counterfeiters?
6. If you know that a product is fake, is it ethical to buy it?

ENDNOTES

1. See Mary Coulter, *Entrepreneurship in Action* (Upper Saddle River, NJ: Prentice Hall, 2001), 9–11.

2. PowerSki's Web site, About PowerSki International section, http://powerski.com/content/psi_index.php (accessed April 18, 2014).

3. "Woody Allen Quotes," *Brainy Quote*, http://www.brainyquote.com/quotes/quotes/w/woodyallen121347.html (accessed April 18, 2014).

4. See Mary Coulter, *Entrepreneurship in Action* (Upper Saddle River, NJ: Prentice Hall, 2001), 9, 206–7.

5. Scott Thurm and Joann S. Lublin, "Peter Drucker's Legacy Includes Simple Advice: It's All about the People," *Wall Street Journal* (November 14, 2005), B1, http://online.wsj.com/news/articles/SB113192826302796041 - Peter Drucker's Legacy.htm (accessed April 18, 2014).

6. Philip Kotler and Gary Armstrong, *Principles of Marketing*, 12th ed. (Upper Saddle River, NJ: Pearson Education, 2008), 253.

7. Seth Godin, *Purple Cow: Transform Your Business by Being Remarkable* (New York: Penguin Group, 2003).

8. See "Fascinating Facts about Dean Kamen Inventor," *The Great Idea Finder*, October, 11, 2006, http://www.ideafinder.com/history/inventors/kamen.htm (accessed April 18, 2014).

9. See "The JD Batball," *The Great Idea Finder*, http://www.ideafinder.com/history/inventions/jdbatball.htm (accessed April 18, 2014); "SolidWorks Software Helps Make an 8-Year-Old's Dream a Home Run," *The Free Library*, http://www.thefreelibrary.com/SolidWorks+Software+Helps+Make+an+8-Year-Old's+Dream+a+Home+Run.-a080152784 (accessed April 18, 2014).

10. PowerSki International, "Awards and Media," http://www.powerski.com/content/psi_index.php (accessed April 18, 2014).

11. See *Eureka!Ranch* at http://www.eurekaranch.com (accessed April 18, 2014).

12. "Success Calls for Creativity," *CNN Money*, February 4, 1997, http://money.cnn.com/1997/02/04/busunu/intv_hall (accessed April 18, 2014).

13. "Why Eureka," *Eureka!Ranch*, http://eurekaranch.com (accessed April 18, 2014).

14. WalletPop, "Top 25 Biggest Product Flops of All Time," http://www.dailyfinance.com/photos/top-25-biggest-product-flops-of-all-time (accessed April 18, 2014).

15. This approach is adapted from Kathleen Allen, *Entrepreneurship for Dummies* (New York: Wiley, 2001), 73–77.

16. See Kathleen Allen, *Entrepreneurship for Dummies* (Foster, CA: IDG Books, 2001), 67.

17. Karl Ulrich and Steven Eppinger, *Product Design and Development*, 2nd ed. (New York: Irwin McGraw-Hill, 2000), 66; and Kathleen Allen, *Entrepreneurship for Dummies* (Foster, CA: IDG Books, 2001), 79.

18. Karl Ulrich and Steven Eppinger, *Product Design and Development*, 2nd ed. (New York: Irwin McGraw-Hill, 2000), 3.

19. Tony Ulwick and John A. Eisenhauer, "Predicting the Success or Failure of a New Product Concept," *The Management Roundtable*, http://www.consensuspoint.com/wp-content/themes/radius/whitepapers/Product_Concept.pdf (accessed April 19, 2014).

20. Steve Hannaford, "Slotting Fees and Oligopolies," http://investorshub.advfn.com/boards/read_msg.aspx?message_id=8975654 (accessed April 19, 2014).

21. U.S. Patent and Trademark Office, "How to Get a Patent," http://www.uspto.gov/web/patents/howtopat.htm (accessed April 19, 20141).

22. Ina Fried, "Microsoft Gets 10,000th Patent," *CNET News*, http://news.cnet.com/8301-13860_3-10157884-56.html (accessed April 19, 2014).

23. U.S. Patent and Trademark Office, "Inventors Resources" http://www.uspto.gov/web/offices/com/iip/index.htm (accessed April 19, 2014).

CHAPTER 11
Operations Management in Manufacturing and Service Industries

THE CHALLENGE: PRODUCING QUALITY JETBOARDS

The product development process can be complex and lengthy. It took sixteen years for Bob Montgomery and others at his company to develop the PowerSki Jetboard, and this involved thousands of design changes. It seemed worth it: the Jetboard, an exciting, engine-propelled personal watercraft that's a cross between a high-performance surfboard and a competition water-ski/wakeboard, received extensive media attention and earned rave reviews. It was showered with honors, including *Time* magazine's "Best Invention of the Year" award. Stories about the Jetboard appeared in more than fifty magazines around the world, and it appeared in several movies, in over twenty-five TV shows, and on YouTube.[1] One reviewer of the Jetboard exclaimed, "Up, up and away. PowerSki's the closest you'll get to being Superman on the water. With 40 hp under your toes, the 100-pound board literally flies. You supply the cape."[2]

Montgomery and his team at PowerSki enjoyed taking their well-deserved bows for the job they did designing the product. But having a product was only the beginning for the company. The next step was developing a system that would produce high-quality Jetboards at reasonable prices. Before putting this system in place, PowerSki managers had to address several questions: What kind of production process should they use to make the Jetboards? How large should their production facilities be, and where should they be located? How should the plant be laid out? Should every component be made in-house, or should some be furnished by subcontractors? Where should they buy the materials they needed to build Jetboards? What systems would they need to ensure that production was as efficient as possible and that quality standards were maintained? Answering these questions helped PowerSki set up a manufacturing system through which it could accomplish the most important task that it had set for itself: efficiently producing quality Jetboards.

1. OPERATIONS MANAGEMENT IN MANUFACTURING

operations management (OM)

Management of the process that transforms resources into products.

Like PowerSki, every organization—whether it produces goods or provides services—sees Job 1 as furnishing customers with quality products. Thus, to compete with other organizations, a company must convert resources (materials, labor, money, information) into goods or services as efficiently as possible. The upper-level manager who directs this transformation process is called an *operations manager*. The job of **operations management (OM)**, then, consists of all the activities involved in transforming a product idea into a finished product, as well as those involved in planning and controlling the systems that produce goods and services. In other words, operations managers manage the process that transforms inputs into outputs. Figure 11.1 illustrates this traditional function of operations management.

FIGURE 11.1 The Transformation Process

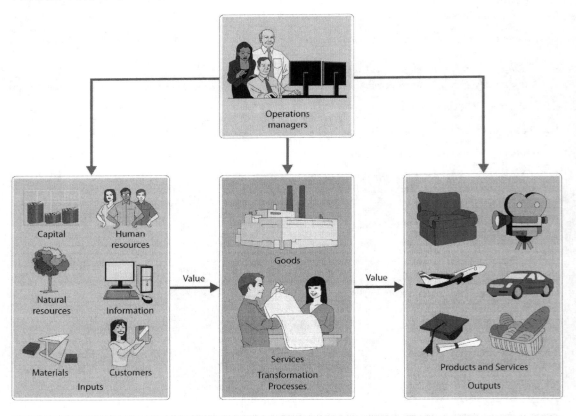

The Transformation Process

Click on this link to experience an active version of this figure.

In the rest of this chapter, we'll discuss the major activities of operations managers. We'll start by describing the role that operations managers play in the various processes designed to produce goods and offer services. Next, we'll look at the production of goods in manufacturing firms; then, we'll describe operations management activities in companies that provide services. We'll wrap up the chapter by explaining the role of operations management in such processes as quality control and outsourcing.

1.1   Operations Management in Manufacturing

Like PowerSki, all manufacturers set out to perform the same basic function: *to transform resources into finished goods.* To perform this function in today's business environment, manufacturers must continually strive to improve operational efficiency. They must fine-tune their production processes to focus on quality, to hold down the costs of materials and labor, and to eliminate all costs that add no value to the finished product. Making the decisions involved in the effort to attain these goals is the job of the operations manager. That person's responsibilities can be grouped as follows:

- *Production planning.* During production planning, managers determine how goods will be produced, where production will take place, and how manufacturing facilities will be laid out.
- *Production control.* Once the production process is under way, managers must continually schedule and monitor the activities that make up that process. They must solicit and respond to feedback and make adjustments where needed. At this stage, they also oversee the purchasing of raw materials and the handling of inventories.
- *Quality control.* Finally, the operations manager is directly involved in efforts to ensure that goods are produced according to specifications and that quality standards are maintained.

Let's take a closer look at each of these responsibilities.

1.2   Planning the Production Process

The decisions made in the planning stage have long-range implications and are crucial to a firm's success. Before making decisions about the operations process, managers must consider the goals set by marketing managers. Does the company intend to be a low-cost producer and to compete on the basis of price? Or does it plan to focus on quality and go after the high end of the market? Perhaps it wants to build a reputation for reliability. What if it intends to offer a wide range of products? To make things even more complicated, all these decisions involve trade-offs. Upholding a reputation for reliability isn't necessarily compatible with offering a wide range of products. Low cost doesn't normally go hand in hand with high quality.

With these factors in mind, let's look at the specific types of decisions that have to be made in the production planning process. We've divided these decisions into those dealing with production methods, site selection, facility layout, and components and materials management.

Production-Method Decisions

The first step in production planning is deciding which type of production process is best for making the goods that your company intends to manufacture. In reaching this decision, you should answer such questions as the following:

- How much input do I receive from a particular customer before producing my goods?
- Am I making a one-of-a-kind good based solely on customer specifications, or am I producing high-volume standardized goods to be sold later?
- Do I offer customers the option of "customizing" an otherwise standardized good to meet their specific needs?

One way to appreciate the nature of this decision is by comparing three basic types of processes or methods: *make-to-order, mass production,* and *mass customization.* The task of the operations manager is to work with other managers, particularly marketers, to select the process that best serves the needs of the company's customers.

Make-to-Order

At one time, most consumer goods, such as furniture and clothing, were made by individuals practicing various crafts. By their very nature, products were *customized* to meet the needs of the buyers who ordered them. This process, which is called a **make-to-order strategy**, is still commonly used by such businesses as print or sign shops that produce low-volume, high-variety goods according to customer specifications.

make-to-order strategy

Production method in which products are made to customer specification.

Mass Production

By the early twentieth century, however, a new concept of producing goods had been introduced: **mass production (or make-to-stock strategy)** is the practice of producing high volumes of identical goods at a cost low enough to price them for large numbers of customers. Goods are made in anticipation of future demand (based on forecasts) and kept in inventory for later sale. This approach is particularly appropriate for standardized goods ranging from processed foods to electronic appliances.

Mass Customization

But there's a disadvantage to mass production: customers, as one contemporary advertising slogan puts it, can't "have it their way." They have to accept standardized products as they come off assembly lines. Increasingly, however, customers are looking for products that are designed to accommodate individual tastes or needs but can still be bought at reasonable prices. To meet the demands of these consumers, many companies have turned to an approach called **mass customization**, which (as the term suggests) combines the advantages of customized products with those of mass production.

This approach requires that a company interact with the customer to find out exactly what the customer wants and then manufacture the good, using efficient production methods to hold down costs. One efficient method is to mass-produce a product up to a certain cut-off point and then to customize it to satisfy different customers.

The list of companies devoting at least a portion of their operations to mass customization is growing steadily. One of the best-known mass customizer is Nike, which has achieved success by allowing customers to configure their own athletic shoes, apparel, and equipment through Nike's iD program. The Web has a lot to do with the growth of mass customization. Levi's, for instance, lets a woman find a pair of perfect fitting jeans by going through an online fitting process that first identifies her "curve" type: *slight* (straight figure), *demi* (evenly proportioned), *bold* (curvy figure, which experiences waist gapping in the back), and supreme (curviest shape, which needs a higher rise in the back). Oakley offers customized sunglasses, goggles, watches, and backpacks, while Mars, Inc. can make M&M's in any color the customer wants (say, school colors) as well as add text and pictures to the candy.[3]

Naturally, mass customization doesn't work for all types of goods. Most people don't care about customized detergents or paper products (although a customized Kleenex tissue box with your picture on it and a statement that says, "go ahead…cry over me!" might come in handy after a relationship breakup with your significant other).[4] And while many of us like the idea of customized clothes, footwear from Nike, or sunglasses from Oakley, we often aren't willing to pay the higher prices they command.

FIGURE 11.2

Automakers produce a high volume of cars in anticipation of future demand.

© 2010 Jupiterimages Corporation

mass production (or make-to-stock strategy)

Production method in which high volumes of products are made at low cost and held in inventory in anticipation of future demand.

mass customization

Production method in which fairly high volumes of customized products are made at fairly low prices.

Production Processes, Technology, and Volume

Take a few minutes to complete an exercise that tests your understanding of the link between volume and standardization.

Facilities Decisions

After selecting the best production process, operations managers must then decide where the goods will be manufactured, how large the manufacturing facilities will be, and how those facilities will be laid out.

Site Selection

In choosing a location, managers must consider several factors:

- To minimize shipping costs, both for raw materials coming into the plant and for finished goods going out, managers often want to locate plants close to suppliers, customers, or both.
- They generally want to locate in areas with ample numbers of skilled workers.
- They naturally prefer locations where they and their families will enjoy living.
- They want locations where costs for resources and other expenses—land, labor, construction, utilities, and taxes—are low.
- They look for locations with a favorable business climate—one in which, for example, local governments might offer financial incentives (such as tax breaks) to entice them to do business in their locales.

Managers rarely find locations that meet all these criteria. As a rule, they identify the most important criteria and aim at satisfying them. In deciding to locate in San Clemente, California, for instance, PowerSki was able to satisfy three important criteria: (1) proximity to the firm's suppliers, (2) availability of skilled engineers and technicians, and (3) favorable living conditions. These factors were more important than operating in a low-cost region or getting financial incentives from local government. Because PowerSki distributes its products throughout the world, proximity to customers was also unimportant.

Capacity Planning

Now that you know *where* you're going to locate, you have to decide on the quantity of products that you'll produce. You begin by *forecasting* demand for your product. As we discussed in Chapter 10, forecasting isn't easy. To estimate the number of units that you're likely to sell over a given period, you have to understand the industry that you're in and estimate your likely share of the market by reviewing industry data and conducting other forms of research.

Once you've forecasted the demand for your product, you can calculate the **capacity** requirements of your production facility—the maximum number of goods that it can produce over a given time under normal working conditions. In turn, having calculated your capacity requirements, you're ready to determine how much investment in plant and equipment you'll have to make, as well as the number of labor hours required for the plant to produce at capacity.

Like forecasting, capacity planning is difficult. Unfortunately, failing to balance capacity and projected demand can be seriously detrimental to your bottom line. If you set capacity too low (and so produce less than you should), you won't be able to meet demand, and you'll lose sales and customers. If you set capacity too high (and turn out more units than you should), you'll waste resources and inflate operating costs.

capacity

Maximum number of products that a facility can produce over a given period under normal working conditions.

KEY TAKEAWAYS

- The job of **operations management** is to oversee the process of transforming resources into goods and services.
- The role of operations managers in the manufacturing sector includes production planning, production control, and quality control.
- During production planning, managers determine how goods will be produced (production process), where production will take place (site selection), and how manufacturing facilities will be laid out (layout planning).
- In selecting the appropriate production process, managers compare three basic methods: **make-to-order strategy** (goods are made to customer specifications), **mass production** or **make-to-stock strategy** (high volumes of goods are made and held in inventory for later sale), and **mass customization** (high volumes of customized goods are made).
- In choosing the site for a company's manufacturing operations, managers look for locations that minimize shipping costs, have an ample supply of skilled workers, provide a favorable community for workers and their families, offer resources at low cost, and have a favorable business climate.
- Managers estimate the quantity of products to be produced by forecasting demand for their product and then calculating the capacity requirements of the production facility—the maximum number of goods that it can produce over a given period under normal working conditions.

Before going to the next section of this chapter, take a few minutes to test your knowledge of the material covered in this section. Quizzes can be found under the "Resources" tab, "Study Aids: Quizzes."

EXERCISES

1. Two former surfers invented a material for surfboards that's lighter and stronger than anything manufacturers now use. They have received funding to set up a production facility, and they want you to help them select a location. In addition to your recommendation, identify the factors that you considered in reaching your decision.

2. Compare and contrast three common types of production processes: make-to-order, make-to-stock, and mass customization. What are the advantages and disadvantages of each? Why are more companies devoting at least a portion of their operations to mass customization? Identify three goods that could probably be adapted to mass customization and three that probably couldn't.

2. FACILITY LAYOUTS

L E A R N I N G   O B J E C T I V E

1. **Describe four major types of facility layouts: process, product, cellular, and fixed position.**

layout

Arrangement in a facility of equipment, machinery, and people to make a production process as efficient as possible.

process layout

Layout that groups together workers or departments that perform similar tasks.

The next step in production planning is deciding on plant **layout**—how equipment, machinery, and people will be arranged to make the production process as efficient as possible. In this section, we'll examine four common types of facility layouts: process, product, cellular, and fixed position.

The **process layout** groups together workers or departments that perform similar tasks. *Goods in process* (goods not yet finished) move from one workstation to another. At each position, workers use specialized equipment to perform a particular step in the production process. To better understand how this layout works, we'll look at the production process at the Vermont Teddy Bear Company. Let's say that you just placed an order for a personalized teddy bear—a "hiker bear" with khaki shorts, a white T-shirt with your name embroidered on it, faux-leather hiking boots, and a nylon backpack with sleeping bag. Your bear begins at the fur-cutting workstation, where its honey-brown "fur" coat is cut. It then moves to the stuffing and sewing workstation to get its insides and have its sides stitched together. Next, it moves to the dressing station, where it's outfitted with all the cool clothes and gear that you ordered. Finally, it winds up in the shipping station and starts its journey to your house. For a more colorful "Online Mini-Tour" of this process, log on to the Vermont Teddy Bear Web site at http://www.vermontteddybear.com/Static/Tour-Welcomestation.aspx (or see Figure 11.3).

FIGURE 11.3 Process Layout at Vermont Teddy Bear Company

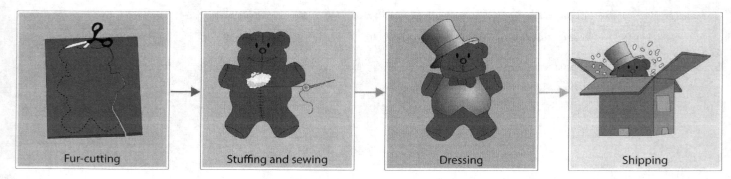

Fur-cutting   Stuffing and sewing   Dressing   Shipping

Process Layout at Vermont Teddy Bear Company

Click on this link to experience an active version of this figure.

product layout

Layout in which products are produced by people, equipment, or departments arranged in an assembly line.

In a **product layout**, high-volume goods are produced efficiently by people, equipment, or departments arranged in an *assembly line*—that is, a series of workstations at which already-made parts are *assembled*. Just Born, a candy maker located in Bethlehem, Pennsylvania, makes a product called Marshmallow Peeps on an assembly line. First, the ingredients are combined and whipped in huge kettles. Then, sugar is added for color. At the next workstation, the mixture—colored warm marshmallow—is poured into baby-chick–shaped molds carried on conveyor belts. The conveyor-belt parade of candy pieces then moves forward to stations where workers add eyes or other details. When the finished candy reaches the packaging area, it's wrapped for shipment to stores around the world. To take an online tour of the Marshmallow Peeps production process, log on to the Just Born Web site at http://www.justborn.com/get-to-know-us/our-factory (or see Figure 11.4).

FIGURE 11.4 Product Layout at Just Born, Inc.

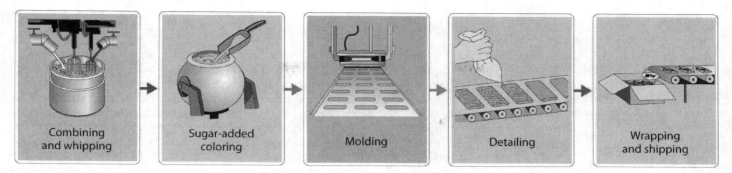

| Combining and whipping | Sugar-added coloring | Molding | Detailing | Wrapping and shipping |

Product Layout at Just Born, Inc.

Click on this link to experience an active version of this figure.

Both product and process layouts arrange work by *function*. At the Vermont Teddy Bear Company, for example, the cutting function is performed in one place, the stuffing-and-sewing function in another place, and the dressing function in a third place. If you're a cutter, you cut all day; if you're a sewer, you sew all day: that's your function. The same is true for the production of Marshmallow Peeps at Just Born: if your function is to decorate peeps, you stand on an assembly line and decorate all day; if your function is packing, you pack all day.

Arranging work by function, however, isn't always efficient. Production lines can back up, inventories can build up, workers can get bored with repetitive jobs, and time can be wasted in transporting goods from one workstation to another. To counter some of these problems, many manufacturers have adopted a **cellular layout**, in which small teams of workers handle all aspects of building a component, a "family" of components, or even a finished product. Each team works in a small area, or cell, equipped with everything that it needs to function as a self-contained unit. Machines are sometimes configured in a U-shape, with people working inside the U. Because team members often share duties, they're trained to perform several different jobs. Teams monitor both the quantity and the quality of their own output. This arrangement often results in faster completion time, lower inventory levels, improved quality, and better employee morale. Cellular manufacturing is used by large manufacturers, such as Boeing, Raytheon, and Pratt & Whitney,[5] as well as by small companies, such as Little Enterprise, which makes components for robots.[6] Figure 11.5 illustrates a typical cellular layout.

cellular layout

Layout in which teams of workers perform all the tasks involved in building a component, group of related components, or finished product.

FIGURE 11.5 Cellular Layout

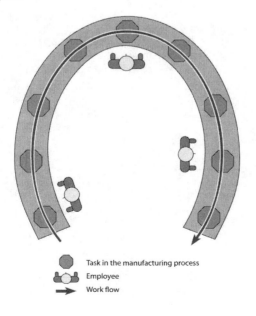

⬡ Task in the manufacturing process

Employee

→ Work flow

Cellular Layout

Click on this link to experience an active version of this figure.

fixed-position layout

Layout in which workers are moved to the product, which stays in one place.

It's easy to move teddy bears and marshmallow candies around the factory while you're making them, but what about airplanes or ships? In producing large items, manufacturers use **fixed-position layout** in which the product stays in one place and the workers (and equipment) go to the product. This is the arrangement used by General Housing Corporation in constructing modular homes. Each house is constructed at the company's factory in Bay City, Michigan, according to the customer's design. Because carpenters, electricians, plumbers, and others work on each building inside the climate-controlled factory, the process can't be hindered by weather. Once it's done, the house is transported in modules to the owner's building site and set up in one day. For a closer view of General Housing Corporation's production process, go to the General Housing Web site at http://www.genhouse.com.

KEY TAKEAWAYS

- Managers have several production **layout** choices, including process, product, cellular, and fixed-position.
- The **process layout** groups together workers or departments that perform similar tasks. At each position, workers use specialized equipment to perform a particular step in the production process.
- In a **product layout**, high-volume goods are produced in assembly-line fashion—that is, a series of workstations at which already-made parts are assembled.
- In a **cellular layout**, small teams of workers handle all aspects of building a component, a "family of components," or even a finished product.
- A **fixed-position layout** is used to make large items (such as ships or buildings) that stay in one place while workers and equipment go to the product.

Before going to the next section of this chapter, take a few minutes to test your knowledge of the material covered in this section. Quizzes can be found under the "Resources" tab, "Study Aids: Quizzes."

EXERCISE

As purchasing manager for a company that flies corporate executives around the world, you're responsible for buying everything from airplanes to onboard snacks. You plan to visit all the plants that make the things you buy: airplanes, passenger seats, TV/DVDs that go in the back of the passenger seats, and the specially designed uniforms (with embroidered company logos) worn by the flight attendants. What type of layout should you expect to find at each facility—process, product, or fixed-position? What will each layout look like? Why is it appropriate for the company's production process? Could any of these plants switch to a cellular layout? What would this type of layout look like? What would be its advantages?

3. MANAGING THE PRODUCTION PROCESS IN A MANUFACTURING COMPANY

LEARNING OBJECTIVES

1. Identify the activities undertaken by the operations manager in overseeing the production process in a manufacturing company.
2. Identify the major materials management decisions made by operations managers.
3. Examine the importance of vendor selection and material acquisition.
4. Discuss the following technology advances that aid the purchasing function: e-purchasing and electronic data interchange (EDI).
5. Explain the following inventory control methods: just-in-time (JIT) production and material requirements planning (MRP).
6. Explain how managers schedule jobs by using a master production schedule (MPS).

Once the production process is in place, the attention of the operations manager shifts to the daily activities of **materials management**, which encompass the following activities: purchasing, inventory control, and work scheduling.

3.1 Purchasing and Supplier Selection

The process of acquiring the materials and services to be used in production is called **purchasing** (or *procurement*). For many products, the costs of materials make up about 50 percent of total manufacturing costs. Not surprisingly, then, materials acquisition gets a good deal of the operations manager's time and attention.

As a rule, there's no shortage of vendors willing to supply parts and other materials, but the trick is finding the *best* suppliers. In selecting a supplier, operations managers must consider such questions as the following:

- Can the vendor supply the needed quantity of materials at a reasonable price?
- Is the quality good?
- Is the vendor reliable (will materials be delivered on time)?
- Does the vendor have a favorable reputation?
- Is the company easy to work with?

Getting the answers to these questions and making the right choices—a process known as supplier selection—is a key responsibility of operations management.

E-Purchasing

Technology is changing the way businesses buy things. Through *e-purchasing* (or *e-procurement*), companies use the Internet to interact with suppliers. The process is similar to the one you'd use to find a consumer good—say, a forty-two-inch LCD high-definition TV—over the Internet. You might start by browsing the Web sites of TV manufacturers, such as Sony or Samsung, or electronics retailers, such as Best Buy. To gather comparative prices, you might go to a comparison-shopping Web site, such as Amazon.com, the world's largest online retailer. You might even consider placing a bid on eBay, an online marketplace where sellers and buyers come together to do business through auctions. Once you've decided where to buy your TV, you'd complete your transaction online, even paying for it electronically.

If you were a purchasing manager using the Internet to buy parts and supplies, you'd follow basically the same process. You'd identify potential suppliers by going directly to private Web sites maintained by individual suppliers or to public Web sites that collect information on numerous suppliers. You could do your shopping through online catalogs, or you might participate in an online marketplace by indicating the type and quantity of materials you need and letting suppliers bid on prices. (Some of these e-marketplaces are quite large. Covisint, for example, which was started by automakers to coordinate online transactions in the auto industry, is used by more than two hundred and fifty thousand suppliers in the auto industry, as well as suppliers in the health care field.)[7] Finally, just as

materials management

All decisions pertaining to the purchase of inputs, the inventory of components and finished products, and the scheduling of production processes.

purchasing

Process of acquiring materials and services to be used in production.

electronic data interchange (EDI)

Computerized exchange of business transaction documents.

you paid for your TV electronically, you could use a system called **electronic data interchange (EDI)** to process your transactions and transmit all your purchasing documents.

The Internet provides an additional benefit to purchasing managers by helping them communicate with suppliers and potential suppliers. They can use the Internet to give suppliers specifications for parts and supplies, encourage them to bid on future materials needs, alert them to changes in requirements, and give them instructions on doing business with their employers. Using the Internet for business purchasing cuts the costs of purchased products and saves administrative costs related to transactions. And it's faster for procurement and fosters better communications.

3.2 Inventory Control

If a manufacturer runs out of the materials it needs for production, then production stops. In the past, many companies guarded against this possibility by keeping large inventories of materials on hand. It seemed like the thing to do at the time, but it often introduced a new problem—wasting money. Companies were paying for parts and other materials that they wouldn't use for weeks or even months, and in the meantime, they were running up substantial storage and insurance costs.

Most manufacturers have since learned that to remain competitive, they need to manage inventories more efficiently. This task requires that they strike a balance between two threats to productivity: losing production time because they've run out of materials, and wasting money because they're carrying too much inventory. The process of striking this balance is called **inventory control**, and companies now regularly rely on a variety of inventory-control methods.

Just-in-Time Production

One method is called **just-in-time (JIT) production**: the manufacturer arranges for materials to arrive at production facilities *just in time* to enter the manufacturing process. Parts and materials don't sit unused for long periods, and the costs of "holding" inventory are significantly cut. JIT, however, requires considerable communication and cooperation between the manufacturer and the supplier. The manufacturer has to know what it needs, and when. The supplier has to commit to supplying the right materials, of the right quality, at exactly the right time.

Material Requirements Planning

Another method, called **material requirements planning (MRP)**, relies on a computerized program both to calculate the quantity of materials needed for production and to determine when they should be ordered or made. Let's say, for example, that you and several classmates are planning a fundraising dinner for the local animal shelter. First, you estimate how many people will attend—say, fifty. Next, you plan the menu—lasagna, garlic bread, salad, and cookies. Then, you determine what ingredients you'll need to make the food. Next, you have to decide when you'll need your ingredients. You don't want to make everything on the afternoon of the dinner; some things—like the lasagna and cookies—can be made ahead of time. Nor do you want to buy all your ingredients at the same time; in particular, the salad ingredients would go bad if purchased too far in advance. Once you've made all these calculations and decisions, you work out a schedule for the production of your dinner that indicates the order and timing of every activity involved. With your schedule in hand, you can determine when to buy each ingredient. Finally, you do your shopping.

Though the production process at most manufacturing companies is a lot more complex than planning a dinner (even for fifty), an MRP system is designed to handle similar problems. The program generates a production schedule based on estimated output (your food-preparation timetable for fifty guests), prepares a list of needed materials (your shopping list), and orders the materials (goes shopping).

FIGURE 11.6

Making lasagna requires decision making and calculations to ensure a yummy final product.

© 2010 Jupiterimages Corporation

The basic MRP focuses on material planning, but there's a more sophisticated system—called **manufacturing resource planning (MRP II)**—that goes beyond material planning to help monitor resources in all areas of the company. Such a program can, for instance, coordinate the production schedule with HR managers' forecasts for needed labor.

3.3 Work Scheduling

As we've seen, manufacturers make profits by transforming inputs (materials and other resources) into outputs (finished goods). We know, too, that production activities, like all business activities, have to be *controlled*: they have to be monitored to ensure that actual performance satisfies planned performance. In production, the control process starts when operations managers decide not only *which* goods and *how many* will be produced, but *when*. This detailed information goes into a **master production schedule (MPS)**. To draw up an MPS, managers need to know where materials are located and headed at every step in the production process. For this purpose, they determine the *routing* of all materials—that is, the work flow of each item based on the sequence of operations in which it will be used.

> **manufacturing resource planning (MRP II)**
>
> System for coordinating a firm's material requirements planning activities with the activities of its other functional areas.

> **master production schedule (MPS)**
>
> Timetable that specifies which and how many products will be produced and when.

KEY TAKEAWAYS

- Once the production process is under way, the attention of the operations manager shifts to the daily activities of **materials management**, which encompasses materials **purchasing**, **inventory control**, and work scheduling.
- Because material costs often make up about 50 percent of total manufacturing costs, vendor selection and material acquisition gets a good deal of the operations manager's time and attention.
- In recent years, the purchasing function has been simplified through technology advances, including e-purchasing and **electronic data interchange (EDI)**, which process transactions and transmit purchasing documents.
- Commonly used inventory control methods include **just-in-time (JIT) production**, by which materials arrive just in time to enter the manufacturing process, and **material requirements planning (MRP)**, which uses computer programming to determine material needs.
- To schedule jobs, managers create a **master production schedule (MPS)**.

Before going to the next section of this chapter, take a few minutes to test your knowledge of the material covered in this section. Quizzes can be found under the "Resources" tab, "Study Aids: Quizzes."

EXERCISE

What is e-purchasing (or e-procurement)? How does it work? What advantages does it give a purchasing manager? How does it benefit a company? How does it change the relationship between purchasing managers and vendors?

4. GRAPHICAL TOOLS: PERT AND GANTT CHARTS

LEARNING OBJECTIVE

1. Explain how to create and use both PERT and Gantt charts.

Because they also need to control the timing of all operations, managers set up *schedules*: They select jobs to be performed during the production process, assign tasks to work groups, set timetables for the completion of tasks, and make sure that resources will be available when and where they're needed. There are a number of scheduling techniques. We'll focus on two of the most common—*Gantt* and PERT *charts*.

4.1 Gantt Charts

A **Gantt chart**, named after the designer, Henry Gantt, is an easy-to-use graphical tool that helps operations managers determine the status of projects. Let's say that you're in charge of making the "hiking bear" that we ordered earlier from the Vermont Teddy Bear Company. Figure 11.7 is a Gantt chart for the production of one hundred of these bears. As you can see, it shows that several activities must be completed before the bears are dressed: the fur has to be cut, stuffed, and sewn; and the clothes and accessories must be made. Our Gantt chart tells us that by day six, all accessories and clothing have been made. The stuffing and sewing, however (which must be finished before the bears are dressed), isn't scheduled for completion until the end of day eight. As operations manager, you'll have to pay close attention to the progress of the stuffing and sewing operations to ensure that finished products are ready for shipment by their scheduled date.

FIGURE 11.7 Gantt Chart for Vermont Teddy Bear

Activity/Day	1	2	3	4	5	6	7	8	9	10	11	12	13
Cut fur	■	■											
Stuff and sew fur			■	■	■	■	■	■					
Cut material	■	■											
Sew clothes			■	■									
Embroider T-shirt					■	■							
Cut accessories	■												
Sew accessories		■	■										
Dress bears									■	■	■		
Package bears												■	
Ship bears													■

Lot size: 100 bears

All activities are scheduled to begin at their earliest start time.

■ Completed work

■ Work to be completed

4.2 PERT Charts

Gantt charts are useful when the production process is fairly simple and the activities aren't interrelated. For more complex schedules, operations managers may use **PERT charts**. PERT (which stands for *Program Evaluation and Review Technique*) is designed to diagram the activities required to produce a good, specify the time required to perform each activity in the process, and organize activities in the most efficient sequence. It also identifies a *critical path*: the sequence of activities that will entail the greatest amount of time. Figure 11.8 is a PERT diagram showing the same process for producing one "hiker" bear at Vermont Teddy Bear.

FIGURE 11.8 PERT Chart for Vermont Teddy Bear

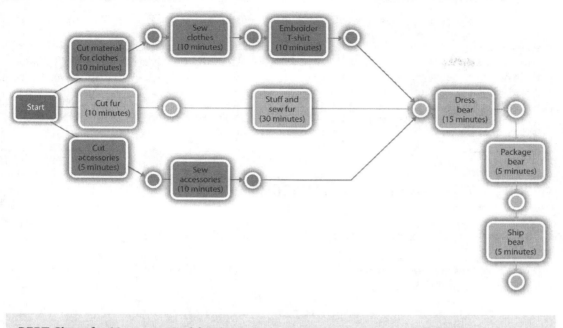

PERT Chart for Vermont Teddy Bear

Click on this link to experience an active version of this figure.

Our PERT chart shows how the activities involved in making a single bear are related. It indicates that the production process begins at the cutting station. Next, the fur that's been cut for this particular bear moves first to the stuffing and sewing stations and then to the dressing station. At the same time that its fur is moving through this sequence of steps, the bear's clothes are being cut and sewn and its T-shirt is being embroidered. Its backpack and tent accessories are also being made at the same time. Note that fur, clothes, and accessories all meet at the dressing station, where the bear is dressed and outfitted with its backpack. Finally, the finished bear is packaged and shipped to the customer's house.

What was the critical path in this process? The path that took the longest amount of time was the sequence that included cutting, stuffing, dressing, packaging, and shipping—a sequence of steps taking sixty-five minutes. If you wanted to produce a bear more quickly, you'd have to save time on this path. Even if you saved the time on any of the other paths—say, the sequence of steps involved in cutting, sewing, and embroidering the bear's clothes—you still wouldn't finish the entire job any sooner: the finished clothes would just have to wait for the fur to be stuffed and sewn and moved to the dressing station. In other words, we can gain efficiency only by improving our performance on one or more of the activities along the critical path.

KEY TAKEAWAYS

- Gantt and PERT charts are two of the most common graphical tools used by operations managers to diagram the activities involved in producing goods.
- A Gantt chart is an easy-to-use graphical tool that helps operations managers determine the status of projects.
- PERT charts are used to diagram the activities required to produce a good, specify the time required to perform each activity in the process, and organize activities in the most efficient sequence.
- A PERT chart identifies a critical path—the sequence of activities that will entail the greatest amount of time.

Before going to the next section of this chapter, take a few minutes to test your knowledge of the material covered in this section. Quizzes can be found under the "Resources" tab, "Study Aids: Quizzes."

Earning a college degree requires not only a lot of hard work but also, as you know, a lot of planning. You must, for example, complete a specified number of credits and take many required courses, particularly in your major. Deciding which courses to take and when to take them can be complicated when some of them have prerequisites. A PERT chart—which diagrams the activities required to complete a goal—might help you determine the order in which you should take courses for your major. Pick a major that interests you and find out what courses you'd need to complete it. Then prepare a PERT chart showing all the courses you'd plan to take each semester to complete your major. (For example, if you select the accounting major, include only accounting courses; don't include your other business courses or your elective courses.) Identify the critical path laid out in your chart. What happens if you fail to take one of your critical-path courses on time?

5. THE TECHNOLOGY OF GOODS PRODUCTION

LEARNING OBJECTIVES

1. **Explain how manufacturing companies use technology to produce and deliver goods in an efficient, cost-effective manner.**
2. **Provide the purpose of the following software systems: computer-aided design (CAD), computer-aided manufacturing (CAM), computer-integrated manufacturing (CIM), and flexible manufacturing systems (FMS).**
3. **Understand how these various software systems can be linked together.**

PowerSki founder and CEO Bob Montgomery spent sixteen years designing the Jetboard and bringing it to production. At one point, in his efforts to get the design just right, he'd constructed thirty different prototypes. Needless to say, this process took a very long time, but even so, Montgomery thought that he could handle the designing of the engine without the aid of a computer. Before long, however, he realized that it was impossible to keep track of all the changes.

5.1 Computer-Aided Design

computer-aided design (CAD)

System using computer technology to create models representing the design of a product.

That's when Montgomery turned to computer technology for help and began using a **computer-aided design (CAD)** software package to design not only the engine but also the board itself and many of its components. The CAD program enabled Montgomery and his team of engineers to test the product digitally and work out design problems before moving to the prototype stage.

The sophisticated CAD software allowed Montgomery and his team to put their design paper in a drawer and to start building both the board and the engine on a computer screen. By rotating the image on the screen, they could even view the design from every angle. Having used their CAD program to make more than four hundred design changes, they were ready to test the Jetboard in the water. During the tests, onboard sensors transmitted data to portable computers, allowing the team to make adjustments from the shore while the prototype was still in the water. Nowadays, PowerSki uses *collaboration software* to transmit design changes to the suppliers of the 340 components that make up the Jetboard.

5.2 Computer-Aided Manufacturing

computer-aided manufacturing (CAM)

System using computer technology to control production processes and equipment.

For many companies, the next step is to link CAD to the manufacturing process. A **computer-aided manufacturing (CAM)** software system determines the steps needed to produce the component and instructs the machines that do the work. Because CAD and CAM programs can "talk" with each other, companies can build components that satisfy exactly the requirements set by the computer-generated model. CAD/CAM systems permit companies to design and manufacture goods faster, more efficiently, and at a lower cost, and they're also effective in helping firms monitor and improve quality. CAD/CAM technology is used in many industries, including the auto industry, electronics, and clothing.

5.3   Computer-Integrated Manufacturing

By automating and integrating all aspects of a company's operations, **computer-integrated manufacturing (CIM)** systems have taken the integration of computer-aided design and manufacturing to a higher level—and are in fact revolutionizing the production process. CIM systems expand the capabilities of CAD/CAM. In addition to design and production applications, they handle such functions as order entry, inventory control, warehousing, and shipping. In the manufacturing plant, the CIM system controls the functions of **industrial robots**—computer-controlled machines used to perform repetitive tasks that are also hard or dangerous for human workers to perform.

5.4   Flexible Manufacturing Systems

Finally, a CIM system is a common element in **flexible manufacturing systems (FMS)**, in which computer-controlled equipment can easily be adapted to produce a variety of goods. An FMS has immense advantages over traditional production lines in which machines are set up to produce only one type of good. When the firm needs to switch a production line to manufacture a new product, substantial time and money are often spent in modifying equipment. An FMS makes it possible to change equipment setups merely by reprogramming computer-controlled machines. Such flexibility is particularly valuable to companies that produce customized products.

computer-integrated manufacturing (CIM)

System in which the capabilities of a CAD/CAM system are integrated with other computer-based functions.

industrial robot

Computer-controlled machine used to perform repetitive tasks that are also hard or dangerous for human workers.

flexible manufacturing system (FMS)

System in which computer-controlled equipment is programmed to handle materials used in manufacturing.

KEY TAKEAWAYS

- In addition to creating high-quality products, companies must produce and deliver goods and services in an efficient, cost-effective manner.
- Sophisticated software systems, including **computer-aided design (CAD)**, **computer-aided manufacturing (CAM)**, **computer-integrated manufacturing (CIM)**, and **flexible manufacturing systems (FMS)**, are becoming increasingly important in this area.
- Computer-aided design software (CAD) is used to create models representing the design of a product.
- Many companies link CAD systems to the manufacturing process through computer-integrated manufacturing (CIM) systems that not only determine the steps needed to produce components but also instruct machines to do the necessary work.
- A CAD/CAM system can be expanded by means of computer-integrated manufacturing (CIM), which integrates various operations (from design through production) with functional activities ranging from order taking to shipping.
- A CIM system is a common element in a flexible manufacturing system (FMS), in which computer-controlled equipment can easily be adapted to produce a variety of goods.

Before going to the next section of this chapter, take a few minutes to test your knowledge of the material covered in this section. Quizzes can be found under the "Resources" tab, "Study Aids: Quizzes."

EXERCISE

The design and production of both goods and services can be facilitated by various high-tech tools, including CAD, CAM, CIM, and FMS. What does CAD software do, and how does it improve a design process? What is CAM, and why is it beneficial to integrate CAD and CAM programs? How do CIM systems expand the capabilities of CAD/CAM? What is an FMS, and what are its advantages over traditional manufacturing systems?

6. OPERATIONS MANAGEMENT FOR SERVICE PROVIDERS

As the U.S. economy has changed from a goods producer to a service provider, the predominance of the goods-producing sector has declined substantially over the last sixty years. Today, only about 14 percent of U.S. workers are employed in the goods-producing sector (including 9 percent in manufacturing),[8] Most of us now hold jobs in the service-producing sector, which employs 86 percent of workers in the U.S.[9] Wal-Mart is now America's largest employer, followed by Yum! Brands (owner of Kentucky Fried Chicken, Taco Bell, and Pizza Hut), McDonald's, International Business Machines (IBM), United Parcel Service (UPS), Target, Kroger, and Home Depot. Not until we drop down to the ninth-largest employer—Hewlett-Packard (HP)—do we find a company with even a manufacturing component.[10]

FIGURE 11.9

Wal-Mart employs more than 1.3 million people in the United States.

© 2010 Jupiterimages Corporation

FIGURE 11.10

Here is just one of the over twelve thousand Burger King restaurants across the globe.

Though the primary function of both manufacturers and service providers is to satisfy customer needs, there are several important differences between the two types of operations. Let's focus on three of them:

- *Intangibility.* Manufacturers produce tangible products—things that can be touched or handled, such as automobiles and appliances. Service companies provide intangible products, such as banking, entertainment, or education.

- *Customization.* Manufactured goods are generally standardized; one twelve-ounce bottle of Pepsi is the same as any other twelve-ounce bottle of Pepsi. Services, by contrast, are often customized to satisfy the specific needs of a customer. When you go to the barber or the hairdresser, you ask for a haircut that looks good on you because of the shape of your face and the texture of your hair. When you go to the dentist, you ask him or her to fill or pull the tooth that's bothering you.

- *Customer contact.* You could spend your entire working life assembling cars in Detroit and never meet a customer who bought a car that you helped to make. But if you were a waitress, you'd interact with customers every day. In fact, their satisfaction with your product would be determined in part by the service that you provided. Unlike manufactured goods, many services are bought and consumed at the same time.

Not surprisingly, operational efficiency is just as important in service industries as it is in manufacturing. To get a better idea of the role of operations management in the service sector, we'll look closely at Burger King (BK), home of the Whopper, and the world's second-largest fast-food hamburger chain.[11] BK has grown substantially since selling the first Whopper (for $0.37) sixty years ago. The instant success of the fire-grilled burger encouraged the Miami founders of the company to expand by selling franchises. Today, there are approximately 13,700 BK company- and independently-owned franchised restaurants in ninety-seven countries (seven thousand of which are in the United States).[12] More than eleven million customers visit BK each day.[13]

6.1 Operations Planning

When starting or expanding operations, businesses in the service sector must make a number of decisions quite similar to those made by manufacturers:

- What services (and perhaps what goods) should they offer?
- How will they provide these services?

- Where will they locate their business, and what will their facilities look like?
- How will they forecast demand for their services?

Let's see how service firms like BK answer questions such as these.[14]

Operations Processes

Service organizations succeed by providing services that satisfy customers' needs. Companies that provide transportation, such as airlines, have to get customers to their destinations as quickly and safely as possible. Companies that deliver packages, such as FedEx, must pick up, sort, and deliver packages in a timely manner. Colleges must provide quality educations. Companies that provide both services and goods, such as Domino's Pizza, have a dual challenge: they must produce a quality good and deliver it satisfactorily.

Service providers that produce goods can, like manufacturers, adopt either a *make-to-order* or a *make-to-stock* approach to manufacturing them. BK, which encourages patrons to customize burgers and other menu items, uses a make-to-order approach. BK can customize products because it builds sandwiches one at a time rather than batch-process them. Meat patties, for example, go from the grill to a steamer for holding until an order comes in. Then the patty is pulled from the steamer and requested condiments are added. Finally, the completed sandwich chutes to a counter worker, who gives it to the customer. In contrast, many of BK's competitors, including McDonald's, rely on a make-to-stock approach in which a number of sandwiches are made at the same time with the same condiments. If a customer wants, say, a hamburger without onions, he or she has to wait for a new batch of patties to be grilled. The procedure could take up to five minutes, whereas BK can process a special order in thirty seconds.

Like manufacturers, service providers must continuously look for ways to improve operational efficiency. Throughout its sixty-year history, BK has introduced a number of innovations that have helped make the company (as well as the fast-food industry itself) more efficient. BK, for example, was the first to offer drive-through service (which now accounts for 70 percent of its sales[15]).

It was also a BK vice president, David Sell, who came up with the idea of moving the drink station from behind the counter so that customers could take over the time-consuming task of filling cups with ice and beverages. BK was able to cut back one employee per day at every one of its more than eleven thousand restaurants. Material costs also went down because customers usually fill cups with more ice, which is cheaper than a beverage. Moreover, there were savings on supply costs because most customers don't bother with lids, and many don't use straws. On top of everything else, most customers liked the system (for one thing, it allowed them to customize their own drinks by mixing beverages), and as a result, customer satisfaction went up, as well. Overall, the new process was a major success and quickly became the industry standard.

Facilities

When starting or expanding a service business, owners and managers must invest a lot of time in selecting a location, determining its size and layout, and forecasting demand. A poor location or a badly designed facility can cost customers, and inaccurate estimates of demand for products can result in poor service, excessive costs, or both.

Site Selection

People in the real estate industry often say that the three most important factors to consider when you're buying a home are location, location, location. The same principle applies when you're trying to locate a service business. To be successful in a service industry, you need to be accessible to your customers. Some service businesses, such as cable-TV providers, package-delivery services, and e-retailers, go to their customers. Many others, however—hotels, restaurants, stores, hospitals, and airports—have to attract customers to their facilities. These businesses must locate where there's a high volume of available customers. Let's see how BK decides where to place a restaurant.

"Through the light and to the right." This is a favorite catchphrase among BK planners who are looking for a promising spot for a new restaurant (at least in the United States). In picking a location, BK planners perform a detailed analysis of demographics and traffic patterns, yet the most important factor is usually *traffic count*—the number of cars or people that pass by a specific location in the course of a day. In the United States, where we travel almost everywhere by car, BK looks for busy intersections, interstate interchanges with easy off and on ramps, or such "primary destinations" as shopping malls, tourist attractions, downtown business areas, or movie theaters. In Europe, where public transportation is much more common, planners focus on subway, train, bus, and trolley stops.

Once planners find a site with an acceptable traffic count, they apply other criteria. It must, for example, be easy for vehicles to enter and exit the site, which must also provide enough parking to handle projected dine-in business. Local zoning must permit standard signage, especially along interstate highways. Finally, expected business must be high enough to justify the cost of the land and building.

Size and Layout

Because manufacturers do business out of plants rarely visited by customers, they base the size and layout of their facilities solely on production needs. In the service sector, however, most businesses must design their facilities with the customer in mind: they must accommodate the needs of their customers while keeping costs as low as possible. Performing this twofold task isn't easy. Let's see how BK has met the challenge.

For its first three decades, almost all BK restaurants were pretty much the same. They all sat on one acre of land (located "through the light and to the right"), had about four thousand square feet of space, and held seating for seventy customers. All kitchens were roughly the same size. As long as land was cheap and sites were readily available, this system worked well enough. By the early 1990s, however, most of the prime sites had been taken, if not by BK itself, then by one of its fast-food competitors or other businesses needing a choice spot, including gas stations and convenience stores. With everyone bidding on the same sites, the cost of a prime acre of land had increased from $100,000 to over $1 million in a few short years.

To continue growing, BK needed to change the way it found and developed its locations. Planners decided that they had to find ways to reduce the size of a typical BK restaurant. For one thing, they could reduce the number of seats, because the business at a typical outlet had shifted over time from 90 percent inside dining and 10 percent drive-through to a 50-50 split. BK customers tended to be in a hurry, and more customers preferred the convenience of drive-through "dining."

David Sell (the same executive who had recommended letting customers fill their own drink cups) proposed to save space by wrapping Whoppers in paper instead of serving them in the cardboard boxes that took up too much space in the back room of every restaurant. So BK switched to a single paper wrapper with the label "Whopper" on one side and "Cheese Whopper" on the other. To show which product was inside, employees just folded the wrapper in the right direction. Ultimately, BK replaced pallets piled high with boxes with a few boxes full of wrappers.

Ideas like these helped BK trim the size of a restaurant from four thousand square feet to as little as one thousand. In turn, smaller facilities enabled the company to enter markets that were once cost prohibitive. Now BK could locate profitably in airports, food courts, strip malls, center-city areas, and even schools. The company even designed 10-foot-by-10-foot kiosks that could be transported to special events, stadiums, and concerts.

Capacity Planning

Estimating capacity needs for a service business isn't the same thing as estimating those of a manufacturer. A manufacturer can predict overall demand, produce the product, store it in inventory, and ship it to a customer when it's ordered. Service providers, however, can't store their products for later use: hairdressers can't "inventory" haircuts, hospitals can't "inventory" operations, and amusement parks can't "inventory" roller-coaster rides. Service firms have to build sufficient capacity to satisfy customers' needs on an "as-demanded" basis. Like manufacturers, service providers must consider many variables when estimating demand and capacity:

- How many customers will I have?
- When will they want my services (which days of the week, which times of the day)?
- How long will it take to serve each customer?
- How will external factors, such as weather or holidays, affect the demand for my services?

Forecasting demand is easier for companies like BK, which has a long history of planning facilities, than for brand-new service businesses. BK can predict sales for a new restaurant by combining its knowledge of customer-service patterns at existing restaurants with information collected about each new location, including the number of cars or people passing the proposed site and the effect of nearby competition.

6.2 Managing Operations

Overseeing a service organization puts special demands on managers, especially those running firms, such as hotels, retail stores, and restaurants, that have a high degree of contact with customers. Service firms provide customers with personal attention and must satisfy their needs in a timely manner. This task is complicated by the fact that demand can vary greatly over the course of any given day. Managers, therefore, must pay particular attention to employee work schedules and (in some cases) inventory management. Let's see how BK deals with these problems.

Scheduling

In manufacturing, managers focus on scheduling the *activities* needed to transform raw materials into finished goods. In service organizations, they focus on scheduling *workers* so that they're available to handle fluctuating customer demand. Each week, therefore, every BK store manager schedules employees to cover not only the peak periods of breakfast, lunch, and dinner, but also the slower periods in between. If he or she staffs too many people, labor cost per sales dollar will be too high. If there aren't enough employees, customers have to wait in lines. Some get discouraged, and even leave, and many may never come back.

Scheduling is made easier by information provided by a point-of-sale device built into every BK cash register. The register keeps track of every sandwich, beverage, and side order sold by the hour, every hour of the day, every day of the week. Thus, to determine how many people will be needed for next Thursday's lunch hour, the manager reviews last Thursday's data, using sales revenue and a specific BK formula to determine the appropriate staffing level. Each manager can adjust this forecast to account for other factors, such as current marketing promotions or a local sporting event that will increase customer traffic.

Inventory Control

Businesses that provide both goods and services, such as retail stores and auto-repair shops, have the same inventory-control problems as manufacturers: keeping levels too high costs money, while running out of inventory costs sales. Technology, such as the point-of-sale registers used at BK, makes the job easier. BK's system tracks everything sold during a given time and lets each store manager know how much of everything should be kept in inventory. It also makes it possible to count the number of burgers and buns, bags and racks of fries, and boxes of beverage mixes at the beginning or end of each shift. Because there are fixed numbers of supplies—say, beef patties or bags of fries—in each box, employees simply count boxes and multiply. In just a few minutes, the manager knows whether the inventory is correct (and should be able to see if any theft has occurred on the shift).

FIGURE 11.11

Retailers have to be prepared to accommodate much heavier traffic than normal during the holiday season.

© 2010 Jupiterimages Corporation

KEY TAKEAWAYS

- Though the primary function of both manufacturers and service providers is to satisfy customer needs, there are several important differences between the two types of operations.
- While manufacturers produce tangible, generally standardized products, service firms provide intangible products that are often customized to satisfy specific needs. Unlike manufactured goods, many services are bought and consumed at the same time.
- Operational efficiency is just as important in service industries as it is in manufacturing.
- Operations managers in the service sector make many decisions that are similar to those made by manufacturers: they decide which services to offer, how to provide these services, where to locate their businesses, what their facilities will look like, and what the demand will be for their services.
- Service providers that produce goods can, like manufacturers, adopt either a make-to-order approach (in which products are made to customer satisfaction) or make-to-stock approach (in which products are made for inventory) to manufacturing them.
- Estimating **capacity** needs for a service business is more difficult than for a manufacturer. Service providers can't store their services for later use: services must be delivered on an as-needed basis.
- Overseeing a service organization puts special demands on managers, especially services requiring a high degree of contact with customers.
- Given the importance of personalized service, scheduling workers is more complex in the service industry than in manufacturing. In manufacturing, operations managers focus on scheduling the *activities* needed to produce goods; in service organizations, they focus on scheduling *workers* to ensure that enough people are available to handle fluctuating customer demand.

Before going to the next section of this chapter, take a few minutes to test your knowledge of the material covered in this section. Quizzes can be found under the "Resources" tab, "Study Aids: Quizzes."

EXERCISE

Starting a new business can be an exciting adventure. Here's your chance to start a "pretend" business. Select a service business that you'd like to open, and answer these questions. Provide an explanation for each answer:

1. What services (and perhaps goods) will I provide?
2. How will I provide these services?
3. Where will I locate my business?
4. What will the facilities look like (how large will the facilities be and what will the layout look like)?
5. How many customers will I serve each day?
6. When will my customers want my services (which days of the week, which times of the day)?
7. How long will it take to serve each customer?
8. Why will my business succeed? Why will my customers return?

7. PRODUCING FOR QUALITY

LEARNING OBJECTIVES

1. Explain how manufacturing and service companies alike use total quality management and outsourcing to provide value to customers.
2. Define total quality management (TQM), and identify the three tasks a company adhering to TQM principles focuses on.
3. Describe how statistical process control (SPC) is used to identify areas for improvement.
4. Explain why outsourcing is an appealing option for companies without the expertise in producing everything needed to make a product.

What do you do if you get it home and your brand-new DVD player doesn't work? What if you were late for class because it took you twenty minutes to get a burger and order of fries at the drive-through window of a fast-food restaurant? Like most people, you'd probably be more or less disgruntled. As a customer, you're constantly assured that when products make it to market, they're of the highest possible quality, and you tend to avoid brands that have failed to live up to your expectations or to producers' claims. You're told that workers in such businesses as restaurants are there to serve you, and you probably don't go back to establishments where you've received poor-quality service.

But what is *quality*? According to the American Society for Quality, **quality** refers to "the characteristics of a product or service that bear on its ability to satisfy stated or implied needs."[16] When you buy a DVD player, you expect it to play DVDs. When it doesn't, you question its quality. When you go to a drive-through window, you expect to be served in a reasonable amount of time. If you're forced to wait, you conclude that you're the victim of poor-quality service.

> **quality**
> Ability of a product to satisfy customer needs.

7.1 Quality Management

To compete today, companies must deliver quality goods and services that satisfy customers' needs. This is the objective of quality management. **Total quality management (TQM)**, or quality assurance, includes all the steps that a company takes to ensure that its goods or services are of sufficiently high quality to meet customers' needs. Generally speaking, a company adheres to TQM principles by focusing on three tasks:

> **total quality management (TQM) (or quality assurance)**
> All the steps taken by a company to ensure that its products satisfy customer needs.

1. Customer satisfaction
2. Employee involvement
3. Continuous improvement

Let's take a closer look at these three principles.

Customer Satisfaction

Companies that are committed to TQM understand that the purpose of a business is to generate a profit by satisfying customer needs. Thus, they let their customers define *quality* by identifying and offering those product features that satisfy customer needs. They encourage customers to tell them how to make the right products, both goods and services, that work the right way.

Armed with this knowledge, they take steps to make sure that providing quality is a factor in every facet of their operations—from design, to product planning and control, to sales and service. To get feedback on how well they're doing, many companies routinely use surveys and other methods to monitor customer satisfaction. By tracking the results of feedback over time, they can see where they need to improve.

Employee Involvement

Successful TQM requires that everyone in the organization, not simply upper-level management, commits to satisfying the customer. When customers wait too long at a drive-through window, it's the responsibility of a number of employees, not the manager alone. A defective DVD isn't solely the responsibility of the manufacturer's quality control department; it's the responsibility of every employee involved in its design, production, and even shipping. To get everyone involved in the drive for quality assurance, managers must communicate the importance of quality to subordinates and motivate them to focus on customer satisfaction. Employees have to be properly trained not only to do their jobs but also to detect and correct quality problems.

quality circle

Employees who perform similar jobs and work as teams to identify quality, efficiency, and other work-related problems; to propose solutions; and to work with management in implementing their recommendations.

continuous improvement

Company's commitment to making constant improvements in the design, production, and delivery of its products.

statistical process control

Technique for monitoring production quality by testing sample outputs to ensure that they meet specifications.

benchmarking

Practice of comparing a company's own performance with that of a company that excels in the same activity.

ISO 9000

Set of international quality standards established by the International Organization for Standardization.

ISO 14000

Set of international standards for environmental management established by the International Organization for Standardization.

In many companies, employees who perform similar jobs work as teams, sometimes called **quality circles**, to identify quality, efficiency, and other work-related problems, to propose solutions, and to work with management in implementing their recommendations.

Continuous Improvement

An integral part of TQM is **continuous improvement**: the commitment to making constant improvements in the design, production, and delivery of goods and services. Improvements can almost always be made to increase efficiency, reduce costs, and improve customer service and satisfaction. Everyone in the organization is constantly on the lookout for ways to do things better.

Statistical Process Control

Companies can use a variety of tools to identify areas for improvement. A common approach in manufacturing is called **statistical process control**. This technique monitors production quality by testing a sample of output to see whether goods in process are being made according to predetermined specifications.

Assume for a moment that you work for Kellogg's, the maker of Raisin Bran cereal. You know that it's the company's goal to pack two scoops of raisins in every box of cereal. How can you test to determine whether this goal is being met? You could use a statistical process control method called a *sampling distribution*. On a periodic basis, you would take a box of cereal off the production line and measure the amount of raisins in the box. Then you'd record that amount on a *control chart* designed to compare actual quantities of raisins with the desired quantity (two scoops). If your chart shows that several samples in a row are low on raisins, you'd shut down the production line and take corrective action.

Benchmarking

Sometimes it also helps to look outside the organization for ideas on how to improve operations and to learn how your company compares with others. Companies routinely use **benchmarking** to compare their performance on a number of dimensions with the performance of other companies that excel in particular areas. Frequent benchmark targets include L.L. Bean, for its superior performance in filling orders; 3M, for its record of introducing innovative products; Motorola, for its success in maintaining consistent quality standards; and Mary Kay Cosmetics, for its skills in inventory control.[17]

7.2   International Quality Standards

As a consumer, wouldn't you like to know which companies ensure that their products meet quality specifications? Some of us would like to know which companies take steps to protect the environment. Some consumers want to know which companies continuously improve their performance in both of these areas—that is, practice both quality management and environmental management. By the same token, if you were a company doing a good job in these areas, wouldn't you want potential customers to know? It might be worth your while to find out whether your suppliers were also being conscientious in these areas—and even your suppliers' suppliers.

ISO 9000 and ISO 14000

Through the International Organization for Standardization (ISO), a nongovernmental agency based in Switzerland, it's possible to find this kind of information. The resources of this organization will enable you to identify those organizations that have people and processes in place for delivering products that satisfy customers' quality requirements. You can also find out which organizations work to reduce the negative impact of their activities on the environment. Working with representatives from various countries, the organization has established the **ISO 9000** family of international standards for quality management and the **ISO 14000** family of international standards for environmental management.

ISO standards focus on the way a company does its work, not on its output (though there's certainly a strong correlation between the way in which a business functions and the quality of its products). Compliance with ISO standards is voluntary, and the certification process is time-consuming and complex. Even so, hundreds of thousands of organizations around the world are ISO 9000 and ISO 14000 certified.[18] ISO certification has become an internationally recognized symbol of quality management and is almost essential to be competitive in the global marketplace.

7.3   Outsourcing

PowerSki's Web site states that "PowerSki International has been founded to bring a new watercraft, the PowerSki Jetboard, and the engine technology behind it, to market."[19] That goal was reached in May 2003, when the firm emerged from a lengthy design period. Having already garnered praise for its innovative product, PowerSki was ready to begin mass-producing Jetboards. At this juncture, the management team made a strategic decision that's not uncommon in manufacturing today. Rather than producing Jetboards in-house, they opted for **outsourcing**: having outside vendors manufacture the engines, fiberglass hulls, and associated parts. Assembly of the final product took place in a manufacturing facility owned by All American Power Sports in Moses Lake, Washington. This decision doesn't mean that the company relinquished control over quality; in fact, every component that goes into the PowerSki Jetboard is manufactured to exact specifications set by PowerSki. One advantage of outsourcing its production function is that the management team can thereby devote its attention to refining its product design and designing future products.

> **outsourcing**
>
> Practice of using outside vendors to manufacture all or part of a company's actual products.

Outsourcing in the Goods-Producing Sector

FIGURE 11.12

Outsourcing the production of its engines, hulls, and other components enables PowerSki to reduce the cost of producing each Jetboard through manufacturing efficiencies and lower labor costs. All components that go into the Jetboard are made to PowerSki's specifications and are inspected upon arrival to ensure that they meet the company's high-quality standards.

Understandably, outsourcing is becoming an increasingly popular option among manufacturers. For one thing, few companies have either the expertise or the inclination to produce everything needed to make a product. Today, more firms, like PowerSki, want to specialize in the processes that they perform best—and outsource the rest. Like PowerSki, they also want to take advantage of outsourcing by linking up with suppliers located in regions with lower labor costs.

Outsourcing in the Service Sector

Outsourcing is by no means limited to the goods-producing (manufacturing) sector. Service companies also outsource many of their noncore functions. Your school, for instance, probably outsources such functions as food services, maintenance, bookstore sales, printing, groundskeeping, security, information-technology (IT) support, and even residence operations.

KEY TAKEAWAYS

- Today, companies that compete in both the manufacturing and service sectors must deliver **quality** goods and services that satisfy customers' needs. Many companies achieve this goal by adhering to principles of **total quality management (TQM)**.
- Companies using a TQM approach focus on customer satisfaction, engage all members of the organization in quality efforts, and strive for **continuous improvement** in the design, production, and delivery of goods and services. They also **benchmark** other companies to find ways to improve their own performance.
- To identify areas for improvement, companies can use a technique called **statistical process control (SPC)**, which monitors quality by testing to see whether a sample of output is being made to predetermined specifications.
- Another cost-saving approach is **outsourcing**—having outside vendors manufacture components or even entire products or provide services, such as information-technology support or service center operations.
- Outsourcing is an appealing option for companies without the expertise in producing everything needed to make a product or those that want to take advantage of low labor costs in developing countries.

Before going to the next chapter, take a few minutes to test your knowledge of the material covered in this section. Quizzes can be found under the "Resources" tab, "Study Aids: Quizzes."

EXERCISES

1. You know that organizations adhering to the principles of TQM focus on three tasks: customer satisfaction, employee involvement, and continuous improvement. Think about the course-registration process at your school. Does the process appear to be managed according to TQM principles? Is it designed to satisfy the customer (you)? Do employees in the registrar's office, as well as others involved in the process, focus on customer satisfaction? Does anyone seem to be on the lookout for ways to do things better?

2. Ever wonder how Jelly Bellys are made? Go to https://jellybelly.com/Info/VirtualTour/virtual_tour to participate in a virtual plant tour and learn how the candy is made. After gaining an understanding of the production process to make the Jelly Belly's, pretend that you've just been hired by the Jelly Belly Candy Company as operations manager for a new candy manufacturing plant. Your first assignment is to set up a plant somewhere in the United States. Next, identify the planning decisions you'd make and indicate what you would decide. Now, fast-forward two years to the point where the plant is up and running. What responsibilities do you have at this point? What technologies do you use to make your job easier? Finally, quality control is vital to the Jelly Belly Candy Company. What activities are you responsible for that ensure that the candy made at your plant meets Jelly Belly's strict quality standards?

8. CASES AND PROBLEMS

LEARNING ON THE WEB

How to Build an Audi

How'd you like to own an Audi A8 model Spyder that lists for $128,400 (http://www.audiusa.com/models/audi-r8-spyder)? How about a convertible Spyder for those warm summer days? Or maybe a less expensive (but still not cheap) A7 coupe for $64,500 or an even less expensive A6 for $43,100? Or, if you just want to use the car for hauling camping equipment, dogs, or kids, maybe you would prefer an even lower priced A4 Saloon for $33,800? We can't help you finance an Audi, but we can show you how they're made. Go to http://www.audi.co.uk/audi-innovation/virtual-factory-tour.html to link to the Audi Web site for a virtual tour of the company's Neckarsulm, Germany, plant that makes these cars.

First click on the Neckarsulm, Germany, location. Then click on "Watch Tour." Once you have reached the "Production" section of the tour, watch the video that zips you through the production steps needed to make an Audi. After watching the brief video describing the work done in a particular area of the plant, pause and answer the following questions. You will answer this set of questions four times—once for each of these areas of the factory: press shop, body shop, paint shop, and assembly.

1. What production steps occurred in this area of the plant?
2. What technology does Audi use in the production process?
3. Approximately what percentage of the work was done by people? What percentage was done by robots? What percentage was accomplished by people and robots working together?

After watching the test drive section of the video, answer this final question: What procedures were followed to ensure the production of high-quality vehicles?

CAREER OPPORTUNITIES

Wanted: Problem Solvers and Creative Thinkers

If you had a time machine plus a craving for a great hamburger, you could return to the early 1950s and swing by Dick and Mac McDonald's burger stand in San Bernardino, California. Take a break from eating and watch the people in the kitchen. You'll see an early application of operations management in the burger industry. Dick and Mac, in an effort to sell more burgers in less time, redesigned their kitchen to use assembly-line procedures. As the number of happy customers grew, word spread about their speedy system, and their business thrived. Curiously, it wasn't Dick and Mac who made McDonald's what it is today, but rather a traveling milkshake-mixer salesman named Ray Kroc. He visited the hamburger stand to learn how they could sell twenty thousand shakes a year. When he saw their operations and the lines of people walking away with bags filled with burgers, fries, and shakes, he knew he had a winner. In cooperation with the McDonald brothers, he started selling franchises around the country, and the rest is history.

So, what does this story have to do with a career in operations management? If you're a problem solver like Dick and Mac (who discovered a way to make burgers faster and cheaper) or a creative thinker like Ray Kroc (who recognized the value in an assembly-line burger production system), then a career in operations management might be for you. The field is broad and offers a variety of opportunities. To get a flavor of the choices available, go to Monster.com to link to the job search site. Enter the job category "operations manager" in the first block of the "I'm looking for" section at the top of the page (there is no need to indicate a company name or location), hit the search button and review the operations management positions listed. Provide a brief description of five positions. Indicate how interesting you find each position by rating it using a five-point scale (with 1 being uninteresting and 5 being very interesting). Based on your assessment, pick the position you find most interesting and the one you find least interesting. Explain why you made your selections.

ETHICS ANGLE

In many ways, Eastman Kodak (a multinational manufacturer and distributor of photographic equipment and supplies) is a model corporate citizen. *Fortune* magazine has ranked it as one of the country's most admired companies, applauding it in particular for its treatment of minorities and women. Its community-affairs programs and contributions have also received praise, but Eastman Kodak remains weak in one important aspect of corporate responsibility: it has consistently received low scores on environmental practices. For example, the watchdog group Scorecard rated Eastman Kodak's Rochester, New York, facility as the third-worst emitter of airborne carcinogens in the United States. Other reports have criticized the company for dumping cancer-causing chemicals into the nation's waters.

Go to http://www.kodak.com/US/en/corp/HSE/homepage.jhtml?pd-path=2879/7196 to link to the Eastman Kodak Web site and read its own assessment of its environmental practices. Then answer the following questions:

- Based on the information provided on its Web site, how favorable do you feel about Eastman Kodak's environmental practices?
- In what ways is the company responding to criticisms of its environmental practices and improving them?
- Do the statements on the Web site mesh with the criticism that the company has received? If not, what accounts for the differences?

TEAM-BUILDING SKILLS

Growing Accustomed to Your Fit

Instead of going to the store to try on several pairs of jeans that may or may not fit, wouldn't it be easier to go online and order a pair of perfect-fitting jeans? Lands' End has made this kind of shopping possible through mass-customization techniques and some sophisticated technology.

To gain some firsthand experience at shopping for mass-customized goods, have each member of your team go to Nike's iD site (http://www.nike.com/us/en_us/c/nikeid). Each team member should go through the process of customizing a different Nike product but stop right before placing an order. After everyone has gone through the process, get together and write a report in which the team explains exactly what's entailed by online mass customization and details the process at Nike. Be sure to say which things impressed you and which didn't. Explain why Nike developed this means of marketing products and, finally, offer some suggestions on how the process could be improved.

THE GLOBAL VIEW

What's the State of Homeland Job Security?

Over the past several decades, more and more U.S. manufacturers began outsourcing production to such low-wage countries as Mexico and China. The number of U.S. manufacturing jobs dwindled, and the United States became more of a service economy. People who were directly affected were understandably unhappy about this turn of events, but most people in this country didn't feel threatened. At least, not until service jobs also started going to countries that, like India, have large populations of well-educated, English-speaking professionals. Today, more technology-oriented jobs, including those in programming and Internet communications, are being outsourced to countries with lower wage rates. And tech workers aren't alone: the jobs of accountants, analysts, bankers, medical technicians, paralegals, insurance adjusters, and even customer-service representatives have become candidates for overseas outsourcing.

Many U.S. workers are concerned about job security (though the likelihood of a particular individual's losing a job to an overseas worker is still fairly low). The issues are more complex than merely deciding where U.S. employers should be mailing paychecks, and politicians, economists, business executives, and the general public differ about the causes and consequences of foreign outsourcing. Some people think it's a threat to American quality of life, while others actually think that it's a good thing.

Spend some time researching trends in outsourcing. Formulate some opinions, and then answer the following questions:

1. About what percentage of U.S. jobs have left the country in the last five years? What percentage will probably leave in the next five years?

2. What kinds of jobs are being outsourced, and where are they going? What kinds of jobs can't be outsourced?

3. How does global outsourcing help U.S. businesses? How does it hinder them?

4. How has the trend in outsourcing manufacturing and service operations to foreign countries helped average Americans? How has it harmed them?

5. Does overseas outsourcing help or hurt the U.S. economy? In what ways?

ENDNOTES

1. "Powerski Jetboard," YouTube video, 1:57, posted by "wannahaves.com," January 14, 2014, http://www.youtube.com/watch?v=Xub5W4QWusM (accessed April 19, 2014); "Liquid Blue Features PowerSki Jetboards," YouTube video, 6:50, posted by "powerskijetboard," March 13, 2008, http://www.youtube.com/watch?v=pyflXBxC0_A (accessed April 19, 2014); Jetboard, "Publicity," http://jetboard.com/marketingpublicity.html (accessed April 19, 2014).

2. Cliff Gromer, "PowerSki Jetboard," *Popular Mechanics*, March 2000, http://www.popularmechanics.com/outdoors/adventures/1277611.html (accessed June 1, 2008).

3. See these Web sites for examples of customized products: Nike (http://www.nike.com/us/en_us/c/nik-eid?cp=usns_kw_AL!1778!3!34161626222!e!!g!nike.id!c), Oakley (http://www.oakley.com/custom), and Mars's M&M's (http://www.mymms.com/?utm_source=-google&utm_medi-um=cpc&utm_term=http+www+mymms+-com&utm_con-tent=MyMMs_Phrase&utm_campaign=S.B.MMs&cvosrc=ppc.google.http www mymms com&matchtype=p&searchntwk=1&gclid=CleAio247b0CFUNqOgodCnAALw) (accessed April 19, 2014).

4. Kleenex, http://www.mykleenextissue.com (accessed April 19, 2014).

5. Wayne Chaneski, "Cellular Manufacturing Can Help You," *Modern Machine Shop*, August 1, 1998, http://www.mmsonline.com/columns/cellular-manufacturing-can-help-you (accessed April 19, 2014).

6. "Better Production—Manufacturing Cell Boosts Profits and Flexibility," *Modern Machine Shop Magazine*, May 2001, http://www.mmsonline.com/articles/manufacturing-cell-boosts-profits-and-flexibility (accessed April 19, 2014), Little Enterprises, Inc., http://www.littleenterprisesinc.com/ (accessed April 19, 2014).

7. Jingzhi Guo, "Covisint.com," http://www.cis.umac.mo/~jzguo/pages/covisint.html (accessed April 19, 2014).

8. Bureau of Labor Statistics, "Data Retrieval: Employment, Hours, and Earnings (CES)," February 7, 2014, http://www.bls.gov/webapps/legacy/cesbtab1.htm (accessed April 19, 2014).

9. Barbara Hagenbaugh, "U.S. Manufacturing Jobs Fading Away Fast," *USA Today*, December 12, 2002, http://usatoday30.usatoday.com/money/economy/2002-12-12-manufacture_x.htm (accessed April 19, 2014).

10. Alexander E. M. Hess, "The Ten Largest Employers in America," *USA Today*, August, 22, 2013, http://www.usatoday.com/story/money/business/2013/08/22/ten-largest-employers/2680249 (accessed April 14, 2014).

11. Burger King, "About BK," http://www.bk.com/en/us/company-info/about-bk.html (accessed April 19, 2014).

12. Burger King, *2013 Annual Report*, February 21, 2014, http://investor.bk.com/download_arquivos.asp?id_arquivo=C0B7F543-DEA6-4852-ACB8-F589DFD66CC7 (accessed April 21, 2014).

13. Burger King, "About BK," http://www.bk.com/en/us/company-info/about-bk.html (accessed April 19, 2014).

14. Information on Burger King was obtained from an interview with David Sell, former vice president of Central, Eastern, and Northern Europe divisions and president of Burger King France and Germany.

15. Bob Krummert, "Burger King: Headed For A Fast-Casual Flameout?" *Restaurant Hospitality*, http://restaurant-hospitality.com/news/burger-king-headed-flameout-1019 (accessed April 21, 2014).

16. American Society of Quality, "Basic Concepts, Definitions," http://asq.org/glossary/q.html (accessed April 19, 2014).

17. Charles J. Nuese, *Building the Right Things Right* (New York: Quality Resources, 1995), 102.

18. International Organization for Standardization, "ISO Survey of Certifications," 2009, http://www.iso.org/iso/survey2009.pdf (accessed April 19, 2014).

19. PowerSki International, "About PowerSki International," http://www.powerski.com/aboutpsi.htm (accessed April 19, 2014).

CHAPTER 12
The Role of Accounting in Business

A NEW FORM OF GPS: THE GREGARIOUS PEOPLE SEEKER

Things are moving so fast we really don't know what's going to happen.

- *Naveen Selvadurai, cofounder of Foursquare*

Let's say that you're doing your homework for your economics class, trying to calculate the effect of a recession on room rates in Fort Lauderdale.[1] For some reason, you start thinking about fun in the sun and wonder if your friends are out somewhere having fun without you. What's a quick way to find out where they are and what they're up to? If you're signed up, you can "check in" with the Foursquare app on your smartphone, iPad, tablet PC, or whatever device you use to connect to a wireless network. Foursquare is a mobile social network, and in addition to the handy "friend finder" feature, you can use it to find new and interesting places to do whatever you and your friends like to do. It even rewards you for doing business with sponsor companies, such as local restaurants.

Foursquare, which has been getting a lot of buzz lately, was started in 2009 by two young entrepreneurs, Dennis Crowley and Naveen Selvadurai. It's already attracted more than 20 million registered users, and Crowley and Selvadurai are understandably enthusiastic about their prospects. Not everybody, however, is as optimistic as they are. Right now, Foursquare is bringing in money and growing, but let's face facts—it's a start-up and it's barely four years old. Among the experts who pay attention to the business of software apps, Foursquare has both optimists and skeptics, and, as usual, there are a lot of people who think that the two entrepreneurs should take the money and run—sell out to a large company and move on.

Clearly, Crowley and Selvadurai have some questions to answer and—at some point, if not necessarily right now—decisions to make. This is where they'll have to rely on an accountant, because they'll need somebody with a knowledge of accounting to help them ask and answer the right questions and formulate and make the right decisions: How much revenue are we bringing in? Can we increase it? What are our expenses? Will they continue to get higher or can we cut them? How much money are we actually making? Are we operating at a profit or a loss? How much do we have invested in the company? How much debt do we have? Can we pay our bills on time? If we need more money, where can we get it? How much cash do we have on hand? How much cash comes in each month and how much goes out? How long will it last? How much is our business really worth? If we decide to sell it, how much should we ask for it? Is it a good idea to put more of our own money into the venture? What are the odds that Foursquare will succeed?

FIGURE 12.1

Foursquare founders Naveen Selvadurai (left) and Dennis Crowley. Selvadurai "checked out" in 2012, three years after the company was started.

Needless to say, the founders of Foursquare will have made a lot of business and financial decisions by the time you've finished this book. When you have finished it, however—along with, perhaps, a few more courses in accounting—you'll know how they gathered, interpreted, and used accounting information to make those decisions.

In this chapter, we'll learn how to gather, summarize, and interpret accounting information and how to use it in making business decisions like the ones facing Crowley and Selvadurai.

1. THE ROLE OF ACCOUNTING

LEARNING OBJECTIVES

1. Define "accounting," and explain the differences between "managerial accounting" and "financial accounting."
2. Identify some of the users of accounting information, and explain how they use it.

1.1 The Language of Business

stakeholders

Parties who are interested in the activities of a business because they're affected by them.

accounting

System for measuring and summarizing business activities, interpreting financial information, and communicating the results to management and other decision makers.

Accounting is often called "the language of business." Why? Because it *communicates* so much of the information that owners, managers, and investors need to evaluate a company's financial performance. These people are all **stakeholders** in the business—they're interested in its activities because they're affected by them. In fact, the purpose of accounting is to help stakeholders make better business decisions by providing them with financial information. Obviously, you wouldn't try to run an organization or make investment decisions without accurate and timely financial information, and it's the accountant who prepares this information. More importantly, accountants make sure that stakeholders understand the *meaning* of financial information, and they work with both individuals and organizations to help them use financial information to deal with business problems. Actually, collecting all the numbers is the easy part—today, all you have to do is start up your accounting software. The hard part is analyzing, interpreting, and communicating the information. Of course, you also have to present everything clearly while effectively interacting with people from every business discipline. In any case, we're now ready to define **accounting** as the process of measuring and summarizing business activities, interpreting financial information, and communicating the results to management and other decision makers.

Fields of Accounting

Accountants typically work in one of two major fields. *Management accountants* provide information and analysis to decision makers *inside* the organization in order to help them run it. *Financial accountants* furnish information to individuals and groups *both inside and outside* the organization in order to help them assess its financial performance.

In other words, management accounting helps you keep your business running while financial accounting tells you how well you're running it.

Management Accounting

management accounting

Branch of accounting that provides information and analysis to decision makers inside the organization to help them operate the business.

Management accounting plays a key role in helping managers carry out their responsibilities. Because the information that it provides is intended for use by people who perform a wide variety of jobs, the format for reporting information is flexible. Reports are tailored to the needs of individual managers, and the purpose of such reports is to supply *relevant*, *accurate*,and *timely information* in a format that will aid managers in making decisions. In preparing, analyzing, and communicating such information, accountants work with individuals from all the *functional areas* of the organization—human resources, operations, marketing, and finance.

Financial Accounting

Financial accounting is responsible for preparing the organization's **financial statements**—including the *income statement*, the *statement of owner's equity*, the *balance sheet*, and the *statement of cash flows*—that summarize a company's past performance and evaluate its current financial condition. In preparing financial statements, financial accountants adhere to a uniform set of rules called **generally accepted accounting principles (GAAP)**—the basic principles for financial reporting issued by an independent agency called the Financial Accounting Standards Board (FASB). Users want to be sure that financial statements have been prepared according to GAAP because they want to be sure that the information reported in them is accurate. They also know that they can compare the statements issued by one company to those of another company in the same industry.

While companies headquartered in the United States follow U.S.-based GAAP, many companies located outside the United States follow a different set of accounting principles called **International Financial Reporting Standards (IFRS)**. These multinational standards, which are issued by the International Accounting Standards Board (IASB), differ from U.S. GAAP in a number of important ways. IFRS, for example, is a little stricter about the ways you can calculate the costs of inventory, but we're not going to dwell unnecessarily on such fine distinctions. Bear in mind, however, that, according to most experts, a single set of worldwide standards will eventually emerge to govern the accounting practices of both U.S. and non-U.S. companies.

FIGURE 12.2

Financial statements provide a snapshot of a company's performance over a specific period.

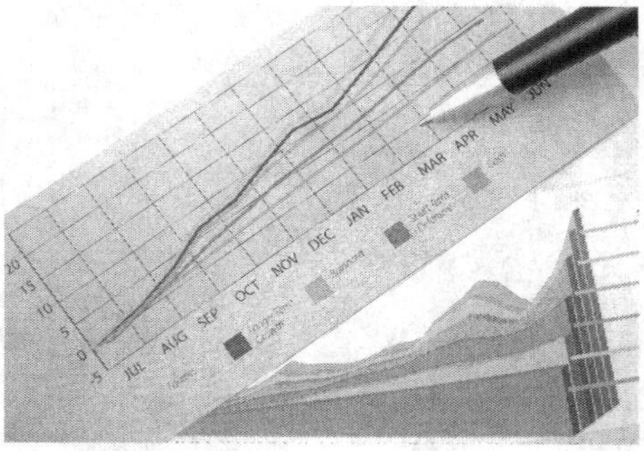

© 2010 Jupiterimages Corporation

1.2   Who Uses Financial Accounting Information?

The users of *managerial* accounting information are pretty easy to identify—basically, they're a firm's *managers*. We need to look a little more closely, however, at the users of *financial* accounting information, and we also need to know a little more about what they do with the information that accountants provide them.

Owners and Managers

In summarizing the outcomes of a company's financial activities over a specified period of time, financial statements are, in effect, report cards for owners and managers. They show, for example, whether the company did or didn't make a profit and furnish other information about the firm's financial condition. They also provide information that managers and owners can use in order to take corrective action.

Investors and Creditors

If you loaned money to a friend to start a business, wouldn't you want to know how the business was doing? Investors and creditors furnish the money that a company needs to operate, and not surprisingly, they feel the same way. Because they know that it's impossible to make smart investment and loan decisions without accurate reports on an organization's financial health, they study financial statements to assess a company's performance and to make decisions about continued investment.

According to the world's most successful investor (and third-richest individual), Warren Buffett, the best way to prepare yourself to be an investor is to learn all the accounting you can. Buffett, chairman and CEO of Berkshire Hathaway, a company that invests in other companies, turned an original investment of $10,000 into a net worth of $35 billion in four decades, and he did it, in large part, by paying close attention to financial accounting reports.[2]

financial accounting

Branch of accounting that furnishes information to individuals and groups both inside and outside the organization to help them assess the firm's financial performance.

financial statements

Financial reports—including the income statement, the balance sheet, and the statement of cash flows—that summarize a company's past performance and evaluate its financial health.

generally accepted accounting principles (GAAP)

Uniform set of rules for financial reporting issued by an independent agency called the Financial Accounting Standards Board (FASB).

International Financial Reporting Standards (IFRS)

A set of worldwide accounting rules and guidelines used by companies to prepare financial statements that can be compared with those of other countries.

FIGURE 12.3 Warren Buffet

Photo by Kevin Parry/WireImage/Getty Images

Government Agencies

Businesses are required to furnish financial information to a number of government agencies. Publicly owned companies, for example—the ones whose shares are traded on a stock exchange—must provide annual financial reports to the Securities and Exchange Commission (SEC), a federal agency that regulates stock trades. Companies must also provide financial information to local, state, and federal taxing agencies, including the Internal Revenue Service.

Other Users

A number of other external users have an interest in a company's financial statements. Suppliers, for example, need to know if the company to which they sell their goods is having trouble paying its bills or may even be at risk of going under. Employees and labor unions are interested because salaries and other forms of compensation are dependent on an employer's performance.

Figure 12.4 summarizes the main differences between the users of management and financial accounting and the types of information issued by accountants in the two areas. In the rest of this chapter, we'll learn how to prepare a set of financial statements and how to interpret them. We'll also discuss issues of ethics in the accounting communities and career opportunities in the accounting profession.

FIGURE 12.4 Management and Financial Accounting

Management Accountants
supply financial information to help...

...Internal Users
answer questions and make decisions.

Owners
Should we sell some of our assets next year?

Managers
Did our prices optimize our profits this year?

Can we afford to expand capacity next year?

Financial Accountants
supply financial information to help both...

**...External Users
and Internal Users**
answer questions and make decisions.

Owners
Did we make a satisfactory profit this year?

Managers
Can we afford to pay dividends to stockholders this year?
Can we afford to give employees raises this year?

Government Agencies
Did the company report correct income to investors?

Investors and Creditors
Did the company generate satisfactory revenues this year?

Employees
Did the company contribute to the pension fund this year?

Questions That Managers and Accountants Must Answer

Management accountants provide relevant, timely information to individuals throughout the business organization. See if you can match typical questions asked of management accountants with the area of the organization seeking advice. Click here to complete the exercise.

KEY TAKEAWAYS

- **Accounting** is a system for measuring and summarizing business activities, interpreting financial information, and communicating the results to management and other **stakeholders** to help them make better business decisions.
- Accounting can be divided into two major fields:
  - **Management accounting** provides information and analysis to decision makers *inside* the organization (such as owners and managers) to help them operate the business.
  - **Financial accounting** provides information not only to internal managers, but also to people *outside* the organization (such as investors, creditors, government agencies, suppliers, employees, and labor unions) to assist them in assessing a firm's financial performance.
- U.S. and non-U.S. companies follow different sets of standards in preparing financial accounting reports:
  - U.S. companies adhere to a uniform set of rules called **generally accepted accounting principles (GAAP)**, which are issued by an independent agency called the Financial Accounting Standards Board (FASB).
  - Many companies outside the United States follow a set of accounting principles called **International Financial Reporting Standards (IFRS)**, which are issued by the International Accounting Standards Board (IASB).
- Experts expect that a single set of worldwide accounting standards will eventually emerge and be followed by both U.S. and non-U.S. companies.

Before going to the next section of this chapter, take a few minutes to test your knowledge of the material covered in this section. Quizzes can be found under the "Resources" tab, "Study Aids: Quizzes."

EXERCISE

1. Who uses accounting information? What do they use it for, and why do they find it helpful? What problems would arise if they weren't provided with accounting information?

2. UNDERSTANDING FINANCIAL STATEMENTS

LEARNING OBJECTIVES

1. Understand the function of the income statement.
2. Understand the function of the balance sheet.
3. Understand the function of the statement of owner's equity.
4. Describe the accounting equation.
5. Identify the order in which financial statements should be prepared.
6. Understand breakeven analysis, and demonstrate how it can be used to determine the level of sales needed to break even.

We hope that, so far, we've made at least one thing clear: If you're in business, you need to understand financial statements. For one thing, the law no longer allows high-ranking executives to plead ignorance or fall back on delegation of authority when it comes to taking responsibility for a firm's financial reporting. In a business environment tainted by episodes of fraudulent financial reporting and other corporate misdeeds, top managers are now being held accountable (so to speak) for the financial statements issued by the people who report to them. For another thing, top managers need to know if the company is hitting on all cylinders or sputtering down the road to bankruptcy. To put it another way (and to switch metaphors): if he didn't understand the financial statements issued by the company's accountants, an executive would be like an airplane pilot who doesn't know how to read the instrument in the cockpit—he might be able keep the plane in the air for a while, but he wouldn't recognize any signs of impending trouble until it was too late.

2.1 The Function of Financial Statements

Put yourself in the place of the woman in Figure 12.5. She runs Connie's Confections out of her home. She loves what she does, and she feels that she's doing pretty well. In fact, she has an opportunity to take over a nearby store at very reasonable rent, and she can expand by getting a modest bank loan and investing some more of her own money. So it's decision time for Connie: She knows that the survival rate for start-ups isn't very good, and before taking the next step, she'd like to get a better idea of whether she's actually doing well enough to justify the risk. As you can see, she has several pertinent questions. We aren't privy to Connie's finances, but we can tell her how basic financial statements will give her some answers.

FIGURE 12.5 What Connie Wants to Know

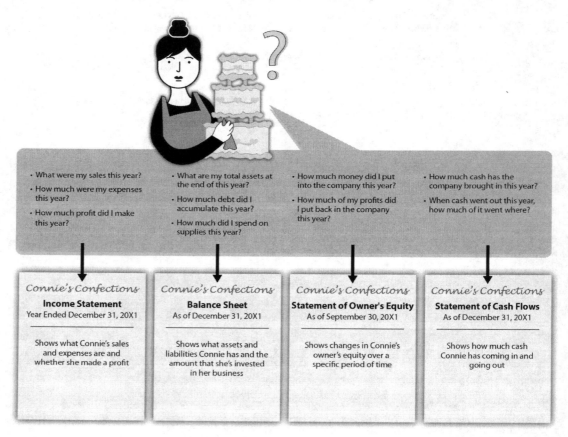

Toying with a Business Idea

We know what you're thinking: It's nice to know that accounting deals with real-life situations, but while you wish Connie the best, you don't know enough about the confectionary business to appreciate either the business decisions or the financial details. Is there any way to bring this lesson a little closer to home? Besides, while knowing what financial statements will tell you is one thing, you want to know how to *prepare* them.

Agreed. So let's assume that you need to earn money while you're in college and that you've decided to start a small business. Your business will involve selling stuff to other college students, and to keep things simple, we'll assume that you're going to operate on a "cash" basis: you'll pay for everything with cash, and everyone who buys something from you will pay in cash.

A Word about Cash. You probably have at least a little *cash* on you right now—some currency, or paper money, and coins. In accounting, however, the term *cash* refers to more than just paper money and coins. It also refers to the money that you have in checking and savings accounts and includes items that you can deposit in these accounts, such as money orders and different types of checks.

Your first task is to decide exactly what you're going to sell. You've noticed that with homework, exams, social commitments, and the hectic lifestyle of the average college student, you and most of the people you know always seem to be under a lot of stress. Sometimes you wish you could just lie back between meals and bounce a ball off the wall. And that's when the idea hits you: Maybe you could make some money by selling a product called the "Stress-Buster Play Pack." Here's what you have in mind: you'll buy small toys and other fun stuff—instant stress relievers—at a local dollar store and pack them in a rainbow-colored plastic treasure chest labeled "Stress-Buster."

And here's where you stand: You have enough cash to buy a month's worth of plastic treasure chests and toys. After that, you'll use the cash generated from sales of Stress-Buster Play Packs to replenish your supply. Each plastic chest will cost $1.00, and you'll fill each one with a variety of five of the following toys, all of which you can buy for $1.00 each:

- A happy face stress ball
- A roomarang (an indoor boomerang)
- Some silly putty
- An inflatable beach ball
- A coil "slinky" spring
- A paddle-ball game
- A ball for bouncing off walls

You plan to sell each Stress-Buster Play Pack for $10 from a rented table stationed outside a major dining hall. Renting the table will cost you $20 a month. Because your own grades aren't what your parents and the dean would like them to be, you decide to hire fellow students (trustworthy people with better grades than yours) to staff the table at peak traffic periods. They'll be on duty from noon until 2:00 p.m. each weekday, and you'll pay them $6 an hour. Wages, therefore, will cost you $240 a month (2 hours × 5 days × 4 weeks = 40 hours × $6). Finally, you'll run ads in the college newspaper at a monthly cost of $40. Thus your total monthly costs will amount to $300 ($20 + $240 + $40).

2.2 The Income Statement

Let's say that during your first month, you sell one hundred play packs. Not bad, you say to yourself, but did I make a *profit*? To find out, you prepare an **income statement** showing **revenues**, or **sales**, and **expenses**—the costs of doing business. You divide your expenses into two categories:

- **Cost of goods sold**: the total cost of the *goods that you've sold*
- **Operating expenses**: the costs of *operating your business* except for the costs of things that you've sold

Now you need to do a little subtracting:

income statement

Financial statement summarizing a business's revenues, expenses, and net income.

revenues

Amount of money earned by selling products to customers.

expenses

Costs incurred by selling products to customers.

cost of goods sold

Cost of the products that a business sells to customers.

operating expenses

Costs of selling products to customers, not including cost of goods sold.

gross profit (or gross margin)

Positive difference between revenues and cost of goods sold.

net income (or net profit)

Positive difference between gross profit and total expenses.

1. The positive difference between *sales* and *cost of goods sold* is your **gross profit or gross margin.**
2. The positive difference between *gross profit* and *operating expenses* is your **net income** or **profit,** which is the proverbial "bottom line." (If this difference is *negative*, you took a *loss* instead of making a profit.)

Figure 12.6 is your income statement for the first month. (Remember that we've made things simpler by handling everything in cash.)

FIGURE 12.6 Income Statement for Stress-Buster Company

Stress-Buster Company

Income Statement
Month Ended September 30, 20X1

Sales (100 × $10)		$1,000
Less cost of goods sold (100 × $6)		600
Gross profit (100 × $4)		400
Less operating expenses		
Salaries	240	
Advertising	40	
Table rental	20	
	300	
Net income (profit)		$100

Did You Make Any Money?

What does your income statement tell you? It has provided you with four pieces of valuable information:

1. You sold 100 units at $10 each, bringing in *revenues* or *sales* of $1,000.
2. Each unit that you sold cost you $6—$1 for the treasure chest plus 5 toys costing $1 each. So your *cost of goods sold* is $600 (100 units × $6 per unit).
3. Your *gross profit*—the amount left after subtracting cost of goods sold from sales—is $400 (100 units × $4 each).
4. After subtracting *operating expenses* of $300—the costs of doing business other than the cost of products sold—you generated a positive *net income* or *profit* of $100.

What If You Want to Make More Money?

You're quite relieved to see that you made a profit during your first month, but you can't help but wonder what you'll have to do to make even more money next month. You consider three possibilities:

1. Reduce your cost of goods sold (say, package four toys instead of five)
2. Reduce your operating costs (salaries, advertising, table rental)
3. Increase the quantity of units sold

In order to consider these possibilities fully, you need to generate new income statements for each option. And to do that, you'll have to play a few "what-if" games.

"What If" Number One—Four Toys Instead of Five

Because possibility number one—packaging four toys instead of five—is the most appealing, you start there. Your cost of goods sold would go down from $6 to $5 per unit (4 toys at $1 each + 1 plastic treasure chest at $1). Figure 12.7 is your hypothetical income statement if you choose this option.

FIGURE 12.7 Proposed Income Statement for Option Number One for Stress-Buster Company

Stress-Buster Company

Income Statement
Month Ended September 30, 20X1
[If cost of goods sold is $5 per unit]

Sales (100 × $10)		$1,000
Cost of goods sold (100 × $5)		500
Gross profit (100 × $5)		500
Less operating expenses		
Salaries	240	
Advertising	40	
Table rental	20	
	300	
Net income (profit)		$200

Possibility number one seems to be a good idea. Under this scenario, your income doubles from $100 to $200 because your per-unit *gross profit* increases by $1 (and you sold 100 stress packs). But there may be a catch: if you cut back on the number of toys, your customers might perceive your product as a lesser value for the money. In fact, you're reminded of a conversation that you once had with a friend whose father, a restaurant owner, had cut back on the cost of the food he served by buying less expensive meat. In the short term, gross profit per meal went up, but customers eventually stopped coming back and the restaurant nearly went out of business.

"What If" Number Two—Reduce Operating Costs

Thus you decide to consider possibility number two—reducing your operating costs. In theory, it's a good idea, but in practice—at least in your case—it probably won't work. Why not? For one thing, you can't do without the table and you need your workers (because your grades haven't improved, you still don't have time to sit at the table yourself). Second, if you cut salaries from, say, $6 to $5 an hour, you may have a hard time finding people willing to work for you. Finally, you could reduce advertising costs by running an ad every two weeks instead of every week, but this tactic would increase your income by only $20 a month and could easily lead to a drop in sales. This possibility isn't attractive enough to justify another hypothetical income statement.

"What If" Number Three—Increase Sales

So you move on to possibility number three—increase sales. The appealing thing about this option is that it has no downside. If you could somehow increase the number of units sold from 100 Stress-Buster packs per month to 150, your income would go up, even if you stick with your original five-toy product. So you decide to crunch some numbers for possibility #3 and come up with the new "what-if" income statement in Figure 12.8.

FIGURE 12.8 Proposed Income Statement for Option Number Three for Stress-Buster Company

Stress-Buster Company

Income Statement
Month Ended September 30, 20X1
[At breakeven level of sales = 75 units]

Sales (75 X $10)	$750
Less cost of goods sold (75 X $6)	450
Gross profit (75 X $4)	300
Less operating expenses	
Salaries	240
Advertising	40
Table rental	20
	300
Net income (profit)	$0

As you can see, this is an attractive possibility, even though you haven't figured out how you're going to increase sales. Maybe you could put up some eye-popping posters and play cool music to attract people to your table. Or maybe your workers could attract buyers by demonstrating relaxation and stress-reduction exercises. Obviously, you'll have to make a few decisions, but at least you have enough accounting information to focus on a specific goal.

Breakeven Analysis

breakeven analysis

Method of determining the level of sales at which the company will break even (have no profit or loss).

fixed costs

Costs that don't change when the amount of goods sold changes.

variable costs

Costs that vary, in total, as the quantity of goods sold changes but stay constant on a per-unit basis.

contribution margin per unit

Excess of revenue per unit over variable cost per unit.

breakeven point in units

Number of sales units at which net income is zero.

Playing these what-if games has started you thinking: is there some way to figure out the level of sales you need to avoid *losing* money—to "break even"? This can be done using **breakeven analysis**. To break even (have no profit or loss), your *total sales revenue must exactly equal all your expenses (both variable and fixed)*. For a merchandiser, like a hypothetical one called The College Shop, this balance will occur when gross profit equals all other (fixed) costs. To determine the level of sales at which this will occur, you need to do the following:

1. Determine your total **fixed costs**, which are so called because the total cost doesn't change as the quantity of goods sold changes:

   - Fixed costs = $240 salaries + $40 advertising + $20 table = $300

2. Identify your **variable costs**. These are costs that vary, in total, as the quantity of goods sold changes but stay constant on a per-unit basis. State variable costs on a per-unit basis:

   - Variable cost per unit = $6 ($1 for the treasure chest and $5 for the toys)

3. Determine your **contribution margin per unit**: selling price per unit – variable cost per unit:

   - Contribution margin per unit = $10 selling price – $6 variable cost per unit = $4

4. Calculate your **breakeven point in units**: fixed costs ÷ contribution margin per unit:

   - Breakeven in units = $300 fixed costs ÷ $4 contribution margin per unit = 75 units

Your calculation means that if you sell 75 units, you'll end up with zero profit (or loss) and will exactly break even. To test your calculation, you can prepare a what-if income statement for 75 units in sales (which is your breakeven number of sales). The resulting statement is shown in Figure 12.9.

FIGURE 12.9   Proposed Income Statement Number Three for Stress-Buster Company

Stress-Buster Company

Income Statement
Month Ended September 30, 20X1
[At breakeven level of sales = 75 units]

Sales (75 X $10)		$750
Less cost of goods sold (75 X $6)		450
Gross profit (75 X $4)		300
Less operating expenses		
Salaries	240	
Advertising	40	
Table rental	20	
	300	
Net income (profit)		$0

What if you want to do better than just break even? What if you want to earn a profit of $200 next month? How many Stress-Buster Pack units would you need to sell? You can find out by building on the results of your breakeven analysis. Note that each additional sale will bring in $4 (contribution margin per unit). If you want to make a profit of $200—which is $200 *above your breakeven point*—you must sell an additional 50 units ($200 desired profit divided by $4 contribution margin per unit) above your breakeven point of 75 units. If you sell 125 units (75 breakeven units + the additional 50), you'll make a profit of $200 a month.

As you can see, breakeven analysis is rather handy. It enables you to determine the level of sales that you must reach to avoid losing money and the level of sales that you have to reach to earn a profit of $200. Such information will help you plan for your business. For example, knowing you must sell 125 Stress-Buster Packs to earn a $200 profit will help you decide how much time and money you need to devote to marketing your product.

2.3   The Balance Sheet

Your **balance sheet** reports the following information:

balance sheet

Report on a company's assets, liabilities, and owner's equity at a specific point in time.

asset

Resource from which a business expects to gain some future benefit.

liability

Debt owed by a business to an outside individual or organization.

owner's equity

Amount which is invested in a business by its owners and which owners can claim from its assets.

fiscal year,

Company's designated business year.

accounting equation

Accounting tool showing the resources of a business (assets) and the claims on those resources (liabilities and owner's equity).

- Your **assets**: the resources from which it expects to gain some future benefit
- Your **liabilities**: the debts that it owes to *outside* individuals or organizations
- Your **owner's equity**: your investment in your business

Whereas your income statement tells you how much income you earned *over some period of time*, your balance sheet tells you what you have (and where it came from) *at a specific point in time.*

Most companies prepare financial statements on a twelve-month basis—that is, for a **fiscal year,** which ends on December 31 or some other logical date, such as June 30 or September 30. Why do fiscal years vary? A company generally picks a fiscal-year end date that coincides with the end of its peak selling period; thus a crabmeat processor might end its fiscal year in October, when the crab supply has dwindled. Most companies also produce financial statements on a quarterly or monthly basis. For Stress-Buster, you'll want to prepare monthly financial statements.

The Accounting Equation

The balance sheet is based on the **accounting equation**:

assets = liabilities + owner's equity

This important equation highlights the fact that a company's *assets* came from somewhere: either from loans (*liabilities*) or from investments made by the owners (*owner's equity*). This means that the asset section of the balance sheet on the one hand and the liability and owner's-equity section on the other must be equal, or *balance*. Thus the term *balance sheet.*

Let's prepare two balance sheets for your company: one for the first day you started and one for the end of your first month of business. We'll assume that when you started Stress-Buster, you borrowed \$400 from your parents and put in \$200 of your own money. If you look at your first balance sheet in Figure 12.10, you'll see that your business has \$600 in cash (your *assets*). Of this total, you borrowed \$400 (your *liabilities*) and invested \$200 of your own money (your *owner's equity*). So far, so good: your assets section *balances* with your liabilities and owner's equity section.

FIGURE 12.10 Balance Sheet Number One for Stress-Buster Company

Stress-Buster Company Balance Sheet As of September 1, 20X1	
Assets	
Cash	$600
Liabilities and owner's equity	
Liabilities	400
Owner's equity	200
Total liabilities and owner's equity	$600

Now let's see how things have changed by the end of the month. Recall that Stress-Buster earned \$100 (based on sales of 100 units) during the month of September and that you decided to leave these earnings in the business. This \$100 profit increases two items on your *balance sheet*: the *assets* of the company (its cash) and your investment in it (its *owner's equity*). Figure 12.11 shows what your balance sheet will look like on September 30. Once again, it *balances*. You now have \$700 in cash: \$400 that you borrowed plus \$300 that you've invested in the business (your original \$200 investment plus the \$100 profit from the first month of operations). Your liabilities are still \$400, and your owner's equity has increased to \$300 (the \$200 you originally invested plus your profit of \$100).

FIGURE 12.11 Balance Sheet Number Two for Stress-Buster Company

Stress-Buster Company

Balance Sheet
As of September 30, 20X1

Assets	
Cash (original $600 plus $100 earned)	$700
Liabilities and Owner's equity	
Liabilities	400
Owner's equity ($200 invested by owner plus $100 profits retained)	300
Total Liabilities and Owner's equity	$700

2.4   The Statement of Owner's Equity

Note that we used the *net income* figure from your *income statement* to update the owner's equity section of your end-of-month balance sheet. Often, companies prepare an additional financial statement, called the **statement of owner's equity**, which details changes in owner's equity for the reporting period. Figure 12.12 shows what this statement looks like.

statement of owner's equity

A financial statement that details changes in owner's equity for a specified period of time.

FIGURE 12.12 Sample Statement of Owner's Equity for Stress-Buster Company

Stress-Buster Company

Statement of Owner's Equity
As of September 30, 20X1

Owner's equity, September 1, 20X1	$200
+ Net income	100
Owner's equity, September 30, 20X1	$300

2.5   How Do Financial Statements Relate to One Another?

When you prepare your financial statements, you should complete them in a certain order:

1. Income statement
2. Statement of owner's equity
3. Balance sheet

Why must they be prepared in this order? Because financial statements are interrelated: numbers generated on one financial statement appear on other financial statements. Figure 12.13 presents Stress-Buster's financial statements for the month ended September 30, 20X1. As you review these statements, note that in two cases, numbers from one statement appear in another statement:

FIGURE 12.13 How Financial Statements Relate to One Another

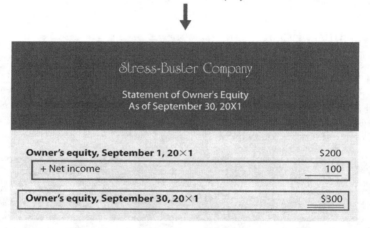

Net income for the month is also on the **Statement of Owner's Equity** as an addition to the beginning *Owner's equity* balance. This addition of $100 increases the balance in *Owner's equity* from $200 to $300:

The ending *Owner's equity* balance of $300 also appears on the Balance Sheet as *Owner's equity*:

If the interlinking numbers are carried forward correctly, and if assets and liabilities are listed correctly, then the balance sheet will *balance*: Total *assets* will equal the total of *liabilities* plus *owner's equity*.

KEY TAKEAWAYS

- Accountants prepare four **financial statements**: *income statement*, *statement of owner's equity*, *balance sheet*, and *statement of cash flows* (which is discussed later in the chapter).
- The **income statement** shows a firm's **revenues** and **expenses** and whether it made a profit.
- The **balance sheet** shows a firm's **assets**, **liabilities** and **owner's equity** (the amount that its owners have invested in it).
- The balance sheet is based on the **accounting equation**:

$$\text{assets} = \text{liabilities} + \text{owner's equity}$$

  This equation highlights the fact that a company's *assets* came from one of two sources: either from loans (its *liabilities*) or from investments made by owners (its *owner's equity*).
- The **statement of owner's equity** reports the changes in owner's equity that have occurred over a specified period of time.
- Financial statements should be competed in a certain order: *income statement*, *statement of owner's equity*, and *balance sheet*. These financial statements are interrelated because numbers generated on one financial statement appear on other financial statements.
- **Breakeven analysis** is a technique used to determine the level of sales needed to break even—to operate at a sales level at which you have neither profit nor loss.
- To break even, total sales revenue must exactly equal all your expenses (both **variable** and **fixed costs**).
- To calculate the **breakeven point in units** to be sold, you divide fixed costs by **contribution margin per unit** (selling price per unit minus variable cost per unit).
- This technique can also be used to determine the level of sales needed to obtain a specified profit.

Before going to the next section of this chapter, take a few minutes to test your knowledge of the material covered in this section. Quizzes can be found under the "Resources" tab, "Study Aids: Quizzes."

EXERCISES

1. Describe the information provided by each of these financial statements: income statement, balance sheet, statement of owner's equity. Identify ten business questions that can be answered by using financial accounting information. For each question, indicate which financial statement (or statements) would be most helpful in answering the question, and why.

2. You're the president of a student organization, and to raise funds for a local women's shelter you want to sell single long-stem red roses to students on Valentine's Day. Each prewrapped rose will cost $3. An ad for the college newspaper will cost $100, and supplies for posters will cost $60. If you sell the roses for $5, how many roses must you sell to break even? Because breaking even won't leave you any money to donate to the shelter, you also want to know how many roses you'd have to sell to raise $500. Does this seem like a realistic goal? If the number of roses you need to sell in order to raise $500 is unrealistic, what could you do to reach this goal?

3. ACCRUAL ACCOUNTING

LEARNING OBJECTIVES

1. Understand the difference between cash-basis and accrual accounting.
2. Understand the purpose of a statement of cash flows and describe its format.
3. Define the following accounting terms used by merchandisers: inventory, cost of goods sold, and gross profit.
4. Describe how depreciation is calculated and where it appears on your financial statements.
5. Understand how a classified balance sheet divides assets and liabilities into current assets and liabilities and long-term assets and liabilities.

In this section, we're going to take a step further into the world of accounting by examining the principles of *accrual accounting*. In our Stress-Buster illustration, we've assumed that all your transactions have been made in *cash*: You paid cash for your inputs (plastic treasure chests and toys) and for your other expenses, and your customers paid cash when they bought Stress-Buster packs. In the real world, of course, things are rarely that simple. In the following cases, timing plays a role in making and receiving payments:

- Customers don't always pay in cash; they often buy something and pay later. When this happens, the seller is owed money and has an **account receivable** (it will *receive* something later).

- Companies don't generally pay cash for materials and other expenses—they often pay later. If this is the case, the buyer has an **account payable** (it will *pay* something later).

- Many companies manufacture or buy goods and hold them in **inventory** before selling them. Under these circumstances, they don't report payment for the goods until they've been sold.

- Companies buy *long-term assets* (also called *fixed assets*), such as cars, buildings, and equipment, which they plan to use over an extended period (as a rule, for more than one year).

3.1 What Is Accrual Accounting?

In situations such as these, firms use **accrual accounting**: a system in which the accountant records a transaction *when it occurs*, without waiting until cash is paid out or received. Here are a few basic principles of accrual accounting:

- Revenue from a sale is recognized on the income statement *when the sale takes place*, regardless of when cash is collected.

- An expense is recognized on the income statement *when it's incurred*, regardless of when payment is made.

- An item manufactured for later sale or bought for resale becomes part of *inventory* and appears on the balance sheet *until it's actually sold*; at that point, it goes on the income statement under *cost of goods sold*.

- A *long-term asset* that will be used for several years—for example, a vehicle, machine, or building—appears on the balance sheet. Its cost is spread *over its useful life*—the number of years that it will be used. Its annual allocated cost appears on the income statement as a **depreciation expense**.

3.2 Going to School on a New Business Idea

As we saw in our Stress-Buster illustration, it's easier to make sense of accounting concepts when you see some real—or at least realistic—numbers being put to realistic use. So let's now assume that you successfully operated the Stress-Buster Company while you were in college. Now fast-forward to graduation, and rather than work for someone else, you've decided to set up a more ambitious business—some kind of retail outlet—close to the college. During your four years in school, you noticed that there was no store near campus that met the wide range of students' specific needs. Thus the mission of your proposed retail business: to provide products that satisfy the specific needs of college students.

---

account receivable

Record of cash that will be received from a customer to whom a business has sold products on credit.

account payable

Record of cash owed to sellers from whom a business has purchased products on credit.

inventory

Goods that a business has made or bought and expects to sell in the process of normal operations.

accrual accounting

Accounting system that records transactions when they occur, regardless of when cash is paid or received.

depreciation expense

Costs of a long-term or fixed asset spread over its useful life.

You've decided to call your store "The College Shop." Your product line will range from things needed to outfit a dorm room (linens, towels, small appliances, desks, rugs, dorm refrigerators) to things that are just plain fun and make student life more enjoyable (gift packages, posters, lava lamps, games, inflatable furniture, bean bag chairs, message boards, shower radios, backpacks). And of course you'll also sell the original Stress-Buster Fun Pack. You'll advertise to students and parents through the college newspaper and your own Web site.

FIGURE 12.14
The College Shop

3.3   Accrual-Basis Financial Statements

At this point, we're going to repeat pretty much the same process that we went through with your first business. First, we'll prepare a *beginning balance sheet* that reflects your new company's assets, liabilities, and owner's equity on your first day of business—January 1, 20X6. Next, we'll prepare an *income statement* and a *statement of owner's equity*. Finally, we'll create a balance sheet that reflects the company's financial state at the end of your first year of business.

Although the process should now be familiar, the details of our new statements will be more complex—after all, your transactions will be more complicated: You're going to sell and buy stuff on credit, maintain an inventory of goods to be sold, retain assets for use over an extended period of time, borrow money and pay interest on it, and deal with a variety of expenses that you didn't have before (rent, insurance, etc.).

Beginning Balance Sheet

Your new beginning balance sheet contains the same items as the one that you created for Stress-Buster—cash, loans, and owner's equity. But because you've already performed a broader range of transactions before you opened for business, you'll need some new categories:

- You've bought furniture and equipment that you'll use over the next five years. You'll allocate the cost of these long-term assets by depreciating them. Because you estimate that this furniture and equipment will have a *useful life* of five years, you allocate one-fifth of the cost per year for five years.
- You've purchased an inventory of goods for later resale.
- You've taken out two types of loans: one that's *current* because it's payable in one year and one that's *long term* because it's due in five years.

Obviously, then, you need to prepare a more sophisticated balance sheet than the one you created for your first business. We call this new kind of balance sheet a **classified balance sheet** because it classifies assets and liabilities into separate categories.

Types of Assets

On a classified balance sheet, assets are listed in order of **liquidity**—how quickly they can be converted into cash. They're also broken down into two categories:

1. **Current assets**—assets that you intend to convert into cash within a year
2. **Long-term assets**—assets that you intend to hold for more than a year

Your current assets will be cash and inventory, and your long-term assets will be furniture and equipment. We'll take a closer look at the assets section of your beginning balance sheet, but it makes sense to analyze your liabilities first.

Types of Liabilities

Liabilities are grouped in much the same manner as assets:

1. **Current liabilities**—liabilities that you'll pay off within one year
2. **Long-term liabilities**—liabilities that don't become due for more than one year

Recall that your liabilities come from your two loans: one that is payable in a year and considered current and one that is long term and due in five years.

Now we're ready to review your beginning balance sheet, which is shown in Figure 12.15. Once again, your balance sheet balances the following: your total assets of $275,000 equal your total liabilities plus owner's equity of $275,000.

classified balance sheet

Balance sheet that totals assets and liabilities in separate categories.

liquidity

Speed with which an asset can be converted into cash.

current asset

Asset that a business intends to convert into cash within a year.

long-term asset (or fixed asset)

Asset that a business intends to hold for more than a year before converting it to cash.

current liability

Liability that a business intends to pay off within a year.

long-term liability

Liability that a business need not pay off within the following year.

FIGURE 12.15 Beginning Balance Sheet for The College Shop

The College Shop
Balance Sheet
As of January 1, 20X6

Assets

Current assets

Cash	$50,000
Inventory	75,000

Long-term assets

Furniture, displays, and equipment	150,000
Total assets	**$275,000**

Liabilities and owner's equity

Current liabilities

Loan payable (due this year)	$25,000

Long-term liabilities

Loan payable (due in 5 years)	100,000
Owner's equity	150,000
Total liabilities and owner's equity	**$275,000**

Liabilities and Owner's Equity

Let's begin our analysis of your beginning balance sheet with the liabilities and owner's-equity sections. We're assuming that, thanks to a strong business plan, you've convinced a local bank to loan you a total of $125,000—a short-term loan of $25,000 and a long-term loan of $100,000. Naturally, the bank charges you *interest* (which is the cost of borrowing money); your rate is 8 percent per year. In addition, you personally contributed $150,000 to the business (thanks to a trust fund that paid off when you turned 21).

Assets

Now let's turn to the assets section of your beginning balance sheet. What do you have to show for your $275,000 in liabilities and owner's equity? Of this amount, $50,000 is in *cash*—that is, money deposited in the company's checking and other bank accounts. You used another $75,000 to pay for *inventory* that you'll sell throughout the year. Finally, you spent $150,000 on several *long-term assets*, including a sign for the store, furniture, store displays, and computer equipment. You expect to use these assets for five years, at which point you'll probably replace them.

Income Statement

Finally, let's look at your income statement, which is shown in Figure 12.16. Like your College Shop balance sheet, your College Shop income statement is more complex than the one you prepared for Stress-Buster, and the amounts are much larger. In addition, the statement covers a full calendar year.

FIGURE 12.16 Income Statement for The College Shop, Year Ended December 31

The College Shop
Income Statement
Year Ended December 31, 20X6

Sales		$500,000
Less cost of goods sold		275,000
Gross profit		225,000
Less operating expenses		
Salaries and employee benefits	75,000	
Depreciation	30,000	
Rent and utilities	20,000	
Advertising	20,000	
Other (insurance, office expenses, miscellaneous)	30,000	
Total operating expenses	$175,000	
Operating income (Income before interest and taxes)		50,000
Less interest expense (8% × loans of $125,000)		10,000
Net income before income taxes		40,000
Less income taxes (25% × income before taxes)		10,000
Net income		30,000

Note, by the way, that the income statement that we prepared for The College Shop is designed for a *merchandiser*—a company that makes a profit by selling goods. How can you tell? Businesses that sell services (such as accounting firms or airlines) rather than merchandise don't have lines labeled *cost of goods sold* on their statements. In addition, their revenue is called "sales."

The format of this income statement also highlights the most important financial fact in running a merchandising company: *you must sell goods at a profit (called* gross profit*) that is high enough to cover your operating costs, interest, and taxes.* Your income statement, for example, shows that The College Shop generated $225,000 in *gross profit* through *sales* of goods. This amount is sufficient to cover your *operating expense*, interest, and taxes and still produce a *net income* of $30,000.

A Few Additional Expenses

Note that The College Shop income statement also lists a few expenses that the Stress-Buster didn't incur:

- *Depreciation expense.* Recall that before opening for business, you purchased some long-term assets (store sign, displays, furniture, and equipment) for a total amount of $150,000. In estimating that you would use these assets for five years (your estimate of their useful lives), you spread the cost of $150,000 over five years. For each of these five years, then, your income statement will show $30,000 in *depreciation expense* ($150,000 ÷ 5 years = $30,000).

- *Interest expense.* When you borrowed money from the bank, you agreed to pay interest at an annual rate of 8 percent. Your *interest expense* of $10,000 ($125,000 × 0.08) is a cost of financing your business and appears on your income statement after the subheading *operating income*.

- *Income taxes.* Your company has to pay income taxes at a rate of 25 percent of *net income before taxes*. This amount of $10,000 ($40,000 × 25%) appears on your income statement after the subheading *net income before income taxes*. It's subtracted from *income before income taxes* before you arrive at your "bottom line," or *net income*.

Statement of Owner's Equity

Our next step is to prepare a statement of owner's equity, which is shown in Figure 12.17. Note that the *net income* of $30,000 from the income statement was used to arrive at the year-end balance in owner's equity.

FIGURE 12.17 Statement of Owner's Equity for The College Shop

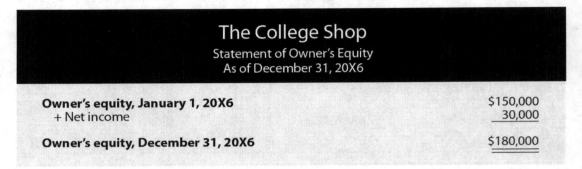

End-of-First-Year Balance Sheet

We'll conclude with your balance sheet for the end of your first year of operations, which is shown in Figure 12.18. First, look at your assets. At year's end, you have a *cash balance* of $70,000 and *inventory* of $80,000. You also have an *accounts receivable* of $90,000 because many of your customers have bought goods on credit and will pay later. In addition, the balance sheet now shows two numbers for *long-term assets*: the original cost of these assets, $150,000, and an *accumulated depreciation* amount of $30,000, which reflects the amount that you've charged as depreciation expense since the purchase of the assets. The carrying value of these long-term assets is now $120,000 ($150,000 – $30,000), which is the difference between their original cost and the amount that they've been depreciated. Your *total assets* are thus $360,000.

FIGURE 12.18 End-of-Year Balance Sheet for The College Shop

The College Shop
Balance Sheet
As of December 31, 20X6

Assets
Current assets

Cash	$70,000
Accounts receivable	90,000
Inventory	80,000
Total current assets	240,000

Long-term assets

Furniture, displays, and equipment	150,000
Less: accumulated depreciation	(30,000)
Total long-term assets	120,000
Total assets	$360,000

Liabilities and owner's equity
Current liabilities

Accounts payable	$80,000

Long-term liabilities

Loan payable (due in 4 years)	100,000

Owner's equity

(150,000 1 30,000)	180,000
Total liabilities and owner's equity	$360,000

The total of your liabilities of $180,000 plus owner's equity of $180,000 also equals $360,000. Your liabilities consist of a long-term loan of $100,000 (which is now due in four years) and *accounts payable* of $80,000 (money that you'll have to pay out later for purchases that you've made on credit). Your owner's equity (your investment in the business) totals $180,000 (the $150,000 you originally put in plus the $30,000 in first-year earnings that you retained in the business).

Statement of Cash Flows

Owners, investors, and creditors can learn a lot from your balance sheet and your income statement. Indeed, each tells its own story. The balance sheet tells what assets your company has now and where they came from. The income statement reports earned income on an accrual basis (recognizing revenues when earned and expenses as incurred regardless of when cash is received or paid). But the key to surviving in business is generating the *cash* you need to keep it up and running. It's not unusual to hear reports about companies with cash problems. Sometimes they arise because the products in which the firm has invested aren't selling as well as it had forecast. Maybe the company tied up too much money in a plant that's too big for its operations. Maybe it sold products to customers who can't pay. Maybe management just overspent. Whatever the reason, cash problems will hamper any business. Owners and other interested parties need a financial statement that helps them understand a company's cash flow.

statement of cash flows

Financial statement reporting on cash inflows and outflows resulting from operating, investing, and financing activities.

operating activity

Activity that creates cash inflows or outflows through day-to-day operations.

investing activity

Activity that creates cash inflows or outflows through the selling or buying of long-term assets.

financing activity

Activity that creates cash inflows or outflows through the obtaining or repaying of borrowed or invested funds.

The **statement of cash flows** tells you where your cash came from and where it went. It furnishes information about three categories of *activities* that cause cash either to come in (*cash inflows*) or to go out (*cash outflows*):

1. Cash flows from **operating activities** come from the day-to-day operations of your main line of business.
2. Cash flows from **investing activities** result from buying or selling long-term assets.
3. Cash flows from **financing activities** result from obtaining or paying back funds used to finance your business.

A cash flow statement for The College Shop would look like the one in Figure 12.19. You generated $45,000 in cash from your company's operations (a cash inflow) and used $25,000 of this amount to pay off your short-term loan (a cash outflow). The net result was an increase in cash of $20,000. This $20,000 increase in cash agrees with the change in your cash during the year as it's reported in your balance sheets: you had an end-of-the-year cash balance of $70,000 and a beginning-of-the-year balance of $50,000 ($70,000 − $50,000 = $20,000). Because you didn't buy or sell any *long-term assets* during the year, your cash flow statement shows no cash flows from investing activities.

FIGURE 12.19 Statement of Cash Flows for The College Shop

The College Shop

Cash Flow Statement
As of December 31, 20X6

Cash inflows from operating activities	$45,000
Cash outflows from financing activities	25,000
Increase in cash during the year	$20,000

Activities That Produce Cash Inflows and Outflows

Take a few moments to reinforce your understanding of the cash flow statement by classifying cash transactions into the three categories highlighted on a cash flow statement: operating, investing and financing activities. Click here to complete the exercise.

KEY TAKEAWAYS

- There are two different methods for reporting financial transactions:
  - Companies using *cash-basis accounting* recognize **revenue** as earned only when cash is received and recognize **expenses** as incurred only when cash is paid out.
  - Companies using **accrual accounting** recognize revenues when they're earned (regardless of when the cash is received) and expenses when they're incurred (regardless of when the cash is paid out).
- An item manufactured for later sale or bought for resale appears on the balance sheet as an asset called **inventory**. When it's sold, it goes on the income statement as an expense under the category *cost of goods sold*.
- The difference between *sales* and *cost of goods* sold is called **gross profit**.
- A merchandising company's gross profit must be high enough to cover its operating costs, interest, and taxes.
- An asset that will be used for several years (say, a truck) appears on the balance sheet as a **long-term asset**. Its cost is allocated over its *useful life* and appears on the income statement as a **depreciation expense**.
- A **classified balance sheet** separates assets and liabilities into two categories—*current* and *long-term*:
  - **Current assets** include those that you intend to convert into cash within a year; **long-term assets** include those that you plan to hold for more than a year.
  - **Current liabilities** include those that you'll pay off within a year; **long-term liabilities** include those that do not become due for more than a year.
- The **statement of cash flows** shows how much cash the business has coming in and going out.
- The *statement of cash flows* furnishes information about three categories of activities that cause cash either to come in or to go out: **operating activities**, **investing activities**, and **financing activities**.

Before going to the next section of this chapter, take a few minutes to test your knowledge of the material covered in this section. Quizzes can be found under the "Resources" tab, "Study Aids: Quizzes."

EXERCISES

1. To earn money to pay some college expenses, you ran a lawn-mowing business during the summer. Before heading to college at the end of August, you wanted to find out how much money you earned for the summer. Fortunately, you kept good accounting records. During the summer, you charged customers a total of $5,000 for cutting lawns (which includes $500 still owed to you by one of your biggest customers). You paid out $1,000 for gasoline, lawn mower repairs, and other expenses, including $100 for a lawn mower tune-up that you haven't paid for yet. You decided to prepare an income statement to see how you did. Because you couldn't decide whether you should prepare a cash-basis statement or an accrual statement, you prepared both. What was your income under each approach? Which method (cash basis or accrual) more accurately reflects the income that you earned during the summer? Why?

2. Identify the categories used on a classified balance sheet to report assets and liabilities. How do you determine what goes into each category? Why would a banker considering a loan to your company want to know whether an asset or liability is current or long term?

3. You review a company's statement of cash flows and find that cash inflows from operations are $150,000, net outflows from investing are $80,000, and net inflows from financing are $60,000. Did the company's cash balance increase or decrease for the year? By what amount? What types of activities would you find under the category investing activities? Under financing activities? If you had access to the company's income statement and balance sheet, why would you be interested in reviewing its statement of cash flows? What additional information can you gather from the statement of cash flows?

4.   FINANCIAL STATEMENT ANALYSIS

LEARNING OBJECTIVES

1. Evaluate a company's financial performance using vertical percentage analysis.
2. Describe the purpose of ratio analysis.
3. Indicate what can be learned by preparing the following categories of ratios: profit margin ratios, management efficiency ratios, management effectiveness ratios, and financial condition ratios.
4. Prepare the following profit margin ratios: gross profit margin and net profit margin.
5. Prepare the following management efficiency ratio: inventory turnover.
6. Explain what can be learned from the following management effectiveness ratio: return on assets.
7. Prepare and explain the meaning of the following financial condition ratios: current ratio, debt-to-equity ratio, and interest coverage ratio.

Now that you know how financial statements are prepared, let's see how they're used to help owners, managers, investors, and creditors assess a firm's performance and financial strength. You can glean a wealth of information from financial statements, but first you need to learn a few basic principles for "unlocking" it.

4.1   The Comparative Income Statement

comparative income statement

Financial statement showing income for more than one year.

Let's fast-forward again and assume that your business—The College Shop—has just completed its second year of operations. After creating your second-year income statement, you decide to compare the numbers from this statement with those from your first statement. So you prepare the **comparative income statement** in Figure 12.20, which shows income figures for year 2 and year 1 (accountants generally put numbers for the most recent year in the inside column).

FIGURE 12.20 Comparative Income Statement for The College Shop

The College Shop

Comparative Income Statement
Years Ended December 31, 20X7 and 20X6

	12/31/20X7	12/31/20X6
Sales	$600,000	$500,000
Less cost of goods sold	387,000	275,000
Gross profit	213,000	225,000
Less operating expenses	180,000	175,000
Operating income	33,000	50,000
Less interest	10,000	10,000
Less income taxes	5,000	10,000
Net income	$18,000	$30,000

Vertical Percentage Analysis

What does this statement tell us about your second year in business? Some things look good and some don't. Your sales went up from $500,000 to $600,000 (a 20 percent increase—not bad). But your profit was down—from $30,000 to $18,000 (a bad sign). As you stare at the statement, you're asking yourself the question: Why did my profit go down even though my sales went up? Does this result make sense? Is there some way of comparing two income statements that will give me a more helpful view of my company's financial health? One way is called **vertical percentage analysis**. It's useful because it reveals the relationship of each item on the income statement to a specified base—generally sales—by expressing each item as a percentage of that base.

Figure 12.21 shows what comparative income statements look like when you use vertical percentage analysis showing each item as a percentage of sales. Let's see if this helps clarify things. What do you think accounted for the company's drop in income even though The College Shop sales went up?

vertical percentage analysis

Analysis of an income statement treating the relationship of each item as a percentage of a base (usually sales).

FIGURE 12.21 Comparative Income Statement Using Vertical Percentage Analysis

The College Shop

Comparative Income Statement
Years Ended December 31, 20X7 and 20X6
[Using vertical percentage analysis
showing each item as a % of sales]

| | 12/31/20X7 | | 12/31/20X6 | |
	Amount	Percent	Amount	Percent
Sales	$600,000	100	$500,000	100
Less cost of goods sold	387,000	64	275,000	55
Gross profit	213,000	36	225,000	45
Less operating expenses	180,000	30	175,000	35
Operating income	33,000	6	50,000	10
Less interest	10,000	2	10,000	2
Less income taxes	5,000	1	10,000	2
Net income	$18,000	3%	$30,000	6%

The percentages help you to analyze changes in the income statement items over time, but it might be easier if you think of the percentages as pennies. In year 1, for example, for every $1.00 of sales, $0.55 went to pay for the goods that you sold, leaving $0.45 to cover your other costs and leave you a profit. Operating expenses (salaries, rent, advertising, and so forth) used up $0.35 of every $1.00 of sales, while interest and taxes took up $0.02 each. After you covered all your costs, you had $0.06 profit for every $1.00 of sales.

Asking the Right Questions

Now, compare these figures to those for year 2. Where is the major discrepancy? It's in *Cost of goods sold*. Instead of using $0.55 of every $1.00 of sales to buy the goods you sold, you used $0.64. As a result, you had $0.09 less ($0.64 – $0.55) to cover other costs. This is the major reason why you weren't as profitable in year 2 as you were in year 1: your *Gross profit as a percentage of sales* was lower in year 2 than it was in year 1. Though this information doesn't give you all the answers you'd like to have, it does, however, raise some interesting questions. Why was there a change in the relationship between *Sales* and *Cost of goods sold*? Did you have to pay more to buy goods for resale and, if so, were you unable to increase your selling price to cover the additional cost? Did you have to reduce prices to move goods that weren't selling well? (If your costs stay the same but your selling price goes down, you make less on each item sold.) Answers to these questions require further analysis, but at least you know what the useful questions are.

4.2   Ratio Analysis

ratio analysis

Technique for financial analysis that shows the relationship between two numbers.

Vertical percentage analysis helps you analyze relationships between items on your income statement. But how do you compare your financial results with those of other companies in your industry or with the industry overall? And what about your balance sheet? Are there relationships on this statement that also warrant investigation? Should you further examine any relationships between items on your income statement and items on your balance sheet? These issues can be explored by using **ratio analysis**, a technique for evaluating a company's financial performance.

First, remember that a *ratio* is just one number divided by another, with the result expressing the relationship between the two numbers. Let's say, for example, that you want to know the relationship between the cost of going to a movie and the cost of renting a DVD movie. You could make the following calculation:

$$\frac{\text{Cost of going to a movie}}{\text{Cost of renting a DVD}} = \frac{\$8}{\$4} = 2 \text{ (or 2 to 1)}$$

Going to a movie costs two times as much as renting a DVD.

Ratio analysis is also used to assess a company's performance over time and to compare one company to similar companies or to the overall industry in which it operates. You don't learn much from just one ratio, or even a number of ratios covering the same period. Rather, the value in ratio analysis lies in looking at the *trend* of ratios over time and in comparing the ratios for several time periods with those of competitors and the industry as a whole. There are a number of different ways to categorize financial ratios. Here's just one set of categories:

- **Profit margin ratios** tell you how much of each sales dollar is left after certain costs are covered.
- **Management efficiency ratios** tell you how efficiently your assets are being managed.
- **Management effectiveness ratios** tell you how effective management is at running the business and measure overall company performance.
- **Financial condition ratios** help you assess a firm's financial strength.

Using each of these categories, we can find dozens of different ratios, but we'll focus on a few examples.

Profit Margin Ratios

We've already determined the two most common profit margin ratios—*gross profit margin* and *net profit margin*—when we used vertical percentage analysis to determine the relationship to *Sales* of each item on The College Shop's income statement. We were examining gross profit when we found that *Gross profit* for year 1 was 45 percent of *Sales* and that, in year 2, it had declined to 36 percent. We can express the same relationships as ratios:

$$\text{Gross profit margin} = \frac{\text{Gross profit}}{\text{Sales}}$$

$$\text{Year 1:} \frac{\$225,000}{\$500,000} = 45\%$$

$$\text{Year 2:} \frac{\$213,000}{\$600,000} = 36\% \text{ (rounded)}$$

We can see that gross profit margin declined (a situation that, as we learned earlier, probably isn't good). But how can you tell whether your gross profit margin for year 2 is appropriate for your company? For one thing, we can use it to compare The College Shop's results to those of its industry. When we make this comparison, we find that the specialized retail industry (in which your company operates) reports an average gross profit margin of 41 percent. For year 1, therefore, we had a higher ratio than the industry; in year 2, though we had a lower ratio, we were still in the proverbial ballpark.

It's worthwhile to track gross profit margin, whether for your company or for companies that you might invest in or lend money to. In particular, you'll gain some insight into *changes* that might be occurring in a business. For instance, what if you discover that a firm's gross profit margin has declined? Is it because it's costing more for the company to buy or make its products, or is it because its competition is forcing it to lower its prices?

Net Profit Margin

Net profit is the money that a company earns *after paying all its expenses*, including the costs of buying or making its products, running its operations, and paying interest and taxes. Look again at Figure 12.21. Using vertical percentage analysis, we found that for The College Shop, net profit as a percentage of sales was 6 percent in year 1 but declined to 3 percent in year 2. Expressed as ratios, these relationships would look like this:

---

profit margin ratio

Financial ratio showing how much of each sales dollar is left after certain costs are covered.

management efficiency ratio

Financial ratio showing how efficiently a company's assets are being used.

management effectiveness ratio

Financial ratio showing how effectively a firm is being run and measuring its overall performance.

financial condition ratio

Financial ratio that helps to assess a firm's financial strength.

$$\text{Net profit margin} = \frac{\text{Net profit}}{\text{Sales}}$$

$$\text{Year 1}: \frac{\$30,000}{\$500,000} = 6\%$$

$$\text{Year 2}: \frac{\$18,000}{\$600,000} = 3\% \text{ (rounded)}$$

You realize that a declining net profit margin isn't good, but you wonder how you compare with your industry. A little research informs you that average net profit margin in the industry is 7 percent. You performed nearly as well as the industry in year 1 but fell further from your target in year 2. What does this information tell you? That a goal for year 3 should be trying to increase your net profit margin.

Management Efficiency Ratios

These ratios reveal the way in which assets (shown on the balance sheet) are being used to generate income (shown on the income statement). To compute this group of ratios, therefore, you must look at both statements. In Figure 12.20, we produced a comparative income statement for The College Shop's first two years. Figure 12.22 is a comparative balance sheet for the same period.

FIGURE 12.22 Comparative Balance Sheet for The College Shop

The College Shop
Comparative Balance Sheet
As of December 31, 20X7 and 20X6

	12/31/20X7	12/31/20X6
Assets		
Current assets		
Cash	$76,000	$70,000
Accounts receivable	92,000	90,000
Inventory	110,000	80,000
Total current assets	278,000	240,000
Long-term assets		
Furniture, equipment, net of depreciation	90,000	120,000
Total assets	368,000	$360,000
Liabilities and owner's equity		
Current liabilities		
Accounts payable	$70,000	80,000
Long-term liabilities		
Loan	100,000	100,000
Total liabilities	170,000	180,000
Owner's equity	198,000	180,000
Total liabilities and owner's equity	$368,000	$360,000

As you can see from Figure 12.22, running even a small business entails a substantial investment in assets. Even if you rent space, for example, you must still buy furniture and equipment. To have products on hand to sell, you need to tie up money in inventory. And once you've sold them, you may have money tied up in accounts receivable while you're waiting for customers to pay you. Thus, investing in assets is a normal part of doing business. Managing your assets efficiently is a basic requirement of business success. Let's look at a representative management efficiency ratio. The **inventory turnover ratio** measures a firm's efficiency in selling its inventory.

You don't make money from unsold inventory. You make money when you sell inventory, and the faster you sell it, the more money you make. To determine how fast your inventory is "turning," you need to examine the relationship between sales and inventory.[3] Let's see how well The College Shop is doing in moving its inventory:

inventory turnover ratio

Financial ratio that shows how efficiently a company turns over its inventory.

$$\text{Inventory turnover} = \frac{\text{Sales}}{\text{Inventory}}$$

$$\text{Year 1}: \frac{\$500,000}{\$80,000} = 6.25 \text{ times}$$

$$\text{Year 2}: \frac{\$600,000}{\$110,000} = 5.45 \text{ times}$$

For year 1, The College Shop converted its inventory into sales 6.25 times: on average, your entire inventory was sold and replaced 6.25 times during the year. For year 2, however, inventory was converted into sales only 5.45 times. The industry did better, averaging turnover of 6.58 times. Before we discuss possible reasons for the drop in The College Shop's inventory turnover ratio, let's look at an alternative way of describing this ratio. Simply convert this ratio into the average number of days that you held an item in inventory. In other words, divide 365 days by your turnover ratio:

$$\text{Year 1}: 365 \ / \ 6.25 = 58 \text{ days}$$

$$\text{Year 2}: 365 \ / \ 5.45 = 67 \text{ days}$$

$$\text{Industry}: 365 \ / \ 6.58 = 55 \text{ days}$$

The College Shop was doing fine in year 1 (relative to the industry), but something happened in year 2 to break your stride. Holding onto inventory for an extra 9 days (67 days for year 2 minus 58 days for year 1) is costly. What happened? Perhaps inventory levels were too high because you overstocked. It's good to have products available for customers, but stocking too much inventory is costly. Maybe some of your inventory takes a long time to sell because it's not as appealing to customers as you thought. If this is the case, you may have a problem for the next year because you'll have to cut prices (and reduce profitability) in order to sell the same slow-moving inventory.

Optimal inventory turnover varies by industry and even by company. A supermarket, for example, will have a high inventory turnover because many of its products are perishable and because it makes money by selling a high volume of goods (making only pennies on each sale). A company that builds expensive sailboats, by contrast, will have a low inventory turnover: it sells few boats but makes a hefty profit on each one. Some companies, such as Dell Computer, are known for keeping extremely low inventory levels. Because computers are made to order, Dell maintains only minimal inventory and so enjoys a very high ratio of sales to inventory.

Management Effectiveness Ratios

"It takes money to make money," goes the old saying, and it's true. Even the smallest business uses money to grow. Management effectiveness ratios address the question: how well is a company performing with the money that owners and others have invested in it?

These ratios are widely regarded as the best measure of corporate performance. You can give a firm high marks for posting good profit margins or for turning over its inventory quickly, but the final grade depends on how much profit it generates with the money invested by owners and creditors. Or, to put it another way, that grade depends on the answer to the question: is the company making a sufficiently high return on its assets?

Like management efficiency ratios, management effectiveness ratios examine the relationship between items on the income statement and items on the balance sheet. From the income statement you always need to know the "bottom line"—net profit. The information that you need from the balance sheet varies according to the ratio that you're trying to calculate, but it's always *some measure of the amount of capital used in the business*. Common measures of capital investment include total equity, total assets, or a combination of equity and long-term debt. Let's see whether The College Shop made the grade. Did it generate a reasonable profit on the assets invested in the company?

$$\text{Return on assets} = \frac{\text{Net Profit}}{\text{Total assets}}$$

$$\text{Year 1}: \frac{\$30,000}{\$360,000} = 8.3\%$$

$$\text{Year 2}: \frac{\$18,000}{\$368,000} = 4.9\%$$

Because the industry average return on assets is 7.9 percent, The College Shop gets an "A" for its first year's performance. It slipped in the second year but is probably still in the "B" range.

Financial Condition Ratios

Financial condition ratios measure the financial strength of a company. They assess its ability to pay its current bills; and to determine whether its debt load is reasonable, they examine the proportion of its debt to its equity.

Current Ratio

Let's look first at a company's ability to meet current obligations. The ratio that evaluates this ability is called the **current ratio**, which examines the relationship between a company's current assets and its current liabilities. The balance of The College Shop's current assets and current liabilities appears on the comparative balance sheet in Figure 12.22. By calculating its current ratio, we'll see whether the business is likely to have trouble paying its current liabilities.

$$\text{Current ratio} = \frac{\text{Current assets}}{\text{Current liabilities}}$$

$$\text{Year 1: } \frac{\$240,000}{\$80,000} = 3 \text{ to } 1$$

$$\text{Year 2: } \frac{\$278,000}{\$70,000} = 4 \text{ to } 1$$

The College Shop's current ratio indicates that, in year 1, the company had $3.00 in current assets for every $1.00 of current liabilities. In the second year, the company had $4.00 of current assets for every $1.00 of current liabilities. The average current ratio for the industry is 2.42. The good news is that The College Shop should have no trouble meeting its current obligations. The bad news is that, ironically, its current ratio might be too high: companies should have enough liquid assets on hand to meet current obligations, but not too many. Holding excess cash can be costly when there are alternative uses for it, such as paying down loans or buying assets that can generate revenue. Perhaps The College Shop should reduce its current assets by using some of its cash to pay a portion of its debt.

Debt-to-Equity Ratio

Now let's look at the way The College Shop is financed. The **debt-to-equity ratio** (also called debt ratio) examines the riskiness of a company's **capital structure**—the relationship between funds acquired from creditors (*debt*) and funds invested by owners (*equity*):

$$\text{Total debt to equity} = \frac{\text{Total liabilities}}{\text{Total equity}}$$

$$\text{Year 1: } \frac{\$180,000}{\$180,000} = 1$$

$$\text{Year 2: } \frac{\$170,000}{\$198,000} = 0.86$$

In year 1, the ratio of 1 indicates that The College Shop has an equal amount of equity and debt (for every $1.00 of equity, it has $1.00 of debt). But this proportion changes in year 2, when the company has more equity than debt: for every $1.00 of equity, it now has $0.85 in debt. How does this ratio compare to that of the industry? The College Shop, it seems, is heavy on the debt side: the industry average of 0.49 indicates that, on average, companies in the industry have only $0.49 of debt for every $1.00 of equity. Its high debt-to-equity ratio might make it hard for The College Shop to borrow more money in the future.

How much difference can this problem make to a business when it needs funding? Consider the following example. Say that you have two friends, both of whom want to borrow money from you. You've decided to loan money to only one of them. Both are equally responsible, but you happen to know that one has only $100 in the bank and owes $1,000. The other also has $100 in the bank but owes only $50. To which one would you lend money? The first has a debt-to-equity ratio of 10 ($1,000 debt to $100 equity) and the second a ratio of 0.50 ($50 debt to $100 equity). You—like a banker—will probably lend money to the friend with the better debt-to-equity ratio, even though the other one needs the money more.

It's possible, however, for a company to make its interest payments comfortably even though it has a high debt-to-equity ratio. Thus, it's helpful to compute the **interest coverage ratio**, which measures the number of times that a firm's operating income can cover its interest expense. We compute this ratio by examining the relationship between interest expense and operating income. A high-interest coverage ratio indicates that a company can easily make its interest payments; a low ratio suggests trouble. Here are the interest coverage ratios for The College Shop:

current ratio

Financial ratio showing the relationship between a company's current assets and current liabilities.

debt-to-equity ratio (or debt ratio)

Financial ratio showing the relationship between debt (funds acquired from creditors) and equity (funds invested by owners).

capital structure

Relationship between a company's debt (funds acquired from creditors) and its equity (funds invested by owners).

interest coverage ratio

Financial ratio showing a company's ability to pay interest on its debts from its operating income.

$$\text{Interest coverage} = \frac{\text{Operating income}}{\text{Interest expense}}$$

$$\text{Year 1}: \frac{\$50,000}{\$10,000} = 5 \text{ times}$$

$$\text{Year 2}: \frac{\$33,000}{\$10,000} = 3.3 \text{ times}$$

As the company's income went down, so did its interest coverage (which isn't good). But the real problem surfaces when you compare the firm's interest coverage with that of its industry, which is much higher—14.5. This figure means that companies in the industry have, on average, $14.50 in operating income to cover each $1.00 of interest that it must pay. Unfortunately, The College Shop has only $3.30.

Again, consider an example on a more personal level. Let's say that following graduation, you have a regular interest payment due on some student loans. If you get a fairly low-paying job and your income is only 3 times the amount of your interest payment, you'll have trouble making your payments. If, on the other hand, you land a great job and your income is 15 times the amount of your interest payments, you can cover them much more comfortably.

4.3   What Have the Ratios Told Us?

So, what have we learned about the performance of The College Shop? What do we foresee for the company in the future? To answer this question, let's identify some of the basic things that every businessperson needs to do in order to achieve success:

- Make a good profit on each item you sell.
- Move inventory: the faster you sell inventory, the more money you make.
- Provide yourself and others with a good return on investment: make investing in your business worthwhile.
- Watch your cash: if you run out of cash and can't pay your bills, you're out of business.

The ratios that we've computed in this section allow us to evaluate The College Shop on each of these dimensions, and here's what we found:

- Profit margin ratios (gross profit margin and net profit margin) indicate that the company makes a reasonable profit on its sales, though profitability is declining.
- One management efficiency ratio (inventory turnover) suggests that inventory is moving quickly, though the rate of turnover is slowing.
- One management effectiveness ratio (return on assets) tells us that the company generated an excellent return on its assets in its first year and a good return in its second year. But again, the trend is downward.
- Financial condition ratios (current ratio, total debt-to-equity, and interest coverage) paint a picture of a company heading for financial trouble. While meeting current bills is not presently a problem, the company has too much debt and isn't earning enough money to make its interest payments comfortably. Moreover, repayment of a big loan in a few years will put a cash strain on the company.

What, then, does the future hold for The College Shop? It depends. If the company returns to year-1 levels of gross margin (when it made $0.45 on each $1.00 of sales), and if it can increase its sales volume, it might generate enough cash to reduce its long-term debt. But if the second-year decline in profitability continues, it will run into financial difficulty in the next few years. It could even be forced out of business when the bank demands payment on its long-term loan.

KEY TAKEAWAYS

- Two common techniques for evaluating a company's financial performance are **vertical percentage analysis** and **ratio analysis**.
- Vertical percentage analysis reveals the relationship of each item on the income statement to a specified base—generally sales—by expressing each item as a percentage of that base.
- The percentages help you to analyze changes in the income statement items over time.
- Ratios show the relationship of one number to another number—for example, **gross profit** to sales or **net profit** to total assets.
- Ratio analysis is used to assess a company's performance and financial condition over time and to compare one company to similar companies or to an overall industry.
- Ratios can be divided into four categories: profit margin ratios, management efficiency ratios, management effectiveness ratios, and debt-to-equity ratios.
- **Profit margin ratios** show how much of each sales dollar is left after certain costs are covered.
    - Two common profitability ratios are the *gross profit margin* (which shows how much of each sales dollar remains after paying for the goods sold) and *net profit margin* (which shows how much of each sales dollar remains after all costs are covered).
- **Management efficiency ratios** tell you how efficiently your assets are being managed.
    - One of the ratios in this category—**inventory turnover**—measures a firm's efficiency in selling its inventory by looking at the relationship between sales and inventory.
- **Management effectiveness ratios** tell you how effective management is at running the business and measure overall company performance by comparing net profit to some measure of the amount of capital used in the business.
    - The **return on assets ratio**, for instance, compares net profit to total assets to determine whether the company generated a reasonable profit on the assets invested in it.
    - **Financial condition ratios** are used to assess a firm's financial strength.
- The **current ratio** (which compares **current assets** to **current liabilities**) provides a measure of a company's ability to meet current liabilities.
- The **debt-to-equity ratio** examines the riskiness of a company's **capital structure** by looking at the amount of debt that it has relative to total equity.
- Finally, the **interest coverage ratio** (which measures the number of times a firm's operating income can cover its interest expense) assesses a company's ability to make interest payments on outstanding debt.

Before going to the next section of this chapter, take a few minutes to test your knowledge of the material covered in this section. Quizzes can be found under the "Resources" tab, "Study Aids: Quizzes."

EXERCISES

1. The accountant for my company just ran into my office and told me that our gross profit margin increased while our net profit margin decreased. She also reported that while our debt-to-equity ratio increased, our interest coverage ratio decreased. She was puzzled by the apparent inconsistencies. Help her out by providing possible explanations for the behavior of these ratios.
2. Which company is more likely to have the higher inventory turnover ratio: a grocery store or an automobile manufacturer? Give an explanation for your answer.

5.   THE PROFESSION: ETHICS AND OPPORTUNITIES

LEARNING OBJECTIVES

1. Understand why it's not a good idea to falsify financial statements.
2. Appreciate the background behind stricter legal and professional standards in U.S. business and accounting practices.
3. Understand ethics and their importance in the accounting profession.
4. Describe the purpose of the Sarbanes-Oxley Act (SOX).
5. Identify career opportunities in accounting.

5.1   Accountant, Audit Thyself?

Consider the following scenario. You feel good that you've managed to create *relevant, accurate,* and *timely* financial statements for your first year in business as The College Shop, but you find that you're disappointed about one thing—your net income figure. For some time now, you've been trying to convince a friend to invest in The College Shop, telling him that the business would bring in at least $40,000 in income during its first year. Every time you review the income statement in Figure 12.16 (shown in abbreviated form below), however, you're forced to face the fact that you earned just $30,000—$10,000 short of your optimistic projection.

$$\text{Revenues} - \text{Expenses (CGS, operating expenses, interest and taxes)} = \text{Net income}$$

$$\$500{,}000 - \$470{,}000 = \$30{,}000$$

As you stare one more time at your bottom line, you're wishing that there was some way to change that single bothersome digit and transform $30,000 into $40,000. Then it hits you. You know that it's not exactly the most upright thing to do, but what if you were to shift half of your first-year advertising expense of $20,000 into your second year of operation? If you did that, then you'd cut the advertising expense on your first-year income statement by $10,000. Now, with your newly acquired understanding of accounting principles, you know that if you reduce expenses on your income statement by $10,000, your net income will increase by the same amount. So just to see what your "revised" income statement would look like, you go ahead and make your hypothetical change. Sure enough, mission accomplished: Your income statement now reports a net income of $40,000—your actual net income of $30,000 plus your upward "adjustment" of $10,000.

$$\text{Revenues} - \text{Expenses (CGS, operating expenses, interest and taxes)} = \text{Net income}$$

$$\$500{,}000 - \$460{,}000 = \$40{,}000$$

Although you now feel even more satisfied than ever with your newfound expertise in accounting strategy, you're once again forced to stop and think. If you merely change your net income and nothing else, the balance sheet in Figure 12.18 won't balance anymore. Why not? Because when you inflated your net income to $40,000 and added it to your beginning owner's equity balance of $150,000, this increased your owner's equity by $10,000—from $180,000 to $190,000. To make sure that you've accurately assessed the snag in your strategy, you plug in the accounting equation—

$$\text{assets} = \text{liabilities} + \text{owner's equity}$$

—and this, unfortunately, is what you get:

$$\$360{,}000 \neq \$180{,}000 + \$190{,}000.$$

So, now what? As you ponder the troublesome ramifications of your balance sheet, yet another accounting strategy pops into your head. At the end of the year, you still owed $6,000 for radio ads and $4,000 for newspaper ads—$10,000 that's included in *accounts payable* on your year-end balance sheet. What if you just reduced your *accounts payable* balance by $10,000? If you did that, you'd also reduce by $10,000 the amount under *liabilities and owner's equity,* cutting it from $370,000 to $360,000. Wouldn't that make everything balance? Plugging in the numbers from your latest brainstorm, you now get:

$$\$360,000 = \$170,000 + \$190,000.$$

That's more like it. Now you can go ahead and "adjust" your financial statements, satisfied that you're well on your way to mastering all the accounting strategy that you'll need to handle the financial-reporting needs of your new business.

Accounting "Strategy," Ethics, and the Law

Unfortunately, you may also be well on your way to becoming the Bernie Ebbers of the small-business set. In 2002, when the giant telecom company WorldCom collapsed under the weight of an $11 billion fraud scheme, CEO Ebbers, who was convicted of securities fraud and conspiracy, got twenty-five years in a federal penitentiary ("I don't know accounting," he told the judge). And Ebbers wasn't the only person on the WorldCom payroll who was charged with illegal activities: Accounting department managers went down with him. Betty Vinson, for example, a forty-seven-year-old midlevel accountant who'd followed orders to falsify accounting records, was sentenced to five months in jail. And she was lucky—she got minimal jail time because she cooperated with federal prosecutors.[4]

The damage done at WorldCom spread to innocent employees as well, not to mention investors, creditors, and business partners. In 2001, when Enron, the seventh-largest company in America, melted down in the heat of an investigation into its financial-reporting practices, it took down an entire accounting firm with it—eighty-nine-year-old Arthur Andersen, then one of the "Big Five" public accounting firms. Volumes have been written about what went wrong, but we can pretty much boil it down to this: *Enron executives behaved unethically and illegally, and Andersen auditors looked the other way.* Instead of performing its role as public watchdog, Andersen was watching its own pocketbook: The accounting firm protected the revenues generated by lucrative consulting contracts with its client instead of protecting the client's stakeholders. In so doing, Andersen not only shirked its responsibilities as a public auditor but also covered up evidence of its own inappropriate actions.

In 2002, Andersen gave up its licenses to practice as certified public accountants in the United States, and a company that had employed 85,000 people only 10 years earlier now employs about 200, most of them to deal with lawsuits and to oversee the process of shutting down the company for good.[5]

Who Can You Trust?

In a very real sense, the issue at the bottom of all this financial misconduct is *trustworthiness.* As we've seen, accountants are supposed to provide *users* with financial reports that are *useful* because they're relevant, timely, and, most important, accurate. It should go without saying that if users—whether internal or external—can't trust these reports to be accurate, they can't rely on them to be as useful as they should be. Would you, for instance, invest in or loan money to a company whose financial reports you can't trust?

Which—appropriately—brings us back to you and your little foray into falsifying accounting records. Let's say that in February of your second year of operations, you have an unexpected opportunity to expand into the vacated store right next to The College Shop. It's too good to pass up, but you'll need quite a bit of money to outfit the space and expand your inventory. First, you go to the friend for whose benefit you "adjusted" your financial statements, but he's just lost a bundle in the stock market and can't help you out. Your only option, then, is to get a bank loan. So you go to your banker, and some version of the following exchange occurs early in the conversation:

> **YOU:**   *I need a loan.*
> **BANKER:** *Let me see your financial statements.*

She means, of course, the first-year statements that you falsified, and if you're offered and accept a loan under these circumstances, you could be guilty of a financial crime that, according to the FBI, is normally characterized by "deceit, concealment, or violation of trust" and committed "to obtain personal or business advantage." The maximum you could get under federal law is twenty years, although your case no doubt calls for a sentence measured in mere months.[6]

Are You Ethical?

We could give you the benefit of the doubt and agree that you wouldn't have gotten yourself into this mess had you known the legal ramifications. We must assume, however, that you knew what you did was *ethically* wrong. **Ethics** refers to the ability and willingness to distinguish right from wrong and to know when you're doing one or the other. Ethical and trustworthy behavior is critical in both business and accounting, and although the vast majority of businesspeople and accountants behave ethically, all of them—especially providers of financial information—constantly face ethical dilemmas in the course of their work.

Sarbanes-Oxley Act (SOX)

It will be helpful to remember that both the law and the accounting profession have taken steps to remind you of your responsibilities when you're reporting financial information. In the wake of corporate scandals like the ones we described above, Congress passed the **Sarbanes-Oxley Act (SOX)** of 2002, which was designed to encourage ethical corporate behavior and to discourage fraud and other forms of corporate wrongdoing. Among other things, SOX requires its top executives to take responsibility for a company's financial statements and subjects them to criminal penalties for falsely certifying its financial reports. SOX also set up the Public Company Accounting Oversight Board (PCAOB) to regulate accounting professionals, especially in the area of auditing standards.

The Profession's Code of Ethics

Finally, you can always turn to the Code of Professional Ethics of the American Institute of Certified Public Accountants (AICPA), which sets down two hallmarks of ethical behavior:[7]

- *Integrity.* An accountant should be "honest and candid" and should never subordinate the "public trust…to personal gain and advantage."
- *Objectivity and independence.* An accountant should be "impartial, intellectually honest, and free of conflicts of interest." He or she is "scrupulous in [the] application of generally accepted accounting principles and candid in all…dealings with members in public practice."

5.2 Careers in Accounting

You may know that Phil Knight is the founder of Nike. But you may not know that he began his business career as an accountant. Another thing that you may not know is that accounting is a "people profession." A lot of people think that accountants spend the day sitting behind desks crunching numbers, but this is a serious misconception. Accountants work with other people to solve business problems. They need strong analytical skills to assess financial data, but they must also be able to work effectively with colleagues. Thus they need good interpersonal skills, and because they must write and speak clearly and present complex financial data in terms that everyone can understand, they need excellent communication skills as well.

Job Descriptions

If you choose a career in accounting, you have two career options:

- Work as a public accountant, whether for a "Big Four" public accounting firm or for a midsize or smaller company
- Work as a private accountant for a business, not-for-profit organization, or government agency

Let's take a closer look at these options. Public accounting firms provide clients with accounting and tax services in return for fees. Most members of such firms are **certified public accountants (CPAs)** who have met educational and work requirements set by the state and passed a rigorous exam. Although public accounting firms offer consulting and tax services, the hallmark of the profession is performing external **audits**: the public accountant examines a company's financial statements and submits an opinion on whether they've been prepared in accordance with GAAP. This "stamp of approval" provides the investing public with confidence that a firm's financial reports are accurate. Typically, public accountants are self-employed, work for small, sometimes regional firms, or are associated with one of the "Big Four" public accounting firms—Deloitte & Touche, Ernst & Young, KPMG, and PricewaterhouseCoopers—or one of the large second-tier public accounting firms, such as BDO Seidman or Grant Thornton.

Often called *management* or *corporate accountants*, **private accountants** may work for specific companies, nonprofit organizations, or government agencies. A firm's chief accounting officer is called a **controller**. As a rule, the controller reports to the organization's *chief financial officer (CFO)*, who's responsible for all of its accounting and other financial activities. The jobs of private accountants vary according to the company or industry in which they're employed. Most private accountants record and analyze financial information and provide support to other members of the organization in such diverse areas as marketing, strategic planning, new product development, operations, human resources, and finance. Private accountants also conduct *internal audits*. In this capacity, they ensure that accounting records are accurate, company policies are adhered to, assets are safeguarded, and operations are efficiently conducted. Finally, they may also provide a variety of specialized services:

- Develop and prepare financial reports
- Prepare tax returns
- Perform cost accounting functions (that is, determine the cost of goods or services)
- Prepare and supervise budgets
- Manage such functions as payroll, accounts payable, and receivables

Accountants who pass a special exam and meet other professional requirements in the field of management accounting are designated *certified management accountants (CMAs)*. CMAs often have greater job responsibilities and receive higher compensation than other accountants.

The Job and Its Prospects

So, what's the job like? For that matter, what's the professional life of an accountant like? Or perhaps even more important, what are your prospects for getting a job in accounting, and what kind of income can you expect if you're able to make a career for yourself in the field? "If you're looking for a career that's challenging and for which the dynamics change constantly…then this is where it's at," advises one practicing CPA.[8] Beatrice Sanders, former director of Academic and Career Development for the American Institute of Certified Public Accountants, agrees: "Whatever form of practice you choose, accounting provides a challenging and rewarding career in which there are no limits on where you can go, or how far."[9]

The Job Market Today

"The one great benefit of choosing accounting as your career is that you will always have a job when you graduate." Or so says one accountant CPA (in fact, the same CPA who promises a challenging career in a dynamic profession). Obviously, we can't make any guarantees, but in order to help you better assess your prospects for a satisfying career in accounting, we can offer you some relevant facts and figures.

First of all, we can confirm that accounting graduates have always faced a favorable job market and that, according to a survey conducted by the National Association of Colleges and Employers (NACE), the year 2013 is no different. According to Dan Black, Ernst & Young's Americas director of campus recruiting and NACE's president-elect, accounting is "still one of the most in-demand majors for new graduates. It's been in the top five for as long as I can remember."[10] And what about the area that probably interests you most right now—salary? For the most part, we can report good news. The NACE survey, for example, reports that, with average salary offers of just over $53,000, 2013 accounting graduates could expect to be among the highest-paid entrants into the workforce.

KEY TAKEAWAYS

- Current statutes and standards governing U.S. business and accounting practice reflect public reaction to a wave of corporate misconduct in the 2000s.
- Ethical and trustworthy behavior is critical in accounting because users trust accountants to provide financial reports that are relevant, timely, and, most important, accurate.
- The federal **Sarbanes-Oxley Act (SOX)** of 2002 was designed to encourage ethical corporate behavior and to discourage fraud and other forms of corporate malfeasance. The Code of Professional Ethics of the American Institute of Certified Public Accountants (AICPA) sets down two hallmarks of ethical behavior: *integrity* and *objectivity and independence.*
- If you choose a career in accounting, you have two career options: work as a public accountant or work as a private accountant.
- **Public accounting firms** provide clients with external **audits** in which they examine a company's financial statements and submit an opinion on whether they've been prepared in accordance with GAAP. They also provide other accounting and tax services.
- Most members of public accounting firms are **certified public accountants (CPAs)** who have met required educational and work requirements.
- **Private accountants**, often called *management* or *corporate accountants*, work for specific companies, nonprofit organizations, or government agencies.
- Most private accountants record and analyze financial information and provide support to other members of the organization. They also conduct *internal audits* as well as a variety of specialized services.
- Accountants who pass a special exam and meet other professional requirements in the field of management accounting are designated **certified management accountants (CMAs)**.

Before going to the next chapter, take a few minutes to test your knowledge of the material covered in this section. Quizzes can be found under the "Resources" tab, "Study Aids: Quizzes."

EXERCISES

1. What is accounting and what purpose does it serve? What do accountants do? What career choices do they have? Which career choice seems most interesting to you? Why?
2. What actions have been taken to help restore the trust that the public once had in the accounting profession? Do you believe these actions will help? Why, or why not? What other suggestions do you have to help the accounting profession and corporate America regain the public trust?

6. CASES AND PROBLEMS

Discounting Retailers

There was a time when Kmart was America's number-one discount retailer and Sears, Roebuck & Co. was the seventh largest corporation in the world. Things have changed since Wal-Mart came on the scene. In the fifty years since Sam Walton opened the first Wal-Mart store in Rogers, Arkansas, the company has propelled itself to the number-one spot in discount retailing, and (even more impressive) has higher sales than *any other company in the world*. Over this same fifty-year period, Target emerged as a major player in the retail industry. The fifty-year period wasn't kind to Kmart and Sears, and both stores watched their dominance in the retail market slip away. In an effort to reverse the downward spiral of both retailers, in November 2004, Sears and Kmart merged into a new company called Sears Holdings. To learn more about how Wal-Mart, Target, and Sears Holdings are doing today, go to the National Retail Federation's Web site (http://www.stores.org/STORES Magazine July 2011/top-100-retailers) to access a report that ranks the 2010 top 100 retailers. After reading the introduction and reviewing the list of top retailers, prepare a report comparing the three retailers on the following:

- U.S. sales and percentage increase or decrease in sales
- Worldwide sales
- Number of stores and percentage increase or decrease in number of stores

Based on your analysis and reading of the introductory write-up, answer the following questions:

1. Do you believe that Target will be able to compete against Wal-Mart in the future? If so, how?
2. What about Sears Holdings? Will the company survive?
3. Some people criticize Wal-Mart for forcing other retailers out of business and for lowering the average wage for retail workers. Is this a legitimate criticism? In your opinion, has Wal-Mart helped the American people or hurt them?

Is a Career in Accounting for You?

Do you want to learn what opportunities are available for people graduating with degrees in accounting? Go to the Web site of the American Institute of Certified Public Accountants (http://www.startheregoplaces.com) and click on "Why Accounting?" (top, left). Then click on "Career Options" (left side bar). Select two areas of interest. Click on each interest area and select a job in that area that interests you. For each of two jobs selected (one from each interest area), answer the following questions:

- What is the job like?
- Why does the job seem interesting to you?

ETHICS ANGLE

Counting Earnings before They Hatch

You recently ran into one of your former high school teachers. You were surprised to learn that he'd left teaching, gone back to school, and, a little more than a year ago, started a business that creates Web sites for small companies. It so happens that he needs a loan to expand his business, and the bank wants financial statements. When he found out that you were studying accounting, he asked whether you'd look over a set of statements that he'd just prepared for his first year in business. Because you're anxious to show off your accounting aptitude, you agreed.

First, he showed you his income statement. It looked fine: revenues (from designing Web sites) were $94,000, expenses were $86,000, and net income was $8,000. When you observed how unusual it was that he'd earned a profit in his first year, he seemed a little uneasy.

"Well," he confessed, "I fudged a little when I prepared the statements. Otherwise, I'd never get the loan."

He admitted that $10,000 of the fees shown on the income statement was for work he'd recently started doing for a client (who happened to be in big trouble with the IRS). "It isn't like I won't be earning the money," he explained. "I'm just counting it a little early. It was easy to do. I just added $10,000 to my revenues and recorded an accounts receivable for the same amount."

You quickly did the math: without the $10,000 payment for the client in question, his profit of $8,000 would become a loss of $2,000 (revenues of $84,000 less expenses of $86,000).

As your former teacher turned to get his balance sheet, you realized that, as his accountant, you had to decide what you'd advise him to do. The decision is troublesome because you agree that if he changes the income statement to reflect the real situation, he won't get the bank loan.

1. What did you decide to do, and why?
2. Assuming that he doesn't change the income statement, will his balance sheet be incorrect? How about his statement of cash flows? What will happen to next year's income: will it be higher or lower than it should be?
3. What would happen to your former teacher if he gave the bank the fraudulent financial statements and the bank discovered the truth? How could the bank learn the truth?

TEAM-BUILDING SKILLS

Taking Stock of Ratios

Your class has been told that each group of three students will receive a share of stock in one of three companies in the same industry. But there's a catch: each group has to decide which of the companies it wants to own stock in. To reach this decision, your team will use ratio analysis to compare the three companies. Each team member will analyze one of the companies using the ratios presented in this chapter. Then, you'll get together, compare your results, and choose a company. Here are the details of the project:

1. The team selects a group of three companies in the same industry. Here are just a few examples:

    - *Auto manufacturers*. Ford, General Motors, Toyota
    - *Airlines*. Southwest, United Airlines, American Airlines
    - *Drug companies*. GlaxoSmithKline, Eli Lilly & Co., Bristol-Myers Squibb
    - *Specialty retailers*. Bed Bath & Beyond, Pottery Barn, Pier 1 Imports
    - *Computers*. Hewlett-Packard, Gateway, Apple Computer

2. Every team member gets a copy of one company's most recent annual report (which includes its financial statements) from the company's Web site (investor section).
3. Every member calculates the following ratios for the company for the last two years: gross profit margin, net profit margin, inventory turnover (if applicable), return on assets, current ratio, debt-to-equity, and interest coverage.
4. Get together as a group and compare your results. Decide as a group which company you want to own stock in.
5. Write a report indicating the company that your team selected and explain your choice. Attach the following items to your team report:

    5.1. A brief explanation of each ratio (how to calculate it and what it means)
    5.2. Detailed calculations showing how each ratio was determined
    5.3. A chart comparing the ratios for the three companies

THE GLOBAL VIEW

Why Aren't Shoes Made in the USA?

Having just paid $70 for a pair of athletic shoes that were made in China, you wonder why they had to be made in that country. Why weren't they made in the United States, where lots of people need good-paying jobs? You also figure that the shoe company must be making a huge profit on each pair it sells. Fortunately, you were able to get a breakdown of the costs for making a pair of $70 athletic shoes:[11]

Production labor	$2.75
Materials	9.00
Rent, equipment	3.00
Supplier's operating profit	1.75
Duties	3.00
Shipping	0.50
Cost to the Manufacturer	**$20.00**
Research and development	0.25
Promotion and advertising	4.00
Sales, distribution, administration	5.00
Shoe company's operating profit	6.25
Cost to the Retailer	**$35.50**
Retailer's Rent	9.00
Personnel	9.50
Other	7.00
Retailer's operating profit	9.00
Cost to Consumer	**$70.00**

You're surprised at a few of these items. First, out of the $70, the profit made by the manufacturer was only $6.25. Second, at $2.75, labor accounted for only about 4 percent of the price you paid. The advertising cost ($4.00) was higher than the labor cost. If labor isn't a very big factor in the cost of the shoes, why are they made in China?

Deciding to look further into this puzzle, you discover that the $2.75 labor cost was for two hours of work. Moreover, that $2.75 includes not only the wages paid to the workers, but also labor-related costs, such as food, housing, and medical care.

That's when you begin to wonder. How much would I have to pay for the same shoes if they were made in the United States? Or what if they were made in Mexico? How about Spain? To answer these questions, you need to know the hourly wage rates in these countries. Fortunately, you can get this information by going to the Foreign Labor section of the Bureau of Labor Statistics Web site (http://www.bls.gov/news.release/ichcc.t08.htm). The table you want is "Production Workers: Hourly Compensation Costs in U.S. Dollars." Use the most recent hourly compensation figures.

To investigate this issue further, you should do the following:

1. Recalculate the cost of producing the shoes in the United States and two other countries of your choice. Because operating profit for the supplier, the shoe company, and the retailer will change as the cost to make the shoe changes, you have decided to determine this profit using the following percentage rates:

   - Supplier's operating profit: 10 percent of its costs
   - Shoe company's operating profit: 20 percent of its costs (including the cost paid to the supplier to make the shoes)
   - Retailer's operating profit: 15 percent of its costs (including the cost paid to the shoe company)

2. Prepare a report that does the following:

   - Shows the selling price of the shoe for each manufacturing country (the United States and the other two countries you selected)
   - Lists any costs other than labor that might change if shoe production was moved to the United States

- Identifies other factors that should be considered when selecting a manufacturing country
- Indicates possible changes to production methods that would make production in the United States less costly

3. Finally, draw some conclusions: Do you, as a U.S. citizen, benefit from shoe production in foreign countries? Does the United States benefit overall? Does the world benefit? Should shoe production return to the United States?

ENDNOTES

1. This vignette is based on the following sources: Diane Brady, "Social Media's New Mantra: Location, Location, Location," *Bloomberg BusinessWeek*, May 6, 2010, http://www.businessweek.com/magazine/content/10_20/b4178034154012.htm (accessed March 26, 2014); Arik Hesseldahl, "Foursquare Tries Broadening Its Appeal," *Bloomberg BusinessWeek*, April 19, 2010, http://www.businessweek.com/technology/content/apr2010/tc20100416_035687.htm (accessed March 26, 2014); Foursquare, http://foursquare.com (accessed March 26, 2014).

2. Robert P. Miles, *Warren Buffett Wealth: Principles and Practical Methods Used by the World's Greatest Investor* (Hoboken, NJ: John Wiley & Sons, 2004), 93.

3. Another way to calculate inventory turnover is to divide *Cost of goods sold* by inventory (rather than dividing *Sales* by inventory). We don't discuss this method here because the available industry data used for comparative purposes reflect *Sales* rather than *Cost of goods sold*.

4. See Susan Pulliam, "How Following Orders Can Harm Your Career," *Wall Street Journal*, June 23, 2003, CareerJournal.com, http://www.cfo.com/article.cfm/3010537/c_3036075 (accessed April 23, 2014).

5. See Michael Moffett, *What Happened at Enron?* (Cambridge, MA: Harvard Business Review, July 2004); and Barbara Ley Toffler with Jennifer Reingold, *Final Accounting: Ambition, Greed, and the Fall of Arthur Andersen* (New York: Broadway Books, 2003), http://books.google.com (accessed March 27, 2014).

6. Federal Bureau of Investigation, *Financial Crimes Report to the Public* (Washington, D.C.: U.S. Dept. of Justice, 2005), http://www.fbi.gov (accessed March 27, 2014).

7. American Institute of Certified Public Accountants, *AICPA Code of Professional Conduct—Current and Historical Versions* (2006–2010), http://www.aicpa.org (accessed March 27, 2014).

8. "Ask a CPA," *Start Here Go Places*, http://www.startheregoplaces.com (accessed March 27, 2014).

9. Gloria A. Gaylord and Glenda E. Reid, *Careers in Accounting*, 4th ed. (New York: McGraw-Hill, 2006), http://books.google.com (accessed March 27, 2014).

10. Danielle Lee, "Hiring, Salaries up for Accounting Graduates," *Accounting Today*, April 30, 2013, http://www.accountingtoday.com/acto_blog/national-association-colleges-employers-nace-job-outlook-salary-guide-2013-66550-1.html (accessed March 27, 2014).

11. From Tom Vanderbilt, *The Sneaker Book: Anatomy of an Industry and an Icon* (New York: The New Press, 1998), 111.

CHAPTER 13

Managing Financial Resources

HOW TO KEEP FROM GOING UNDER

How can you manage to combine a fantastic business idea, an efficient production system, a talented management team, and a creative marketing plan…and still go under? It's not so hard if you don't understand finance. Everyone in business—not finance specialists alone—needs to understand how the U.S. financial system operates and how financial decisions affect an organization. Businesspeople also need to know how securities markets work. In this chapter, we'll discuss these three interrelated topics. Let's start by taking a closer look at one of the key ingredients in any business enterprise—money.

1. THE FUNCTIONS OF MONEY

LEARNING OBJECTIVES

1. Identify and explain the three functions of money.
2. Identify and describe the two government measures of the money supply.

Finance is about money. So our first question is, what is money? If you happen to have one on you, take a look at a $5 bill. What you'll see is a piece of paper with a picture of Abraham Lincoln on one side and the Lincoln Memorial on the other. Though this piece of paper—indeed, money itself—has no intrinsic value, it's certainly in demand. Why? Because money serves three basic functions. **Money** is the following:

1. A medium of exchange
2. A measure of value
3. A store of value

money

Anything commonly accepted as a medium of exchange, measure of value, and store of value.

To get a better idea of the role of money in a modern economy, let's imagine a system in which there is no money. In this system, goods and services are *bartered*—traded directly for one another. Now, if you're living and trading under such a system, for each barter exchange that you make, you'll have to have something that another trader wants. For example, say you're a farmer who needs help clearing his fields. Because you have plenty of food, you might enter into a barter transaction with a laborer who has time to clear fields but not enough food: he'll clear your fields in return for three square meals a day.

This system will work as long as two people have exchangeable assets, but needless to say, it can be inefficient. If we identify the functions of money, we'll see how it improves the exchange for all the parties in our hypothetical set of transactions.

1.1 Medium of Exchange

Money serves as a medium of exchange because people will accept it in exchange for goods and services. Because people can use money to buy the goods and services that they want, everyone's willing to trade something for money. The laborer will take money for clearing your fields because he can use it to buy food. You'll take money as payment for his food because you

FIGURE 13.1

Money itself has no intrinsic value.

© 2010 Jupiterimages Corporation

can use it not only to pay him but also to buy something else you need (perhaps seeds for planting crops).

For money to be used in this way, it must possess a few crucial properties:

1. It must be *divisible*—easily divided into usable quantities or fractions. A $5 bill, for example, is equal to five $1 bills. If something costs $3, you don't have to rip up a $5 bill; you can pay with three $1 bills.

2. It must be *portable*—easy to carry; it can't be too heavy or bulky.

3. It must be *durable*. It must be strong enough to resist tearing and the print can't wash off if it winds up in the washing machine.

4. It must be *difficult to counterfeit*; it won't have much value if people can make their own.

1.2 Measure of Value

Money simplifies exchanges because it serves as a measure of value. We state the price of a good or service in monetary units so that potential exchange partners know exactly how much value we want in return for it. This practice is a lot better than bartering because it's much more precise than an ad hoc agreement that a day's work in the field has the same value as three meals.

1.3 Store of Value

Money serves as a store of value. Because people are confident that money keeps its value over time, they're willing to save it for future exchanges. Under a bartering arrangement, the laborer earned three meals a day in exchange for his work. But what if, on a given day, he skipped a meal? Could he "save" that meal for another day? Maybe, but if he were paid in money, he could decide whether to spend it on food each day or save some of it for the future. If he wanted to collect on his "unpaid" meal two or three days later, the farmer might not be able to "pay" it; unlike money, food could go bad.

1.4 The Money Supply

demand deposits

Checking accounts that pay given sums to "payees" when they demand them.

money market mutual funds

Accounts that pay interest to investors who pool funds to make short-term loans to businesses and the government.

M-1

Measure of the money supply that includes only the most liquid forms of money, such as cash and checking-account funds.

M-2

Measure of the money supply that includes everything in M-1 plus near-cash.

Now that we know what money does, let's tackle another question: How much money is there? How would you go about "counting" all the money held by individuals, businesses, and government agencies in this country? You could start by counting the money that's held to pay for things on a daily basis. This category includes *cash* (paper bills and coins) and funds held in **demand deposits**—checking accounts, which pay given sums to "payees" when they demand them.

Then, you might count the money that's being "saved" for future use. This category includes *interest-bearing accounts, time deposits* (such as *certificates of deposit*, which pay interest after a designated period of time), and **money market mutual funds**, which pay interest to investors who pool funds to make short-term loans to businesses and the government.

M-1 and M-2

Counting all this money would be a daunting task (in fact, it would be impossible). Fortunately, there's an easier way—namely, by examining two measures that the government compiles for the purpose of tracking the money supply: M-1 and M-2.

- The narrowest measure, **M-1**, includes the most *liquid* forms of money—the forms, such as cash and checking-accounts funds, that are spent immediately.

- **M-2** includes everything in M-1 plus *near-cash items* invested for the short term—savings accounts, time deposits below $100,000, and money market mutual funds.

So what's the bottom line? How much money *is* out there? To find the answer, you can go to the Federal Reserve Board Web site. The Federal Reserve reports that in March 2014, M-1 was about $2.7 trillion and M-2 was $11.2 trillion.[1] Figure 13.2 shows the increase in the two money-supply measures since 1980.

FIGURE 13.2 The U.S. Money Supply, 1980–2014

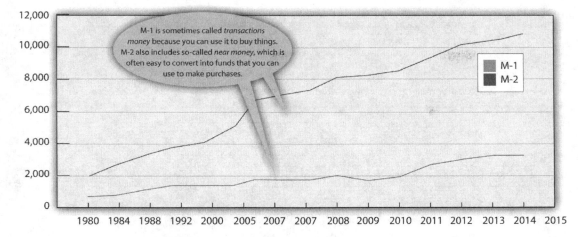

If you're thinking that these numbers are too big to make much sense, you're not alone. One way to bring them into perspective is to figure out how much money *you'd* get if all the money in the United States were redistributed equally. According to the U.S. Census Population Clock,[2] there are more than three hundred million people in the United States. Your share of M-1, therefore, would be about $8,500 and your share of M-2 would be about $35,000.

What, Exactly, Is "Plastic Money"?

Are credit cards a form of money? If not, why do we call them plastic money? Actually, when you buy something with a credit card, you're not spending money. The principle of the credit card is buy-now-pay-later. In other words, when you use plastic, you're taking out a loan that you intend to pay off when you get your bill. And the loan itself is not money. Why not? Basically because the credit card company can't use the asset to buy anything. The loan is merely a promise of repayment. The asset doesn't become money until the bill is paid (with interest). That's why credit cards aren't included in the calculation of M-1 and M-2.

KEY TAKEAWAYS

- Money serves three basic functions:
    1. *Medium of exchange*: because you can use it to buy the goods and services you want, everyone's willing to trade things for money.
    2. *Measure of value*: it simplifies the exchange process because it's a means of indicating how much something costs.
    3. *Store of value*: people are willing to hold onto it because they're confident that it will keep its value over time.

- The government uses two measures to track the money supply: **M-1** includes the most liquid forms of money, such as cash and checking-account funds. **M-2** includes everything in M-1 plus near-cash items, such as savings accounts and time deposits below $100,000.

Before going to the next section of this chapter, take a few minutes to test your knowledge of the material covered in this section. Quizzes can be found under the "Resources" tab, "Study Aids: Quizzes."

2. FINANCIAL INSTITUTIONS

LEARNING OBJECTIVES

1. Distinguish among different types of financial institutions.
2. Discuss the services that financial institutions provide and explain their role in expanding the money supply.
3. Explain how the money multiplier effect impacts the money supply.

For financial transactions to happen, money must change hands. How do such exchanges occur? At any given point in time, some individuals, businesses, and government agencies have more money than they need for current activities; some have less than they need. Thus, we need a mechanism to match up savers (those with surplus money that they're willing to lend out) with borrowers (those with deficits who want to borrow money). We could just let borrowers search out savers and negotiate loans, but the system would be both inefficient and risky. Even if you had a few extra dollars, would you lend money to a total stranger? If you needed money, would you want to walk around town looking for someone with a little to spare?

2.1 Depository and Nondepository Institutions

Now you know why we have financial institutions: they act as intermediaries between savers and borrowers and they direct the flow of funds between them. With funds deposited by savers in checking, savings, and money market accounts, they make loans to individual and commercial borrowers. In the next section, we'll discuss the most common types of depository institutions (banks that accept deposits), including *commercial banks, savings banks*, and *credit unions*. We'll also discuss several nondepository institutions (which provide financial services but don't accept deposits), including finance companies, insurance companies, brokerage firms, and pension funds.

Commercial Banks

Commercial banks

Financial institution that generates profits by lending funds and providing customers with services, such as check processing.

Commercial banks are the most common financial institutions in the United States, with total financial assets of about $12.6 trillion (which, together with savings banks, account for 80 percent of the total assets of the banking institutions).[3] They generate profit not only by charging borrowers higher interest rates than they pay to savers but also by providing such services as check processing, trust- and retirement-account management, and electronic banking. The country's 6,300 commercial banks range in size from very large (Bank of America Corporation and J.P. Morgan Chase and Company) to very small (local community banks). Because of mergers and financial problems, the number of banks has declined significantly in recent years, but, by the same token, surviving banks have grown quite large. If you've been with one bank over the past ten years or so, you've probably seen the name change at least once or twice.

Savings Banks

Savings banks (also called *thrift institutions* and *savings and loan associations*, or *S&Ls*) were originally set up to encourage personal saving and provide mortgages to local home buyers. Today, however, they provide a range of services similar to those offered by commercial banks. Though not as dominant as commercial banks, they're an important component of the industry, holding total financial assets of almost $1.2 trillion.[4] Hudson City Savings Bank, one of the largest U.S.-controlled savings banks, has close to 135 branches in the New York metropolitan area.[5] Savings banks can be owned by their depositors (mutual ownership) or by shareholders (stock ownership).

Credit Unions

To bank at a **credit union**, you must be linked to a particular group, such as employees of Southwest Airlines, employees of the state of North Carolina, teachers in Pasadena, California, or current and former members of the U.S. Navy. Credit unions are owned by their members, who receive shares of their profits. They offer almost anything that a commercial bank or savings and loan does, including savings accounts, checking accounts, home and car loans, credit cards, and even some commercial loans. Collectively, they hold about $962 billion in financial assets (around 6 percent of the total assets of the financial institutions).[6]

Figure 13.3 summarizes the distribution of assets among the nation's depository institutions.

FIGURE 13.3 Where Our Money Is Deposited

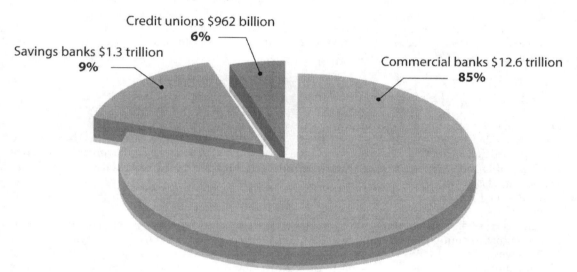

Credit unions $962 billion
6%

Savings banks $1.3 trillion
9%

Commercial banks $12.6 trillion
85%

Finance Companies

Finance companies are nondeposit institutions because they don't accept deposits from individuals or provide traditional banking services, such as checking accounts. They do, however, make loans to individuals and businesses, using funds acquired by selling securities or borrowed from commercial banks. They hold about $1.5 trillion in assets.[7] Those that lend money to businesses, such as General Electric Capital, are *commercial finance companies*, and those that make loans to individuals or issue credit cards, such Citgroup, are *consumer finance companies*. Some, such as Ally Financial (formerly General Motors Acceptance Corporation), provide loans to both consumers (car buyers) and businesses (GM dealers).

Insurance Companies

Insurance companies sell protection against losses incurred by illness, disability, death, and property damage. To finance claims payments, they collect premiums from policyholders, which they invest in stocks, bonds, and other assets. They also use a portion of their funds to make loans to individuals, businesses, and government agencies.

Brokerage Firms

Companies like Charles Schwab and BlackRock, which buy and sell stocks, bonds, and other investments for clients, are **brokerage firms** (also called *securities investment dealers*). A **mutual fund** invests money from a pool of investors in stocks, bonds, and other securities. Investors become part owners of the fund. Mutual funds reduce risk by diversifying investment: because assets are invested in dozens of companies in a variety of industries, poor performance by some firms is usually offset by good performance by others. Mutual funds may be stock funds, bond funds, and **money market funds**, which invest in safe, highly liquid securities. (Recall our definition of *liquidity* in Chapter 12 as the speed with which an asset can be converted into cash.)

Finally, **pension funds**, which manage contributions made by participating employees and employers and provide members with retirement income, are also nondeposit institutions.

2.2   Financial Services

You can appreciate the diversity of the services offered by commercial banks, savings banks, and credit unions by visiting their Web sites. For example, Wells Fargo promotes services to four categories of customers: individuals, small businesses, corporate and institutional clients, and affluent clients seeking "wealth management." In addition to traditional checking and savings accounts, the bank offers automated teller machine (ATM) services, credit cards, and debit cards. It lends money for homes, cars, college, and other personal and business needs. It provides financial advice and sells securities and other financial products, including **individual retirement account (IRA)**, by which investors can save money that's tax free until they retire. Wells Fargo even offers life, auto, disability, and homeowners insurance. It also provides electronic banking for customers who want to check balances, transfer funds, and pay bills online.[8]

2.3   Bank Regulation

How would you react if you put your life savings in a bank and then, when you went to withdraw it, learned that the bank had failed—that your money no longer existed? This is exactly what happened to many people during the Great Depression. In response to the crisis, the federal government established the **Federal Depository Insurance Corporation (FDIC)** in 1933 to restore confidence in the banking system. The FDIC insures deposits in commercial banks and savings banks up to $250,000. So today if your bank failed, the government would give you back your money (up to $250,000). The money comes from fees charged member banks.

To decrease the likelihood of failure, various government agencies conduct periodic examinations to ensure that institutions are in compliance with regulations. Commercial banks are regulated by the FDIC, savings banks by the Office of Thrift Supervision, and credit unions by the National Credit Union Administration. As we'll see later in the chapter, the Federal Reserve System also has a strong influence on the banking industry.

2.4   Crisis in the Financial Industry (and the Economy)

What follows is an interesting, but scary, story about the current financial crisis in the banking industry and its effect on the economy. In the years between 2001 and 2005, lenders made billions of dollars in subprime adjustable-rate mortgages (ARMs) to American home buyers. Subprime loans are made to home buyers who don't qualify for market-set interest rates because of one or more risk factors—income level, employment status, credit history, ability to make only a very low down payment. In 2006 and 2007, however, housing prices started to go down. Many homeowners with subprime loans, including those with ARMs whose rates had gone up, were able neither to refinance (to lower their interest rates) nor to borrow against their homes. Many of these homeowners got behind in mortgage payments, and foreclosures became commonplace—1.3 million in 2007 alone.[9] By April 2008, 1 in every 519 American households had received a foreclosure notice.[10] By August, 9.2 percent of the $12 trillion in U.S. mortgage loans was delinquent or in foreclosure.[11]

The repercussions? Banks and other institutions that made mortgage loans were the first sector of the financial industry to be hit. Largely because of mortgage-loan defaults, profits at more than 8,500 U.S. banks dropped from $35 billion in the fourth quarter of 2006 to $650 million in the corresponding quarter of 2007 (a decrease of 89 percent). Bank earnings for the year 2007 declined 31 percent and dropped another 46 percent in the first quarter of 2008.[12]

Losses in this sector were soon felt by two publicly traded government-sponsored organizations, the Federal National Mortgage Association (Fannie Mae) and the Federal Home Loan Mortgage

Corporation (Freddie Mac). Both of these institutions are authorized to make loans and provide loan guarantees to banks, mortgage companies, and other mortgage lenders; their function is to make sure that these lenders have enough money to lend to prospective home buyers. Between them, Fannie Mae and Freddie Mac backed approximately half of that $12 trillion in outstanding mortgage loans, and when the mortgage crisis hit, the stock prices of the two corporations began to drop steadily. In September 2008, amid fears that both organizations would run out of capital, the U.S. government took over their management.

Freddie Mac also had another function: to increase the supply of money available in the country for mortgage loans and new home purchases, Freddie Mac bought mortgages from banks, bundled these mortgages, and sold the bundles to investors (as mortgage-backed securities). The investors earned a return because they received cash from the monthly mortgage payments. The banks that originally sold the mortgages to Freddie Mac used the cash they got from the sale to make other loans. So investors earned a return, banks got a new influx of cash to make more loans, and individuals were able to get mortgages to buy the homes they wanted. This seemed like a good deal for everyone, so many major investment firms started doing the same thing: they bought individual subprime mortgages from original lenders (such as small banks), then pooled the mortgages and sold them to investors.

But then the bubble burst. When many home buyers couldn't make their mortgage payments (and investors began to get less money and consequently their return on their investment went down), these mortgage-backed securities plummeted in value. Institutions that had invested in them—including investment banks—suffered significant losses.[13] In September 2008, one of these investment banks, Lehman Brothers, filed for bankruptcy protection; another, Merrill Lynch, agreed to sell itself for $50 billion. Next came American International Group (AIG), a giant insurance company that insured financial institutions against the risks they took in lending and investing money. As its policyholders buckled under the weight of defaulted loans and failed investments, AIG, too, was on the brink of bankruptcy, and when private efforts to bail it out failed, the U.S. government stepped in with a loan of $85 billion.[14] The U.S. government also agreed to buy up risky mortgage-backed securities from teetering financial institutions at an estimated cost of "hundreds of billions."[15] And the banks started to fail—beginning with the country's largest savings and loan, Washington Mutual, which had 2,600 locations throughout the country. The list of failed banks kept getting longer: by November 2008, it had grown to nineteen. In response, Congress passed, and the President signed into law, the Dodd-Frank Wall Street Reform and Consumer Protection Act, which was designed to lessen the chance of a recurrence of the 2008 financial crisis.

The economic troubles that began in the banking industry as a result of the subprime crisis spread to the rest of the economy. Credit markets froze up, and it became difficult for individuals and businesses to borrow money. Consumer confidence plummeted, people reduced their spending, businesses cut production, sales dropped, company profits fell, and many lost their jobs. It would be nice if this story had a happy ending. At this point in time, all we do know is that the economy is recovering at a slow pace, consumer confidence is rebounding, and the unemployment rate is slowly decreasing (though long-term unemployment has increased).

2.5 How Banks Expand the Money Supply

When you deposit money, your bank doesn't set aside a special pile of cash with your name on it. It merely records the fact that you made a deposit and increases the balance in your account. Depending on the type of account, you can withdraw your share whenever you want, but until then, it's added to all the other money held by the bank. Because the bank can be pretty sure that all its depositors won't withdraw their money at the same time, it holds on to only a fraction of the money that it takes in—its *reserves*. It lends out the rest to individuals, businesses, and the government, earning interest income and expanding the money supply.

The Money Multiplier

Precisely how do banks expand the money supply? To find out, let's pretend you win $10,000 at the blackjack tables of your local casino. You put your winnings into your savings account immediately. The bank will keep a fraction of your $10,000 in reserve; to keep matters simple, we'll use 10 percent. The bank's reserves, therefore, will increase by $1,000 ($10,000 × 0.10). It will then lend out the remaining $9,000. The borrowers (or the parties to whom they pay it out) will then deposit the $9,000 in their own banks. Like your bank, these banks will hold onto 10 percent of the money ($900) and lend out the remainder ($8,100). Now let's go through the process one more time. The borrowers of the $8,100 (or, again, the parties to whom they pay it out) will put this amount into their banks, which will hold onto $810 and lend the remaining $7,290. As you can see in Figure 13.4, total bank deposits would now be $27,100. Eventually, bank deposits would increase to $100,000, bank reserves to $10,000, and

money multiplier

The amount by which an initial bank deposit will expand the money supply.

loans to $90,000. A shortcut for arriving at these numbers depends on the concept of the **money multiplier**, which is determined using the following formula:

$$\text{Money multiplier} = 1/\text{Reserve requirement}$$

In our example, the money multiplier is $1/0.10 = 10$. So your initial deposit of $10,000 expands into total deposits of $100,000 ($10,000 × 10), additional loans of $90,000 ($9,000 × 10), and increased bank reserves of $10,000 ($1,000 × 10). In reality, the multiplier will actually be less than 10. Why? Because some of the money loaned out will be held as currency and won't make it back into the banks.

FIGURE 13.4 The Effect of the Money Multiplier

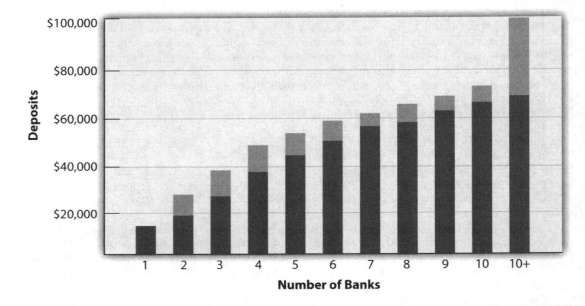

The Effect of the Money Multiplier

Click on this link to experience an active version of this figure.

KEY TAKEAWAYS

- Financial institutions serve as financial intermediaries between savers and borrowers and direct the flow of funds between the two groups.
- Those that accept deposits from customers—depository institutions—include **commercial banks**, **savings banks**, and **credit unions**; those that don't—nondepository institutions—include **finance companies**, **insurance companies**, and **brokerage firms**.
- Financial institutions offer a wide range of services, including checking and savings accounts, ATM services, and credit and debit cards. They also sell securities and provide financial advice.
- A bank holds onto only a fraction of the money that it takes in—an amount called its **reserves**—and lends the rest out to individuals, businesses, and governments. In turn, borrowers put some of these funds back into the banking system, where they become available to other borrowers. The **money multiplier** effect ensures that the cycle expands the money supply.

Before going to the next section of this chapter, take a few minutes to test your knowledge of the material covered in this section. Quizzes can be found under the "Resources" tab, "Study Aids: Quizzes."

3.   THE FEDERAL RESERVE SYSTEM

LEARNING OBJECTIVES

1. **Identify the goals of the Federal Reserve System.**
2. **Examine how the Federal Reserve System uses monetary policy to control the money supply and influence interest rates.**

Who decides how much banks should keep in reserve? The decision is made by the Federal Reserve System (popularly known as "the Fed"), a central banking system established in 1913. Most large banks belong to the Federal Reserve System, which divides the country into twelve districts, each with a member-owned Federal Reserve Bank. The twelve banks are coordinated by a board of governors.

3.1   The Tools of the Fed

The Fed has three major goals:

1. Price stability
2. Sustainable economic growth
3. Full employment[16]

Recall our definition of *monetary policy* in Chapter 1 as the efforts of the Federal Reserve System to regulate the nation's money supply. We also defined *price stability* as conditions under which the prices for products remain fairly constant. Now, we can put the two concepts together: the Fed seeks to stabilize prices by regulating the money supply and interest rates. In turn, stable prices promote economic growth and full employment—at least in theory. To conduct monetary policy, the Fed relies on three tools: *reserve requirements*, the *discount rate*, and *open market operations*.

Reserve Requirements

Under what circumstances would the Fed want to change the reserve requirement for banks? The purpose of controlling the money supply is primarily to lessen the threat of *inflation* (a rise in the overall price level) or *recession* (an economic slowdown gauged by a decline in gross domestic product). Here's how it works (again, in theory). If the Fed *raises* the reserve requirement (for example, from 10 percent to 11 percent), banks must set aside more money. Consequently, they have *less to lend* and so raise their interest rates. Under these conditions, it's harder and more expensive for people to borrow money, and

FIGURE 13.5

The Federal Reserve Building in Washington, DC.

© 2010 Jupiterimages Corporation

Federal Reserve System (the Fed)

U.S. central banking system, which has three goals: price stability, sustainable economic growth, and full employment.

if they can't borrow as much, they can't spend as much, and if people don't spend as much, prices don't go up. Thus, the Fed has lessened the likelihood of inflation.

Conversely, when the Fed *lowers* the reserve requirement (for example, from 10 percent to 9 percent), banks need to set aside less money. Because they have *more money to lend*, they keep interest rates down. Borrowers find it easier and cheaper to get money for buying things, and the more consumers buy, the higher prices go. In this case, the Fed has reduced the likelihood of a recession.

A 1 percent change in the reserve requirement, whether up to 11 percent or down to 9 percent, may not seem like much, but remember our earlier discussion of the *money multiplier*: because of the money-multiplier effect, a small change in the reserve requirement has a dramatic effect on the money supply. (For the same reason, the Fed changes reserve requirements only rarely.)

The Discount Rate

discount rate

Rate of interest the Fed charges member banks when they borrow reserve funds.

To understand how the Fed uses the discount rate to control the money supply, let's return to our earlier discussion of reserves. Recall that banks must keep a certain fraction of their deposits as reserves. The bank can hold these reserve funds or deposit them into a Federal Reserve Bank account. Recall, too, that the bank can lend out any funds that it doesn't have to put on reserve. What happens if a bank's reserves fall below the required level? The Fed steps in, permitting the bank to "borrow" reserve funds from the Federal Reserve Bank and add them to its reserve account at the Bank. There's a catch: the bank must pay interest on the borrowed money. The rate of interest that the Fed charges member banks is called the **discount rate**. By manipulating this rate, the Fed can make it appealing or unappealing to borrow funds. If the rate is high enough, banks will be reluctant to borrow. Because they don't want to drain their reserves, they cut back on lending. The money supply, therefore, decreases. By contrast, when the discount rate is low, banks are more willing to borrow because they're less concerned about draining their reserves. Holding fewer excess reserves, they lend out a higher percentage of their funds, thereby increasing the money supply.

Even more important is the carryover effect of a change in the discount rate to the overall level of interest rates.[17] When the Fed adjusts the discount rate, it's telling the financial community where it thinks the economy is headed—up or down. Wall Street, for example, generally reacts unfavorably to an increase in the discount rate. Why? Because the increase means that interest rates will probably rise, making future borrowing more expensive.

Open Market Operations

open market operations

The sale and purchase of U.S. government bonds by the Fed in the open market.

The Fed's main tool for controlling the money supply and influencing interest rates is called **open market operations**: the sale and purchase of U.S. government bonds by the Fed in the open market. To understand how this process works, we first need to know a few facts:

- The Fed's assets include a substantial dollar amount of government bonds.
- The Fed can buy or sell these bonds on the open market (consisting primarily of commercial banks).
- Because member banks use cash to buy these bonds, they decrease their reserve balances when they buy them.
- Because member banks receive cash from the sale of the bonds, they increase their reserve balances when they sell them.
- Banks must maintain a specified balance in reserves; if they dip below this balance, they have to make up the difference by borrowing money.

If the Fed wants to decrease the money supply, it can *sell* bonds, thereby reducing the reserves of the member banks that buy them. Because these banks would then have less money to lend, the money supply would decrease. If the Fed wants to increase the money supply, it will *buy* bonds, increasing the reserves of the banks that sell them. The money supply would increase because these banks would then have more money to lend.

The Federal Funds Rate

federal funds rate

The interest rate that a Federal Reserve member bank pays when it borrows from other member banks to meet reserve requirements.

In conducting open market operations, the Fed is trying to do the same thing that it does in using its other tools—namely, to influence the money supply and, thereby, interest rates. But it also has something else in mind. To understand what that is, you need to know a few more things about banking. When a bank's reserve falls below its required level, it may, as we've seen, borrow from the Fed (at the discount rate). But it can also borrow from other member banks that have excess reserves. The rate that banks pay when they borrow through this channel is called the **federal funds rate**.[18]

How does the federal funds rate affect the money supply? As we've seen, when the Fed sells bonds in the open market, the reserve balances of many member banks go down. To get their reserves back to the required level, they must borrow, whether from the Fed or from other member banks. When Bank 1 borrows from Bank 2, Bank 2's supply of funds goes down; thus, it increases the interest rate that it charges. In short, the increased demand for funds drives up the federal funds rate.

All this interbank borrowing affects you, the average citizen and consumer. When the federal funds rate goes up, banks must pay more for their money, and they'll pass the cost along to their customers: banks all over the country will raise the interest rates charged on mortgages, car loans, and personal loans. Figure 13.6 charts ten-year fluctuations in the discount rate, federal funds rate, and **prime rate**—the rate that banks charge their best customers. Because all three rates tend to move in the same direction, borrowers—individuals, as well as organizations—generally pay more to borrow money when banks have to pay more and less when banks have to pay less. Notice that the prime rate (which banks charge their customers) is higher than both the federal funds and discount rates (which banks must pay when they need to borrow). That's why banks make profits when they make loans. Note, too, that the Fed lowered the discount rate and federal funds rate drastically in 2008 in an attempt to stimulate a weakening economy. The Fed has elected to keep these low rates until the economy no longer needs them.

> **prime rate**
>
> Rate that banks charge their best customers.

FIGURE 13.6   Key Interest Rates, 2002–2013

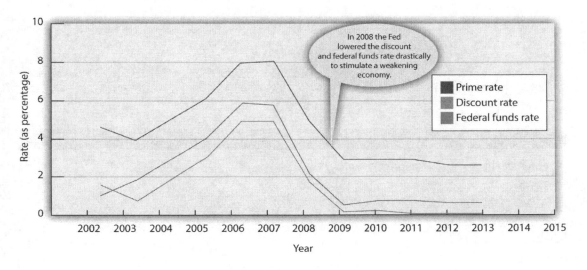

3.2   The Banker's Bank and the Government's Banker

The Fed performs another important function: it serves its member banks in much the same way as your bank serves you. When you get a check, you deposit it in your checking account, thereby increasing your balance. When you pay someone by check, the dollar amount of the check is charged to your account, and your balance goes down. The Fed works in much the same way, except that its customers are member banks. Just as your bank clears your check, the Fed clears the checks that pass through its member banks. The monumental task of clearing more than fifteen billion checks a year is complicated by the fact that there are twelve district banks. If someone in one district (for example, Boston) writes a check to a payee in another district (say, San Francisco), the check must be processed through both districts.[19]

Prior to 2004, clearing checks took days because the checks themselves needed to be physically moved through the system. But thanks to the passage of Check 21 (a U.S. federal law), things now move much more quickly. Instead of physically transporting checks, banks are allowed to make an image of the front and back of a check and send the digital version of the original check, called a "substitute" check, through the system electronically.[20] The good news is that Check 21 shortened the time it takes to clear a check, often down to one day. The bad news is that Check 21 shortened the time it takes to clear a check, which increases the risk that a check you write will bounce. So be careful: don't write a check unless you have money in the bank to cover it.

In performing the following functions, the Fed is also the U.S. government's banker:

- Holding the U.S. Treasury's checking account
- Processing the paperwork involved in buying and selling government securities
- Collecting federal tax payments
- Lending money to the government by purchasing government bonds from the Treasury

The Fed also prints, stores, and distributes currency and destroys it when it's damaged or worn out. Finally, the Fed, in conjunction with other governmental agencies, supervises and regulates financial institutions to ensure that they operate soundly and treat customers fairly and equitably.[21]

KEY TAKEAWAYS

- Most large banks are members of the central banking system called the **Federal Reserve System** (commonly known as "the Fed").
- The Fed's goals include price stability, sustainable economic growth, and full employment. It uses *monetary policy* to regulate the money supply and the level of interest rates.
- To achieve these goals, the Fed has three tools:
    1. it can raise or lower reserve requirements—the percentage of its funds that banks must set aside and can't lend out;
    2. it can raise or lower the **discount rate**—the rate of interest that the Fed charges member banks to borrow "reserve" funds;
    3. it can conduct **open market operations**—buying or selling government securities on the open market.

Before going to the next section of this chapter, take a few minutes to test your knowledge of the material covered in this section. Quizzes can be found under the "Resources" tab, "Study Aids: Quizzes."

EXERCISE

Answer this three-part question on the Federal Reserve:

1. What is the Federal Reserve?
2. What is the purpose of the Federal Reserve? What are its goals?
3. How does the Federal Reserve affect the U.S. economy?

4. THE ROLE OF THE FINANCIAL MANAGER

LEARNING OBJECTIVES

1. Define the term "financial plan," and identify its purpose.
2. Identify and describe three common sources of funding for new businesses.
3. Distinguish among the following loan maturities: short-term, intermediate-term, and long-term loans.
4. Identify the purpose of a line of credit.
5. Explain why a bank might ask a borrower to provide security for a loan, and identify different forms of security.
6. Identify approaches used by existing companies to finance operations and growth, and differentiate between angels and venture capitalists.
7. Describe the process required to take a privately-held company public.

So far, we've focused our attention on the financial environment in which U.S. businesses operate. Now let's focus on the role that finance plays within an organization. In Chapter 1, we defined *finance* as all the activities involved in planning for, obtaining, and managing a company's funds. We also explained that a *financial manager* determines how much money the company needs, how and where it will get the necessary funds, and how and when it will repay the money that it has borrowed. The financial manager also decides what the company should do with its funds—what investments should be made in plant and equipment, how much should be spent on research and development, and how excess funds should be invested.

4.1   Financing a New Company

Because new businesses usually need to borrow money in order to get off the ground, good financial management is particularly important to start-ups. Let's suppose that you're about to start up a company that you intend to run from your dorm room. You thought of the idea while rummaging through a pile of previously worn clothes to find something that wasn't about to get up and walk to the laundry all by itself. "Wouldn't it be great," you thought, "if there was an on-campus laundry service that would come and pick up my dirty clothes and bring them back to me washed and folded." Because you were also in the habit of running out of cash at inopportune times, you were highly motivated to start some sort of money-making enterprise, and the laundry service seemed to fit the bill (even though washing and folding clothes wasn't among your favorite activities—or skills).

4.2   Developing a Financial Plan

Because you didn't want your business to be so small that it stayed under the radar of fellow students and potential customers, you knew that you'd need to raise funds to get started. So what are your cash needs? To answer this question, you need to draw up a **financial plan**—a document that performs two functions:

1. Calculating the amount of funds that a company needs for a specified period
2. Detailing a strategy for getting those funds

> **financial plan**
>
> Planning document that shows the amount of funds a company needs and details a strategy for getting those funds.

Estimating Sales

Fortunately, you can draw on your newly acquired accounting skills to prepare the first section—the one in which you'll specify the amount of cash you need. You start by estimating your *sales* (or, in your case, revenue from laundering clothes) for your first year of operations. This is the most important estimate you'll make: without a realistic sales estimate, you can't accurately calculate equipment needs and other costs. To predict sales, you'll need to estimate two figures:

1. The number of loads of laundry that you'll handle
2. The price that you'll charge per load

You calculate as follows: You estimate that 5 percent of the ten thousand students on campus will use the service. These five hundred students will have one large load of laundry for each of the thirty-five weeks that they're on campus. Therefore, you'll do 17,500 loads (500 × 35 = 17,500 loads). You decide to price each load at $10. At first, this seemed high, but when you consider that you'll have to pick up, wash, dry, fold, and return large loads, it seems reasonable.

Perhaps more important, when you projected your costs—including salaries (for some student workers), rent, utilities, depreciation on equipment and a truck, supplies, maintenance, insurance, and advertising—you found that each load would cost $8, leaving a profit of $2 per load and earning you $35,000 for your first year (which is worth your time, though not enough to make you rich).

What things will you have to buy in order to get started? Using your estimate of sales, you've determined that you'd need the following:

- Five washers and five dryers
- A truck to pick up and deliver the clothes (a used truck will do for now)
- An inventory of laundry detergent and other supplies, such as laundry baskets
- Rental space in a nearby building (which will need some work to accommodate a laundry)

And, you'll need cash—cash to carry you over while the business gets going and cash with which to pay your bills. Finally, you'd better have some extra money for contingencies—things you don't expect, such as a machine overflowing and damaging the floor. You're mildly surprised to find that your cash needs total $33,000. Your next task is to find out where you can get $33,000. In the next section, we'll look at some options.

4.3 Getting the Money

Figure 13.8 summarizes the results of a survey in which owners of small and medium-size businesses were asked where they typically acquired their financing. To simplify matters, we'll work on the principle that new businesses are generally financed with some combination of the following:

- Owners' personal assets
- Loans from families and friends
- Bank loans (including those guaranteed by the Small Business Development Center)

FIGURE 13.8 Where Small Businesses Get Funding

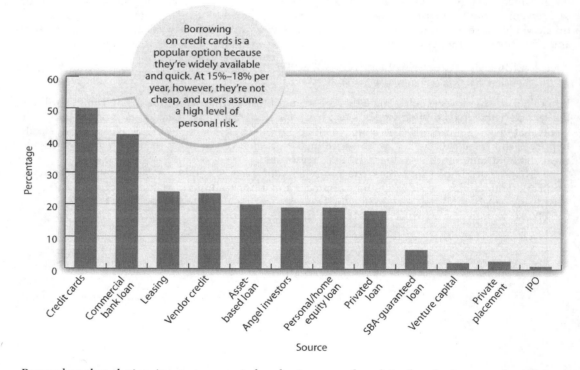

Remember that during its start-up period, a business needs a lot of cash: it not only will incur substantial start-up costs, but may even suffer initial operational losses.

Personal Assets

Its owners are the most important source of funds for any new business. Figuring that owners with substantial investments will work harder to make the enterprise succeed, lenders expect owners to put up a substantial amount of the start-up money. Where does this money come from? Usually through personal savings, credit cards, home mortgages, or the sale of personal assets.

Loans from Family and Friends

For many entrepreneurs, the next stop is family and friends. If you have an idea with commercial potential, you might be able to get family members and friends either to invest in it (as part owners) or to lend you some money. Remember that family and friends are like any other creditors: they expect to be repaid, and they expect to earn interest. Even when you're borrowing from family members or friends, you should draw up a formal loan agreement stating when the loan will be repaid and specifying the interest rate.

Bank Loans

The financing package for a start-up company will probably include bank loans. Banks, however, will lend you some start-up money only if they're convinced that your idea is commercially feasible. They also prefer you to have some combination of talent and experience to run the company successfully. Bankers want to see a well-developed business plan, with detailed financial projections demonstrating your ability to repay loans. Financial institutions offer various types of loans with different payback periods. Most, however, have a few common characteristics.

Maturity

The period for which a bank loan is issued is called its **maturity**. A **short-term loan** is for less than a year, an **intermediate loan** for one to five years, and a **long-term loan** for five years or more. Banks can also issue **lines of credit** that allow you to borrow up to a specified amount as the need arises (it's a lot like the limit on your credit card).

In taking out a loan, you want to match its term with its purpose. If, for example, you're borrowing money to buy a truck that you plan to use for five years, you'd request a five-year loan. On the other hand, if you're financing a piece of equipment that you'll use for ten years, you'll want a ten-year loan. For short-term needs, like buying inventory, you may request a one-year loan.

With any loan, however, you must consider the ability of the business to repay it. If you expect to lose money for the first year, you obviously won't be able to repay a one-year loan on time. You'd be better off with intermediate or long-term financing. Finally, you need to consider **amortization**—the schedule by which you'll reduce the balance of your debt. Will you be making periodic payments on both principal and interest over the life of the loan (for example, monthly or quarterly), or will the entire amount (including interest) be due at the end of the loan period?

Security

A bank won't lend you money unless it thinks that your business can generate sufficient funds to pay it back. Often, however, the bank takes an added precaution by asking you for **security**—business or personal assets, called **collateral**, that you pledge in order to guarantee repayment. You may have to secure the loan with company assets, such as inventory or accounts receivable, or even with personal assets. (Likewise, if you're an individual getting a car loan, the bank will accept the automobile as security.) In any case, the principle is pretty simple: if you don't pay the loan when it's due, the bank can take possession of the collateral, sell it, and keep the proceeds to cover the loan. If you don't have to put up collateral, you're getting an **unsecured loan**, but because of the inherent risk entailed by new business ventures, banks don't often make such loans.

Interest

Interest is the cost of using someone else's money. The rate of interest charged on a loan varies with several factors—the general level of interest rates, the size of the loan, the quality of the collateral, and the debt-paying ability of the borrower. For smaller, riskier loans, it can be as much as 6 to 8 percentage points above the prime rate—the rate that banks charge their most creditworthy borrowers. It's currently around 3 percent per year.

4.4   Making the Financing Decision

Now that we've surveyed your options, let's go back to the task of financing your laundry business. You'd like to put up a substantial amount of the money you need, but you can only come up with a measly $1,000 (which you had to borrow on your credit card). You were, however, able to convince your parents to lend you $10,000, which you've promised to pay back, with interest, in three years. (They were wavering until you pointed out that Fred DeLuca started SUBWAY as a way of supporting himself through college).

---

maturity

Period of time for which a bank loan is issued.

short-term loan

Loan issued with a maturity date of less than one year.

intermediate loan

Loan issued with a maturity date of one to five years.

long-term loan

Loan issued with a maturity date of five years or more.

lines of credit

Commitment by a bank that allows a company to borrow up to a specified amount of money as the need arises.

amortization

Schedule by which you'll reduce the balance of your debt.

security

Collateral pledged to secure repayment of a loan.

collateral

Specific business or personal assets that a bank accepts as security for a loan.

unsecured loan

Loan given by a bank that doesn't require the borrower to put up collateral.

interest

Cost charged to use someone else's money.

So you still need $22,000 ($33,000 minus the $11,000 from you and your parents). You talked with someone at the Small Business Development Center located on campus, but you're not optimistic about getting them to guarantee a loan. Instead, you put together a sound business plan, including projected financial statements, and set off to your local banker. To your surprise, she agreed to a five-year loan at a reasonable interest rate. Unfortunately, she wanted the entire loan secured. Because you're using some of the loan money to buy washers and dryers (for $15,000) and a truck (for $6,000), you can put up these as collateral. You have no accounts receivable or inventories, so you agreed to put up some personal assets—namely, the shares of Microsoft stock that you got as a high-school graduation present (now worth about $5,000).

4.5   Financing the Business During the Growth Stage

Flash-forward two and a half years: much to your delight, your laundry business took off. You had your projected five hundred customers within six months, and over the next few years, you expanded to four other colleges in the geographical area. Now you're serving five colleges and some three thousand customers a week. Your management team has expanded, but you're still in charge of the company's finances. In the next sections, we'll review the tasks involved in managing the finances of a high-growth business.

Managing Cash

cash-flow management

Process of monitoring cash inflows and outflows to ensure that the company has the right amount of funds on hand.

Cash-flow management means monitoring cash inflows and outflows to ensure that your company has sufficient—but not excessive—cash on hand to meet its obligations. When projected cash flows indicate a future shortage, you go to the bank for additional funds. When projections show that there's going to be idle cash, you take action to invest it and earn a return for your company.

Managing Accounts Receivable

Because you bill your customers every week, you generate sizable *accounts receivable*—money that you'll receive from customers to whom you've sold your service. You make substantial efforts to collect receivables on a timely basis and to keeping nonpayment to a minimum.

Managing Accounts Payable

trade credit

Credit given to a company by its suppliers.

Accounts payable are records of cash that you owe to the suppliers of products that you use. You generate them when you buy supplies with **trade credit**—credit given you by your suppliers. You're careful to pay your bills on time, but not ahead of time (because it's in your best interest to hold on to your cash as long as possible).

Budgeting

budget

A document that itemizes the sources of income and expenditures for a future period (often a year).

cash budget

Financial plan that projects cash inflows and outflows over a period of time.

capital budget

Budget that shows anticipated expenditures for major equipment.

A **budget** is a preliminary financial plan for a given time period, generally a year. At the end of the stated period, you compare actual and projected results and then you investigate any significant discrepancies. You prepare several types of budgets: projected financial statements, a **cash budget** that projects cash flows, and a **capital budget** that shows anticipated expenditures for major equipment.

4.6   Seeking Out Private Investors

So far, you've been able to finance your company's growth through internally generated funds—profits retained in the business—along with a few bank loans. Your success, especially your expansion to other campuses, has confirmed your original belief that you've come up with a great business concept. You're anxious to expand further, but to do that, you'll need a substantial infusion of new cash. You've poured most of your profits back into the company, and your parents can't lend you any more money. After giving the problem some thought, you realize that you have three options:

1. Ask the bank for more money.
2. Bring in additional owners who can invest in the company.
3. Seek funds from a private investor.

Angels and Venture Capitalists

Eventually, you decide on the third option. First, however, you must decide what type of private investor you want—an "angel" or a venture capitalist. **Angels** are usually wealthy individuals willing to invest in *start-up ventures* they believe will succeed. They bet that a business will ultimately be very profitable and that they can sell their interest at a large profit. **Venture capitalists** pool funds from private and institutional sources (such as pension funds and insurance companies) and invest them in *existing businesses* with strong growth potential. They're typically willing to invest larger sums but often want to cash out more quickly than angels.

There are drawbacks. Both types of private investors provide business expertise, as well as financing, and, in effect, both become partners in the enterprises that they finance. They accept only the most promising opportunities, and if they do decide to invest in your business, they'll want something in return for their money—namely, a say in how you manage it.

When you approach private investors, you can be sure that your business plan will get a thorough going-over. Under your current business model, setting up a new laundry on another campus requires about $50,000. But you're a little more ambitious, intending to increase the number of colleges that you serve from five to twenty-five. So you'll need a cash inflow of $1 million. On weighing your alternatives and considering the size of the loan you need, you decide to approach a venture capitalist. Fortunately, because you prepared an excellent business plan and made a great presentation, your application was accepted. Your expansion begins.

4.7   Going Public

Fast-forward another five years. You've worked hard (and been lucky), and even finished your degree in finance. Moreover, your company has done amazingly well, with operations at more than five hundred colleges in the Northeast. You've financed continued strong growth with a combination of venture-capital funds and internally generated funds (that is, reinvested earnings).

Up to this point, you've operated as a privately held corporation with limited stock ownership (you and your parents are the sole shareholders). But because you expect your business to prosper even more and grow even bigger, you're thinking about the possibility of selling stock to the public for the first time. The advantages are attractive: not only would you get a huge influx of cash, but because it would come from the sale of stock rather than from borrowing, it would also be interest free and you wouldn't have to repay it. Again there are some drawbacks. For one thing, going public is quite costly—often exceeding $300,000—and time-consuming. Second, from this point on, your financial results would be public information. Finally, you'd be responsible to shareholders who will want to see the kind of short-term performance results that boosts stock prices.

After weighing the pros and cons, you decide to go ahead. The first step in the process of becoming a publicly traded corporation is called an **initial public offering (IPO)**, and you'll need the help of an **investment banking firm**—a financial institution (such as Goldman Sachs or Morgan Stanley) that specializes in issuing securities. Your investment banker advises you that now's a good time to go public and determines the best price at which to sell your stock. Then, you'll need the approval of the Securities and Exchange Commission (SEC), the government agency that regulates securities markets.

angel

Wealthy individual willing to invest in start-up ventures.

venture capitalist

Individual who pools funds from private and institutional sources and invests them in businesses with strong growth potential.

initial public offering (IPO)

Process of taking a privately held company public by selling stock to the public for the first time.

investment banking firm

Financial institution that specializes in issuing securities.

KEY TAKEAWAYS

- If a new business hopes to get funding, it should prepare a financial plan—a document that shows the amount of capital that it needs for a specified period, how and where it will get it, and how and when it will pay it back.

- Common sources of funding for new businesses include personal assets, loans from family and friends, and bank loans.

- Financial institutions offer business loans with different **maturities**. A **short-term loan** matures in less than a year, an **intermediate loan** in one to five years, and a **long-term loan** after five years or more.

- Banks also issue **lines of credit** that allow companies to borrow up to a specified amount as the need arises.

- Banks generally require **security** in the form of **collateral**, such as company or personal assets. If the borrower fails to pay the loan when it's due, the bank can take possession of these assets.

- Existing companies that want to expand often seek funding from private investors. **Angels** are wealthy individuals who are willing to invest in ventures that they believe will succeed. **Venture capitalists**, though willing to invest larger sums of money, often want to cash out more quickly than angels. They generally invest in existing businesses with strong growth potential.

- Successful companies looking for additional capital might decide to go public, offering an initial sale of stock called an **initial public offering (IPO)**.

Before going to the next section of this chapter, take a few minutes to test your knowledge of the material covered in this section. Quizzes can be found under the "Resources" tab, "Study Aids: Quizzes."

EXERCISES

1. The most important number in most financial plans is projected revenue. Why? For one thing, without a realistic estimate of your revenue, you can't accurately calculate your costs. Say, for example, that you just bought a condominium in Hawaii, which you plan to rent out to vacationers. Because you live in snowy New England, however, you plan to use it yourself from December 15 to January 15. You've also promised your sister that she can have it for the month of July. Now, in Hawaii, condo rents peak during the winter and summer seasons—December 15 to April 15, and June 15 to August 31. They also vary from island to island, according to age and quality, number of rooms, and location (on the beach or away from it). The good news is that your relatively new two-bedroom condo is on a glistening beach in Maui. The bad news is that no one is fortunate enough to keep a condo rented for the entire time that it's available. What information would you need to estimate your rental revenues for the year?

2. You're developing a financial plan for a retail business that you want to launch this summer. You've determined that you need $500,000, including $50,000 for a truck, $80,000 for furniture and equipment, and $100,000 for inventory. You'll use the rest to cover start-up and operating costs during your first six months of operation. After considering the possible sources of funds available to you, create a table that shows how you'll obtain the $500,000 you need. It should include all the following items:

   - Sources of all funds
   - Dollar amounts to be obtained through each source
   - The maturity, annual interest rate, and security of any loan

   The total of your sources must equal $500,000. Finally, write a brief report explaining the factors that you considered in arriving at your combination of sources.

3. For the past three years, you've operated a company that manufactures and sells customized surfboards. Sales are great, your employees work hard, and your customers are happy. In lots of ways, things couldn't be better. There is, however, one stubborn cloud hanging over this otherwise sunny picture: you're constantly short of cash. You've ruled out going to the bank because you'd probably be turned down, and you're not big enough to go public. Perhaps the solution is private investors. To see whether this option makes sense, research the pros and cons of getting funding from a venture capitalist. Write a brief report explaining why you have, or haven't, decided to seek private funding.

5.   UNDERSTANDING SECURITIES MARKETS

LEARNING OBJECTIVES

1. **Indicate the two key functions provided by the securities market.**
2. **Distinguish between the primary market and the secondary market.**
3. **Identify the best known stock exchanges.**
4. **Show how the securities market operates and how it's regulated.**
5. **Understand how market performance is measured.**
6. **Contrast a bull market and a bear market.**
7. **Understand how to read a stock quote.**

So, before long, you're a publicly traded company. Fortunately, because your degree in finance comes with a better-than-average knowledge of financial markets, you're familiar with the ways in which investors will evaluate your company. Investors will look at the overall quality of the company and ask some basic questions:

- How well is it managed?
- Is it in a growing industry? Is its market share increasing or decreasing?
- Does it have a good line of products? Is it coming out with innovative products?
- How is the company doing relative to its competitors?
- What is its future? What is the future of its industry?

Investors also analyze the company's performance over time and ask more-specific questions:

- Are its sales growing?
- Is its income going up?
- Is its stock price rising or falling?
- Are earnings per share rising?

They'll assess the company's financial strength, asking another series of specific questions:

- Can it pay its bills on time?
- Does it have too much debt?
- Is it managing its productive assets (such as inventory) efficiently?

5.1   Primary and Secondary Markets and Stock Exchanges

Security markets serve two functions:

1. They help companies to raise funds by making the initial sale of their stock to the public.
2. They provide a place where investors can trade already issued stock.

When you went through your IPO, shares were issued through a **primary market**—a market that deals in new financial assets. As we've seen, the sale was handled by an investment banking firm, which matched you, as a corporation with stock to sell, with investors who wanted to buy it.

primary market

Market that deals in the sale of newly issued securities.

Organized Exchanges

After a certain time elapsed, investors began buying and selling your stock on a **secondary market**. The proceeds of sales on this market go to the investor who sells the stock, not to your company. The best-known of these markets is the **New York Stock Exchange (NYSE)**,[22] where the stocks of the largest, most prestigious corporations in the world are traded. Other exchanges, including the **American Stock Exchange (AMEX)** and regional exchanges located in places like Chicago and Boston, trade the stock of smaller companies.

OTC Markets

Note that a "market" doesn't have to be a physical location. In the **over-the-counter (OTC) market**, securities are traded among dealers over computer networks or by phone rather than on the floor of an organized exchange. Though there are exceptions, stocks traded in the OTC market are generally those of smaller (and often riskier) companies. The best-known OTC electronic-exchange system is the **NASDAQ** (National Association of Securities Dealers Automated Quotation system). It's home to almost five thousand corporations, many of them technology companies. Unlike other OTC markets, the NASDAQ lists a variety of companies, ranging from small start-ups to such giants as Google, Microsoft, and Intel.

5.2 Regulating Securities Markets: The SEC

Because it's vital that investors have confidence in the securities markets, Congress created the **Securities and Exchange Commission (SEC)** in 1934. The SEC is charged with enforcing securities laws designed to promote full public disclosure, protecting investors against misconduct in the securities markets, and maintaining the integrity of the securities markets.[23]

Before offering securities for sale, the issuer must register its intent to sell with the SEC. In addition, the issuer must provide prospective buyers with a **prospectus**—a written offer to sell securities that describes the business and operations of the issuer, lists its officers, provides financial information, discloses any pending litigation, and states the proposed use of funds from the sale.

The SEC also enforces laws against **insider trading**—the illegal buying or selling of its securities by a firm's officers and directors or anyone else taking advantage of valuable information about the company before it's made public. The intent of these laws is to prevent insiders from profiting at the expense of other investors.

5.3 Measuring Market Performance: Market Indexes

Throughout the day, you can monitor the general drift of the stock market by watching any major news network and following the band at the bottom of your TV. News channels and broadcasts generally feature a market recap in the evening. Even music-oriented radio stations break for a minute of news every now and then, including a quick review of the stock market. Almost all these reports refer to one or more of the **market indexes** with which investors can track trends in stock price. Let's look more closely at some of these indicators.

The Dow

By far the most widely reported market index is the **Dow Jones Industrial Average (DJIA)**, or "the Dow." The Dow is the total value of a "market basket" of thirty large companies headquartered in the United States. They aren't the thirty largest or best-performing companies, but rather a group selected by the senior staff members at the *Wall Street Journal* to represent a broad spectrum of the U.S. economy, as well as a variety of industries. The thirty selected stocks change over time, but the list usually consists of household names, such as AT&T, Nike, Disney, IBM, General Electric, and Wal-Mart.

The graph in Figure 13.9 tracks the Dow for the ten-year period ended March 2014. The market measured by the Dow was on an upward swing from 2002 until it peaked in October 2007 at 14,200. At that point, it headed down until it reached a low point in March 2008 of 6,500 (a 54 percent drop). It has since reversed its drop and moved up to 16,400 (15 percent above its previous high). The path of the DOW during this ten-year period has been very volatile (subject to up and down movements in response to unstable worldwide economic and political situations).[24]

---

secondary market

Market in which investors buy previously issued securities from other investors.

New York Stock Exchange (NYSE)

Best-known stock market where stocks of the largest, most prestigious corporations are traded.

American Stock Exchange (AMEX)

Stock market where shares of smaller companies are traded.

over-the-counter (OTC) market

Market in which securities are traded over computer networks and phones rather than on the trading floor of an exchange.

NASDAQ

Best-known over-the-counter, electronic exchange system.

Securities and Exchange Commission (SEC)

Government agency that enforces securities laws.

prospectus

Written offer to sell securities that provides useful information to prospective buyers.

insider trading

Practice of buying or selling of securities using important information about the company before it's made public.

market index

Measure for tracking stock prices.

Dow Jones Industrial Average (DJIA)

Market index that reflects the total value of a "market basket" of thirty large U.S. companies.

FIGURE 13.9 DJIA for Ten-Year Period Ended March 2014

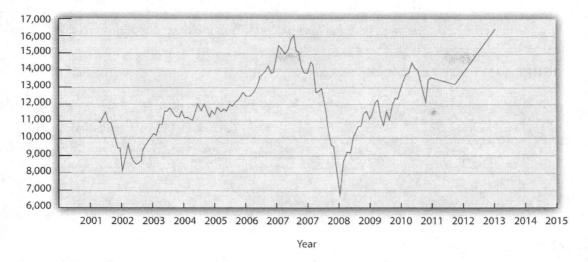

The NASDAQ Composite and the S&P 500

Also of interest is the performance of the **NASDAQ Composite Index**, which includes many technology companies. Note in Figure 13.10 that the NASDAQ peaked in early 2000 at an index of over 5,000, but as investors began reevaluating the prospects of many technologies and technology companies, prices fell precipitously and the NASDAQ shed more than 80 percent of its value. It rebounded somewhat over the next seven years, only to be shot down again when difficult economic times in 2008 spelled trouble, and it declined by 45 percent. Another broad measure of stock performance is **Standard & Poor's Composite Index (S&P 500)**, which lists the stocks of five hundred large U.S. companies. It followed the same pattern as the Dow and the NASDAQ Composite and declined by 37 percent in 2008.

NASDAQ Composite Index

Market index of all stocks listed on the NASDAQ Stock Exchange.

Standard & Poor's Composite Index (S&P 500)

Market index of the stocks of five hundred large U.S. companies.

FIGURE 13.10 NASDAQ for Ten-Year Period Ended March 2014

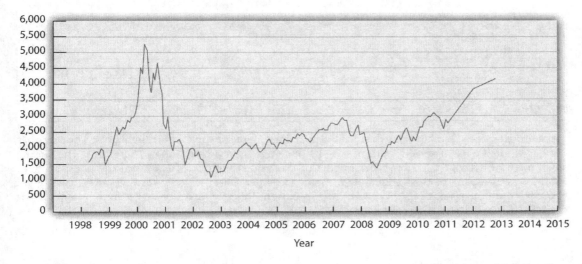

When the stock market is enjoying a period of large stock-price increases, we call it a **bull market**; when it's declining or sluggish, we call it a **bear market**. The year 2008 was definitely a bear market.

bull market

Period of large stock-price increases.

bear market

Period of declining or sluggish stock prices.

5.4 How to Read a Stock Listing

Businesspeople—both owners and managers—monitor their stock prices on a daily basis. They want the value of their stock to rise for both professional and personal reasons. Stock price, for example, is a sort of "report card" on the company's progress, and it reflects the success of its managers in running the company. Many managers have a great deal of personal wealth tied directly to the fortunes of the companies for which they work.

If you have any interest in investing, you'll want to know how to interpret stock market information. Step one is learning how to read a stock listing like those printed daily in the *Wall Street Journal* and other newspapers as well as online at sites such as Yahoo! Finance and CNBC.[25] Figure 13.11 reports the information on Hershey Foods for April 16, 2014. Let's use the explanations in Table 13.1 to examine each item in greater detail.

FIGURE 13.11 Stock Listing for Hershey Foods

	1		2	3	4	5	6	7	8
52-WEEK		STOCK (SYMBOL)		DIV	YLD %	EPS	PE	CLOSE	NET CHG
HI	LO								
108.69	85.14	HSY		1.94	1.97	3.61	28	100.47	+.54

TABLE 13.1 Interpreting a Stock Quotation

52-WEEK HI	The highest price during the past year (April 16, 2013, to April 16, 2014) was $108.69.
52-WEEK LO	The lowest price during the past year was $85.14.
STOCK (SYMBOL)	The listing is for Hershey Foods, whose stock symbol is "HSY."
DIV	HSY pays an annual *dividend* of $1.94 on each share of stock.
YLD %	HSY's dividend provides each investor with a 1.93 percent return (or *dividend yield*), as based on the day's closing stock price ($1.94 ÷ $100.47 = 1.93%).
EARNINGS PER SHARE	EPS is total profits divided by the number of shares of common stock outstanding. EPS for Hershey for 2008 is $3.61.
PE	The *price-earnings (PE) financial ratio* determines the amount that an investor would be willing to pay for every dollar of the company's earnings. This is a relative measure for comparing companies. For every $1 of HSY's *earnings per share* (the company's annual income divided by the number of shares of stock), investors are willing to pay $28 per share. High-growth firms usually have higher PE ratios, and vice versa.
CLOSE	HSY is traded on the New York Stock Exchange, which opens at 9:30 a.m. and closes at 4:00 p.m. every business day. Throughout the day, the price of HSY stock fluctuates, and at the end of the day, it stood at $100.47.
NET CHG	The price of $100.47 is up by $0.54 from the previous trading day's close, which was $99.93

What, exactly, does Hershey Foods's stock listing tell us? Here are some of the highlights: The stock has done well for the past twelve-month period. Its price has risen by more than 18 percent. The closing stock price of $100.47 falls above the middle of the annual high of $108.69 and the annual low of $85.14. The company pays an annual dividend of $1.94 per share (which gives investors a fairly good cash return on their stock of 1.93 percent). At its current PE ratio, investors are willing to pay $28 for every $1 of Hershey's earnings per share.

KEY TAKEAWAYS

- Securities markets provide two functions:
    1. They help companies raise funds by making the initial sale of stock to the public.
    2. They provide a place where investors can trade previously issued stock.
- Stock sold through an IPO is issued through a **primary market** with the help of an **investment banking firm**.
- Previously issued securities are traded in a **secondary market**, where the proceeds from sales go to investors rather than to the issuing companies.
- The best-known exchanges are the **New York Stock Exchange**, the **American Stock Exchange**, and the **NASDAQ**.
- They're all regulated by the **Securities and Exchange Commission (SEC)**, a government agency that is charged with enforcing securities laws designed to protect the investing public.
- Stock market trends are measured by **market indexes**, such as the **Dow Jones Industrial Average (DJIA)**, the **NASDAQ Composite Index**, and **Standard & Poor's Composite Index (S&P 500)**.
- When the stock market is enjoying a period of large increases in prices, it's said to be in a **bull market**. When prices are declining, it's often called a **bear market**.

Before going to the next section of this chapter, take a few minutes to test your knowledge of the material covered in this section. Quizzes can be found under the "Resources" tab, "Study Aids: Quizzes."

1. The three most commonly used stock indices are the DJIA, the NASDAQ composite index, and the S&P 500. To create charts that compare these three indices, go to http://bigcharts.marketwatch.com to link to the BigCharts Web site and take the following steps. (*Note*: These steps might change if the BigCharts Web site is changed.)

   Repeat this process to compare the DJIA with the S&P 500. Then, answer the following questions:

   - Type the letters "DJIA" in the box about a quarter of the way down the page.
   - Click on "Advanced Chart" on the top bar.
   - For time frame (left sidebar), do the following:
     - Click on "Time" and then select "1 decade"
     - Click on "Frequency" and then select "Quarterly"
   - For "Compare," go to "Index" and select "NASDAQ."
   - Chart Style:
     - Click on "Price/Display" and then select "Close"
     - Click on "Chart Background" and then select "Blue and White"
     - Click on "Size" and then select "Medium"
   - Click on "Draw Chart."
   - Print out the chart using the "Printer Friendly" format option.

   a. Which two indices tend to follow similar patterns—DJIA and NASDAQ, or DJIA and S&P?
   b. What accounts for this similarity? What types of companies does each index track? How many companies does each cover?
   c. Which index had a large peak? What accounts for that peak?
   d. Which index do you prefer for tracking the movement of the stock market? Why?

2. Below is a stock listing for P&G for April 16, 2014. This information appears daily in the *Wall Street Journal* and other newspapers. It's also available online on such Web sites as Yahoo! Finance.

52 WEEK HI	52 WEEK LO	STOCK (SYMBOL)	DIV	YLD %
85.82	73.61	Procter & Gamble PG	2.57	3.15%
PE		**CLOSE**	**NET CHG**	**EPS**
22		81.65	1.00	$3.70

To assess your ability to read and interpret this information, explain each item in the stock listing.

6. FINANCING THE GOING CONCERN

1. Define equity financing and debt financing, and discuss the advantages and disadvantages of each financing approach.
2. Explain the differences among various types of stock: common stock, preferred stock, cumulative stock, and convertible preferred stock.
3. Identify the advantages and disadvantages of common stock and preferred stock.
4. Understand the term "dividend."
5. Explain what a bond is, and describe the advantages and disadvantages of financing a company through the issuance of bonds.

Let's assume that taking your company public was a smart move: in posing questions like those that we've just listed, investors have decided that your business is a good buy. With the influx of investment capital, the little laundry business that you started in your dorm ten years ago has grown into a very large operation with laundries at more than seven hundred colleges all across the country, and you're opening two or three laundries a week. But there's still a huge untapped market out there, and you've just left a meeting with your board of directors at which it was decided that you'll seek additional funding for further growth. Everyone agrees that you need about $8 million for the proposed expansion, yet there's a difference of opinion among your board members on how to go about getting it. You have two options:

1. **Equity financing**: raising the needed capital through the sale of stock
2. **Debt financing**: raising the needed capital by selling bonds

Let's review some of the basics underlying your options.

6.1 Stock

If you decide to sell stock to finance your expansion, the proceeds from the sale will increase your **stockholders' equity**—the amount invested in the business by its owners (which is the same thing that we called *owner's equity* in Chapter 12). In general, an increase in stockholders' equity is good. Your *assets*—specifically, your cash—will increase because you'll have more money with which to expand and operate your business (which is also good). But if you sell additional shares of stock, you'll have more stockholders—a situation that, as we'll see later, isn't always good.

6.2 The Risk/Reward Trade-Off

To issue additional shares of stock, you'll need to find buyers interested in purchasing them. You need to ask yourself this question: Why would anyone want to buy stock in your company? Stockholders, as we know, are part owners of the company and, as such, share in the risks and rewards associated with ownership. If your company does well, they may benefit through **dividends**—distributed earnings—or through appreciation in the value of their stock, or both. If your company does poorly, the value of their stock will probably decline. Because the risk/reward trade-off varies according to the type of stock—*common* or *preferred*—we need to know a little more about the difference between the two.

Common Stock

Holders of **common stock** bear the ultimate rewards and risks of ownership. Depending on the extent of their ownership, they could exercise some control over the corporation. They're generally entitled to vote on members of the board of directors and other important matters. If the company does well, they benefit more than holders of preferred stock; if it does poorly, they take a harder hit. If it goes out of business, they're the last to get any money from the sale of what's left and can in fact lose their investments entirely.

So who would buy common stock? It's a good option for individuals and institutions that are willing to take an investment roller-coaster ride: for a chance to share in the growth and profits of a company (the ups), they have to be willing to risk losing all or part of their investments (the downs).

Preferred Stock

Preferred stock is safer, but it doesn't have the upside potential. Unlike holders of common stock, whose return on investment depends on the company's performance, preferred shareholders receive a fixed dividend every year. As usual, there are disadvantages and advantages. They don't usually have voting rights, and unless the company does extremely well, their dividends are limited to the fixed amount. On the other hand, they're *preferred* as to dividends: the company can pay no dividends to common shareholders until it's paid all preferred dividends. If the company goes under, preferred stockholders also get their money back before common shareholders get any of theirs. In many ways, they're more like creditors than investors in equity: though they can usually count on a fixed, relatively safe income, they have little opportunity to share in a company's success.

equity financing

Process of raising capital for a company through the sale of stock.

debt financing

Process of raising capital for a company through the sale of bonds.

stockholders' equity

Amount invested in a corporation by its shareholders.

dividends

Earnings distributed to stockholders.

common stock

Stock whose owners bear the ultimate rewards and risks of ownership.

preferred stock

Stock that pays owners a fixed dividend annually.

Cumulative and Convertible Preferred Stock

cumulative preferred stock

Preferred stock that requires a corporation to pay all current and missed preferred dividends before it can pay common dividends.

convertible preferred stock

Preferred stock that gives its owner the option of exchanging it for common stock.

There are a couple of ways to make preferred stock more attractive. With **cumulative preferred stock**, if a company fails to make a dividend payment to preferred shareholders in a given year, it can pay no common dividends until preferred shareholders have been *paid in full for both current and missed dividends*. Anyone holding **convertible preferred stock** may exchange it for common stock. Thus, preferred shareholders can convert to common stock when and if the company's performance is strong—when its common stock is likely to go up in value.

6.3 Bonds

Now, let's look at the second option: debt financing—raising capital through the sale of bonds. As with the sale of stock, the sale of bonds will increase your assets (again, specifically your cash) because you'll receive an inflow of cash (which, as we said, is good). But as we'll see, your *liabilities*—your debt to outside parties—will also increase (which is bad). And just as you'll need to find buyers for your stock, you'll need to find buyers for your bonds. Again, we need to ask the question: Why would anyone want to buy your company's bonds?

bonds

Debt securities that require annual interest payments to bondholders.

Your financial projections show that you need $8 million to finance your expansion. If you decide to borrow this much money, you aren't likely to find one individual or institution that will loan it to you. But if you divided up the $8 million loan into eight thousand smaller loans of $1,000 each, you'd stand a better chance of getting the amount you need. That's the strategy behind issuing **bonds**: debt securities that obligate the issuer to make interest payments to bondholders (generally on a periodic basis) and to repay the principal when the bond matures. In other words, a bond is an IOU that pays interest. Like equity investors, bondholders can sell their securities on the financial market.

From the investor's standpoint, buying bonds is a way to earn a fairly good rate of return on money that he or she doesn't need for a while. The interest is better than what they'd get on a savings account or in a money market fund. But there is some risk. Investors who are interested in your bonds will assess the financial strength of your company: they want to feel confident that you'll be able to make your interest payments and pay back the principal when the time comes. They'll probably rely on data supplied by such bond-rating organizations as Moody's and Standard & Poor's, which rate bonds from AAA (highly unlikely to default) to D (in default).

Treasuries and Munis

Remember, too, that if you decide to issue bonds, you'll be competing with other borrowers, including state and local governments and the federal government. In fact, the U.S. government, which issues bonds through the Treasury Department, is the country's largest debtor. *Treasury bills*, for example, mature in one year, *Treasury notes* in one to ten years, and *Treasury bonds* in more than ten years. State and local governments issue bonds (often called *munis*, for "municipals") to support public services such as schools and roads or special projects. Both treasuries and munis are attractive because the income earned on them is generally tax free at the state and local levels.

6.4 Choosing Your Financing Method

Let's say that after mulling over your money-raising options—equity financing versus debt financing—you decide to recommend to the board that the company issue common stock to finance its expansion. How do you explain your decision? Issuing bonds is an attractive option because it won't dilute your ownership, but you don't like the idea of repaying interest-bearing loans: at this point, you're reluctant to take on any future financial obligation, and money obtained through the sale of stock doesn't have to be paid back. Granted, adding additional shareholders will force you to relinquish some ownership interest: new shareholders will vote on your board of directors and could have some influence over major decisions. On balance, you prefer the option of selling stock—specifically, common stock. Why not preferred stock? Because it has drawbacks similar to those of debt financing: you'd have to make periodic dividend payments, requiring an outflow of cash. Once the matter has been settled, you take a well-deserved vacation. Unfortunately, you can't stop thinking about what you'll do the next time you want to expand. In particular, franchising seems to be a particularly attractive idea. It's something you'll need to research when you get a chance.

Before going to the next section of this chapter, take a few minutes to test your knowledge of the material covered in this section. Quizzes can be found under the "Resources" tab, "Study Aids: Quizzes."

EXERCISE

You've been out of college for fifteen years, and now you're the CFO for a large corporation. Your CEO just showed you plans for a multimillion-dollar plant expansion and reminded you that it's your job to raise the money. You have three choices: sell bonds, issue common stock, or issue preferred stock. Write a brief report that explains the advantages and disadvantages of each option. Conclude by stating your opinion on the best choice in today's economic environment.

7.   CAREERS IN FINANCE

LEARNING OBJECTIVES

1. **Discuss career opportunities in finance.**
2. **Indicate the education you will need to pursue a career in finance.**

A financial career path offers a number of interesting, entry-level jobs that can develop into significant senior-level positions. In addition to a strong finance education, you'll need to be familiar with both accounting and economics. Along with possessing strong analytical skills and the ability to assess financial data, you'll need to work effectively with colleagues throughout an organization. So you'll need good interpersonal and communication skills: you'll have to write and speak clearly and, in particular, you'll have to be able to present complex financial data in terms that everyone can understand.

Generally, most positions in finance fall into one of three broad areas: *commercial banking, corporate finance*, and the *investment industry*.

7.1   Positions in Commercial Banking

Commercial banks employ finance professionals as loan officers to work with clients requesting personal or business loans. It's the borrower's responsibility, of course, to present a clear and coherent application, and it's the loan officer who evaluates it—who decides whether the borrower will be able to meet the terms of the loan. Finance professionals also manage the deposits made at commercial banks, providing the bank with additional revenue by investing funds that don't go into loans.

7.2   Positions in Corporate Finance

Every organization needs financial expertise. Large companies need finance professionals to manage their cash, their debt requirements, and their pension investments. They're responsible for securing capital (whether through debt or equity), and they may be called on for any of the following tasks:

- Analyzing industry trends
- Evaluating corporate investment in new plants, equipment, or products

- Conducting financial planning
- Evaluating acquisitions (deciding, for example, whether to buy another company)
- Reviewing the financial needs of top management

In smaller firms, all these tasks may fall to a single finance professional. In addition, both large and small companies may occasionally use the services of financial consultants. They may be provided by investment bankers, by specialized consulting firms, or by the financial-advisory departments of a major accounting firm.

From an entry-level position—usually called *analyst* or *junior analyst*—the finance professional will advance from *senior analyst* to a managerial position. With each step, you'll have greater exposure to senior management and face more important and more complex issues. Within ten to fifteen years, you may become a director or vice president. The rungs on the career ladder are pretty much the same in consulting and investment banking.

7.3   Positions in the Investment Industry

In the investment industry, finance professionals can be stockbrokers, investment analysts, or portfolio managers. Each of these positions requires an ability to assimilate great quantities of information, not only about specific companies and their securities, but also about entire industries and, indeed, the economy itself.

Some investment professionals work directly with individual clients. Others provide support to those who make sell or buy recommendations. Still others manage portfolios in the mutual fund industry. A mutual fund gathers money—ranging upward from a few hundred dollars—from thousands or even millions of investors and invests it in large portfolios of stocks and other investment securities. Finance professionals review and recommend prospective investments to company managers.

Because real estate (both commercial and personal) and insurance are investment fields, many financial professionals can be found working in these areas, as well.

7.4   Graduate Education and Certification

After completing the undergraduate degree with a major or concentration in finance, accounting, or economics, a finance professional may start to think about graduate school. The typical path is an MBA with a finance track. Though some schools offer a master's in finance degree, such a program is highly specialized, with rigorous math requirements that may not appeal to everyone with an interest in finance.

Certification is a means of achieving professional distinction in a finance career. The most popular certifications include the following:

- CFA or *Chartered Financial Analyst* (usually an investment-analyst designation)
- CFM or *Certified Financial Manager* (usually a corporate-finance designation)
- CCM or *Certified Cash Manager* (usually a corporate-treasury designation)
- CFP or *Certified Financial Planner* (usually an individual stockbroker designation)

The insurance and real estate industries have their own certifications. In addition, because the federal government requires anyone who sells securities to be licensed, there is an entire set of licensing procedures that must be followed.

KEY TAKEAWAYS

- Most positions in finance fall into one of these three areas: commercial banking, corporate finance, and the investment industry.
- Finance professionals employed in commercial banking help clients obtain personal or business loans. They also invest the bank's excess funds.
- Those employed in corporate finance obtain and manage their employing company's cash, debt, and investments. They provide financial analysis and advice to management.
- Financial professionals in the investment industry provide financial advice to their clients and help them buy and sell stocks.
- To pursue a career in finance, you'll need a strong finance education, as well as familiarity with both accounting and finance.

EXERCISE

When you hear on the news that banks around the world are cutting 330,000 jobs and expect to give pink slips to another eighteen thousand in the next eighteen months, you have to wonder whether it makes sense to major in finance. If you are thinking of majoring in finance, these two articles will cheer you up: "Finance: Post-Crisis, Still a Hot Major" (http://www.businessweek.com/bschools/content/sep2010/bs20100920_625085.htm), and "2011 Finance Employment Outlook" (http://career-advice.monster.com/job-search/company-industry-research/2011-finance-hiring-outlook/article.aspx). Read these articles and answer the following questions:

1. If you had your choice, what type of finance position would you want after graduation? Why?
2. If you were not able to find a position in your preferred area, what would be your second choice? Why?
3. What could you do as a student to differentiate yourself and be more competitive in a tough job market?

---

8. CASES AND PROBLEMS

LEARNING ON THE WEB

How Much Should You Reveal in *Playboy***?**

What can you do if you're sitting around your dorm room with nothing else to do (or at least nothing else you want to do)? How about starting a business? It worked for Michael Dell, who found assembling and selling computers more rewarding than attending classes at the University of Texas. It also worked for two Stanford graduate students, Sergey Brin and Larry Page. They came up with a novel (though fairly simple) idea for a search engine that ranked Web sites according to number of hits and online linkages. Because their goal was to organize massive amounts of electronic data, they wanted a name that connoted seemingly infinite volumes of information. They liked the word "googol" (a child's coinage for a very big number—1 followed by a hundred zeros), but, unfortunately, someone already owned the domain name "Googol." So Brin and Page did a little letter juggling and settled (as we all know by now) for "Google."

By 2004, the company that they'd started in 1998 was the number-one search engine in the world. Their next step, like that of so many successful entrepreneurs before them, was to go public, and that's where our exercise starts. To learn more about this episode in the epic story of Google—and to find out what role *Playboy* magazine plays in it—read the article "Google Sets $2.7 Billion IPO" (http://money.cnn.com/2004/04/29/technology/google), read Google's *Playboy* interview (http://kottke.org/plus/misc/google-playboy.html), and read the *BusinessWeek* article "Google Dodges a Bullet" (http://www.businessweek.com/stories/2005-01-13/google-dodges-a-bullet).

When you've finished reading the articles, answer the following questions:

1. What's an IPO? Why did Brin and Page take their company public? What disadvantages did they incur by going public? Are they likely to lose control of their company?
2. How does a *Playboy* interview enter into the Google story? What did Brin and Page do wrong? (By the way, the interview appeared in the August 2004 issue of *Playboy*; because Google incorporated the text into its revised IPO filing, it's now in the public domain and available online.)
3. Did the Google founders get off the hook? Was the punishment (or lack of it) appropriate? Quitting school to run Google paid off big for Brin and Page. Their combined net worth as a result of the IPO suddenly skyrocketed to $8 billion. But how about you? Could you have gotten rich if you'd jumped on the Google bandwagon just as it started to roll? Could you at least have earned enough to pay another year's tuition? To respond to these questions, you need to know two things: (1) the IPO price of Google stock—$85—and (2) Google's current stock price. To find the current price, go to http://finance.yahoo.com to link to the finance section of the Yahoo.com Web site. Enter Google's stock symbol—GOOG—and click "Go." When you find the current stock price, answer the following questions:
   a. If you'd bought Google stock on the IPO date and sold it today, how many shares of Google would you have had to buy in order to make enough to cover this year's tuition?
   b. If you owned Google stock today, would you sell it or hold it? Explain your answer.

CAREER OPPORTUNITIES

Financial Futures

One advantage of a finance major is that it prepares you for a wide range of careers. Some graduates head for Wall Street to make big bucks in investment banking. Others prefer the security of working in the corporate finance department of a large firm, while still others combine finance and selling in fields such as insurance or real estate. If you like working with other people's finances, you might end up in commercial banking or financial planning. To better acquaint yourself with the range of available finance careers, go to http://www.careers-in-finance.com/ to link to the Careers in Finance Web site. After reviewing the descriptions of each career option, select two areas that you find particularly interesting and two that you find unattractive. For each of your four selections, answer the following questions:

1. Why do you find a given area interesting (or unattractive)?
2. What experience and expertise are entailed by a career in a given area?

ETHICS ANGLE

The Inside Story

You're the founder and CEO of a publicly traded biotech firm that recently came up with a promising cancer drug. Right now, life on Wall Street is good: investors are high on your company, and your stock price is rising. On top of everything else, your personal wealth is burgeoning because you own a lot of stock in the company. You're simply waiting to hear from the FDA, which is expected to approve the product. But when the call comes, the news is bad: the FDA has decided to delay approval because of insufficient data on the drug's effectiveness. You know that when investors hear the news, the company's stock price will plummet. The family and friends that you encouraged to buy into your company will lose money, and you'll take a major hit.

Quickly, you place an order to sell about $5 million worth of your own stock. Then you start making phone calls. You tell your daughter to dump her stock, and you advise your friends to do the same thing. When you tell your stockbroker the news, he gets on the phone and gives a heads-up to his other clients. Unfortunately, he can't reach one client (who happens to be a good friend of yours), so he instructs his assistant to contact her and tell her what's happened. As a result, the client places an order to sell four thousand shares of stock at a market value of $225,000.

Let's pause at this point to answer a few questions:

1. Are you being a nice guy or doing something illegal?
2. Is your stockbroker doing something illegal?
3. Is the assistant doing something illegal or merely following orders?
4. Is the stockbroker's client acting illegally?

Fast-forward a few months. Federal investigators are interested in the sale of your stock and the sale of your daughter's stock. Because all signs point to the truth as being an invitation to trouble, you lie. When they talked with your friend about her sale, say investigators, she explained a standing agreement that instructed her broker to sell the stock when the market price went below a specified level. It sounds like a good explanation, so you go along with it.

Now, answer this question.

1. What have you done wrong? What has your client friend done wrong?

The Reality Version of the Story

At this point, let's stop protecting the not-so-innocent and name some names. The biotech company is ImClone, and its founder and CEO is Dr. Samuel Waksal. The Merrill Lynch broker is named Peter Bacanovic and his assistant Douglas Faneuil. The client friend who dumped her stock is Martha Stewart.

Let's focus on Stewart, who is the founder of Martha Stewart Living Omnimedia, a prosperous lifestyle empire. Her actions and their consequences are detailed in an article titled "Martha's Fall," which you can access by going to http://www.newsweek.com/id/53363 and linking to the MSNBC Web site. Read the article and then answer the following questions:

1. Do you believe Stewart's story that she sold the stock because of a preexisting sell order and not because she learned that the cancer drug wouldn't be approved? What did she do that was illegal? What was she actually *convicted* of doing?
2. Waksal got seven years in prison for insider trading (and a few other illegal schemes). Bacanovic (Stewart's broker) got five months in jail and five months of home confinement for lying and obstructing the investigation into the sale of ImClone stock. In return for helping the prosecutors convict Stewart, Faneuil (the broker's assistant) got a federal "get-out-of-jail" card but was fined $2,000 for accepting a payoff (namely, an extra week of vacation and a bump in his commission) to stonewall investigators. Stewart went to prison for five months and spent another five under house arrest. Was her punishment too lenient? Too harsh? If you'd been the judge, what sentence would you have given her?
3. How could Stewart have avoided prison? Did her celebrity status or reputation help or hurt her? Did she, as some people claim, become a poster CEO for corporate wrongdoing?
4. Why are government agencies, such as the SEC, concerned about insider trading? Who's hurt by it? Who's helped by government enforcement of insider-trading laws?

TEAM-BUILDING SKILLS

Looking for a High-Flying Stock

Congratulations! Your team has just been awarded $100,000 in hypothetical capital. There is, however, a catch: you have to spend the money on airline stocks. Rather than fly by the seat of your pants, you'll want to research a number of stocks. To familiarize yourself with the airline industry, go to http://adg.stanford.edu/aa241/intro/airlineindustry.html to read the article "The Airline Industry."

Each team member is responsible for researching and writing a brief report on a different company. Don't duplicate your research. Be sure to include low-cost airlines as well as larger carriers. To cover the industry, pick airlines from the following list. The URLs bring you to each airline's information page on Yahoo! Finance.

- AMR Corporation (American Airlines) (http://biz.yahoo.com/ic/10/10021.html)
- Delta Air Lines (http://finance.yahoo.com/q?s=DAL)
- U.S. Airways (http://biz.yahoo.com/ic/11/11527.html)
- Spirit Airlines (http://finance.yahoo.com/q?s=S)
- Jet Blue Airways (http://finance.yahoo.com/q?s=JBLU)
- Southwest Airlines (http://biz.yahoo.com/ic/11/11377.html)

Each member should prepare a report detailing the following information about his or her chosen company:

- A description of the airline
- The percentage change in revenue over the last fiscal year
- The percentage change in net income over the last fiscal year
- A chart comparing the movement in the company's stock price over the past year with the movement of the DJIA
- Current earnings per share (EPS): net income divided by number of common shareholders
- Current PE ratio
- Current stock price

Here are some hints for finding this information on the Yahoo! page devoted to a given company:

- The company will be described in a "Company Profile" appearing toward the top of the page.
- You can get the remaining information by going to the bottom of the page and clicking on the following:
- "Financials" for changes in revenues and net income
- "Chart" for trends in stock prices
- "Quote" for EPS, PE ratio, and current stock price
- When reviewing financial statements to calculate percentage changes in revenues and net income, be sure you click on "Annual Data" to get information for the entire year rather than for just the quarter.

Team Report

Once each member has researched one airline, the team should get together and decide how to invest its $100,000. Announce your decision in a final report that includes the following items:

1. An overall description and assessment of the airline industry, including a report on opportunities, threats, and future outlook
2. A decision on how you'll invest your $100,000, including the names of the stock or stocks that you plan to purchase, current market prices, and numbers of shares
3. An explanation of the team's investment decision
4. Individual member reports on each researched company

Follow-Up

A few weeks later, you might want to check on the stock prices of your picks to see how you'd have done if you'd actually invested $100,000.

THE GLOBAL VIEW

Where's the Energy in the Chinese Stock Market?

Warren Buffett is the third-richest man in the world (behind Bill Gates). As CEO of Berkshire Hathaway, a holding company with large stakes in a broad portfolio of investments, Buffett spends a lot of his time looking for companies with promising futures. His time has been quite well spent: the market price of a share in Berkshire Hathaway now tops $115,000—up from $16 a share in 1964.

In 2002 and 2003, Berkshire Hathaway paid $488 million for two million shares in PetroChina, an energy firm 90 percent owned by the Chinese government. In 2007, he sold the stock for $4 billion, realizing an incredible more than 700 percent gain. To evaluate Buffett's thinking in buying and then selling stock in PetroChina, you'll need to do some research.

First, find out something about the company by going to http://www.petrochina.com.cn/ptr and linking to the English version of the PetroChina Web site. Explore the sections "About PetroChina" and "Investor Relations." Look for answers to the following questions:

1. What does the company do? What products and services does it provide? How does it distribute its products?
2. On which stock exchanges are its shares sold?

Next, to learn about the company's financial performance, go to http://finance.yahoo.com to link to the Finance section of the Yahoo.com Web site. Enter the company's stock symbol—PTR—and review the information provided on the site. To see what analysts think of the stock, for example, click on "Analyst Opinion." To gain insight into why Buffett sold his stock and whether it was a good or a bad move, read these articles: "Should We Buy the PetroChina Stock Warren Buffett Sold?" (http://www.peridotcapitalist.com/2008/03/should-we-buy-petrochina-stock-warren.html) and "Buffett's PetroChina Sale: Fiscal or Social Move," (http://investorsagainstgenocide.net/page1001126)

Now, answer the following questions:

1. What do analysts think of the stock?
2. Should Buffett have bought the stock in PetroChina? Was it a good decision at the time? Why, or why not?
3. Should Buffett have sold his stock in the company? Why do you think he sold the stock? Was it a good decision at the time? Why, or why not?
4. If you personally had $50,000 to invest, how likely is it that you'd buy stock in PetroChina? What factors would you consider in making your decision?

To learn more about the pros and cons of buying stock in Chinese companies, go to http://www.newsweek.com/id/54174 to link to the MSNBC Web site and read the article "Nice Place to Visit." Then answer these final questions:

1. What are the advantages of investing in the stock of Chinese companies? What are the disadvantages?
2. In your opinion, should the average investor put money in Chinese stock? Why, or why not?

ENDNOTES

1. Federal Reserve, "Money Stock Measures," *Federal Reserve Statistical Release*, http://www.federalreserve.gov/releases/h6/current (accessed April 14, 2014).

2. U.S. Census Bureau, "U.S. World Population Clocks," http://www.census.gov/main/www/popclock.html (accessed April 14, 2014).

3. Insurance Information Institute, "Banking: Commercial Banks," *Online Financial Services Fact Book 2013*, http://www2.iii.org/financial-services-fact-book/banking/commercial-banks.html (accessed April 14, 2014).

4. Insurance Information Institute, "Banking: Commercial Banks," *Online Financial Services Fact Book 2013*, http://www2.iii.org/financial-services-fact-book/banking/commercial-banks.html (accessed April 14, 2014).

5. "Hudson City Bancorp, Inc. (HCBK) Profile," *Yahoo! Finance*, http://finance.yahoo.com/q/pr?s=HCBK+Profile (accessed April 14, 2014).

6. Insurance Information Institute, *Online Financial Services Fact Book 2013*, http://www2.iii.org/financial-services-fact-book (accessed April 14, 2014).

7. Insurance Information Institute, "Banking: Commercial Banks," *Online Financial Services Fact Book 2013*, http://www2.iii.org/financial-services-fact-book/banking/commercial-banks.html (accessed April 14, 2014).

8. See Wells Fargo, https://www.wellsfargo.com (accessed April 14, 2014).

9. Justin Lahart, "Egg Cracks Differ in Housing, Finance Shells," *Wall Street Journal*, July 13, 2008, http://online.wsj.com/article/SB119845906460548071.html?mod=googlenews_wsj (accessed April 14, 2014).

10. RealtyTrac Inc., "Foreclosure Activity Increases 4 Percent in April According to RealtyTrac(R) U.S. Foreclosure Market Report," news release, *PR Newswire*, May 14, 2008, http://www.prnewswire.com/news-releases/foreclosure-activity-increases-4-percent-in-april-according-to-realtytracr-us-foreclosure-market-report (accessed April 14, 2014).

11. Mortgage Bankers Association, "Delinquencies and Foreclosures Increase in Latest MBA National Delinquency Survey," news release, September 5, 2008, http://www.mbaa.org/NewsandMedia/PressCenter/64769.htm (accessed April 14, 2014); Charles Duhigg, "Loan-Agency Woes Swell from a Trickle to a Torrent," *nytimes.com* http://www.nytimes.com/2008/07/11/business/11ripple.html?ex=1373515200&en=8ad220403fcfdf6e&ei=5124&partner=permalink&exprod=permalink (accessed April 14, 2014).

12. Federal Deposit Insurance Corporation, *Quarterly Banking Profile* (Fourth Quarter 2007), http://www2.fdic.gov/qbp/qbpSelect.asp?menuItem=QBP (accessed April 14, 2014); FDIC, *Quarterly Banking Profile* (First Quarter 2008), at http://www2.fdic.gov/qbp/qbpSelect.asp?menuItem=QBP (accessed April 14, 2014).

13. Shawn Tully, "Wall Street's Money Machine Breaks Down," *Fortune, CNNMoney.com*, November 12, 2007, http://money.cnn.com/magazines/fortune/fortune_archive/2007/11/26/101232838/index.htm (accessed April 14, 2014).

14. See Greg Robb et al., "AIG Gets Fed Rescue in Form of $85 Billion Loan," *MarketWatch*, September 16, 2008, http://www.marketwatch.com/story/aig-gets-fed-rescue-in-form-of-85-billion-loan (accessed April 14, 2014).

15. Mortgage Bankers Association, "Delinquencies and Foreclosures Increase in Latest MBA National Delinquency Survey," news release, September 5, 2008, http://www.mbaa.org/NewsandMedia/PressCenter/64769.htm (accessed April 14, 2014).

16. Federal Reserve System, "Monetary Policy Basics," http://federalreserveeducation.org/about-the-fed/structure-and-functions/monetary-policy (accessed April 14, 2014).

17. Robert Heilbroner and Lester Thurow, *Economics Explained* (New York: Simon & Schuster, 1998), 134.

18. Federal Reserve System, "Monetary Policy Basics," http://federalreserveeducation.org/about-the-fed/structure-and-functions/monetary-policy (accessed April 14, 2014).

19. Federal Reserve System, "Financial Services," http://federalreserveeducation.org/about-the-fed/structure-and-functions/financial-services (accessed April 14, 2014).

20. Privacy Rights Clearinghouse, "Fact Sheet 30: Check 21: Paperless Banking," https://www.privacyrights.org/fs/fs30-check21.htm (accessed April 14, 2014).

21. Federal Reserve System, "Banking Supervision," http://federalreserveeducation.org/about-the-fed/structure-and-functions/banking-supervision (accessed April 14, 2014).

22. The official name of the New York Stock Exchange is the "NYSE Euronext." Its name was formed following its merger with the fully electronic stock exchange Euronext. The exchange tends to go by its old and very familiar name—the New York Stock Exchange.

23. U.S. Securities and Exchange Commission, http://www.sec.gov (accessed April 14, 2014).

24. MD Leasing Corporation, "History of the Dow Jones Industrial Average," http://www.mdleasing.com/djia.htm (accessed April 14, 2014).

25. Yahoo! Finance is accessed by going to http://www.yahoo.com and clicking on "Finance" in the left side bar. CNBC Real-Time Quotes is accessed by going to http://www.cnbc.com and entering the company's name or stock symbol (HSY) in the box on the top bar.

Personal Finances

Do you wonder where your money goes? Do you have trouble controlling your spending? Have you run up the balances on your credit cards or gotten behind in your payments and hurt your credit rating? Do you worry about how you'll pay off your student loans? Would you like to buy a new car or even a home someday and you're not sure where the money will come from? If you do have extra money, do you know how to invest it? Do you know how to find the right job for you, land an offer, and evaluate the company's benefits? If these questions seem familiar to you, you could benefit from help in managing your personal finances. This chapter will provide that help.

Carefully managing your personal finances makes it possible for you to buy a new car, go on a vacation, or afford your dream home.

© 2010 Jupiterimages Corporation

1.   WHERE DOES YOUR MONEY GO?

L E A R N I N G   O B J E C T I V E S

1. Offer advice to someone who is burdened with debt.
2. Offer advice to someone whose monthly bills are too high.
3. Identify the five criteria used to compile your Fair Isaac Company (FICO) score.
4. Identify actions a young person should take to build a good credit history that will produce a high FICO score.
5. Discuss actions you could take to raise your credit score.
6. Explain what you should do if you can't pay your debt.
7. Recognize the effect the interest rate has on the overall cost of a loan.
8. Identify and define the costs associated with using a credit card.

Let's say that you're single and twenty-eight. You have a good education and a good job—you're pulling down $60K working with a local accounting firm. You have $6,000 in a retirement savings account, and you carry three credit cards. You plan to buy a house (maybe a condo) in two or three years, and you want to take your dream trip to the world's hottest surfing spots within five years (or, at the most, ten). Your only big worry is the fact that you're $70,000 in debt, mostly from student loans, your car loan, and credit card debt. In fact, even though you've been gainfully employed for a total of six years now, you haven't been able to make a dent in that $70,000. You can afford the necessities of life and then some, but you've occasionally wondered if you're ever going to have enough income to put something toward that debt.[1]

Now let's suppose that while browsing through a magazine in the doctor's office, you run across a short personal-finances self-help quiz. There are two sets of three statements each, and you're asked to check off each statement with which you *agree*:

Part 1

- If I didn't have a credit card in my pocket, I'd probably buy a lot less stuff.
- My credit card balance usually goes up at the holidays.
- If I really want something that I can't afford, I put it on my credit card or sign up for a payment plan.

Part 2

- I can barely afford my apartment.
- Whenever something goes wrong (car repairs, doctors' bills), I have to use my credit card.
- I almost never spend money on stuff I don't need, but I always seem to owe a balance on my credit card bill.

At the bottom of the page, you're asked whether you agreed with *any* of the statements in Part 1 and *any* of the statements in Part 2. It turns out that you answered yes in both cases and are thereby informed that you're probably jeopardizing your entire financial future.

Unfortunately, personal-finances experts tend to support the author of the quiz: if you agreed with any statement in Part 1, you have a problem with splurging; if you agreed with any statement in Part 2, your monthly bills are too high for your income.

1.1 Building a Good Credit Rating

So, you have a financial problem: according to the quick test you took, you're a splurger and your bills are too high for your income. How does this put you at risk? If you get in over your head and can't make your loan or rent payments on time, you risk hurting your credit—your ability to borrow in the future.

Let's talk about your credit. How do potential lenders decide whether you're a good or bad credit risk? If you're a poor credit risk, how does this affect your ability to borrow, or the rate of interest you have to pay, or both? Here's the story. Whenever you use credit, those you borrow from (retailers, credit card companies, banks) provide information on your debt and payment habits to three national credit bureaus: Equifax, Experian, and TransUnion. The credit bureaus use the information to compile a numerical credit score, generally called a FICO score; it ranges from 300 to 850, with the majority of people falling in the 600–700 range. (Here's a bit of trivia to bring up at a dull party: FICO stands for Fair Isaac Company—the company that developed the score.) In compiling the score, the credit bureaus consider five criteria: payment history—do you pay your bills on time? (the most important), total amount owed, length of your credit history, amount of new credit you have, and types of credit you use. The credit bureaus share their score and other information about your credit history with their subscribers.

So what does this do for you? It depends. If you paid your bills on time, carried only a reasonable amount of debt, didn't max out your credit cards, had a history of borrowing, hadn't applied for a bunch of new loans, and borrowed from a mix of lenders, you'd be in good shape. Your FICO score would be high and lenders would like you. Because of your high credit score, they'd give you the loans you asked for at reasonable interest rates. But if your FICO score is low (perhaps you weren't so good at paying your bills on time), lenders won't like you and won't lend you money (or would lend it to you at high interest rates). A low FICO score can raise the amount you have to pay for auto insurance and cell phone plans and can even affect your chances of renting an apartment or landing a particular job. So it's very, very, very (the last "very" is for emphasis) important that you do everything possible to earn a high credit score. If you don't know your score, here is what you should do: go to https://www.quizzle.com/ and request a free copy of your credit report.

As a young person, though, how do you build a credit history that will give you a high FICO score? Your means for doing this changed in 2009 with the passage of the Credit CARD Act, federal legislation designed to stop credit card issuers from treating its customers unfairly.[2] Based on feedback from several financial experts, Emily Starbuck Gerson and Jeremy Simon of CreditCards.com compiled the following list of ways students can build good credit.[3]

1. *Become an authorized user on your parents' account.* According to the rules set by the Credit CARD Act, if you are under age twenty-one and do not have independent income, you can get a credit card in your own name **only** if you have a cosigner (who is over twenty-one and does have an income). This is a time when a parent can come in handy. Your parent could add you to his or her credit card account as an authorized user. Of course, this means your parent will know what you're spending your money on (which could make for some interesting conversations). But, on the plus side, by piggybacking on your parent's card you are building good credit (assuming, of course, that your parent pays the bill on time).

2. *Obtain your own credit card.* If you can show the credit card company that you have sufficient income to pay your credit card bill, you might be able to get your own card. It isn't as easy to get a card as it was before the passage of the Credit CARD Act, and you won't get a lot of goodies for signing up (as was true before), but you stand a chance.

3. *Get the right card for you.* If you meet the qualifications to get a credit card on your own, look for the best card for you. Although it sounds enticing to get a credit card that gives you frequent flyer miles for every dollar you spend, the added cost for this type of card, including higher interest charges and annual fees, might not be worth it. Look for a card with a low interest rate and no annual fee. As another option, you might consider applying for a retail credit card, such as a Target or Macy's card.

4. *Use the credit card for occasional, small purchases.* If you do get a credit card or a retail card, limit your charges to things you can afford. But don't go in the other direction and put the card in a drawer and never use it. Your goal is to build a good credit history by showing the credit

reporting agencies that you can handle credit and pay your bill on time. To accomplish this, you need to use the card.

5. *Avoid big-ticket buys, except in case of emergency.* Don't run up the balance on your credit card by charging high-cost, discretionary items, such as a trip to Europe during summer break, which will take a long time to pay off. Leave some of your credit line accessible in case you run into an emergency, such as a major car repair.

6. *Pay off your balance each month.* If you cannot pay off the balance on your credit card each month, this is likely a signal that you're living beyond your means. Quit using the card until you bring the balance down to zero. When you're first building credit, it's important to pay off the balance on your card at the end of each month. Not only will this improve your credit history, but it will save you a lot in interest charges.

7. *Pay all your other bills on time.* Don't be fooled into thinking that the only information collected by the credit agencies is credit card related. They also collect information on other payments including phone plans, Internet service, rental payments, traffic fines, and even library overdue fees.

8. *Don't cosign for your friends.* If you are twenty-one and have an income, a nonworking, under-age-twenty-one friend might beg you to cosign his credit card application. Don't do it! As a cosigner, the credit card company can make you pay your friend's balance (plus interest and fees) if he fails to meet his obligation. And this can blemish your own credit history and lower your credit rating.

9. *Do not apply for several credit cards at one time.* Just because you can get several credit cards, this doesn't mean that you should. When you're establishing credit, applying for several cards over a short period of time can lower your credit rating. Stick with one card.

10. *Use student loans for education expenses only, and pay on time.* For many, student loans are necessary. But avoid using student loans for noneducational purposes. All this does is run up your debt. When your loans become due, consolidate them if appropriate and don't miss a payment.

What if you've already damaged your credit score—what can you do to raise it? Do what you should have done in the first place: pay your bills on time, pay more than the minimum balance due on your credit cards and charge cards, keep your card balances low, and pay your debts off as quickly as possible. Also, scan your credit report for any errors. If you find any, work with the credit bureau to get them corrected.

1.2   Understand the Cost of Borrowing

Because your financial problem was brought on, in part, because you have too much debt, you should stop borrowing. But, what if your car keeps breaking down and you're afraid of getting stuck on the road some night? So, you're thinking of replacing it with a used car that costs $10,000. Before you make a final decision to incur the debt, you should understand its costs. The rate of interest matters a lot. Let's compare three loans at varying interest rates: 6, 10, and 14 percent. We'll look at the monthly payment, as well as the total interest paid over the life of the loan.

$10,000 Loan for 4 Years at Various Interest Rates			
Interest Rate	6%	10%	14%
Monthly Payment	$235	$254	$273
Total Interest Paid	$1,272	$2,172	$3,114

If your borrowing interest rate is 14 percent, rather than 6 percent, you'll end up paying an additional $1,842 in interest over the life of the loan. Your borrowing cost at 14 percent is more than twice as much as it is at 6 percent. The conclusion: search for the best interest rates and add the cost of interest to the cost of whatever you're buying before deciding whether you want it and can afford it. If you have to borrow the money for the car at the 14 percent interest rate, then the true cost of the car isn't $10,000, but rather $13,114.

Now, let's explore the complex world of credit cards. First extremely important piece of information: not all credit cards are equal. Second extremely important piece of information: watch out for credit card fees! Credit cards are a way of life for most of us. But they can be very costly. Before picking a credit card, do your homework. A little research can save you a good deal of money. There are a number of costs you need to consider:

- *Finance charge.* The interest rate charged to you often depends on your credit history; those with good credit get the best rates. Some cards offer low "introductory" rates—but watch out; these rates generally go up after six months.

- *Annual fee.* Many credit cards charge an annual fee: a yearly charge for using the card. You can avoid annual fees by shopping around (though there can be trade-offs: you might end up paying a higher interest rate to avoid an annual fee).

- *Over-limit fee.* This fee is charged whenever you exceed your credit line.

- *Late payment fee.* Pretty self-explanatory, but also annoying. Late payment fees are common for students; a study found students account for 6 percent of all overdraft fees.[4] One way to decrease the chance of paying late is to call the credit card company and ask them to set your payment due date for a time that works well for you. For example, if you get paid at the end of the month, ask for a payment date around the 10th of the month. Then you can pay your bill when you get paid and avoid a late fee.

- *Cash advance fee.* While it's tempting to get cash from your credit card, it's pretty expensive. You'll end up paying a fee (around 3 percent of the advance), and the interest rate charged on the amount borrowed can be fairly high.

debit card

Pulls money out of your checking account whenever you use the card to buy something or get cash from an ATM.

An alternative to a credit card is a **debit card**, which pulls money out of your checking account whenever you use the card to buy something or get cash from an ATM. These cards don't create a loan when used. So, are they better than credit cards? It depends—each has its advantages and disadvantages. A big advantage of a credit card is that it helps you build credit. A disadvantage is that you can get in over your head in debt and possibly miss payments (thereby incurring a late payment fee). Debit cards help control spending. Theoretically, you can't spend more than you have in your checking account. But be careful—if you don't keep track of your checking account balance, it's easy to overdraft your account when using your debit card. Prior to July 2010, most banks just accepted purchases or ATM withdrawals even if a customer didn't have enough money in his or her account to cover the transaction. The banks didn't do this to be nice, and they didn't ask customers if they wanted this done—they just overdrafted the customer's account and charged the customer a hefty overdraft fee of around $35 through what they call an "overdraft protection program."[5] Overdraft fees can be quite expensive, particularly if you used the card to purchase a hamburger and soda at a fast-food restaurant.

The Federal Reserve changed the debit card rules in 2010, and now banks must get your permission before they enroll you in an overdraft protection program.[6] If you opt in (agree), things work as before: You can spend or take out more money through an ATM machine than you have in your account, and the bank lets you do this. But it charges you a fee of about $30 plus additional fees of $5 per day if you don't cover the overdraft in five days. If you don't opt in, the bank will not let you overdraft your account. The downside is that you could get embarrassed at the cash register when your purchase is rejected or at a restaurant when trying to pay for a meal. Obviously, you want to avoid being charged an overdraft fee or being embarrassed when paying for a purchase. Here are some things you can do to decrease the likelihood that either would happen:[7]

- Ask your bank to e-mail or text you when your account balance is low.

- Have your bank link your debit card account to a savings account. If more money is needed to cover a purchase, the bank will transfer the needed funds from your savings to your checking account.

- Use the online banking feature offered by most banks to check your checking account activity.

Before going to the next section of this chapter, take a few minutes to test your knowledge of the material covered in this section. Quizzes can be found under the "Resources" tab, "Study Aids: Quizzes."

1.3 A Few More Words about Debt

What should you do now to turn things around—to start getting out of debt? According to many experts, you need to take two steps:

1. Cut up your credit cards and start living on a cash-only basis.

2. Do whatever you can to bring down your monthly bills.

Step 1 in this abbreviated two-step personal-finances "plan" is probably the easier of the two, but taking even this step can be hard enough. In fact, a lot of people would find it painful to give up their credit cards, and there's a perfectly logical reason for their reluctance: the degree of pain that one would suffer from destroying one's credit cards probably stands in direct proportion to one's reliance on them.

A 2013 report puts average credit card debt, per person, in the United States at $8,220.[8] Why is the average credit card debt per person important? Primarily because, *on average*, too many consumers have debt that they simply can't handle. "Credit card debt," says one expert on the problem, "is clobbering millions of Americans like a wrecking ball,"[9] and if you're like most of us, you'd probably like to know whether your personal-finances habits are setting you up to become one of the clobbered.

If, for example, you're worried that your credit card debt may be overextended, the American Bankers Association suggests that you ask yourself a few questions:[10]

- Do I pay only the minimum month after month?
- Do I run out of cash all the time?
- Am I late on critical payments like my rent or my mortgage?
- Am I taking longer and longer to pay off my balance(s)?
- Do I borrow from one credit card to pay another?

FIGURE 14.1

Living on a cash-only basis is the first step in getting debt under control.

© 2010 Jupiterimages Corporation

If such habits as these have helped you dig yourself into a hole that's steadily getting deeper and steeper, experts recommend that you take three steps as quickly as possible:[11]

1. *Get to know the enemy.* You may not want to know, but you should collect all your financial statements and figure out exactly how much credit card debt you've piled up.

2. *Don't compound the problem with late fees.* List each card, along with interest rates, monthly minimums, and due dates. Bear in mind that paying late fees is the same thing as tossing what money you have left out the window.

3. *Now cut up your credit cards (or at least stop using them).* Pay cash for everyday expenses, and remember: swiping a piece of plastic is one thing (a little too easy), while giving up your hard-earned cash is another (a little harder).

And, if you find you're unable to pay your debts, don't hide from the problem, as it will not go away. Call your lenders and explain the situation. They should be willing to work with you in setting up a payment plan. If you need additional help, contact a nonprofit credit assistance group such as the National Foundation for Credit Counseling (http://www.nfcc.org).

1.4 Why You Owe It to Yourself to Manage Your Debts

Now, it's time to tackle step 2 of our recommended personal-finances miniplan: do whatever you can to bring down your monthly bills. As we said, many people may find this step easier than step 1—cutting up your credit cards and starting to live on a cash-only basis.

If you want to take a gradual approach to step 2, one financial planner suggests that you perform the following "exercises" for one week:[12]

- Keep a written record of everything you spend and total it at week's end.
- Keep all your ATM receipts and count up the fees.
- Take $100 out of the bank and don't spend a penny more.
- Avoid gourmet coffee shops.

Among other things, you'll probably be surprised at how much of your money can become somebody else's money on a week-by-week basis. If, for example, you spend $3 every day for one cup of coffee at a coffee shop, you're laying out nearly $1,100 a year. If you use your ATM card at a bank other than your own, you'll probably be charged a fee that can be as high as $3. The average person pays more than $60 a year in ATM fees, and if you withdraw cash from an ATM twice a week, you could be racking up $300 in annual fees. As for your ATM receipts, they'll tell you whether, on top of the fee that you're charged by that other bank's ATM, your *own* bank is *also* tacking on a surcharge.[13]

If this little exercise proves enlightening—or if, on the other hand, it apparently fails to highlight any potential pitfalls in your spending habits—you might devote the next week to another exercise:

- Put all your credit cards in a drawer and get by on cash.
- Take your lunch to work.
- Buy nothing but groceries and gasoline.
- Use coupons whenever you go to the grocery store (but don't buy anything just because you happen to have a coupon).

The obvious question that you need to ask yourself at the end of week 2 is, "how much did I save?" An equally interesting question, however, is, "what can I do without?" One survey asked five thousand financial planners to name the two expenses that most consumers should find easiest to cut back on. Figure 14.2 shows the results.

FIGURE 14.2 Reducible Expenses

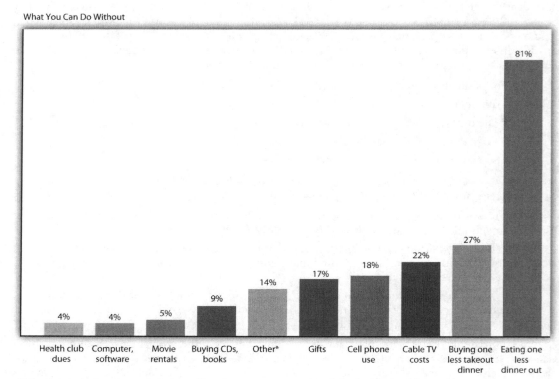

*Other Includes buying a less expensive car, taking a less extravagant vacation, eliminating impulse clothes purchases.

You may or may not be among the American consumers who buy thirty-five million cans of Bud Light each and every day, or 150,000 pounds of Starbucks coffee, or 2.4 million Burger King hamburgers, or 628 Toyota Camrys. Yours may not be one of the 70 percent of U.S. households with an unopened consumer-electronics product lying around.[14] And you may or may not be ready to make some major adjustments in your personal-spending habits, but if, at age twenty-eight, you have a good education and a good job, a $60,000 income, and a $70,000 debt—by no means an implausible scenario—there's a very good reason why you should think hard about controlling your modest share of that $11.3 trillion in U.S. consumer debt:[15] your level of indebtedness will be a key factor in your ability—or inability—to reach your longer-term financial goals, such as home ownership, a dream trip, and, perhaps most important, a reasonably comfortable retirement.

The great English writer Samuel Johnson once warned, "Do not accustom yourself to consider debt only as an inconvenience; you will find it a calamity." In Johnson's day, you could be locked up for failing to pay your debts; there were even so-called debtors' prisons for the purpose, and we may suppose that the prospect of doing time for owing money was one of the things that Johnson had in mind when he spoke of debt as a potential "calamity." We don't expect that you'll ever go to prison on account of indebtedness, and we won't suggest that, say, having to retire to a condo in the city instead of a tropical island is a "calamity." We'll simply say that you're more likely to meet your lifetime financial goals—whatever they are—if you plan for them. What you need to know about planning for and reaching those goals is the subject of this chapter.

KEY TAKEAWAYS

- Before buying something on credit, ask yourself whether you really need the goods or services, can afford them, and are willing to pay interest on the purchase.
- Whenever you use credit, those you borrow from provide information on your debt and payment habits to three national credit bureaus.
- The credit bureaus use the information to compile a numerical credit score, called a FICO score, which they share with subscribers.
- The credit bureaus consider five criteria in compiling the score: payment history, total amount owed, length of your credit history, amount of new credit you have, and types of credit you use.
- As a young person, you should do the following to build a good credit history that will give you a high FICO score.
    - Become an authorized user on your parents' account.
    - Obtain your own credit card
    - Get the right card for you.
    - Use the credit card for occasional, small purchases
    - Avoid big-ticket buys, except in case of emergency.
    - Pay off your balance each month.
    - Pay all your other bills on time.
    - Don't cosign for your friends.
    - Do not apply for several credit cards at *one time*.
    - Use student loans for education expenses only, and pay on time.
- To raise your credit score, you should pay your bills on time, pay more than the minimum balance due, keep your card balances low, and pay your debts off as quickly as possible. Also, scan your credit report for any errors and get any errors fixed.
- If you can't pay your debt, explain your situation to your lenders and see a credit assistance counselor.
- Before you incur a debt, you should understand its costs. The interest rate charged by the lender makes a big difference in the overall cost of the loan.
- The costs associated with credit cards include finance charges, annual fees, over-limit fees, late payment fees, and cash advance fees.
- The Federal Reserve changed the debit card rules in 2010 and now banks must get your permission before they enroll you in an overdraft protection program.
- If you have a problem with splurging, cut up your credit cards and start living on a cash-only basis.
- If your monthly bills are too high for your income, do whatever you can to bring down those bills.

EXERCISE

There are a number of costs associated with the use of a credit card, including finance charges, annual fee, over-limit fee, late payment fee, and cash advance fee. Identify these costs for a credit card you now hold. If you don't presently have a credit card, go online and find an offer for one. Check out these costs for the card being offered.

2. FINANCIAL PLANNING

personal finance

The application of financial principles to the monetary decisions of an individual or a family.

financial planning

The process of managing your personal finances to meet goals that you've set for yourself or your family.

Before we go any further, we need to nail down a couple of key concepts. First, just what, exactly, do we mean by personal finances? *Finance* itself concerns the flow of money from one place to another, and your personal finances concern your money and what you plan to do with it as it flows in and out of your possession. Essentially, then, **personal finance** is the application of financial principles to the monetary decisions that you make either for your individual benefit or for that of your family.

Second, as we suggested in Section 1—and as we'll insist in the rest of it—monetary decisions work out much more beneficially when they're planned rather than improvised. Thus our emphasis on **financial planning**—the ongoing process of managing your personal finances in order to meet goals that you've set for yourself or your family.

Financial planning requires you to address several questions, some of them relatively simple:

- What's my annual income?
- How much debt do I have, and what are my monthly payments on that debt?

Others will require some investigation and calculation:

- What's the value of my assets?
- How can I best budget my annual income?

Still others will require some forethought and forecasting:

- How much wealth can I expect to accumulate during my working lifetime?
- How much money will I need when I retire?

2.1 The Financial Planning Life Cycle

Another question that you might ask yourself—and certainly would do if you were a professional in financial planning—is something like, "How will my financial plans change over the course of my life?" Figure 14.3 illustrates the financial life cycle of a typical individual—one whose financial outlook and likely outcomes are probably a lot like yours.[16] As you can see, our diagram divides this individual's life into three stages, each of which is characterized by different life events (such as beginning a family, buying a home, planning an estate, retiring). At each stage, too, there are recommended changes in the focus of the individual's financial planning:

- In stage 1, the focus is on building wealth.
- In stage 2, the focus shifts to the process of preserving and increasing the wealth that one has accumulated and continues to accumulate.
- In stage 3, the focus turns to the process of living on (and, if possible, continuing to grow) one's saved wealth.

FIGURE 14.3 Financial Life Cycle

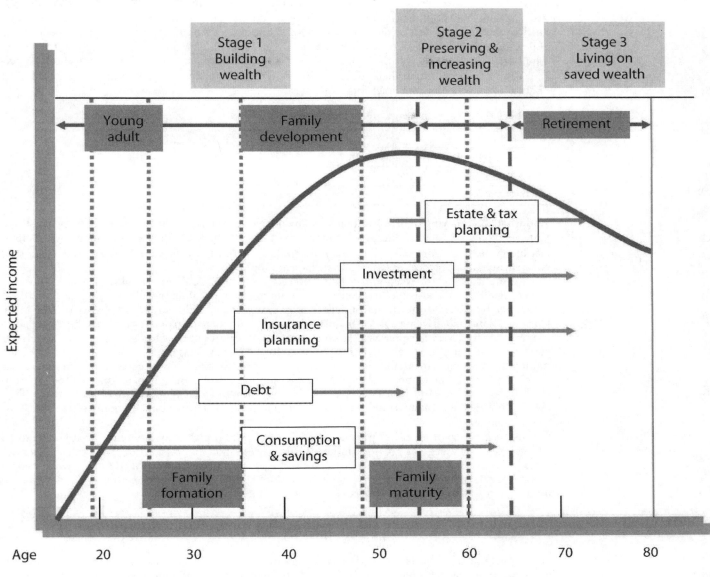

At each stage, of course, complications can set in—say, changes in such conditions as marital or employment status or in the overall economic outlook. Finally, as you can also see, your financial needs will probably peak somewhere in stage 2, at approximately age fifty-five, or ten years before typical retirement age.

Choosing a Career

Until you're eighteen or so, you probably won't generate much income; for the most part, you'll be living off your parents' wealth. In our hypothetical life cycle, however, financial planning begins in the individual's early twenties. If that seems like rushing things, consider a basic fact of life: this is the age at which you'll be choosing your career—not only the sort of work you want to do during your prime income-generating years, but also the kind of lifestyle you want to live in the process.[17]

What about college? Most readers of this book, of course, have decided to go to college. If you haven't yet decided, you need to know that college is an extremely good investment of both money and time.

A recent study by Pew Research Center shows that those who do not finish college can expect to earn only 62 percent of what a college graduate earns. This difference equates to a substantial difference in salary—for example, a young college graduate earns about $17,500 a year more than those with only a high school diploma.[18] Over the course of the financial life cycle, families headed by college graduates will earn about $1.6 million more than families headed by high school graduates who didn't attend college. (With better access to health care—and, studies show, with better dietary and health practices—college graduates will also live longer. And so will their children.)[19] Also, college graduates are more likely to be employed—the Pew Research Center study reports a 3.8 percent unemployment rate for college graduates versus a 12.2 percent unemployment rate for those with only a high school degree.[20] But what about the cost of going to college—do the benefits outweigh the cost? The answer, according to those surveyed by the Pew Research Center is "yes." About 90 percent of young people with college degrees indicate that their education has already paid off or will pay off in the future. Even those who borrowed money to get through college were positive about the value of their education: 86 percent of this group said that their education has paid off or will pay off in the future.[21] See Table 14.1 "Education and Average Income" for a comparison of income by level of education.

TABLE 14.1   Education and Average Income

Education	Average income
High school graduate	$28,000
Two-year degree/some college	$30,000
Bachelor's degree	$45,500

And what about paying off the debt that so many people accumulate to finish college? For every $1 that you spend on your college education, you can expect to earn about $35 during the course of your financial life cycle.[22] At that rate of return, you should be able to pay off your student loans (unless, of course, you fail to practice reasonable financial planning).

Naturally, there are exceptions to these average outcomes. You'll find English-lit majors stocking shelves at 7-Eleven, and you'll find college dropouts running multibillion-dollar enterprises. Microsoft cofounder Bill Gates dropped out of college after two years, as did his founding partner, Paul Allen. Current Microsoft CEO Steve Ballmer finished his undergraduate degree but quit his MBA program to join Microsoft (where he apparently fit in among the other dropouts in top management). It's always good to remember, however, that though exceptions to rules (and average outcomes) occasionally modify the rules, they invariably fall far short of disproving them: in entrepreneurship as in most other walks of adult life, the better your education, the more promising your financial future. One expert in the field puts the case for the average person bluntly: educational credentials "are about being employable, becoming a legitimate candidate for a job with a future. They are about climbing out of the dead-end job market."[23]

As far as your future career prospects and income, does it make any difference what you study in college? Yes. Some degrees provide graduates with better job prospects and higher pay than other degrees. A survey by the National Association of Colleges and Employers identified the following majors that offered the highest starting salaries for the graduating class of 2013: engineering, computer science, information systems, business, and logistics/materials management.

2.2 Financing a College Education

Let's revisit one of the facts included in the earlier discussion: for every $1 that you spend on your college education, you can expect to earn about $35 during the course of your financial life cycle. And let's say you're convinced (as you should be) that getting a college degree is a wise financial choice. You still have to deal with the cost of getting your degree. We're sure this won't come as a surprise: attending college is expensive—tuition and fees have gone up sharply, the cost of books has skyrocketed, and living expenses have climbed. Many students can attend college only if they receive some type of financial aid. Though the best way to learn what aid is available to you is to talk with a representative in the financial aid office at your school, this section provides an overview of the types of aid offered to students. Students finance their education through scholarships, grants, education loans, and work-study programs.[24] We'll explore each of these categories of aid:

Work-study

Federally sponsored program that provides students with paid, part-time jobs on campus.

- *Scholarships*, which don't have to be repaid, are awarded based on a number of criteria, including academic achievement, athletic or artistic talent, special interest in a particular field of study, ethnic background, or religious affiliation. Scholarships are generally funded by private donors such as alums, religious institutions, companies, civic organizations, professional associations, and foundations.

- *Grants*, which also don't have to be repaid, are awarded based on financial need. They're funded by the federal government, the states, and academic institutions. An example of a common federal grant is the Pell Grant, which is awarded to undergraduate students based on financial need. The maximum Pell Grant award for the 2014–15 award year (July 1, 2014, to June 30, 2015) is $5,730.[25]

- *Education loans*, which must be repaid, are available to students from various sources, including the federal government, states, and academic institutions. While recent problems in the credit markets have made college loans more difficult to obtain, most students are able to get the loans they need.[26] The loans offered directly to undergraduate students by the federal government include the need-based, subsidized Federal Stafford, the non–need-based unsubsidized Federal Stafford, and the need-based Federal Perkins loans. With the exception of the unsubsidized Federal Stafford, no interest accrues while the student is enrolled in college at least part time. There are also a number of loans available to parents of students, such as the Federal Parent PLUS program. Under this program, parents can borrow federally guaranteed low-interest loans to fund their child's education.

- **Work-study** is a federally sponsored program that provides students with paid, part-time jobs on campus. Because the student is paid based on work done, the funds received don't have to be repaid.

2.3   Find a Great Job

As was highlighted earlier, your financial life cycle begins at the point when you choose a career. Building your career takes considerable planning. It begins with the selection of a major in college and continues through graduation as you enter the workforce full time. You can expect to hold a number of jobs over your working life. If things go as they should, each job will provide valuable opportunities and help you advance your career. A big challenge is getting a job offer in your field of interest, evaluating the offer, and (if you have several options) selecting the job that's right for you.[27]

Getting a Job Offer

Most likely your college has a career center. The people working there can be a tremendous help to you as you begin your job search. But most of the work has to be done by you. Like other worthwhile projects, your job search project will be very time-consuming. As you get close to graduation, you'll need to block out time to work on this particularly important task.

The first step is to prepare a **résumé**, a document that provides a summary of educational achievements and relevant job experience. Its purpose is to get you an interview. A potential employer will likely spend less than a minute reviewing your résumé, so its content should be concise, clear, and applicable to the job for which you're applying. For some positions, the person in charge of hiring might read more than a hundred résumés. If you don't want your résumé kicked out right away, be sure it contains no typographical or grammatical errors. Once you've completed your résumé, you can use it to create different versions tailored to specific companies you'd like to work for. Your next step is to write a **cover letter**, a document accompanying your résumé that explains why you're sending your résumé and highlights your qualifications. You can find numerous tips on writing résumés and cover letters (as well as samples of both) online. Be sure your résumé is accurate: never lie or exaggerate in a résumé. You could get caught and not get the job (or—even worse—you could get the job, get caught, and then get fired). It's fairly common practice for companies to conduct background checks of possible employees, and these checks will point out any errors. In effect, says one expert, "you jeopardize your future when you lie about your past."[28]

After writing your résumé and cover letter, your next task is to create a list of companies you'd like to work for. Use a variety of sources, including your career services office and company Web sites, to decide which companies to put on your list. Visit the "career or employment" section of the company Web sites and search for specific openings.

You could also conduct a general search for positions that might be of interest to you, by doing the following:

- Visiting career Web sites, such as Monster.com, Wetfeet.com, or Careerbuilder.com (which maintain large databases of openings for all geographical areas)
- Searching classified ads in online and print newspapers
- Attending career fairs at your college and in your community
- Signing up with career services to talk with recruiters when they visit your campus
- Contacting your friends, family, and college alumni and letting them know you're looking for a job and asking for their help

Once you spot a position you want, send your résumé and cover letter (tailored to the specific company and job). Follow up in a few days to be sure your materials got to the right place, and offer to provide any additional information. Keep notes on all contacts.

résumé

A document that provides a summary of educational achievements and relevant job experience.

cover letter

A document accompanying your résumé that explains why you're sending your résumé and highlights your qualifications.

FIGURE 14.4

Preparing well for an interview can make it easier to relax and help the interviewer get to know you.

© 2010 Jupiterimages Corporation

When you're invited for an interview, visit to the company's Web site and learn as much as you can about the company. Practice answering questions you might be asked during the interview, and think up a few pertinent questions to ask your interviewer. Dress conservatively—males should wear a suit and tie and females should wear professional-looking clothes. Try to relax during the interview (though everyone knows this isn't always easy). Your goal is to get an offer, so let the interviewer learn who you are and how you can be an asset to the company. Send a thank-you note (or thank-you e-mail) to the interviewer after the interview.

Evaluating Job Offers

Let's be optimistic and say that you did quite well in your interviews, and you have two job offers. It's a great problem to have, but now you have to decide which one to accept. Salary is important, but it's clearly not the only factor. You should consider the opportunities the position offers: will you learn new things on the job, how much training will you get, could you move up in the organization (and if so, how quickly)? Also consider quality of life issues: how many hours a week will you have to work, is your schedule predictable (or will you be asked to work on a Friday night or Saturday at the last minute), how flexible is your schedule, how much time do you get off, how stressful will the job be, do you like the person who will be your manager, do you like your coworkers, how secure is the job, how much travel is involved, where's the company located, and what's the cost of living in that area? Finally, consider the financial benefits you'll receive. These could include health insurance, disability insurance, flexible spending accounts, and retirement plans. Let's talk more about the financial benefits, beginning with health insurance.

- **Employer-sponsored health insurance** plans vary greatly. Some cover the employee only, while others cover the employee, spouse, and children. Some include dental and eye coverage while others don't. Most plans require employees to share some of the cost of the medical plan (by paying a portion of the insurance premiums and a portion of the cost of medical care). But the amount that employees are responsible for varies greatly. Given the rising cost of health insurance, it's important to understand the specific costs associated with a health care plan and to take these costs into account when comparing job offers. More important, it's vital that you have medical insurance. Young people are often tempted to go without medical insurance, but this is a major mistake. An uncovered, costly medical emergency (say you're rushed to the hospital with appendicitis) can be a financial disaster. You could end up paying for your hospital and doctor care for years.

- **Disability insurance** isn't as well known as medical insurance, but it can be as important (if not more so). Disability insurance pays an income to an insured person when he or she is unable to work for an extended period. You would hope that you'd never need disability insurance, but if you did it would be of tremendous value.

- A **flexible spending account** allows a specified amount of pretax dollars to be used to pay for qualified expenses, including health care and child care. By paying for these costs with pretax dollars, employees are able to reduce their tax bill.

- There are two main types of *retirement plans*. One, called a **defined benefit retirement plan**, provides a set amount of money each month to retirees based on the number of years they worked and the income they earned. This form of retirement plan was once very popular, but it's less common today. The other, called a **defined contribution retirement plan**, is a form of savings plan. The employee contributes money each pay period to his or her retirement account, and the employer matches a portion of the contribution. Even when retirement is exceedingly far into the future, it's financially wise to set aside funds for retirement.

---

employer-sponsored health insurance

Insurance plan paid for by the employer that covers medical care for the employee only, or for the employee, spouse, and children.

disability insurance

Pays an income to an insured person when he or she is unable to work for an extended period.

flexible spending account

Allows a specified amount of pretax dollars to be used to pay for qualified expenses, including health care and child care.

defined benefit retirement plan

Provides a set amount of money each month to retirees based on the number of years they worked and the income they earned.

defined contribution retirement plan

A form of retirement savings plan in which both the employee and the employer may contribute.

KEY TAKEAWAYS

- *Finance* concerns the flow of money from one place to another; your *personal finances* concern your money and what you plan to do with it as it flows in and out of your possession. **Personal finance** is thus the application of financial principles to the monetary decisions that you make, either for your individual benefit or for that of your family.

- **Financial planning** is the ongoing process of managing your personal finances to meet goals that you've set for yourself or your family.

- The *financial life cycle* divides an individual's life into three stages, each of which is characterized by different life events. Each stage also entails recommended changes in the focus of the individual's financial planning:

  1. In stage 1, the focus is on *building* wealth.
  2. In stage 2, the focus shifts to the process of *preserving and increasing* the wealth that one has accumulated and continues to accumulate.
  3. In stage 3, the focus turns to the process of *living on* (and, if possible, continuing to grow) one's saved wealth.

- According to the model of the financial life cycle, financial planning begins in the individual's early twenties, the age at which most people choose a *career*—both the sort of *work* they want to do during their income-generating years and the kind of *lifestyle* they want to live in the process.

- College is a good investment of both money and time. People who graduate from high school can expect to improve their average annual earnings by about 49 percent over those of people who don't, and those who go on to finish college can expect to generate 82 percent more annual income than that. The area of study designated on your degree often doesn't matter when you're applying for a job: when poring over résumés, employers often look for the degree and simply note that a candidate has one.

- The first step in your job search is to prepare a **résumé**, a document that provides a summary of educational achievements and relevant job experience. Your résumé should be concise, clear, applicable to the job for which you are applying, and free of errors and inaccuracies.

- A **cover letter** is a document that accompanies your résumé and explains why you're sending your résumé and highlights your qualifications.

- To conduct a general search for positions that might be of interest to you, you could:

  1. Visit career Web sites, such as Monster.com, Wetfeet.com, or Careerbuilder.com.
  2. Search classified ads in online and print newspapers.
  3. Attend career fairs at your college and in your community.
  4. Talk with recruiters when they visit your campus.
  5. Contact people you know, tell them you're looking for a job, and ask for their help.

- When you're invited for an interview, you should research the company, practice answering questions you might be asked in the interview, and think up pertinent questions to ask the interviewer.

- When comparing job offers, consider more than salary. Also of importance are quality of life issues and benefits. Common financial benefits include health insurance, disability insurance, flexible spending accounts, and retirement plans.

  1. *Employer-sponsored health insurance* plans vary greatly in coverage and cost to the employee.
  2. Disability insurance pays an income to an insured person when he or she is unable to work for an extended period of time.
  3. A *flexible spending account* allows a specified amount of pretax dollars to be used to pay for qualified expenses, including health care and child care. By paying for these costs with pretax dollars, employees are able to reduce their tax bill.

- There are two main types of *retirement plans*: a defined benefit plan, which provides a set amount of money each month to retirees based on the number of years they worked and the income they earned, and a defined contribution plan, which is a form of savings plan into which both the employee and employer contribute. A well-known defined contribution plan is a 401(k).

Before going to the next section of this chapter, take a few minutes to test your knowledge of the material covered in this section. Quizzes can be found under the "Resources" tab, "Study Aids: Quizzes."

EXERCISE

Think of the type of job you'd like to have. Describe the job and indicate how you'd go about getting a job offer for this type of job. How would you evaluate competing offers from two companies? What criteria would you use in selecting the right job for you?

---

3. TIME IS MONEY

LEARNING OBJECTIVES

1. **Explain compound interest and the time value of money.**
2. **Discuss the value of getting an early start on your plans for saving.**

The fact that you have to choose a career at an early stage in your financial life cycle isn't the only reason that you need to start early on your financial planning. Let's assume, for instance, that it's your eighteenth birthday and that on this day you take possession of $10,000 that your grandparents put in trust for you. You could, of course, spend it; in particular, it would probably cover the cost of flight training for a private pilot's license—something you've always wanted but were convinced that you couldn't afford for another ten or fifteen years. Your grandfather, of course, suggests that you put it into some kind of savings account. If you just wait until you finish college, he says, and if you can find a savings plan that pays 5 percent interest, you'll have the $10,000 plus another $2,209 to buy a pretty good used car.

The total amount you'll have— $12,209—piques your interest. If that $10,000 could turn itself into $12,209 after sitting around for four years, what would it be worth if you actually held on to it until you did retire—say, at age sixty-five? A quick trip to the Internet to find a compound-interest calculator informs you that, forty-seven years later, your $10,000 will have grown to $104,345 (assuming a 5 percent interest rate). That's not really enough to retire on, but after all, you'd at least have some cash, even if you hadn't saved another dime for nearly half a century. On the other hand, what if that four years in college had paid off the way you planned, so that (once you get a good job) you're able to add, say, another $10,000 to your retirement savings account every year until age sixty-five? At that rate, you'll have amassed a nice little nest egg of slightly more than $1.6 million.

3.1 Compound Interest

In your efforts to appreciate the potential of your $10,000 to multiply itself, you have acquainted yourself with two of the most important concepts in finance. As we've already indicated, one is the principle of **compound interest**, which refers to the effect of earning interest on your interest.

Let's say, for example, that you take your grandfather's advice and invest your $10,000 (your *principal*) in a savings account at an annual interest rate of 5 percent. Over the course of the first year, your investment will earn $512 in interest and grow to $10,512. If you now reinvest the entire $10,512 at the same 5 percent annual rate, you'll earn another $537 in interest, giving you a total investment at the end of year 2 of $11,049. And so forth. And that's how you can end up with $104,345 at age sixty-five.

> **compound interest**
>
> Interest earned on your savings is added to the money in your savings account, and the new total (principle plus interest) earns more interest.

3.2 Time Value of Money

You've also encountered the principle of the **time value of money**—the principle whereby a dollar received in the present is worth more than a dollar received in the future. If there's one thing that we've stressed throughout this chapter so far, it's the fact that, for better or for worse, most people prefer to consume now rather than in the future. This is true for both borrowers and lenders. If you borrow money from me, it's because you can't otherwise buy something that you want at the present time. If I lend it to you, it's because I'm willing to postpone the opportunity to purchase something I want at the present time—perhaps a risk-free, ten-year U.S. Treasury bond with a present yield rate of 3 percent.

I'm willing to forego my opportunity, however, only if I can get some compensation for its loss, and that's why I'm going to charge you interest. And you're going to pay the interest because you need the money to buy what you want to buy. How much interest should we agree on? In theory, it could be just enough to cover the cost of my lost opportunity, but there are, of course, other factors. Inflation, for example, will have eroded the value of my money by the time I get it back from you. In addition,

> **time value of money**
>
> The principle whereby a dollar received in the present is worth more than a dollar received in the future.

while I would be taking no risk in loaning money to the U.S. government (as I would be doing if I bought that Treasury bond), I am taking a risk in loaning it to you. Our agreed-on rate will reflect such factors.[29]

Finally, the time value of money principle also states that a dollar received today starts earning interest sooner than one received tomorrow. Let's say, for example, that you receive $2,000 in cash gifts when you graduate from college. At age twenty-three, with your college degree in hand, you get a decent job and don't have an immediate need for that $2,000. So you put it into an account that pays 10 percent compounded *and* you add another $2,000 ($167 per month) to your account every year for the next eleven years.[30] The left panel of Table 14.2 shows how much your account will earn each year and how much money you'll have at certain ages between twenty-three and sixty-seven. As you can see, you'd have nearly $52,000 at age thirty-six and a little more than $196,000 at age fifty; at age sixty-seven, you'd be just a bit short of $1 million. The right panel of the same table shows what you'd have if you hadn't started saving $2,000 a year until you were age thirty-six. As you can also see, you'd have a respectable sum at age sixty-seven—but less than half of what you would have accumulated by starting at age twenty-three. More important, even to accumulate that much, *you'd have to add $2,000 per year for a total of thirty-two years, not just twelve.*

TABLE 14.2 Why to Start Saving Early (I)

Age	Savings accumulated from age 23, with deposits of $2,000 annually until age 67			Savings accumulated from age 36, with deposits of $2,000 annually until age 67		
	Annual deposit	Annual interest earned	Total saved at the end of the year	Annual deposit	Annual interest earned	Total saved at the end of the year
23	$0.00	$0.00	$0.00	$0.00	$0.00	$0.00
24	$2,000	$200.00	$2,200	$0.00	$0.00	$0.00
25	$2,000	$420.00	$4,620	$0.00	$0.00	$0.00
30	$2,000	$1,897.43	$20,871.78	$0.00	$0.00	$0.00
35	$2,000	$4,276.86	$47,045.42	$0.00	$0.00	$0.00
36	$0.00	$4,704.54	$51,749.97	$2,000	$200.00	$2,200.00
40	$0.00	$6,887.92	$75,767.13	$2,000	$1,221.02	$13,431.22
45	$0.00	$11,093.06	$122,023.71	$2,000	$3,187.48	$35,062.33
50	$0.00	$17,865.49	$196,520.41	$2,000	$6,354.50	$69,899.46
55	$0.00	$28,772.55	$316,498.09	$2,000	$11,455.00	$126,005.00
60	$0.00	$46,338.49	$509,723.34	$2,000	$19,669.41	$216,363.53
65	$0.00	$74,628.59	$820,914.53	$2,000	$32,898.80	$361,886.65
67	$0.00	$90,300.60	$993,306.53	$2,000	$40,277.55	$442,503.09

Source: Data from Consumer Credit Counseling Service of Maryland and Delaware Inc., "Power of Saving Early" (2008), http://www.cccs-inc.org/ tools/tools_saving_early.php (accessed April 27, 2014).

Here's another way of looking at the same principle. Suppose that you're twenty years old, don't have $2,000, and don't want to attend college full-time. You are, however, a hard worker and a conscientious saver, and one of your (very general) financial goals is to accumulate a $1 million retirement nest egg. As a matter of fact, if you can put $33 a month into an account that pays 12 percent interest compounded,[31] you can have your $1 million by age sixty-seven. That is, *if you start at age twenty*. As you can see from Table 14.3, if you wait until you're twenty-one to start saving, you'll need $37 a month. If you wait until you're thirty, you'll have to save $109 a month, and if you procrastinate until you're forty, the ante goes up to $366 a month.[32]

TABLE 14.3 Why to Start Saving Early (II)

First Payment When You Turn	Required Monthly Payment	First Payment When You Turn	Required Monthly Payment
20	$33	30	$109
21	$37	31	$123
22	$42	32	$138
23	$47	33	$156
24	$53	34	$176
25	$60	35	$199
26	$67	40	$366
27	$76	50	$1,319
28	$85	60	$6,253
29	$96		

Source: Arthur J. Keown, Personal Finance: Turning Money into Wealth, 4th ed. (Upper Saddle River, NJ: Pearson Education, 2007), 23.

The moral here should be fairly obvious: a dollar saved today not only starts earning interest sooner than one saved tomorrow (or ten years from now) but also can ultimately earn a lot more money in the long run. Starting early means in your twenties—early in stage 1 of your financial life cycle. As one well-known financial advisor puts it, "If you're in your 20s and you haven't yet learned how to delay gratification, your life is likely to be a constant financial struggle."[33]

KEY TAKEAWAYS

- The principle of **compound interest** refers to the effect of earning interest on your interest.
- The principle of the **time value of money** is the principle whereby a dollar received in the present is worth more than a dollar received in the future.
- The principle of the time value of money also states that a dollar received today starts earning interest sooner than one received tomorrow.
- Together, these two principles give a significant financial advantage to individuals who begin saving early during the financial-planning life cycle.

Before going to the next section of this chapter, take a few minutes to test your knowledge of the material covered in this section. Quizzes can be found under the "Resources" tab, "Study Aids: Quizzes."

EXERCISE

Everyone wants to be a millionaire (except those who are already billionaires). To find out how old you'll be when you become a millionaire, go to http://www.bankrate.com/calculators/savings/save-million-calculator.aspx?ec_id=m1108556&s_kwcid=AL!1325!3!41196367568!b!!s!!save a million dollars calculator&ef_id=Ut8OegAAAHfYQWSi:20140427173744:s&MSA=0240 and input these assumptions:

Age: your actual age

Millionaire target age: 65

Amount currently invested: $10,000

Savings per month: $500

Expected rate of return (interest rate): 7 percent

Expected inflation rate: 3 percent

Click "calculate" and you'll learn when you'll become a millionaire (given the previous assumptions). Click "view report" to receive advice on ways to become a millionaire earlier.

Now, let's change things. We'll go through this process three times. Change only the items described. Keep all other assumptions the same as those listed previously.

1. Change the interest rate to 3 percent and then to 6 percent.
2. Change the savings amount to $200 and then to $800.
3. Change your age from "your age" to "your age plus 5" and then to "your age minus 5."

Write a brief report describing the sensitivity of becoming a millionaire, based on changing interest rates, monthly savings amount, and age at which you begin to invest.

4. THE FINANCIAL PLANNING PROCESS

LEARNING OBJECTIVES

1. **Identify the three stages of the personal-finances planning process.**
2. **Explain how to draw up a personal net-worth statement, a personal cash-flow statement, and a personal budget.**

We've divided the financial planning process into three steps:

1. Evaluate your current financial status by creating a net worth statement and a cash flow analysis.
2. Set short-term, intermediate-term, and long-term financial goals.
3. Use a budget to plan your future cash inflows and outflows and to assess your financial performance by comparing budgeted figures with actual amounts.

4.1 Step 1: Evaluating Your Current Financial Situation

Just how are you doing, financially speaking? You should ask yourself this question every now and then, and it should certainly be your starting point when you decide to initiate a more or less formal financial plan. The first step in addressing this question is collecting and analyzing the records of what you *own* and what you *owe* and then applying a few accounting terms to the results:

- Your personal *assets* consist of what you *own*.
- Your personal *liabilities* are what you *owe*—your obligations to various creditors, big and small.

Preparing Your Net-Worth Statement

Your **net worth** (accounting term for your *wealth*) is the difference between your assets and your liabilities. Thus the formula for determining net worth is:

$$\text{Assets} - \text{Liabilities} = \text{Net worth}$$

net worth

The difference between an individual's assets and liabilities.

If you own more than you owe, your net worth will be *positive*; if you owe more than you own, it will be *negative*. To find out whether your net worth is on the plus or minus side, you can prepare a personal **net worth statement** like the one in Figure 14.5, which we've drawn up for a fictional student named Joe College. (Note that we've included lines for items that may be relevant to some people's net worth statements but left them blank when they don't apply to Joe.)

net worth statement

A personal balance sheet that lists the value of the things you own, the amounts owed to others, and the difference, called "net worth."

FIGURE 14.5   Net Worth Statement

Joe College's Personal Net Worth Statement as of August 31, 2012

ASSETS (what you own)	Value
Cash	$ 200
Checking accounts	1,000
Savings accounts/CDs/money market accounts	400
Market value of investments (stocks, bonds, mutual funds)	—
Retirement accounts	—
Market value of real estate	—
Cars	8,000
Furniture and appliances	1,500
Computers	900
Stereo/video equipment/cell phones	400
Jewelry	—
Clothing	300
Other assets	—
Total Assets	**12,700**
LIABILITIES (what you owe)	Amount
Credit card balances	1,200
Charge account balances	200
Student loans	7,000
Car loans	2,300
Home mortgage	—
Other liabilities	—
Total Liabilities	**10,700**

Assets − Liabilities = Net worth

Total Net Worth	**$ 2,000**

Assets

Joe has two types of assets:

- First are his *monetary* or *liquid assets*—his cash, the money in his checking accounts, and the value of any savings, CDs, and money market accounts. They're called *liquid* because either they're cash or they can readily be turned into cash.

- Everything else is a *tangible asset*—something that Joe can use, as opposed to an investment. (We haven't given Joe any *investments*—such financial assets as stocks, bonds, or mutual funds—because people usually purchase these instruments to meet such long-term goals as buying a house or sending a child to college.)

fair market value

The price you could get by selling assets at their present price.

Note that we've been careful to calculate Joe's assets in terms of their **fair market value**—the price he could get by selling them at present, not the price he paid for them or the price that he could get at some future time.

Liabilities

Joe's net worth statement also divides his liabilities into two categories:

- Anything that Joe owes on such items as his furniture and computer are *current liabilities*—debts that must be paid within one year. Much of this indebtedness no doubt ends up on Joe's credit card balance, which is regarded as a current liability because he *should* pay it off within a year.
- By contrast, his car payments and student-loan payments are *noncurrent liabilities*—debt payments that extend for a period of more than one year. Joe is in no position to buy a house, but for most people, their mortgage is their most significant noncurrent liability.

Finally, note that Joe has positive net worth. At this point in the life of the average college student, positive net worth may be a little unusual. If you happen to have negative net worth right now, you're technically *insolvent*, but remember that a major goal of getting a college degree is to enter the workforce with the best possible opportunity for generating enough wealth to reverse that situation.

Preparing Your Cash-Flow Statement

cash-flow statement

Shows where your money has come from and where it's slated to go.

Now that you know something about your financial status *on a given date*, you need to know more about it *over a period of time*. This is the function of a **cash-flow or income statement**, which shows where your money has come from and where it's slated to go.

Figure 14.6 is Joe College's cash-flow statement. As you can see, Joe's *income* (his cash *inflows*—money coming in) is derived from two sources: student loans and income from a part-time job. His expenditures (cash *outflows*—money going out) fall into several categories: housing, food, transportation, personal and health care, recreation/entertainment, education, insurance, savings, and other expenses. To find out Joe's *net cash flow*, we subtract his expenditures from his income:

$$\$25,700 - \$25,300 = \$400$$

FIGURE 14.6 Cash-Flow Statement

Joe College's Personal Cash-Flow Statement as of August 31, 2012	
CASH INFLOWS (cash coming in)	
Wages (full time in summer/part time during semester)	$ 18,700
Student loan	7,000
Total inflow of cash	**25,700**
CASH OUTFLOWS (cash going out)	
Housing	
Rent	5,400
Utilities (electricity, heat, water, cable)	700
Communication (phone and internet access)	900
Food	
Groceries	2,300
Eating out	1,200
Transportation	
Gas and maintenance	1,400
Car loan payments	1,400
Personal and healthcare	
Medical co-payments and dental	200
Clothing	200
Laundry/cleaning supplies/miscellaneous	100
Recreation/Entertainment	
Night life/movies/concerts	900
Magazines/music/miscellaneous	200
Education	
Tuition	5,500
Books	1,000
Student loan payments	—
Insurance	
Car, health, renter's	1,900
Savings	1,200
Other expenses	800
Total outflow of cash	**25,300**
Cash inflow – Cash outflow = Net cash flow **Net Cash Flow**	**$ 400**

Joe has been able to maintain a positive cash flow for the year ending August 31, 2012, but he's cutting it close. Moreover, he's in the black only because of the inflow from student loans—income that, as you'll recall from his net worth statement, is also a noncurrent liability. We are, however, willing to give Joe the benefit of the doubt: Though he's incurring the high costs of an education, he's willing to commit himself to the debt (and, we'll assume, to careful spending) because he regards education as an investment that will pay off in the future.

Remember that when constructing a cash-flow statement, you must record only income and expenditures that pertain to a given period, whether it be a month, a semester, or (as in Joe's case) a year.

Remember, too, that you must figure both inflows and outflows *on a cash basis*: you record income only when you receive money, and you record expenditures only when you pay out money. When, for example, Joe used his credit card to purchase his computer, he didn't actually pay out any money. Each monthly payment on his credit card balance, however, is an outflow that must be recorded on his cash-flow statement (according to the type of expense—say, recreation/entertainment, food, transportation, and so on).

Your cash-flow statement, then, provides another perspective on your *solvency*: if you're *insolvent*, it's because you're spending more than you're earning. Ultimately, your net worth and cash-flow statements are most valuable when you use them together. While your net worth statement lets you know what you're worth—how much wealth you have—your cash-flow statement lets you know precisely what effect your spending and saving habits are having on your wealth.

4.2　Step 2: Set Short-Term, Intermediate-Term, and Long-Term Financial Goals

We know from Joe's cash-flow statement that, despite his limited income, he feels that he can save $1,200 a year. He knows, of course, that it makes sense to have some cash in reserve in case of emergencies (car repairs, medical needs, and so forth), but he also knows that by putting away some of his money (probably each week), he's developing a habit that he'll need if he hopes to reach his long-term financial goals.

Just what are Joe's goals? We've summarized them in Figure 14.7, where, as you can see, we've divided them into three time frames: short-term (less than two years), intermediate-term (two to five years), and long-term (more than five years). Though Joe is still in an early stage of his financial life cycle, he has identified and structured his goals fairly effectively. In particular, they satisfy four criteria of well-conceived goals: they're *realistic* and *measurable*, and Joe has designated both *definite time frames* and *specific courses of action*.[34]

FIGURE 14.7 Joe's Goals

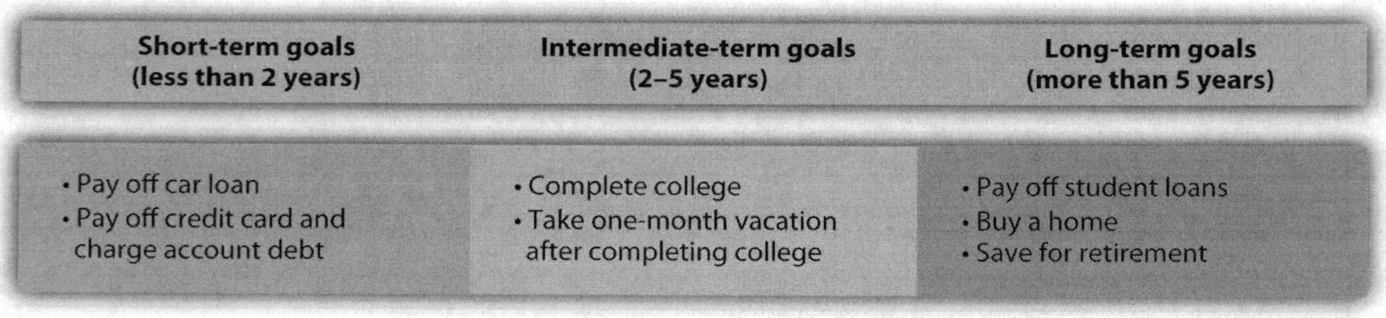

Short-term goals (less than 2 years)	Intermediate-term goals (2–5 years)	Long-term goals (more than 5 years)
• Pay off car loan • Pay off credit card and charge account debt	• Complete college • Take one-month vacation after completing college	• Pay off student loans • Buy a home • Save for retirement

They're also sensible. Joe sees no reason, for example, why he can't pay off his car loan, credit card, and charge account balances within two years. Remember that, with no income other than student-loan money and wages from a part-time job, Joe has decided (rightly or wrongly) to use his credit cards to pay for much of his personal consumption (furniture, electronics equipment, and so forth). It won't be an easy task to pay down these balances, so we'll give him some credit (so to speak) for regarding them as important enough to include paying them among his short-term goals. After finishing college, he'll splurge and take a month-long vacation. This might not be the best thing to do from a financial point of view, but he knows this could be his only opportunity to travel extensively. He is realistic in his classification of student loan repayment and the purchase of a home as long-term. But he might want to revisit his decision to classify saving for his retirement as a long-term goal. This is something we believe he should begin as soon as he starts working full-time.

4.3   Step 3: Develop a Budget and Use It to Evaluate Financial Performance

Once he has reviewed his cash-flow statement, Joe has a much better idea of what cash flowed in for the year that ended August 31, 2012, and a much better idea of where it went when it flowed out. Now he can ask himself whether he's satisfied with his annual inflow (income) and outflow (expenditures). If he's anything like most people, he'll want to make some changes—perhaps to increase his income, to cut back on his expenditures, or, if possible, both. The first step in making these changes is drawing up a personal **budget**—a document that itemizes the sources of his income and expenditures for the coming year, along with the relevant money amounts for each.

> **budget**
>
> A document that itemizes the sources of income and expenditures for a future period (often a year).

Having reviewed the figures on his cash-flow statement, Joe did in fact make a few decisions:

- Because he doesn't want to jeopardize his grades by increasing his work hours, he'll have to reconcile himself to just about the same wages for another year.

- He'll need to apply for another $7,000 student loan.

- If he's willing to cut his spending by $1,200, he can pay off his credit cards. Toward this end, he's targeted the following expenditures for reduction: rent (get a cheaper apartment), phone costs (switch plans), auto insurance (take advantage of a "good-student" discount), and gasoline (pool rides or do a little more walking). Fortunately, his car loan will be paid off by midyear.

Revising his figures accordingly, Joe developed the budget in Figure 14.8 for the year ending August 31, 2013. Look first at the column headed "Budget." If things go as planned, Joe expects a cash surplus of $1,600 by the end of the year—enough to pay off his credit card debt and leave him with an extra $400.

FIGURE 14.8 Joe's Budget

Item	Budget	Actual	Variance (actual vs. budgeted)
Joe College's Budget **for year ending August 31, 2013.**			
CASH INFLOW			
Wages	$ 18,700	$ 19,000	$ 300 favorable
Student loan	7,000	7000	—
Total	**25,700**	**26,000**	**300 favorable**
CASH OUTFLOW			
Housing			
Rent	5,100	5,100	—
Utilities (electricity, heat, water, TV cable)	700	800	100 unfavorable
Communication (phone and internet)	800	800	—
Food			
Groceries	2,300	2,100	200 favorable
Eating out	1,200	1,300	100 unfavorable
Transportation			
Gas and maintenance	1,300	1,400	100 unfavorable
Car loan payments	900	900	—
Personal and healthcare			
Medical co-payments and dental	200	300	100 unfavorable
Clothing	200	300	100 unfavorable
Laundry/cleaning supplies/miscellaneous	100	100	—
Recreation/Entertainment			
Night life/movies/concerts	900	1,000	100 unfavorable
Magazines/music/miscellaneous	200	200	—
Education			
Tuition	5,500	5,500	—
Books	1,000	1,000	—
Insurance			
Car, health, renter's	1,700	1,700	—
Savings	1,200	1,200	—
Other expenses	800	600	200 favorable
Total	**24,100**	**24,300**	**200 unfavorable**
Surplus (Deficit)	**$ 1,600**	**$ 1,700**	**$ 100 favorable**

Figuring the Variance

Now we can examine the two remaining columns in Joe's budget. Throughout the year, Joe will keep track of his actual income and actual expenditures and will enter the totals in the column labeled "Actual." Like most reasonable people, however, Joe doesn't really expect his actual figures to match with his budgeted figures. So whenever there's a difference between an amount in his "Budget" column and the corresponding amount in his "Actual" column, Joe records the difference, whether plus or minus, as a **variance**. Two types of variances appear in Joe's budget:

- *Income variance.* When actual *income* turns out to be higher than expected or budgeted income, Joe records the variance as "favorable." (This makes sense, as you'd find it favorable if you earned more income than expected.) When it's just the opposite, he records the variance as "unfavorable."

- *Expense variance.* When the actual amount of an *expenditure* is more than he had budgeted for, he records it as an "unfavorable" variance. (This also makes sense, as you'd find it unfavorable if you spent more than the budgeted amount.) When the actual amount is less than budgeted, he records it as a "favorable" variance.

> **variance**
>
> Difference between the actual amount and the budgeted amount.

4.4   Setting Mature Goals

Before we leave the subject of the financial-planning process, let's revisit the topic of Joe's goals. Another look at Figure 14.7 reminds us that, at the current stage of his financial life cycle, Joe has set fairly simple goals. We know, for example, that Joe wants to buy a home, but when does he want to take this major financial step? And of course, Joe wants to retire, but what kind of lifestyle does he want in retirement? Does he expect, like most people, a retirement lifestyle that's more or less comparable to that of his peak earning years? Will he be able to afford both the cost of a comfortable retirement and, say, the cost of sending his children to college? As Joe and his financial circumstances mature, he'll have to express these goals (and a few others) in more specific terms.

Levels of Mature Goals

Let's fast-forward a decade or so, when Joe's picture of stages 2 and 3 of his financial life cycle have come into clearer focus. If he hasn't done so already, Joe is now ready to identify a primary goal to guide him in identifying and meeting all his other goals.[35] Suppose that because Joe's investment in a college education has paid off the way he'd planned ten years ago, he's in a position to target a primary goal of financial independence—by which he means a certain financially secure life not only for himself but for his children, as well. Now that he's set this *primary* goal, he can identify a more specific set of goals—say, the following:

- A standard of living that reflects a certain level of comfort—a level associated with the possession of certain assets, both tangible and intangible.
- The ability to provide his children with college educations.
- A retirement lifestyle comparable to that of his peak earning years.

Having set this *secondary* level of goals, Joe's now ready to make specific plans for reaching them. As we've already seen, Joe understands that plans are far more likely to work out when they're focused on specific goals. His next step, therefore, is to determine the goals on which he should focus this next level of plans.

As it turns out, Joe already knows what these goals are, because he's been setting the appropriate goals every year since he drew up the cash-flow statement in Figure 14.6. In drawing up that statement, Joe was careful to create several line items to identify his various expenditures: *housing, food, transportation, personal and health care, recreation/entertainment, education, insurance, savings,* and *other expenses.* When we introduced these items, we pointed out that each one represents a cash outflow—something for which Joe expected to pay. They are, in other words, things that Joe intends to *buy* or, in the language of economics, *consume.* As such, we can characterize them as *consumption goals.* These "purchases"—what Joe wants in such areas as housing, insurance coverage, recreation/entertainment, and so forth—make specific his secondary goals and are therefore his *third-level* goals.

Figure 14.9 gives us a full picture of Joe's three-level hierarchy of goals.

FIGURE 14.9 Three-Level Goals/Plans

Present and Future Consumption Goals

A closer look at the list of Joe's consumption goals reveals that they fall into two categories:

1. We can call the first category *present* goals because each item is intended to meet Joe's present needs and those (we'll now assume) of his family—housing, health care coverage, and so forth. They must be paid for as Joe and his family take possession of them—that is, when they use or consume them. All these things are also necessary to meet the first of Joe's secondary goals—a certain standard of living.

2. The items in the second category of Joe's consumption goals are aimed at meeting his other two secondary goals: sending his children to college and retiring with a comfortable lifestyle. He won't take possession of these purchases until sometime in the *future*, but (as is so often the case) there's a catch: they must be paid for out of *current* income.

4.5 A Few Words about Saving

Joe's desire to meet this second category of consumption goals—*future* goals such as education for his kids and a comfortable retirement for himself and his wife—accounts for the appearance on his list of the one item that, at first glance, may seem misclassified among all the others: namely, *savings*.

Paying Yourself First

It's tempting to glance at Joe's budget and cash-flow statement and assume that he shares with most of us a common attitude toward saving money: when you're done allotting money for various spending needs, you can decide what to do with what's left over—save it or spend it. In reality, however, Joe's budgeting reflects an entirely different approach. When he made up the budget in Figure 14.8, Joe *started out* with the decision to save $1,600—or at least to avoid spending it. Why? Because he had a goal: to be free of credit card debt. To meet this goal, he planned to use $1,200 of his *current* income to pay off what would continue to hang over his head as a *future* expense (his credit card debt). In addition, he *planned* to have $400 left over after he'd paid his credit card balance. Why? Because he had still longer-term goals, and he intended to get started on them early—as soon as he finished college. Thus his intention from the outset was to put $400 into savings.

In other words, here's how Joe went about budgeting his money for the year ending August 31, 2013 (as shown in Figure 14.8):

1. He calculated his income—total cash inflows from his student loan and his part-time job ($25,700).

2. He subtracted from his total income two targeted consumption goals—credit card payments ($1,200) and savings ($400).

3. He allocated what was left ($24,100) to his remaining consumption goals: housing ($6,600), food ($3,500), education ($6,500), and so forth.

If you're concerned that Joe's sense of delayed gratification is considerably more mature than your own, think of it this way: *Joe has chosen to pay himself first*. It's one of the key principles of personal-finances planning and an important strategy in doing something that we recommended earlier in this chapter—starting early.[36]

KEY TAKEAWAYS

- The financial planning process consists of three steps:
    1. Evaluate your current financial status by creating a net worth statement and a cash flow analysis.
    2. Set short-term, intermediate-term, and long-term financial goals.
    3. Use a budget to plan your future cash inflows and outflows and to assess your financial performance by comparing budgeted figures with actual amounts.

- In step 1 of the financial planning process, you determine what you *own* and what you *owe*:
    1. Your personal *assets* consist of what you own.
    2. Your personal *liabilities* are what you owe—your obligations to various creditors.

- Most people have two types of assets:
    1. *Monetary* or *liquid assets* include cash, money in checking accounts, and the value of any savings, CDs, and money market accounts. They're called *liquid* because either they're cash or they can readily be turned into cash.
    2. Everything else is a *tangible asset*—something that can be used, as opposed to an investment.

- Likewise, most people have two types of liabilities:
    1. Any debts that should be paid within one year are *current liabilities*.
    2. *Noncurrent liabilities* consist of debt payments that extend for a period of more than one year.

- Your **net worth** is the difference between your assets and your liabilities. **Your net worth statement** will show whether your net worth is on the plus or minus side on a given date.

- In step 2 of the financial planning process, you create a **cash-flow** or **income statement**, which shows where your money has come from and where it's slated to go. It reflects your financial status over a period of time. Your cash *inflows*—the money you have coming in—are recorded as *income*. Your cash *outflows*—money going out—are itemized as *expenditures* in such categories as housing, food, transportation, education, and savings.

- A good way to approach your financial goals is by dividing them into three time frames: short-term (less than two years), intermediate-term (two to five years), and long-term (more than five years). Goals should be realistic and measurable, and you should designate definite time frames and specific courses of action.

- Net worth and cash-flow statements are most valuable when used together: while your net worth statement lets you know what you're worth, your cash-flow statement lets you know precisely what effect your spending and saving habits are having on your net worth.

- If you're not satisfied with the effect of your spending and saving habits on your net worth, you may want to make changes in future inflows (income) and outflows (expenditures). You make these changes in step 3 of the financial planning process, when you draw up your personal **budget**—a document that itemizes the sources of your income and expenditures for a future period (often a year).

- In addition to the itemized lists of inflows and outflows, there are three other columns in the budget:
    1. The "Budget" column tracks the amounts of money that you *plan* to receive or to pay out over the budget period.
    2. The "Actual" column records the amounts that did in fact come in or go out.
    3. The final column records the **variance** for each item—the difference between the amount in the "Budget" column and the corresponding amount in the "Actual" column.

- There are two types of variance:
    1. An *income variance* occurs when actual income is higher than budgeted income (or vice versa).
    2. An *expense variance* occurs when the actual amount of an expenditure is higher than the budgeted amount (or vice versa).

Before going to the next section of this chapter, take a few minutes to test your knowledge of the material covered in this section. Quizzes can be found under the "Resources" tab, "Study Aids: Quizzes."

Using your own information (or made-up information if you prefer), go through the three steps in the financial planning process:

1. Evaluate your current financial status by creating a net worth statement and a cash flow analysis.
2. Identify short-term, intermediate-term, and long-term financial goals.
3. Create a budget (for a month or a year). Estimate future income and expenditures. Make up "actual" figures and calculate a variance by comparing budgeted figures with actual amounts.

5. A HOUSE IS NOT A PIGGY BANK: A FEW LESSONS FROM THE SUBPRIME CRISIS

LEARNING OBJECTIVES

1. Discuss the trend in the U.S. savings rate.
2. Define a subprime loan and explain the difference between a fixed-rate mortgage and an adjustable-rate mortgage.
3. Discuss what can go wrong with a subprime loan at an adjustable rate. Discuss what can go wrong with hundreds of thousands of subprime loans at adjustable rates.
4. Define "risk" and explain some of the risks entailed by personal financial transactions.

Joe isn't old enough to qualify, but if his grandfather had deposited $1,000 in an account paying 7 percent interest in 1945, it would now be worth $64,000. That's because money invested at 7 percent compounded will double every ten years. Now, $64,000 may or may not seem like a significant return over fifty years, but after all, the money did all the heavy lifting, and given the miracle of compound interest, it's surprising that Americans don't take greater advantage of the opportunity to multiply their wealth by saving more of it, even in modest, interest-bearing accounts. Ironically, with $683 billion in credit card debt,[37] it's obvious that a lot of American families are experiencing the effects of compound interest—but in reverse.[38]

As a matter of fact, though Joe College appears to be on the right track when it comes to saving, many people aren't. A lot of Americans, it seems, do indeed set savings goals, but in one recent survey, nearly 70 percent of the respondents reported that they fell short of their monthly goals because their money was needed elsewhere. About one-third of Americans say that they're putting away something but not enough, and another third aren't saving anything at all. Almost one-fifth of all Americans have net worth of zero—or less.[39]

As we indicated in the opening section of this chapter, this shortage of savings goes hand in hand with a surplus in spending. "My parents," says one otherwise gainfully employed American knowledge worker, "are appalled at the way I justify my spending. I think, 'Why work and make money unless you're going to enjoy it?' That's a fine theory," she adds, "until you're sixty, homeless, and with no money in the bank."[40] And indeed, if she doesn't intend to alter her personal-finances philosophy, she has good reason to worry about her "older adult" years. Sixty percent of Americans over the age of sixty-five have less than $100,000 in savings, and only 30 percent of this group have more than $25,000; 45 percent have less than $15,000. As for income, 75 percent of people over age sixty-five generate less than $35,000 annually, and 30 percent are in the "poverty to near-poverty" range of $10,000 to $20,000 (as compared to 12 percent of the under-sixty-five population).[41]

5.1 Disposing of Savings

Figure 14.10 shows the U.S. *savings rate*—which measures the percentage of disposable income devoted to savings for the period 1960 to 2014. As you can see, it suffered a steep decline from 1980 to 2005 and remained at this negligible savings rate until it started moving up in 2008. But after that, the savings rate declined and, by 2014, had fallen below the long-term rate of 7 percent.[42]

FIGURE 14.10 U.S. Savings Rate

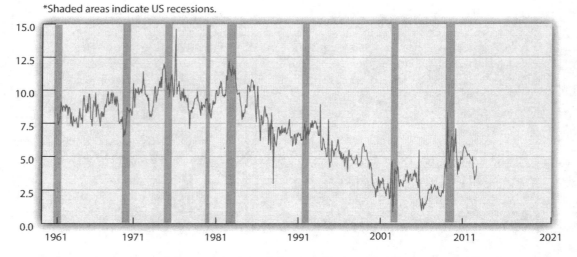

*Shaded areas indicate US recessions.

Not surprisingly, as Americans save less, they spend more. A recent study by the Federal Reserve of New York shows that consumer spending in 2014 rose to its highest level since 2007.[43] Now, a widespread tendency on the part of Americans to spend rather than save doesn't account entirely for the downward shift in the savings rate. The Federal Reserve has cited at least two other (closely related) factors in the decline of savings:[44]

- An increase in the ratio of stock-market wealth to disposable income
- An increase in the ratio of residential-property wealth to disposable income

Assume, for example, that, in addition to your personal savings, you own some stock and have a mortgage on a home. Both your stock and your home are (supposedly) *appreciable assets*—their value used to go up over time. (In fact, if you had taken out your mortgage in 2000, by the end of 2005 your home would have appreciated at double the rate of your disposable personal income.) The decline in the personal savings rate during the mid-2000s, suggested the Fed, resulted in part from people's response to "long-lived bull markets in stocks and housing"; in other words, a lot of people had come to rely on the appreciation of such assets as stocks and residential property as "a substitute for the practice of saving out of wage income."

Subprime Rates and Adjustable Rate Mortgages

subprime mortgage loan

Mortgage loans made to borrowers who don't qualify for market-set interest rates because of one or more risk factors.

adjustable-rate mortgage (ARM)

Mortgage that's pegged to the increase or decrease of certain interest rates that your lender has to pay.

Let's assume that you weren't ready to take advantage of the boom in mortgage loans in 2000 but did set your sights on 2005. You may not have been ready to buy a house in 2005 either, but there's a good chance that you got a loan anyway. In particular, some lender might have offered you a so-called **subprime mortgage loan**. Subprime loans are made to borrowers who don't qualify for market-set interest rates because of one or more risk factors—income level, employment status, credit history, ability to make only a very low down payment. As of March 2007, U.S. lenders had written $1.3 trillion in mortgages like yours.[45]

Granted, your terms might not have been very good. For one thing, interest rates on subprime loans may run from 8 percent to 10 percent and higher.[46] In addition, you probably had to settle for an **adjustable-rate mortgage (ARM)**—one that's pegged to the increase or decrease of certain interest rates that your lender has to pay. When you signed your mortgage papers, you knew that if those rates went up, your mortgage rate—and your monthly payments—would go up, too. Fortunately, however, you had a plan B: with the value of your new asset appreciating even as you enjoyed living in it, it wouldn't be long before you could refinance it at a more manageable and more predictable rate.

5.2　The Meltdown

Now imagine your dismay when housing prices started to go *down* in 2006 and 2007. As a result, you weren't able to refinance, your ARM was set to adjust upward in 2008, and foreclosures were already happening all around you—1.3 million in 2007 alone.[47] By April 2008, one in every 519 American households had received a foreclosure notice.[48] By August, 9.2 percent of the $12 trillion in U.S. mortgage loans was delinquent or in foreclosure.[49]

The repercussions? Banks and other institutions that made mortgage loans were the first sector of the financial industry to be hit. Largely because of mortgage-loan defaults, profits at more than 8,500 U.S. banks dropped from $35 billion in the fourth quarter of 2006 to $650 million in the corresponding quarter of 2007 (a decrease of 89 percent). Bank earnings for the year 2007 declined 31 percent and dropped another 46 percent in the first quarter of 2008.[50]

Losses in this sector were soon felt by two publicly traded government-sponsored organizations, the Federal National Mortgage Association (Fannie Mae) and the Federal Home Loan Mortgage Corporation (Freddie Mac). Both of these institutions are authorized to make loans and provide loan guarantees to banks, mortgage companies, and other mortgage lenders; their function is to make sure that these lenders have enough money to lend to prospective home buyers. Between them, Fannie Mae and Freddie Mac backed approximately half of that $12 trillion in outstanding mortgage loans, and when the mortgage crisis hit, the stock prices of the two corporations began to drop steadily. In September 2008, amid fears that both organizations would run out of capital, the U.S. government took over their management.

Freddie Mac also had another function: to increase the supply of money available for mortgage loans and new home purchases, Freddie Mac bought mortgages already written by lenders, pooled them, and sold them as mortgage-backed securities to investors on the open market. Many major investment firms did much the same thing, buying individual subprime mortgages from original lenders (such as small banks), pooling the projected revenue—payments made by the original individual home buyers—and selling securities backed by the pooled revenue.

But when their rates went too high and home buyers couldn't make these payments, these securities plummeted in value. Institutions that had invested in them—including investment banks—suffered significant losses.[51] In September 2008, one of these investment banks, Lehman Brothers, filed for bankruptcy protection; another, Merrill Lynch, agreed to sell itself for $50 billion. Next came American International Group (AIG), a giant insurance company that insured financial institutions against the risks they took in loaning and investing money. As its policyholders buckled under the weight of defaulted loans and failed investments, AIG, too, was on the brink of bankruptcy, and when private efforts to bail it out failed, the U.S. government stepped in with a loan of $85 billion.[52] The U.S. government also agreed to buy up risky mortgage-backed securities from teetering financial institutions at an estimated cost of "hundreds of billions."[53]

Subprime Directives: A Few Lessons from the Subprime Crisis

If you were one of the millions of Americans who took out subprime mortgages in the years between 2001 and 2005, you probably have some pressing financial problems. If you defaulted on your subprime ARM, you may have suffered foreclosure on your newly acquired asset, lost any equity that you'd built up in it, and taken a hit in your credit rating. (We'll assume that you're not one of the people whose eagerness to get on the subprime bandwagon caused fraudulent mortgage applications to go up by 300 percent between 2002 and 2006.)[54]

On the other hand, you've probably learned a few lessons about financial planning and strategy. Let's conclude with a survey of three lessons that you should have learned from your hypothetical adventure in the world of subprime mortgages.

Lesson 1: All mortgages are not created equal. Despite (or perhaps because of) the understandable enticement of home ownership, your judgment may have been faulty in this episode of your financial life cycle. Generally speaking, you're better off with a **fixed-rate mortgage**—one on which the interest rate remains the same regardless of changes in market interest rates—than with an ARM.[55] As we've explained at length in this chapter, planning is one of the cornerstones of personal-finances management, and ARMs don't lend themselves to planning. How well can you plan for your future mortgage payments if you can't be sure what they're going to be?

In addition, though interest rates may go up or down, planning for them to go *down* and to take your mortgage payments with them doesn't make much sense. You can wait around to get lucky, and you can even try to get lucky (say, by buying a lottery ticket), but you certainly can't *plan* to get lucky. Unfortunately, the only thing you can really *plan* for is higher rates and higher payments. An ARM isn't a good idea if you don't know whether you can meet payments higher than your initial payment. In fact, if you have reason to believe that you can't meet the *maximum* payment entailed by an ARM, you probably shouldn't take it on.

Lesson 2: It's risky out there. You now know—if you hadn't suspected it already—that planning your personal finances would be a lot easier if you could do it in a predictable economic environment. But you can't, of course, and virtually constant instability in financial markets is simply one economic fact of life that you'll have to deal with as you make your way through the stages of your financial life cycle.

FIGURE 14.11

In 2008, nearly one out of five hundred households in the United States received a foreclosure notice.

© 2010 Jupiterimages Corporation

fixed-rate mortgage

A mortgage on which the interest rate remains the same regardless of changes in market interest rates.

In other words, any foray into financial markets is risky. Basically, *risk* is the possibility that cash flows will be variable.[56] Unfortunately, volatility in the overall economy is directly related to just one category of risks. There's a second category—risks related to the activities of various organizations involved in your financial transactions. You've already been introduced to the effects of these forms of financial risk, some of which have affected you directly, some of which have affected you indirectly, and some of which may affect you in the future:[57]

- *Management risk* is the risk that poor management of an organization with which you're dealing may adversely affect the outcome of your personal-finances planning. If you couldn't pay the higher rate on your ARM, managers at your lender probably failed to look deeply enough into your employment status and income.

- *Business risk* is the risk associated with a product that you've chosen to buy. The fate of your mortgagor, who issued the original product—your subprime ARM—and that of everyone down the line who purchased it in some form (perhaps Freddy Mac and Merrill Lynch) bear witness to the pitfalls of business risk.

- *Financial risk* refers to the risk that comes from ill-considered indebtedness. Freddie Mac, Fannie Mae, and several investment banks have felt the repercussions of investing too much money in financial instruments that were backed with shaky assets (namely, subprime mortgages).

In your own small way, of course, you, too, underestimated the pitfalls of all three of these forms of risk.

Lesson 3: Not all income is equally disposable. Figure 14.12 shows the increase in the ratio of debt to disposable income among American households between 1985 and 2007. As you can see, the increase was dramatic—from 80 percent in the early 1990s to about 130 percent in 2007.[58] This rise was made possible by greater access to credit—people borrow money in order to spend it, whether on consumption or on investments, and the more they can borrow, the more they can spend.

In the United States, greater access to credit in the late 1990s and early 2000s was made possible by rising housing prices: the more valuable your biggest asset, the more lenders are willing to lend you, even if what you're buying with your loan—your house—*is* your biggest asset. As the borrower, your strategy is twofold: (1) Pay your mortgage out of your wage income, and (2) reap the financial benefits of an asset that appreciates in value. On top of everything else, you can count the increased value of your asset as *savings*: when you sell the house at retirement, the difference between your mortgage and the current value of your house is yours to support you in your golden years.

FIGURE 14.12 Debt-Income Ratio

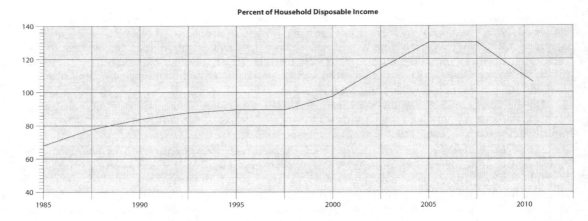

As we know, however, housing prices had started to fall by the end of 2006. From a peak in mid-2006, they had fallen 8 percent by November 2007, and by April 2008 they were down from the 2006 peak by more than 19 percent—the worst rate of decline since the Great Depression. And most experts expected it to get worse before it gets better, and unfortunately they were right. Housing prices have declined by 33 percent from the mid-2006 peak to the end of 2010 (but fortunately the prices started to climb back up again in 2011).[59]

So where do you stand? As you know, your house is worth no more than what you can get for it on the open market; thus the asset that you were counting on to help provide for your retirement has *depreciated* substantially in little more than a decade. If you're one of the many Americans who tried to substitute equity in property for traditional forms of income savings, one financial specialist explains the unfortunate results pretty bluntly: your house "is a place to live, not a brokerage account."[60] If it's any consolation, you're not alone: a recent study by the Security Industries Association reports that, for many Americans, nearly half their net worth is based on the value of their home. Analysts fear that many of these people—a significant proportion of the baby-boom generation—won't be able to retire with the same standard of living that they've been enjoying during their wage-earning years.[61]

KEY TAKEAWAYS

- Personal saving suffered a steep decline from 1980 to 2005 and remained at this negligible savings rate until it started moving up in 2008. The recent increase in the savings rate, however, is still below the long-term average of 7 percent.

- In addition to Americans' tendency to spend rather than save, the Federal Reserve observed that a lot of people had come to rely on the appreciation of such assets as stocks and residential property as a substitute for the practice of saving out of wage income.

- **Subprime loans** are made to would-be home buyers who don't qualify for market-set interest rates because of one or more risk factors—income level, employment status, credit history, ability to make only a very low down payment. Interest rates may run from 8 percent to 10 percent and higher.

- An **adjustable-rate mortgage (ARM)** is a home loan pegged to the increase or decrease of certain interest rates that the lender has to pay. If those rates go up, the mortgage rate and the home buyer's monthly payments go up, too. A **fixed-rate mortgage** is a home loan on which the interest rate remains the same regardless of changes in market interest rates.

- In the years between 2001 and 2005, lenders made billions of dollars in subprime ARM loans to American home buyers. In 2006 and 2007, however, housing prices started to go down. Homeowners with subprime ARM loans weren't able to refinance, their mortgage rates began going up, and foreclosures became commonplace.

- In 2006 and 2007, largely because of mortgage-loan defaults, banks and other institutions that made mortgage loans began losing huge sums of money. These losses carried over to Fannie Mae and Freddie Mac, publicly traded government-sponsored organizations that make loans and provide loan guarantees to banks and other mortgage lenders.

- Next to be hit were major investment firms that had been buying subprime mortgages from banks and other original lenders, pooling the projected revenue—payments made by the original individual home buyers—and selling securities backed by the pooled revenue. When their rates went too high and home buyers couldn't make their house payments, these securities plummeted in value, and the investment banks and other institutions that had invested in them suffered significant losses.

- *Risk* is the possibility that cash flows will be variable. Three types of risk are related to the activities of various organizations that may be involved in your financial transactions:

  1. *Management risk* is the risk that poor management of an organization with which you're dealing may adversely affect the outcome of your personal-finances planning.
  2. *Business risk* is the risk associated with a product that you've chosen to buy.
  3. *Financial risk* refers to the risk that comes from ill-considered indebtedness.

Before going to the next chapter, take a few minutes to test your knowledge of the material covered in this section. Quizzes can be found under the "Resources" tab, "Study Aids: Quizzes."

EXERCISE

Write a report giving your opinion on how we got into the subprime mortgage crisis and how we got out of it.

---

6. CASES AND PROBLEMS

LEARNING ON THE WEB

Go to https://www.quizzle.com and request a free copy of your credit report. Review the report. If you identify any errors, get them fixed. Write a brief report explaining the value of good credit.

ETHICS ANGLE

Go online and read this article at *Forbes*: "Most Common Resume Lies," by Kate DuBose Tomassi at http://www.forbes.com/workspecial/2006/05/20/resume-lies-work_cx_kdt_06work_0523lies.html. View the slide show of common résumé lies. Answer these questions: What are the most common lies made in résumés? Why is it a bad idea to lie on such a document? What are the potential consequences of misstating facts on your résumé?

TEAM-BUILDING SKILLS

It's becoming more difficult for individuals to buy homes. This has meant that many people who would have bought a home have remained in apartments. In big cities, such as New York, sharing an apartment with roommates is a good way to save money. Yet it has some disadvantages. Get together as a team and identify the pros and cons of sharing housing. Pretend that each member of the group has agreed to share one apartment. Create a document that details each member's rights and responsibilities. Decide as a group whether the lease should be in one person's name or in all your names. Explain the pros and cons of both approaches.

THE GLOBAL VIEW

You're looking forward to taking a month-long vacation to Australia when you graduate from college in two years. Create a budget for this trip after researching likely costs. Determine how much you'll need for the trip and calculate how much you'd have to save each month to afford the trip.

ENDNOTES

1. This vignette is adapted from a series titled *USA TODAY's Financial Diet*, which ran in *USA Today* in 2005 (accessed April 26, 2014). Go to http://www.usatoday.com/money/perfi/basics/2005-04-14-financial-diet-excercise1_x.htm and use the embedded links to follow the entire series.

2. LaToya Irby, "10 Key Changes of the New Credit Card Rules," *About.com*, http://credit.about.com/od/consumercreditlaws/tp/new-credit-card-rules.htm (accessed April 26, 2014).

3. Emily Starbuck Gerson and Jeremy M. Simon, "10 Ways Students Can Build Good Credit," *CreditCards.com*, http://www.creditcards.com/credit-card-news/help/10-ways-students-get-good-credit-6000.php (accessed April 26, 2014).

4. Harriet Johnson Brackey, "Students Burdened by Overdraft Charges, Group Says," *Wisdom of the Rich Dad*, http://www.richdadwisdom.com/2007/12/students-burdened-by-overdraft-charges (accessed April 26, 2014).

5. Kathy Chu, "Debit Card Overdraft Fees Hit Record Highs," *USA Today*, January 24, 2007, http://www.usatoday.com/money/perfi/credit/2007-01-24-debit-card-fees_x.htm (accessed April 26, 2014).

6. Board of Governors of the Federal Reserve System, "What You Need to Know: Bank Account Overdraft Fees," http://www.federalreserve.gov/consumerinfo/wyntk_overdraft.htm (accessed April 26, 2014).

7. Connie Prater, "Consumers to Fed: Stop Debit Card Overdraft Opt-In 'Scare' Tactics: New Debit Card Overdraft Rules Slated to Start July 1, 2010," *CreditCards.com*, http://www.creditcards.com/credit-card-news/debit-card-overdraft-fee-opt-in-rules-1282.php (accessed April 26, 2014).

8. Fred O. Williams, "Average Credit Card Debt? Take Your Pick," CreditCards.com, July 8, 2011, http://www.creditcards.com/credit-card-news/average-credit_card_debt-1276.php (accessed February 26, 2014). As of February 2014, these cards carry an average interest rate of 13.14 percent, according to the Board of Governors of the Federal Reserve, "Consumer Credit—G.19," June 6, 2014, http://www.federalreserve.gov/releases/g19/current (accessed April 26, 2014).

9. U.S. Senator Ron Wyden, quoted in "Avoiding the Pitfalls of Credit Card Debt," Center for American Progress Action Fund, February 25, 2008, http://www.americanprogressaction.org/issues/regulation/news/2008/02/25/4031/avoiding-the-pitfalls-of-credit-card-debt (accessed April 26, 2014).

10. Joshua Lipton, "Choking On Credit Card Debt," *Forbes.com*, September 12, 2008, http://www.forbes.com/2008/09/12/credit-card-debt-pf-ii-in_jl_0911creditcards_inl.html (accessed April 26, 2014).

11. Joshua Lipton, "Choking On Credit Card Debt," *Forbes.com*, September 12, 2008, http://www.forbes.com/2008/09/12/credit-card-debt-pf-ii-in_jl_0911creditcards_inl.html (accessed April 26, 2014).

12. Financial planner Elissa Buie helped to develop *USA TODAY's Financial Diet*.

13. Marshall Loeb, "The High Cost of ATM Convenience," *Market Watch*, June 14, 2007, http://www.marketwatch.com/news/story/four-ways-keep-atm-fees/story.aspx?guid={EFB2C425-B7F8-40C4-8720-D684A838DBDA (accessed April 26, 2014).

14. Michael Arrington, "eBay Survey Says Americans Buy Crap They Don't Want," *TechCrunch*, August 21, 2008, http://techcrunch.com/2008/08/21/ebay-survey-says-americans-buy-crap-they-dont-want (accessed April 26, 2014).

15. Federal Reserve Bank of New York, *Quarterly Report on Household Debt and Credit*, November 2013, http://www.newyorkfed.org/householdcredit/2013-q3/data/pdf/HHDC_2013Q3.pdf (accessed April 26, 2014).

16. This section is based on Arthur J. Keown, *Personal Finance: Turning Money into Wealth*, 4th ed. (Upper Saddle River, NJ: Pearson Education, 2007), 8–11.

17. See Arthur J. Keown, *Personal Finance: Turning Money into Wealth*, 4th ed. (Upper Saddle River, NJ: Pearson Education, 2007), 11.

18. Pew Research Center, "The Rising Cost of Not Going to College," February 11, 2014, http://www.pewsocialtrends.org/2014/02/11/the-rising-cost-of-not-going-to-college (accessed April 26, 2014).

19. Adapted from U.S. Census Bureau, "One-Third of Young Women Have Bachelor's Degrees," *U.S. Department of Commerce*, http://www.census.gov/newsroom/releases/archives/education/cb08-10.html (accessed April 26, 2014).

20. Pew Research Center, "The Rising Cost of Not Going to College," February 11, 2014, http://www.pewsocialtrends.org/2014/02/11/the-rising-cost-of-not-going-to-college (accessed April 26, 2014).

21. Pew Research Center, "The Rising Cost of Not Going to College," February 11, 2014, http://www.pewsocialtrends.org/2014/02/11/the-rising-cost-of-not-going-to-college (accessed April 26, 2014).

22. See Katharine Hansen, "What Good Is a College Education Anyway?" *Quintessential Careers*, http://www.quintcareers.com/college_education_value.html (accessed April 26, 2014).

23. John G. Ramsay, Perlman Center for Learning and Teaching, quoted by Katharine Hansen, "What Good Is a College Education Anyway?" *Quintessential Careers*, http://www.quintcareers.com/college_education_value.html (accessed April 26, 2014).

24. Denise Witmer, "The Basics of Financial Aid for College," *About.com*, http://parentingteens.about.com/od/collegeinfo/a/financial_aid.htm (accessed April 26, 2014).

25. Federal Student Aid, "Federal Pell Grant," http://studentaid.ed.gov/types/grants-scholarships/pell (accessed April 26, 2014).

26. Susan Snyder, "College lending tight but available," *The Philadelphia Inquirer*, August 18, 2008, http://www.philly.com/inquirer/education/20080818_College_lending_tight_but_available.html (accessed April 26, 2014).

27. This section is based in part on sections 13 and 14 of the Playbook for Life by The Hartford. The Playbook can be found on line at http://http.vitalstreamcdn.com/hartford_vitalstream_com/main.html (accessed April 26, 2014).

28. Kim Isaacs, "Lying on Your Resume: What Are the Career Consequences?" *Inside Tech*, December 8, 2008, http://insidetech.monster.com/careers/articles/3574-lying-on-your-resume-what-are-the-career-consequences (accessed April 26, 2014)

29. See Timothy J. Gallager and Joseph D. Andrews Jr., *Financial Management: Principles and Practice*, 3rd ed. (Upper Saddle River, NJ: Prentice Hall, 2003), 34, 196.

30. This 10 percent interest rate is not realistic for today's economic environment. It's used for illustrative purposes only.

31. This 12 percent rate is unrealistic in today's economic environment. It's used for illustrative purposes only.

32. See Arthur J. Keown, *Personal Finance: Turning Money into Wealth*, 4th ed. (Upper Saddle River, NJ: Pearson Education, 2007), 23.

33. Jonathan Clements, quoted in "An Interview with Jonathan Clements—Part 2," *All Financial Matters*, February 10, 2006, http://allfinancialmatters.com/2006/02/10/an-interview-with-jonathan-clements-part-2 (accessed April 27, 2014).

34. Jack R. Kapoor, Les R. Dlabay, and Robert J. Hughes, *Personal Finance*, 8th ed. (New York: McGraw-Hill, 2007), 81.

35. See Bernard J. Winger and Ralph R. Frasca, *Personal Finance: An Integrated Planning Approach*, 6th ed. (Upper Saddle River, NJ: Prentice Hall, 2003), 57–58.

36. See Arthur J. Keown, *Personal Finance: Turning Money into Wealth*, 4th ed. (Upper Saddle River, NJ: Pearson Education, 2007), 22 et passim.

37. Sam Frizell, "Americans Are Taking On Debt at Scary High Rates," *Time*, February 19, 2014, http://time.com/8740/federal-reserve-debt-bankrate-consumers-credit-card (accessed April 27, 2014).

38. Robert H. Frank, "Americans Save So Little, but What Can Be Done to Change That?" *New York Times*, March 17, 2005, http://www.robert-h-frank.com/PDFs/ES.3.17.05.pdf (accessed April 27, 2014).

39. Don Taylor, "Two-Thirds of Americans Don't Save Enough," *Bankrate.com*, October 2007, http://www.bankrate.com/brm/news/retirement/Oct_07_retirement_poll_results_a1.asp (accessed November 11, 2011); Robert H. Frank, "Americans Save So Little, but What Can Be Done to Change That?" *New York Times*, March 17, 2005, http://www.robert-h-frank.com/PDFs/ES.3.17.05.pdf (accessed April 27, 2014).

40. Quoted by Marilyn Gardner, "Why Can't Americans Save a Dime?" *Christian Science Monitor* (2008), http://www.mrshultz.com/webpages/whycantamericanssave.htm (accessed April 27, 2014).

41. Rose M. Rubin, Shelley I. White-Means, and Luojia Mao Daniel, "Income Distribution of Older Americans," *Monthly Labor Review*, November 2000, http://www.bls.gov/opub/mlr/2000/11/art2full.pdf (accessed April 27, 2014).

42. Economic Research, Federal Reserve Bank of St. Louis, "Personal Savings Rate (PSAVERT)," August 28, 2008, http://research.stlouisfed.org/fred2/series/PSAVERT (accessed April 27, 2014); Andrea Dickson, "U.S. Personal Savings Rate Close to Depression-Era Rates," *Wisebread*, February 2, 2007, http://www.wisebread.com/u-s-personal-savings-rate-close-to-depression-era-rates (accessed April 27, 2014).

43. Sam Frizell, "Americans Are Taking On Debt at Scary High Rates," *Time*, February 19, 2014, http://time.com/8740/federal-reserve-debt-bankrate-consumers-credit-card (accessed April 27, 2014).

44. Federal Reserve Bank of San Francisco, "Spendthrift Nation," *Economic Research and Data*, November 10, 2005, http://www.frbsf.org/publications/economics/letter/2005/el2005-30.html (accessed April 27, 2014).

45. Associated Press, "How Severe Is Subprime Mess?" *MSNBC.com*, March 13, 2007, http://www.msnbc.msn.com/id/17584725/ns/business-real_estate/t/will-subprime-mess-ripple-through-economy/#.Tr2hFvKuI2I (accessed November 11, 2011).

46. "Subprime Mortgage Pricing Varies Greatly among U.S. Cities," *consumeraffairs.com*, September 13, 2005, http://www.consumeraffairs.com/subprime-lending-and-mortgages (accessed April 27, 2014).

47. Justin Lahart, "Egg Cracks Differ in Housing, Finance Shells," *Wall Street Journal*, July 13, 2008, http://online.wsj.com/article/SB119845906460548071.html?mod=googlenews_wsj (accessed April 14, 2014).

48. RealtyTrac Inc., "Foreclosure Activity Increases 4 Percent in April According to RealtyTrac(R) U.S. Foreclosure Market Report," news release, *PR Newswire*, May 14, 2008, http://www.prnewswire.com/news-releases/foreclosure-activity-increases-4-percent-in-april-according-to-realtytracr-us-foreclosure-ma (accessed April 14, 2014).

49. Mortgage Bankers Association, "Delinquencies and Foreclosures Increase in Latest MBA National Delinquency Survey," news release, September 5, 2008, http://www.mbaa.org/NewsandMedia/PressCenter/64769.htm (accessed April 27, 2014); Charles Duhigg, "Loan-Agency Woes Swell from a Trickle to a Torrent," *nytimes.com*, July 11, 2008, http://www.nytimes.com/2008/07/11/business/11ripple.html?ex=1373515200&en=8ad220403fcfdf6e&ei=5124&partner=permalink&expr (accessed April 27, 2014).

50. Federal Deposit Insurance Corporation, *Quarterly Banking Profile* (Fourth Quarter 2007), http://www.2.fdic.gov/qbp/2007dec/qbp.pdf (accessed September 25, 2008); FDIC, *Quarterly Banking Profile* (First Quarter 2008), http://www.2.fdic.gov/qbp/2008mar/qbp.pdf (accessed September 25, 2008).

51. Shawn Tully, "Wall Street's Money Machine Breaks Down," *Fortune, CNNMoney.com*, November 12, 2007, http://money.cnn.com/magazines/fortune/fortune_archive/2007/11/26/101232838/index.htm (accessed April 27, 2014).

52. See Greg Robb et al., "AIG Gets Fed Rescue in Form of $85 Billion Loan," *MarketWatch*, September 16, 2008, http://www.marketwatch.com/News/Story/aig-gets-fed-rescue-form/story.aspx?guid={E84A4797-3EA6-40B1-9DB5-F07B5A7F5BC2} (accessed April 27, 2014).

53. Mortgage Bankers Association, "Delinquencies and Foreclosures Increase in Latest MBA National Delinquency Survey," news release, September 5, 2008, http://www.mbaa.org/NewsandMedia/PressCenter/64769.htm (accessed April 27, 2014).

54. Financial Crimes Enforcement Network, *Mortgage Loan Fraud: An Industry Assessment Based upon Suspicious Activity Report Analysis*, November 2006, http://www.fincen.gov/news_room/rp/reports/pdf/MortgageLoanFraud.pdf (accessed April 27, 2014).

55. See Arthur J. Keown, *Personal Finance: Turning Money into Wealth*, 4th ed. (Upper Saddle River, NJ: Pearson Education, 2007), 253–54.

56. See esp. Arthur J. Keown et al., *Foundations of Finance: The Logic and Practice of Financial Management*, 6th ed. (Upper Saddle River, NJ: Pearson Education, 2008), 174.

57. This section is based on Bernard J. Winger and Ralph R. Frasca, *Personal Finance: An Integrated Planning Approach*, 6th ed. (Upper Saddle River, NJ: Prentice Hall, 2003), 250–51.

58. "Getting Worried Downtown," *Economist.com*, November 15, 2007, http://www.economist.com/world/unitedstates/displaystory.cfm?story_id=10134077 (accessed April 27, 2014).

59. David Streitfeld, "Bottom May Be Near for Slide in Housing," *The New York Times*, May 31, 2011, http://www.nytimes.com/2011/06/01/business/01housing.html (accessed April 27, 2014); Nadeem Walayat, "U.S. House Prices Forecast 2008–2010," *Market Oracle*, June 29, 2008, http://www.rnarketoracle.co.uk/Article5257.html (accessed April 27, 2014).

60. Sherman L. Doll, of Capital Performance Advisors, quoted by Amy Hoak, "Why a House Is Not a Piggy Bank to Tap Into for Your Retirement," *Wall Street Journal*, July 19, 2006, http://appraisalnewsonline.typepad.com/appraisal_news_for_real_e/2006/07/why_a_house_is_.html (accessed April 27, 2014).

61. Amy Hoak, "Why a House Is Not a Piggy Bank to Tap Into for Your Retirement," *Wall Street Journal*, July 19, 2006, http://appraisalnewsonline.typepad.com/appraisal_news_for_real_e/2006/07/why_a_house_is_.html (accessed April 27, 2014).

CHAPTER 15
Managing Information and Technology

A WINNING HAND FOR CAESARS

If you enjoy gambling and want to be pampered, the Las Vegas Strip is the place for you.[1] The four-mile stretch is home to some of the world's most lavish hotels and casinos, each competing for its share of the forty million visitors who pack the city each year.[2] The Strip is a smorgasbord of attractions. At the luxurious Mirage, you can witness the eruption of a seventy-foot volcano every quarter hour. The five-star Bellagio resort boasts a $300 million art collection (including Picassos and Van Goghs). There are star-studded shows, upscale retailers, and posh restaurants with award-winning chefs. You can relax at pools and spas or try your luck in the casinos.

So how does a gaming and entertainment company compete in this environment? If you've ever been to Las Vegas, you know that a lot of them erect mammoth, neon-bathed, brick-and-mortar casino-resorts. A few, however, do what Caesars did in the late 1990s: they invest heavily in technology and compete through the effective use of information. What kind of information? Marketers at Caesars collect information about the casino's customers and then use it to entice the same people to return. Does the strategy work? Caesars is the world's largest casino entertainment company in the world.[3]

Throughout this chapter, we'll discuss the information needs of Caesars's top executives, managers, and other employees. We'll examine the ways in which the company uses technology to collect data and process them into information that can be used at every level of the organization.

Caesars Entertainment, formerly called Harrah's Entertainment, has become an industry leader in the gaming and entertainment industry by effectively using technology.

© 2010 Jupiterimages Corporation

1. DATA VERSUS INFORMATION

LEARNING OBJECTIVES

1. Distinguish between data and information.
2. Define information system (IS), and identify the tasks of the information systems manager.
3. Identify the tasks handled by information managers.
4. Compare the information needs of top managers, middle managers, and first-line managers.
5. Describe the advantages of an enterprise resource planning (ERP) system.

By the time the company took the plunge and committed $100 million to marketing-related information technology (IT), Caesars had been collecting and storing data about customers for almost a decade. "While the company thought it important to collect customer information," recalls a senior marketing executive, "the problem was we had millions of customers to collect information on, but we had no systematic way of turning it into a marketing decision. We didn't know what to do with it." In other words, Caesars was collecting a lot of *data* but not necessarily any *information*. So what's the difference?

As an example, suppose that you want to know how you're doing in a particular course. So far, you've taken two 20-question multiple-choice tests. On the first, you got questions 8, 11, and 14 wrong; on the second, you did worse, missing items 7, 15, 16, and 19. The items that you got wrong are merely **data**—unprocessed facts. What's important is your total score. You scored 85 on the first exam and 80 on the second. These two numbers constitute **information**—data that have been processed, or turned into some useful form. Knowing the questions that you missed simply supplied you with some data for calculating your scores.

Now let's fast-forward to the end of the semester. At this point, in addition to taking the two tests, you've written two papers and taken a final. You got a 90 and 95 on the papers and a 90 on the final. You now have more processed data, but you still want to organize them into more useful information. What you want to know is your average grade for the semester. To get the information you want, you need yet more data—namely, the weight assigned to each graded item. Fortunately, you've known from day one that each test counts 20 percent, each paper 10 percent, and the final exam 40 percent. A little math reveals an average grade of 87.

Though this is the information you're interested in, it may be mere data to your instructor, who may want different information: an instructor who intends to scale grades, for example, will want to know the average grade for the entire class. You're hoping that the class average is low enough to push your average of 87 up from a B+ to an A– (or maybe even an A—it doesn't hurt to hope for the best). The moral of the story is that what constitutes *information* at one stage can easily become *data* at another: or, one person's information can be another person's data.

As a rule, you want information; data are good only for generating the information. So, how do you convert data into information that's useful in helping you make decisions and solve problems? That's the question we'll explore in the next section.

1.1 Information Systems

To gather and process data into information and distribute it to people who need it, organizations develop an **information system (IS)**—the combination of technologies, procedures, and people who collect and distribute the information needed to make decisions and coordinate and control company-wide activities. In most large organizations, the IS is operated by a senior management team that includes a **chief information officer (CIO)** who oversees information and telecommunications systems. There may also be a **chief technology officer** who reports to the CIO and oversees IT planning and implementation. As for **information managers**, their tasks include the following:

- Determining the information needs of members of the organization
- Collecting the appropriate data
- Applying technology to convert data into information
- Directing the flow of information to the right people

Differences in Information Needs

The job is complicated by the fact that information needs vary according to different levels, operational units, and functional areas. Consider, for instance, the information needs of managers at several levels:

- *Top managers* need information for planning, setting objectives, and making major strategic decisions.
- *Middle managers* need information that helps them allocate resources and oversee the activities under their control.
- *First-line managers* require information that helps them supervise employees, oversee daily operations, and coordinate activities.

Figure 15.1 illustrates a hypothetical hierarchy of information needs at Caesars. The president, for example, needs information to determine whether profitability is up or down or if the organization is facing any new competitive threats. At the vice-presidential level, executives need information that will help them in controlling and planning for specific areas of operations. The VP of casino operations, for example, might need to know which operations are most profitable—slots, table games, or other gaming activities. The VP of hotel operations might want to know whether room revenues are going up or down.

data

Unprocessed facts.

information

Data that have been processed or turned into some useful form.

information system (IS)

Computer system for gathering and processing data into information and distributing it to people who need it.

chief information officer (CIO)

Senior executive who oversees information and telecommunications systems.

chief technology officer

High-level executive who reports to the CIO and oversees information technology planning and implementation.

information manager

Manager with responsibility for determining the information needs of members of the organization and meeting those needs.

FIGURE 15.1 Information Needs and Flows

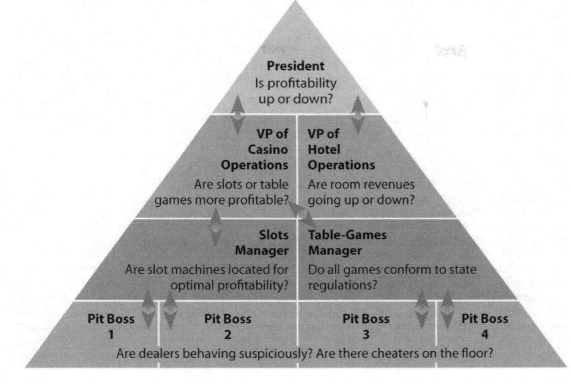

The information needs of middle-level and lower-level managers are different still. The slot-machine manager might want to know whether the placement of machines on the casino floor affects profitability. The poker manager might want to know whether all table games comply with state regulations. At a lower level, the pit manager (who's in charge of table games in a particular area) needs to know whether there's a card-counter at his blackjack table or whether a dealer's activities are suspicious.

Even at a given level, information needs can vary. A manager on the hotel side of the business, for instance, doesn't care much about profitability at the poker tables, while a pit manager doesn't have much use for hotel housekeeping reports. The reports that an accountant needs would hardly be the same as those needed by a human resources manager.

The Need to Share Information

Having stressed the differences in information needs, we should pause to remind ourselves that the managerial levels, operations, and functions of every organization are intertwined, to a greater or lesser degree. If you'll glance again at Figure 15.1, you'll be reminded that organizations need to share information, that information must flow, and that it must flow in both directions, bottom-up and top-down. At Caesars, for instance, both casino and hotel managers are concerned about security, which is also of interest to managers in different functional areas. Information supplied by the security group is obviously vital to managers in the gaming areas, but HR managers also need it to screen potential employees. Marketing information is clearly important to both casino and hotel operations: to maximize overall profits, the company uses marketing data to fill hotel rooms with customers who spend big in the casinos.[4]

Caesars's information needs entail more than allowing individuals in a given casino to share information; information has to be shared among all of Caesars's thirty-nine casinos. Thus, Caesars relies on an *integrated IT system* that allows real-time communication among all its properties. Installing the system (in the mid-1990s) was complicated, and not everyone in the organization liked the idea. Some managers felt that information sharing threatened their independence. Others, including some in the IT group, doubted that a large number of separate IT systems could be adequately integrated. To get everyone on board, John Bushy, then senior VP of information technology, pledged that he wouldn't cut his hair until the system was up and running. By the time it was operational in 1997, Bushy had hair down to his shoulders, but it was worth it: Caesars's ability to share real-time information across all its properties has been a major factor in the company's success. Caesars's new system cut costs by $20 million a year, increased brand recognition, and increased the number of customers playing at more than one Caesars property by 72 percent.[5]

Enterprise Systems

Many large and mid-size companies rely on a highly integrated system called an **enterprise resource planning (ERP) system** to channel information to multiple users. To understand what an ERP system does, forget about the P for *planning* (it really doesn't have much to do with planning) and the R for *resource* (it's an imprecise term). Focus on the E for *enterprise*.[6] An ERP system integrates the computer needs of all activities *across the enterprise* into a single system that serves all users. Such broad integration isn't a simple task, and you wouldn't be the first person to wonder whether it wouldn't be easier to give each department its own computer system. Salespeople, for example, need a system that tracks sales and generates sales reports. Meanwhile, manufacturing personnel don't need to track sales but do need to track inventory. What's the problem with stand-alone computer systems? Quite simply, users in various departments can't share information or communicate with each other.

What If You Don't Have ERP?

Imagine that you're a sales manager for a fairly large manufacturing company that produces and sells treadmills. Like every other department in the organization, you have your own computer system. A local sporting-goods store orders one hundred treadmills through a regional sales representative. It's your job to process the order. It wouldn't be much of a problem for you to go into your computer and place the order. But how would you know if the treadmills were actually in stock and when they could be delivered? How would you know if the customer's credit was any good? You could call the warehouse and ask if the treadmills are in stock. If they are, you'd tell the warehouse manager that you're placing an order and hope that the treadmills are still in stock by the time your order gets there two days later. While you're at it, you'd better ask for an expected delivery date. As a final precaution, you should probably call the finance department and ask about your customer's credit rating. So now you've done your job, and it can hardly be your fault that because the cost of manufacturing treadmills has gone up, accounting has recommended an immediate price increase that hasn't shown up in your computer system yet.

What If You Do Have ERP?

Wouldn't it be easier if you had an ERP system like the one illustrated in Figure 15.2—one that lets you access the same information as every other department? Then you could find out if there were one hundred treadmills in stock, the expected delivery date, your customer's credit rating, and the current selling price—without spending most of the day exchanging phone calls, e-mails, text messages, and faxes. You'd be in a better position to decide whether you can give your customer credit, and you could promise delivery (at a correct price) on a specified date. *Then*, you'd enter the order into the system. The information that you entered would be immediately available to everyone else. The warehouse would know what needs to be shipped, to whom, and when. The accounting department would know that a sale had been made, the dollar amount, and where to send the bill. In short, everyone would have up-to-date information, and no one would have to reinput any data.

FIGURE 15.2 ERP System

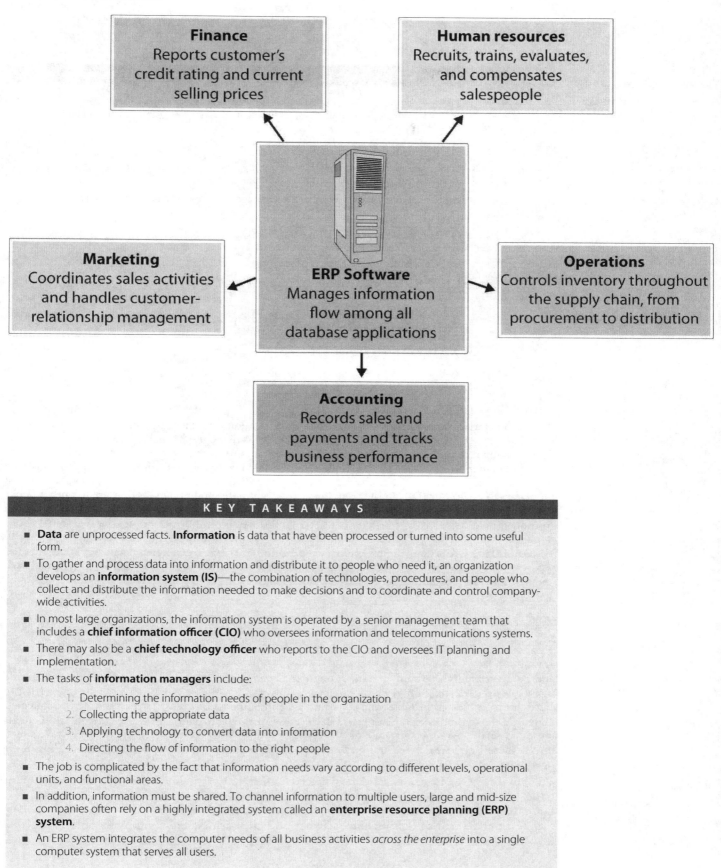

Before going to the next section of this chapter, take a few minutes to test your knowledge of the material covered in this section. Quizzes can be found under the "Resources" tab, "Study Aids: Quizzes."

EXERCISES

1. Using the college-application process as an example, explain the difference between *data* and *information*. Identify the categories of data that you supplied on your college application and the information generated from them by the admissions department.

2. Consider these three positions at Starbucks: retail store manager (in charge of the day-to-day operations at one store), district manager (responsible for the operations at multiple stores), and president of Starbucks North America (in charge of operations throughout the United States, Canada, and Mexico). Identify the information needs of managers at each level.

3. In what ways could a large automobile dealership, with a service shop and a body shop, benefit from an ERP system?

---

2. MANAGING DATA

LEARNING OBJECTIVES

1. **Explain how IS managers capture, store, and analyze data.**
2. **Explain the purpose of data mining.**

Did you ever think about how much data you yourself generate? Just remember what you went through to start college. First, you had to fill out application forms asking you about test scores, high school grades, extracurricular activities, and finances, plus demographic data about you and your family. Once you'd picked a college, you had to supply data on your housing preferences, the curriculum you wanted to follow, and the party who'd be responsible for paying your tuition. When you registered for classes, you gave more data to the registrar's office. When you arrived on campus, you gave out still more data to have your ID picture taken, to get your computer and phone hooked up, to open a bookstore account, and to buy an on-campus food-charge card. Once you started classes, data generation continued on a daily basis: your food card and bookstore account, for example, tracked your various purchases, and your ID tracked your coming and going all over campus. And you generated grades.

And all these data apply to just one aspect of your life. You also generated data every time you used your credit card and your cell phone. Who uses all these data? How are they collected, stored, analyzed, and distributed in organizations that have various reasons for keeping track of you?

2.1 Data and Databases

To answer such questions, let's go back to our Caesars example. As we've seen, Caesars collects a vast amount of data. Its hotel system generates data when customers make reservations, check in, buy food and beverages, purchase stuff at shops, attend entertainment events, and even relax at the spa. In the casino, customers apply for rewards programs, convert cash to chips (and occasionally chips back to cash), try their luck at the tables and slots, and get complimentary drinks. Then, there are the data generated by the activities of the company itself: employees, for instance, generate payroll and benefits data, and retail operations generate data every time they buy or sell something. Moreover, if we added up all these data, we'd have only a fraction of the amount generated by the company's gaming operations.

database

Electronic collection of related data accessible to various users.

How does Caesars handle all these data? First of all, it captures and stores them in several **databases**—electronic collections of related data that can be accessed by various members of the organization. Think of databases as filing cabinets that can hold massive amounts of organized information, such as revenues and costs from hotel activities, casino activities, and events reservations at each of Caesars facilities.

Warehousing and Mining Data

What if Caesars wants to target customers who generate a lot of revenue, by using a program designed to entice return visits? How would it identify and contact these people? Theoretically, it could search through the relevant databases—those that hold customer-contact information (such as name and address) and information about customer activity in the company's hotels, casinos, and entertainment venues. It would be a start, perhaps, but it wouldn't be very efficient. First of all, it would be time-consuming. Plus, what if the same data weren't stored in a similar fashion in each database? In that case, it would be quite hard to combine the data in a meaningful way. To address this problem, Caesars managers will rely on a system like the one illustrated in Figure 15.3, which calls for moving all the relevant data into a **data warehouse**—a centralized database in which data from several databases are consolidated and organized so that they can be easily analyzed.

data warehouse

Centralized database that stores data from several databases so they can be easily analyzed.

FIGURE 15.3 The Data Mining Process

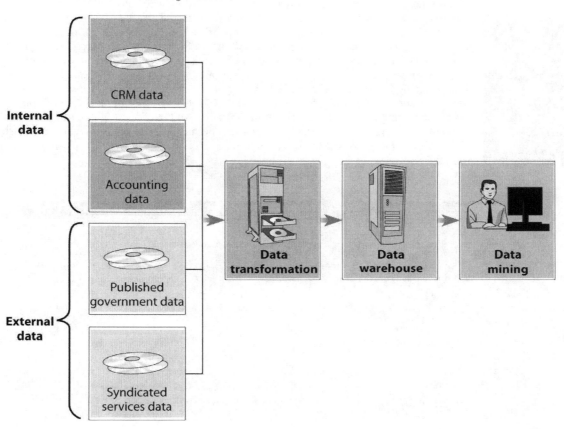

Data Mining

With the data in one central location, management can find out everything it needs to about a particular group of customers. It can also use the data to address some pretty interesting questions. Why do people come to our casinos? How can we keep customers coming back? How can we increase the number of visits per customer? How can we increase the amount they spend on each visit? What incentives (such as free dinners, hotel rooms, or show tickets) do our customers like most? To come up with answers to these questions, they'll perform a technique called **data mining**—the process of searching and analyzing large amounts of data to reveal patterns and trends that can be used to predict future behavior.

data mining

Technique used to search and analyze data to reveal patterns and trends that can be used to predict future behavior.

Data Mining and Customer Behavior

By data-mining its customer-based data warehouse, Caesars's management can discover previously unknown relationships between the general behavior of its customers and that of a certain group of customers (namely, the most profitable ones). Then, it can design incentives to appeal specifically to those people who will generate the most profit for the company.

To get a better idea of how data mining works, let's simplify a description of the process at Caesars. First, we need to know how the casino gathered the data to conduct its preliminary analysis. Most customers who play the slots use a Caesars player's card that offers incentives based on the amount of money that they wager on slot machines, video poker, and table games.[7] To get the card, a customer must supply some personal information, such as name, address, and phone number. From Caesars's standpoint, the card is extremely valuable because it can reveal a lot about the user's betting behavior: actual wins and losses, length of time played, preferred machines and coin denominations, average amount per bet, and—most important—the speed with which coins are deposited and buttons pushed.[8] As you can see from Figure 15.3, Caesars's primary data source was *internal*—generated by the company itself rather than provided by an outside source—and drew on a marketing database developed for *customer relationship management* (CRM).

FIGURE 15.4

Caesars collects data on its customers by using players' cards to gather information and to track betting behavior.

© 2010 Jupiterimages Corporation

What does the casino do with the data that it's mined? Caesars was most interested in "first trippers"—first-time casino customers. In particular, it wanted to know which of these customers should be enticed to return. By analyzing the data collected from player's-card applications and from customer's actual play at the casino (even if for no more than an hour), Caesars could develop a profile of a profitable customer. Now, when a first-timer comes into any of its casinos and plays for a while, Caesars can instantly tell whether he or she fits the profitable-customer profile. To lure these people back for return visits, it makes generous offers of free or reduced-rate rooms, meals, entertainment, or free chips (the incentive of choice for Caesars's preferred customers). These customers make up 26 percent of all Caesars's customers and generate 82 percent of its revenues. Surprisingly, they're not the wealthy high rollers to whom Caesars had been catering for years. Most of them are regular working people or retirees with available time and income and a fondness for slots. They generally stop at the casino on the way home from work or on a weekend night and don't stay overnight. They enjoy the thrill of gambling, and you can recognize them because they're the ones who can't push the button or pump tokens in fast enough.[9]

KEY TAKEAWAYS

- Organizations capture and store data in **databases**—electronic collections of related data that can be accessed by various people in the organization.
- To facilitate data analysis, IS managers may move data from various databases into a **data warehouse**—a centralized database in which data are consolidated and organized for efficient analysis.
- To come up with answers to a huge range of questions, managers perform a technique called **data mining**—the process of searching and analyzing large amounts of data to reveal patterns and trends that can be used to predict future behavior.

Before going to the next section of this chapter, take a few minutes to test your knowledge of the material covered in this section. Quizzes can be found under the "Resources" tab, "Study Aids: Quizzes."

EXERCISE

Caesars uses data mining to identify its most profitable customers and predict their future behavior. It then designs incentives to appeal specifically to these customers. Do you see any ethical problems with this process? Is it ethical to encourage people to gamble? Explain your answer.

3. TYPES OF INFORMATION SYSTEMS

As we saw earlier, different managers, operational units, and functional areas have different information needs. That's why organizations often tailor information systems to meet particular needs. Caesars's IT group, for example, developed the Player Contact System[10] to help its casino salespeople connect to top customers on a more personal basis. Working from a prioritized list of customer names displayed on a computer screen, the salesperson clicks on a name to view relevant information about the customer, such as background and preferred casino activities. There's even a printed script that can be used to guide the conversation. Such a system isn't very helpful, however, to middle or top-level managers, who need systems to help them carry out their oversight and planning responsibilities. To design marketing programs, for instance, marketing managers rely on summary information gleaned from a dedicated customer-relationship management system. Let's look at some of the widely available information systems designed to support people at the operational and upper-management levels.

3.1 Operations Support Systems

Operations support systems are generally used by managers at lower levels of the organization—those who run day-to-day business operations and make fairly routine decisions. They may be *transaction processing systems, process control systems,* or *design and production systems.*

Transaction Processing Systems

Most of an organization's daily activities are recorded and processed by its **transaction processing system,** which receives input data and converts them into output—information—intended for various users. Input data are called **transactions**—events that affect a business. A *financial transaction* is an economic event: it affects the firm's assets, is reflected in its accounting statements, and is measured in monetary terms. Sales of goods to customers, purchases of inventory from suppliers, and salaries paid to employees are all financial transactions. Everything else is a *nonfinancial transaction.* The marketing department, for example, might add some demographic data to its customer database. The information would be processed by the firm's transaction processing system, but it wouldn't be a financial transaction.

Figure 15.5 illustrates a transaction processing system in which the transaction is a customer's electronic payment of a bill. As you can see, transaction processing system output can consist not only of documents sent to outside parties (in this case, notification of payment received), but also of information circulated internally (in the form of reports), as well as of information entered into the database for updating.

operations support system

Information system used by lower-level managers to assist them in running day-to-day operations and making routine decisions.

transaction processing system

Information system used to record and process an organization's daily activities or transactions.

transactions

Financial and nonfinancial events that affect a business.

FIGURE 15.5 Transaction Processing System

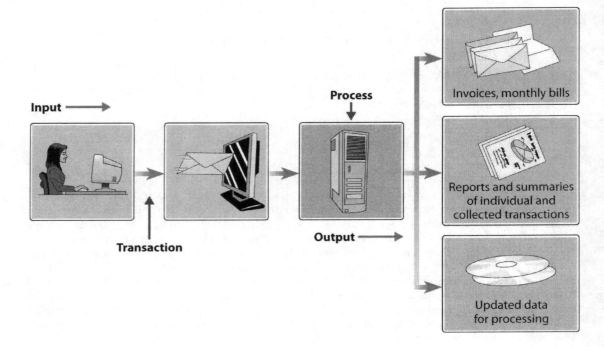

Process Control Systems

process control

Application of technology to monitor and control physical processes.

Process control refers to the application of technology to monitor and control physical processes. It's useful, for example, in testing the temperature of food as it's being prepared or gauging the moisture content of paper as it's being manufactured. Typically, it depends on sensors to collect data periodically. The data are then analyzed by a computer programmed either to make adjustments or to signal an operator.

Caesars uses process-control technology to keep customers happy. At any given point, some slot machines are down, whether because a machine broke or ran out of money or somebody hit the jackpot. All these contingencies require immediate attention by a service attendant. In the past, service personnel strolled around looking for machines in need of fixing. Now, however, a downed slot machine sends out an "I need attention" signal, which is instantly picked up by a monitoring and paging system called MessengerPlus and sent to a service attendant.

Design and Production Systems

As we saw in Chapter 11, modern companies rely heavily on technology to design and make products. **Computer-aided design (CAD)** software, for instance, enables designers to test computer models digitally before moving new products into the prototype stage. Many companies link CAD systems to the manufacturing process through **computer-aided manufacturing (CAM)** systems that not only determine the steps needed to produce components but also instruct machines to do the necessary work. A CAD/CAM system can be expanded by means of **computer-integrated manufacturing (CIM)**, which integrates various operations (from design through manufacturing) with functional activities ranging from order taking to final shipment. The CIM system may also control industrial robots—computer-run machines that can perform repetitive or dangerous tasks. A CIM system is a common element in a **flexible manufacturing system**, which makes it possible to change equipment setups by reprogramming computer-controlled machines that can be adapted to produce a variety of goods. Such flexibility is particularly valuable to makers of customized products.

3.2   Management Support Systems

Mid- and upper-level managers rely on a variety of information systems to support decision-making activities, including *management information systems, decision support systems, executive support systems,* and *expert systems.*

Management Information Systems

A **management information system** extracts data from a database to compile reports, such as sales analyses, inventory-level reports, and financial statements, to help managers make routine decisions. The type and form of the report depend on the information needs of a particular manager. At Caesars, for example, several reports are available each day to a games manager (who's responsible for table-game operations and personnel): a customer-analysis report, a profitability report, and a labor-analysis report.[11]

Decision Support Systems

A **decision support system** is an interactive system that collects, displays, and integrates data from multiple sources to help managers make nonroutine decisions. For example, suppose that a gaming company is considering a new casino in Pennsylvania (which has recently legalized slot machines). To decide whether it would be a wise business move, management could use a decision support system like the one illustrated in Figure 15.6. The first step is to extract data from internal sources to decide whether the company has the financial strength to expand its operations. From external sources (such as industry data and Pennsylvania demographics), managers might find the data needed to determine whether there's sufficient demand for a casino in the state. The decision support system will apply both types of data as variables in a quantitative *model* that managers can analyze and interpret. People must make the final decision, but in making sense of the relevant data, the decision support system makes the decision-making process easier—and more reliable.[12]

---

computer-aided design (CAD)

System using computer technology to create models representing the design of a product.

computer-aided manufacturing (CAM)

System using computer technology to control production processes and equipment.

computer-integrated manufacturing (CIM)

System in which the capabilities of a CAD/CAM system are integrated with other computer-based functions.

flexible manufacturing system

System in which computer-controlled equipment is programmed to handle materials used in manufacturing.

management information system

System used to extract data from a database and compile reports that help managers make routine decisions.

decision support system

Interactive system that extracts, integrates, and displays data from multiple sources to help managers make nonroutine decisions.

FIGURE 15.6 Decision Support System

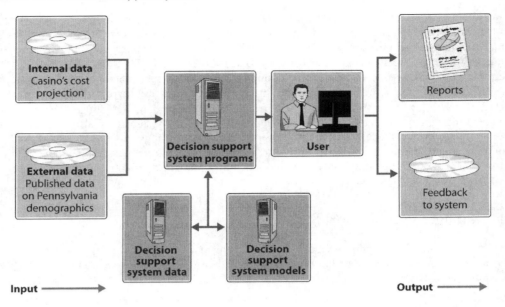

Executive Information Systems

As we observed in Chapter 6, senior managers spend a good deal of their time planning and making major decisions. They set performance targets, determine whether they're being met, and routinely scan the external environment for opportunities and threats. To accomplish these tasks, they need relevant, timely, easily understood information. Often, they can get it through an **executive information system**, which provides ready access to strategic information that's customized to their needs and presented in a convenient format. Using an executive information system, for example, a gaming-company executive might simply touch a screen to view key summary information that highlights in graphical form a critical area of corporate performance, such as revenue trends. After scanning this summary, our executive can "drill down" to retrieve more detailed information—for example, revenue trends by resort or revenue trends from various types of activities, such as gaming, hotel, retail, restaurant, or entertainment operations.

Artificial Intelligence

Artificial intelligence is the science of developing computer systems that can mimic human behavior. Ever since the term was coined in 1956, artificial intelligence has always seemed on the verge of being "the next big thing." Unfortunately, optimistic predictions eventually collided with underwhelming results, and many experts began to doubt that it would ever have profitable applications.[13] In the last two decades, however, some significant advances have been made in artificial intelligence—albeit in the area of game playing, where activities are generally governed by small sets of well-defined rules. But even the game-playing environment is sometimes complex enough to promote interesting developments. In 1997, for example, IBM's Deep Blue—a specialized computer with an advanced chess-playing program—defeated the world's highest-ranked player.[14]

More recently, several artificial intelligence applications have been successfully put to commercial use. Let's take a brief look at two of these: *expert systems* and *face-recognition technology*.

Expert Systems

Expert systems are programs that mimic the judgment of experts by following sets of rules that experts would follow. They're useful in such diverse areas as medical diagnosis, portfolio management, and credit assessment. For example, you've called the customer-service department of your credit card company because you want to increase your credit line. Don't expect to talk to some financial expert who's authorized to say yes or no. You'll be talking to a service representative with no financial expertise whatsoever. He or she will, however, have access to an expert system, which will give you an answer in a few seconds. How does it work? The expert system will prompt the representative to ask you certain questions about your salary and living expenses. It will also check internal corporate data to analyze your purchases and payment behavior, and, based on the results, it will determine whether you get an increase and, if so, how much.

At Caesars, an expert system called the Revenue Management System helps to optimize the overall profitability of both hotel and casino operations. When a customer requests a room, the program accesses his or her profile in the database and consults certain "rules" for assessing the application.[15] One rule, for example, might be, "If the customer has wagered more than $100,000 in the past year, add 10 points." Eventually, the system decides whether your application will be accepted (and at what rate) by adding up points determined by the rules. While a tightwad may not get a room even when there are vacancies, a high roller may get a good rate on a luxury suite even if the hotel is nearly full.

Systematic Review

Take a few minutes to complete an exercise that reinforces your understanding of seven different types of information-management systems.

Face-Recognition Technology

Caesars uses another particularly interesting, and sophisticated, application of artificial intelligence. In the hotel-casino business, it's crucial to identify and turn away undesirable visitors. One tool for this task is a digital camera-surveillance system that uses *face-recognition technology*. Using this technology, a program classifies a person's face according to the presence/absence or extent of certain unique features, such as dimpled chins, receding jaws, overbites, and long or short noses. If there's a match on, for example, fifteen features between a person being scanned and someone in the company database, a staff member decides whether the two people are the same. If a security manager then concludes that the face belongs to a skilled card-counter, the customer will be discouraged from playing blackjack; if it belongs to a known cheater, the individual will be escorted out of the casino. The system, however, does more than spot undesirables. It can also identify high rollers and send information about customers to managers on the floor. That's why a Caesars manager can greet a preferred customer at the door with his favorite drink and a personalized greeting, such as "Hi, Bill! How's Karen? Did you ever get that vintage Corvette? Here, have a gin rickey on the house."[16]

KEY TAKEAWAYS

- Information needs vary according to managerial level (top, middle, or first-line).
- An IS, or information system, can be divided into two categories:
  1. Those that meet the needs of low-level managers
  2. Those that meet the needs of middle- and upper-level managers
- Low-level managers—those who run day-to-day operations and make routine decisions—use **operations support systems**, which usually fall into three categories: transaction processing systems, process control systems, and computer-aided design software.
  1. Most daily activities are recorded and processed by a **transaction processing system**, which receives input data and converts them into output—information—intended for various users.
  2. **Process control** refers to the application of technology to monitor and control physical processes, such as food preparation. The system depends on sensors to collect data for analysis by a computer programmed either to make adjustments or to signal an operator.
  3. Technology can be used to design and make products. **Computer-aided design (CAD)** software, for instance, enables designers to test computer models digitally before moving new products into the prototype stage.
- Mid- and upper-level managers may use one of four types of **management support system** to assist in decision-making activities: management information systems, decision support systems, executive information systems, and expert systems.
  1. A **management information system** extracts data from a database to compile reports, such as sales analyses, needed for making routine decisions.
  2. A **decision support system** is an interactive system that collects and integrates data from multiple sources to assist in making nonroutine decisions.
  3. To develop plans and make major decisions, managers may gather relevant, timely, easily understood information through an **executive information system**; an EIS provides ready access to strategic information that's customized to their needs and presented in a convenient format.
  4. An **expert system** mimics expert judgment by following sets of rules that experts would follow; it relies on **artificial intelligence**—the science of developing computer systems that can mimic human behavior.

Before going to the next section of this chapter, take a few minutes to test your knowledge of the material covered in this section. Quizzes can be found under the "Resources" tab, "Study Aids: Quizzes."

EXERCISE

For each of the following situations, select the appropriate management support system to aid the user: decision support system, executive support system, or expert system. In each case, describe the management support system that you recommend.

- You're trying to identify a rash on your arm.
- You own two golf courses in the Northeast, and you're thinking about building one in Florida. You need to gather and analyze information about your current operations in the Northeast, as well as external information about the golf industry in Florida.
- You own three McDonald's franchises. Every morning, you want to know the revenues and costs at each store. You're also interested in a breakdown of revenues by product and costs by category of expense (salaries, food and ingredients, maintenance, and so on).

---

4. COMPUTER NETWORKS AND CLOUD COMPUTING

LEARNING OBJECTIVES

1. Describe the main systems for sharing information through networked computers.
2. Compare and contrast a local area network (LAN) and a wide area network (WAN).
3. Define cloud computing and identify its advantages and disadvantages.
4. Discuss these categories of cloud computing: software as a service (SaaS), infrastructure as a service (IaaS), and platform as a service (PaaS).

Once it's grown beyond just a handful of employees, an organization needs a way of sharing information. Imagine a flower shop with twenty employees. The person who takes phone orders needs access to the store's customer list, as do the delivery person and the bookkeeper. Now, the store may have one computer and everyone could share it. It's more likely, however, that there are a number of computers (several for salespeople, one for delivery, and one for bookkeeping). In this case, everyone needs to be sure that customer records have been updated on all computers every time that a change is required.

4.1 Networks

applications software

Software that performs a specific task, such as word processing or spreadsheet creation.

local area network (LAN)

Network that links computers that are in close proximity.

Likewise, many companies want their personal computers to run their own software and process data independently. But they also want people to share databases, files, and printers, and they want them to share **applications software** that performs particular tasks, including word processing, creating and managing spreadsheets, designing graphical presentations, and producing high-quality printed documents (*desktop publishing*).

The solution in both cases is *networking*—linking computers to one another. The two major types of networks are distinguished according to geographical coverage:

- A **local area network (LAN)** links computers that are in close proximity—in the same building or office complex. They can be connected by cables or by wireless technology. Your university might have a LAN system that gives you access to resources, such as registration information, software packages, and printers. Figure 15.7 illustrates a LAN that's connected to another network by means of a *gateway*—a processor that allows dissimilar networks to communicate with one another.

FIGURE 15.7 Local Area Network (LAN)

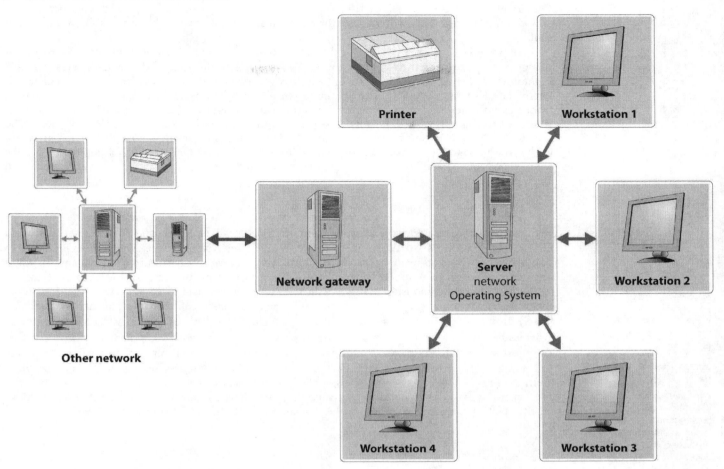

- Because a **wide area network (WAN)** covers a relatively large geographical area, its computers are connected by telephone lines, wireless technology, or even satellite.

Like the one in Figure 15.7, some networks are **client-server systems**, which include a number of client machines (the ones used by employees for data input and retrieval) and a server (which stores the database and the programs used to process the data). Such a setup saves time and money and circulates more-accurate information.

4.2 Cloud Computing

A cloud is a "visible mass of condensed water vapor floating in the atmosphere, typically high above the ground."[17] The term "**cloud computing**" means performing computer tasks using services provided over the Internet.[18] So how do you connect the two definitions? When IT professionals diagrammed computer systems, they used a cloud symbol to represent the Internet. So when you hear or read that an individual or company is using the "cloud" or technology firms, such as IBM, Hewlett-Packard, and Salesforce.com, are offering cloud services, just substitute the word "Internet" for "cloud" and things will make sense.

You might be surprised to learn that you're already using the cloud—that is if you use Facebook (which is very likely—in fact, just mentioning Facebook here might prompt you to stop studying and check out your friends' pages). How do you know that Facebook is a cloud application? Remember the trick: just substitute the word "Internet" for "cloud." The Facebook computer application lets you store information about yourself and share it with others using the Internet.

Business Applications

Think about the functional areas of business you've explored in this text: accounting, finance, human resources, management, marketing, operations, and product design. Now imagine you're Katrina Lane, senior vice president and chief technology officer for Caesars Entertainment, who is responsible for the information technology needed to handle multiple tasks in all these functional areas. You're sitting at

---

wide area network (WAN)

Network that links computers that are spread over a relatively large geographical area.

client-server system

System connecting client machines (which are used by employees for data input and retrieval) and a server (that stores shared databases and programs).

cloud computing

Cloud computing means performing computer tasks using services provided over the Internet.

your desk when Gary Loveman, chief executive officer of Caesars, walks in and gives you the news. Caesars just purchased the Planet Hollywood Casino and Resort in Las Vegas and will open up two new casinos in Ohio. This is good news for the company, but it means a lot of work for you and your staff.

You wonder whether this might be the time to outsource some of your computing tasks to a technology firm specializing in cloud computing. You remember an example that really makes sense:[19] Right now, whenever Microsoft comes out with a new version of Word, Caesars has to pay $350 per PC for the latest version. Wouldn't it make more sense to rent the use of the Microsoft Word program from a cloud vendor for say $5 a month (or $60 a year)? Given that the average time between new releases of Word is two years, your total cost per PC would be $120 (2 × $60)—a savings of about $230 per PC ($350 − $120). Your employees wouldn't mind; instead of working offline, they would just login to the Internet and work with their online version using the files that were saved for them. And the members of your IT staff would be pleased that they wouldn't need to install the new version of Word on all your PCs.

The As-A-Service Group

software as a service (SaaS)

The software as a service category of cloud computing gives companies access to a large assortment of software packages without having to invest in hardware or install and maintain software on its own computers.

infrastructure as a service (IaaS)

A technology firm offering infrastructure as a service provides users with hardware, including servers, central processing units, network equipment, and disk space.

platform as a service (PaaS)

Those offering the platform as a service category of cloud computing provide services that enable users to develop customized web applications.

Companies can contract for various cloud computing services. The Microsoft Word example discussed previously is classified as **software as a service (SaaS)**. This type of service gives companies access to a large assortment of software packages without having to invest in hardware or install and maintain software on its own computers. The available software, which includes e-mail and collaboration systems and customer relationship management programs, can be customized and used by an individual client or shared among several clients. A second type of service is called **infrastructure as a service (IaaS)**. Instead of providing users with software, a technology firm offering infrastructure as a service provides hardware, including servers, central processing units, network equipment, and disk space.[20] The most successful IaaS provider is Amazon Web Services.[21] The company rents computer power and storage to users who access their data via the Internet. The last as-a-service model is called **platform as a service (PaaS)**. Those offering platform as a service provide services that enable users to develop customized web applications. Because they don't have to start from scratch but rather build on existing platforms made available by the service provider, the web applications can be developed quickly.

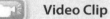

Video Clip

"Traditional business applications and platforms are too complicated and expensive. They need a data center, a complex software stack, and a team of experts to run them."

View the video online at: http://www.youtube.com/embed/ae_DKNwK_ms

Advantages and Disadvantages of Cloud Computing

In making your final decision (as the pretend chief technology officer for Caesars) you should consider these advantages and disadvantages of cloud computing:

Advantages

Shifting some of Caesars's IT functions to the cloud would produce a number of advantages:

1. *Cost Savings*—By "renting" software rather than buying it, Caesars can reduce its costs. The monthly fee to "use" the software is generally less than the combined cost of buying, installing, and maintaining the software internally. On the hardware site, housing Caesars's data in a service

provider's facilities, rather than in-house, reduces the large outlay of cash needed to build and maintain data centers.

2. *Speed of Delivery*—Purchasing and installing software and data processing equipment can be time consuming. A cloud computing service provider could get Caesars's applications up and running in only a few weeks.

3. *Scalable*—Caesars is constantly expanding both in the number of casinos it owns and geographically. In this ever-changing environment, it's difficult to gauge the level of our technology needs. If we overestimate our requirements, we end up paying for technology we don't need. If we underestimate, efficiency goes down, and the experience for our customers diminishes. By using cloud computing we are able to have exactly what we need at our disposal at any point in time.

4. *Employees Can Be Mobile*—The use of cloud computing will free workers from their desks and allow them to work wherever they are. As applications move to the cloud, all that is needed for our employees to connect to their "offices" is the Internet. This mobility benefit also makes it easier for employees to collaborate on projects and connect with others in the company.

5. *Information Technology Staff*—Although our current staff is extremely qualified and dedicated, finding experienced and knowledgeable staff is a continuing problem particularly in the casino industry which suffers from historically high turnover. By using cloud computing, we reduce our human resource needs by shifting some of our work to outside vendors who are able to hire and keep well qualified individuals (in part because IT professionals enjoy working for technology companies).

Disadvantages

Although the advantages of moving to a cloud environment outnumber the disadvantages, the following disadvantages are cause for concern:

1. *Disruption in Internet Service*—If Caesars moves some of its applications to the cloud, its employees can work on these applications on any device and in any location as long as they have an Internet connection. But what if the Internet is unavailable because of a disruption? Depending on the length of the disruption, this could create serious problems for Caesars.

2. *Security*—Many companies are reluctant to trust cloud service providers with their data because they're afraid it might become available to unauthorized individuals or criminals. This is a particular problem for Caesars, which collects and stores sensitive client information and has to constantly be on the lookout for fraudulent activity of staff and customers.[22]

3. *Service Provider System Crash*—Organizations considering moving to the cloud are justifiably concerned about the possibility of a computer service crash at their service providers' facilities. It looks like this concern was warranted. In April of 2011, Amazon Web Service (a leading cloud services provider) experienced an outage in one of its large web-connected data centers. The outage crashed its system and brought down the Web sites of a number of companies, including the location-based social network, Foursquare.[23] It took more than thirty-six hours to get all seventy or so of the crashed sites up and running.

Go or No Go?

So, pretend chief technology officer for Caesars, what's your decision: will you get on the cloud or stay on the ground? If you are curious about what the real chief technology officer did, she took the high road and transferred a number of applications to Salesforce.com's Web-based Force.com's cloud applications service.[24]

KEY TAKEAWAYS

- Once an organization has grown to more than a few employees, it needs to network individual computers to allow them to share information and technologies.
- A **client-server system** links a number of client machines (for data input and retrieval) with a server (for storing the database and the programs that process data).
- Many companies want personal computers to run their own software and process data independently.
- But they also want individuals to share databases, files, printers, and **applications software** that perform particular types of work (word processing, creating and managing spreadsheets, and so forth).
- There are two systems that can satisfy both needs.

    1. A **local area network (LAN)** links computers in close proximity, connecting them by cables or by wireless technology.
    2. A **wide area network (WAN)** covers a relatively large geographical area and connects computers by telephone lines, wireless technology, or satellite.

- The term "**cloud computing**" means performing computer tasks using services provided over the Internet.
- The **software as a service (SaaS)** category of cloud computing gives companies access to a large assortment of software packages without having to invest in hardware or install and maintain software on its own computers.
- A technology firm offering **infrastructure as a service** provides users with hardware, including servers, central processing units, network equipment, and disk space.
- Those offering the **platform as a service** category of cloud computing provide services that enable users to develop customized web applications.
- Shifting IT functions to the cloud produces a number of advantages, including cost savings, speedy delivery of software, scalability (you pay for only what you need), employee mobility, and a reduction in information technology staff.
- The following disadvantages of cloud computing are cause for concern: disruption in internet service, security issues, and unreliability of service provider systems.

Before going to the next section of this chapter, take a few minutes to test your knowledge of the material covered in this section. Quizzes can be found under the "Resources" tab, "Study Aids: Quizzes."

EXERCISES

1. What's the difference between a LAN and a WAN? Give an example of the use to which each type of system can be put. Does your college maintain either type of computer network?
2. In what ways could your college benefit from cloud computing? In responding, consider the three types of services offered by cloud service providers: software as a service, infrastructure as a service, and platform as a service. What type of security issues might your college administrators be concerned with?

5. DATA COMMUNICATIONS NETWORKS

LEARNING OBJECTIVES

1. Explain how four networking technologies—the Internet, the World Wide Web, intranets, and extranets—make data communication possible.
2. Identify and discuss reasons why businesses use the Internet.
3. Determine the difference between the Internet, an intranet, and an extranet.

In addition to using networks for information sharing within the organization, companies use networks to communicate and share information with those outside the organization. All this is made possible by **data communication networks**, which transmit digital data (numeric data, text, graphics, photos, video, and voice) from one computer to another using a variety of wired and wireless communication channels. Let's take a closer look at the networking technologies that make possible all this electronic communication—in particular, the *Internet* (including the *World Wide Web*), *intranets*, and *extranets*.

data communication network

Large network used to transmit digital data from one computer to another using a variety of wired and wireless communication channels.

5.1   The Internet and the World Wide Web

Though we often use the terms *Internet* and *World Wide Web* interchangeably, they're not the same thing. The **Internet** is an immense global network comprising smaller interconnected networks linking millions of computers around the world. Originally developed for the U.S. military and later adapted for use in academic and government research, the Internet experienced rapid growth in the 1990s, when companies called **Internet service providers** were allowed to link into the Internet infrastructure in order to connect paying subscribers. Today, Internet service providers, such as Comcast and Verizon, enable us to use the Internet to communicate with others through e-mail, texting, instant messaging, online conferencing, and so on. These services also connect us with third-party providers of information, including news stories, stock quotes, and magazine articles.

Internet

Global network comprising smaller interconnected networks linking millions of computers around the world.

Internet service providers

Company, such as America Online, that links into the Internet infrastructure to connect paying subscribers.

The **World Wide Web** (or simply "the Web") is just a portion of the Internet—albeit a large portion. The Web is a subsystem of computers that can be accessed on the Internet using a special protocol, or language, known as *hypertext transfer protocol* (HTTP). What's the difference between the Internet and the Web? According to Tim Berners-Lee (one of the small team of scientists who developed the concept for the Web in 1989), the Internet is a network of networks composed of cables and computers. You can use it to send "packets" of information from one computer to another, much like sending a postcard. If the address on the packet is accurate, it will arrive at the correct destination in much less than a second. Thus, the Internet is a packet-delivery *service* that delivers such items as e-mail messages all over the globe. The Web, by contrast, is composed of *information*—documents, pictures, sounds, streaming videos, and so on. It's connected not through cables, but rather through *hypertext links* that allow users to navigate between resources on the Internet.[25]

World Wide Web

Subsystem of computers on the Internet that communicate with each other using a special language called HTTP.

Because it's driven by programs that communicate between computers connected to the Internet, the Web couldn't exist without the Internet. The Internet, on the other hand, could exist without the Web, but it wouldn't be nearly as useful. The Internet itself is enormous, but it's difficult to navigate, and it has no pictures, sounds, or streamed videos. They exist on computers connected to the Web, which also makes it much easier to retrieve information. The creation of Web **browsers**—software, such as Microsoft's Internet Explorer and Netscape Navigator, that locates and displays Web pages—opened up the Internet to a vast range of users. Almost 80 percent of individuals in the United States use the Internet regularly.[26] So, who's in charge of the Web? No one owns it, but an organization called the World Wide Web Consortium (W3C) oversees the development and maintenance of standards governing the way information is stored, displayed, and retrieved on it.[27]

browsers

Software (such as Internet Explorer) that locates and displays Web pages.

The Technology of the Web

FIGURE 15.8 Google

Tsunami Alert for New Zealand, the Philippines, Indonesia, Papua New Guinea, Hawaii, and others. Waves expected over the next few hours, caused by 8.9 earthquake in Japan.

Advertising Programs   Business Solutions   About Google   **Go to Google Danmark**

© 2011 - Privacy

Web server

Computer that retrieves Web pages.

search engine

Software program that scans Web pages for specified keywords and provides a list of documents containing them.

Let's look a little more closely at some of the technologies that enable us to transmit and receive data over the Web. Documents on the Web are called *Web pages*, and they're stored on *Web sites*. Each site is maintained by a *Webmaster* and opens with a *home page*. Each Web page is accessed through a unique address called a *uniform resource locator (URL)*. For example, if you want to find statistics on basketball star LeBron James, you could type in the URL address http://www.nba.com/playerfile/ lebron_james/career_stats.html. The prefix *http://* is the protocol name, *http://www.nba.com* the domain name, *playerfile* the subdirectory name, and *lebron_james/career_stats* the document name (or Web page). A computer that retrieves Web pages is called a **Web server**. A **search engine** is a software program that scans Web pages containing specified keywords and provides a list of documents containing them. The most popular search engine is Google; others include Bing and Yahoo!

5.2 Intranets and Extranets

intranet

Private network using Internet technologies that are available only to employees.

firewall

Software program that controls access to a company's intranet.

extranet

Intranet that's partially available to certain parties outside the organization.

What's the difference among the Internet, an intranet, and an extranet? It depends on who can and can't access the information on the network. The Internet is a public network that anyone can use. A company's **intranet**, on the other hand, is a private network using Internet technologies that's available only to employees; access is controlled by a software program called a **firewall**. The information available on an intranet varies by company but may include internal job postings, written company policies, and proprietary information, such as price lists meant for internal use only.

An **extranet** is an intranet that's partially available to certain parties outside the organization. Say, for example, you've posted the following information on your intranet: company policies, payroll and benefit information, training programs, parts specifications and inventories, and production schedules. To allow suppliers to bid on contracts, you might give them access to sections of the site disclosing parts specifications, inventories, and production schedules. All other sections would be off limits. You'd control access to employee-only and supplier-accessible sections by means of usernames and passwords. As you can see from Figure 15.9, which illustrates some of the connections made possible by an extranet, access can be made available to customers and business partners, as well.

FIGURE 15.9 How an Extranet Works

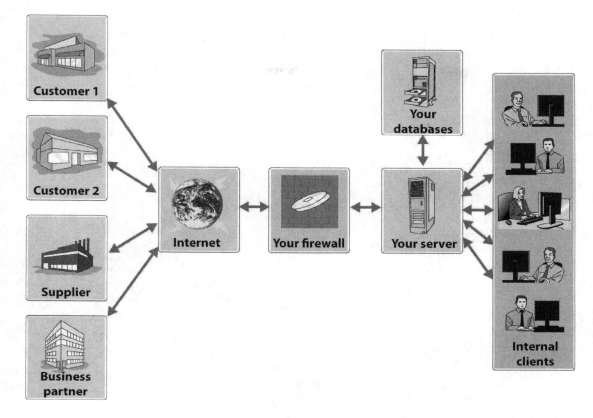

5.3   E-Commerce

The level of **e-commerce**—conducting business over the Internet—varies by company. Some companies, such as Amazon.com, rely on the Internet for their existence. Others, especially smaller firms, have yet to incorporate the Internet into their business models, but these companies belong to a dwindling group: about half of small companies and 90 percent of large companies have Web sites, and a third of the companies that maintain Web sites sell products through them.[28]

Why Business Uses the Internet

Businesses use the Internet for four purposes: presenting information, selling products, distributing digital products, and acquiring goods and services.

1. *Presenting information.* By posting a Web site, a company can tell people about itself, its products, and its activities. Customers can also check the status of orders or account balances. Information should always be current, complete, and accurate. Customers should be able to find and navigate the site, which should be able to accommodate them during high-use periods.

2. *Selling products.* Selling over the Internet—whether to individuals or to other businesses—enables a business to enlarge its customer base by reaching buyers outside its geographical area. A company selling over the Internet must attract customers to its site, make the buying process simple, assure customers that the site is secure, and provide helpful information.

3. *Distributing digital products.* Some companies use the Internet to sell and deliver such digital products as subscriptions to online news services, software products and upgrades, and music and video products. In these businesses, the timely delivery of products is crucial. Sales of digital products over the Internet are expected to increase substantially in the future, particularly sales of digital music.[29]

4. *Acquiring goods and services.* E-purchasing (which was introduced in Chapter 11 "Operations Management in Manufacturing and Service Industries") saves time, speeds up delivery, reduces administrative costs, and fosters better communications between a firm and its suppliers. Most importantly, it cuts the costs of purchased products because it's now feasible for buyers to request competitive bids and do comparative shopping. Many companies now use a technology called **electronic data interchange** to process transactions and transmit purchasing documents directly from one IS to another. Figure 15.10 shows an electronic data interchange system at a

e-commerce

Business conducted over the Internet.

electronic data interchange

Computerized exchange of business transaction documents.

company that subscribes to a *value-added network*—a private system supplied by a third-party firm—over which it conducts a variety of transactions.

FIGURE 15.10 Electronic Data Interchange System and Value-Added Networks

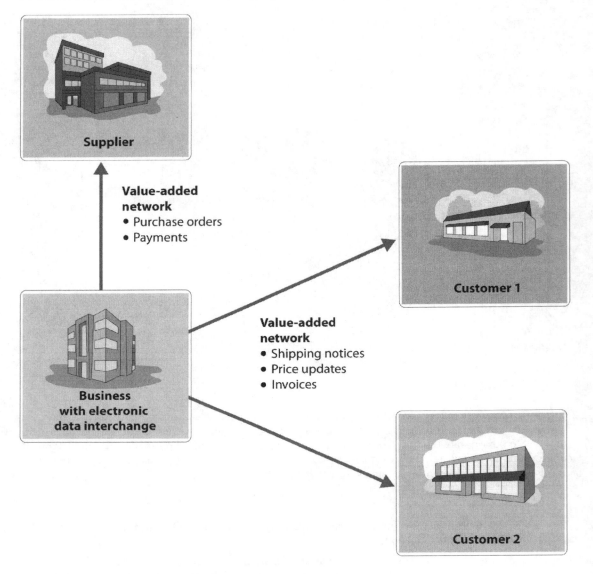

The Virtual Company

Imagine a company that retails products for schoolteachers over the Internet—for example, books, software, and teaching supplies purchased from various manufacturers and distributors. It would need facilities to store inventories and personnel to handle inventories and fill customer orders. But what if this company decided to get out of the traditional retail business? What if it decided instead to team up with three trading partners—a book publisher, a software developer, and a manufacturer of office supplies? Our original company could re-create itself as a Web site for marketing the books, software, and supplies provided by its partners, without taking physical possession of them. It would become a **virtual company**. Its partners would warehouse their own products and furnish product descriptions, prices, and delivery times. Meanwhile, the virtual company, besides promoting all three lines of products, would verify customer orders and forward them to its partners, who would ship their own products directly to customers. All four partners would be better off, because they'd be competing in a business in which none of them could compete by itself. This business approach has allowed Spun.com, a CD, DVD, and game Internet retailer, to avoid carrying the $8 million inventory that it would have needed to support its sales. Rather than hold its own inventory, Spun.com merely passes the orders on to Alliance Entertainment (a home entertainment products wholesale distributor), which ships them directly to customers.[30]

KEY TAKEAWAYS

- **Data communication networks** transmit digital data from one computer to another computer using a variety of wired and wireless communication channels.
- One such network, the **Internet**, is an immense global network of smaller interconnected networks linking millions of computers.
- By connecting paying subscribers into the Internet infrastructure, a company called an **Internet service provider** provides services, such as e-mail, online conferencing, and instant messaging.
- A large portion of the Internet, the **World Wide Web** ("the Web"), is a subsystem of computers that can be accessed by means of a special protocol known as *hypertext transfer protocol (HTTP)*.
- Computers on the Web are connected with **hypertext links** that permit users to navigate among Internet resources.
- A Web **browser** is software that locates and displays Web pages.
- Though the Web couldn't exist without the Internet, it's the Web that provides such multimedia material as pictures, sounds, and streaming videos.
- Businesses use the Internet for four purposes: presenting information, selling products, acquiring goods and services, and distributing digital products.
- While the Internet is a public network that anyone can use, a company's **intranet** is a private network that's available only to its employees; access is controlled by a software program called a *firewall*.
- An **extranet** is an intranet that's partially available to certain outside parties, such as suppliers.

Before going to the next section of this chapter, take a few minutes to test your knowledge of the material covered in this section. Quizzes can be found under the "Resources" tab, "Study Aids: Quizzes."

EXERCISES

1. If asked by your instructor, how would you explain the difference between the Internet and the World Wide Web?
2. Identify ten specific ways in which your college uses the Internet.

6. SECURITY ISSUES IN ELECTRONIC COMMUNICATION

LEARNING OBJECTIVES

1. **Identify and discuss challenges faced by companies engaged in e-commerce, particularly in the area of security.**
2. **Explain what a firewall does.**
3. **Identify illegal activities companies face when conducting business over the Internet.**
4. **Explain how encryption is accomplished.**
5. **Identify the purpose of a certificate authority.**

E-commerce has presented businesses with opportunities undreamt of only a couple of decades ago. But it also has introduced some unprecedented challenges. For one thing, companies must earmark a substantial portion of their information technology budgets for protecting themselves against disrupted operations and theft due to computer crime and sabotage. The costs resulting from cyber-crimes—criminal activity done using computers or the Internet—are substantial and increasing at an alarming rate. The "2013 Cost of Cyber Crime Study" reports that cybercrime attacks doubled during the last four years while the cost of these crimes rose by nearly 78 percent. The companies in its sample experienced more than one hundred cyberattacks a year at an average cost per company of $12 million.

Some unfortunate companies, such as Target, have suffered costs considerably higher than that average.[31] In December 2013, a group of criminals gained access to Target's database and stole debit and credit card information belonging to forty million people. Consumers were afraid their financial information (which was likely sold in the underground market) would be used by others and were, therefore, afraid to shop at Target. This resulted in a 46 percent decline in profits at Target during the critical holiday season. The company was under fire by consumer groups and lawyers representing banks that suffered losses due to credit card fraud. It's too early to tally up the cost to Target of the "holiday" cyberattack, but it's estimated by some at $1 billion.[32]

It is common to worry about cybercrime when buying something online from Internet companies such as Amazon, Overstock.com, or eTrade (an online discount stock brokerage service), but it is argued that the brick-and-mortar (physical) stores such as Target are more susceptible to cybercrime than the Internet companies. Why might this be true? One reason is that the Internet companies stake their reputations on being very careful with their customers' financial information. Another reason is that cybercriminals can get a lot more financial information from a brick-and-mortar computer system than from an Internet computer system. Internet companies often collect credit card information only, whereas brick-and-mortar companies capture additional financial information from its customers, such as social security numbers, household incomes, and so on.[33]

The cost of cybercrime in the United States was recently estimated at $100 billion.[34] Most of these costs are absorbed by U.S. businesses, who either accept lower profits or push up prices to cover these added costs. In addition to protecting their own operations from computer crime, companies engaged in e-commerce must clear another hurdle: they must convince consumers that it's safe to buy things over the Internet—that credit card numbers, passwords, and other personal information are protected from theft or misuse. In this section, we'll explore some of these challenges and describe a number of the efforts being made to meet them.

6.1   Data Security

In some ways, life was simpler for businesspeople before computers. Records were produced by hand and stored on paper. As long as you were careful to limit access to your records (and remembered to keep especially valuable documents in a safe), you faced little risk of someone altering or destroying your records. In some ways, storing and transmitting data electronically is a little riskier. Let's look at two data-security risks associated with electronic communication: *malicious programs* and *spoofing*.

Malicious Programs

Some people get a kick out of wreaking havoc with computer systems by spreading a variety of destructive programs. Once they're discovered, they can be combated with antivirus programs that are installed on most computers and that can be updated daily. In the meantime, unfortunately, they can do a lot of damage, bringing down computers or entire networks by corrupting operating systems or databases.

Viruses, Worms, and Trojan Horses

The cybervandal's repertory includes "viruses," "worms," and "Trojan horses." Viruses and worms are particularly dangerous because they can copy themselves over and over again, eventually using up all available memory and closing down the system. Trojan horses are viruses that enter your computer by posing as some type of application. Some sneak in by pretending to be virus-scanning programs designed to rid your computer of viruses. Once inside, they do just the opposite.

Viruses that can spread rapidly from computer to computer create enormous damage. It's estimated, for example, that damage to 50,000 personal computers and corporate networks from the so-called Blaster worm in August 2003 totaled $2 billion, including $1.2 billion paid by Microsoft to correct the problem.[35]

Spoofing

It's also possible for unauthorized parties to gain access to restricted company Web sites—usually for the purpose of doing something illegal. Using a technique called "spoofing," culprits disguise their identities by modifying the address of the computer from which the scheme has been launched. Typically, the point is to make it look as if an incoming message has originated from an authorized source. Then, once the site's been accessed, the perpetrator can commit fraud, spy, or destroy data. You could, for example, spoof a manufacturing firm with a false sales order that seems to have come from a legitimate customer. If the spoof goes undetected, the manufacturer will incur the costs of producing and delivering products that were never ordered (and will certainly never be paid for).

Every day, technically savvy thieves (and dishonest employees) steal large sums of money from companies by means of spoofing or some other computer scheme. It's difficult to estimate the dollar amount because many companies don't even know how much they've lost.

6.2   Revenue Theft

In addition to the problems of data security faced by every company that stores and transmits information electronically, companies that sell goods or provide services online are also vulnerable to activities that threaten their revenue sources. Two of the most important forms of computer crime are *denial of service* and *piracy*.

Denial of Service

A denial-of-service attack does exactly what the term suggests: it prevents a Web server from servicing authorized users. Consider the following scenario. Dozens of computers are whirring away at an online bookmaker in the offshore gambling haven of Costa Rica. Suddenly a mass of blank incoming messages floods the company's computers, slowing operations to a trickle. No legitimate customers can get through to place their bets. A few hours later, the owner gets an e-mail that reads, "If you want your computers to stay up and running through the football season, wire $40,000 to each of 10 numbered bank accounts in Eastern Europe."

You're probably thinking that our choice of online gambling as an example of this scheme is a little odd, but we chose it because it's real: many companies in the online-gambling industry suffer hundreds of such attacks each year.[36] Because most gambling operations opt to pay the ransom and get back to business as usual, denial of service to businesses in the industry has become a very lucrative enterprise.

Online gambling operations are good targets because they're illegal in the United States, where they can't get any help from law-enforcement authorities. But extortionists have been known to hit other targets, including Microsoft and the Recording Industry Association of America. The problem could become much more serious if they start going after e-commerce companies and others that depend on incoming orders to stay afloat.

Piracy

Technology makes it easier to create and sell intellectual property, but it also makes it easier to steal it. Because digital products can be downloaded and copied almost instantly over the Internet, it's a simple task to make perfect replicas of your favorite copyright-protected songs, movies, TV shows, and computer software, whether for personal use or further distribution. When you steal such materials, you're cheating the countless musicians, technicians, actors, programmers, and others involved in creating and selling them. Theft cuts into sales and shrinks corporate profits, often by staggering amounts. Entertainment-industry analysts estimate that $30 billion worth of songs were illegally downloaded in the five year period ending in 2009.[37] The software industry estimates that the global market for pirated software reached $59 billion in 2010.[38]

So, what's being done to protect the victimized companies? Actually, quite a lot, even though it's a daunting task, both in the United States and abroad.[39] In 1998, Congress passed the Digital Millennium Copyright Act, which outlaws the copying of copyright-protected music (unless you're copying legally acquired music for your own use). The penalties are fairly stiff: up to three years in prison and $250,000 in fines.[40] To show that it means business, the music industry is also hauling offenders into court, but legal action is costly and prosecuting teenage music lovers doesn't accomplish much. Some observers believe that the best solution is for the industry to accelerate its own efforts to offer its products online.[41] Initial attempts seem to be working: people who are willing to obey copyright laws have downloaded more than ten billion songs from the iTunes site alone.[42]

Firewalls

Builders install firewalls (or fireproof walls) in structures to keep a fire that starts in one part of a building from entering another part. Companies do something similar to protect their computer systems from outside intruders: they install virtual firewalls—software and hardware systems that prevent unauthorized users from accessing their computer networks.

You can think of the firewall as a gatekeeper that stands at the entry point of the company's network and monitors incoming and outgoing traffic. The firewall system inspects and screens all incoming messages to prevent unwanted intruders from entering the system and causing damage. It also regulates outgoing traffic to prevent employees from inappropriately sending out confidential data that shouldn't leave the organization.

Who Does the Most Hacking?

Have any of your accounts been hacked? Did you ever wonder what a profile of a hacker would look like? Take this exercise and find out.

6.3 Risks to Customers

Many people still regard the Internet as an unsafe place to do business. They worry about the security of credit card information and passwords and the confidentiality of personal data. Are any of these concerns valid? Are you really running risks when you shop electronically? If so, what's being done to make the Internet a safer place to conduct transactions? Let's look a little more closely at the sort of things that tend to bother some Internet users (or, as the case may be, nonusers), as well as some of the steps that companies are taking to convince people that e-commerce is safe.

credit card Theft

One of the more serious barriers to the growth of e-commerce is the perception of many people that credit card numbers can be stolen when they're given out over the Internet. Though virtually every company takes considerable precautions, they're not entirely wrong. Cybercriminals, unfortunately, seem to be tirelessly creative. One popular scheme involves setting up a fraudulent Internet business operation to collect credit card information. The bogus company will take orders to deliver goods—say, Mother's Day flowers—but when the day arrives, it will have disappeared from cyberspace. No flowers will get delivered, but even worse, the perpetrator can sell or use all the collected credit card information.

Password Theft

Many people also fear that Internet passwords—which can be valuable information to cybercriminals—are vulnerable to theft. Again, they're not altogether wrong. There are schemes dedicated entirely to stealing passwords. In one, the cyberthief sets up a Web site that you can access only if you register, provide an e-mail address, and select a password. The cybercriminal is betting that the site will attract a certain percentage of people who use the same password for just about everything—bank accounts, e-mail, employer networks. Having finagled a password, the thief can try accessing other accounts belonging to the victim. So, one day you have a nice cushion in your checking account, and the next you're dead broke.

Invasion of Privacy

If you apply for a life-insurance policy online, you may be asked to supply information about your health. If you apply for a mortgage online, you may be asked questions about your personal finances. Some people shy away from Internet transactions because they're afraid that such personal information can be stolen or shared with unauthorized parties. Once again, they're right: it does happen.

How Do "Cookies" Work?

In addition to data that you supply willingly, information about you can be gathered online without your knowledge or consent.[43] Your online activities, for example, can be captured by something called a *cookie*. The process is illustrated in Figure 15.11. When you access a certain Web site, it sends back a unique piece of information to your browser, which proceeds to save it on your hard drive. When you go back to the same site, your browser returns the information, telling the site who you are and confirming that you've been there before. The problem is not that the cookie can identify you in the same way as a name or an address. It is, however, linked to other information about you—such as the goods you've bought or the services you've ordered online. Before long, someone will have compiled a profile of your buying habits. The result? You'll soon be bombarded with advertisements targeted to your interests. For example, let's suppose you check out the Web site for an online diet program. You furnish some information but decide that the program is not for you. The next time you log on, you may be greeted by a pop-up pushing the latest miracle diet.

FIGURE 15.11 How Cookies Work

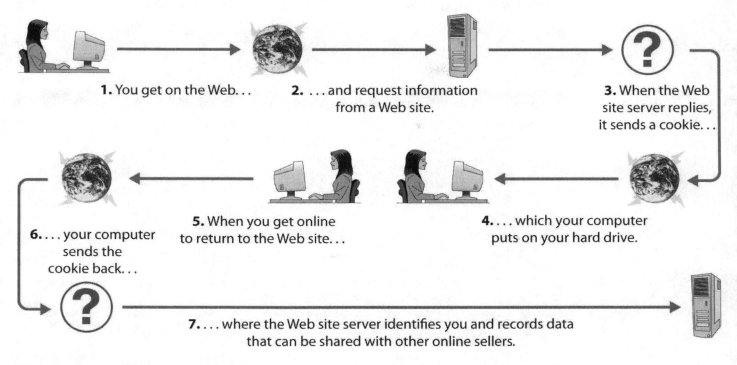

1. You get on the Web...

2. ...and request information from a Web site.

3. When the Web site server replies, it sends a cookie...

4. ...which your computer puts on your hard drive.

5. When you get online to return to the Web site...

6. ...your computer sends the cookie back...

7. ...where the Web site server identifies you and records data that can be shared with other online sellers.

Cookies aren't the only form of online espionage. Your own computer, for example, monitors your Internet activities and keeps track of the URLs that you access.

6.4   Shoring Up Security and Building Trust

So, what can companies do to ease concerns about the safety of Internet transactions? First, businesses must implement internal controls for ensuring adequate security and privacy. Then, they must reassure customers that they're competent to safeguard credit card numbers, passwords, and other personal information. Among the most common controls and assurance techniques, let's look at *encryption* and *seals of assurance*.

Encryption

The most effective method of ensuring that sensitive computer-stored information can't be accessed or altered by unauthorized parties is **encryption**—the process of encoding data so that only individuals (or computers) armed with a secret code (or key) can decode it. Here's a simplified example: You want to send a note to a friend on the other side of the classroom, but you don't want anyone else to know what it says. You and your friend could devise a code in which you substitute each letter in the message with the letter that's two places before it in the alphabet. So you write A as C and B as D and so on. Your friend can decode the message, but it'll look like nonsense to anyone else. This is an oversimplification of the process. In the real world, it's much more complicated: data are scrambled using a complex code, the key for unlocking it is an algorithm, and you need certain computer hardware to perform the encryption/decryption process.

encryption

Process of encoding data so that only individuals or computers armed with a secret code (or key) can decode it.

Certificate Authorities

The most commonly used encryption system for transmitting data over the Internet is called *secure sockets layer* (SSL). You can tell whether a Web site uses SSL if its URL begins with *https* instead of *http*. SSL also provides another important security measure: when you connect to a site that uses SSL (for example, your bank's site), your browser will ask the site to authenticate itself—prove that it is who it says it is. You can be confident that the response is correct if it's verified by a **certificate authority**—a third-party vendor (such as VeriSign) that verifies the identity of the responding computer and sends you a digital certificate of authenticity stating that it trusts the site.

certificate authority

Third-party vendor (such as VeriSign) that verifies the identity of a computer site.

What Web Shoppers Want

Do you conduct many purchases on the Internet? Take a minute to complete an exercise that lets you identify the features most Web shoppers value. Then compare the most popular features with your own picks.

KEY TAKEAWAYS

- Though a source of vast opportunities, **e-commerce**—conducting business over the Internet—also presents some unprecedented challenges, particularly in the area of security.

    1. *Malicious programs*, such as viruses and worms, can wreak havoc with computer systems.
    2. Unauthorized parties may gain access to restricted company Web sites in order to steal funds or goods.
    3. **Firewalls**—software and hardware systems that prevent unauthorized users from accessing computer networks—help to reduce the risks of doing business online.

- Companies that do business online are also vulnerable to illegal activities.

    1. A *denial-of-service attack*, for example, prevents a Web server from servicing authorized users; the culprit demands a ransom to stop the attack.
    2. Companies that use the Internet to create and sell intellectual property (such as songs, movies, and software) face the problem of *piracy*.
    3. The theft of digital products, which can be downloaded and copied almost instantly over the Internet, not only cheats the individuals and organizations that create them, but also reduces sales and shrinks corporate profits.

- Finally, online businesses must convince consumers that it's safe to buy things over the Internet—that credit card numbers, passwords, and other personal information are protected from theft.

- One effective method for protecting computer-stored information is **encryption**—the process of encoding data so that only individuals (or computers) armed with a secret code (or key) can decode it.

    1. A commonly used encryption scheme is a *secure sockets layer* (SSL), which directs the user's browser to ask a site to authenticate itself.
    2. Often, the user receives a digital certificate of authenticity, verifying that a third-party security provider called a **certificate authority** has identified a computer.

Before going to the next section of this chapter, take a few minutes to test your knowledge of the material covered in this section. Quizzes can be found under the "Resources" tab, "Study Aids: Quizzes."

EXERCISE

Reflective Skills

Are you, or is someone you know, hesitant to buy things over the Internet? What risks concern you? What are companies doing to ease consumers' concerns about the safety of Internet transactions?

7. CAREERS IN INFORMATION MANAGEMENT

LEARNING OBJECTIVE

1. Identify career opportunities in information management.

The number and variety of opportunities in the IS field have grown substantially as organizations have expanded their use of IT. In most large organizations, the senior management team includes a *chief information officer (CIO)* who oversees information and telecommunications systems. A large organization might also have a *chief technology officer* who reports to the CIO and oversees IT planning and implementation.

Most entry-level IS jobs require a business degree with a major in information systems. Many people supplement their IS majors with minors in computer science or some other business area, such as accounting, finance, marketing, or operations management.

If you're starting out with an IS degree, you may choose to follow either a management path or a technical path. At Kraft Foods, for example, IS professionals can focus on one of two areas: applications development (a management focus) and information technology (a technology focus). "Applications development," according to the company itself, "calls for an ability to analyze [Kraft's] clients' needs and translate them into systems applications. Information technology calls for the ability to convert business systems specifications into technical specifications and to provide guidance and technical counsel to other Kraft professionals."[44] Despite the differences in focus, Kraft encourages IS specialists to develop expertise in both areas. After all, it's the ability to apply technical knowledge to business situations that makes IS professionals particularly valuable to organizations. (By the way, if you want a career in casinos, you can major in casino management at a number of business schools.)

KEY TAKEAWAYS

- The number and variety of opportunities in the information systems (IS) field have grown substantially as companies have expanded their use of information technology.
- The senior management team in large organizations includes a chief information officer who oversees information and a chief technology officer who oversees IT planning and implementation.
- Most entry-level IS jobs require a business degree with a major in information systems.
- Many supplement their IS majors with computer science or some other business area, such as accounting, finance, marketing, or operations management.
- Those entering organizations with IS degrees may choose to follow either a management or a technology path.

EXERCISE

Reflective Skills

Why is studying IT important to you as a student? How will competency in this area help you get and keep a job in the future?

8. CASES AND PROBLEMS

LEARNING ON THE WEB

Taking Care of Your Cyberhealth

It seems that some people have nothing better to do than wreak havoc by spreading computer viruses, and as a computer user, you should know how to protect yourself from malicious tampering. One place to start is by reading the article "How Computer Viruses Work," by Marshall Brain, which you can access by going to the How Stuff Works Web site (http://computer.howstuffworks.com/virus.htm). After reading the article, answer the following questions:

1. Why do people create viruses?
2. What can you do to protect yourself against viruses?

CAREER OPPORTUNITIES

Could You Manage a Job in IT or IS?

Do you have an aptitude for dealing with IT? Would you enjoy analyzing the information needs of an organization? Are you interested in directing a company's Internet operations or overseeing network security? If you answered yes to any of these questions, then a career in computer and information technology might be for you. Go to the U.S. Department of Labor Web site (http://www.bls.gov/oco/ocos258.htm) and learn more about the nature of the work, qualifications, and job outlook in computer and information technology. Bearing in mind that many people who enter the IT field attain middle-management positions, look for answers to the following questions:

1. What kinds of jobs do computer and information technology managers perform?
2. What educational background, work experience, and skills are needed for positions in computer and information technology management?
3. What's the current job outlook for computer and information technology managers? What factors drive employment opportunities?
4. What's the median annual income of a midlevel computer and information technology manager?

ETHICS ANGLE

Campus Commando or Common Criminal?

Do you want to be popular (or at least more prominent) on campus? You could set up a Web site that lets fellow students share music files over the campus network. All you have to do is seed the site with some of your own downloaded music and let the swapping begin. That's exactly what Daniel Peng did when he was a sophomore at Princeton. It was a good idea, except for one small hitch: it was illegal, and he got caught. Unimpressed with Peng's technological ingenuity, the Recording Industry Association of America (RIAA) sued him, and he was forced to settle for $15,000. Instead of delivering music, Peng's Web site now asks visitors to send money to help defray the $15,000 and another $8,000 in legal costs.

To learn more about the case, read these articles from the Daily Princetonian: "Peng, RIAA Settle Infringement Case" (http://dailyprincetonian.com/news/2003/05/peng-riaa-settle-infringement-case), and "Peng '05 Sued by Recording Industry for 'Wake' Site" (http://dailyprincetonian.com/news/2003/04/peng-05-sued-by-recording-industry-for-wake-site).

After researching the topic, answer the following questions:

1. The practice of sharing commercial music files is illegal. Do you think that it's also unethical? Why, or why not?
2. What steps to curb the practice are being taken by the music industry? By college administrators? By the government? Do you approve of these steps? Have they been effective?
3. What, ultimately, do you see as the solution to the problem?

Source: Josh Brodie, "Peng, RIAA Settle Infringement Case," *The Daily Princetonian*, http://www.dailyprincetonian.com/2003/05/02/8154/ (accessed November 14, 2011); Zachary Goldfarb and Josh Brodie, "Peng '05 Sued by Recording Industry for 'Wake' Site," *The Daily Princetonian* http://www.dailyprincetonian.com/2003/04/04/7791/ (accessed November 14, 2011).

TEAM-BUILDING SKILLS

CampusCupid.com

It's no secret that college can be fun. For one thing, you get to hang around with a bunch of people your own age. Occasionally, you want to spend time with just one special someone, but finding that special person on a busy campus can take some of the fun out of matriculating. Fortunately, you're in the same love boat with a lot of other people, so one possible solution—one that meshes nicely with your desire to go into business—is to start an online dating service that caters to your school. Inasmuch as online dating is nothing new, you can do some preliminary research. For example, go to the Internetnews Web site (http://www.internetnews.com/ec-news/article.php/2228891/Online+Personals+Big+Profits+Intense+Competition.htm) and read the article "Online Personals: Big Profits, Intense Competition."

Next, you and several of your classmates should work as a team to create a business model for an online dating service at your school. After working out the details, submit a group report that covers the following issues:

1. *Services*. How will you earn revenues? What services will you offer? How will you price these services? What forms of payment will you accept? Will you sell ads? If so, what kinds?

2. *Appearance*. What will your site look like? Will it have graphics? Sound? Video? What will your domain name be? What information will you collect from customers? What information will you provide to visitors?

3. *Operations*. What criteria will you use to match customers? How will your customers interface with the Web site? How will they connect with each other? Will you design your own software or buy or lease it from vendors? Before you answer, go to these vendors' Web sites and check out their dating software:

   - WebDate (http://www.webscribble.com/products/webdate/index.shtml)
   - PG Dating (http://www.datingpro.com/dating)

4. *Attracting Customers*. How will you attract customers to the site? How will you monitor and analyze site activity?

5. *Security*. How will you guarantee confidentiality? How will you ensure that your site is secure? How will you limit access to students at your school?

6. *Opportunities and Challenges*. What opportunities do e-businesses offer? What challenges do they create? How would your business model change if you decided to run it as a traditional business rather than as an e-business?

THE GLOBAL VIEW

"Hong Kong—Traditional Chinese"

Hewlett-Packard (HP) provides technology solutions to individuals, businesses, and institutions around the world. It generates annual revenues of $112 billion from the sale of IT products, including computers, printers, copiers, digital photography, and software. Anyone in the United States who wants to buy an HP product, get technical support, download software, learn about the company, or apply for a job can simply go to the HP Web site. But what if you live in Hong Kong? How would you get answers to your questions? You'd do the same thing as people in this country do—go to HP's Web site.

Try to imagine, however, the complex process of developing and maintaining a Web site that serves the needs of customers in more than seventy countries. To get a better idea, go to the HP Web site (http://www.hp.com). Start by looking at HP's line of laptops ("Laptops & Hybrids" under "Shop HP") and checking their prices. Then, look for a job—it's good practice (click on "Jobs" in the bottom of the home page).

Now pretend that you live in Hong Kong and repeat the process. Start by going to the same HP Web site (http://www.hp.com). Click on the United States (next to U.S. flag in the bottom left) and then "Hong Kong." The page will still be in English (which would be great if you don't speak Chinese). But now pretend you are fluent in Chinese—you can switch to Chinese by clicking on "Chinese Only" on the right side of the page next to the words, "Find Out More." Then, answer the following questions (if you need to return to the U.S. version, just use the back arrow):

1. How easy was it to navigate the site and to switch back and forth between the U.S. and Hong Kong sections of the site?

2. Identify at least five differences between the two sections.

3. Does HP's Web site meet the needs of customers in both the United States and Hong Kong? Why, or why not? How could it be improved?

ENDNOTES

1. In November 2010, Harrah's Entertainment, Inc. changed its name to Caesars Entertainment Corporation. The Harrah's name will still be one of the newly named company's primary brands, in addition to Caesars and Horseshoe.

2. Las Vegas Convention and Visitors Authority, "Las Vegas Stats and Facts," http://www.lvcva.com/stats-and-facts (accessed April 30, 2014).

3. Caesars, "Company Information," http://www.caesars.com/corporate (accessed April 30, 2014).

4. Jim Kilby, Jim Fox, and Anthony F. Lucas, *Casino Operations and Management*, 2nd ed. (Hoboken, NJ: John Wiley & Sons, 2005), 183–84.

5. Meridith LeVinson, "Jackpot! Harrah's Big Payoff Came from Using IT to Manage Customer Information," *CIO Magazine*, February 1, 2001, http://www.google.com/url?sa=t&rct=j&q=&esrc=s&source=web&cd=3&ved=0CDsQFjAC&url=http://kennedyonline.us/downloads/Jackpot-KOL.docx&ei=0pBhU7ePH-zRsQTXp4HoBg&usg=AFQjCNF4DRzuaaLt1VBkTwwMz9uHc9snAQ&sig2=NnTVtEIJeiZdZGAPAXFZhQ&bvm=bv.65860765,d.cWc (accessed April 30, 2014); Global Supply Chain Management Forum, Stanford Graduate School of Business, "Harrah's Entertainment Inc.: Real-Time CRM in a Service Supply Chain," https://gsbapps.stanford.edu/cases/detail1.asp?Document_ID=2838 (accessed April 30, 2014).

6. Christopher Koch, "The ABCs of ERP," *CIO.com*, http://wikifab.dimf.etsii.upm.es/wikifab/images/d/da/The_ABCs_of_ERP.pdf (accessed April 30, 2014).

7. Caesars, "Total Rewards," https://www.totalrewards.com/TotalRewards/RewardsAndBenefits.do?page=overview (accessed April 30, 2014).

8. Robert L. Shook, *Jackpot! Harrah's Winning Secrets for Customer Loyalty* (Hoboken, NJ: John Wiley & Sons, 2003), 228–29.

9. Gary Loveman, "Diamonds in the Data Mine," *Harvard Business Review*, May 2003, 3.

10. Darrell Dunn, "Personal Touch For VIPs," *Information Week*, November 4, 2003, http://www.informationweek.com/news/16000115 (accessed April 30, 2014); Darrell Dunn, "Personal Touch for VIPs—Client-Tracking System Helps Harrah's Tailor Sales Efforts for Frequent Visitors," *Information Week*, November 4, 2003, http://www.informationweek.com/story/showArticle.jhtml?articleID=16000115 (accessed April 30, 2014).

11. Robert L. Shook, *Jackpot! Harrah's Winning Secrets for Customer Loyalty* (Hoboken, NJ: John Wiley & Sons, 2003), 248–52.

12. "Decision Support System," *Webopedia*, http://www.webopedia.com/TERM/D/decision_support_system.html (accessed April 30, 2014).

13. "Artificial Intelligence," *Webopedia*, http://www.webopedia.com/TERM/A/artificial_intelligence.html (accessed April 30, 2014).

14. "Artificial Intelligence," *Webopedia*, http://www.webopedia.com/TERM/A/artificial_intelligence.html (accessed April 30, 2014).

15. John Goff, "Head Games: Businesses Deploying Analytical Software to Get a Better Fix on Customer Behavior," *CFO Magazine for Senior Financial Executives* 20:9, July 1, 2004, http://www.cfo.com/printable/article.cfm/3014815/c_3046615?f=options (accessed April 30, 2014).

16. See Daintry Duffy, "Catching Casino Cheats: Technology's Winning Hand," *CSO.online*, October 1, 2003, http://www.csoonline.com/article/2116624/loss-prevention/catching-casino-cheats--technology-s-winning-hand.html (accessed April 30, 2014); Larry Barrett Gallagher and Sean Gallagher, "NORA and ANNA: Non-Obvious Relationship Awareness," *Baseline*, April 4, 2004, http://www.baselinemag.com/c/a/Past-News/NORA-and-ANNA (accessed April 30, 2014).

17. "Cloud," *Dictionary.com*, http://dictionary.reference.com/browse/cloud (accessed April 30, 3014).

18. Melanie Pinola, "What Is Cloud Computing?" *About.com*, http://mobileoffice.about.com/od/workingontheroad/f/cloudcomputing.htm (accessed April 30, 2014).

19. Paul Gil, "What Is Cloud Computing?" *About.com*, http://netforbeginners.about.com/od/c/f/cloudcomputing.htm (accessed April 30, 2014).

20. "Software as a Service/ Infrastructure as a Service," *Thrive Networks*, March 2009, http://www.thrivenetworks.com/resources/march-2009-software-as-a-service.html (accessed April 30, 2014).

21. Best Price Computers, "Infrastructure as a Service," http://www.bestpricecomputers.co.uk/glossary/infrastructure-as-a-service.htm (accessed April 30, 2014).

22. Joseph Eve, "Cloud Computing as a Security Asset," *Indian Gaming*, www.indiangaming.com/istore/Apr11_JosephEve.pdf (accessed April 30, 2014), 60–61.

23. Steve Lohr, "Amazon's Trouble Raises Cloud Computing Doubts," *The New York Times*, April 22, 2011, http://www.nytimes.com/2011/04/23/technology/23cloud.html?_r=1 (accessed April 30, 2014).

24. "Caesars Entertainment Hits the Efficiency Jackpot with Force.com," *Salesforce.com*, http://www.salesforce.com/showcase/stories/caesars.jsp (accessed April 30, 2014).

25. Richard T. Griffiths, "Chapter Two: The World Wide Web (WWW)," *The History of the Internet*, http://www.let.leidenuniv.nl/history/ivh/chap2.htm (accessed April 30, 2014).

26. "Internet Users by Country," *Internet Live Stats*, April 30, 2014, http://www.internetlivestats.com/internet-users/#bycountry (accessed April 30, 2014); Sarah Kessler, "Study: 80 Percent of Children under 5 Use Internet Weekly," *Mashable*, March 15, 2011, http://content.usatoday.com/communities/technologylive/post/2011/03/study-80-percent-of-children-under-5-use-internet-weekly/1 (accessed April 30, 2014).

27. "World Wide Web," *Wikipedia*, http://en.wikipedia.org/wiki/World_Wide_Web (accessed April 30, 2014).

28. Erika Andersen, "How Small Business Owners Are Wrecking Their Own Chances of Success," *Forbes*, October 7, 2013, http://www.forbes.com/sites/erikaandersen/2013/10/07/how-small-business-owners-are-wrecking-their-own-chances-of-success (accessed April 30, 2014).

29. Ben Sisario, "Digital Music Leads Boost in Record Sales," *The New York Times*, July 6, 2011, http://artsbeat.blogs.nytimes.com/2011/07/06/digital-music-leads-boost-in-record-sales (accessed April 30, 2014).

30. "Can E-Tailers Find Fulfillment with Drop Shipping?" *Kowledge@Wharton*, July 17, 2002, http://knowledge.wharton.upenn.edu/article/can-e-tailers-find-fulfillment-with-drop-shipping (accessed April 30, 2014).

31. Ponemon Institute, "2013 Cost of Cyber Crime Study Report," HP Enterprise Security, http://www.hpenterprisesecurity.com/ponemon-2013-cost-of-cyber-crime-study-reports (accessed April 30, 2014).

32. Susan Berfield, "From Cyber Crime to Canada, Target Had a Very Bad Year," *Businessweek Online*, February 16, 2014, http://www.businessweek.com/articles/2014-02-26/from-cyber-crime-to-canada-target-had-a-very-bad-year.

33. Victor Luckerson, "Target Breach Shows You Can Be a Victim of Cybercrime at a Brick-and-Mortar Store," *Time*, December 20, 2013, http://business.time.com/2013/12/20/target-credit-card-breach-shows-expansion-of-cybercrime (accessed April 30, 2014).

34. Siobhan Gorman, "Annual U.S. Cybercrime Costs Estimated at $100 Billion," *Wall Street Journal*, July 22, 2013, http://online.wsj.com/news/articles/SB10001424127887324238904578621880966242990 (accessed April 30, 2014).

35. Paul Shukovsky, "Blaster Worm Attacker Gets 18 Months," *Seattle Post-Intelligencer*, http://www.seattlepi.com/local/article/Blaster-worm-attacker-gets-18-months-1165231.php (accessed April 30, 2014).

36. Stephen Baker and Brian Grow, "Gambling Sites, This Is a Holdup," *BusinessWeek Online*, August 9, 2004, http://www.businessweek.com/magazine/content/04_32/b3895106_mz063.htm (accessed April 30, 2014).

37. Recording Industry Association of America, "For Students Doing Reports," http://www.riaa.com/faq.php (accessed April 30, 2014).

38. Zach Epstein, "Global Market for Pirated Software Reaches $59 billion," *BGR Innovation*, http://bgr.com/2011/05/12/global-market-for-pirated-software-reaches-59-billion (accessed April 30, 2014).

39. "Can't Stop Piracy," *AudioMicro*, May 20, 2010, http://www.audiomicro.com/royalty-free-music-blog/2010/05/can%E2%80%99t-stop-piracy/ (accessed April 30, 2014).

40. Recording Industry Association of America, "The Law," http://www.riaa.com/physicalpiracy.php?content_selector=piracy_online_the_law (accessed November 14, 2011); "Is Downloading Music Illegal?" *World Law Direct*, http://www.worldlawdirect.com/article/1395/downloading-music-legal.html (accessed April 30, 2014).

41. Heather Green, "Digital Media: Don't Clamp Down Too Hard," *BusinessWeek Online*, October 14, 2002, http://www.businessweek.com/magazine/content/02_41/b3803121.htm (accessed April 30, 2014).

42. Apple, "Apple's App Store Downloads Top 10 Billion," http://www.apple.com/pr/library/2011/01/22Apples-App-Store-Downloads-Top-10-Billion.html (accessed April 30, 2014).

43. "Are Cookies Jeopardizing Your Online Privacy?" Reputation.com, http://www.reputation.com/reputationwatch/articles/are-cookies-jeopardizing-your-online-privacy (accessed April 30, 2014).

44. Kraft Foods, "Kraft Foods Information Systems: A World of Opportunity," http://www.google.com/url?sa=t&rct=j&q=&esrc=s&source=web&cd=1&sqi=2&ved=0CCkQFjAA&url=http://www.indian~jobtalk/ppt/SCOOPs/2000-2001/09-21/KraftFoods.ppt&ei=Pk9kU7u4JKvJsQTjzYLABw&usg=AFQjCNFYE994D7TUkShusN3EZ1YX5A_QUg (accessed April 30, 2014).

CHAPTER 16

The Legal and Regulatory Environment of Business

WHATEVER HAPPENED TO…GEORGE MCGOVERN?

You may or may not have heard of George McGovern.[1] A professor of history in his home state of South Dakota, he was elected to Congress in 1956 and to the U.S. Senate in 1962. He was a prominent opponent of the war in Vietnam and became the Democratic Party nominee for president in 1972. His run for the presidency failed (he lost in a landslide), and he remained in the Senate until 1980. After more than a quarter century as a lawmaker, he then entered private life, serving on a few boards and giving a lot of lectures.

In 1988, McGovern and his wife Eleanor decided to go into business, so they purchased a small hotel in the city of Stratford, Connecticut. At first, the onetime politician was enlightened by life as a small business owner. "I wish I'd done this before I'd run for president," he said in early 1990, "It would have given me insight into the anxiety any independent businessman…must have….Now I've had to meet a payroll every week. I've got to pay the bank every month. I've got to pay the state of Connecticut taxes….It gives you a whole new perspective on what other people worry about."

Before the end of the year, the Stratford Inn went bankrupt and McGovern's otherwise educational venture into the world of small-business ownership had come to an abrupt end. What happened? McGovern observed in retrospect that the terms of his lease weren't particularly good and that New England was on the verge of severe recession just as he was starting up his enterprise. But the knockout blow, he maintains, was delivered in the legal arena. During McGovern's tenure as owner, the Stratford was sued twice under laws governing **premises liability**—the duty of innkeepers to take reasonable care in preventing customers and third parties from being injured on their property. There's a subcategory called "slip-and-fall," laws because slipping and falling are at the heart of so many premises-liability lawsuits.

In McGovern's case, one lawsuit actually did involve a slip and fall (and an allegedly serious injury) in the parking lot of the hotel. In the other incident, a patron got into a fight when he came out of the hotel bar and sued the Stratford for failure to provide adequate security. A security guard was in fact on duty, but McGovern argues that few small businesses can furnish the kind of protection needed to prevent fights outside a bar. Both lawsuits were dismissed, but, as McGovern points out, "not without a first-rate legal defense that did not come cheaply."

premises liability
The duty of innkeepers to take reasonable care in preventing customers and third parties from being injured on their property.

George McGovern gained a new perspective, and appreciation, for the complex legal environment of U.S. business during his brief tenure as a small business owner.

© 2010 Jupiterimages Corporation

administrative law

Body of law dealing with statutes and regulations related to the activities of administrative agencies.

statutory law

Body of law made by legislative bodies.

tort reform

A movement to stem the swelling tide of personal-injury litigation in the United States.

In an article written for *Inc.* magazine a couple of years later, McGovern acknowledged a few more lessons from his brief experience as a small businessman: "I learned first of all that over the past 20 years, America has become the most litigious society in the world." He acknowledged the rationale behind premises-liability laws, "but it does seem to me," he suggested, "that not every accident or fall or misfortune is the fault of the business at which it occurs." Recalling that the Stratford was also required to meet "fire regulations more appropriate to the Waldorf-Astoria," McGovern went on to report the second lesson he learned as owner of the Stratford Inn: that "legislators and government regulators must more carefully consider the economic and management burdens we have been imposing on U.S. business."

McGovern's eyes, it seems, had been opened after forty months as a small-business proprietor, and in the aftermath, he narrowed his focus to two problem areas for the small-business owner trying to survive in the highly complex legal environment of the United States. The first area falls under the heading of **administrative law**—law pertaining to rules set down by any of the numerous agencies and departments created to administer federal or local law. McGovern happily confirms his commitment to such worthy social goals as worker safety and a clean environment, but he's also convinced that we can pursue these goals "and still cut down vastly on the incredible paperwork, the complicated tax forms, the number of tiny regulations, and the seemingly endless reporting requirements that afflict American business."

He's also targeted what he regards as unnecessary burdens placed on business by **statutory law**—laws enacted by legislative branches of government (such as the U.S. Congress, of which he was a member for nearly three decades). In particular, as a survivor of two premises-liability suits, McGovern has become an advocate of **tort reform**—a movement to stem the swelling tide of personal-injury litigation in the United States. Americans, he charges, "sue one another at the drop of a hat, [and] lawsuits without merit…are hurting both the economy and decency of our society." Business suffers because businesses hold most of the insurance policies at which liability litigation is aimed. With each settlement, premiums surge, and many businesses, especially smaller ones, argues McGovern, "simply can't pass such costs on to their customers and remain competitive or profitable….If I were back in the U.S. Senate or in the White House," he concludes, "I would ask a lot of questions before I voted for any more burdens on the thousands of struggling businesses across the nation."

1. LAW AND THE LEGAL SYSTEM

LEARNING OBJECTIVES

1. Define "law," and explain how it differs from a "legal system."
2. Explain the concept of "the rule of law," and discuss the role of flexibility and fairness in a legal system governed by the rule of law.
3. Discuss the primary functions of law in the United States.

In the eighteenth century, when the legal and regulatory environment of everything was a lot simpler than it is today, the great Irish satirist Jonathan Swift likened laws to cobwebs because they seem to stretch in every direction to catch innocent flies while failing utterly to stop wasps and other creatures responsible for much greater crimes against human comfort. Like George McGovern, many people no doubt find this comparison at least as true today as it was in Swift's time. After all, in order to be law-abiding innkeepers (or just plain citizens), we must negotiate a vast web of constitutional law, federal law, regulatory law, and state and local law; criminal law, civil law, and common law; substantive law and procedural law; public law and private law; and business law, which includes contract law, product-liability law, patent law, consumer-protection law, environmental law, employment and labor law, insurance law, cyberlaw, agency law, and a host of other forms of law. In fact, being a truly law-abiding citizen is virtually out of the question. According to one estimate, the average American driver deserves ten speeding tickets a day. Other underpenalized violations range from stealing cable TV and scalping tickets to exhibitionism and illegal fishing and hunting.[2]

1.1 A System of Rules and Principles

Perhaps, however, we should examine the issue of the laws in our lives from a more positive perspective. As a veteran lawmaker, for example, George McGovern certainly appreciates the value of **law**, which is basically a body of enforceable rules and principles of conduct. Clearly, his criticisms are directed not at the existence of laws, but rather at certain facets of administrative and statutory law—in particular, the way specific statutes can be applied to the activities of a small business owner in the state of Connecticut. What he calls for, in effect, is a little more flexibility in the enforcement of certain rules and principles.

In a very basic—and very important—sense, McGovern's point about legal obstacles to daily business-related activities is well taken. In the United States, as in all complex societies, we've entrusted the responsibility for adopting and enforcing legal rules and principles to government. In so doing, we've approved the formation of a **legal system**—the institutions and processes that actually enforce our rules and principles.[3] That system, like any other, works because its key elements are stable and interact in reliable ways. When it's applied systematically, in other words, law isn't always as flexible as it should be in doing what it's supposed to do—namely, preserving peace and stability so that members of society can pursue their various social and economic activities.

Flexibility

At the same time, however, we should point out that, on a certain level, *flexibility* is a hallmark of law in the United States. Why do we say "on a certain level"? For one thing, it apparently isn't sufficiently flexible on the level on which George McGovern was obliged to deal with it. In all probability, a small hotel like the Stratford Inn doesn't need to meet the same fire regulations as a hotel with 1,500 guest rooms, 100,000 square feet of meeting space, three four-star restaurants, and a five-story parking garage. Laws, however, can't be written to take care of each and every contingency that arises during the course of life in the real world—the one in which millions of people and organizations are constantly pursuing different social and economic activities. When it comes to law, therefore, we settle for general "rules and principles," and the key to flexibility in a legal system is flexibility on the level at which rules and principles are *applied*. In the United States, the legal system evolves to respond to changes in social norms and commercial activities, and through the court system, it's prepared to address each issue or dispute on its own terms.[4]

Fairness

There are, of course, abuses and mistakes by judges and juries, and procedural mishaps occasionally tip the scales of justice in the wrong direction. Sometimes—as in George McGovern's case—innocent parties are forced to bear the cost of defending themselves in court. On the whole, however, the U.S. legal system is remarkably fair.

The Rule of Law: Predictability and Fairness. How do we know what's legally "fair" and what isn't?[5] Granted, depending on who's enforcing the rules of the game, just about anything can be "fair" and just about anything can be "foul." Legal tradition in the United States, however, rests on the principle of the **rule of law**—the principle by which government legitimately exercises its authority only in accordance with publicly declared laws that are adopted and enforced according to established procedure. All members of society know what the laws are and the conditions under which they should be applied. Under the rule of law, then, the legal system establishes the rules of the game, adopting and enforcing them in a reasonably *predictable* manner.

Unfortunately, the principle of predictability doesn't in itself guarantee that a legal system is committed to *fairness*. If, for example, the law allows only certain people to vote—say, property owners—it extends a guarantee of fairness in the electoral process only to property owners. People who don't own property would have a good reason to complain of social injustice in electoral matters, but only property owners could claim a right to fairness in the courts. Even under the rule of law, therefore, a legal system can achieve a reasonable degree of fairness in any given social or economic activity only if it also guarantees *equal treatment* of all members of society. Admittedly, the U.S. legal system hasn't always

---

law

Body of enforceable rules and principles of conduct.

legal system

Institutions and processes that enforce laws.

rule of law

Principle by which government legitimately exercises its authority only in accordance with publicly declared laws that are adopted and enforced according to established procedure.

been successful in guaranteeing equal treatment under the law—the original thirteen states, for example, granted the vote only to white male property owners, and women couldn't vote in every state until 1920. Since 1868, however, U.S. courts have used the Equal Protection Clause of the Fourteenth Amendment to the Constitution to check a range of potentially discriminatory and unfair actions by governments at every level.

Functions of Law

Laws such as the Equal Protection Clause are designed to serve a general function—namely, the promotion of social justice. This is just one of several primary functions served by law in the United States:[6]

crime

Violation of statute for which the law imposes punishment.

- *Keeping the peace* (e.g., designating some activities as **crimes**—violations of statutes for which the law imposes punishment)
- *Shaping moral standards* (e.g., laws discouraging such activities as drug or alcohol abuse)
- *Promoting social justice* (e.g., laws prohibiting discrimination in such areas as voting and employment)
- *Maintaining the status quo* (e.g., laws preventing the forcible overthrow of the government)
- *Facilitating orderly change* (e.g., laws and practices requiring public scrutiny of proposed statutes)
- *Facilitating planning* (e.g., laws that enable businesses to evaluate the risks that they may be taking in a commercial venture)
- *Providing a basis for compromise* (e.g., laws and practices making it possible to resolve disputes without taking them to trial)
- *Maximizing individual freedom* (e.g., laws ensuring such rights as freedom of speech and religion)

KEY TAKEAWAYS

- *Law* is a body of enforceable rules and principles of conduct. When we entrust the responsibility for adopting and enforcing legal rules and principles to government, we approve the formation of a *legal system*—the institutions and processes that actually enforce our laws. That system works because its key elements are stable and interact in reliable ways.
- U.S. legal tradition rests on the principle of the **rule of law**—the principle by which government legitimately exercises its authority only in accordance with publicly declared laws that are adopted and enforced according to established procedure. Under the rule of law, the legal system adopts and enforces laws in a reasonably predictable manner. The principle of *predictability*, however, doesn't in itself guarantee that a legal system is fair. A legal system can achieve a reasonable degree of *fairness* only if it also guarantees *equal treatment* of all members of society.
- When it's applied systematically, law isn't always as flexible as it should be in preserving the peace and stability that members of society need to pursue their various social and economic activities. But because laws can't be written to cover each and every contingency, we settle for general "rules and principles." The key to *flexibility* in a legal system is flexibility in *applying* legal rules and principles.
- U.S. law serves several primary functions:
    1. Keeping the peace
    2. Shaping moral standards
    3. Promoting social justice
    4. Maintaining the status quo
    5. Facilitating orderly change
    6. Facilitating planning
    7. Providing a basis for compromise
    8. Maximizing individual freedom

Before going to the next section of this chapter, take a few minutes to test your knowledge of the material covered in this section. Quizzes can be found under the "Resources" tab, "Study Aids: Quizzes."

EXERCISE

Individuals in the United States are guaranteed equal treatment under the law. Do you believe that all individuals do in fact receive equal treatment? Support your answer with examples.

2. CRIMINAL VERSUS CIVIL LAW

LEARNING OBJECTIVES

1. Distinguish between criminal law and civil law, and understand the roles of plaintiffs and defendants in both criminal and civil cases.
2. Define a "tort," explain tort law, and discuss an intentional tort.

In the case of George McGovern and his Stratford Inn, we saw what sort of legal entanglements could discourage even a veteran lawmaker from pursuing a modest dream of business ownership. What about you? How easily discouraged would you be? Put yourself in the following scenario, which could happen to anybody:

> When you were in high school, you worked part time and over the summers for your father, a house painter. Now that you're in college, you've decided to take advantage of that experience to earn some money during your summer vacation. You set yourself up as a house-painting business and hire your college roommate to help you out. One fine summer day, the two of you are putting a coat of Misty Meadow acrylic latex on the exterior of a two-story Colonial. You're working on the ground floor around the door of the house while your roommate is working from scaffolding over the garage. Looking up, you notice that, despite several warnings, your roommate has placed his can of paint at his feet rather than fixed it to the ladder bracing the platform. You're about to say something yet one more time, but it's too late: he accidentally kicks the bucket (so to speak), which bounces off the homeowner's red sports car, denting the hood and splattering it with Misty Meadow. As luck would have it, the whole episode is witnessed by the homeowner's neighbor, who approaches the scene of the disaster just as your roommate has climbed down from the scaffold. "Man, you must be dumber than a bag of hammers," says the neighbor to your roommate, who's in no mood for unsolicited opinions, and before you know what's happening, he breaks the neighbor's nose with a single well-placed punch.

> The homeowner sues you and your roommate for negligence, and the neighbor sues you and your roommate for assault and battery.[7]

Clearly, being an employer—even of just one person—isn't nearly as simple as you thought it would be. What should you have known about the basics of *employment law* in the state where you intended to paint houses? What should you have known about *tort law*? What about *tax law*? If you have to pay damages as a result of the homeowner's negligence claim, can you at least deduct them as business expenses?

Welcome to the *legal environment of business*—the place where business interacts with the legal system. Besides the fact that these interactions are usually quite complicated, what valuable lessons should you learn from your experience once your case has been *adjudicated* (resolved in court)? You probably won't be surprised to learn that your roommate is liable for negligence in kicking over the paint bucket, but you may be dismayed to learn that you are, too. When it comes to the claim of assault and battery, your roommate is also liable for that, but you may be protected from liability. As for the damages that you'll probably have to pay in order to settle the homeowner's negligence suit, you'll be pleased to learn that you can indeed write them off as "ordinary" business expenses (unless they're paid by your insurance company).

As we work our way through this chapter, we'll look a little more closely at the types of law involved in your case, but we'll start by observing that, in at least one respect, your roommate's

predicament can be more instructive than yours. That's because assault and battery violates statutes established by two different types of law—*criminal* and *civil.*

2.1 Criminal Law

criminal law

Body of law that prohibits and punishes wrongful conduct.

plaintiff

Party filing a legal complaint; in criminal law, usually a government body acting as a representative of society; in civil law, party suing to obtain compensation for wrong allegedly done by the defendant.

defendant

Party charged in a legal complaint; in criminal law, party against whom a criminal charge is brought; in civil law, party being sued for compensation for wrong allegedly done to plaintiff.

It's a *crime* to make unauthorized and harmful physical contact with another person (*battery*). In fact, it's a crime even to *threaten* such contact (*assault*). **Criminal law** prohibits and punishes wrongful conduct, such as assault and battery, murder, robbery, extortion, and fraud. In criminal cases, the **plaintiff**—the party filing the complaint—is usually a government body acting as a representative of society. The **defendant**—the party charged in the complaint—may be an individual (such as your roommate) or an organization (such as a business). Criminal punishment includes fines, imprisonment, or both.

FIGURE 16.1

2.2 Civil Law

civil law

Body of law governing disputes between private parties.

Assault and battery may also be a matter of **civil law**—law governing disputes between private parties (again, individuals or organizations). In civil cases, the *plaintiff* sues the *defendant* to obtain compensation for some wrong that the defendant has allegedly done the plaintiff. Thus your roommate may be sued for monetary damages by the homeowner's neighbor, with whom he made unauthorized and harmful physical contact.

Tort Law

Complaints of assault and battery fall under a specific type of civil law called *tort law*. A **tort** is a civil wrong—an injury done to someone's person or property. The punishment in tort cases is the monetary compensation that the court orders the defendant to pay the plaintiff.

Intentional Torts

In categorizing the offense for which your roommate may be sued, we can get even more specific: assault and battery is usually an **intentional tort**—an intentional act that poses harm to the plaintiff. Note that *intent* here refers to the *act* (directing a blow at another person), not to the *harm caused* (the broken nose suffered as a result of the blow).

Intentional torts may also pose harm to a party's property or economic interests:[8]

- *Intentional torts against property* may take three forms: (1) entering another person's land or placing an object on another person's land without the owner's permission; (2) interfering with another person's use or enjoyment of personal property; or (3) permanently removing property from the rightful owner's possession.

- *Intentional torts against economic interests* are the most common torts when it comes to disputes in business. The three most important forms are (1) making a false statement of material fact about a business product; (2) enticing someone to breach a valid contract; and (3) going into business for the sole purpose of taking business from another concern (i.e., not for the purpose of making a profit).

On a more personal note, you may want to avoid *defamation*—communicating to a third party information that's harmful to someone's reputation. If you put the information in some permanent form (e.g., write it or present it on TV or on the Internet), it's called *libel*; if you deliver it orally, it's called *slander*. You can also be held liable for *intentional infliction of emotional distress* if you direct outrageous conduct at someone who's likely to suffer extreme emotional pain as a result.[9]

Table 16.1 provides a more complete list of intentional torts, along with the types of compensatory damages normally awarded in each type of case. As we'll see in the following sections of this chapter, intentional torts comprise just one category of torts. The others are *negligence torts* and *strict liability torts*.

tort

Civil wrong; injury done to someone's person or property.

intentional tort

Intentional act that poses harm to another person or another person's property.

TABLE 16.1 Categories of Intentional Torts

Category	Type	Definition	Compensatory Damages Usually Awarded
Against persons	Assault	Threatening immediate harm or offensive contact	For medical bills, lost wages, and pain and suffering
	Battery	Making unauthorized harmful or offensive contact with another person	
	Defamation	Communicating to a third party information that's harmful to someone's reputation	For measurable financial losses
	Invasion of privacy	Violating someone's right to live his or her life without unwarranted or undesired publicity	For resulting economic loss or pain and suffering
	False imprisonment	Restraining or confining a person against his or her will and without justification	For treatment of physical injuries and lost time at work
	Intentional infliction of emotional distress	Engaging in outrageous conduct that's likely to cause extreme emotional distress to the party toward whom the conduct is directed	For treatment of physical illness resulting from emotional stress
Against property	Trespass to realty	Entering another person's land or placing an object on another person's land without the owner's permission	For harm caused to property and losses suffered by rightful owner
	Trespass to personalty	Interfering with another person's use or enjoyment of personal property	For harm to property
	Conversion	Permanently removing property from the rightful owner's possession	For full value of converted item
Against economic interests	Disparagement	Making a false statement of material fact about a business product	For actual economic loss
	Intentional interference with a contract	Enticing someone to breach a valid contract	For loss of expected benefits from contract
	Unfair competition	Going into business for the sole purpose of taking business from another concern	For lost profits
	Misappropriation	Using an unsolicited idea for a product or marketing method without compensating the originator of the idea	For economic losses

Source: Adapted from Nancy A. Kubasek, Bartley A. Brennan, and M. Neil Browne, The Legal Environment of Business: A Critical Thinking Approach, 5th ed. (Upper Saddle River, NJ: Pearson Education, 2009), 348.

As we indicated, your roommate may have committed assault and battery in violation of both criminal and civil statutes. Consequently, he may be in double trouble: not only may he be sued for a civil offense by the homeowner's neighbor, but he may also be prosecuted for a criminal offense by the proper authority in the state where the incident took place. It's also conceivable that he may be sued but not prosecuted, or vice versa. Everything is up to the discretion of the complaining parties—the homeowner's neighbor in the civil case and the prosecutor's office in the criminal case.

Why might one party decide to pursue a case while the other decides not to? A key factor might be the difference in the burden of proof placed on each potential plaintiff. Liability in civil cases may be established by a *preponderance of the evidence*—the weight of evidence necessary for a judge or jury to decide in favor of the plaintiff (or the defendant). Guilt in criminal cases, however, must be established by *proof beyond a reasonable doubt*—doubt based on reason and common sense after careful, deliberate consideration of all the pertinent evidence. Criminal guilt thus carries a tougher standard of proof than civil liability, and it's conceivable that even though the plaintiff in the civil case believes that he can win by a preponderance of the evidence, the prosecutor may feel that she can't prove criminal guilt beyond a reasonable doubt.

Finally, note that your roommate would be more likely to face criminal prosecution if he had committed assault and battery with *criminal intent*—with the intent, say, to kill or rob the homeowner's neighbor or to intimidate him from testifying about the accident with the paint bucket. In that case, in most jurisdictions, his action would be not only a crime but a **felony**—a serious or "inherently evil" crime punishable by imprisonment. Otherwise, if he's charged with criminal wrongdoing at all, it will probably be for a **misdemeanor**—a crime that's not "inherently evil" but that is nevertheless prohibited by society.[10]

Table 16.2 summarizes some of the key differences in the application of criminal and civil law.

felony

Serious or "inherently evil" crime punishable by imprisonment.

misdemeanor

Crime that's not "inherently evil" but that's nevertheless prohibited by society.

TABLE 16.2 Civil versus Criminal Law

	Civil Law	Criminal Law
Parties	Individual or corporate plaintiff vs. individual or corporate defendant	Local, state, or federal prosecutor vs. individual or corporate defendant
Purpose	Compensation or deterrence	Punishment/deterrence/rehabilitation
Burden of proof	Preponderance of the evidence	Beyond a reasonable doubt
Trial by jury/ jury vote	Yes (in most cases)/specific number of votes for judgment in favor of plaintiff	Yes/unanimous vote for conviction of defendant
Sanctions/ penalties	Monetary damages/equitable remedies (e.g., injunction, specific performance)	Probation/fine/imprisonment/capital punishment

Source: Adapted from Henry R. Cheesman, Contemporary Business and Online Commerce Law: Legal, Internet, Ethical, and Global Environments, 5th ed. (Upper Saddle River, NJ: Pearson Education, 2006), 127.

KEY TAKEAWAYS

- The *legal environment of business* is the area in which business interacts with the legal system.
- **Criminal law** prohibits and punishes wrongful conduct. The **plaintiff**—the party filing the complaint—is usually a government body acting as a representative of society. The **defendant**—the party charged in the complaint—may be an individual or an organization. Criminal punishment includes fines, imprisonment, or both. **Civil law** refers to law governing disputes between private parties. In civil cases, the plaintiff sues the defendant to obtain compensation for some wrong that the defendant has allegedly done the plaintiff.
- Tort law covers **torts**, or civil wrongs—injuries done to someone's person or property. The punishment in tort cases is the monetary compensation that the court orders the defendant to pay the plaintiff.
- An **intentional tort** is an intentional act that poses harm to the plaintiff. Intentional torts may be committed against a person, a person's property, or a person's economic interests. In addition to intentional torts, the law recognizes *negligence torts* and *strict liability torts*.
- Liability in civil cases may be established by a *preponderance of the evidence*—the weight of evidence necessary for a judge or jury to decide in favor of the plaintiff (or the defendant). Guilt in criminal cases must be established by *proof beyond a reasonable doubt*—doubt based on reason and common sense after careful, deliberate consideration of all the pertinent evidence.
- A crime may be a **felony**—a serious or "inherently evil" crime punishable by imprisonment—or a **misdemeanor**—a crime that's not "inherently evil" but that is nevertheless prohibited by society.

Before going to the next section of this chapter, take a few minutes to test your knowledge of the material covered in this section. Quizzes can be found under the "Resources" tab, "Study Aids: Quizzes."

EXERCISE

You own a moving company. One of your workers let go of a chair he was carrying up a staircase. Unfortunately, a tenant of the building was walking up the stairs at the time and was seriously hurt in the incident. Can your company be sued? Would the case fall under criminal or civil law?

Now, let's say that your worker was going up the stairs with a chair when the tenant yelled at him for blocking her way. In anger, your worker threw the chair at her and cases serious harm. What actions can be taken against your employee?

3. NEGLIGENCE TORTS

LEARNING OBJECTIVES

1. Define a "negligence tort," and discuss the elements of a negligence claim.
2. Explain a contract, and discuss the requirements of an enforceable contract.
3. Explain the concepts of "respondeat superior" and "scope of employment," and discuss their roles in an employment contract.

negligence tort

Tort resulting from carelessness.

We can now get back to your role in this case, though doing so means first taking a closer look at further aspects of your roommate's role. You and your roommate are being sued by the homeowner for a different type of tort—a **negligence tort**, which results not from intentional wrongdoing, but from *carelessness*. When he placed that can of paint at his feet, where he might easily dislodge it as he moved around the platform, your roommate allowed his conduct to fall below a certain standard of care—namely, the degree of care necessary to protect others from an unreasonable likelihood of harm.

3.1 Elements of a Negligence Claim

To prove that the act in question was negligent, the homeowner must demonstrate the four elements of a negligence claim:[11]

duty of care

Basic obligation that one person owes another; duty not to cause harm or unreasonable risk of harm.

1. *That the defendant (your roommate and, ultimately, you) owed a* duty of care *to the plaintiff (the homeowner).* **Duty of care** refers simply to the basic obligation that one person owes another—the duty not to cause harm or an unreasonable risk of harm.

2. *That the defendant* breached *his duty of care.* Once it has been determined that the defendant owed a duty of care, the court will ask whether he did indeed fail to perform that duty. Did he, in other words, fail to act as a reasonable person would act? (In your roommate's case, by the way, it's a question of acting as a reasonable *professional* would act.)

3. *That the defendant's* breach of duty of care *caused injury to the plaintiff or the plaintiff's property.* If the bucket of paint had fallen on his own car, your roommate's carelessness wouldn't have been *actionable*—wouldn't have provided cause for legal action—because the plaintiff (the homeowner) would have suffered no injury to person or property. What if the paint bucket had hit and shattered the homeowner's big toe, thus putting an end to his career as a professional soccer player? In that case, you and your roommate would be looking at much higher damages. As it stands, the homeowner can seek compensation only to cover the damage to his car.

4. *That the defendant's action did in fact cause the injury in question.* There must be a direct cause-and-effect relationship between the defendant's action and the plaintiff's injury. In law, this relationship is called a *cause in fact* or *actual cause*. For example, what if the homeowner had taken one look at his dented, paint-spattered car and collapsed from a heart attack? Would your roommate be liable for this injury to the plaintiff's person? Possibly, though probably not. Most actions of any kind set in motion a series of consequent actions, and the court must decide the point beyond which a defendant is no longer liable for these actions. The last point at which the defendant is liable for negligence is called a *proximate cause* or *legal cause*. The standard for determining proximate cause is generally *foreseeability*. Your roommate couldn't reasonably foresee the possibility that the owner of the car beneath his platform might have a heart attack as a result of some mishap with his paint bucket. Thus he probably wouldn't be held liable for this particular injury to the plaintiff's person.

3.2 Negligence and Employer Liability

At this point, you yourself may still want to ask an important question: "*Why me?*" Why should *you* be held liable for negligence? Undoubtedly you owed your client (the homeowner) a duty of care, but you personally did nothing to breach that duty. And if you didn't breach any duty of care, how could you have been the cause, either actual or proximate, of any injury suffered by your client? Where does he get off suing *you* for negligence?

The Law of Contracts

To answer these questions, we must enter an extremely important area of civil law—the law of contracts. A **contract** is an exchange of promises or an exchange of a promise for an act, and because it involves an *exchange*, it obviously involves at least two parties. As you can see in Figure 16.2, an *offeror* makes an offer to enter into a contract with an *offeree*. The offeror offers to do something in particular (or to refrain from doing something in particular), and if the offeree accepts this offer, a contract is created. As you can also see, both offer and acceptance must meet certain conditions.

> **contract**
>
> Exchange of promises or exchange of a promise for an act.

FIGURE 16.2 Parties to a Contract

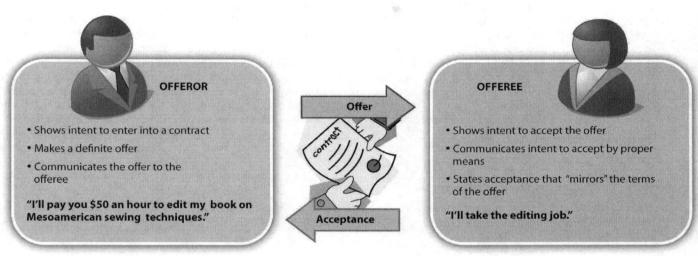

A contract is *legally enforceable*: if one party fails to do what he or she has promised to do, the other can ask the courts to enforce the agreement or award damages for injury sustained because the contract has been *breached*—because a promise made under the contract hasn't been kept or an act hasn't been performed. A contract, however, can be enforced only if it meets four requirements:[12]

- *Agreement*. The parties must have reached a mutual agreement. The offeror must have made an *offer*, and the offeree must have replied with an *acceptance*.
- *Consideration*. Each promise must be made in return for the performance of a legally sufficient act or promise. If one party isn't required to exchange something of legal value (e.g., money, property, a service), an agreement lacks sufficient consideration.
- *Contractual capacity*. Both parties must possess the full legal capacity to assume contractual duties. Limitations to full capacity include mental illness and such diminished states as intoxication.[13]
- *Lawful object*. The purpose of the contract must be legal. A contract to commit an unlawful act or to violate public policy is *void* (without legal force).

Employment Contracts

Here's where you come in: an employment relationship like the one that you had with your roommate is a contract. Under this contract, both parties have certain duties (you're obligated to compensate your roommate, for instance, and he's obligated to perform his assigned tasks in good faith). The law assumes that, when performing his employment duties, your employee is under your *control*—that you control the time, place, and method of the work.[14] This is a key concept in your case.

Respondeat Superior

U.S. law governing employer-employee contracts derives, in part, from English common law of the seventeenth century, which established the doctrine known as *respondeat superior*—"Let the master answer [for the servant's actions]." This principle held that when a servant was performing a task for a master, the master was liable for any damage that the servant might do (a practical consideration, given that servants were rarely in any position to make financial restitution for even minor damages).[15] Much the same principle exists in contemporary U.S. employment law, which extends it to include the "servant's" violations of tort law. Your client—the homeowner—has thus filed a *respondeat superior* claim of negligence against you as your roommate's employer.

Scope of Employment

In judging your responsibility for the damages done to the homeowner's car by your employee, the court will apply a standard known as *scope of employment*: an employee's actions fall within the scope of his employment under two conditions: (1) if they are performed in order to fulfill contractual duties owed to his employer and (2) if the employer is (or could be) in some control, directly or indirectly, over the employee's actions.[16]

If you don't find much support in these principles for the idea that your roommate was negligent but you weren't, that's because there isn't much. Your roommate was in fact your employee; he was clearly performing contractual duties when he caused the accident, and as his employer, you were, directly or indirectly, in control of his activities. You may argue that the contract with your roommate isn't binding because it was never put in writing, but that's irrelevant because employment contracts don't have to be in writing.[17] You could remind the court that you repeatedly told your employee to put his paint bucket in a safer place, but this argument won't carry much weight: in general, courts consider an employee's forbidden acts to be within the scope of his employment.[18]

On the other hand, the same principle protects you from liability in the assault-and-battery case against your roommate. The court will probably find that his aggressive response to the neighbor's comment wasn't related to the business at hand or committed within the scope of his employment; in responding to the neighbor's insult to his intelligence, he was acting independently of his employment contract with you.

Finally, now that we've taken a fairly detailed look at some of the ways in which the law works to make business relationships as *predictable* as possible, let's sum up this section by reminding ourselves that the U.S. legal system is also *flexible*. In its efforts to resolve your case, let's say that the court assesses the issues as follows:

> *The damage to the homeowner's car amounts to $3,000. He can't recover anything from your roommate, who owns virtually nothing but his personal library of books on medieval theology. Nor can he recover anything from your business-liability insurer because you never thought your business would need any insurance (and couldn't afford it anyway). So that leaves you: Can the homeowner recover damages from you personally? Legally, yes: although you didn't go through the simple formalities of creating a sole proprietorship (see Chapter 4), you are nevertheless liable for the contracts and torts of your business. On the other hand, you're not worth much more than your roommate, at least when it comes to financial assets. You have a six-year-old stereo system, a seven-year-old panel truck, and about $200 in a savings account—what's left after you purchased the two ladders and the platform that you used as scaffolding. The court could order you to pay the $3,000 out of future earnings but it doesn't have to. After all, the homeowner knew that you had no business-liability insurance but hired you anyway because he was trying to save money on the cost of painting his house. Moreover, he doesn't have to pay the $3,000 out of his own pocket because his personal-property insurance will cover the damage to his car.*

You should probably consider yourself lucky. Had your case gone to court, it would have been subject to the *rules of civil procedure* outlined in Figure 16.3. As you might suspect, civil suits are time-consuming. Research shows that litigation takes an average of 24.2 months from the time a complaint is filed until a judgment is rendered (25.6 months if you're involved in a tort lawsuit).

FIGURE 16.3 Stages in a Civil Lawsuit

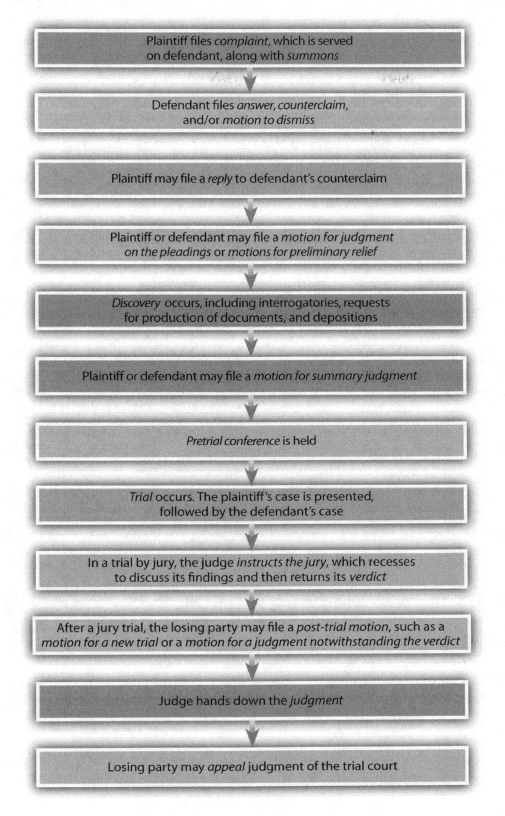

Plaintiff files *complaint,* which is served on defendant, along with *summons*

Defendant files *answer, counterclaim,* and/or *motion to dismiss*

Plaintiff may file a *reply* to defendant's counterclaim

Plaintiff or defendant may file a *motion for judgment on the pleadings* or *motions for preliminary relief*

Discovery occurs, including interrogatories, requests for production of documents, and depositions

Plaintiff or defendant may file a *motion for summary judgment*

Pretrial conference is held

Trial occurs. The plaintiff's case is presented, followed by the defendant's case

In a trial by jury, the judge *instructs the jury,* which recesses to discuss its findings and then returns its *verdict*

After a jury trial, the losing party may file a *post-trial motion,* such as a *motion for a new trial* or a *motion for a judgment notwithstanding the verdict*

Judge hands down the *judgment*

Losing party may *appeal* judgment of the trial court

And of course it's expensive. Let's say that you have a $40,000-a-year job and decide to file a civil suit. Your lawyer will charge you between $200 and $350 an hour. At that rate, he or she will consume your monthly net income of about $1,800 in nine hours' worth of work. But what about your jury award? Won't that more than compensate you for your legal fees? It depends, but bear in mind that, according to one study, the median award in civil cases is $33,000.[19] And you could lose.

KEY TAKEAWAYS

- A **negligence tort** results from *carelessness*. In order to prove a negligence claim, a plaintiff must demonstrate four elements:

  1. *That the defendant owed a* duty of care *to the plaintiff*. **Duty of care** refers to the basic obligation not to cause harm or an unreasonable risk of harm.
  2. *That the defendant* breached *his duty of care*. Did the defendant fail to act as a reasonable person would act?
  3. *That the defendant's* breach of duty of care *caused injury to the plaintiff or the plaintiff's property*.
  4. *That the defendant's action did in fact cause the injury in question*. The direct cause-and-effect relationship between the defendant's action and the plaintiff's injury is called a *cause in fact* or *actual cause*. The point beyond which a defendant is no longer liable for the actions set in motion by his or her carelessness is called a *proximate cause* or *legal cause*. The standard for determining proximate cause is generally *foreseeability*: could the defendant reasonably foresee the possibility of the injury suffered by the plaintiff?

- A **contract** is an exchange of promises or an exchange of a promise for an act. An *offeror* makes an offer to enter into a contract with an *offeree*—that is, to do something in particular (or to refrain from doing something in particular). If the offeree accepts this offer, a contract is created.

- A contract is *legally enforceable*: if one party fails to do what he or she has promised to do, the other can ask the courts to enforce the agreement or award damages for injury sustained because the contract has been *breached*. An enforceable contract must meet four requirements:

  1. *Agreement*. The parties must have reached a mutual agreement.
  2. *Consideration*. Each promise must be made in return for the performance of a legally sufficient act or promise.
  3. *Contractual capacity*. Both parties must possess the full legal capacity to assume contractual duties.
  4. *Lawful object*. The purpose of the contract must be legal.

- The law assumes that, in an employer–employee contract, the employer *controls* the time, place, and method of the employee's work. The doctrine of *respondeat superior*—"Let the master answer [for the servant's actions]"—applies to employer–employee contracts. In judging an employer's responsibility for the damages caused by an employee's negligence, the court will apply the standard of *scope of employment*: an employee's actions fall within the scope of his employment under two conditions: (1) if they are performed in order to fulfill contractual duties owed to his employer and (2) if the employer is (or could be) in some control, directly or indirectly, over the employee's actions.

Before going to the next section of this chapter, take a few minutes to test your knowledge of the material covered in this section. Quizzes can be found under the "Resources" tab, "Study Aids: Quizzes."

EXERCISE

Let's say you own a used car business and offer to sell a customer a used car for $5,000. What is needed to create a binding contract for the sale of the car?

If, when the customer wants to go for a test drive, the salesperson drives into a tree and is injured, is your company liable? Why, or why not?

4.   PRODUCT LIABILITY

> ## LEARNING OBJECTIVES
>
> 1. Define "product liability," and discuss the three grounds, or "theories of recovery," for a claim of product liability.
> 2. Discuss the three forms of manufacturer's negligence that may be claimed in a product-liability case.
> 3. Define "strict liability," and explain the doctrine of strict liability in tort.
> 4. Define a "warranty," and distinguish between express warranties and implied warranties.
> 5. Identify the primary goal of tort law, and distinguish between compensatory damages and punitive damages.

In addition to intentional and negligence torts, U.S. law recognizes a third category of torts: **strict liability torts** involve actions that are inherently dangerous and for which a party may be liable no matter how carefully he or she (or it) performs them. To better appreciate the issues involved in cases of strict liability, let's take up the story of your legal adventures in the world of business where we left off:

strict liability tort

Tort resulting from actions that are inherently dangerous and for which a party may be liable no matter how carefully he or she performs them.

> *Having escaped the house-painting business relatively unscathed, you head back home to rethink your options for gainful employment over your summer vacation. You've stored your only remaining capital assets—the two ladders and the platform that you'd used for scaffolding—in your father's garage, where one afternoon, your uncle notices them. Examining one of the ladders, he asks you how much weight it's designed to hold, and you tell him what the department manager at Ladders 'N' Things told you—three hundred pounds per rung. He nods as if this is a good number, and, sensing that he might want to buy them, you hasten to add that though you got them at a cut-rate price because of a little rust, they're virtually brand-new. As it turns out, he doesn't want to buy them, but he does offer to pay you $35 an hour to take them to his house and help him put up new roofing. He's easygoing, he's family, and he probably won't sue you for anything, so you jump at the opportunity.*
>
> *Everything goes smoothly until day two, when you're working on the scaffolding two stories off the ground. As you're in the process of unwrapping a bundle of shingles, one of the ladders buckles, bringing down the platform and depositing you on your uncle's stone patio with a cervical fracture.*

Fortunately, there's no damage to your spinal cord, but you're in pain and you need surgery. Now it's your turn to sue somebody. But whom? And for what?

4.1   Pursuing a Claim of Product Liability

It comes as no surprise when your lawyer advises an action for **product liability**—a claim of injury suffered because of a defective product (in your case, of course, the ladder). The legal concept of product liability, he explains, developed out of the principles of tort law. He goes on to say that in cases of product liability, there are three grounds for pursuing a claim and seeking damages—what lawyers call three "theories of recovery":

product liability

Claim of injury suffered because of a defective product.

- Negligence
- Strict liability
- Breach of warranty

As the plaintiff, he emphasizes, you'll want to use as many of these three grounds as possible.[20]

Grounds of Negligence

In selecting defendants in your case, you'll start with the manufacturer of the ladder. Manufacturer's negligence—carelessness—can take three different forms:[21]

- *Negligent failure to warn.* The manufacturer may be liable if the company knew (or should have known) that, without a warning, the ladder would be dangerous in ordinary use or in any reasonably foreseeable use. It's possible, for example, that you made the ladder's collapse more likely by placing it at a less than optimal angle from the wall of the house. That mistake, however, is a reasonably foreseeable use of the product, and if the manufacturer failed to warn you of this possibility, the company is liable for failure to warn.

    - *Negligent failure to warn.* The manufacturer may be liable if the company knew (or should have known) that, without a warning, the ladder would be dangerous in ordinary use or in any reasonably foreseeable use. It's possible, for example, that you made the ladder's collapse more likely by placing it at a less than optimal angle from the wall of the house. That mistake, however, is a reasonably foreseeable use of the product, and if the manufacturer failed to warn you of this possibility, the company is liable for failure to warn.[22]

    - *Negligent design.* As the term suggests, this principle applies to defectively designed products. In law, a product is defective if, despite any warnings, the risk of harm outweighs its usefulness in doing what it's designed to do. If, for example, your ladder left the manufacturer's facility with rivets that were likely to break when weight was placed on it, the ladder may be judged defective in its design.

- *Negligent design.* As the term suggests, this principle applies to defectively designed products. In law, a product is defective if, despite any warnings, the risk of harm outweighs its usefulness in doing what it's designed to do. If, for example, your ladder left the manufacturer's facility with rivets that were likely to break when weight was placed on it, the ladder may be judged defective in its design.

FIGURE 16.4

The U.S. Consumer Product Safety Commission has overseen the recall of thousands of baby cribs that it determined to have defective designs.

- *Negligence per se.* The manufacturer may be liable if the ladder fails to meet legal standards. According to standards set by the Occupational Safety and Health Administration (OSHA), for example, the rungs on your ladder should be corrugated or covered with skid-resistant material to minimize slipping. If you're injured because they're not, the manufacturer may be liable on grounds of negligence per se.[23]

If you decide to apply the concept of negligence in suing the manufacturer of the ladder, you must prove the four elements of a negligence case that we detailed above—namely, the following:

1. That the defendant (the manufacturer) owed you a duty of care
2. That the defendant breached this duty of care
3. That the defendant's breach of duty of care caused injury to you or your property
4. That the defendant's action did in fact cause the injury in question

© 2010 Jupiterimages Corporation

Grounds of Strict Liability

For the sake of argument, let's say that your lawyer isn't very confident about pursuing a claim of negligence against the manufacturer of your ladder. The company doesn't appear to have been careless in any of the three forms prescribed by law, and it will in any case be difficult to demonstrate all four elements required in negligence cases. He suggests instead that you proceed on grounds of strict liability, pointing out that the principle of strict liability often makes the plaintiff's legal task less exacting. But (you ask) if the company wasn't *negligent*, how can it be *liable*, either "strictly" or in any other sense? Under the *doctrine of strict liability in tort*, he replies, you don't have to prove negligence on the manufacturer's part. He goes on to explain that under this doctrine, your right to compensation for injury is based on two legal suppositions:

1. Certain products put people at risk of injury no matter how much care is taken to prevent injury.
2. Consumers should have some means of seeking compensation if they're injured while using these products.[24]

Day in and day out, of course, people use ladders quite successfully. According to the Consumer Product Safety Commission (CPSC), however, every year accidents involving ladders cause three hundred deaths and one hundred thirty thousand injuries requiring emergency medical treatment.[25] In a certain number of these instances, the ladder is defective, and in cases of strict liability, it doesn't matter how much care was taken by the manufacturer to prevent defects. This seems a little harsh to you, but your lawyer explains that, in establishing the doctrine of strict liability in tort, the court cited two reasons for making the grounds of liability so strict:[26]

- The manufacturer can protect itself by taking steps to anticipate and prevent hazardous product features, but the public can't.
- The manufacturer can protect itself by purchasing insurance and passing the cost on to the public in the form of higher product prices. Again, the public enjoys no such protection.

Under these conditions, the manufacturer is willing to take a risk—namely, the risk of making available a product that's potentially dangerous, especially if defective. The manufacturer thus takes the first step in a process whereby this product reaches a consumer who may suffer "overwhelming misfortune" by using it, especially if it has become defective *during the process that takes it from the manufacturer to the user*. "Even if he is not negligent in the manufacture of the product," declared the court, the manufacturer "is *responsible for its reaching the market*" (italics added). There's no way of telling when or how a product will become defective or of predicting how or how many people will be injured by it. Defects and injuries, however, are "constant" dangers when people use such products, and users must therefore have some form of "constant protection" under law. That protection is established by the doctrine of strict liability in tort. Why should the manufacturer be held responsible for such defects and injuries? Because, reasoned the court, "the manufacturer is best situated to afford…protection."

And this, explains your lawyer, is why you're going to sue the manufacturer of your ladder on grounds of strict liability.

Strict Liability in the Distribution Chain

You're excited about the prospect of recovering monetary damages from the manufacturer of your ladder, but you continue to wonder (on completely hypothetical grounds, of course) whether the doctrine of strict liability is as fair as it should be. What about all the other businesses involved in the process of getting the product from the manufacturer to the user—especially the one that did in fact introduce the defect that caused all the trouble? Does the doctrine of strict liability relieve them of all liability in the case? Indeed not, your lawyer assures you. The concept of strict liability not only provides more practical grounds for suing the manufacturer but also supports your right to pursue claims against members of the manufacturer's distribution chain (see Chapter 9).[27] That's one reason, he points out, why product-liability lawsuits against businesses that sell such "unreasonably dangerous" products as ladders (or even deliver them to worksites) went up a hundredfold between 1950 and 2001, to a total of $205 billion.[28]

Now, let's say that your lawyer has given your defective ladder to a forensic laboratory in order to find out exactly what caused it to buckle and you to fall. As it turns out, the clue to the problem is the small patch of rust that brought down the price you paid for the ladder when you bought it. The ladder, concludes the lab, had for some time been in close proximity to liquid nitrogen, which can corrode various metals, including aluminum.[29] Sure enough, further investigation reveals that the entire shipment of ladders had been stored for nearly two years in a Ladders 'N' Things warehouse next to an inventory of liquid-nitrogen–based fertilizer. Your lawyer advises you that, in addition to your strict-liability case against the manufacturer of the ladder, you have a strong negligence case against the retailer from which you purchased it.

Figure 16.5 provides a simplified overview of the difference between negligence and strict liability as grounds for a product-liability claim.

FIGURE 16.5 Negligence versus Strict Liability

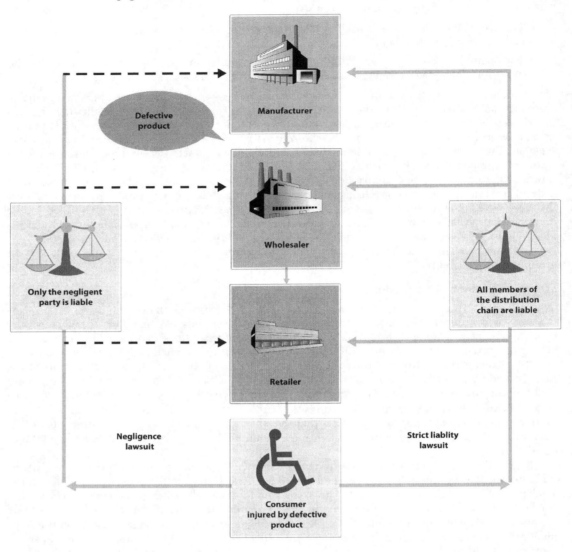

Grounds of Breach of Warranty

Moreover, adds your lawyer, there's one more matter to be considered in determining liability for your injury. Had not the department manager at Ladders 'N' Things assured you that the ladder would support a weight of three hundred pounds per rung? Your uncle had asked you about the weight capacity of the ladder because he knew that the roofing job meant putting heavy bundles of shingles on the scaffold. A ladder that holds three hundred pounds per rung is a Type IA extra-heavy–duty ladder suitable for such jobs as roofing and construction. According to the lab, however, the construction of your ladder is that of a Type II medium-duty–commercial ladder made for lighter-weight tasks.[30] The manager at Ladders 'N' Things, explains your lawyer, may have been guilty of *breach of warranty*—yet further grounds for holding the retailer liable in your product-liability case.

Types of Warranties

A **warranty** is a guarantee that a product meets certain standards of performance. In the United States, warranties are established by the **Uniform Commercial Code (UCC)**, a system of statutes designed to make commercial transactions consistent in all fifty states. Under the UCC, a warranty is based on contract law and, as such, constitutes a binding promise. If this promise—the promise that a product meets certain standards of performance—isn't fulfilled, the buyer may bring a claim of product liability against the seller or maker of the promise.

warranty

Guarantee that a product meets certain standards of performance.

Uniform Commercial Code (UCC)

U.S. system of statutes designed to make commercial transactions consistent in all fifty states.

Express Warranties

An **express warranty** is created when a seller affirms that a product meets certain standards of quality, description, performance, or condition. The seller can make an express warranty in any of three ways:

- By describing the product
- By making a promise of fact about the product
- By providing a model or sample of the product

Sellers aren't obligated to make express warranties. When they do make them, it's usually made through advertisements, catalogs, and so forth, but they needn't be made in writing; they can be oral or even inferred from the seller's behavior. They're valid even if they're made by mistake.

Implied Warranties

There are two types of **implied warranties**—that is, warranties that arise automatically out of transactions:

- In making an *implied warranty of merchantability*, the seller states that the product is reasonably fit for ordinary use. In selling you a ladder, for example, Ladders 'N' Things affirms that it satisfies any promises made on its packaging, meets average standards of quality, and should be acceptable to other users.

- An *implied warranty of fitness for a particular purpose* affirms that the product is fit for some specific use. Let's say, for example, that you had asked the manager at Ladders 'N' Things whether the ladder you had in mind was fit for holding a scaffolding platform for painting a house; if the manager had assured you that it was, he would have created an implied warranty of fitness for a particular purpose.

Table 16.3 provides a more complete overview of the different types of warranties, including more-detailed descriptions of the promises that may be entailed by each.

express warranty

Warranty created when a seller affirms that a product meets certain standards of quality, description, performance, or condition.

implied warranty

Warranty arising automatically out of a transaction.

TABLE 16.3 What Warranties Promise

Type of Warranty	Means by Which the Warranty May Be Created	Promises Entailed by the Warranty
Express warranty	Seller confirms that product conforms to the following: ■ All statements of fact or promise made about it ■ Any description of it ■ Any model or sample of it	Product meets certain standards of quality, description, performance, or condition
Implied warranty of merchantability	Law implies certain promises	Product: ■ Is fit for ordinary purposes for which it's used ■ Is adequately contained, packaged, and labeled ■ Is of an even kind, quality, and quantity within each unit ■ Conforms to any promise or statement of fact made on container or label ■ Passes without objection in the trade ■ Meets a fair, average, or middle range of quality
Implied warranty of fitness for a particular purpose	Law implies certain promises	Product is fit for the purpose for which the buyer acquires it *if* ■ Seller has reason to know the particular purpose for which it will be used ■ Seller makes a statement that it will serve that purpose ■ Buyer relies on seller's statement and purchases it

Source: Adapted from Henry R. Cheesman, Contemporary Business and Online Commerce Law: Legal, Internet, Ethical, and Global Environments, 5th ed. (Upper Saddle River, NJ: Pearson Education, 2006), 366.

What kinds of warranties did you receive when you bought your ladder? Naturally, you received implied warranties of merchantability, which arose out of your transaction with Ladders 'N' Things. You also received an implied warranty of fitness for a particular purpose (that the ladder would hold a scaffolding platform) and an express warranty (that it would a bear a weight of three hundred pounds per rung).

Do you have a case for product liability on grounds of breach of warranty? Arguably, says your lawyer, Ladders 'N' Things breached an implied warranty of merchantability because it sold you a ladder with a defect (corrosion damage) that made it unfit for ordinary use. It's also possible that the retailer breached an express warranty—the manager's assurance that the ladder would bear a weight of three hundred pounds per rung. First, the court will want to know whether that express warranty was a contributing factor—not necessarily the sole factor—in your decision to buy the ladder. If not, you probably can't recover for breach of the express warranty.

Second, there's the complex issue of whether that express warranty was tantamount to an assurance that the ladder could be used for such a job as roofing. Apparently your uncle thought it was, but that will be a matter for your lawyer to argue and the court to decide. It will all depend, in other words, on the flexibility and fairness of the legal system.

Product Liability and Agency Law

agency

Legal relationship in which one party acts on behalf of, and under the control of, another.

When your lawyer has wrapped up his explanation of warranties and ways of breaching them, you feel compelled to ask one last question: Why is Ladders 'N' Things, an entire corporate chain of retail stores, liable for breach of warranty committed by one department manager at one local outlet? Your lawyer replies that it's a matter of **agency**, which he defines for you as a legal relationship between two parties in which one party acts on behalf of, and under the control of, another. In a *principal-agent relationship* like the one diagrammed in Figure 16.6 the *agent* is acting on behalf of the *principal*.

FIGURE 16.6 Agency Relationship

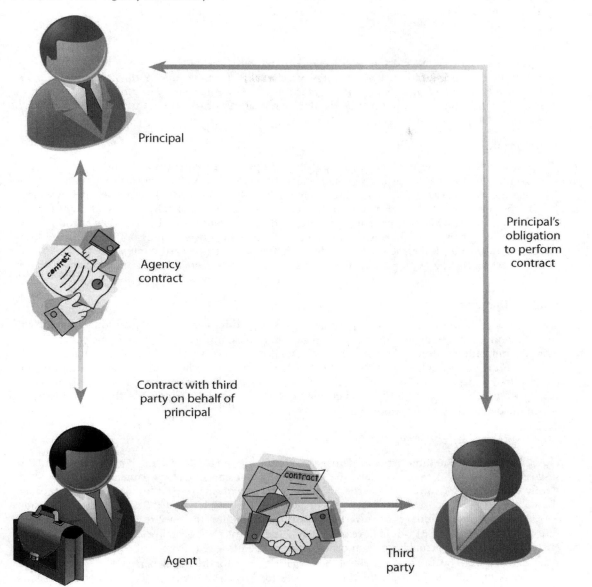

A lawyer acting on behalf of a client is an agent, as is a real estate broker acting on behalf of a homeowner or a partner acting on behalf of a partnership. Perhaps the most common type of agency relationship is the one that applies to your case—the salesperson who's acting on behalf of a retailer. If this sort of legal arrangement sounds familiar, that's probably because employer-employee relationships are also agency relationships.

Agency law is actually a mixture of contract law and tort law.[31] In order to appoint an agent, for example, a person must possess the *capacity*—the legal ability—to make a contract, and agency agreements must in general meet the four elements of a valid contract that we discussed in an earlier section of this chapter. As we've also seen, an agent (such as the department manager at your local Ladders 'N' Things outlet) can make the principal for whom he or she is acting liable for such torts as breach of warranty. The same thing is true of the warehouse manager who stored your ladder next to a shipment of liquid-nitrogen–based fertilizer; acting on behalf of Ladders 'N' Things, he or she exposed the company to liability for negligence.

4.2 Seeking Damages

So, what's your best course of action? You could sue both the manufacturer and the retailer, but to streamline things, your lawyer files only a strict-liability suit against the manufacturer, who agrees to settle out of court and pay damages. The manufacturer subsequently sues Ladders 'N' Things, charging that the retailer's negligence and breach of warranty were contributing causes of your injury. The jury agrees that the retailer's actions were proximate causes of your injury and orders Ladders 'N' Things to contribute to the fund of damages that the manufacturer has agreed to pay you.[32]

The Goals of Tort Law

Imposing damages is the chief means by which the legal system meets the primary goal of tort law—compensating injured parties, or, more precisely, *restoring victims to the conditions that they would have been in had their injuries never taken place.* As we just saw, you settled out of court, but only after your attorney had notified the ladder manufacturer of your intent to seek damages. As the victim of a tort, you may have sought two major types of damages.[33]

Compensatory Damages

compensatory damages
Monetary awards intended to restore tort victims to the conditions that they would have been in had their injuries never taken place.

The most common type of damages sought by plaintiffs, **compensatory damages** are monetary awards intended to meet the primary goal of legal action in tort cases. Some measures of compensatory damages are easier to establish than others—say, such expenses as medical costs. Likewise, if your injury keeps you from working at your job or profession, the court can calculate the amount that you would have earned while you were incapacitated. Things get more complicated when plaintiffs make claims involving pain and suffering or emotional distress (which may include both present and future physical and mental impairment). In deciding whether or not to award compensatory damages for such claims, it's the job of judges and juries to use common sense, good judgment, and general experience.[34]

Punitive Damages

punitive damages
Monetary awards to tort victims intended to deter similar injurious conduct in the future.

Awarded in addition to compensatory damages, **punitive damages** are intended to deter similar injurious conduct in the future. Some experts regard punitive damages as particularly useful in discouraging manufacturers from making unsafe products: if there were no risk of punitive damages, they argue, a manufacturer might find it cheaper to market an unsafe product and compensate injured consumers than to develop a safer product. To determine whether punitive damages are called for, a court usually considers "the degree of reprehensibility of the defendant's conduct"—that is, the extent to which the defendant's action was flagrant or unconscionable.[35]

The Goals of Contract Law

Note that basically the same types of damages are available in cases involving contract law, which we discussed previously. In contract law, the purpose of imposing monetary damages is to correct the wrong done when a contract is breached. *Compensatory damages* are paid by the party that breached the contract to compensate for losses suffered by the nonbreaching party. As in tort law, in other words, compensatory damages are awarded to restore the victim (the nonbreaching party) to the condition that he or she (or it) would have been in had the contract not been breached. Because each party entered into the contractual bargain in order to receive some benefit from it, the purpose of compensatory damages is to restore the "benefit of the bargain" to the nonbreaching party.[36]

Courts typically don't award *punitive damages* for breach of contract. They may be considered, however, if the breaching of the contract is accompanied by some kind of intentional tort, such as fraud or intentional failure to act fairly in discharging the contract.[37] The purpose of punitive damages is to punish the breaching party, to deter it from similar conduct in the future, and to set an example for other parties to legal contracts.

As you can see from Figure 16.7, there are two categories of contractual breach. A *minor breach* occurs when the breaching party has achieved a level of *substantial performance*—that is, completed nearly all the terms of the contract. In the event of a minor breach, the nonbreaching party may seek damages. A *material break* occurs when one party renders *inferior performance*—performance that destroys the value of the contract. In such cases, the nonbreaching party may seek to rescind the contract and to recover damages to compensate for any payments made to the breaching party.[38]

FIGURE 16.7 Remedies for Breach

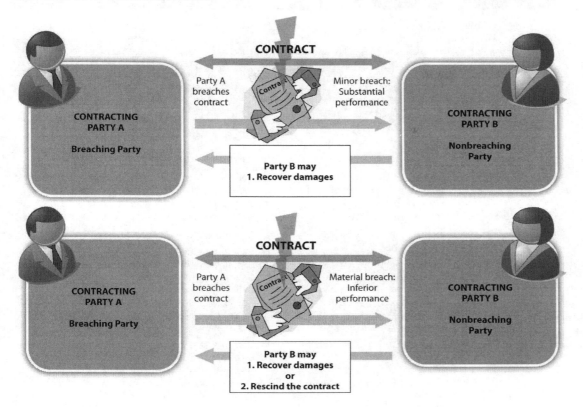

KEY TAKEAWAYS

- **Product liability** is a claim of injury suffered because of a defective product. In such cases, there are three grounds for pursuing a claim and seeking damages (that is, three "theories of recovery"): negligence, strict liability, and breach of warranty. Most plaintiffs use as many of these three grounds as possible.

- In a product-liability case, a manufacturer's negligence can take three different forms:

  1. *Negligent failure to warn*. The manufacturer may be liable if the company knew (or should have known) that, without a warning, the ladder would be dangerous in ordinary use or in any reasonably foreseeable use.
  2. *Negligent design*. A product is defective if, despite any warnings, the risk of harm outweighs its usefulness in doing what it's designed to do.
  3. *Negligence per se*. The manufacturer may be liable if the ladder fails to meet legal standards.

- **Strict liability torts** involve actions that are inherently dangerous and for which a party may be liable no matter how carefully he or she performs them. Under the *doctrine of strict liability in tort*, the plaintiff doesn't have to prove negligence on the manufacturer's part, nor does it matter how much care was taken by the manufacturer to prevent defects. The doctrine of strict liability rests on two legal conclusions:

  1. The manufacturer can protect itself by taking steps to anticipate and prevent hazardous product features, but the public can't.
  2. The manufacturer can protect itself by purchasing insurance and passing the cost on to the public in the form of higher product prices; the consumer has no such protection. The manufacturer is liable under the doctrine of strict liability for any harm that comes to a person from using the product, especially if it has become defective during the process of getting the product from the manufacturer to the user. The concept of strict liability also supports the plaintiff's right to pursue claims against members of the manufacturer's distribution chain.
  3. Breaching a **warranty**—a guarantee that a product meets certain standards of performance—is grounds for recovering in a product-liability case. An **express warranty** is created when a seller affirms that a product meets certain standards of quality, description, performance, or condition. An **implied warranty** arises automatically out of a transaction and takes one of two forms: (1) an *implied warranty of merchantability* (which states that the product is reasonably fit for ordinary use) and (2) an *implied warranty of fitness for a particular purpose* (which states that the product is fit for some specific use).
  4. **Agency** is a legal relationship between two parties in which one party acts on behalf of, and under the control of, another. In a *principal–agent relationship*, the *agent* is acting on behalf of the *principal*. Employer-employee relationships are also agency relationships.
  5. The primary goal of tort law is restoring the victim to the condition that he or she would have been in had no injury ever taken place. Likewise, the primary goal of contract law is restoring the nonbreaching party to the condition that he or she would have been in had the contract not been breached. To achieve these goals, the legal system provides for monetary awards in the form of **compensatory damages**. Another form of monetary award, **punitive damages**, is intended to punish, to deter similar injurious conduct in the future, or to set an example.

Before going to the next section of this chapter, take a few minutes to test your knowledge of the material covered in this section. Quizzes can be found under the "Resources" tab, "Study Aids: Quizzes."

EXERCISE

Upbeat Pharmaceutical Company manufactures a flu vaccine. Several people who got the vaccine became ill. One of them required hospitalization for two weeks. Medical experts believe the vaccine was the cause of their illnesses. Do the people who got sick after taking the vaccine have a valid claim against Upbeat? On what basis?

5.   SOME PRINCIPLES OF PUBLIC LAW

> ## LEARNING OBJECTIVES
>
> 1. Explain the difference between private law and public law.
> 2. Define "statutory law," and give examples of statutory laws at various governmental levels.
> 3. Explain externalities, and show why taxation is used as a means of addressing them.
> 4. Discuss the idea of "market failure" and the principle of "efficiency" as a foundation of law.
> 5. Define "administrative law," and discuss the role of federal administrative agencies in making and enforcing administrative laws.
> 6. Define "case law," and explain the concepts of "precedent" and "judicial review."

Both tort law and contract law fall into the larger domain of **private law**, which deals with private relationships among individuals and organizations. In addition, of course, there are numerous types of law that deal with the relationship of government to private individuals and other private entities, including businesses. This is the area of **public law**, which falls into three general categories:[39]

- *Criminal law*, which we've already introduced, prohibits and punishes wrongful conduct.
- *Constitutional law* concerns the laws and basic legal principles set forth by the U.S. Constitution.
- *Administrative law* refers to statutes and regulations related to the activities of certain legal bodies known as *administrative agencies*. We'll have more to say about administrative agencies and administrative law later in the chapter.

Public law obviously has a major impact on the activities of both individuals and businesses in the United States. We'll discuss the nature of this impact and the reasons why so many private activities are subject to the rules and principles of public law. Like most areas of the law, public law is an extremely complex field of study, and to keep things manageable we're going to explore this field by focusing on three less-than-glamorous legal issues: *why cigarette littering is against the law, why cigarettes cost so much*, and *why businesses ban smoking in the workplace*.

private law

Body of law dealing with private relationships among individuals and organizations.

public law

Body of law dealing with the relationship of government to private individuals and other private entities.

5.1   Why Cigarette Littering Is against the Law

Having sold the Stratford Inn in 1991, former senator George McGovern didn't have to worry about the Connecticut Clean Indoor Air Act of 2004, which banned smoking in such places as the bar of his hotel.[40] Like similar statutes in many states, the Connecticut law was enacted in response to the health hazards of secondary smoke in closed environments (an estimated three thousand nonsmokers die from smoke-related lung cancer every year).

Interestingly, shortly after the new statewide antismoking law went into effect, officials in Connecticut noticed a curious phenomenon: cigarette litter—packaging, lighting materials, and, especially, butts—had begun to accumulate at an unprecedented rate in outdoor areas surrounding drinking establishments, exacerbating an already serious environmental problem. Unless you've lived your entire life indoors, you have undoubtedly noticed that cigarette butts are a fixture of the great American outdoors: Americans smoke about 360 billion cigarettes a year and discard 135 million pounds of butts, much of which ends up as litter.[41] In fact, cigarettes account for 20 percent of all the litter in the United States, 18 percent of which ends up in local streams and other waterways.

FIGURE 16.8

Cigarettes account for 20 percent of all litter.

© 2010 Jupiterimages Corporation

In 2006, U.S. Senator Joseph Lieberman of Connecticut introduced the Cigarette Litter Prevention Act, a federal statute that would require cigarette producers to attach environmental warnings to their packaging.[42] In Connecticut itself, however, statewide antilittering law covers only state property, land, and waters.[43] When it comes to private property, such as most areas adjacent to restaurants and bars, it's left to local communities to police littering violations. The town council of Wallingford, for example, recently took action on a proposed ordinance to fine business owners who fail to clean up the litter on their doorsteps and in their parking lots. The law also targets proprietors who continue to sweep cigarette and other litter into storm drains—a major source of waterway pollution. "I'm not a big fan of making laws to do stuff like this," admitted one town councilor, "but if people don't do it, then they have to be told to do it."[44]

The Wallingford ordinance calls for a written warning followed by a fine of $90 for each day that the offending litter isn't removed. Connecticut state law carries a maximum fine of $199 plus a surcharge of half the fine. As for litter "thrown, blown, scattered, or spilled" from a motor vehicle, Connecticut law regards it as evidence that the driver has in fact littered, but the statute applies only to state land and waters. The issue of litterbug drivers, however, is a much bigger concern to lawmakers in certain other states. In California, for example, Vehicle Code Section 23111 states that "no person in any vehicle and no pedestrian shall throw or discharge from or upon any road or highway or adjoining area, public or private, any lighted or nonlighted cigarette, cigar, match, or any flaming or glowing substance." The statute carries a fine of $380 but could run as high as $1,000. In addition, you may spend eight hours picking up roadside trash, and because the violation goes on your driving record, your insurance premiums may increase.[45] Despite such vigorous preventive measures, the state of California spends $62 million a year of the taxpayers' money to clean up roadside litter.[46]

Besides the cleanup cost, there's another reason why California law regarding motor vehicles and cigarette litter is so stiff: at certain times of the year and under certain conditions, much of the state is a tinderbox. In January 2001, for example, a cigarette tossed from a car onto a grassy highway median near San Diego sparked a brush fire that soon spread across eleven thousand acres of rural forestland. As columns of acrid, ash-filled smoked billowed some thirty thousand feet into the air, officials closed down a twelve-mile stretch of Interstate highway and evacuated 350 homes. Suffering from eye, nose, and lung irritation, hundreds of residents rushed to safety with no time to rescue personal possessions, and before an army of two thousand federal, state, and local emergency workers had contained the blaze a week later, the firefighting effort had cost California taxpayers $10 million.[47]

Statutory Responses to Littering

Clearly the problem of cigarette litter has attracted the attention of lawmakers at every level. All the laws that we mentioned in this section are current or proposed *statutory laws*—laws made by legislative bodies. Enacted by the Connecticut General Assembly, the Clean Indoor Air Act of 2004 and Littering Law (amended 2005) are *state statutes*, as is California's Vehicle Code, which was enacted by the California State Legislature. The antilittering law in Wallingford is a local law, or *municipal ordinance*, passed by the Town Council, whose authority derives from the state General Assembly. If Senator's Lieberman's proposed Cigarette Litter Prevention Act is passed by the U.S. Congress, it will become a *federal statute*. Note, by the way, that each of these laws is a *criminal* statute designed to prohibit and punish wrongful conduct (usually by fine).

5.2 Why Cigarettes Cost So Much

As any smoker will tell you, cigarette littering, and smoking itself, isn't cheap. The cost of a pack of cigarettes varies depending on where you live, but they're higher than they used to be everywhere in the United States. A pack of cigarettes today ranges from $11.90 in New York State (and $14.00 in New York City) to $4.74 in West Virginia.[48] If you're a pack-a-day smoker who lives in New York City, $5,000 of your money goes up in smoke each year. Even if you're lucky enough to be paying the lower West Virginia price, you're still laying out more than $1,700 a year (roughly a nice house payment). Prices vary in large part because of taxes. On top of state taxes, the federal government levies a tax of $1.01 and some municipalities add on their own taxes. New York City, for example, charges $1.50 per pack in addition to the New York State levy of $4.35 (the nation's highest) for a total tax rate of $6.86 per pack (in contrast to a tax rate of $1.56 in West Virginia).[49]

Excises and Externalities

These taxes are *excise taxes*, a rather vague term that refers to taxes placed on "goods" produced within a country. Traditionally, excise taxes have been levied on a wide variety of products, and today they're often placed on items and activities with which people may harm themselves (such as cigarettes), those around them (alcohol when overused), or the general environment (activities that pollute the air we all breathe).

In talking about taxes, we're talking about one means of covering the *costs* of these items and activities, and economists have a word for such costs: **externalities** are costs that don't show up as part of the market price for a product.[50] Actually, externalities can be either bad (i.e., costs) or good (i.e., benefits), but in detailing the negative effects of cigarette littering, we're obviously focusing on *negative externalities*. Think of externalities as spillover effects: they're costs or benefits that result from marketplace transactions—payments of certain prices for certain products—but that aren't borne by the sellers or buyers of the products exchanged in those transactions. The price of a pack of cigarettes, for example, doesn't include the cost of cigarette-litter cleanup or the cost of extinguishing wildfires. These costs are borne by *other people*—people who are outside or *external to* the basic transactions.[51]

Because these costs don't affect the seller's total cost in making the product available, they don't affect the price that the seller charges the buyer. And because the smoker doesn't pay these costs when he or she pays the price of a pack of cigarettes, the product is, in effect, cheaper than it would be otherwise. How much cheaper? As we've just seen, the answer to that question depends on the total cost of externalities. We can't pretend to trace every penny required to cover the total cost of having cigarettes for sale in the United States, but we can draw some conclusions from a few well-researched estimates. It's estimated, for example, that the total cost of public and private cigarette-related health care in the United States is approximately $96 billion annually; it's also estimated that the total cost to U.S. businesses in cigarette-related lost productivity is *another* $97 billion per year.[52] According to the U.S. Centers for Disease Control and Prevention, the combined cost of cigarette-related health care and lost productivity comes to $10.47 per pack.[53]

If you're a smoker, in other words, it could be (and from an economic standpoint, should be) worse. Why isn't it worse? Because the taxes attached to cigarette prices are, as we've explained, excise taxes, and excise taxes cover only a part of external costs.

> **externalities**
>
> Cost that doesn't show up as part of the market price for a product.

5.3   Government and the Economic Environment of Business

These costs aren't simply figments of the economist's imagination: if you suspect that nobody actually pays them, ask the taxpayers of Connecticut and California. Or consider your own tax bill: even if you're a nonsmoker in an average American household, you pay $630 a year in smoking-related federal and state taxes.[54] Taxation is obviously one means by which governments collect money to defray the costs to the taxpayers of an undesirable activity. In many instances, the tax bill is shared by sellers and buyers, but in the cigarette market, sellers merely pass along the added cost to the price paid by buyers. Thus, most of the money raised by the excise tax on cigarettes is paid by smokers.

Government Intervention in the Marketplace

This brings us to a crucial question among political theorists, economists, policymakers, business owners, and consumers—just about every member of society who has social and economic activities to pursue: Why does government intervene in marketplace transactions? Or, perhaps more accurately, Why have most of us come to expect and accept government intervention in our economic activities?

Market Failure: Theory versus Reality

There is, of course, no single answer to this question, but our discussion of the negative externalities of smoking leads us to one of the more important explanations: government may intervene in economic activity to "correct" *market failure*. Recall, for example, our discussion of economic competition in Chapter 1, where we explained that, under conditions of *perfect competition*, all prices would be determined by the rules of supply and demand. If the market for cigarettes were perfectly competitive, cigarettes would cost $10.47 per pack, not $3.11—the average cost of a pack of cigarettes if we subtract the federal tax of $1.01 and the average state tax of $1.46 from the average cost per pack of $5.58.[55] Clearly the market for cigarettes isn't as *efficient* as it might be. We can tell, for example, that it doesn't operate at minimal cost because some of its costs—its negative externalities—spill outside the market and have to be borne by people who don't buy or sell cigarettes.[56]

Here's another way of looking at the issue.[57] *In theory*—that is, according to the principle of supply and demand—the demand for cigarettes will go down as added taxes drive up the price. *In reality*, however, it takes a fairly large increase in price to reduce demand by even a small amount. Moreover, because cigarettes are addictive, demand for the product pays relatively less attention to price than does demand for most products—smokers continue to buy cigarettes regardless of the price. Thus it takes a 10 percent hike in prices to cut cigarette consumption by 4 percent, while the same increase will cut consumption by young people—who presumably aren't yet addicted—by 7 percent.[58]

Law and Economic Decision Making

In the United States, the principle that government intervention is the best means of correcting market failure supported most government regulation of economic activity during the twentieth century.[59] As the response to the subprime crisis makes clear, it continues to support government economic intervention into the twenty-first century.

Perhaps this fact should come as no surprise. In a very real sense, economics is the basic business of law and the legal system. How so? Arguably, we establish laws and legal systems because all resources are not equally available to everybody. If they were, we wouldn't need rules for allocating them—rules for determining who possesses them and how they should be transferred. In using taxation, for example, to allocate economic resources in order to pay for the negative externalities of smoking, the legal system—the set of institutions that enforce our rules of efficient resource allocation—is basically performing a modern version of one of its oldest functions.

Efficiency and the Law

Efficiency, therefore, is one foundation of law: the rule of law encourages "efficiency" in the sense that it requires us to act within certain well-defined limits. It prohibits activities that take place outside those limits—such as stealing resources—because they make the process of allocating resources more wasteful and expensive.

Let's say, for example, that you (hereinafter "Party A") enter into a contract with Party B.[60] The grid in Figure 16.9 shows all the possible outcomes of this agreement. If you both perform as contracted, you both benefit from the bargain, each realizing a profit of $X. This is the result in the upper-left–hand box of the grid. Let's say, however, that Party B takes your money but fails to live up to her end of the bargain. In that case, we get the outcome in the upper-right–hand box: because you've lost your money, you end up with –$X, and because Party B got your money without spending hers, she ends up with $2X. Understandably, you don't intend for this to happen and so stipulate that Party B must perform her end of the bargain before you hand over your money. Fearing that you might not pay after she's lived up to her part of the contract, Party B demands payment before she performs her part. The inevitable result of the contract is now displayed in both lower boxes of the grid: no one does anything and no one earns any profit. In completely wasting the value of every resource committed to the agreement by Party A and Party B, the business process has reached the ultimate level of inefficiency; it's actually ground to a halt.

FIGURE 16.9 Contract Game

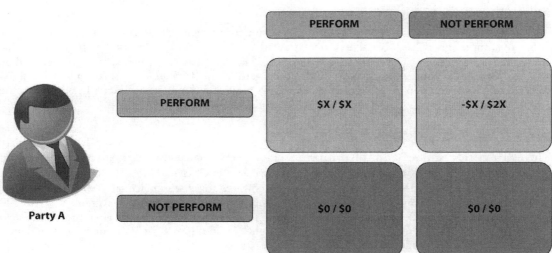

Party B

	PERFORM	NOT PERFORM
PERFORM	$X / $X	-$X / $2X
NOT PERFORM	$0 / $0	$0 / $0

Party A

The only thing that prevents this scenario from playing out in any (or every) contractual situation is the existence of a legal system that can enforce contractual agreements. When such a system is in place, nonperformance makes very little sense. Had Party B taken your money and then failed to perform, the legal system would have required her either to pay back your $X or to live up to the contract, whereby you would earn your expected $X in profit. As a matter of fact, because she would also have been required to pay court costs, she'd end up with less than her original $X—in which case, she'd be worse off than had she performed her part of the bargain in the first place.

Contracting and the Law

As this illustration suggests, contractual relationships are the building blocks of a modern economy. Just about every activity that we pursue in the business environment is based on a contract, and as we've seen throughout this chapter, producers of goods and services make contracts with consumers, other producers, and the government. Moreover, there's often only a very fine line between the business environment and one's private life: you enter into a contract when you take a job, rent an apartment, get a bank loan, use a credit card, and even when you get married.

All these relationships are possible because our legal system provides for the reliable enforcement of contracts. There are countries where the legal system fails to provide reliable contract enforcement, and it should come as no surprise that economic growth in these countries has been severely hampered.

Ethics and the Law

"Efficiency," of course, isn't the only foundation of law. We don't punish murder because it wastes human resources. Law has an essentially *ethical* underpinning as well. We regard some activities, such as killing another human being, as *mala per se* (inherently bad). Other activities, such as filling the air with secondary cigarette smoke, we regard as *mala prohibita* (bad because we declare them to be bad).[61]

Naturally, the distinction between what's inherently bad and what's bad because we declare it bad isn't always clear. We may, for example, punish failure to remove certain chemical compounds (including those in secondhand smoke) from workplace air because they're hazardous to human health and life: according to the American Lung Association, people exposed to smoke in the workplace are 17 percent more likely to develop lung cancer than people who aren't. We may also punish the same failure because we regard certain consequences to be bad—economically inefficient, for example:

research shows that secondhand-smoke exposure in the United Sates costs $10 billion a year, $5 billion in direct medical costs.[62]

5.4 Why Businesses Ban Smoking in the Workplace

A closer look at the ways in which the U.S. legal system approaches the problem of secondhand smoke in the workplace will allow us to focus on some important aspects of that system that we haven't yet encountered. In particular, we'll learn something about the difference between federal *statutory law* and *administrative law*, and we'll see how the *judiciary branch* of the legal system—the courts—may affect the enforcement of law.

Federal Statutory Law: OSHAct

As most of us learned if we studied American government in high school, Article I, Section 1 of the U.S. Constitution gives "all legislative powers granted herein"—that is, all lawmaking powers set aside for the federal government—to Congress.[63] So that's where we'll start—with a specific law enacted by Congress under its constitutional powers. Congress passed the *Occupational Safety and Health Act (OSHAct)* in 1970 to establish standards of safety and health for American workers. In particular, the statute requires employers to keep workplaces free from occupational hazards.

Federal Administrative Law: OSHA

administrative agency

Body created by legislative act to carry out specific duties.

Occupational Health and Safety Administration (OSHA)

Federal administrative agency empowered to set workplace safety and health standards and to ensure that employers take appropriate steps to meet them.

The OSHAct created three **administrative agencies**—bodies created by legislative act to carry out specific duties. The most important agency established by the OSHAct is the **Occupational Health and Safety Administration (OSHA)**, which is empowered to set workplace safety and health standards and to ensure that employers take appropriate steps to meet them. OSHA was among a number of agencies created during the so-called rights revolution of 1960–1980, in which government acted to protect workplace, consumer, and environmental rights in addition to rights against discrimination based on race, sex, age, and national origin.

Responsibility for implementing the OSHAct is delegated to the Department of Labor, making OSHA one of more than fifty agencies managed by the executive branch of the federal government. Figure 16.10 shows the growth of federal administrative agencies from the end of the nineteenth century to the present. As you can see, periods of significant increase in the creation of such agencies tend to correspond to eras of perceived market failure—that is, the failure of unregulated market activity to maintain certain levels of fairness or social responsibility.[64]

FIGURE 16.10 Administrative Agencies

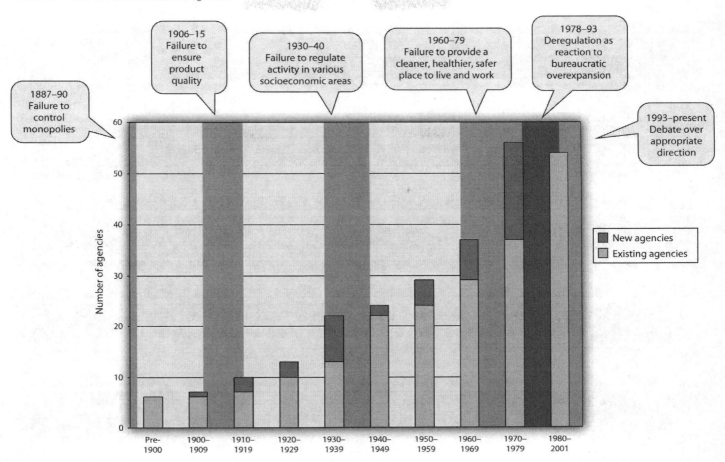

Administrative Rulemaking: OSHA's General Duty Clause

In passing the OSHAct, Congress didn't determine appropriate standards of safety and health, nor did it designate specific occupational hazards. It stipulated only a so-called General Duty Clause requiring an employer to provide "employment and a place of employment which are free from recognized hazards that are causing or are likely to cause death or serious physical harm to his employees."[65] In setting more specific standards for satisfying this "general duty," OSHA may choose to adopt those of recognized industry groups or it may set its own standards, usually relying on research conducted by a sister agency, the National Institute of Occupational Safety and Health (NIOSH). In either case, proposed regulations must go through the five-step process summarized in Figure 16.11. When a regulation has passed through this process, it becomes administrative law, which, as we've seen, refers generally to statutes and regulations related to the activities of such agencies as OSHA.

FIGURE 16.11 Administrative Rulemaking Procedure

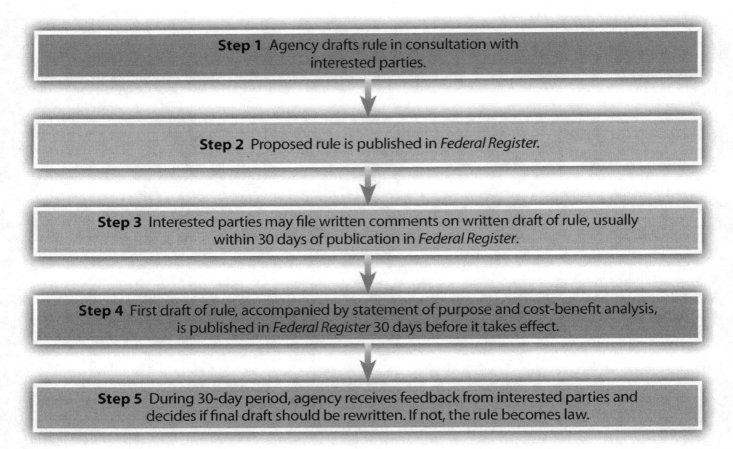

Step 1 Agency drafts rule in consultation with interested parties.

Step 2 Proposed rule is published in *Federal Register.*

Step 3 Interested parties may file written comments on written draft of rule, usually within 30 days of publication in *Federal Register.*

Step 4 First draft of rule, accompanied by statement of purpose and cost-benefit analysis, is published in *Federal Register* 30 days before it takes effect.

Step 5 During 30-day period, agency receives feedback from interested parties and decides if final draft should be rewritten. If not, the rule becomes law.

Administrative Law and Judicial Review

OSHA Regulation 29 CFR 1910.1000 deals with air contaminants but doesn't address cigarette smoke itself. Rather, it limits exposure to some of the forty-seven thousand chemical compounds contained in *environmental tobacco smoke*. Based in part on NIOSH studies, OSHA has set *permissible exposure limits* for such compounds and stipulated that employee exposure to them shall not exceed designated permissible exposure limits.[66] OSHA continues to use permissible exposure limits to assess levels of specific contaminants, and up until the early 1990s, it also relied on the General Duty Clause to deal with cases involving the hundreds of substances not covered by specific permissible exposure limits. Since then, however, the agency has been forced to restrict its use of both the General Duty Clause and permissible exposure limits in enforcing air-contaminant standards.[67] What's responsible for this change in policy? What could possibly prevent a federal executive agency from enforcing authority explicitly granted to it by Congress?

Case Law

case law

Body of law resulting from judicial interpretations of statutory and other forms of law.

precedent

Rule of case law that must be used by lower courts in deciding future cases.

To answer this question, we must understand an extremely important source of law known as **case law**—law resulting from judicial interpretations of statutory and other forms of law. The business of the courts is resolving disputes, and when a dispute involves an interpretation of law, the court's decision in the case may establish a **precedent**—a rule of law that must be used by lower courts in deciding future cases. The principle behind case law is known as *judicial review*, and it permits the judicial branch of government to "check and balance" the actions both of the legislative branch in making laws and of the executive branch in enforcing them.

At what point may judicial review affect the process of enforcing administrative law? After an agency rule has passed through the rulemaking process outlined in Figure 16.11, it usually becomes law. Typically, the courts accept these rules as law by upholding actions taken by agencies to enforce them. But not automatically. In a 1973 case involving a fine based on OSHA's General Duty Clause, a federal court carefully translated the terms of the clause into three "necessary elements of a violation" and ruled that OSHA could win such cases only if it showed that a violation met all three requirements. A fourth requirement was later added, and OSHA now cites these four requirements in its official interpretation the General Duty Clause, issuing violations only "when the four components of this provision are present."[68]

In another case, the U.S. Supreme Court confirmed the opinion of a lower court that the OSHAct did not give OSHA "the unbridled discretion to adopt standards designed to create absolutely risk-free workplaces regardless of costs." In this 1980 case involving workplace exposure to a cancer-causing substance, the Court set down much stricter requirements for the validity of OSHA-issued *permissible exposure limits* and other standards.[69]

Today, therefore, because it's difficult to meet the stringent requirements set by judicial precedent, OSHA rarely resorts either to the General Duty Clause or to permissible exposure limits established later than the 1970s.[70] In the case of cigarette smoke, OSHA rules are applied only in rare and extreme cases, usually when cigarette smoke combines with some other contaminant produced by a manufacturing process.[71]

Beyond OSHA: Public Law, Public Policy, and Environmental Tobacco Smoke

And yet, if you've spent much time recently around American workplaces, you've no doubt observed that a lot of employers have instituted complete or partial restrictions on smoking. In 1985, for example, 27 percent of U.S. worksites with fifty or more employees either were smoke free or limited smoking to separately ventilated areas. According to recent data, the number had risen to nearly 90 percent by 2000.[72] If OSHA standards aren't responsible for this trend toward smoke-free worksites, to what can we attribute it?

For one thing, of course, national attitudes toward smoking have undergone significant changes in the last three or four decades. Few people would be surprised to find that the percentage of U.S. adults who smoke declined from just over 42 percent in 1965 to 22 percent in 2009.[73] In addition, more and more American workers are aware of the effects of secondhand smoke. In one study, 76.5 percent of respondents said they believed that secondhand smoke causes heart damage, and 84.5 percent said they believed that it causes lung cancer.[74] (Interestingly, the conviction that secondhand smoke harms nonsmokers doubles the likelihood that a smoker will succeed in quitting.[75])

Naturally, public attitudes show up in public policy. In the legal environment of business, we can identify at least two areas that reflect public policy toward smoke-free workplaces:

- *Other federal statutes*. In particular, two federal laws support civil suits against employers that fail to take action against environmental tobacco smoke or secondhand smoke:

  - The *Americans with Disabilities Act* protects people with impairments that affect "major life activities." The law requires employers to provide "reasonable accommodation" that allows impaired employees to perform their jobs. An employee with a respiratory impairment that prevents him or her from working in the presence of cigarette smoke may sue an employer that fails to provide appropriate working conditions.

  - The *Rehabilitation Act of 1973* bars employment discrimination on the basis of disability. A worker with a respiratory disability can sue an employer that fails to limit workplace smoke for unlawful discrimination.

- *State laws*. Currently, twenty-four states have laws governing smoke-free workplaces (up from just two states in 2002), and these and related laws in many states have become more stringent in the past few years. According to the Centers for Disease Control, between 2004 and 2007, the following statistics were true:

  - Eighteen states strengthened restrictions for private-sector worksites, eighteen strengthened restrictions for restaurants, and twelve strengthened restrictions for bars.

  - The number of states requiring all three settings to be smoke free climbed from three to twelve.

  - The number of states with no restrictions on any of the three settings decreased from sixteen to eight.[76]

Connecticut law, for example, restricts smoking in most workplaces with at least five employees to specially ventilated smoking rooms.[77]

In addition, we shouldn't underestimate the role played by business itself in the campaign to curb workplace smoking. In Connecticut, for example, the workplace smoking ban applies only to indoor areas, but many companies in the state take advantage of a provision allowing them to ban smoking anywhere on their properties. Businesses, of course, aren't motivated strictly by civic responsibility. Workplace smoking increases employer costs in numerous ways. Smokers are absent from work 50 percent more often than nonsmokers, and they have twice as many accidents. Smoke-free firms often pay 25 percent to 35 percent less for health and fire insurance, and one government report calculates that U.S. businesses could save from $4 billion to $8 billion annually in building operations and maintenance costs if workplace smoking bans were enforced nationwide.[78]

And last but not least, both for-profit and nonprofit organizations must always contend with lawsuits:[79]

- A man suffering from asthma repeatedly asked Olympic Airways flight attendants to change his seat because of persistent secondhand smoke. They refused, he died, and his widow sued the airline for negligence. A U.S. District Court awarded the plaintiff damages of $1.4 million.

- After sharing an office with a chain smoker for twenty-six years, a nonsmoking New Jersey teacher contracted tonsilar cancer and sought workers' compensation benefits for a temporary disability caused by secondhand smoke. A workers' compensation judge and a state appeals panel ordered the Middletown Board of Education to pay the plaintiff $45,000 in disability benefits, $53,000 in medical costs, and $20,000 in legal fees and to provide for any future treatment that he might require.

- When her employer refused to provide reasonable accommodation to protect her from secondhand smoke, a woman suffering from severe respiratory allergies sued under the Americans with Disabilities Act. A U.S. Appeals Court agreed with her contention that her disability interfered with a "major life activity"—namely, breathing. The case is still under consideration.

5.5 Law and the "Public Interest"

It's probably tempting to see the current status of public policy and law on both environmental tobacco smoke and secondhand smoke as a logical convergence of private and public interest.[80] Many political scientists and economists, however, argue that the idea of "the public interest" is difficult to pin down. Is there really a set of underlying principles reflecting what society regards as good or right? Can a society actually come to any general agreement about what these principles are? And who speaks for these principles? We hear lawmakers talk about "the public interest" all the time, but we suspect that they're often motivated by private interests and cite "the public interest" for rhetorical purposes.

Now, we're not necessarily criticizing politicians, whose job description includes an ability to balance a bewildering array of private interests. According to many people who are skeptical of the term "public interest," public policy and law reflect not an imaginary consensus about what's good or right but rather a very real interplay among *competing* interests. Public policy and law on environmental tobacco smoke and secondhand smoke, for example, reflect the long-term interaction of interest groups as diverse as the American Lung Association and the Tobacco Institute. Likewise, the record of OSHA's shifting policy on how to address environmental tobacco smoke as a workplace hazard reflects an interplay of competing interests within the U.S. political and legal systems.

As for businesses, they must, of course, negotiate the resulting shifts in the political and legal environment. In addition, a firm's response to such a problem as air contamination in the workplace will reflect an interplay of competing fiscal demands. On the one hand, a company must consider the losses in productivity that result from smoking and secondhand smoke in its workplace; on the other hand, it must consider the cost of controlling air contaminants and other hazards in its workplace. Every company, therefore, must participate more or less actively in the interplay of competing interests that shape public policy and law. After all, its own interests are inherently bound up with the diverse, often conflicting interests of groups that have a stake in its performance: namely, its *stakeholders*—employees, shareholders, customers, suppliers, and the communities in which they do business.

KEY TAKEAWAYS

- **Private law** deals with private relationships among individuals and organizations. **Public law**, which concerns the relationship of government to private individuals and other private entities, including businesses, falls into three general categories:

    1. *Criminal law* prohibits and punishes wrongful conduct.
    2. *Constitutional law* concerns the laws and basic legal principles set forth by the U.S. Constitution.
    3. *Administrative law* refers to statutes and regulations related to the activities of certain legal bodies known as administrative agencies.

- **Statutory laws** are laws made by legislative bodies.

- **Externalities** are costs that don't show up as part of the market price for a product. Negative externalities result from marketplace transactions—payments of certain prices for certain products—but aren't borne by the sellers or buyers of the products exchanged in those transactions; rather, they're borne by people who are outside or *external to* them.

- Government may intervene in economic activity in order to "correct" *market failure*, which is perceived to occur when markets aren't as efficient as they should be in theory. Efficiency is thus one foundation of law: the rule of law encourages "efficiency" in the sense that it requires us to act within certain well-defined limits, and it prohibits activities that take place outside those limits—such as stealing resources—because they make the process of allocating resources more wasteful and expensive.

- Law also has an ethical underpinning. We regard some activities as inherently bad and others as bad because society declares them to be bad.

- Contractual relationships, which are the building blocks of a modern economy, are possible when a legal system provides for the reliable enforcement of contracts.

- In passing the Occupational Safety and Health Act (OSHAct) to establish standards of safety and health for American workers, Congress created **administrative agencies**—bodies established by legislative act to carry out specific duties. The **Occupational Health and Safety Administration (OSHA)** is empowered to set workplace safety and health standards and to ensure that employers take appropriate steps to meet them. Once they've passed through a five-step rulemaking process, administrative regulations become **administrative law**, which refers generally to statutes and regulations related to the activities of administrative agencies.

- **Case law** is law resulting from judicial interpretations of statutory and other forms of law. When the decision of a court involves an interpretation of law, it may establish a **precedent**—a rule of law that must be used by lower courts in deciding future cases. The principle behind case law is known as *judicial review*, which permits the judicial branch of government to "check and balance" the actions of the legislative branch in making laws and of the executive branch in enforcing them.

Before going to the next chapter, take a few minutes to test your knowledge of the material covered in this section. Quizzes can be found under the "Resources" tab, "Study Aids: Quizzes."

EXERCISE

If you were able to set the price of a pack of cigarettes, how much would you charge? Would your price include excise taxes? What other costs would your price cover?

Do you think it's right to ban smoking in the workplace? Why, or why not?

6. CASES AND PROBLEMS

CAREER OPPORTUNITIES

Would You Like to Be a Lawyer?

Are you interested in a career in law? To learn what lawyers do, read the article on About.com, "Lawyer" by Sally Kane, http://legalcareers.about.com/od/careerprofiles/p/Lawyer.htm

As a follow-up (and because getting a job is a good thing), read a second article on About.com, "Who Hires Lawyers?" by Tara Kuther, http://gradschool.about.com/od/lawschool/f/lawjobs.htm. Then, answer the following questions, being sure to provide an explanation for each of your answers:

- What about being a lawyer interests you?
- What might discourage you from pursuing a career in law?
- Overall, does a career in law appeal to you? Why, or why not?

ETHICS ANGLE

The Product Liability Debate

The article "Who Should Pay? The Product Liability Debate," by Claire Andre and Manuel Velasquez, provides the pros and cons of the current product liability legal environment. Read the article, which can be found at http://www.scu.edu/ethics/publications/iie/v4n1/pay.html, and answer these questions:

1. Should consumers bear more responsibility for product injuries?
2. Should drug manufacturers bear more responsibility?
3. Is the current product-liability legal system broken? Why, or why not? If you believe it is broken, how would you fix it?

TEAM-BUILDING SKILLS

Get together as a team and debate these two related issues: "How much should a pack of cigarettes cost?" and "Should businesses ban smoking the workplace?" Write a "position" paper explaining your group's opinion. If the group doesn't reach an agreement on the issues, include a "minority report"—the opinion of a minority of the group.

THE GLOBAL VIEW

What issues would you encounter as a businessperson negotiating a sales contract with a company in China? How would you overcome these issues?

ENDNOTES

1. This vignette is based on the following sources: George McGovern, "What I Know Now: Nibbled to Death," *Inc*, December 1993, http://www.inc.com/magazine/19931201/3809.html (accessed April 4, 2014); McGovern, "Freedom Means Responsibility," *Wall Street Journal Online*, March 7, 2008, http://online.wsj.com/article/SB120485275086518279.html (accessed April 4, 2014); Jack Schultz, "Being a Small Business Owner Isn't Easy—Ask George," *BoomtownUSA*, February 28, 2005, http://boomtownusa.blogspot.com/2005_02_01_archive.html (accessed November 11, 2011).

2. See Timothy Sexton, "Millions of Americans Break the Law Several Times a Day without Being Punished," *Associated Content*, September 9, 2008, http://www.associatedcontent.com/article/979756/millions_of_americans_break_the_law.html (accessed November 12, 2011).

3. Mark E. Roszkowski, *Business Law: Principles, Cases, and Policy*, 5th ed. (Upper Saddle River, NJ: Prentice Hall, 2002), 4.

4. This section is based on Henry R. Cheesman, *Contemporary Business and Online Commerce Law: Legal, Internet, Ethical, and Global Environments*, 5th ed. (Upper Saddle River, NJ: Pearson Education, 2006), 4.

5. This section is based on Monroe E. Price and Peter Krug, *The Enabling Environment for Free and Independent Media* (Washington, DC: USAID Center for Democracy and Governance, December 2000), Chapter 3.

6. See Henry R. Cheesman, *Contemporary Business and Online Commerce Law: Legal, Internet, Ethical, and Global Environments*, 5th ed. (Upper Saddle River, NJ: Pearson Education, 2006), 3–4.

7. This case is inspired by John Jude Moran, *Employment Law: New Challenges in the Business Environment* (Upper Saddle River, NJ: Pearson Education, 2008), 27.

8. This section is based on Nancy A. Kubasek, Bartley A. Brennan, and M. Neil Browne, *The Legal Environment of Business: A Critical Thinking Approach*, 5th ed. (Upper Saddle River, NJ: Pearson Education, 2009), 360–63.

9. See Nancy A. Kubasek, Bartley A. Brennan, and M. Neil Browne, *The Legal Environment of Business: A Critical Thinking Approach*, 5th ed. (Upper Saddle River, NJ: Pearson Education, 2009), 349–50, 360.

10. See Henry R. Cheesman, *Contemporary Business and Online Commerce Law: Legal, Internet, Ethical, and Global Environments*, 5th ed. (Upper Saddle River, NJ: Pearson Education, 2006), 126.

11. See Henry R. Cheesman, *Contemporary Business and Online Commerce Law: Legal, Internet, Ethical, and Global Environments*, 5th ed. (Upper Saddle River, NJ: Pearson Education, 2006), 79–83.

12. See Henry R. Cheesman, *Contemporary Business and Online Commerce Law: Legal, Internet, Ethical, and Global Environments*, 5th ed. (Upper Saddle River, NJ: Pearson Education, 2006), 172.

13. See Mark E. Roszkowski, *Business Law: Principles, Cases, and Policy*, 5th ed. (Upper Saddle River, NJ: Prentice Hall, 2002), 181.

14. See John Jude Moran, *Employment Law: New Challenges in the Business Environment* (Upper Saddle River, NJ: Pearson Education, 2008), 3.

15. See Nancy A. Kubasek, Bartley A. Brennan, and M. Neil Browne, *The Legal Environment of Business: A Critical Thinking Approach*, 5th ed. (Upper Saddle River, NJ: Pearson Education, 2009), 446; "Respondeat Superior," *Law Library: American Law and Legal Information* (2008), http://encyclopedia.thefreedictionary.com/respondeat+superior (accessed April 3, 2014).

16. "Scope of Employment," *Law Library: American Law and Legal Information* (2008), http://law.jrank.org/pages/10039/Scope-Employment.html (accessed April 3, 2014).

17. John Jude Moran, *Employment Law: New Challenges in the Business Environment* (Upper Saddle River, NJ: Pearson Education, 2008), 11.

18. "Scope of Employment," *Law Library: American Law and Legal Information* (2008), http://law.jrank.org/pages/10039/Scope-Employment.html (accessed April 3, 2014).

19. Judicial Council of California, "Unlimited Civil Cases," *California Courts* (2008), http://www.courtinfo.ca.gov/reference/documents/retrounlimited.pdf; Thomas H. Cohen and Steven K. Smith, "Civil Trial Cases and Verdicts in Large Counties, 2001," *Bureau of Justice Statistics Bulletin* (Washington, DC: U.S. Dept. of Justice, April 2004), http://www.bjs.gov/content/pub/pdf/ctcvlc01.pdf (accessed April 3, 2014).

20. Nancy A. Kubasek, Bartley A. Brennan, and M. Neil Browne, *The Legal Environment of Business: A Critical Thinking Approach*, 5th ed. (Upper Saddle River, NJ: Pearson Education, 2009), 376.

21. This section is based on Nancy A. Kubasek, Bartley A. Brennan, and M. Neil Browne, *The Legal Environment of Business: A Critical Thinking Approach*, 5th ed. (Upper Saddle River, NJ: Pearson Education, 2009), 377–81.

22. This example is borrowed from Scott Baldwin, Francis Hare, and Francis E. McGovern, *The Preparation of a Product Liability Case* (New York: Aspen Publishers Online, 1998), 2–38, http://books.google.com/books?id=KOvn3Dz5-HAC&pg=PA76&lpg=PA76&dq=ladder+defective+design&source=web&q&f=false (accessed April 3, 2014).

23. Occupational Safety and Health Administration, *Stairways and Ladders: A Guide to OSHA Rules* (Washington, DC: U.S. Dept. of Labor, 2003), 7, 7, http://www.freeoshainfo.com/pubpages/Files/Walking Working Surfaces (Slips Trips Falls)/StairsLaddersHandbook.pdf (accessed April 3, 2014).

24. See Henry R. Cheesman, *Contemporary Business and Online Commerce Law: Legal, Internet, Ethical, and Global Environments*, 5th ed. (Upper Saddle River, NJ: Pearson Education, 2006), 93.

25. American Ladder Institute, "Ladder Safety and Education" (2002), at http://www.laddersafety.org (accessed November 12, 2011); see also "Ladder Injuries Climbing, Study Finds," *ConsumerAffairs.com*, May 1, 2007, http://www.consumeraffairs.com/news04/2007/05/ladder_safety.html (accessed April 3, 2014).

26. See *Greenman v. Yuba Power Products* (1963), http://online.ceb.com/CalCases/C2/59C2d57.htm (accessed April 3, 2014).

27. See Henry R. Cheesman, *Contemporary Business and Online Commerce Law: Legal, Internet, Ethical, and Global Environments*, 5th ed. (Upper Saddle River, NJ: Pearson Education, 2006), 370.

28. Conrad Shawn, "Tackling Product Liability: NLBMDA to Introduce Product Liability Legislation," *AllBusiness*, January 1, 2006, http://www.highbeam.com/doc/1G1-140954968.html (accessed April 3, 2014).

29. See David E. Baker and Rusty Lee, "Portable Ladder Safety," *National Ag Safety Database*, October 1993, http://nasdonline.org/document/1091/d000877/portable-ladder-safety.html (accessed November 12, 2011).

30. "Ladders: A Ladder for Every Task: Ladder Types and Industry Ratings," *Guide4Home* (2008), http://www.guide4home.com/rem-lad (accessed April 3, 2014).

31. See Henry R. Cheesman, *Contemporary Business and Online Commerce Law: Legal, Internet, Ethical, and Global Environments*, 5th ed. (Upper Saddle River, NJ: Pearson Education, 2006), 509.

32. This hypothetical outcome is based on *Economy Engineering v. Commonwealth* (1992), http://masscases.com/cases/sjc/413/413mass791.html (accessed April 3, 2014).

33. See Nancy A. Kubasek, Bartley A. Brennan, and M. Neil Browne, *The Legal Environment of Business: A Critical Thinking Approach*, 5th ed. (Upper Saddle River, NJ: Pearson Education, 2009), 339–47.

34. See "Compensatory Damages," *Law Library: American Law and Legal Information* (2008), http://law.jrank.org/pages/5947/Damages-Compensatory-Damages.html (accessed April 3, 2014).

35. *BMW of North America v. Gore* (1996), http://www.casebriefs.com/blog/law/constitutional-law/constitutional-law-keyed-to-chemerinsky/economic-liberties/bmw-of-north-america-inc-v-gore-2 (accessed April 3, 2014); Nancy A. Kubasek, Bartley A. Brennan, and M. Neil Browne, *The Legal Environment of Business: A Critical Thinking Approach*, 5th ed. (Upper Saddle River, NJ: Pearson Education, 2009), 341–43.

36. See Henry R. Cheesman, *Contemporary Business and Online Commerce Law: Legal, Internet, Ethical, and Global Environments*, 5th ed. (Upper Saddle River, NJ: Pearson Education, 2006), 270–71.

37. See Henry R. Cheesman, *Contemporary Business and Online Commerce Law: Legal, Internet, Ethical, and Global Environments*, 5th ed. (Upper Saddle River, NJ: Pearson Education, 2006), 277.

38. See Henry R. Cheesman, *Contemporary Business and Online Commerce Law: Legal, Internet, Ethical, and Global Environments*, 5th ed. (Upper Saddle River, NJ: Pearson Education, 2006), 267–68.

39. See Nancy A. Kubasek, Bartley A. Brennan, and M. Neil Browne, *The Legal Environment of Business: A Critical Thinking Approach*, 5th ed. (Upper Saddle River, NJ: Pearson Education, 2009), 30–31.

40. Saul Spigel, "Statewide Smoking Ban," *OLR Research Report*, June 9, 2003, http://cga.ct.gov/2003/rpt/2003-R-0466.htm (accessed April 4, 2014).

41. "How Many Discarded Cigarette Butts Are There?" *Cigarette Butt Litter* (Clean Virginia Waterways, Longwood University, 2008), http://www.longwood.edu/cleanva/cigbutthowmany.htm (accessed April 4, 2014).

42. "Lieberman Lauds Legislation to Eradicate Tobacco Trash," news release, May 8, 2006, http://votesmart.org/public-statement/171383/lieberman-lauds-legislation-to-eradicate-tobacco-trash#.U0DF9BvQflU (accessed April 4, 2014).

43. Paul Frisman, "Connecticut's Littering Law," *OLR Research Report*, May 20, 2008, http://www.cga.ct.gov/2008/rpt/2008-R-0314.htm (accessed April 4, 2014).

44. "Litter Law Would Target Smokers outside Bars," *The Record-Journal*, August 22, 2008, http://forums.ctrecord.com/showthread.php?t=2181 (accessed November 12, 2011).

45. California Department of Motor Vehicles, "Throwing Substances on Highways or Adjoining Areas" (2007), http://www.dmv.ca.gov/pubs/vctop/d11/vc23111.htm (accessed April 4, 2014).

46. "The High Cost of Litter—Millions of Taxpayer $$$$," *Green Eco Services*, September 7, 2008, http://www.greenecoservices.com/the-high-cost-of-litter-millions-of-taxpayer (accessed April 4, 2014).

47. "Viejas Fire Almost 100 Percent Contained," *10News.com*, January 7, 2001, http://www.10news.com/news/407147/detail.html (accessed November 12, 2011); "Crews Work Overnight against Wind-Fueled Fire near San Diego," *CNN.com*, January 3, 2001, http://archives.cnn.com/2001/US/01/03/wildfire.04 (accessed October 23, 2008); "Brush Fire Burns Homes in S. California," *USAToday.com*, January 3, 2001, http://www.usatoday.com/weather/news/2001/scalifire0103.htm (accessed October 23, 2008).

48. Nate Hopper, "What a Pack of Cigarettes Costs, State by State," *The Awl*, June 8, 2011, http://www.theawl.com/2011/06/what-a-pack-of-cigarettes-costs-state-by-state (accessed April 4, 2014).

49. Campaign for Tobacco-Free Kids, "State Cigarette Excise Tax Rates and Rankings," Campaign for Tobacco-Free Kids, http://www.tobaccofreekids.org/research/factsheets/pdf/0267.pdf (accessed April 4, 2014); Wendy Koch, "Biggest U.S. Tax Hike on Tobacco Takes Effect," *USA Today*, April 3, 2009, http://www.usatoday.com/money/perfi/taxes/2009-03-31-cigarettetax_N.htm#table (accessed April 4, 2014).

50. See Robert S. Pindyck and Daniel L. Rubinfeld, *Microeconomics*, 7th ed. (Upper Saddle River, NJ: Pearson Education, 2009), 315–16.

51. See Daniel H. Cole and Peter Z. Grossman, *Principles of Law and Economics* (Upper Saddle River, NJ: Pearson Education, 2005), 14–15.

52. Campaign for Tobacco-Free Kids, "Toll of Tobacco in the United States of America," Campaign for Tobacco-Free Kids, http://www.tobaccofreekids.org/research/factsheets/pdf/0072.pdf (accessed April 4, 2014).

53. Centers for Disease Control and Prevention, "Economic Costs Associated with Smoking, Economic Facts about U.S. Tobacco Production and Use," http://www.cdc.gov/tobacco/data_statistics/fact_sheets/economics/econ_facts/index.htm (accessed April 4, 2014).

54. Hilary Smith, "The High Cost of Smoking," *MSN Money*, September 3, 2008, http://money.bundle.com/article/the-high-cost-of-smoking-7269 (accessed November 12, 2011).

55. Campaign for Tobacco-Free Kids, "State Cigarette Excise Tax Rates and Rankings," Campaign for Tobacco-Free Kids, http://www.tobaccofreekids.org/research/factsheets/pdf/0097.pdf (accessed April 4, 2014).

56. See Daniel H. Cole and Peter Z. Grossman, *Principles of Law and Economics* (Upper Saddle River, NJ: Pearson Education, 2005), 13.

57. See Robert S. Pindyck and Daniel L. Rubinfeld, *Microeconomics*, 7th ed. (Upper Saddle River, NJ: Pearson Education, 2009), 337–38.

58. Campaign for Tobacco-Free Kids, "Higher Cigarette Taxes" (2008), http://www.tobaccofreekids.org/reports/prices (accessed April 4, 2014).

59. See Daniel H. Cole and Peter Z. Grossman, *Principles of Law and Economics* (Upper Saddle River, NJ: Pearson Education, 2005), 19.

60. This section is based on Daniel H. Cole and Peter Z. Grossman, *Principles of Law and Economics* (Upper Saddle River, NJ: Pearson Education, 2005), 156.

61. See Henry R. Cheesman, *Contemporary Business and Online Commerce Law: Legal, Internet, Ethical, and Global Environments*, 5th ed. (Upper Saddle River, NJ: Pearson Education, 2006), 126.

62. American Lung Association, "Smoking Policies in the Workplace Fact Sheet," July 2008, http://no-smoke.org/document.php?id=209 (accessed April 4, 2014).

63. This section is based on John Jude Moran, *Employment Law: New Challenges in the Business Environment* (Upper Saddle River, NJ: Pearson Education, 2008), 450–53. See also "Occupational Safety and Health Administration (OSHA)," *Encyclopedia of Small Business*, 2nd ed. (2002), http://findarticles.com/p/articles/mi_gx5201/is_/ai_n19121420 (accessed November 26, 2008).

64. See Kenneth F. Warren, *Administrative Law in the Political System*, 4th ed. (Boulder, CO: Westview Press, 2004), 41–43, http://books.google.com/books?id=AZVD_QM1QIYC&ie=ISO-8859-1&output=html (accessed November 12, 2011).

65. Occupational Safety and Health Administration, "SEC. 5 Duties" (U.S. Dept. of Labor, 2008), http://www.osha.gov/pls/oshaweb/owadisp.show_document?p_table=OSHACT&p_id=3359 (accessed April 4, 2014).

66. Occupational Safety and Health Administration, "Air Contaminants—1910.1000" (U.S. Dept. of Labor, 2008), at http://www.osha.gov/pls/oshaweb/owadisp.show_document?p_id=9991&p_table=STANDARDS (accessed April 4, 2014).

67. See Occupational Safety and Health Administration, "Reiteration of Existing OSHA Policy on Indoor Air Quality" (U.S. Dept. of Labor, 2003), at http://www.osha.gov/pls/oshaweb/owadisp.show_document?p_table=INTERPRETATIONS&p_id=24602 (accessed April 4, 2014).

68. See *National Realty and Construction v. OSHRC* (1973), http://cases.justia.com/us-court-of-appeals/F2/489/1257/152788 (accessed April 4, 2014); OSHA, "Reiteration of Existing OSHA Policy on Indoor Air Quality"; OSHA, "Elements Necessary for a Violation of the General Duty Clause" (U.S. Dept. of Labor, 2003), at http://www.osha.gov/pls/oshaweb/owadisp.show_document?p_table=INTERPRETATIONS&p_id=24784 (accessed April 4, 2014).

69. See Mark Robson and William Toscano, *Risk Assessment for Environmental Health* (Hoboken, NJ: John Wiley & Sons, 2007), 209–12, http://books.google.com/books?id=s_ih18SnrvcC&pg=PA212&lpg=PA208&ots=aiV5C-1chP&dq=Industrial+Union+PELs&i (accessed November 12, 2011); Randy Rabinowitz, *Occupational Safety and Health Law* (Washington, DC: BNA Books, 2004), 387, http://books.google.com/books?id=11e2Q2zABmIC&pg=PA91&lpg=PA91&dq=National+Realty+and+Construction+Co,+H (accessed November 12, 2011).

70. OSHA, "Enforcement Policy for Respiratory Hazards Not Covered by OSHA Permissible Exposure Limits" (U.S. Dept. of Labor, 2003), http://www.osha.gov/pls/oshaweb/owadisp.show_document?p_table=INTERPRETATIONS&p_id=24749 (accessed April 4, 2014).

71. *Nolo's Encyclopedia of Everyday Law: Answers to Your Most Frequently Asked Legal Questions*, ed. Shea Irving (Berkeley, CA: Nolo Press, 2007), 63, http://books.google.com/books?id=mvIXStpeSVEC&dq=OSHA+rules+apply+to+tobacco+smoke+only+in+rare+and+extr (accessed November 12, 2011).

72. Nell H. Gottlieb, "Workplace Smoking Policies and Programs," *Encyclopedia of Public Health* (New York: Macmillan Reference USA, 2002), http://www.answers.com/topic/workplace-smoking-policies-and-programs (accessed November 12, 2011); Jon Jenney, "Clean Indoor Air Ordinances," *Encyclopedia of Public Health* (New York: Macmillan Reference USA, 2002), http://www.novelguide.com/a/discover/eph_01/eph_01_00186.html (accessed November 12, 2011).

73. Campaign for Tobacco-Free Kids, "Number of Smokers and Number of Smokers Who Have Quit," Campaign for Tobacco-Free Kids, http://www.cdc.gov/tobacco/quit_smoking/how_to_quit/you_can_quit/alone (accessed April 4, 2014).

74. "Smoking Prevalence among U.S. Adults, 1955–2007" (2007), *Information Please Database*, http://www.infoplease.com/ipa/A0762370.html (accessed April 4, 2014); data from Centers for Disease Control and Prevention. Ellen Striebel, "Marion County Residents' Attitudes toward Secondhand Smoke in Public Places," December 8, 2005, http://www.bowenresearchcenter.iupui.edu/brc_lectures/BowenLecture2005-12-08.pdf (accessed April 4, 2014).

75. Stanton A. Glantz and Patrick Jamieson, "Attitudes toward Secondhand Smoke, Smoking, and Quitting among Young People," *Pediatrics* 106:6 (December 2000), http://pediatrics.aappublications.org/cgi/content/full/106/6/e82 (accessed April 4, 2014).

76. Centers for Disease Control and Prevention, "State Smoking Restrictions for Private-Sector Worksites, Restaurants, and Bars—United States, 2004 and 2007," *Morbidity and Mortality Weekly Reports (MMWRs)*, May 23, 2008), http://www.cdc.gov/mmwr/preview/mmwrhtml/mm5720a3.htm#content_area (accessed April 4, 2014); Centers for Disease Control and Prevention, "New Study Shows Tobacco Control Programs Cut Adult Smoking Rates" (U.S. Dept. of Health and Human Services, January 30, 2008), http://www.cdc.gov/media/pressrel/2008/r080130.htm?s_cid=mediarel_r080130_x (accessed November 12, 2011).

77. Saul Spigel, "Statewide Smoking Ban," *OLR Research Report*, June 9, 2003, http://cga.ct.gov/2003/rpt/2003-R-0466.htm (accessed April 4, 2014).

78. "Smoking in the Workplace Costs Employers Money" (Washington, DC: Action on Smoking and Health, 2005), http://www.ash.org/papers/h100.htm (accessed November 12, 2011); American Lung Association, "Smoking Policies in the Workplace Fact Sheet." http://no-smoke.org/document.php?id=209 (accessed April 4, 2014).

79. See E. L. Sweda Jr., "Lawsuits and Secondhand Smoke," *Tobacco Control* (London: BMJ Publishing Group, 2004), http://tobaccocontrol.bmj.com/cgi/content/full/13/suppl_1/i61 (accessed April 4, 2014).

80. This section is based on David P. Baron, *Business and Its Environment*, 5th ed. (Upper Saddle River, NJ: Pearson Education, 2006), 158–59, 199–200.

Index